About the Author

Robert Stedall was educated at Marlborough College and McGill University, Montreal.

Following his career as a chartered accountant, he has researched genealogy of the Scottish peerage resulting in a two-volume history of Mary Queen of Scots. He was master of the Ironmongers' Livery Company in 1989. He lives near Petworth, West Sussex.

Also by the same author:

Hunting From Hampstead, Book Guild Publishing, 2002
The Challenge to the Crown, Book Guild Publishing, 2012
The Survival of the Crown, Book Guild Publishing, 2014

Robert Stedall

MEN OF SUBSTANCE

THE LONDON LIVERY COMPANIES'
RELUCTANT PART IN
THE PLANTATION OF ULSTER

'The Colonists should be men of substance with the wherewithal to
implement the works necessary to ensure the success of the venture.'
Sir Francis Bacon

AUSTIN MACAULEY
PUBLISHERS LTD.

A CIP catalogue record for this title is available from the British Library.

ISBN 9781786124562 (Paperback)
ISBN 9781786124555 (Hardback)
ISBN 9781786124579 (E-Book)

www.austinmacauley.com

First Published (2016)
Austin Macauley Publishers Ltd.
25 Canada Square
Canary Wharf
London
E14 5LQ

Acknowledgments

The history of the Livery Companies in Northern Ireland is not well known, but there is a wealth of information among their records. I have received assistance from many sources among the Companies and from The Honourable the Irish Society. I particularly wish to mention Edward Montgomery, DL, the Society's Secretary and Representative (Ireland) for his support and encouragement, and Penny Fussell, Archivist of the Drapers' Company, for her extraordinary understanding of their Irish records and artefacts. My son, Oliver, has travelled with me through County Londonderry persevering with my thirst for photographs of the fine buildings that still remain in the proportions, in the City of Londonderry and in Coleraine. My cousin, Maria Bremridge has, as always, unearthed some fascinating portraits of the personalities in the story, many in armour. The *doyen* of the earlier research into this extraordinary subject has been James Stevens Curl, and this book makes numerous references to the works that he has undertaken and to the sources, which his scholarship has identified.

Francis Bacon, writing in 1608, 'believed that the scheme [for the Plantation of Ulster] would be even more significant than the Plantation of Virginia because it was regarded as strategically and politically more sensitive, and was clearly capable of supporting a very considerable population. Ulster was geographically less remote, and so would be more attractive to settlers, while the cost of colonisation would be less. It had large tracts of potentially good farmland: they were richly endowed with rivers teeming with fish; they were well stocked with animal life including varieties of game; they had minerals, good building stone, clay and other resources; and (most attractive to builders) they possessed substantial areas covered with fine forests.' (Curl 1986, p. 22)

Contents

The Honourable The Irish Society

Foreword

A largely unremarked feature of English history from the Norman Conquest onwards has been the relationship between the City of London and the monarchy: the monarch, long on political power but short on cash, recognised the City, long on cash but short on political power, as the business centre and, in return, the City recognised the monarchy as the political head.

This understanding enabled the monarch to call on the City for funds when needed for military purposes. The best known example is the loan by the City to Henry V personally to finance the Agincourt campaign, secured on a deposit of the King's gold chain.

A far more complex example is the involvement, now over four hundred years long, of the Livery Companies of the City in Ireland. As Governor of The Honourable The Irish Society, the body set up to oversee the Companies' arrival and subsequent operations there, and as a past Lord Mayor of the City, I very much welcome this book, the first authoritative account of that involvement, set in the context of the longer history of the relationship of England, Scotland and Ireland.

An excellent work, both for its historical perspective and as an aid to understanding events much more recent.

David Wootton

Alderman Sir David Wootton
Governor, The Honourable The Irish Society 2015 - 2018
Lord Mayor of London 2011-2012

Map of Ireland showing the showing the provinces divided into counties with their principal towns. *Drawn by David Atkinson, Handmade Maps Limited*

12

List of illustrations

Preface

If 19th Century colonisation is epitomised by pioneers on wagon trains fighting their way through Indian country, the 'Wild West' of the 16th and 17th Centuries was Ireland. British settlers saw the native Irish as 'Indians', alien in language, clothing, custom and religion. The difference was that the Irish had powerful allies in Continental Europe, who threatened to turn Ireland into England's Achilles heel. It was the favoured launching pad for pretenders hoping to establish themselves on the English throne, particularly those who were Catholic. It was always the bridgehead for Catholic Continental powers to launch invasions into England with every expectation of garnering local support and was used to provide a second front with which to temper English aggression on the Continent. Its smouldering unrest forced the English to deploy a sizeable army of seasoned troops to protect its backside.

The English quickly discovered that they could not tame the native Irish by pressurising them into adopting English ways. James I's solution was to swamp them with colonists and to maintain control by weight of numbers. By this means, he hoped to induce them to adopt English language, dress, religious dogma, farming methods and customs. Yet the Irish were passionately determined to maintain their traditions; they resented being ousted from their ancestral lands to make way for new arrivals. When they fought back against the injustices being meted out against them, they committed appalling atrocities against their heretic invaders, only to be treated with the utmost cruelty by bigoted English troops egged on by Anglican churchmen.

Faced with the prohibitive cost of maintaining a sufficient English force to protect its growing population of settlers, the Crown turned to wealthy English and Scottish landowners with the clout to control their own estates. In Ulster this was not enough. James I found it necessary to coerce the wealthy citizens of London through their Livery Companies[1] to fortify and establish control of

---

[1] Livery Companies take their name from the distinctive mode of dress worn by members of each Company. They are ancient Guilds with their own halls set up by each trade within London for its own supervision. Their role was (and sometimes still is) to set trade standards, register apprentices, charge fees and 'fines' and resolve disputes between members. They also acted as collectors of taxes imposed on their membership and levied armed 'yeomen' to support the royal armies in times of war. Over time, many of the Livery Companies have become wealthy and act as trustees for charitable benefactions often administered on behalf of deceased members. Each Company is managed by its Clerk, supervised by a Court

this most belligerent area. The Londoners were only most reluctant participants and were forced to provide ever-increasing amounts of money in an attempt to protect their initial investment, and to provide their colonists with an infrastructure of housing, protestant churches and fortifications.

On 28 January 1610, the Court of Common Council[2] of the City of London authorised a committee, acting on behalf of the Mayor and Commonalty, to sign a document with the English Privy Council for the City to acquire an area of 256,000 statute acres[3] in Ulster around Derry (or The Derry) and Coleraine. This was to be renamed the County of Londonderry. The City was required to provide £20,000, of which £5,000 was to buy out existing interests and £15,000 was to be expended on a Protestant 'plantation' of London settlers. The expenditure was to include the cost of building houses and churches at Derry (to be renamed Londonderry) with further accommodation at Coleraine. Both centres were to be provided 'with convenient fortifications'.[a] Plans for this 'plantation' were not new, but the English Government knew that the required investment was likely to exceed, by some margin, the initial tranche of £15,000. James I had concluded that it was only the wealthy merchants of the City of London who had the wherewithal to finance a settlement on a scale capable of bringing order to the area. Yet the wealthy City merchants showed little enthusiasm for the project and were persuaded to become involved only after some of their number had been imprisoned and fined for their intransigence.

The one imported culture, which had gained a complete hold with the indigenous Celtic population of Ireland was Roman-Catholicism, so much so, that even while the Reformation swept through the rest of northern Europe, Ireland remained a bastion of papal dogma. Reformist inducements to persuade the Irish to convert to Protestantism proved a complete failure. These efforts had been entirely political, and a plantation of loyal Protestants was seen as a simpler means to maintain control by diluting the local Catholic population in remoter areas.

To hold together its settlements on Irish soil and to enforce its rule, the English provided a strong military presence to prop up a Protestant Government in Dublin and it established an Anglican Church, the Church of Ireland, with a diocesan structure throughout the country. This 'Establishment' was continuously in fear of losing control. For years, it put about propaganda laying the blame for Irish insurgency on Popery. Yet Irish Government administrators were often corrupt and their motives were self-seeking. The English religious

---

of Assistants elected from among its Livery. The Court is chaired by a Master (or Prime Warden), who holds office for one year, supported by two or more Wardens.

[2] The City of London is managed by twenty-six Aldermen, each elected for life to represent one of the City wards. Each year, one of their number becomes Lord Mayor. They have responsibility for the maintenance and administration of the City and its port, supported by the Court of Common Council, members of which are also elected by each ward.

[3] The original survey undertaken by Sir Josias Bodley measured the area as 45,520 acres, but this proved to be woefully inaccurate.

crusade was always half-hearted, but both Church and State used religion to justify their usurpation of territory from the indigenous Catholics.

As plantations started to develop, life in Ireland was made even more complicated by the arrival in large numbers of Scottish Presbyterian settlers. It was unfortunate that these included their most bigoted clergy, who left Scotland in the face of the Crown's efforts to impose Anglican dogma, which they found abhorrent. This left the Church of Ireland at odds, not only with Irish Catholics but also with Scottish Presbyterians, neither of whom would conform.

Part 1

The historical background

Chapter 1

Early Ireland – the Celtic inheritance

By its very remoteness, Ireland was always relatively unaffected by developments in the rest of Europe. The Iron Age Celtic arrival appears to have been a gradual one over several centuries starting in about 500 BCE, perhaps being pushed into Britain and later into Ireland by progressive Roman conquest of the Celts' former continental European heartland. Any Irish population before the Celtic arrival was quickly subsumed into the Celts' Gaelic culture. Despite conquering Britain, the Romans never landed an army in Ireland, although there was certainly some trading activity between Roman Britain and its Celtic neighbour. Then, in the 5th Century CE, St. Patrick arrived, probably from Cumbria, to set up a Roman-Catholic Church, initially as a monastic institution. By the 9th Century the great majority of the Irish were Christian, and Catholicism had become fully integrated with Celtic custom.

Starting in about 800 CE, the arrival of Vikings from Norway resulted in the port of Dublin becoming one of the main Viking centres outside Scandinavia. Just as in the rest of Britain, Vikings 'raped and pillaged', until they were finally ousted from Ireland after the Battle of Clontarf in 1014, during which many of the Viking settlers were killed. Their removal did not bring peace. The country became divided into a 'shifting hierarchy of petty kingdoms and over-kingdoms'. While retaining their traditional Celtic customs, their Catholicism encouraged the Irish to have greater links with the English Catholic Church, and rival warlords turned to the Plantagenet kings of England for assistance in restoring their fiefdoms.

After the Norman conquest of England, the Norman Kings granted fiefdoms to their knights to induce them to establish control over the outer reaches of the British Isles. It took some time for them to reach Ireland, but, in 1169, Henry II sent Richard de Clare, Earl of Pembroke, ('Strongbow') with a party of Norman knights to gain sway on the Crown's behalf. Having landed at Waterford, Strongbow formed an alliance with Diarmait Mac Murchada, King of Leinster, and, after marrying Diarmait's daughter, was named as heir to his Kingdom. When Strongbow inherited Leinster in 1171, Henry began to doubt his loyalty, fearing that a rival Norman state was being established in Ireland. The Irish clans were to prove powerful adversaries after years of honing their skills in attacking Viking settlements and in generations of squabbling among themselves, during which chieftains formed complex alliances to gain military support against rivals.

Henry II needed to assert his position. Backed by the *Laudabiliter,* a papal bull provided by Pope Adrian IV (Cardinal Nicholas Breakspear – the only English Pope), he claimed Ireland as a papal possession and won the Pope's support to subjugate what was already a Catholic country. Yet Irish Catholicism had become eccentric and the Irish needed to be brought to heel. Henry landed a large fleet at Waterford and was the first English king to set foot on Irish soil. He promptly set about seeking the submission of the Irish Kings and awarded the Lordship of Ireland to his younger son, John Lackland, with Strongbow being appointed his 'custos' or deputy.[a] When John's elder brother, Richard I, died unexpectedly, John succeeded to the English throne as King John; this brought his Irish dominions directly under the English crown, but this did not pacify the Irish, who remained in conflict.

John Lackland (King John) (1166-1216), granted the Lordship of Ireland as a papal possession by his father Henry II. On the unexpected death of his brother Richard I, his Irish dominions came directly under the English Crown. *British School before 1620 oil on panel. By permission of the Trustees of Dulwich Picture Gallery, London DPG526*

Having gained control of Ireland's east coast and pushed its way deep into the country, the initial Anglo-Norman invasion was followed by others. John de Courcy, a knight from Cumbria, had invaded northwards in 1177 and conquered the coastlands of Down and Antrim. Those who came after him extended the Earldom of Ulster along the north coast and even built a fortress at Greencastle in Inish Owen, arguably the most remote Norman castle in Western Europe.[b]

King John's visits to Ireland in 1185 and in 1210 helped to consolidate Norman-controlled areas and caused many Irish kings to swear fealty to him. In 1197, the Normans razed Coleraine, so that Norman 'power extended over north

Antrim and into the valleys of the Bann and Roe'.[c] Despite also controlling an area round the Foyle estuary, they never succeeded in gaining sway in western Ulster and, in 1199, were defeated at Donaghmore by a Gaelic army led by the O'Neills. This left the Province of Ulster 'virtually intact under the O'Neills',[d] who preserved its Gaelic identity.

The Norman knights installed a Catholic episcopacy and priesthood, and initially the Papacy supported them in power. Yet they 'never attempted a systematic conquest of Ireland, and survived within the Pale[4] or in their coastal strongholds largely by fomenting strife among the Irish themselves'.[e] By 1219, their descendants had 'gone native'. They had intermarried with the families of their adversaries, and joined with them in clan warfare aimed at establishing local supremacy. The continuance of constant civil war, to which Ireland was no stranger, had the effect of weakening Gaelic culture.

When the Papacy realised it was losing control of the Irish Catholic Church, which the Anglo-Normans had set up, it had a change of heart and 'the rights of the English Crown in Irish episcopal elections were recognised'.[f] Ireland's Catholic Church was suddenly sided with England 'against the ambition and avarice of the Anglo-Norman Barons'.[g] With support from both England and the Papacy, it now became too influential to be overthrown. Throughout the 13th Century, England's policy was to weaken the authority of the Norman knights originally sent to establish control on their behalf. With their power being progressively reduced, the Normans faced stiff resistance from rival Gaelic chieftains, who regained some of the lands originally lost to the English invaders. The Pale around Dublin was the only part of Ireland that remained assuredly under English control. Within this area, a derivation of English became the common language. The rest of Ireland remained in the hands of feudal Gaelic chieftains and their fully integrated Anglo-Norman allies, now established with their own clans.

'More than any other part of Ireland, Ulster was beyond the Pale. It remained the most Gaelic, least anglicised and most independent of the four provinces.'[h] To officials in Dublin, it was known as the 'Great Irishry'. With the total Irish population being about 750,000, it is estimated (with great uncertainty) that the population of Ulster was no more than 150,000. Few Gaelic families lived in townships, which were at most 'modest villages, such as Strangford, Downpatrick and Coleraine. The only Norman foundation of any size was Carrickfergus, by far the largest town in Ulster.'[i] At Carlingford Lough, 'the Bagenals were making Newry into a successful urban development'.[j] Despite only a few villages, there were some settlements clustered round castles such as at Dungiven and Limavady, and 'there were small developments associated with

---

[4] This was an area of fertile lowlands around Dublin, between Dundalk and Bray and inland to Naas, which was easier to garrison and defend than the wooded hills beyond. It took its name from the fenced earthen rampart and ditch which was built to surround and protect it.

the ancient religious foundations at Derry and Coleraine'.[k] The O'Neills[5] of Tír Eóghain (Ter Owen or Tyrone) remained Ulster's most powerful native rulers, to whom many of the smaller clans or 'septs' owed allegiance. The Tir Chonaill (O'Donnell) sept was second in importance, controlling an area, rather larger than the present Donegal, and holding sway over a similar group of smaller septs. The principal families occupied fortified tower houses, rectangular keeps at least twelve metres high, constructed for defence with entrances under a 'bold arch' flanked by two towers.

> The extent of each lordship … was in a constant state of flux. Partly this was the result of expansion of the ruling family from the top downwards. … As the sons and families of the rulers multiplied, so their subjects and followers were squeezed out and withered away. This process could be rapid because Gaelic lords practiced serial monogamy, sending one wife back to her father after a few years and taking on another. … This could lead to fierce disputes on the death of a lord: primogeniture was not yet the norm, and the successor could in theory be chosen as the 'worthiest' by the high-born from any member of the [ruling] family … which included first cousins and extended over four generations. The Reality was that a man from the ruling family might make himself lord so long as he was popular enough and powerful enough to do so.[l]

'Illegitimate male children were not excluded from the right of succession'[m] and maintained a place in the society of their clans. Crown officials strongly disapproved of this, as it resulted in a land distribution system where parcels regularly changed hands. This 'acted as a strong disincentive to improve lands or to erect permanent buildings'.[n] According to Fynes Moryson, secretary to Lord Deputy Mountjoy in the final years of Elizabeth's reign, 'Gaelic lords regarded labourers and tenants at will as 'born slaves to till their ground and do them all services''.[o] Rather than receiving rent, 'a Gaelic lord expected to have his party and his retinue fed, accommodated and entertained by the proprietor of the lands he was visiting or passing through'.[p] The costs were high. 'In wartime, the great lords ordered an … uprising of able bodied men, the upper classes serving as horsemen and the freemen as footsoldiers'.[q] Tributes 'were almost always levied in kind',[r] often in cattle, other farm produce or the provision of labour. Yet labourers were not serfs and were free to move from one proprietor to another. When Ulster proprietors became short of labour, they often attempted to attract families to the north from the Pale.

'Ulster in Elizabeth's time was overwhelmingly rural'[s] and dependent on agriculture. If unable to afford tower houses, farmers lived in what the English called 'coupled houses', post-and-wattle single storey dwellings with curved load-bearing timbers springing from the side walls to support a hipped, thatched roof. Chimneys were rare 'and smoke from the hearth in the middle of the house

---

[5] The O'Neills are the oldest traceable family in Europe, dating from about AD 360. Members of the family had frequently been Kings of Ireland, and produced the most important of the Ulster chieftains.

had to pass through the door'.[t] 'Methods of cultivation were primitive in the extreme. The people ate dairy products, oatmeal, and wild vegetables: if they ate meat at all, it was usually pork.'[u] The basis of the rural economy was cattle. Herds were driven onto the hills, drying fens and bogland in spring where herdsmen erected temporary dwellings and retained hounds to protect their calves from wolves. In autumn, they returned to graze the stubble and manure the arable land. Much of this was in ridges to assist drainage and was cultivated using horse-drawn ploughs and wooden spades sheathed in iron. Corn (principally oats, rye and some barley) was broadcast on the fields and was harvested with primitive equipment. Only cattle reserved for breeding survived the slaughter before winter set in. Gaelic lords jealously guarded their fishing rights: trapping and salting salmon, which found a ready market abroad. There was a smaller trading activity in tanned hides, coarse woollen mantles, linen, horses and wolfhounds. These were bartered for wine from Bordeaux and Spain, and for clothing and arms.

Irish peasants were primitive. Spanish sailors seeking refuge after the Armada saw them as 'savages'. Captain Francisco de Cuéllar, who resided in the far north-west of Ireland for more than a year reported:

> The men are all large-bodied, and of handsome features and limbs; and as active as the roe-deer. The most of the women are very beautiful, but badly got up. They do not eat oftener than once a day, and this is at night; and that which they usually eat is butter with oaten bread. They drink sour milk, for they have no other drink; they don't drink water, although it is the best in the world. On feast days they eat some flesh half-cooked without bread or salt, as that is their custom.[v]

Moryson commented: 'When they come to any market to sell a cow or a horse, they never return home, till they have drunk the price in Spanish wine … or [whiskey] till they have outslept two or three days' drunkenness'.[w] This may account for the report of a Bohemian nobleman, Jaroslav z Donina, who

> encountered sixteen high-born women, all naked, with 'which strange sight his eyes being dazzled, they led him into the house' to converse politely in Latin in front of the fire. Joining them, the Lord O'Cahan threw all his clothes off and was surprised that the Czech baron was too bashful to do likewise.[x]

The English found the Irish 'odd and barbarous' with fighting being a popular pastime. Crimes could be compensated by making payment under Brehon Law. Yet there was also an impressive level of education and intelligence, with Latin being spoken among the educated classes. 'The rich legacy of poetry, music and learning' survived late into the 17th Century.[y]

Chapter 2

English efforts to bring Ireland to heel Middle ages – 1585

Throughout the Middle Ages, the English Crown had remained so pre-occupied with threats to its French dominions and to its northern border with Scotland that control of Ireland remained of less pressing importance. In 1315, Edward Bruce landed a Scottish invasion force at Olderfleet in Ulster. Within three years, he had destroyed local English settlements, and had even captured the fort at Carrickfergus.[a]

The Castle at Carrickfergus which overlooks the harbour of Ulster's principal mediaeval town

In 1333, William de Burgh, Earl of Ulster, who had offered the English a degree of protection, was murdered. Many of the remaining English fled, though some adopted native customs to save their lives and property.[b] In 1348, the Black Death swept through Ireland. This was far worse for the Normans and English living in townships than for the natives in their rural communities. With their power weakened, the English formed a Parliament at Kilkenny in an attempt to assert authority. Parliamentary statute now forbade intermarriage between English settlers and Irish natives, and prohibited the use of the Gaelic language, clothing and customs. Such dictats were completely unenforceable even within the Pale, so that Irish language and custom regained most of the territory originally lost to the colonists and intermarriage became the norm. By 1430,

English authority was precarious; the only parts of Ulster under English control were County Down and a few places along the coast, but even these decreased as the Century continued.

Although it might be assumed that Gaelic Ireland remained a single political union of provinces, there was no cohesion among Irish clans, and inter-clan warfare was endemic. In some periods there were nominal monarchs of Ireland able to call warriors from each province to arms in some great cause, but they never achieved political unification. It was Henry VIII who attempted this for the first time. Although there were 'common links of language, religion, custom and culture' throughout the rest of the country,[c] Ulster remained quite distinct. Its proximity to the Western Isles of Scotland brought close economic links 'between the Glens of Antrim and the west of Gaelic Scotland.'[d] Ties with the Isles and the ports in Ayrshire and Galloway predated, by a long period, the arrival of lowland Scots as settlers.

Following the Wars of the Roses, the descendants of the Anglo-Norman knights supported Plantagenet pretenders in revolts against Henry VII's rule. In 1487, the Fitzgeralds invited Burgundian troops to Ireland to crown the Yorkist Lambert Simnel as King. In 1494, Henry tried to enforce Tudor authority by introducing Poyning's law, which required all statutes passed in the Irish Parliament to be sent to Westminster for approval. This placed it under English control. Initially both Henry VII and Henry VIII appointed the more powerful Irish earls as their Lords Deputy. When the leaders of the Fitzgerald clan, the Earls of Kildare, were given the role, they needed alliances with other Gaelic chieftains to maintain authority. Rivalry between Gerald Fitzgerald, 8th Earl of Kildare, who had been brought up in England, and Piers Butler, 8th Earl of Ormonde, was such that, when either was appointed, it began inter-clan fighting. This resulted in a reduction in the areas under English supervision and a consequent shrinkage in tax revenue, causing the Lords Deputy to fall out with their Tudor masters.

After the English Reformation, Henry VIII realised that he had to establish authority in both Ireland and Scotland to prevent them from becoming bases for future Catholic invasions of England. In 1534, in an effort to establish better control, he tried to frighten the Irish by recalling Kildare to London and placing him in the Tower. Kildare's son, 'Silken' Thomas Fitzgerald, who was appointed deputy by his father in his absence, heard rumours (which turned out to be false) that his father had been executed. Fearing a similar fate, he renounced allegiance to the English King and started a rebellion. When his troops attacked Dublin Castle, they were routed, and, having retreated to his stronghold at Maynooth in Kildare, he was attacked by an English force under Sir William Skeffington. When Maynooth fell, he was put to death with his garrison. After hearing this tragedy, his distraught father died in the Tower.

In 1542, Henry's conciliatory Lord Deputy, Anthony St Leger came to terms with the principal Gaelic chieftains and Anglo-Norman earls. He induced them to attend the Irish Parliament at Kilkenny and to pass the Crown of Ireland Act, which proclaimed Henry as King. This legitimised his position, which previously derived from Papal grants and the *Laudabiliter* of Pope Adrian IV. To enforce allegiance in both Scotland and Ireland, Henry embarked on a series of punitive military campaigns. In Scotland, these became known as the 'rough wooings', as they were designed to put pressure on the Scots to agree that the Infant Mary Queen of Scots should marry Prince Edward, thereby subsuming the Scottish Crown under that of England. His belligerence was counter-productive and caused both Scots and Irish to seek assistance in Continental Europe. With Henry running out of money, he financed a group of Protestant preachers to travel round Scotland to show up the excesses of the Scottish Catholic Church. With Scottish bishops enjoying an extravagant and sometimes dissolute lifestyle his approach brought about the Scottish Reformation, and despite the Scottish Regency's efforts to retain its Catholic alliance with France, it was a Protestant alliance with England that prevailed. He had no similar success in Ireland. There had been no corruption in the Irish Catholic church and it proved a bastion against Protestantism. Henry focused on bringing

> Irish captains to further obedience ... [by] circumspect and political ways ... which thing must as yet rather be practiced by sober ways, political drifts and amiable persuasions.[e]

With a mixture of 'carrot and stick', Henry began reintegrating Ireland under English control. He was able to restore English authority over much of the country, helped by the continuance of internecine strife between clans. To subdue Ulster, he granted the Earldom of Tyrone to Conn Bacach O'Neill out of what had previously been the Kingdom of Tír Eóghain. By restoring key Gaelic chieftains, his aim was to establish subservience not expropriation.[f] When Irish and Anglo-Irish Lords surrendered their lands, they immediately became tenants-in-chief under the Crown in accordance with English law and custom. By 1543, nearly all Irish chiefs had submitted and had visited England to be granted earldoms and other titles. There was no choice in the matter. Chiefs, who resisted Henry's offers, found him confiscating their lands and arranging grants to waves of English colonists and opportunists in an effort to 'break the overgrown power of the Anglo-Irish aristocracy' and to establish 'an English interest in Ireland'.[g] 'This policy of 'surrender and regrant' enjoyed considerable success, and Elizabeth continued to implement it when it seemed appropriate,'[h] but Henry's scheme conflicted with Gaelic practice. English titles were inherited by eldest sons in accordance with primogeniture, while, under the Irish Law of Tanistry, successors to chieftains were elected by clans as the person best qualified. The traditional Irish practice was reinforced by local warlords continuing to maintain a substantial army of clan members to settle conflicts with neighbours and to impose laws in their own fiefdom.

When Jesuits led a Papal intervention to Ulster in 1542, they were 'given short shrift by Tyrone and his allies'[i] who owed their positions to the English Crown. Despite this success for English policies, Roman-Catholicism remained a major stumbling block. The accession of Edward VI heralded an aggressive

Protestant campaign to implement an Irish Reformation, but Ireland remained aloof from Protestantism as it was sweeping through the rest of Northern Europe. Edward VI's Lord Protectors followed Henry's policy, but were motivated by the need to establish Tudor authority rather than religious consideration. Irish Catholics argued that, as Henry owed his status in Ireland to the original Papal grant, his authority was forfeited when he became a heretic. Despite making progressively more brutal efforts to subjugate local clans, English officials faced harsh resistance.

The English had some notable successes. In 1539, Sir Nicholas Bagenal from Staffordshire arrived in the south of Ulster and made some progress in establishing English control, particularly by becoming Tyrone's military adviser. When Elizabeth became Queen, she confirmed Bagenal in his occupation of the abbey lands at Newry, where he developed a settlement, and was appointed Marshal of the Queen's Army in Ireland, a role which he passed on to his son, Sir Henry. Sir Nicholas had some success in Ulster, putting down rebellions and expelling Scottish[6] arrivals, who had settled at Dufferin. He made a point of fostering a better relationship with the O'Neills, who remained Ulster's dominant Gaelic clan.

It might have been expected that 'Bloody' Mary Tudor's accession would be welcomed in Ireland. There was great enthusiasm among Irish Catholics at England's Counter-Reformation and its links to the Habsburg Empire through her marriage to Philip II. Yet her desire for Ireland to maintain the Catholic faith was tempered by a need to establish English authority. In 1555, she appointed Hugh Curwen as Archbishop of Dublin, making him responsible for supervising the restoration of Roman-Catholicism, notwithstanding his earlier support for Henry's marriage to Anne Boleyn. Curwen also became the Irish Lord Chancellor and his Protestant sympathies made him lukewarm about his new role, particularly when he found that 'anti-Protestant policies alienated influential members of the Dublin administration'.[j] [7] Although existing Established Church Bishops were required to adhere to Roman-Catholic dogma, a change that they no doubt found more appealing than the prospect of martyrdom, they undertook their new roles with a minimum of conviction and made no effort to communicate with their greatly increased flock by learning

---

[6] In 1476, James IV of Scotland received help from the powerful Campbell clan, who policed Gaelic Scotland on his behalf, to force the ruling Gaelic MacDonald family into surrender, thus bringing the Islands under Royal control. One branch of the MacDonald clan, the Lords of Islay and Kintyre, fought a desperate rearguard action and took refuge in the Glens of Antrim, acquired as a result of a marriage alliance in 1399 between John Mór MacDonald and Margery Bisset, the last heiress of a Norman family long settled there. 'In Ireland they became known as the MacDonnells.'[n] They brought with them other Scottish Highland clans and soon expanded their Ulster lands by further marriage alliances. This caused conflict with the O'Neills, and the Establishment in Dublin saw them as a serious threat to local stability.
[7] There can be little surprise that, in 1558, Curwen was reconfirmed as Protestant Archbishop and Lord Chancellor. 'The English seemed to hope that vagueness in matters of doctrine would ensure an inperceptible change from Catholicism'[o]

Gaelic. The Restoration of Catholic institutions moved slowly, and Catholic administrators found that the Irish clergy were 'unreliable with low standards of religious observance',[k] so that such efforts as were made to improve and stabilise them failed. The bishops were more comfortable when Mary gave 'full support to those at court who thought that tough military action was the only lesson the rebellious Irish would understand'.[l] In 1556, she appointed Thomas Radclyffe, 3rd Earl of Sussex, as Lord Deputy. He inherited a situation where there was no 'consistent and thoroughgoing policy to bring the island under an orderly system of administration'.

Thomas Radclyffe, 3rd Earl of Sussex (c.1526-1583) Having been appointed Lord Deputy of Ireland by Mary Tudor, he found no 'consistent and thorough-going policy to bring the island under an orderly system of administration'.
British (English) School oil on panel Anglesey Abbey © National Trust No. 985182

It was under Mary that the plantation of English settlers as a means of maintaining control became the cornerstone of English policy. When a scheme for planting Ulster was proposed, Mary sent Radclyffe a plan 'to settle the north-east … with Roman-Catholic English in order to keep the Scots out'.[m] He immediately passed laws to suppress Protestantism and to forbid the immigration of Scots to Ireland. The strongly Protestant Bagenal was demoted, despite his considerable military experience gained largely in France, but he remained in Ulster occupying his lands at Newry. Sussex brought from England his young brother-in-law, Henry Sidney. From the first, Sidney played a key part in supporting his policies. He, too, was 'a persuasive advocate of plantation'.[p] Yet he was 'deeply critical'[q] of Mary Tudor's initial efforts; her scheme to plant English Catholics in Ulster never succeeded, and Scots returned to Antrim in greater numbers than before.

Until Mary's attention became diverted by the outbreak of war between England and France, her most ambitious plan for plantation was to expand the

Pale westward by creating colonies of loyal subjects in Laois and Offally, which, in 1557, were renamed Queen's County and King's County (after Philip II). She abandoned Henry VIII's policy of surrender and re-grant, and arranged for the execution or expulsion of indigenous Gaelic nobles, although a proposal to drive out or slaughter all the native inhabitants was rejected. The land was offered to 'Englishmen born in England or Ireland', but most of them arrived from the Pale, so that there was little overall increase in settlers. 'The principal Gaelic families in the [new plantation area] rebelled at least a dozen times in the ensuing decades',[r] only to be put down with increasing savagery. If the English Government had expected to achieve a profit from this plantation, 'in practice, the cost of protecting the colonists, and crushing the surviving dispossessed was ruinous'.[s]

On Elizabeth's accession to the English throne in 1558, the Catholics in Ireland became confused. With the doubts over her legitimacy, she had turned to Mary's widow, Philip II, for support, even dangling the prospect of marriage before him in an effort to avoid a Continental Catholic crusade against her. The Papacy sent large numbers of travelling friars (mostly Jesuits) to Ireland. These were often Irish, but there were Englishmen among them, and all were educated men who were greatly superior in quality to the clergy of Ireland of the first half of the 16th Century. As storm-troopers of the Counter-Reformation they brought many Irish back to Rome, and gave succour to the faithful; they were to be found in the courts of the chieftains[8]; they were advisers and scribes to the mass of the populace; and they helped to unite national feelings with the old religion against English ambitions in Ireland.[t] Yet, when Elizabeth's Protestantism became clear, the Catholic Irish were soon calling for a Roman-Catholic Monarch to restore ecclesiastical and temporal traditions. They approached Philip II, but he was not prepared to risk having England and France joining forces against him, particularly as, between them, they controlled both sides of the Channel, upon which he was dependent for communication between the two parts of his Empire in Spain and the Low Countries. Although some Catholics saw Philip as the rightful King of Ireland, he broke off negotiations in 1564, and delegated any claims that he might have had to Mary Queen of Scots, who was soon to be imprisoned in England.

Elizabeth countered Catholic threats in Ireland by establishing the English form of Communion Service, with provision for a Latin version, for those who did not speak English. She also clarified the authority of her Viceroys (sometimes Lords Lieutenant and sometimes Lords Deputy). They could 'confer knighthoods, levy forces, and had most of the powers of Royalty, except that of minting coinage'.[u] In effect they were Ireland's governors.

---

[8] As late as 1590, the O'Neills, O'Donnells and Maguires were able to offer sufficient protection for Redmond O'Gallagher, the Roman-Catholic Bishop of Derry, to ordain a priest in the Catholic church of Derry. Bishops nominated by the Papacy remained in control of the sees of Derry and Raphoe until the end of the 16th Century. Monastries continued to function in Ulster until well into the reign of James I.

The Viceroy was assisted by a Council, which included the Lord Chancellor, the Chief Justice, a Treasurer at Wars, Marshal of the Army, and noblemen such as the Earls of Ormonde or Kildare.[v] Parliament met only for special purposes and it role was minimal. Each region had a Governor, with Sheriffs for each county and Mayors in the Corporate towns. The judiciary maintained varying degrees of control, although this proved minimal in Ulster.

Sidney was given particular responsibility for Ulster and for dealing with the O'Neills, who, without Bagenal working with them, were proving troublesome. In accordance with Gaelic law, Tyrone had drawn up an entail to his will, which nominated his illegitimate (or more likely adopted) son Matthew, Baron of Dungannon, to succeed him, rather than his belligerent legitimate son, Shane. It would appear that the Dublin authorities had persuaded him to make this change and conveniently forgot Shane's dynastic rights under primogeniture. Shane armed his followers and, in the ensuing conflict, killed Matthew, whose son Brian now became Tyrone's heir. When Shane also overran Tyrone's estates, Sussex had to assist Tyrone to recover them, and they, in turn, ravaged Shane's lands.

In the autumn of 1558, with Elizabeth having firmly established her authority in England, Sussex sailed to Scotland where he laid Kintyre and the southern Hebridean islands to waste to deter any further highland Scottish incursions into Ireland; on his return, he ravished the Scottish settlements in Antrim. He needed help to deal with the MacDonnells, and unwisely sought it from Shane, who had succeeded to the Lordship of O'Neill on the death of his father, thinking that he too would be anxious to see Scottish incursions into traditional O'Neill territory brought to an end. By this time, Shane had murdered most of his O'Neill rivals, and was powerfully positioned to oust the unwelcome Scots. Yet he promptly sided with the MacDonnells and turned on the English. Having gathered a sizeable force about him, he linked with the Geraldine (Fitzgerald) Earls in the south and hired Scots mercenaries. When the O'Donnells objected to his claim of paramountcy, he challenged them by imprisoning Calvagh O'Donnell and forcing Calvagh's wife, Catherine Maclean, widow of the 4th Earl of Argyll, to become his mistress. Having established control, he was determined to keep his territories free of the English and provocatively claimed the Earldom of Ulster, a title already merged with the English Crown.

When Sussex returned to England to attend Elizabeth's Coronation, he was instructed by the ever-cautious Queen to come to terms with Shane and the MacDonnells. Not surprisingly, Shane refused to meet with him without being assured of his security and proposed terms that Elizabeth would not accept. Despite her reluctance to take aggressive action, Sussex, in 1561, sent a small army into Ulster, but his limited force was defeated by Shane at Red Saguns, and an English attempt to assassinate Shane also failed. Elizabeth recalled Sussex to England and instructed Gerald 'The Wizard' FitzGerald, 11th Earl of Kildare to negotiate. In 1562, she invited Shane, who was now in league with the Spanish, to meet her in London and, on arrival, he brought both Ormonde and Kildare with him to guarantee his protection. He was also surrounded by a bodyguard of Gallowglass mercenaries[9] with long hair down to their shoulder blades wearing long-sleeved tunics of linen dyed with saffron, over which woollen mantles were worn. Camden reported 'that they smelled of urine'.[w] Hitherto Elizabeth had only met the upper echelons of Irish Society, who dressed like English aristocrats, except for bare legs and feet. She considered Shane to be a savage. After denouncing the murdered Dungannon as a bastard, he confessed his rebellion to Elizabeth on his knees, emitting ear-splitting yells of anguish as he did so. This noisy and unnerving means of showing contrition was peculiarly Irish, and doubtless caused ructions at Court.[x] When she offered him concessions, he demanded, tongue in cheek, the hand of Sussex's half-sister, Lady Frances Radclyffe in marriage.[10] To stop any further intriguing, Elizabeth recognised him as 'The O'Neill'[11], which confirmed his position as head of the O'Neill clan[12], and gave him a verbal assurance that he would be recognised as heir to the Earl of Tyrone. This was never honoured and the meeting achieved nothing. On his return to Ireland, he continued raiding, plundering and burning. Having murdered Dungannon's eldest son, Brian, it was now Brian's 12-year-old brother, Hugh, who became Lord Dungannon and, in English eyes, was heir to the Tyrone earldom. To provide him with protection, the English whisked Hugh off to the Pale for his upbringing.

When Sussex returned as Lord Deputy in 1563, he embarked on a new expedition against Shane and tried unsuccessfully to divide and rule by persuading Turlough Luineach O'Neill, who after Shane, was the O'Neill strong man, to renounce him. He built new fortifications at Armagh, Carrickfergus and Newry and planned to fortify the garrison at the old religious settlement of Derry. His efforts had little effect, as Elizabeth was still providing insufficient troops for him to act decisively. After a few skirmishes, Shane submitted but, as a sop, it was agreed that the English would recognise the O'Donnells' subservience to him. Sussex now turned to Sorley Boy MacDonnell, leader of the MacDonnells, for help against Shane, but, in 1565, Shane attacked the MacDonnells, slaughtering a great many, although he spared Sorley Boy and some of their other leaders. With the MacDonnell stronghold of Dunluce

---

[9] The gallowglass (or gallóglaigh) were fierce warriors of Norse-Gaelic origin, who arrived as mercenaries from Highland Scotland in support of Gaelic chieftains. They were 'picked and selected men of great and mighty bodies, cruel without compassion ... choosing rather to die than to yield the field'.[y]

[10] This was in accordance with the Gaelic practice of seeking wives from among their enemies to assure their future loyalty.

[11] This made him the most powerful man in Ulster and gave him a mystique that had no parallel in the other Irish provinces.

[12] The archaeic inauguration ritual for Irish chiefs usually involved ceremonies at ancient Neolithic sites. The O'Neill chiefs were 'inaugurated standing on the 'Stone of Kings' shaped like a huge chair at Tullahogue – when he smashed it to pieces in 1601 Lord Deputy Mountjoy knew the symbolic importance of his act'.[z]

together with the Glynns having fallen to him, Shane now controlled most of Ulster.

Sir Henry Sidney KG (1529-1586)
Having replaced Sussex as Lord Deputy in 1565, he played on the rivalries between Gaelic clans and appointed English Lord Presidencies, which challenged their authority with great brutality.
Arnold van Bronckhorst (c. 1566-86) oil on canvas 1573 Petworth Park ©National Trust Images No. 1000115

In 1565, Sidney replaced Sussex as Lord Deputy and immediately pressed Elizabeth to take more vigorous action. He realised that his best hope was to play on the rivalry between the O'Neills and O'Donnells by supporting the O'Donnells and their allies. To restore authority, he strengthened the garrison at Derry and re-appointed Bagenal as Marshal of the Army, although he proved too old to be effective. The English scored several victories and were able to restore Calvagh O'Donnell in Tyrconnell. In the face of concerted opposition, Shane asked Charles IX of France for support, but the French reacted slowly. On the basis that attack was the best form of defence, he focused on the English garrison at Derry, where an explosion in the magazine stored in St Columba's church destroyed the English encampment. The demoralised English troops retired to Carrickfergus, leaving Derry, despite its strategic location, without a garrison until 1600. Buoyed up by this success, Shane led his army into the Pale, but failed in an attempt to capture Dundalk. On his return, the O'Donnells, with an inferior force, defeated him at Farsetmore. Although he was able to escape the field, he threw himself on the mercy of the MacDonnells, who assassinated him. His pickled head was sent to Carrickfergus, from whence it was taken to Dublin to be set up on a spike over the Castle. In 1569, he was attainted posthumously and his O'Neill lordship was abolished; his clan immediately recognised Turlough Luineach O'Neill as 'The O'Neill' and continued efforts to destroy English influence in Ulster.

The English found Turlough to be a formidable adversary. He formed an alliance with the MacDonnells, cementing it by marriage to Agnes Campbell, widow of James MacDonnell of the Glynns and the Isles. As an illegitimate daughter of Colin Campbell, 3rd Earl of Argyll, she arrived with a contingent of Scottish mercenaries from Kintyre. Her daughter, Finola 'the dark daughter', married Hugh O'Donnell, Lord of Tyrconnell. By linking with his fomer enemies, the MacDonnells and O'Donnells, Turlough posed a real threat. A memorandum sent from Carrickfergus in 1580 warned Elizabeth:

> Here is a great bruit of 2000 Scots landed in Clandeboye. Turlough Luineach's marriage with the Scot is the cause of all this, and if her Majesty does not provide against her devices, this Scottish woman will make a new Scotland of Ulster. She hath already planted a good foundation; for she in Tyrone, and her daughter in Tyrconnell, do carry all the sway in the north.[aa]

In an effort to curb Turlough's power, the English refused to recognise him as Earl of Tyrone and continued to support Dungannon as the rightful claimant. Sidney did not believe that Turlough would live long, given his 'ill diet, and continual surfeit'[bb] and it was reported that 'Sir Turlough is very old and what with decay of nature through his age and overrun with drink which daily he is in, he is utterly past government'.[cc] Yet he survived until 1595, by when he had established a formidable Gaelic coalition against the English.

Elizabeth was powerless against Turlough, but continued to offer Dungannon protection to retain his loyalty to the English. As their protégé, he was sent to England for training in the hope that he would return to 'introduce English law, culture and speech'.[dd] He did not let them down. In 1580, he supported English forces against the second Desmond Rebellion in Munster. In 1584, he assisted Perrot's forces against the Scots in Ulster.

Sidney now turned his attention to the south. He concentrated on settling quarrels between rival clans, who were tearing themselves apart in almost continuous warfare. Most disagreements were between chiefs and their septs rather than with the English. In an effort to re-establish authority in Munster and Connaught, he replaced local chieftains with 'Lord Presidencies' (provincial military governors), and disbanded the chieftains' armies. This was easier said than done and the locals, particularly the FitzGeralds of Desmond (sometimes called FitzThomas, and only very remotely connected to the FitzGeralds of Kildare), saw the English presence as an intrusion. Internecine warfare continued, but Sidney made progress by offering to support those who would submit to the English. In 1565, there was a pitched battle at Affane in County Waterford between the FitzGeralds led by Gerald 'The Rebel' FitzGerald, 14th Earl of Desmond, and the Butlers, led by the Anglo-Norman Thomas Butler, 10th Earl of Ormonde ('The Black Earl'), whose family, since the time of Edward I, had received the duty on all wine imported into Ireland. Sidney treated the Butlers severely, but Elizabeth I, having called both sides to London to explain themselves, supported them. Desmond and his brother, John FitzGerald, were imprisoned in London. This left their Captain General, James FitzMaurice FitzGerald, Earl of Clanclare, ("FitzMaurice") to uphold their cause. With the English confiscating their ancestral lands and providing them as grants to settlers, FitzMaurice received widespread support from Irish Catholics in his attempt to stop further incursions by the mainly Protestant English arrivals intent on watering down Irish conflict and opposition.

Thomas Butler, 10th Earl of Ormonde, 'the Black Earl' (1532-1614) In 1569, he supported English efforts to expropriate the lands of his rivals, the Fitzgeralds of Desmond, who gained widespread Gaelic and Continental backing to devastate the new English colony.
Attributed to Steven van der Meulen, Netherlandish, fl. 1543-1568 oil on panel
Photo ©National Gallery of Ireland NGI.4687

In 1569, the English expropriated FitzMaurice's lands at Kerrycurihy, south of Cork. As a devout Catholic, he despised the Protestant English governors opposing him and was provoked into inciting what became known as the First Desmond Rebellion to re-establish Geraldine authority over Ormonde and the Butlers. This became much more threatening, when he sought Philip II's help to curb further Protestant infiltration, and Archbishop MacGibbon of Cashel offered Philip the allegiance of Irish Roman-Catholics. FitzMaurice gathered 4,500 troops against the new English colony at Kerrycurihy and later attacked the Ormonde stronghold at Kilkenny, projecting his action as a Counter-Reformation against English heresy. This was part of a broader Papal plan, which included support for the Northern Rising in 1569 led by English Earls in northern England, Elizabeth's excommunication by Pope Pius V in the following year designed to free her subjects from allegiance to her, and the Massacre of St-Bartholomew against the Huguenots in France. The English had to move fast. With help from Ormonde and other clans hostile to the Geraldines, they mustered six hundred men, including the young Dungannon in command of a troop of horse; a further four hundred arrived by sea. They adopted terror tactics, devastating the lands of FitzMaurice's allies and killing civilians at random. By 1570, most of his allies had been forced into submission, but he soldiered on with guerrilla tactics for a further three years. Although he was supported by a small contingent of French troops, which landed at Dingle, the Spanish failed to send an invasion force, despite their recent defeat of the Ottoman fleet at Lepanto.

Sir John Perrot In 1571, as Lord President of Munster, his aggression led to the defeat the Geraldines. In 1584, he became Lord Deputy, but, despite his administrative skills, he fell out with his colleagues.
Courtesy of Haverfordwest Town Museum

Believing that he lacked Elizabeth's full support, Sidney retired as Lord Deputy and left Ireland; in 1571, he was replaced by Sir William Fitzwilliam. Sir John Perrot was appointed Lord President of Munster and continued Sidney's brutal tactics. He forced Fitzmaurice back into the mountains of Kerry with his few remaining supporters and, in 1573, cornered him at Castlemaine. Perrot was never a man to offer quarter. Although FitzMaurice was permitted to submit with security of his life, eight hundred of his followers were hanged, and the use of Gaelic customs and private armies was banned. When FitzMaurice continued to incite opposition, his lands were again confiscated. In 1575, he left for France to seek help from European Catholic powers. This caused such concern in England that, against Perrot's advice, Desmond and his brother, John, were released from the Tower to stabilise the Geraldines and were allowed to rebuild their estates. Their private armies were to be limited to twenty horsemen, and their tenants were to pay rent rather than provide military service. When Perrot temporarily left Ireland, Ormonde took the opportunity to establish himself as the most powerful magnate in the south on the back of his loyalty to the English Crown.

The plantation of settlers was still considered the most appropriate means for the English to maintain control. While settlements generally took place on lands expropriated from rebellious chieftains, this was not always the case. In November 1571, Sir Thomas Smith, a Privy Councillor and close political ally of William Cecil, the Secretary of State, persuaded Elizabeth to allow him to colonise the Ards peninsula and Upper Clandeboye in eastern Ulster. This was one of a number of occasions when Elizabeth meddled with her Government's efforts to settle Ireland without consulting her advisers on the ground. Her motive, as always, was to save the Royal Exchequer from having to foot the bill. Smith's objective was to cut Gaelic Ireland off from Gaelic Scotland by creating a plantation of 'loyal English subjects who would bring civility, order and the Protestant faith to the barbarous people there'.[ee] He hoped 'to sweep away the native Irish, except for 'churls' to plough the soil',[ff] insisting that:

> every Irishman shall be forbidden to wear English apparel or weapon upon pain of death. That no Irishman, born of Irish race and brought up Irish, shall purchase land, bear office, be chosen of any jury.[gg]

Even Cecil invested £33 6s. 8d. in Smith's scheme, and about one hundred prospective planters arrived at Strangford, led by Smith's son, another Thomas. As soon as they advanced north they faced ferocious opposition. The land granted was the 'Country' of the Lord of Upper Clandeboye, Sir Brian MacPhelim O'Neill, who had recently been knighted by the Lord Deputy, Sir William Fitzwilliam, in gratitude for his loyal service against Shane and Turlough. No one warned either Fitzwilliam or Sir Brian of the impending expedition. Sir Brian furiously destroyed every building that might offer the settlers shelter. Having taken refuge at Ringhaddy Castle, they appealed to Dublin for help. Fitzwilliam was equally angry and 'resented the intrusion on his own authority'.[hh] He feared that their arrival would cause an Ulster insurrection at a time when he was still trying to deal with unrest in Munster. In October 1573, the younger Smith was stabbed to death by Irish members of his own household, and his body was boiled and fed to the dogs. The planned plantation came to nothing.

In August 1573, Walter Devereux, 1st Earl of Essex set out from Liverpool, after raising £10,000 for a second expedition, to occupy a similar grant of land made by Elizabeth encompassing Clandeboye, the Route, the Glynns of Antrim and Rathlin Island. It extended as far inland as Lough Neagh and the River Bann into land occupied by the O'Neills, MacDonnells and MacQuillans and was in direct contravention of their rights. Elizabeth financed half of the cost of one thousand British troops sent with Essex. After a stormy crossing, he reached Carrickfergus with his imposing force. When Sir Brian submitted, Essex took possession of 10,000 head of his cattle. This was too much. After bribing the guards at Carrickfergus, he escaped with his cattle to Massereene. Faced with mounting hostility, Essex wrote to the Queen that many of the colonists had lost heart and returned home. When some of his troops threatened to desert without better pay, he hanged them. In an effort to give him encouragement, Elizabeth appointed him Governor of Ulster. Despite promising her that he 'would not willingly imbrue his hands with more blood than the necessity of the cause requireth', he shed a great deal of it. When he was called away to deal with the Desmond rebellion, he left the young Dungannon in command. Despite having shown loyalty in Munster, Dungannon was horrified at the way Essex was treating his fellow Ulstermen. In November 1574, Essex invited Sir Brian and his family to join him in Belfast 'to parley over the disputed colonisation'.[ii] After spending three days feastling pleasantly together, he arranged to have all Sir Brian's men slaughtered. Sir Brian was sent with his wife and brother to Dublin, where they were hung, drawn and quartered. In an effort to retain Dungannon's loyalty, he was granted large parts of Tyrone and Armagh, but he was losing faith with the English and, in 1584, secretly became Turlough's Tanist (heir).

Walter Devereux, 1st Earl of Essex In 1573, Elizabeth funded half the £10,000 cost of his failed settlement in County Antrim. The Lord Deputy, Sir William Fitzwilliam, was furious not to be pre-warned of the plan.
Artist unknown c. 1575 oil on panel © *National Portrait Gallery, London NPG No. 4984*

Essex did not stop there. In the following year, he slaughtered other O'Neill clan members, who had taken refuge on an island at Banbridge and wreaked havoc deep into Tyrone by declaring war on Turlough. Three frigates, led by Sir Francis Drake, were sent to the Glynns to break the power of the MacDonnells. After landing three hundred and eighty men at Arkill Bay on the east end of Rathlin Island, Drake's men were instructed by Essex to storm the castle where the MacDonnells' women and children were being protected by fifty men. After a four-day pounding from the ships' cannon, the castle's wooden ramparts were destroyed. Although the garrison surrendered after being granted security of their lives, the furious attackers killed everyone, leaving the distraught Sorley Boy MacDonnell watching from the shore.

Far from reproving Essex's cruelty, Elizabeth praised the 'good services' of his men. He reported to her: 'I will not leave the enterprise as long as I have any foot of land in England unsold.' Yet Sidney, recently restored as Lord

Lieutenant with increased powers, had no confidence that Essex would succeed. In September, he arrived at Clandeboye to find it 'utterly disinhabited', with Kinelarty 'desolated and waste' and Carrickfergus 'much decayed and impoverished'. He observed that Rathlin was 'very easy to be wonne at any tyme but very chardgious and hard to be held'.[ii] Although Essex was now Earl Marshall of Ireland, he was suffering from dysentery and retired to Dublin, where he died. Sidney reported that a better man might have been more successful and urged the Queen to promote

> the introduction of collonys of English and other loyal subjects, whereby a perpetual inhabitation would have ensued to be a recompense as well of that which was spent

and to build up the 'strength of the country against all forreyne invasion'. He argued that a plantation was 'no subject's enterprise, a prince's purse and power must do it'.[kk] He 'believed that all Ireland should be brought to adopt English law and the reformed religion, and to submit to the power of the Crown'.[ll] He began breaking up lands previously controlled by Irish chieftains into shires along English lines, but was still limited by the meagre resources that Elizabeth would make available to him. His only means of maintaining control was by funding a substantial army out of the Cess, a tax levied on landowners in the Pale. When they complained at this, she censured him for his extravagance and, in 1578, recalled him to London. On arrival he was received coldly and retired to Ludlow after being appointed President of the Welsh Marches. It was only when she faced war with Spain that she realised that Ireland, with its many natural harbours, was a potential bridgehead for an invasion of England and took concerted steps to force it into submission.

In 1579, Fitzmaurice, reinvented as a soldier of the Counter-Reformation, returned from Europe to initiate another Catholic revolt against Elizabeth. He had persuaded both Pope Gregory XIII and Philip II to support a new Irish uprising by funding an expedition with Italian and Spanish troops. This became known as 'the Second Desmond Rebellion'. After landing at Smerwick on the Dingle peninsula, he established a fortified enclave and linked up with John FitzGerald and other clans still threatened with the loss of their ancestral estates. When Fitzmaurice was killed in a skirmish in August, John assumed the leadership. Although his brother, Desmond, had initially remained neutral, the English proclaimed him a traitor, and he joined the rebels, sacking Youghal, Kinsale and the new English settlements. The new Lord Deputy, Arthur, 14th Lord Grey de Wilton, sent William Pelham with English troops to deal with the insurgency. With Ormonde's support, Pelham laid Geraldine lands to waste and killed their tenants, rapidly bringing it under control. At Easter 1580, he captured the Desmond fortress of Carrigafoyle at the mouth of the Shannon, cutting off the Geraldine forces further west from the rest of Ireland.

This did not settle matters. A second Catholic rebellion broke out in Leinster in the south east . On 25 August, insurgents ambushed and massacred a large English force under Grey at Glenmalure. Yet they failed to capitalise on their victory or to link up with the Geraldines holed up at the Shannon. Elizabeth sent the respected Admiral William Winter with a fleet, which included Richard Bingham as Captain of the *Swiftsure*, to prevent more foreign troops from landing at Munster ports. On arriving at Smerwick, Winter bombarded six hundred Italian and Spanish troops, who had landed to assist the Geraldines. Within two days, they surrendered, and Grey reported their execution to Elizabeth. With Ormonde's continued help, the English now brought the rebellion under control and, in mid-1581, Elizabeth broke its momentum by offering a general pardon. Although John FitzGerald retained a few followers, he was killed north of Cork in the following year, and Desmond was pursued by English forces, but, in November 1583, he too was killed near Tralee by the local clan O'Moriarty, who claimed the prize of £1,000 of silver placed on his head.

With each side having adopted a scorched earth policy, all the crops had been destroyed. This resulted in famine, and, with plague breaking out in Cork, an estimated 30,000 Irish died. Grey's secretary, Edmund Spenser (the poet), described their suffering:

> They looked like anatomies of death, they spake like ghosts crying out of their graves; they did eat of the dead carrions, happy were they if they could find them, yea, and one another soon after ... In short space there were almost none left, and a most populous and plentiful country suddenly made void of man and beast.[mm]

With the Geraldine axis of power now broken, Walter Raleigh, who had been involved in the assault on Smerwick, joined the clamour for people of English birth to be settled on Desmond's confiscated estates. In 1584, with an uneasy peace having been restored, Perrot returned as Lord Deputy to oversee the settlement of 600,000 acres of Desmond's former lands in Munster. They were to be divided among thousands of English soldiers and administrators, and Protestant colonists arriving from England. Raleigh was granted 30,000 acres, but quickly sold them to fund his extravagant lifestyle. Most of the land was parcelled out to undertakers in portions of between 4,000 and 12,000 acres for subdivision among colonists. Munster and Leinster still contained a sizeable population of Old English, the bilingual descendants of the Norman knights, and these created a buffer to bridge the cultural gap with the native Irish. Thirty-five separate areas were established with plans 'to bring in a specified number of families to work the land'.[nn] There was soon trouble. Despite reasonable demand from settlers, the area proved too extensive for the new English arrivals to manage, and they could not cover the whole area, which left them exposed to the war between England and Spain, which broke out in 1585. The new settlers tried to enforce Protestantism in a language that the thoroughly discontented Irish did not understand. Efforts to convert them were quickly abandoned. It proved simpler to water down the native Irish by expanding the colonisation. This became the template for future plantations.

43

Although the Munster plantation started slowly, Perrot was successful in coming to an 'unusually even-handed' arrangement for a land purchase in western Connaught. This was overseen by Bingham, who was appointed Governor and was knighted by Perrot at Dublin Castle. With rebellion breaking out in all quarters, Perrot and Bingham approached rival clans for help in putting down insurgencies, but could not agree on which clans to support. The principal rivalry was between the MacDonnells in Antrim and the Anglo-Norman MacWilliam Burkes in Connaught. Perrot led troops into Ulster to deal with an influx of MacDonnells from Scotland and, in 1586, reached a 'mutually beneficial' arrangement with them. Bingham, meanwhile, challenged the MacWilliam Burkes. When he prosecuted their leaders, Perrot became concerned at his destructive tactics and offered them three months protection, but banned the future use of the MacWilliam name. The Burkes used this window of opportunity to rise up in even greater numbers against the MacDonnells and sent a force into Ulster against them. Although Bingham had the military strength to make the Burkes submit, Perrot tried to prevent him from interfering. This made Bingham furious. He hanged Edmund Burke, their leader, and installed John Bingham, his brother, at their stronghold at Castlebarry. He seized their cattle and imposed fines to cover the costs of his campaign; by 1586, he had arranged seventy executions at Galway assizes on grounds of disloyalty. When he captured Castle Cloonoan in County Clare from the O'Briens, Connaught was in general rebellion. Although Perrot wanted a truce, Bingham was determined to receive proper assurances from the Burkes. Meanwhile the MacDonnells brought a strong force to Connaught from Ulster to challenge the apparently weakened Burkes. Despite his inferior numbers, Bingham routed them at Ardnarea, forcing them back into the River Erne. He gave no quarter; of the 3,000 Scottish troops, including women and children, only eighty escaped the battle and even these were killed by the local Irish.

Despite their opposing tactics, Perrot and Bingham achieved some semblance of peace. Yet Perrot remained unhappy with Bingham and charged him with brutality. He also asked for Bagenal to be withdrawn on grounds of age, causing lasting antagonism between them. When Walsingham in England was asked to mediate between Perrot and Bingham, he dismissed Perrot's case, particularly because the ending of hostilities in Connaught had made it prosperous again. Bingham showed no contrition. When Spanish sailors were forced ashore after the Armada in 1588, he arranged their wholesale slaughter.

The Armada was a further Spanish effort to achieve a Counter-Reformation in England, but it proved a turning point in England's policy towards Ireland. Before her execution, Mary Queen of Scots had nominated Philip II as her heir on the Scottish, English and Irish thrones (although she later revoked this will in favour of her son James, if he should become a Catholic). Philip delegated his claim to his daughter, the Infanta Isabella, and it was on her behalf that the Armada set sail in May 1588 with many Irish emigrés on board. After battling through the channel, twenty-five great Spanish galleons journeyed up the North Sea and around northern Scotland, only to be wrecked on Ireland's west coast.

3,000 Spanish castaways landed on Irish soil, at a time when the Lord Deputy had only 1,000 men under his command. Providentially they 'were too exhausted, sick and demoralised to pose a serious threat'.ᵒᵒ The English Government had already concluded that its security could only be assured if the whole of Ireland was subjugated to English rule. Yet European superpowers now saw Ireland as England's Achilles heel, and decisive action was required if English control was not to be compromised.

In 1593, Bingham found himself having to deal with Grace O'Malley from a powerful family of west coast pirates. He had arrested two of her sons, Tibbot Burke and Murrough O'Flaherty and her half-brother, Donal-na-Piopa, all of whom had been involved in the Connaught rebellions. Grace set off to London to complain to Elizabeth at Bingham's brutality and to petition for their release. She arrived at Court wearing a fine gown with a dagger concealed in it (which had to be removed), but she claimed it was entirely for her own protection. Bingham reported that she had been 'nurse to all rebellions in the province for this forty years', and she refused to bow before the Queen as she did not recognise her as her sovereign. Luckily for Grace, Elizabeth was amused. Grace was three years the elder and, with their only common language being Latin, they came to an understanding. Elizabeth agreed to release her kinsmen and even to recall Bingham, if she would end her support for the Irish rebels and piracy against English ships. Although Bingham was temporarily recalled, the rebellion recurred, and he was quickly restored. Grace believed that she had been duped.

Perrot was becoming increasingly eccentric and Bingham was not his only target for abuse. He fell out with Adam Loftus, who was both Archbishop of Dublin and Lord Chancellor, over a plan to divert church funds to build two colleges, and, in 1587, he struck Bagenal to the ground in the Council Chamber, although both seem to have been drunk. His belligerence made him many enemies, and, in January 1588, Elizabeth granted his request to be recalled. Back in England, he joined the Privy Council, but was accused of corresponding with Philip II over the future of England, Ireland and Wales, on what were almost certainly trumped up charges. His enemies also reported derogatory comments that he had apparently made about Elizabeth, who he reputedly described as a 'base bastard piskitchin'[13]. This resulted in him facing a treason trial, which found him guilty. Although Elizabeth was expected to grant him a pardon, he died in the Tower in 1592, before it could be arranged.

Despite the cruelty meted out by the English, it would be an over-simplification to blame the Tudors and the English for the destruction of Gaelic Irish civilisation. Yet the collapse of Gaelic social organisation caused lawlessness, which threatened the stability of the whole country.ᵖᵖ Although the Irish remained Roman-Catholic, they scrambled for booty following the dissolution of the Irish monasteries. It was the ambition of Irish chieftains 'to

---

[13] Although this is quoted in many sources, the meaning of 'piskitchin' is not explained, but was self-evidently derogatory.

emulate aristocratic grandeur, privilege and land tenure as existing in England',[qq] and many of them 'exercised power without responsibility … and tyranny without scruple'.[rr] It was interminable sequences of revolt between Gaelic chiefs and their followers which damaged crops, farming, property, and ancient foundations, and spelt the end of an ancient order.[ss]

Ancient settlements in Ulster were greatly damaged during outbreaks of strife. Only in the east were some 'poor towns inhabited'.[tt] 'Sir John Davies considered Ulster to be a wilderness, where the people had 'no certain habitation in any towns or villages'.'[uu] The English had great difficulty campaigning in the province, as there were no centres of population to attack, and nomadic Ulstermen challenged English columns without warning. Following on from Sidney's efforts to split Ireland into divisions, Perrot divided the western part of Ulster into six administrative counties. (Antrim and Down, where the English retained some influence, had already existed as counties since de Courcy's time.) This was the prelude to attempts to establish control.

Chapter 3

The rise to pre-eminence of
Hugh O'Neill, Earl of Tyrone
1585 – 1603

By the early 1590s, the English had formed a provincial presidency in Ulster led by Sir Henry Bagenal, Sir Nicholas's son. He became particularly riled when Dungannon eloped with his sister, Mabel, writing to Cecil (now Lord Burghley): 'I can but accurse myself and fortune that my blood, which my father and myself have often spilled in repressing this rebellious race, should now be mingled with so traitorous a stock and kindred.'[a]

Hugh O'Neill, Lord Dungannon, Earl of Tyrone (c.1540-1616)
Having been protected by the English after his father's and brother's murders, he was shocked at English brutality, and sought Spanish and Papal support to rebel against them.
Artist unknown oil on canvas 19th Century © National Museums Northern Ireland BELUM.U2300

Bagenal refused to pay Mabel's dowry, but, despite his distaste for him, the English were still hoping to mould Dungannon to maintain control. In 1585, he had at last been summoned to the Irish Parliament as Earl of Tyrone, and, two years' later, came to Court in London to receive a grant of his grandfather's estates. The English insisted on his lands being surveyed to reserve areas where they could install garrisons, over which he would have no authority.

Tyrone did not enjoy the complete trust of the English, who continued to incite O'Neill rivalries to weaken the clan's power. They adopted a policy of 'divide and rule', breaking up larger clans into smaller groupings. In mid-1586, they came to terms with Sorley Boy MacDonnell, who had recaptured Dunluce Castle from the O'Neills. This resulted in The Route being divided between the MacDonnells and the MacQuillans. In 1587, Perrot seized the fifteen-year-old Hugh Roe O'Donnell, imprisoning him in Dublin Castle in an attempt to prevent an alliance between the O'Donnell and O'Neill clans. By now, Tyrone was beginning to distrust the English, fearing that they had the power to seize back the lands they had granted to him. He believed it would be a better course to build his authority among the Gaelic chieftains and to maintain a dialogue with the Spanish. In 1588, he made a point of offering food and shelter to the crew of a Spanish ship from the Armada wrecked at Inishowen and spared those who landed.

With his authority among the O'Neills growing, Tyrone took the law into his own hands by arranging to kill Shane's son, Gaveloc, who disputed his rights to some of Shane's former lands. In 1592, he assisted the escape of Hugh Roe O'Donnell from Dublin Castle. It was the dead of winter and, although Hugh Roe lost his two big toes from frostbite, he got away with help from Tyrone's allies. On returning to Ulster, his father abdicated in his favour, allowing him to become The O'Donnell and Lord of Tyrconnell. He supported the Catholic Bishops in Tyrconnell, who had held a Synod, after which James O'Hely, Archbishop of Tuam, had called on Irish nobles to seek Spanish aid for a great rebellion, claiming Philip II as their rightful Monarch under Mary Queen of Scots' will. This induced Hugh (or Cuconnach) Maguire of Fermanagh to raise an army, which attacked Sligo and Roscommon.

Tyrconnell realised that, if a rebellion in Ulster was to be successful, it would require Tyrone's support, but Tyrone was cautious of adopting the mantle to champion his fellow Gaelic lords and did not sever his English connections immediately. When Bagenal called on him, as his brother-in-law, to assist in putting down Maguire's rebellion, Tyrone demonstrated his loyalty by joining him in Fermanagh. In 1593, despite making an unsuccessful siege of Enniskillen, they defeated Maguire at Belleek, where Tyrone was wounded. Despite this, Tyrconnell supported Tyrone's efforts to establish prominence among the O'Neills and led two attacks to try to force Turlough to abdicate. This resulted in Tyrone being inaugurated as The Great O'Neill on the remains of the chair at Tullahogue, and he secretly pledged support for Tyrconnell against the English. This encouraged Tyrconnell to mount a counter-attack. In June 1594, Maguire helped Tyrconnell to recapture Enniskillen and to force the Crown Sheriff out of Donegal. English reinforcements under Bingham were later ambushed and destroyed.

With Tyrconnell's encouragement, Tyrone progressively shed his natural diffidence and began to listen to Spanish offers of support. After being warned of rumours of an English plot to take his life, he considered Fitzwilliam and other members of the Dublin Establishment 'unscrupulous and unchivalrous'.[b] He was also riled when he did not receive any reward or compensation for providing Bagenal with support. Mabel soon became disenchanted with Tyrone and returned to her brother, but died shortly after. Tyrone now concluded that his efforts to gain supremacy over rival O'Neill interests would be better served by allying with the Highland Scots and the Spanish. When Fitzwilliam heard rumours of this, he summoned him to Dundalk and accused him of disloyalty, but he had no evidence with which 'to proceed against him on a charge of foreign conspiracy'.[c]

Following the fall of Enniskillen, the English sent Sir John Norris, a soldier with a fearsome record of cruelty, and, in August 1594, he retook it with a strong force. Although Tyrone travelled to Dublin to assure the new Lord Deputy, Sir William Russell, of his loyalty, he was continuing to plot with the Spanish and other Gaelic lords to launch a Counter-Reformation. When he was allowed to return to Ulster unmolested, he made ready for his rebellion. While returning from Enniskillen, Norris turned on Tyrone to try to nip any Spanish invasion plans in the bud and to prevent the arrival of Scottish troops promised by the Catholic Earl of Huntly. Yet Tyrone was warned and galvanised the other Gaelic lords as never before. In February 1595, his half-brother, Art O'Neill captured the Blackwater Fort before Norris could challenge him. Tyrone was no longer reliant on gallowglass mercenaries; he had received gunpowder and equipment from Spain[14] and from the Highland Scots, and had trained a sizeable force from among his own peasantry. News reached Dublin that he had 6,000 men in arms, including 4,000 musketeers and 1,000 cavalry. In May, the O'Donnells, Maguires and O'Neills attacked Longford and recaptured Enniskillen. Shortly after this, Tyrone at last forced Turlough to abdicate, thereby becoming The O'Neill, although he had for some time had this status, and Turlough died soon after. This cemented all the O'Neill interests behind him. In 1596, he ravaged Louth as far as Drogheda, and defeated a small English army under Bagenal at Clontibret. The English rushed troops to Ireland and proclaimed him a traitor. To the Irish, he was now 'the last and greatest of Gaelic Kings', the last King of Ulster. With support from former rival chieftains, he promoted himself as champion of the Roman-Catholic Church, despite lacking any strong religious conviction and having been brought up as an Anglican.

With Tyrone able to rely on continuous supplies of arms and money from Spain, the stage was set for what became known as the Nine Years' War. In April 1596, Alonso Cobos led a Spanish mission to Ireland to treat with Tyrone and Tyrconnell. Tyrone offered to make Ireland a Spanish vassal, suggesting that Archduke Albert, Governor of the Spanish Netherlands, should be crowned

---

[14] The Spanish motive for backing Tyrone was to deflect English troops away from their support for the Dutch rebels in the Netherlands.

as Prince of Ireland, but Philip II turned this down. His forces were hard pressed in the Low Countries and, while he wanted to encourage the rebels, he could not afford to deploy Spanish troops on a second front in Ireland. Yet in July 1596, two Spanish ships landed arms and ammunition at Killybegs in Donegal. In October, a second Spanish fleet carrying Irish noblemen, soldiers and priests was wrecked in a storm. This caused the English to embargo trade with Spain.

Without having Spanish soldiers on the ground, Tyrone used guerrilla tactics. Although his forces were linked with those of Tyrconnell and Maguire, he would not risk a pitch battle with Norris's well-trained British troops; the rebels remained 'elusive, and would strike without warning.'[d] Tyrone's tactic was to temporise with the English authorities, while harassing the supply lines of their forward garrisons positioned to maintain peace. Pledges to heretics meant nothing, after all, and the holy war continued:

> each truce was followed by an attack; each undertaking was broken; and each sworn statement gave way to perjury. Every lull was the signal for an atrocity, an incendiary attack, an investment of a fortress, or a cattle raid.[e]

By these means, he continued for two years to disrupt the English, while managing to defer their incursion onto his estates.

In 1598, a cessation of hostilities was agreed, and Tyrone was formally pardoned. He used the lull in hostilities to build up his forces. In August, he was joined by Tyrconnell and Maguire in an attack on Portmore fort in Armagh. When Bagenal led a large English army to relieve its garrison, he was ambushed at the Yellow Ford on the Blackwater River. Bagenal was killed and his force was crushingly defeated. This was a serious English setback. Tyrone's success led to renewed outbreaks of unrest further south in King's and Queen's Counties, where planters again came under attack. In Munster, the settlers were driven out. In Ulster, only Carrickfergus and Newry remained under English control. Yet Tyrone allowed the British troops remaining from the Yellow Ford to retire to Newry and failed to drive home his advantage. Although he had the opportunity to march on Dublin, his objectives were limited to becoming 'the unchallenged ruler of Ulster, not of Ireland as a whole'.[f]

Tyrone believed that foreign intervention was needed to drive the English out. Despite his growing reputation, he was not an experienced field commander and his army made itself unpopular by feeding on plunder as it moved. Being at risk of losing English control of Ireland, Elizabeth was exasperated with him. With great reluctance, she invested huge sums there, rising to a staggering £2,000,000 by the end of her reign, about a half of her total wartime expenditure between 1585 and 1603.[g] She was in no mood to take prisoners. Her 1598 instruction to Sir George Carew, Deputy of Munster, when sent to carry 'her gracious pleasure' into effect, authorised him and her officers, 'to put suspected Irish to the rack, and to torture them, when they should find it convenient'.[h] In 1599, urgently needing to restore order, she appointed her favourite, Robert Devereux, 2nd Earl of Essex, as Earl Marshal of England and sent him to Ireland with 12,000 troops, the greatest army ever seen there.

Robert Devereux, 2nd Earl of Essex (1566-1601) In 1599, as Elizabeth's favourite, he became Lord Lieutenant with 12,000 troops to defeat Tyrone. Yet disease reduced them to 2,500, and he was forced into ignominious terms. *Marcus Geeraerts, the younger, (1562-1636) oil on panel 1599 Anglesey Abbey © National Trust No. 985187*

Tyrone and Tyrconnell were desperate and again sought help from Spain. On the death of his father, Philip II, in September 1597, the inexperienced Prince of Asturias, now Philip III, was determined to send support. After protracted negotiations, he acted against the advice of his reluctant ministers and agreed to launch a Spanish expedition, despite his pressing need for Spanish reinforcements in the Low Countries. He argued that it would deflect English troops away from supporting the Dutch and would denude Elizabeth's hard-pressed resources. (She had already lost 40,000 troops in Ireland.) When France at last made peace with Savoy, Spanish troops could be spared, and preparations for the Irish expedition began. The plan was to land 6,000 experienced troops, making Ireland the base for a renewed attempt to place the Infanta Isabella on the English throne. Tyrone and Tyrconnell had already agreed that a force of this magnitude should land at Cork or Waterford, but, if in lesser numbers, it should disembark at Limerick or Donegal.

On his arrival in Ireland in March 1599, Essex was appointed Lord Lieutenant. His new English forces were deployed to strengthen the Pale and regarrison the castles in Meath and Louth. When Essex levied further troops, he received seasoned soldiers from the Low Countries. To Elizabeth's fury, he began his counter-attack in Leinster and Munster, despite being aware that his main challenge was in Ulster. Yet he hoped to detach the Leinster and Munster Lords in the South from supporting Tyrone. This proved fruitless. An English detachment was routed by the O'Byrnes in Wicklow, and a larger force under Sir Conyers Clifford was destroyed by Tyrconnell in the Curlew Hills in County Roscommon. With Tyrconnell having established control of Connaught, in 1600, Tyrone brought his army south to Munster, where he completely destroyed the fragile English plantation. When the FitzGeralds and Butlers joined him, the Irish rebel forces attacked the suburbs of Dublin. On returning to Donegal, he received tokens of encouragement from the Pope. More tangibly, he also received Spanish supplies. Don Martin de la Cerdá delivered 2,000 Spanish arquebuses with powder and 20,000 ducats to resupply the O'Neill and O'Donnell forces, but he also came with news of another delay in the Spanish expedition, *La Jornada de Irlanda*.

When Essex at last came north, he had only 2,500 men and, despite involvement in a few inconclusive skirmishes, his troops were starting to desert. This forced him into a humiliating truce, offering terms, which allowed Tyrone to retain control of all the lands he had acquired without having fought a battle. Inexplicably, the terms were not written down, but, if Tyrone is to be believed (and he was an arch-dissembler), they were completely one-sided. No more English garrisons were to be established; English and Irish 'zones of influence' were agreed; the Roman-Catholic faith was to be openly taught and churches were to return to the old faith; there were to be no English clergy in Ireland; the Pope was to be recognised as Governor of the Church in Ireland; a Roman-Catholic University was to be established; all great offices of state were to be held by Irishmen, who were free to travel to the Continent at will; and those whose lands had been forfeited were to have them restored. Elizabeth was furious, and Essex was in a desperate personal situation. He deserted his post and returned to England to lead an ill-advised rebellion against the English Government. In 1601, he lost his head at the Tower of London. Tyrone had every opportunity to capitalise on his success, but again failed to march on Dublin, preferring to wait for the Spanish invasion, although this was hardly needed. By September 1599, when he at last asked Pope Clement VIII for financial support, he was losing his advantage.

Essex was replaced as Lord Lieutenant by Charles Blount, 8th Lord Mountjoy[15], who was sworn in as Lord Deputy on 28 February 1600. Despite a fetish for excessive clothing to ward off the cold, Mountjoy was an inspired and fearless commander. He was surrounded by able subordinates, including Sir George (later Lord) Carew, President of Munster, Sir Arthur Chichester, Governor of Carrickfergus, and the military commander, Sir Henry Docwra. Mountjoy was determined to break the Ulster rebellion by laying waste the countryside and starving the people.

> He preferred to fight in winter, when it was more difficult for the Irish to hide in the leafless woods, when their stores of corn and butter could be burned and when their cattle down from their summer pastures could more easily be slaughtered.[i]

---

15 Mountjoy had been involved in a longstanding affair with Essex's sister, Penelope, who was estranged from her husband, Sir Robert Rich. He was also implicated in Essex's rebellion against the English Government, having offered to send troops from Ireland to support him, but this seems to have remained undiscovered and he was unscathed by his treasonable actions.

Charles Blount, 8th Lord Mountjoy, Earl of Devonshire Having replaced Essex as Lord Lieutenant, he proved an inspired and fearless commander, preventing Tyrone and his allies from linking up with a powerful Spanish force cornered in Kinsale.
The Weiss Gallery, London

Early in 1600, Tyrone began to campaign in Munster, but faced a setback in March when Maguire was killed. Mountjoy managed to break his links with the southern insurgents, and Carew, having systematically captured castles in rebel hands, moved on to campaign in Limerick. In April 1600, the Spanish Mateo de Oviedo, appointed titular Archbishop of Dublin, landed in Donegal with arms, money and ammunition for Tyrone and Tyrconnell. Mountjoy moved quickly. On 7 May 1600, he sent Sir Henry Docwra with a powerful fleet from Carrickfergus carrying an army of 4,000 men and 200 cavalry to drive a wedge between the O'Neills and the O'Donnells. Docwra landed at Culmore on Lough

Foyle and, when his troops murdered the Roman-Catholic Bishop, set up headquarters at Derry, an old ecclesiastical site which he fortified. Although Tyrconnell harassed him, if he ventured out, and stole two hundred of his horses, Docwra accessed reinforcements by sea and won the support of Niall Garbh O'Donnell, who claimed as good a right to the chieftaincy of the O'Donnells as Tyrconnell. Niall Garbh later captured the O'Donnell castle at Lifford. Docwra was also successful in playing on the desire of the O'Cahans in Coleraine and the O'Dohertys in Inishowen to be freed from their O'Neill and O'Donnell overlords. He was soon able to overrun Inishowen and fight on towards Strabane. With Tyrconnell needing help, Tyrone was forced to call off his campaign in the South and to return north by forced marches. Chichester led an attack from the East, while Mountjoy approached from the South to intercept Tyrone at the Moyry Pass, between Dundalk and Newry.

Sir George Carew, Lord Carew, Earl of Totnes His appointment as Lord Deputy of Munster in 1598 was key to Mountjoy's success in settling southern Ireland. He later criticised the Londoners' progress in their plantations in Londonderry.
George Geldorp (attributed)) oil on canvas © Shakespeare Birthplace Trust

Sir Henry Docwra landing at Culmore From the stained glass at Londonderry Guildhall.

SIR·HENRY·DOCWRA·LANDED·AT·CULMORE·16ᵗʰ·APRIL·1600·A.D.

Despite weeks of intense fighting, the English failed to break Tyrone's defences and were forced back in confusion. Mountjoy offered a large reward for Tyrone's capture and provided renewed inducements to gain alliances with rival Irish clans. With his Gaelic and Anglo-Norman support starting to dwindle, Tyrone was forced back to Armagh. By now, Docwra had brokered an alliance with Sir Art O'Neill, Turlough's eldest son, who was ambitious to replace Tyrone as The O'Neill. Mountjoy built strategically placed forts behind enemy lines to limit Tyrone's ability to adopt hit and run tactics. During August, he joined Carew for a successful campaign in Offaly, Kerry and Leinster, but, in the autumn, he broke through between Dundalk and Newry and returned to the offensive against Tyrone.

In December 1600, more Spanish gold and arms were landed in Donegal. Yet the English were continuing to make progress. As reprisals for attacks on English settlers, Chichester's terror tactics caused much slaughter around Coleraine. With Carew driving any remaining Ulster troops out of Munster, English supremacy was gradually restored. Mountjoy offered £2,000 for Tyrone's capture (and £1,000 for his head), but was forced to withdraw his cavalry to Carlingford for lack of fodder. As soon as the winter was over, he pressed back as far as Benburb in Ulster, and Niall Garbh captured Donegal Abbey.

At last, news arrived that *La Jornada de Irlanda* was on its way. With Cerdá having contracted malaria, Don Diego de Brochero y Añaya took over as Spanish naval commander with the experienced Don Juan de Águila in control of their land forces. They argued over where to land; while Brochero favoured the south, Águila wanted to link up with Tyrone and Tyrconnell by landing in Donegal. 'It might have seemed obvious that they should join Tyrone and Tyrconnell in Donegal, as it was now the best defended part of Ireland with its Gaelic and Catholic culture still intact.'[j] Yet, with the objective being a Counter-Reformation, Mathew de Oviedo, the titular Archbishop of Dublin, who was with them, believed that they were arriving in sufficient strength to march in triumph straight to the Capital.[k] As soon as the troops were landed, Brochero was instructed to return his fleet to Spain.

The Spanish fleet of thirty-three ships set out from Lisbon, where further Spanish troops had been embarked, but they carried only 4,432 combatants on departure. A further eleven ships joined them from Andalusia under the command of the Basque Admiral Pedro de Zubiaur. These included the *San Felipe* of nine hundred and sixty tons, carrying most of the expedition's powder and match for the arquebuses. Three hundred leagues from Ireland, Brochero called a conference at sea, at which Águila was out-voted and they agreed to land at Kinsale. They had been at sea for a month and atrocious weather had pushed them a long way off course. The fleet was then scattered by a violent storm off Ireland's west coast. Zubiaur on the *San Felipe* with six accompanying vessels made an abortive attempt to sail north to Donegal before returning to Spain. Águila, with 3,500 troops, eventually landed at Kinsale, from where he issued a proclamation to tell every Irishman that they were attacking heresy, as Elizabeth had been excommunicated by the Pope.[l] Meanwhile, Zubiaur received permission to set out again from Spain with a small force and he landed a further six hundred and twenty-one men further west near Castlehaven.

Mountjoy acted quickly. He arranged for two of Tyrone's more powerful Munster allies, who were expected to reinforce the Spanish, to be seized and sent to the Tower of London. After drawing troops from garrisons around the Pale, he moved south to besiege Kinsale and to prevent Tyrone and Tyrconnell from linking up with the Spanish. Further regiments arrived from England, so that there were soon 12,000 English troops under his command, although illness left only 7,500 combatants. With insufficient men to surround Kinsale, he subjected the Spanish to constant artillery fire from the higher ground above the town, while his cavalry destroyed crops and livestock in the surrounding area.

'Neither Mountjoy [in the south] nor Docwra [in the north] relaxed their campaigns of attrition during the winter of 1600/01.'[m] Docwra was receiving crucial help from Niall Garbh O'Donnell and was joined by Cahir O'Doherty, Lord of Inishowen. Mountjoy captured the crannog [timber-structured] fortress of Lough Lurgan, which held much of the enemy's foodstores and gunpowder, causing famine to set in. Chichester moved from his base at Carrickfergus to ravage Clandeboye. He kept the MacDonnells at bay by crossing Lough Neagh in boats, laying its western shore to waste and murdering its inhabitants.

In the face of continuing threats in Ulster, Tyrone and Tyrconnell were reluctant to leave the north in the depths of winter on a long march to join the Spanish. They were unsure of local support and did not want to risk open battle while travelling through the territory being defended by Carew. Yet, after several weeks of hesitation, they had no choice. The Spanish desperately needed help, and they feared that a further Spanish expedition would not be forthcoming if it was defeated. They set out on their 300 mile trek in two groups to ease supply problems. They had 5,000 infantry and 700 cavalry. Tyrconnell, who left on 23 October 1601, managed to give Carew the slip by making a forced march of forty miles through the frozen Slievephelim Mountains. Having linked up with Gaelic contingents from the south he made contact with Zubiaur's small force at Bandon, north-west of Kinsale. Tyrone, who left seven days later, ravaged Leinster as he went in the hope of cutting Mountjoy's supply lines from the Pale. He then joined Tyrconnell at Bandon.

On 5 December, the combined Gaelic army was encamped a few miles north of Kinsale, in good spirits and confident of victory. Tyrone contacted Àguila, who was desperate for provisions. With the port of Kinsale being blockaded by an English fleet under Admiral Richard Leveson, Àguila had no expectation of Spanish reinforcements. With time being of the essence, he proposed that Tyrone and Tyrconnell should advance on the English at night. With the English turned to face this threat, he would sally out from Kinsale to attack them from behind. With Zubiaur having sent only eighty men from Castlehaven, with the remainder protecting the forts that he had captured, the Gaelic lords still had misgivings about meeting the English in open conflict, but Àguila's advice prevailed.

English morale was not good. They had lost 6,000 men from severe winter cold and dysentery. They feared that their war horses, which were short of forage, would be too weak for effective action. The Irish planned their attack in three columns, but Mountjoy had intelligence of this from captured dispatches and from interrogating prisoners. His position on a ridge to the north west of Kinsale, allowed his scouts to monitor the Gaelic army's movements. Before dawn on 6 December, Sir Henry Power, commanding the English advanced force, saw the Irish lighting slow matches and worked out their likely route. As soon as Tyrone moved forward, the English were called to arms, although Mountjoy left a small force to guard his camp and cover Kinsale. The Irish lacked coordination, and Tyrconnell's men failed to reach their destination by dawn. With Tyrone nervous of facing open warfare on his own, under the cover of a violent squall, he called his men back behind boggy ground, hoping to mire the English cavalry. Despite being under fire from Tyrone's men, the English cavalry, having successfully cleared the bog, were reinforced by a regiment of foot and embarked on a frontal assault. Tyrone's cavalry galloped forward on their inferior lightweight horses, but, when they stalled in traditional fashion brandishing their spears, the English charged. They turned tail, closely followed by O'Neill's foot. A small Spanish contingent was left to make a stand before it was hacked down. When Tyrconnell's men at last arrived, they too joined the flight, 'throwing away their arms 'to run the lighter''.[n] Terrible slaughter was inflicted by the English in pursuit; Mountjoy's surgeon estimated 1,200 Irish casualties with many more dying from wounds and exposure in the ensuing days. The English hanged any Irish prisoners, but the Spanish were spared. The English apparently lost three men.

From his base in Kinsale, Àguila heard the firing. Thinking that the Irish had been victorious, he sallied out from the walls, but was quickly driven back. After seeing the English carrying Irish colours, he knew that the battle was lost. He was permitted to surrender with honour after his men's three month defence of the town and was granted terms to allow his 3,500 survivors to return to Spain with others from the smaller Spanish garrisons round about. Mountjoy treated him with great civility, but Àguila remained very critical of the Irish, seeing them as 'barbarous, untrustworthy and weak'.[o] He did not know that Spanish reinforcements coming to his assistance only turned back on hearing of his garrison's departure.

Tyrconnell joined Zubiaur at Castlehaven, from where, on 27 December, he travelled to Spain to seek further assistance, but he died soon after arrival, possibly as a result of poison. Tyrone escaped north with only sixty men ostensibly to seek a pardon, but was determined to fight on. Yet Mountjoy's policy of destroying his cattle and crops had fatally weakened his power. Large numbers of his supporters died of starvation and were enraged at his failure. He burned his stronghold at Dungannon and retired into the forests of Glenconkeyne.

To end the crippling cost of his campaign[16], Elizabeth and her Government, led by Robert Cecil, instructed Mountjoy to negotiate with Tyrone and to spare his life. The English feared that calls for his unconditional surrender would push him into escaping to Spain at a time when Cecil was trying to negotiate a Spanish peace. It was also feared that Elizabeth did not have long to live, and her likely successor, James VI of Scotland, was expected to show Tyrone mercy. Tyrone was granted safe passage to meet with Mountjoy at Mellifont, near Drogheda, but was kept unaware of Elizabeth's death until negotiations were concluded. He prostrated himself in submission to Mountjoy, resigning all his lands and his title of The O'Neill. Mountjoy insisted on him putting all this in writing, before providing a pardon and restoring his English earldom. The Gaelic chieftains, who had assisted the English, were infuriated at this leniency, but he now recovered much of his former property. With negotiations completed, Mountjoy went to Tullahogue where he pulverised the O'Neills' inauguration chair. With Tyrone's Irish armies having melted away, Mountjoy was left free to deal with

---

[16] To pay the English troops, Cecil had been forced to devalue the Irish currency by one quarter. Large parts of England had been denuded of men of fighting age to join Mountjoy's army.

an outbreak of violence in Kilkenny and Cork, where Carew had imposed the Protestant religion on the locality. When the rebels in the south agreed to swear allegiance to James I, Mountjoy permitted them to practice their religion privately. He now had a breathing place to return to England.

To the horror of senior English officers, Tyrconnell's brother, Rory, was confirmed as Earl of Tyrconnell, and most of his estates were restored. This countermanded Docwra's promises (previously confirmed by Mountjoy) to provide the earldom to Niall Garbh O'Donnell with other lands to go to Cahir O'Doherty[17] and Donal Ballagh O'Cahan[18], who had helped him to gain control. Docwra was incensed, and, in April 1603, took Niall Garbh to Dublin to establish Mountjoy's intentions, but Mountjoy ignored his former promises and rudely dismissed Niall Garbh. It is probable that he believed that control of Ulster would prove easier if magnates like Tyrone and Tyrconnell remained the principal landowners. He may well have been acting on instructions from James I, newly arrived from Scotland. James had faced similar problems on his Gaelic frontier in the Highlands and Islands and his attempts at a plantation in Lewis and later in Kintyre had proved disastrous. He always preferred to work through magnates to maintain peace. With Tyrone having had an English upbringing, it was in keeping with James's style to seek to win him over. Other clan members and smaller clans could then negotiate formal tenancies to avoid future disagreements. English officials became even more enraged when Mountjoy took Tyrone and Rory O'Donnell to Hampton Court to meet James. James received them well, and Tyrone was reconfirmed in his title and core estates, even though most were settled on his tenants; both were reconfirmed in their Earldoms and pardoned, but James would not countenance Catholic worship in Ireland, even in private. 'Any prospect of a further Spanish intervention to achieve a Counter-Reformation in Ireland was now at an end, and it sounded Gaelic Ireland's death knell.'[p] James was full of praise for Mountjoy. In July 1603, he was granted the Earldom of Devonshire and remained Lord Lieutenant, but was not required to return to Ireland. He died in 1606 aged forty-three, as an early addict of tobacco.

---

[17] Niall Garbh O'Donnell was later granted the Finn Valley; O'Doherty was knighted and received the Inishowen Peninsula including the island of Inch.

[18] O'Cahan was told to deny Tyrone's right of overlordship on his estates, thus forgoing rental payments. He also set aside his wife, Tyrone's daughter. When Tyrone threatened him with court action, Sir John Davies, the Solicitor General of Ireland, offered to defend him.

Part 2

Plans to colonise Ulster

Chapter 4

Early steps in colonisation
c.1592 – c.1613

Following Mountjoy's departure from Ireland, his two most able lieutenants in Ulster, Chichester and Docwra, remained as military 'servitors', supervising the areas they had controlled in the war against Tyrone and Tyrconnell.

Sir Arthur Chichester, Lord Chichester As a fearsome military commander, he controlled eastern Ulster on Mountjoy's behalf. In 1604, he became Lord Deputy, and was closely involved in planning the Londoners' plantation.
© *The Belfast Harbour Commissioners*

Chichester came from a minor landowning family in Devon with strong Puritan beliefs. In 1588, aged twenty-five, he had joined *HMS Larke* to fight against the Armada, where he rose to Captain of Marines. In 1592, he arrived in Ireland with his younger brother, John, after a fracas involving a land dispute with servants of the Earl of Bath which forced them to leave England. When eventually restored to favour, Arthur, in 1595, joined Sir Francis Drake on his last expedition to the Americas, commanding 500 men and showing outstanding bravery setting fire to a Spanish frigate. He also commanded a company during Drake's raid on Cadiz, after which he was knighted. In 1597, he served as a mercenary for the French, receiving a French knighthood from Henry IV for his valour at the siege of Amiens, where he was wounded. In 1598, he returned to Ireland to command a large contingent in Essex's ill-fated expedition. A year earlier, his brother, John, who had remained as Governor of Carrickfergus in Ireland, was killed while making an attack with unsufficient men on James MacDonnell, Lord of the Glynns and the Route. John's severed head was sent to Tyrone, where it was kicked around the Irish camp like a football.

In June 1598, MacDonnell brought eight hundred men to besiege Carrickfergus and Belfast, which was commanded by the experienced Sir Ralph Lane. Burning to avenge his brother's death, Arthur Chichester petitioned to be appointed Governor of Carrickfergus, still Ulster's most important township. He then ruthlessly arranged for James MacDonnell to be poisoned. As one of Mountjoy's key lieutenants, he was given command of the Crown's forces in Ulster and was the principal architect of Mountjoy's practice of starving out any garrisons still supporting Tyrone. This caused 'much of south Antrim and north Down [to be] greatly depopulated by slaughter and famine'.[a] 'He was completely unapologetic in the regular despatches he wrote describing the slaughter, hunger and destruction his force inflicted.'[b] In 1603, following Lane's death, he was granted Belfast Castle and its surrounding lands. As the senior English representative in eastern Ulster, he did not consider this adequate reward for his achievements. He complained to the Irish Council that the going rate for selling what he had been granted was only five pounds.

At this time, Belfast was little more than a village clustered round a castle guarding the low tide crossing of the Lagan estuary. Both the castle and village were in ruins, but Chichester could see their potential as a market centre. Despite long absences from Belfast when he became Lord Deputy, he set about building it into a town. He ordered one million bricks to be fired and constructed a Jacobean mansion[19] as his home on the site of the castle. By 1611, there were 'many masons, bricklayers and other labourers' constructing a municipal building. Yet Carrickfergus and Newry remained Ulster's principal urban centres. To increase the Protestant population, Chichester granted leases in Lower Clandeboye to officers serving under him. When these were converted into outright grants, many settled there permanently. Yet the loss was keenly felt by the native Irish so recently expelled from their ancestral lands, particularly as they tended to be in the more fertile areas, and local hostility made them less attractive to British colonists, who were in need of continuing protection from nearby garrisoned strongholds.

As another soldier of fortune, Docwra had a similar background to Chichester. He had arrived in Ireland in 1586 to serve under Bingham, who appointed him constable of Dungarvan Castle on Ireland's south coast. He then returned to England where, like Chichester, he served under Drake at the capture of Cadiz and he, too, was knighted. In 1599, he returned to Ireland with Essex

---

[19] This was accidentally destroyed by fire in 1708.

in command of 4,200 men, who were landed at Carrickfergus to subdue the north. After improving the fortifications at several strategic forts, he was positioned by Mountjoy at Derry, where he was appointed Governor with the task of keeping Tyrone separated from Tyrconnell. Despite failing to deliver the rewards he had promised to his Gaelic allies, when he met Mountjoy in 1603, he pressed his own case for appointment as Lord President of Ulster, but this was turned down. Yet he joined the Irish Privy Council and received an outright grant of lands at Derry, including the right to hold markets and a fair for his own benefit. He was also permitted to hold a market at Lifford nearby. In 1604, James I appointed him Provost of Derry for life with a pension of 20 shillings per day, hoping that he would convert Derry and its surrounding area into a colonial centre by creating a borough with its own corporation, law courts and jail.

With Mountjoy remaining in England, the elderly Sir George Carey was appointed Lord Deputy, although Mountjoy continued as Lord Lieutenant. Initially Carey upheld the terms of the Treaty of Mellifont, and Tyrone gave him no reason to do otherwise. Yet both Chichester and Docwra were critical of the terms of Mountjoy's settlement with Tyrone and Tyrconnell and were determined to undermine their power by dismantling some of the concessions they had received. They began by exploiting divisions between the Earls and minor Gaelic chiefs. The new Solicitor-General, Sir John Davies, who arrived in Ireland in 1603 (and became Attorney-General in 1606), argued that land once forfeited by the Crown belonged to the Crown, 'a dictum that threatened Tyrone as heir to the posthumously attainted Shane O'Neill'. On Davies's advice, Carey began appointing lesser Gaelic chieftains as freeholders in their own right, freed from traditional obligations of allegiance to magnates. This had the effect of enforcing English property rights in Ulster as already implemented in Monaghan and imposing primogeniture to replace the traditional practice under Tanistry of property being left to the lord considered most worthy, which Davies declared 'utterly void in law'.[c] In 1604, with peace restored in Ulster, Derry was incorporated as a city and sheriffs were appointed for the counties of Donegal and Tyrone. With Tyrone still demonstrating model behaviour, the English military presence was cut back from 17,500 men in April 1602, to 4,300 by October 1604 and to 1,014 men in April 1606. Despite being based in England, Mountjoy retained an active interest in Irish affairs and persuaded the Government to appoint his former officers as servitors to supervise an orderly return to peace. James I wisely withdrew the debased currency which, from 1601, had been issued to the army as an economy. Those soldiers paid with it would have found themselves destitute on returning to England, causing many to prefer to remain in Ireland to maintain control, in the hope of being granted land as servitors.

In 1604, rumours started to circulate that Carey had had his fingers in the till during the currency devaluation, and he deemed it wise to resign. With senior English politicians jockeying for position around the new English King in London, the post of Lord Deputy was offered to Chichester. Despite being in debt and worrying whether he had the resources to fulfil the role, he eventually accepted. This positioned him to undo the injustices of the Treaty of Mellifont. He systematically eroded Tyrone's economic position, by 'depriving him of rent and traditional forms of tribute such as hospitality and the right to billet men without payment'.[d]

Chichester still saw the Irish as 'more beasts than men' and realised that Ireland's security was dependent on retaining martial law administered through a network of forts erected both during and after the war. There were seventeen in Ulster, each commanded by an English captain with a ward of between forty and a hundred men. Captains became known as provosts-martial. Although unpaid, they had authority to execute anyone opposing them and were entitled to one-third of each victim's possessions. This positioned them to collect protection money from those they spared. County sheriffs had similar powers and made great efforts to disarm the locality. Even travellers were forbidden from carrying weapons.

At least ten thousand of Tyrone's and Tyrconnell's former fighting men left Ireland to seek employment with Catholic armies on the Continent. Philip III established a permanent Irish regiment in Flanders commanded by Tyrone's sons, Henry and John. Others served in the Holy Roman Empire, France, Bavaria and Poland. Those left in Ireland lived by banditry, taking refuge in the mountains and forests as 'wood-kerne'. Chichester responded by rounding up 'idle swordsmen' and shipping them off in their thousands to fight as mercenaries for Gustavus Adolphus in Sweden, thereby assisting efforts to maintain control at home.

Chichester and Davies also insisted on making the Established Church 'the sole ecclesiastical authority throughout Ireland'.[e] 'Negotiations with Chieftains were aimed at seeking cooperation rather than confrontation in order to bring Ulster safely into the Kingdom as a pacified unit.'[f] There was no choice in the matter. Not only did they face the loss of their estates, but they were required to conform to Anglican dogma. In February 1605, George Montgomery, Dean of Norwich, the King's confidant, was appointed Bishop of the combined dioceses of Derry, Raphoe and Clogher. (see footnote 23 on page 70) From the outset, he employed high-handed efforts to impose Protestantism. On his arrival 'there were very few [Protestant] churches throughout the Province of Ulster, and most of these were in poor repair'.[g] Docwra considered him an irritant, who would unsettle the locality. Like other Protestant bishops, he expanded the Church's money collection process.

> Formerly, small chiefries were paid to Bishops by Ulster Lords, but the new Protestant Bishops claimed huge tracts of lands in demesne, so putting a further strain on the Ulster social order. Coersion was applied to make religious conformity work: Jesuits and seminary Priests were ordered to leave Ireland in June [1605], and the laity was required to attend Divine Worship in accordance with the law.[h]

As Lord Deputy, Chichester subdivided each county into baronies and hundreds. Agreeing boundaries took a considerable time, but, by 1607, each was divided into ten military districts with a fortress at its centre under the command of a governor. At last, 'English organisation and law began to supersede Irish customs.'[i] He appointed justices, sheriffs, coroners and constables, although Tyrone insisted on his trusted kinsmen being appointed as constables on his own estates. 'The aim was to transform Gaelic chieftains from warlords to landed gentlemen in order to promote demilitarisation and create political stability.'[j] 'Both the principal lords and the freeholders would be obliged to pay a yearly tax, or quit rent, to the Crown.'[k] In 1606, with jails and sessions houses having been set up, the area became far more peaceful. Chichester stamped heavily on those who resisted, but those who conformed were treated leniently, to the chagrin of former English soldiers still seeking areas of land on which to settle, and they continued to regard the Irish with suspicion. The chieftains' traditional powers were stripped away, and native Ulstermen soon realised that the network of forts commanded by servitors provided a previously unseen level of security. This laid the foundation for a future plantation in Ulster, which Chichester believed would improve stability and undermine the system of Gaelic authority.

In September 1605, Chichester visited Derry and 'observed there many good buildings, and that, because it was a place of great importance', hoped 'so good a work may not be suffered to decay'.[l] This was an implied criticism of Docwra's slow progress in developing the City. There was a shortage of settlers and he wanted to see speedy growth to encourage more

> merchants, tradesmen, and artificers from England and Scotland which must be commanded by authority to come over and compelled to remain and set up their trades and occupations.[m]

Without more settlers, Chichester was worried about security, recording that 'there are such wastes round that robbers harbour in them and rob and murder merchants and travellers going from Derry and Lifford to the Pale'.[n] On a second visit in the following year, he recorded that 'if the infant city was not supported it was liable to decay, as it was situated 'among neighbours who long for nothing more than the ruin thereof'.[o] Docwra seemed to have lost heart. He had been piqued at Chichester being elevated to Lord Deputy ahead of himself, believing that he had played the more important role, initially at least, in helping Mountjoy to subdue Ulster. He reckoned that he had been overlooked only because he was so remote from the centre of power. There was certainly no love lost between him and Chichester and he decided to leave. With Government approval, he sold his interests in Derry to Sir George Paulet, a younger son of the Marquess of Winchester, and 'a gentleman of good sufficiency and of service in the wars'.[p] Paulet did not prove the 'well-chosen' man that Chichester needed. 'Arrogant and blundering, the new governor would ensure by his actions his own untimely death and that Docwra's infant city would be reduced to ashes.'[q] He even fell out with Bishop Montgomery by laying claim to the Bishop's Palace and the Parish Church.

It was more than fifty years since the dissolution of monasteries in 1550, when Sir Nicholas Bagenal had been granted the lease (and later outright possession) of the abbey of Newry. His family also enjoyed income from the Lordships of Newry, Mourne, and Carlingford. With most of their tenants being Irish, they made a point of keeping on good terms with the Magennis clan, who had traditionally controlled the adjacent Lordship of Iveagh[20]. Sir Henry Bagenal had described Sir Hugh Magennis as 'the civillist of all the Irishry', who lived 'very civilly and English-like in his house and every festival day weareth English garments amongst his followers'.[r] Yet when Bagenal fell out with Tyrone, resulting in the start of the Nine Years' War, Sir Hugh's son, Art Roe Magennis, joined other Gaelic chieftains against the English. When Mountjoy's troops began its war of attrition with famine and slaughter, Art Roe quickly submitted, hoping to retain his lands, and applied to be appointed Lord Iveagh. When Arthur Bagenal came of age in 1603, he started rebuilding Newry, which, in 1600, had been largely destroyed by a fire at a Whiskey distillery. With Newry having become a focal point for British colonisation, servitors hoped to extend their holdings there, and demobilised soldiers had eyes on the former Magennis lands nearby. In 1605, when Chichester set up a Commission for the Division and Bounding of the Lords' and Gentlemen's Livings, they at last hoped for their reward. Yet Art Roe became Lord Iveagh and received twelve of the fifteen Magennis townlands with much of the remainder being granted to other leading members of his family. In all, 85 per cent was granted to native Irish, although some was set aside for the see of Dromore, where John Todd[21] became Bishop in 1608.

> Only a small amount was available for allocation to servitors, including Sir Toby Caulfeild, who had served under Sir Samuel Bagenal in the closing years of the Nine Years War.[s]

Prominent among veterans granted land as servitors in Ulster was Sir Thomas Phillips, a protégé of Cecil. Like Chichester, Phillips had a distinguished military record and arrived in Ireland in the winter of 1598 to serve under Sir Thomas Norris (brother of Sir John Norris) at Kinsale, where he temporarily commanded the garrison, which successfully repulsed an attack by Tyrone's Munster allies. He had previously spent twenty years as a mercenary in France earning the 'special favour' of Henry of Navarre, later Henry IV. In 1601, Cecil arranged for him to be sent with his Company of Foot to augment Chichester's forces at Carrickfergus. He quickly gained Chichester's respect for his 'judgement and valour' and, in July 1602, was given command of the Castle of Toome, strategically placed on the northern side of Loch Neagh on the main road from Carrickfergus to Londonderry, from where he captured Tyrone's fort on the other side of the Bann River. In October, after Docwra had occupied

---

[20] The Guinness family claim descent from the Magennis clan and became the Earls of Iveagh in 1919.
[21] Bishop Todd made fee farm grants of his diocesan lands to his friends. When Chichester heard of this he had Todd arrested and the Bishop's brother-in-law was forced to return what he had acquired improperly. Other beneficiaries were forced to convert what they had acquired into sixty-year freeholds.[t]

Coleraine[22], Robert Cecil arranged for Phillips to be stationed there to keep a watchful eye on the MacDonnells while the treaty of Mellifont was being signed. In June 1604, Cecil also gave him custody of Coleraine Abbey in addition to his continuing role supervising the garrisons at the fort and castle at Toome. It was hoped that he would attract settlers to Coleraine to maintain peace. He progressively expanded his interests, acquiring leases over both the castle and fort at Toome with thirty acres. He purchased a licence to manufacture spirits and acquired a twenty-one year lease over the customs at Portrush, Portballintrae and the Barns with control of all the ferries crossing the Bann River. He later bought the freehold of Coleraine Abbey, within the grounds of which he built his home. He also acquired six adjacent 'townlands' from James Hamilton (see page 72), who had begun the process of colonising the northern part of County Down. Phillips had soon established a small settlement of thatched houses at Coleraine with a watermill and a church with its own minister, all surrounded with fortifications. He acquired timber cutting rights in Killetra from Tyrone in exchange for providing a tun of claret and a half tun of [fortified] wine. He carved roads through the woods to deliver timber for building and was granted permission to hold a weekly market and annual fair at Coleraine to sell his timber and other goods. These were frequented by merchants arriving from Scotland. In 1607, he was knighted for his part in the incursions, which led to the flight of the Earls, and became Coleraine's military superintendent. Despite Salisbury's (Cecil became Earl of Salisbury in 1605) respect for his achievements, Phillips's resources were seriously overextended, and Salisbury concluded that he needed an investor with much deeper pockets.

The Plantations in Ulster did not begin with any well-formulated plan, but individuals were encouraged to become undertakers as land became available, generally the result of confiscation from some rebellious chieftain. They were often financed by the Crown in return for which they agreed to bring in English, or more usually Scottish, farmers as tenants to develop and work the land. As the number of settlers started to grow, so did animosity from traditional Gaelic farmers whose lands had been usurped. Townships were little more than garrisons surrounded by 'aliens in language, religion and blood'.[u] There was a need for a network of support among different settler communities. In 1608, when Derry was destroyed in a rebellion by the O'Doherty clan, Phillips offered shelter to fugitive settlers at Coleraine. He was also responsible for arresting the belligerent Sir Donal Ballagh O'Cahan, and took possession of his castle on the banks of the Bann opposite to Coleraine. He then petitioned Salisbury to be granted the castle with 3,000 to 4,000 acres, so that he could continue his settlement project so well begun. This made him a key figure in the events leading to the Plantation of Londonderry, at the start of which he developed his own colony at Limavady, between Coleraine and Derry.

---

[22] Although Coleraine had been a small township in the 13th Century, in more recent times it had been reduced to an ecclesiastical centre surrounding its abbey.

Among the earliest undertakers were two hard-headed Scots, Hugh Montgomery, 6th Laird of Braidstaine in Ayrshire, a cadet branch of the Montgomeries of Eglinton, and James Hamilton, the son of the minister of Dunlop in Ayrshire, who had graduated from Glasgow University. Both of them were well-known to James I although the reason for this is not entirely clear, but both seem to have been involved in intelligence gathering on his behalf, while he remained in Scotland awaiting the expected call from England, which would follow the death of Elizabeth I. What is certain is that James owed each of them a favour.

In the hope of making his fortune, Montgomery had become a Captain of Foot fighting for Henry IV in France and later for the Prince of Orange in the Netherlands. While there, he was imprisoned after fighting a duel with one of the Cunninghams, in a continuation of the interminable feud between these two rival Ayrshire clans. Yet he escaped after being freed by the jailer's daughter, who was being 'romanced' by one of his compatriots. Throughout his imprisonment, he continued to correspond with his brother George, then a clergyman in Somerset.[23] George had contacts at Court in London, and, after Hugh's return to Scotland, he received intelligence from George to keep the Scottish King abreast of news of Elizabeth and her Government. Although James chastised him for reopening the feud between the Montgomeries and Cunninghams, he recognised his value as a provider of helpful information.

On James's accession to the English throne, Hugh Montgomery remained at Braidstaine Castle in Ayrshire, but George continued to keep his brother informed of events in London. George reported that Conn Mac Néill O'Neill, now Lord of Clandeboye and the Great Ards, had been jailed for treason at Carrickfergus after one of his servants killed a soldier in Belfast. Hugh saw this as an opportunity to gain some of Conn's forfeited estates for himself. In 1604, he approached Conn's wife offering to arrange a jailbreak for Conn and to gain for him a Royal pardon, if, in return, he was granted a substantial part of Upper Clandeboye. He sent another kinsman, Thomas Montgomery, a ship-owner trading grain to Carrickfergus, to arrange Conn's escape. Thomas used the ploy of making love to the Town Marshall's daughter and even gained her father's consent for their marriage. With her help, he smuggled Conn onto his ship, and took him to Largs. After travelling on to Braidstaine Castle, Conn confirmed his undertaking to provide Hugh with half his lands, if Hugh could obtain a pardon for him. Conn and Hugh travelled to Westminster, where they met with George Montgomery, now a chaplain to James I. James received Conn graciously and knighted Hugh. He agreed to confirm their arrangement by Letters Patent, provided that the land was planted with British Protestants and not with people of Irish extraction.

For opportunistic cheek, Montgomery's plan had seemed to take the biscuit! Yet before the patent was signed, a second equally brazen attempt was made to

---

[23] He later became Dean of Norwich and in 1605 was appointed Bishop of the combined dioceses of Derry, Raphoe and Clogher (see page 66).

share in the spoils. The King was approached by Sir James Fullerton from Dunlop in Ayrshire, who suggested that the lands now being granted to Montgomery and Conn O'Neill were too large for them to administer; he proposed a tripartite division, allowing his close associate, Hamilton, to be granted a one-third share.

Fullerton was a long-time friend of Hamilton. After university, Hamilton had returned to Dunlop to teach at its school. In 1587, with Fullerton in tow, he decided to seek his fortune elsewhere. Having set sail from Ayr, their ship arrived in Dublin seeking shelter from a storm. Hamilton decided to set up a school there and employed Fullerton as his assistant. In 1595, Hamilton was invited to become a fellow of the newly formed Trinity College and, after being closely involved with its fund raising, was, in 1598, appointed bursar.

All was not as it seemed. Hamilton and Fullerton were involved in events leading to James VI's accession to the English throne, and were acting as his agents in Dublin. Their intelligence must have been important to James[24]. In 1600, he invited Hamilton to move to London to monitor events at Elizabeth's Court. On James's accession in 1603, Fullerton also moved to London, where he was knighted and appointed a Gentleman of the Bedchamber. From his position so near the King, he was able to promote Hamilton to a one-third share of Conn O'Neill's former lands as reward for having 'furnished himself [the King] for some years last past with intelligences from Dublin'.[v] In the original draft of the patent, the King seemed to overlook that he had already, in December 1604, promised some of the land in the Ards to a London merchant, Thomas Ireland. On 25 February 1605, Ireland assigned his rights to Hamilton and on 10 April the Letters Patent confirmed the tripartite division of the lands between Conn O'Neill, Montgomery and Hamilton. To placate Montgomery, the King granted him all the former abbey lands in the area and insisted that Hamilton and Montgomery should receive the whole of the Great Ards, which included the sea coast. Their grants confirmed that they should introduce only Scottish and English tenants. This is the first record of Scottish immigrants being treated on an equal footing with the English. It was, perhaps, overlooked that they would be Presbyterian and would not conform to the Establish Church of Ireland.

James failed to forewarn Chichester, his Lord Deputy, of this new agreement, and it was not until Hamilton arrived in Dublin to present his Letters Patent that Chichester heard of it. He was appalled. He wrote to Salisbury that Hamilton had been granted more lands than the greatest lords in the Kingdom. To make matters worse, on the day following Hamilton's arrival in Dublin, he

---

[24] It is not at all clear what form their intelligence took, but it is likely that their roles as schoolmasters in Dublin were covers for an intelligence gathering role planned before they left Scotland. It is known that James was considering giving support to Essex's rebellion, in return for an assurance that he would be recognised as Elizabeth's heir, and it is possible that they warned him not to become too closely associated after his disastrous campaign in Ireland.

was also granted Coleraine, Kells and Massereene in County Antrim, and Newtown [Newtownards], Holywood, Movilla, Black Abbey, Greyabbey and Bangor in County Down. When Chichester travelled north, in July 1605, Hamilton felt he should placate him by giving him Massereene.

For Conn O'Neill to retain any part of his estates was considered both by his followers and himself as a triumph, and he settled at Castlereagh. As Elizabeth had previously granted his estates to Sir Thomas Smith and later to Essex, his expectation of recovery had seemed remote. The new landlords had to juggle their assets to raise enough ready money to begin their projects. Conn sold valuable woods in Slut Neale to Montgomery, who sold timber to generate sufficient income to pay his rents. Montgomery seems to have raised money by mortgaging Braidstaine and later had access to facilities from Edinburgh banks. Hamilton sold his abbey lands at Movilla, Newtown and Greyabbey to Montgomery and, in September, sold an area at Coleraine (as outlined on page 69) to Phillips. In February, 1606, he had sufficient resources to acquire Thomas Ireland's fishing rights on the Bann River between Lough Neagh and the Salmon Leap above Coleraine, together with a number of other areas. The fishing rights were to become the focus of a later dispute.

Montgomery and Hamilton both returned to Scotland to recruit settlers and had considerable success in their Ayrshire localities. By the spring of 1607, Scots were beginning to arrive in Ireland. With the land in poor condition after the depredations of the Nine Years' War, they could find little shelter. There were only thirty native Irish cabins[25] in the three counties around Donaghadee and Newtown, and the settlers were forced to camp in roofless churches, the ruined castle at Newtown or in the vaults at Greyabbey. Montgomery brought in teams of builders to erect thatched cottages, and provide him with shelter at Newtown Castle. (He later roofed the priory walls to make a more fitting home for his family.) He established a market, supplied with deliveries from Scottish kinsmen, and built Port Montgomery on the Mull of Galloway only three hour's sail away in Scotland. This later became Port Patrick, from where goods were delivered to Donaghadee on The Great Ards coast. He improved the harbours on each side of the North Channel, erecting large churches with bell towers at each of them. Until the work at Donaghadee[26] was completed in 1626, he was authorised to travel to Scotland to acquire building materials and victuals free of duty. Building work gathered pace, and Hamilton expanded the area under his control by acquiring the barony of Dufferin and, in 1616, he purchased eighteen townlands between Saintfield and Belfast from Conn O'Neill, taking a half-interest in forty more. He built homes for himself at Bangor and at Holywood, three miles further south. After completing his own mansions, he

---

[25] Cabins 'were elliptical on plan, had one room, with a fire in the centre, and were roofed with turf or thatch through a hole in the centre of which smoke was allowed to escape'.[w]

[26] Such was the importance of Donaghadee as a port for Scottish undertakers that it remained the busiest point of arrival for those travelling from Scotland for the next hundred years.

repaired and re-roofed the churches at Newtownards, Greyabbey and Kilmore. Each was supplied with bells bearing his coat of arms and with bibles and prayer books. He also built a 'great school' for both sexes at Newtownards and endowed it with £20 to pay a 'Master of Arts', who taught 'Latin, Greek and Logycks, allowing the scholars a green for recreation at goff[27], football, and archery.'[x] A music master was also employed, and he established it with a tradition in choral music. A picture of domestic improvement began to present itself. Work on manuring the land and planting crops continued apace, and the women spun or knitted to make clothing. With old Scottish feuds being forgotten, everyone lived peaceably.

In May 1622, in recognition of their extraordinary achievements, Hamilton was created Viscount Claneboye and Montgomery became Viscount Montgomery of the Great Ards. They were always looking for new opportunities. With his estates generating cash surpluses, Montgomery borrowed more money in Edinburgh and bought up much of Conn's remaining estates, which Conn was selling off piecemeal until left with nothing. Montgomery always claimed that he treated Conn fairly, having provided him with £2,000 and

> beside this, Conn has received continual and daily benefits from me in money, horses, clothes and other provisions of good value and also has been chargeable unto me in divers other disbursements'.[y]

Hamilton and Montgomery might have been even more successful, if they had been able to avoid some expensive disputes. Sir William Smith, a descendant of Sir Thomas, tried to revive his family's claim to the lands in the Ards granted to Sir Thomas about forty years earlier. Although an inquisition of 1612 found that the Smiths had forfeited their rights for failure to fulfil the terms of their grant, Sir William pressed ahead with a claim against Hamilton and Montgomery. Although this failed, it involved them in considerable legal expenditure. They also disputed land boundaries with each other, mainly over acquisitions made by Montgomery from Conn. Eventually, in 1614, James Hamilton, Earl of Abercorn was asked to arbitrate and in the following year made an award, which favoured Hamilton. They were required to share the woodlands acquired from Conn, and Hamilton was obliged to return abbey lands apportioned to Montgomery in 1605. Montgomery considered the outcome unfair and accused Abercorn of favouring his Hamilton kinsman. Yet if Hamilton was a kinsman, the relationship must have been very remote and, in 1616, James I confirmed Abercorn's award. Bad feeling between Hamilton and Montgomery rumbled on and, in 1621, Hamilton was forced to sell a proportion in County Cavan to pay mounting legal costs. Yet they set aside their differences sufficiently to share in the cost of reconstructing the church on abbey lands at Comber. By the standards of plantations elsewhere, they were extraordinarily successful; the muster of

---

[27] This is the first reference to golf being played in Ireland.

1630 showed 1,401 British males on Hamilton's lands and 1,317 on Montgomery's.

James was also generous to Randal MacDonnell, Sorley Boy's son, a lucky Celtic survivor of the Nine Years' War. Randal was married to Tyrone's third daughter, Éilís, and had marched across Ireland to fight beside him at the battle for Kinsale, when almost his entire contingent of several hundred well-armed men were slaughtered. On returning north, he found Chichester smarting to avenge the death of his brother. Chichester had ravished his lands, destroying houses and crops and driving out any cattle he could find in the extreme snow. Being reduced in state, Randal found his leadership of the MacDonnells being challenged by Sir James MacDonnell of Knockrinsay, who occupied Dunluce Castle. In the autumn of 1602, Tyrone had advised Randal to submit to the English, and, at his own expense, Randal provided five hundred foot and forty horse to fight for Chichester in Fermanagh. When later introduced to Mountjoy, he was knighted.

As a Scot, James I was much better placed than Elizabeth to pressurise the MacDonnells to maintain the peace. In May 1603, shortly after his accession to the English throne, he instructed Mountjoy to confer the Route and the Glynns, amounting to 333,907 acres, to Randal, despite him being a devout Catholic. This made him the largest landowner in County Antrim, and provided him with far more land than the MacDonnells had previously held. James remained confident that he would not ally with the Crown's enemies, and Mountjoy also seemed to trust him. Randal had previously assisted James in Scotland against Angus MacDonnell of Dunyveg, a rival claimant for the lands granted to him in Antrim. He now became a model supporter of the Crown in Ulster. Yet James put a sting in the tail. Randal was required to pay rent or face being forfeited. With his estates in poor condition after the Nine Years' War and a dearth of inhabitants to work the land, he struggled to generate a return. In desperation, he pleaded for a reduction in his rents, and James again obliged him. In 1604, his previous patent was returned and a new one issued on more favourable terms. He was now instructed to subdivide his estates into areas for let, each having its own manor house to be built within seven years. This became a template for apportioning lands in the plantations that were to come. When he agreed to hand over nine townlands near Coleraine to form part of the Londonderry plantations, James compensated him by halving the rents on his remaining estates.

To manage such a huge area, Randal quickly adopted farming practices 'in a modern commercial way'. He followed Montgomery and Hamilton in seeking Scottish tenants. Hebridean Scots arrived in numbers and remained mainly Catholic. He also attracted lowlanders, generally Presbyterians from Renfrew, Dumbarton and Ayr, who, seven years earlier, at James's behest, had been planted by the Earl of Argyll on the MacDonnell lands of Dunyveg on Kintyre. In 1607, Dunyveg retaliated by making a ferocious attack on them, and they moved with all their cattle, seed corn and farm equipment to Antrim. Randal ingratiated himself with the King by offering his land on long leases[28], and this assured him of good rents. In 1611, the number of Scots settled on his lands was already being noted. Other Lowland Scots arrived, and he provided grants to encourage industry and develop market towns, such as Glenarm. He was careful not to drive out the few remaining native Irish and even financed a Franciscan friary at Bonamargy near Ballycastle.

There was considerable jealousy at Randal's success, but he had made it his business to keep abreast of the King's priorities and to respond promptly to his wishes. Although his estates were outside the scope of the Articles of the Plantation of Londonderry, he followed its practice of erecting fortifications. He and his tenants built 'defended' houses at Kilwaughter, Glenarm and Ballycastle, but his focus was on Dunluce. Although originally built as his stronghold, he later converted it into an elegant English-style manor house, surrounded with 'a fayre stone walle'. In 1618, he became Viscount Dunluce and, in 1620, was created Earl of Antrim.

Despite their respective successes, Randal and Hamilton disputed the lucrative fishing rights on the Bann River. Hamilton already owned the rights from Toome to the Salmon Leap above Coleraine, but on 2 March 1606, John Wakeman, a merchant, acquired the valuable rights from the Salmon Leap to the sea. On the following day, he sold them to Hamilton, who now controlled both sides of the river running through Randal's estates. Randal was outraged as he believed the rights formed part of his patent from the King. To make matters worse, Hamilton sold his interest from Toome to the Salmon Leap to Chichester together with a half share in the rights from the Leap to the sea. Although Chichester remained hostile to the MacDonnells, his acquisition was warmly supported by Phillips, who also had territorial ambitions in the area, after having leased land at Portrush. Chichester and Phillips told Salisbury that there was not 'a more cancred and malicious person than Sir Randal, who from a beggar is made great and yet rests unthankful'.[z] Phillips also accused Randal of provoking his tenants into 'stealths, robberies, and other evils' along the Bann, while Randal blamed Phillips for terrorising them and forcing them from their homes. Randal gained the unlikely support of Montgomery's brother, George, now Bishop of Derry, Raphoe and Clogher. George advised Randal to visit James in London to confirm his determination to attract more Scottish settlers. On arrival in 1607, he seems to have won James's approval, as Chichester was instructed to assist him in converting his tenants to freeholders.

Randal's son, also Randal, was extremely extravagant. He had been brought up speaking Gaelic, wearing 'neither hat, cap, nor shoe, nor stocking' until he was seven or eight years old.[aa] At the age of four, he was betrothed to Abercorn's daughter, Lucy. This was designed to confirm him as the legitimate heir, as his father had at least one illegitimate elder son. In 1627, Randal Jr., now Viscount Dunluce, set off for France to gain exposure to Catholicism. On reaching

---

[28] The leases generally varied in length from fifty-one to a hundred and one years, although one was for three hundred and one years.

75

London, he was presented to Charles I at Court, where he made a favourable impression as 'a tall, clean-limbed, handsome man with red hair',[bb] and was retained by the King at Court. He jilted Lucy Hamilton and started to look for a wife. As Tyrone's grandson, he was regarded with some suspicion, but he attracted the recently widowed Lady Katherine Manners, Duchess of Buckingham. Despite being nine years older, she was extremely wealthy and the most eligible widow in England. On their marriage in 1635, she became Catholic. By this time, he had already amassed £3,000 of debts from gambling. On his father's death in 1636, he was determined to make Dunluce Castle fit for Katherine and spent large sums on improving and extending it.[29] By 1639, according to Wentworth, his debts were £50,000. He remained a prodigious gambler, reputedly losing £2,000 playing ninepins during one evening at Tunbridge Wells. At this point, parts of the domestic and kitchen quarters of Dunluce collapsed into the sea, killing some of his servants. Many artisans, including Anthony van Dyck, remained unpaid, and he was forced to lease out his remaining unencumbered lands at low rents to receive high entry fines. His debts were so large that he 'became too big to be allowed to fail',[cc] but he retained the goodwill of Charles I, who made him Marquess of Antrim in 1644. He, at least, was not contemplating rebellion.

Randal MacDonnell, Viscount Dunluce, 2nd Earl and later Marquess of Antrim Despite his Catholicism and close links with Tyrone, James I restored him to his Antrim estates. He was an inveterate gambler, but, in 1635, married Buckingham's very eligible widow, Katherine Manners. *John Michael Wright (attributed to) oil on canvas. Courtesy of Viscount Dunluce, Glenarm Castle*

[29] He spent £22,000 on furnishing Dunluce and Bramshill, his home in Hampshire.

Lady Katherine Manners, Duchess of Buckingham and later Marchioness of Antrim
Following Buckingham's assassination, his extremely wealthy widow Katherine Manners married the much younger 2nd Earl of Antrim, who rebuilt Dunluce Castle for her. *Sir Anthony van Dyck (1599-1641) oil on canvas c. 1633 © Belvoir Castle, Leicestershire, UK, Bridgeman Images*

The ruins of Dunluce Castle The castle was extended by the Marquess of Antrim for Lady Katherine Manners, formerly Duchess of Buckingham.

Chapter 5

The flight of the Earls
1605 – 1608

With Plantations in Ulster starting to gather pace, Tyrone and Tyrconnell sat back and hoped that they would be treated more leniently under the Stuart Kings. This was not to be. Unlike his son Charles, James took a firm stand on strict religious conformity, no doubt being reinforced in his views by Salisbury and the English Parliament. Although Mountjoy had permitted 'Old English' families in Ireland to continue to practice their religion in the privacy of their homes, in July 1605, James diminished his hopes of retaining Catholic loyalty by declaring 'that he would fight to his knees in blood rather than grant toleration'.[a] 'Chichester now launched a programme of religious persecution on a scale never witnessed before in Ireland.'[b] He 'fined ordinary Catholics a shilling for every Sunday they failed to attend a Protestant church'.[c] Those who failed to attend Protestant services were jailed; those failing to pay their fines had their houses ransacked. 'Letters were delivered to sixteen leading Catholic gentlemen in Dublin fining them a hundred pounds each.'[d] Anti-Catholic paranoia was reinforced by the Gunpowder Plot in England in November 1605, which involved a Catholic attempt on the King's life, and there were rumours of Tyrone being party to it.

Chichester continued his efforts to water down the terms granted by Mountjoy to Tyrone and Tyrconnell. He was exultant when Tyrconnell's authority was reduced by the granting of freeholds to lesser Gaelic chieftains, reporting: 'Now the laws of England, and the Ministers thereof, were shackles and handlocks unto him, and the garrisons planted in his country were as pricks in his side.'[e] Under the terms of his new Patent, Tyrconnell was obliged to pay two hundred pounds quit rent to the Crown and to provide the Royal Armies with one hundred and twenty foot soldiers and sixty horse. Yet, without overlordships in north Connaught and Fermanagh, Tyrconnell was being starved of income. A special injunction called on the O'Donnells to 'renounce and relinquish all claim or right which they had or might pretend to have over O'Dohertie's and O'Connor Sligoe's countries',[f] and many smaller clans were relieved of their obligations to pay rent to Tyrconnell. He had lost control of 'the naturally rich agricultural land [in] the lower river valleys', and large parts of his remaining estates proved infertile.[g] Inishowen Peninsula (including the fertile island of Inch) was now held independently by Sir Cahir O'Doherty; Docwra and his successors controlled Derry; other lands were occupied by Bishop George Montgomery on behalf of the dioceses of Derry, Raphoe and Clogher; garrisons of Crown forces usually occupied the surrounding farmland; and Niall Garbh O'Donnell held the Finn Valley. With insufficient tenants to work their lands, all landowners were short of income. The salmon fishing on the river Erne, previously a major source of Tyrconnell's income, had been granted to another servitor, Sir Henry Folliott. In his weakened state, Tyrconnell was being challenged by Niall Garbh O'Donnell with a growing band of followers, so that 'the earl seems to hold it not safe to return thither, but lies here within the Pale very meanly attended'.[h] Following Mountjoy's death in 1606, Chichester was on his travels through Ulster, when he learned that Tyrconnell was planning to flee Ireland with Maguire, whose lands in Fermanagh were also under threat. When Maguire was arrested, Tyrconnell realised that Chichester was aware of the plan. Although he remained in Ireland, he faced the Lord Deputy's continuing hostility. Davies made himself very unpopular by questioning Maguire's title to his Fermanagh estates, but, in 1607, Maguire managed to slip out of Ireland to Flanders.

By comparison to Tyrconnell, Tyrone remained extremely rich. This made Chichester all the more determined to reduce his authority. He encouraged the belligerent Donnell Ballagh O'Cahan to become an independent chief on lands which Docwra had restored to him around Coleraine as a reward for deserting Tyrone. Tyrone argued that O'Cahan's independence did not accord with the terms for the restoration of his earldom. He was furious with O'Cahan and, in April 1607, was summoned to Dublin to answer charges that he was attempting to force him to submit. In the summer of 1607, James, who had hitherto been on cordial terms with Tyrone, instructed him to come to London with O'Cahan. Being unable to win over the 'Old English' Catholic knights to his cause, he became extremely nervous and was warned that, if he went to London, he risked being thrown in the Tower and beheaded. After meeting up with Tyrconnell, they again sought Philip III's help. It was rumoured that Maguire was negotiating with Archduke Albert in Brussels in a renewed attempt to launch a Counter-Reformation in Ulster. Chichester 'was convinced that Tyrone had never ceased to be a traitor and that he was assiduously plotting against the Crown',[i] but could establish no evidence against him. With help from Davies, he did all he could to limit Tyrone's powerbase, and was in no doubt that, like Maguire, Tyrone and Tyrconnell were in contact with Spain. Yet the Spanish needed to avoid being seen to be offering help. In August 1604, a peace treaty had been signed between James I and Philip III in London, stipulating 'that neither monarch would give any help to the rebellious subjects of the other, [although] neither ruler adhered strictly to that stipulation.'[j] Yet plans for another Irish uprising were finalised early in 1607 when Tyrconnell went to London to meet the Spanish ambassador, and a first tranche of four thousand ducats was released to him.

By this time, Tyrone was using Christopher St. Lawrence, heir to Lord Howth, as his conduit for communicating with Spain. St. Lawrence was a devious character. He had been one of the Crown's most experienced army colonels, commanding its largest regiment at the battle of Kinsale, despite having been involved in Essex's rebellion. With the battle over, he was disappointed only to be appointed a servitor as Governor of Monaghan Fort. He then spent several months in Flanders, where he befriended Tyrone's son, Henry O'Neill, now a mercenary with the Spanish army. They were reported to be 'very familiar and inward friends and were oftentimes bedfellows'.[k] St. Lawrence seems to have been the conduit to deliver a grant of three hundred crowns from Spain. Yet, in July, he came to London for an urgent meeting with Salisbury, and it is clear that he was a double agent. He warned Salisbury of 'a general revolt intended by many of the nobility and principal persons of this land … and that they will shake off the yoke of the English government, as they term it, and adhere to the Spaniard.'[l] On St. Lawrence's return to Dublin, he confirmed to Chichester that Tyrconnell and Richard Nugent, Baron of Delvin, were the leaders of the planned rebellion. Although he could provide no evidence, St. Lawrence was sure that Tyrone 'is as deep in the treason as any'.[m] Yet when he refused to present his evidence in court, no immediate action could be taken, although it is probable that the King was advised.

With Philip III lukewarm about supporting an Irish rebellion, Maguire sought his assistance to enable Tyrone and Tyrconnell to escape with their families and followers. The Spanish sent a ship of eighty tons from France disguised as a fishing boat, and Tyrone received news of its arrival whilst he was meeting Chichester. He took his leave and, in September 1607, Tyrone and Tyrconnell boarded the ship at Rathmullan in Lough Swilly. In what became known as 'the flight of the Earls', about forty persons, representing 'the cream of Ulster's Gaelic aristocracy',[n] joined them, but Tyrconnell was forced to leave his pregnant seventeen-year-old wife, Brigid FitzGerald, daughter of the 12th Earl of Kildare at Maynooth, where she was being cared for by her grandmother, as he could not risk making the journey to collect her.

The rebel Earls' plan was unclear. Despite setting out for Spain, the ship faced dangerously bad weather and was forced to make for France, landing at Quillebeuf at the mouth of the River Seine. The French harbour authorities viewed their arrival with deep suspicion, as they had no licence. Although Sir George Carew, the former Lord President of Munster and now English ambassador in Paris, demanded their extradition to England, they were taken to Rouen, where Henry IV, who had converted to Catholicism to become King of France, allowed them to follow their Spanish instructions by sailing on to Flanders. On arrival, they were fêted as champions of the Catholic faith. The Archduke Albert, with his wife, the Infanta Isabella, provided them with luxurious apartments in their palace and they were sent with a military escort to Brussels, where Marqués Ambrosio de Spínola, the commander-in-chief of the Spanish forces, greeted them and held a sumptuous banquet in their honour.

Back in Ireland, Chichester was caught out by the Earls' departure, but Davies was dismissive. He claimed that 'O'Neill and his train of barbarous men, women and children … will be taken for a company of gypsies and be exceedingly scorned.'º Davies could not have been more wrong, but with James having established alliances with many European Catholic powers, Philip III considered their arrival an embarrassment. He dared not imperil his new peace with England at a time when Spain was teetering on the brink of bankruptcy and could not afford another invasion of Ireland. He would not allow them to come to Spain and, to the astonishment of the Earls and their families, he transferred them to the Pope's protection. On 28 February 1608, after leaving their children in Flanders with nurses, tutors and servants, the Earls set off for Italy on horseback, followed by their wives in coaches. On reaching the Alps in ice and snow, one of their horses carrying most of their money fell over a high frozen cliff into a deep glen known as the Devil's Bridge, and its load disappeared into the torrent below. After making a futile attempt to recover it, they travelled on through the St Gotthard Pass to Italy. Despite receiving a warm greeting from the governor of Milan (then a Spanish possession), who held a feast for them, they were in great distress and had no means to pay for their accommodation. The British Ambassador to Spain, Sir Charles Cornwallis, complained at their favourable treatment, and the Milanese were obliged to send them on to Rome, where they arrived on 29 April 1608. Although the Spanish Ambassador had asked the Pope to protect them, he offered only an unfurnished house, but calls for Philip III to provide financial assistance were to no avail.

After arriving in Rome, the Earls received news that O'Doherty had rebelled in Ulster, and they called on Philip III to send a military expedition to support him in defending the Catholic faith. They claimed that the Irish Catholics' only wish 'is to be free of their troubles and to become subjects of Your Majesty'.ᴾ Philip III briefly contemplated combining an expedition with Pius V, but soon dropped the idea. In desperation, Tyrone approached James I to seek reconciliation and to gain the return of his lands, but James was by then committed to a full plantation of Ulster. In January 1609, James issued a printed order for all escheated land to be repopulated with settlers.

In July 1608, Tyrconnell and Maguire tried to escape Rome's summer heat by travelling fifteen miles to Ostia with Tyrconnell's son, and Tyrone's son, Hugh. On their second evening there, Tyrconnell developed a fever, which spread to the rest of the party. On his death eleven days later, the Pope arranged a grand procession for his burial in the monastery of San Pietro Montorio.[30] Both Tyrconnell's son and Maguire also died, so that only Tyrone's son, Hugh, re-joined his father in Rome. Even Hugh died in the following year, and Tyrone's eldest son, Henry, died in Spain at about the same time. Tyrone was now the only survivor of any prominence from those who had sailed from Lough Swilly.

---

[30] This church had been erected in c. 1472 at the expense of Ferdinand and Isabella of Spain. This demonstrates that it was the Spanish, in addition to the Papacy, who were supporting the exiles while they were in Italy.

Although there were frequent rumours in Ulster of his impending return, both the Spanish and the Papacy seem to have lost faith in him and, in 1616, he too died in Rome. Yet, so long as he lived, he remained a threat to the Ulster settlers from Britain.

Chapter 6

O'Doherty's rebellion
1607 – 1608

Having been in fear of a general rising in Ulster, Chichester's initial reaction to the departure of the Earls was to

> issue a proclamation to assure the inhabitants of Tyrone and Tyrconnell that they will not be disturbed in the peaceable possession of their lands provided they remained dutiful and loyal subjects of the King.[a]

Yet the Earls were charged with high treason, and their forfeiture had huge implications for their tenants. Realising the opportunity being offered, Chichester wrote to James I:

> If his Majesty will, during their absence, assume the countries into his possession, divide the lands amongst the inhabitants … and will bestow the rest upon servitors and men of worth here, and withal bring in colonies of civil people of England and Scotland … the country will ever be happily settled.[b]

Both James and Salisbury agreed with him, and James arranged the attainder of all the Earls' estates, covering most of the six western counties of Ulster ("the escheated counties"). Salisbury planned a large settlement of English Protestants on the lines of the earlier plantations in Munster and Connaught. Settlers were to include servitors and other soldiers involved in Tyrone's defeat, who had remained in Ireland in hope of being recompensed for their wartime efforts. Chichester saw Catholicism as the great threat to Irish stability and, although the area was 'more utterly depopulated and poor than ever before',[c] he was determined that it should be filled with a community ready to support the Established Church of Ireland, and wanted settlers positioned as buffers between rival Irish factions to maintain peace.

Although Chichester reported that Ireland was well rid of the Earls, in London their departure was viewed only with concern. There were fears that it would jeopardise the newly signed peace with Spain, and Chichester was criticised for having forced their hand. A Spanish invasion to restore them was expected to receive assistance from 'Old English' Catholic families and would disturb the fragile truce being fostered with other Gaelic Lords, who might sympathise with their plight. Only eight hundred and eighty English soldiers remained in Ireland and recruits sent to supplement them were often conscripted outlaws, who were of poor quality and inadequately armed. Thirty of the new arrivals were returned to England, deemed 'old persons or otherwise disabled and insufficient, and who, for mere debility of body, will soon be consumed here without any other adversary'.[d]

Chichester moved quickly to arrest the rebel Earls' former allies. Tyrone's nephew, Brian MacArt O'Neill, was taken to Dublin for trial and execution. Tyrone's young son, Conn, who had been unable to join his father at Lough Swilly, was sent to England, where he was enrolled at Eton College, but with fears growing that he could become a future rebel leader, he was moved to the Tower of London. Conn was joined by his uncle, Sir Cormac O'Neill, and they spent the rest of their lives there. Every Gaelic chieftain was under suspicion, even those who had supported the Crown during the Nine Years' War. Although O'Cahan and Niall Garbh O'Donnell had been firm supporters of the Crown, they had served their purpose. They, too, ended up in the Tower and were never released. Sir Cahir O'Doherty, Lord of Inishowen, had been Docwra's staunchest ally, and, after fighting bravely beside him, had been knighted by Mountjoy. Although he offered his full cooperation to Chichester, he was treated contemptuously by Paulet at Derry, who believed he was preparing to rise in revolt. O'Doherty arrived in Dublin, confident of clearing his name, but Chichester preferred to 'mistrust many in whose care and honesty I could before that time have reposed my life and safety'.[e] O'Doherty was arrested and forced to provide an outrageously large recognisance of £1,000 for his release. Yet he continued to cooperate and was made foreman of the jury at Lifford which found Tyrconnell guilty of treason. Despite a letter of recommendation from Bishop George Montgomery, his application to join the household of Henry, Prince of Wales, in London was turned down. On arriving in Derry on business, Paulet insulted him in a stormy exchange and punched him in the face. O'Doherty was not going to take this lying down. On returning to Inishowen, he consulted his friends to find a means of taking his revenge. Although Niall Garbh O'Donnell was co-operating with the Crown, it is thought that he incited him to rebel, hoping to gain Inishowen for himself. O'Doherty was certainly egged on by his foster-father, Phelim Reagh MacDavitt, who had faced constant harassment from Crown judges over petty offences. Yet O'Doherty had no ambition to change Ulster's political future; he was entirely focused against Paulet.

On 18 April 1608, O'Doherty invited the governor of Culmore Fort, Captain Henry Hart to join him with his wife for dinner at Buncrana. On arrival, O'Doherty arrested them and told them to hand over the fort. To save her husband's life, Mrs. Hart lured the warders into an ambush, which allowed O'Doherty to gain control of Culmore and its arsenal. With assistance from MacDavitt and seventy men, he now made a surprise assault on Derry. Despite Derry's small garrison showing some resistance, it had been caught napping, and he gained control when MacDavitt shot Paulet dead. Although the townspeople barricaded themselves into the Bishop's house and other adjacent dwellings, they were without arms or victuals. When a piece of ordnance was brought to bear, the occupants, including the Bishop's wife and her sister, surrendered. They were arrested and the City was set on fire, which destroyed all eighty-five houses and the Bishop's library of 'heretical' books. O'Doherty was joined by five hundred men from supportive clans, who gained control of several surrounding forts and villages. There was a further outbreak of rebellion in south Armagh, and rumours spread that, in the autumn, Tyrone and Tyrconnell would return at the head of a Spanish force.

Although Chichester recognised that O'Doherty had been wronged by Paulet, he criticised him for inciting rebellion. Phillips, who received many Londonderry residents at Coleraine, called for urgent assistance, and, despite having only 1,700 men at his disposal, Chichester moved quickly, sending north Sir Richard Wingfield, the King's Marshal, with eight hundred men from the Pale. The King issued instructions in western Scotland to have any Irishmen fleeing from justice arrested and he diverted Andrew Stewart, 3rd Lord Ochiltree with two hundred Scottish troops from a planned expedition in the Scottish Isles. Ochiltree landed at Carrickfergus[31] and joined up with Wingfield to outflank O'Doherty and crush him at Kilmacrenan. Although O'Doherty escaped south, vainly hoping that a Spanish force would arrive to support him, Philip III had no such plans. Wingfield took control of what remained of Derry and captured Buncrana, which was burned by his troops in revenge. He used his cannon on Burt, where O'Doherty's wife and son had taken refuge with some of the prisoners from Derry including the Bishop's wife, and it quickly surrendered. Chichester rounded up the rebels in Armagh, hanging most of them. On his return from the south, O'Doherty made a last stand with one thousand men at the Rock of Doon, but was killed by a chance shot. Wingfield was determined to make an example of him. His dismembered body was put on display in Derry, and his head, skewered on a spike, was brought to Newgate in Dublin. One by one, clans still supporting the Gaelic cause were brought to submission and survivors were brought to trial. MacDavitt and his men were captured after being cornered in a wood, and were tried for treason at Lifford. They were 'dragged through the streets tied to horses, hanged, disembowelled, decapitated and cut into quarters'.[f] When hostilities eventually ended in September 1609, Chichester was granted the Lordship of Inishowen. He was now convinced that the only means of restoring peace was a grandiose scheme to outnumber the remaining Catholic Gaelic inhabitants by repopulating Ulster with Protestant settlers loyal to the Crown. A vast proportion of the Province was confiscated, and, as a first step, Chichester persuaded James I to invite undertakers to take over tracts of land and to establish stability and religious conformity by 'planting' large numbers of British settlers. In an effort to strengthen the economy and keep rival interests in order, even native Irish landlords offered parts of their estates. 'The Irish system of allegiance was seen

---

[31] Chichester considered that Ochiltree's men were inexperienced, being both poorly clothed and armed, but, as soon as O'Doherty's rebellion had been put down, he sent Captain Richard Bingley with a galley to support their postponed expedition in Scotland.

to have exacerbated inter-clan rivalries.'[g] Plantation was now seen as the means whereby chronic tribal warfare among a rebellious population would be stamped out and a vast territory (wasted by inefficient agriculture and by the interminable ravages of revengeful plunderers) would be brought within the rule of English law and become, at last, a prosperous land. At the same time, all the Realm would be protected against the possibility of invasion from the north and the west. The Protestant religion would be spread and legally enforced among a people the Elizabethan and Jacobean English regarded as lost in superstition, and Irish 'lawlessness and depravity' would give way to English 'civility'.[h]

With the lands to the west of the Bann River being occupied by the most belligerent of the Irish, fears that Tyrone would return 'cooled men's affections' for the plantation'.[i] In April 1609, Robert Jacob, the Solicitor-General wrote:

> There are great probabilities that all the people of that province would easily run into rebellion if Tyrone should return, or if any munition or aid should be sent to them from foreign parts; for they are generally diseased with the rumour of the new plantation that is intended … They want no men, notwithstanding the late wars, the famine and the great plague that was amongst them.[j]

It was always known that plantation presented risks.

Chapter 7

Planning of the plantation of Ulster
1608 – 1609

The idea of a plantation in Ulster appealed to both James I and Salisbury, but the decision was taken only after the flight of the Earls and O'Doherty's rebellion. They concluded that the Crown could no longer afford the cost of maintaining a sizeable military presence, and the concept of establishing a 'civilised' community in what had traditionally been the most remote and belligerent part of Ireland strongly appealed to them. The issue was to find undertakers of substance to fund the required investment in buildings and infrastructure. This was no different from colonisation in the Americas. As James Stevens Curl has explained:

> In May 1607 the first settlers had reached the mainland of Virginia, and schemes of colonisation were occupying men's minds to a remarkable degree. ... Expansionist policies in an England with a growing population encouraged the formation of colonies across the seas, and Ulster, like Virginia, was an obvious choice for a settlement. ... Ulster was geographically less remote, and so would be more attractive to settlers, while the costs of colonisation would be less.[a]

Despite so much focus on plantation, many issues remained unresolved. The escheated counties provided 'a greater extent of land than any prince in Europe had to dispose of'.[b] 'James saw it as the greatest project of his reign.'[c] In July 1608, Chichester and Davies set out from Dublin 'to garner all the evidence they could to give legal justification for their confiscation'.[d] In the light of Doherty's rebellion, they were convinced that their initial plan to break up the great lordships into smaller freeholds to be owned by lesser Gaelic clansmen was unlikely to bring peace; it was preferable to attract British colonists and to clear the land of natives. Davies wrote to the King that there was a danger 'to this plantation if the number of civil persons to be planted do not exceed the number of natives, who will quickly overgrow them, as weeds overgrow good corn'.[e]

The land was literally uncharted territory and would need to be surveyed. The native Irish had never measured their lands in acres; provincial kingdoms were organised into a hierarchical structure, which identified areas of profitable land, varying in size according to their fertility. In the 1570s, when the English started the division of Irish land into shires along English lines, each shire was subdivided into baronies, which tended to equate to the previous Irish feudal divisions. The smallest subdivisions, referred to in much of Ulster as 'balliboes', were renamed by the English as 'townlands'. In line with Gaelic practice, these were not uniform in size but varied in accordance with the land's fertility, and were deemed to be capable of supporting two families. To provide a measurement in acres, townlands were generally described as '60 acres of profitable land' (although the deemed acreage varied from county to county). It was only during Mountjoy's expedition that Richard Bartlett had first provided a series of maps to show the route taken by his expeditionary force. To save time, he had established the location of ecclesiastical, temporal lands and fisheries by talking to local informants. He also assumed that each barony was 1,000 acres, although no actual measurement was undertaken and this area rarely bore any semblance to reality. Collaboration was not always peaceful, and Bartlett was murdered while surveying in Donegal. At the same time, the warship *Tremontana* had started to chart Donegal's coastline.

No land transfers could take place without establishing the areas and locations involved. Chichester set up a Commission to survey the six counties of Coleraine, Tyrone, Armagh, Fermanagh, Cavan and Donegal, and their work was completed in September. This followed many of the earlier systems of measurement. In its final analysis, it established that there were 459,110 notional acres in the six counties available for allocation by the Crown. This compares with a modern measurement of 3,690,714 statute acres.

Although Chichester's initial reaction to Doherty's rebellion had been to remove all native Irish from the areas to be planted, he soon considered that it would be politic to make reasonable provision for some of them, and he opposed Davies's calls, which were supported by Sir James Ley, the Chief Justice, for their removal. He no longer sought to segregate native Irish and new British settlers completely and made a list of proposals, entitled *'Certain Notes and Remembrances'*, hoping that the native Irish would be 'prised away from their disloyal inclinations 'if they might be induced by entertainment, or gifts of land, with some reasonable help to stock and manure it''.[f] Without a substantial allocation of territory, he feared that they 'will kindle a new fire in those parts at one time or other, if they be not well looked to or provided for in some reasonable measure'.[g] He was particularly concerned to ensure that the Government honoured agreements already entered into with many of the lesser lords, who were 'worthy the cherishing'. Disregarding them, he felt, would only lead to bitter resentment. He suggested that Counties Cavan and Fermanagh could be divided between Irish freeholders, but wanted lesser clans, for practical reasons, left where they were. He believed that they would become loyal subjects if required to run their estates on English lines and were prevented from ranging their cattle across the countryside in traditional Irish manner. He also hoped that they would become Protestant. He pressed the claims of servitors, particularly those commanding garrison forts in Ulster (of which he was one), but believed they would need financial inducement to position themselves in areas of strategic military importance or those exposed and vulnerable. Servitors would provide security for less experienced settlers against future troubles.

Chichester had been extremely concerned at the King's large grants to Scottish suitors at Court. He was horrified that great estates were being allocated to favourites and others, who lacked the commitment and resources required. He feared that the arrival of yet more Scottish islanders would only cause trouble. In fact, James shared Chichester's concerns in this respect and was deeply suspicious of feuding among Scotland's Gaelic speaking islanders. Yet he wanted to encourage the plantation of lowland Scots. He had the good sense to advise Chichester not to offer any land until a final plan was agreed and the survey completed; he particularly wanted to avoid offers being made to rebels likely to disturb the peace.

The King set up a Committee, the Commissioners for Irish Cases, to provide a detailed plan. Its members included Davies, Ley, Sir Anthony St Leger, Master of the Rolls, Sir Oliver St John, Master of the Ordnance, Docwra and Fullerton. When Chichester was not included, he worried that his advice would be ignored. Yet it moved forward with urgency before further outbreaks of rebellion had time to develop and it considered a range of different views. Salisbury wanted English and Scottish settlers intermingled on land near rivers, with Irish being kept on the plains, and servitors occupying the boundaries near to the Irish. He also wanted to keep proportions appropriate in size to the means and standing of undertakers (although he then proposed allocating the land by lot).

In January 1609, the committee at last published its comprehensive plan, 'The Orders and Conditions'. These were well received. Florence Conry, Archbishop of Tuam, declared that the King is graciously pleased to distribute the said lands to such of his subjects, as well of Great Britain as of Ireland, as being of merit and ability shall seek the same, with a mind not only to benefit themselves but to do service to the crown and commonwealth.[h]

Undertakers were to be offered estates in three different sizes, containing 2,000, 1,500 and 1,000 (notional) acres with additional bog and woodland as the country could 'conveniently afford'. There were to be three classes of grantees: English and Scottish undertakers, who were required to plant their areas with English or inland Scottish inhabitants; servitors, who were free to accept Irish, English or inland Scottish inhabitants; and native Irish, who would be made freeholders. Each undertaker was to 'be responsible for the enclosure and development of land for agricultural purposes according to the latest techniques'.[i] In the expectation of considerable demand, the King confirmed that proportions would be allocated by lot 'to avoid Emulation and Controversy', although he 'was to have the final say in which county any Planter should have his Proportion'.[j] Undertakers were to pay an annual rent of £5 6s. 8d. (English) for every 1,000 acres, to be waived for the first two years. Servitors with larger proportions were to provide military service, if required, and to pay a quit rent of £8 for every 1,000 acres, reduced to £5 6s. 8d. if they had no native Irish tenants. The native Irish were obliged to pay a rent of £10 13s. 4d., waived for the first year only, and were to abandon their nomadic and subsistence farming methods by living in villages and adopting English practice in tillage and husbandry. It was argued that the higher charge made to the native Irish was justified as they did not face the same costs of removal, but they faced the same building obligations as the settlers. 'Chichester was especially keen to educate the natives in the skill of building houses like those found in the Pale',[k] so that the 'rude and primitive cabins' found all over Ulster were replaced. The natives risked forfeiture if involved in rebellion, and 'armed followers of Gaelic chieftains were to be banished into the wilder parts of the west or forced into military service'.[l] Many took 'to the hills, woods and bogs whence they waged unremitting guerrilla warfare.'[m]

Each undertaker faced building obligations. Those holding 2,000 acres were required to build a castle with a strong court or 'bawn' (earthen-banked enclosure) about it; those with 1,500 acres were to provide a stone or brick house with a strong bawn, and those with 1,000 acres had at least to provide a strong bawn. Tenants were to pay rent in accordance with English law without further (Irish) exactions. For mutual protection, houses (including arms stores) were to be built in settlements near their bawn. Undertakers were to swear an Oath of Allegiance to the King and to be Protestant. They were required to have available at all times a convenient store of arms that were to be supplied to competent, able-bodied men. Reviews and musters of armed men were to take place every six months 'according to the manner of England'.[n]

Undertakers (or their competent agents) were required to reside on their proportions for at least five years, after which they could sell, but not to the native Irish. They could import victuals, 90, , tools and stock into Ireland free of customs duty. Tenants were to be in residence within two years. Land was to be set aside to support Trinity College, Dublin, and to maintain a free school. Church lands were to be assigned to the Established Church.

There were to be sufficient parish churches in every proportion with incumbents to be remunerated from a tithe paid in kind by each parishioner. Far from conquering the hearts and minds of the Catholic native Irish, the tithe caused great resentment. It was Irish determination to remain united in their Catholicism, which would galvanise their resistance to the colonisation that was to come. It was perhaps overlooked that Scottish undertakers and settlers were likely to be Presbyterian and would not readily support the payment of tithes to the Established (Anglican) Church of Ireland with its panoply of Bishops.

A second publication clarified and amended some of the terms. These included a requirement for a mix in the size of proportions in each county. Locations for towns were identified and it was agreed that, when established, these should send burgesses to the Irish Parliament. Each proportion was to be a self-contained parish with its own church, with sixty acres of glebe lands allocated to the incumbent. The mix of undertakers, servitors and native Irish was also to be controlled. A seven hundred and fifty acre area was allocated to fund a free school at Mountjoy.

From a Protestant viewpoint and by the standards of the day, the scheme seemed admirable in its objective of creating a settled community in Ulster. Great credit must be given to James, who personally supervised much of its direction. Yet Victorian commentators have argued that the confiscation of an overlord's ancestral lands was a travesty of justice for its occupiers, who had not been accused or convicted of participation in any rebellion. Although the overlord might have taken up arms against the English or otherwise transgressed against its Government, he was not the land's proprietor. 'It became clear that the inhabitants of those escheated counties were going to have to pay for the behaviour of their overlords,'[o] Curl has explained:

> An Irish Chief was the supreme authority in the area where he ruled, but, unlike a feudal lord in England, was not a major landowner in the English or Continental sense, for he enjoyed only an interest for life in demesne lands that were associated with the chieftainship. He did have the right to levies on lands, however, and he could call upon his subjects for moneys or services in times of war.[p]

'This made the old order in Gaelic Ireland aristocratic rather than feudal.'[q] Madden has added:

> According to English law, the ultimate property of all estates is in the crown, and land is held only by virtue of a royal grant: according to the Irish law, the property of land was vested in the sept, tribe or community, who were co-partners with their chief, rather than his tenants or vassals. Whenever a change was made from Irish to English tenure, an obvious injustice was done to the inferior occupants, for they were reduced from the rank of proprietors to that of tenants at will.[r]

Yet the sept, tribe or community had always acted in accordance with the will of its chief and provided him with men. If their chief was rebelling, then it is reasonable to assume that they were a part of it. The whole purpose of the plantation was to achieve a change to English law, where farmers became tenants and paid rent without further obligation to their landlord.

Although large numbers of prospective undertakers lodged sureties to obtain proportions of land, it became clear to the Committee that the new maps were still inadequate for the purpose of making allocations. Sir Josias Bodley, the Director General and Overseer of Fortifications in Ireland, was asked to lead a second more 'exact' survey, which was begun in the summer of 1609, even though this would delay allocations until April 1610. The objective was to name each townland and show its boundaries. Time still did not permit proper measurement of the lands and the surveyors again relied heavily on local advice, mainly from former Irish rent gatherers, who helpfully identified boundaries from venerated trees, streams, Neolithic remains and other markers. Eight men were involved, including the able cartographer, Thomas Raven, who was appointed the City of London's Surveyor in Ireland and an Alderman of Londonderry. After the survey's completion, Davies and Ley brought it to London.

Despite Chichester's concern that he would not be listened to, the Committee heeded his advice not to grant excessively large estates. Davies's father-in-law, the Catholic George Touchet, Lord Audley, made an initial application to plant 100,000 acres in Tyrone and Armagh[32], but this was eventually turned down. It was considered essential for security that settlers should reside in villages of towns, and this required estates to remain close knit. The Committee also accepted Chichester's view that removing 'Swordsmen' (local brigands) from Ulster to Connaught or Munster would only spread disturbances further afield.

Notwithstanding his earlier misgivings, Chichester had been impressed with Montgomery's and Hamilton's progress in bringing lowland Scots into Antrim and Down, and recommended that Scots as well as English should become undertakers, a proposal which appealed to James I. James wanted Scots to plant Strabane (south of Derry), which had been burned during O'Doherty's rebellion. The Scottish Privy Council actively encouraged Scots to invest, and seventy-seven applicants offered sureties to occupy over 141,000 acres of Ulster. There was no shortage of English applicants, despite recent calls for settlers to plant Virginia. 'Underpopulated and underdeveloped Ulster offered prospective colonists a secure title to cheap land, bountiful fisheries and great tracts of valuable woodland.'[u] The Privy Council soon feared that there would be insufficient land available. 'Yet the principal anxiety of the King and his ministers was whether or not there were enough *men of substance* with the resources needed to implement the plantation conditions.'[v]

He was disappointed at the dearth of English and Scottish peers among applicants. Sir Francis Bacon pointed out that servitors 'will not be able to go through with the charge of good and substantial plantations'.[w] He believed that 'settlers should congregate in defensible walled towns for security and not in isolated farms, arguing that the planning and creation of urban developments, highways, places of worship, forts, bridges and other 'public' buildings should be carried out by the State, and not left to individuals working in an uncoordinated way and in a piecemeal fashion'.[x]

---

[32] Audley proposed that, in return for a grant of 100,000 acres, he and his son Sir Mervyn Touchet would build thirty-three castles and thirty-three towns, allocating 600 acres to each castle and 2,400 acres to each town. They would settle thirty families in each town, and offered to pay £533 per year in rent, starting after the fourth year. 'He asked for manorial rights and permits to hold markets and fairs and for a licence to set up iron mills and to make iron and glass for forty-one years.'[s] It was only because Davies had lobbied Salisbury on his father-in-law's behalf that his scheme was not rejected out of hand. Chichester was appalled when the Privy Council recommended it. Audley had not made a success of his earlier settlement near Castlehaven in Munster and had expended insufficient money to make his home there habitable. This was a last gasp attempt to restore his family's fortune. He petitioned James for help to prevent 'the ruin and downfall of an old and decayed house'.[t] Yet despite Chichester's opposition, he was eventually made Chief Undertaker of the Barony of Omagh.

The Privy Council also wanted to demonstrate the moral justification for the plantation. It argued that the native population was so reduced that it could not maintain more than one-third of the farm land. It was also poor and unskilled, making it unable to meet the building requirements or to stock and improve the waste land. The Council drew on biblical and historic precedent including the allocation of the Promised Land to the Israelites coming out of Egypt and Roman settlement of its conquered territories. Although the timing of Irish plantations coincided with those in Virginia, they were potentially far larger and of far greater significance for Britain's security. With Britain remaining overpopulated, emigration would reduce tensions at home.

> Once achieved, Ireland would become another Britain endowed with so many dowries of nature (<u>considering</u> the fruitfulness of the soil, the ports, the rivers, the fishings, the quarries, the woods, or other materials, and especially the race and generation of men, valiant hard and active), as it is not easy, no not upon the continent, to find such a confluence of commodities, if the hand of man did join with the hand of nature.[y]

Although the proposed arrangements called for most native Irish to move to locations controlled by servitors, the Church or 'deserving' Irish freeholders, they were determined to stay put on their ancestral lands. Yet the escheated counties were to be divided so that 36 per cent was granted to undertakers, 12 per cent to servitors, 16 per cent to the Church, 20 per cent to Irish freeholders, 3 per cent to University College, Dublin, and 3 per cent to schools, towns and forts. This left a balance of 10 per cent, which was to be allocated, under an arrangement still being negotiated, to the City of London.

Chapter 8

The plantation of the escheated lands in Ulster is begun
1609 – c. 1611

The detailed planning for the plantation took time, and the King's schedule proved impossibly tight.

> The major grantees had to be given their patents and to be escorted to their allotted lands before large numbers of ordinary people could be persuaded to risk crossing the North Channel and the Irish Sea to become colonists in an unfamiliar land.[a]

Once they had been accepted, undertakers had until 24 June 1610 to present themselves either personally or through representatives to the Lord Deputy and the Plantation Commissioners and were required to be in occupation by 30 September. Assigning each estate and preparing patents was time consuming. Bishop George Montgomery and Sir James Fullerton were made responsible for allocating each parcel of land. In November 1609, they began drawing up a scheme for County Tyrone. Once approved by the Council, plans were produced for each of the other escheated counties, except County Coleraine and its adjacent areas including Derry, where plans were well-advanced for a grant to the City of London. The King's concept of mixing settlers from different locations in the same precinct proved impracticable. They tended to arrive in groups of relatives, tenants or neighbours from one location and wanted to remain together. Yet the King still hankered after mixing English and Scots and retained areas for combined occupation. Undertakers cast lots for the areas on offer, but could allocate proportions within each precinct as they chose. With each undertaker having first choice, he was likely to pick land with access to rivers and loughs. Some coastal soil was thin and acid after centuries of storms and would need much manuring to make it usable.

> Chichester worried that the summer was coming to an end and no undertakers had arrived. Yet he was required to issue warrants of possession and

to preside over the swearing of the Oath of Supremacy. He feared that the Commissioners would not tolerate the cold winter weather in open fields without accommodation. Some of them were reluctant to travel, and he expressed gratitude to the Marshal of the Army, who accompanied them

> for they shall find many stubborn and stiff-necked people to oppose them and to hinder the free passage thereof, the word of removing and transplanting being to the natives as welcome as the sentence of death.[b]

He also feared that settlers would struggle on such desolate land, while having to compete with the warlike natives they were displacing. They needed enough provisions to survive the first winter before being able to plant their spring corn. They would need shelter before their more permanent dwellings were erected. They had to enlist natives to guide them to their lands and to build their houses. This resulted in many being in an Irish style. With no boats or bridges, crossing rivers was difficult and dangerous. Thomas Blennerhasset, a member of a wealthy East Anglian farming family, which became prominent undertakers and landowners, warned settlers coming to his estates to have their weapons ready to deal with 'the cruel wood-kerne, the devouring wolf, and other suspicious Irish', who might well 'put on the smiling countenance' but did 'threaten every hour'.[c]

The wood-kerne, who were generally former Gaelic soldiers living rough, proved a real menace. Until his death in 1616, they still had hopes that Tyrone would return at the head of a Spanish army to kick out the British. Armed men posed a great danger and were particularly numerous in Armagh and in the wooded uplands. Sir Toby Caulfeild had to lock in his cattle at night, but 'the woolfe and the wood-kerne (within caliver shot of his forte) have often times a share'.[d] Labourers cutting timber in woodlands were forced to travel in groups of ten or twelve. 'Again and again wood-kerne emerged from their forest and mountain retreats to plunder the settlers.'[e] There was a second problem. 'The waters between Scotland and Ireland were infested with pirates.'[f] Thus travel by both land and sea was fraught with danger and there were problems in moving large sums of money to and from Britain until Bills of Exchange became the normal mode of payment.

Although Chichester had made great efforts to send Irish rebels to Sweden as mercenaries, plenty were still at large. The Government attempted to bribe Gaelic communities to hand over any in their midst. Although many were rounded up, they were reluctant to go to Sweden and often escaped back into hiding. There were fears that as soon as they reached Scandinavia to fight for Gustavus Adolphus, they would change sides. In the autumn of 1609, Chichester rounded up nine hundred of them. They set out for Sweden in four ships, but were delayed both by bad weather in the English Channel and mutinies on board. When the captain of one ship put in to Milford-on-Sea in Hampshire, they terrorised the local populace stealing '30 or 40 muttons'.[g] On reaching Tilbury, the 'swordsmen' were holding the captain and crew as prisoners. In February 1610, Salisbury sent Phillips, who was in England, to investigate. He reported back that they were complaining of being underpaid, under-victualled and having poor clothing, all of which the captain admitted. When these problems were resolved, it would seem that they went on their way. Although Chichester was eventually able to report that 6,000 swordsmen had arrived in Sweden, many quickly left to meander round Europe. Some even visited Tyrone in Rome; he described them as 'another race of gypsies, they now wander through the world, lost'.[h] Most reached Flanders, where they joined compatriots fighting for the Spanish. Some even returned to Ireland to renew the fight against British settlers.

The Commissioners started the plantation in County Cavan, where Chichester hoped the native Irish might prove more amenable than in other areas. The natives immediately claimed that their lands were freeholds, which could not be forfeited by their chieftain's attainder. They engaged the services of a lawyer from the Pale, who claimed that they held their estates in accordance with the rules of Common Law, but Davies overruled him and argued that they were being treated reasonably as they were being offered alternative lands. Warrants for possession were eventually issued to undertakers without further resistance.

Undertakers came from all walks of life. There were the younger sons of gentlemen seeking lands of their own, Scottish nobles, like the Earl of Abercorn, who was 'induced' into taking land to encourage others, men of the King's household, servitors, who often accepted estates in lieu of arrears of pay from the Crown, merchants, sea captains, Protestant clergy, veterans of the European wars, artisans, artificers, and dispossessed farmers from Scotland. Many of the English, particularly the servitors, came from the West Country. Chichester noted that the English had more capital [but were reluctant to spend it], but the Scots [who tended to come from south-west Scotland, where land was hard to come by – often feuding border reivers fleeing from justice] were the more determined planters.[i]

The Grahams from the Scottish Borders arrived in Roscommon, but, finding the land there laid waste, drifted over the rest of Ulster. Chichester reported them as 'ill neighbours, for they are a fractious and naughty people'.[j] Many borderers of humble origin followed the Grahams' example and arrived in Ireland to escape justice. Most ended up in Donegal and Fermanagh, where they formed the majority of settlers. Those with no strong religious affiliation found it 'economically advantageous'[k] to conform to the Established Church, although their descendants often became Methodists or Dissenters.

Chichester noted that settlers with money were scared off at the first sign of trouble. No one attempted to clear out the remaining Irish, but negotiated with them for supplies and promised to apply to the King to let them stay. With so much work required, the Irish were indispensable as labourers, even though the terms of the settlers' grants required their departure by May 1611.

The King took great care in his choice of undertakers for the nine Scottish precincts, particularly to ensure that they had adequate financial resources, always a scarce commodity at home. He appointed his young cousins, Ludovick Stuart, 2nd Duke of Lennox and his brother, Esmé, Seigneur d'Aubigny, as his Chief Undertakers. Both had fulfilled senior diplomatic and military roles on his behalf and he considered them as heirs to the Scottish Crown after his own children. James Hamilton, who had become Earl of Abercorn[33] in 1603, was also chosen. All three were well able to finance the development of their precincts. Yet, in 1611, d'Aubigny sold his interest in County Cavan to Hamilton of Claneboye.

Abercorn, who was Protestant, was granted 10,217 acres at Dunnalong and a small proportion at Strabane in County Tyrone, where he built a castle. He arranged for two of his younger brothers to be granted adjacent areas. The Protestant Sir Claude Hamilton of Shawfield received Killeny, adjacent to Dunnalong, and Eden in the Plumbridge proportion. He also acquired part of Tirenmurietagh in County Tyrone. The other brother, Sir George Hamilton of Greenlaw, acquired lands at Leckpatrick and Ardstraw nearby, but was an ardent Catholic. James turned a blind eye to Sir George's Catholicism (just as he had to his father Lord Claud Hamilton in Scotland). When Sir Claude died in 1614, his children, who were still minors, were brought up by Sir George, but he insisted on William, the eldest son, becoming Catholic. When Abercorn died in 1618, he was succeeded as 2nd Earl by his eldest son, James, then aged fifteen. James's younger brothers, Claude and George were also placed in Sir George's guardianship, and also became Catholic. Claude inherited Strabane, later becoming Lord Strabane, while George, received Dunnalong, where they nurtured enclaves of Scottish Catholics. Charles I followed his father's lead and ignored this pocket of recusancy. George Downham, Bishop of Derry, writing in 1630, reported:

> Sir George Hamilton, who is otherwise a courteous and civil gentleman, has tried to draw people into popery. Claude [his nephew] would be a hopeful young gentleman were he not poisoned with popery, but maintains Papists so much that there will be a revolt in Strabane if any more of the Scotch Papists come there. The Archbishop of Glasgow has sent to me hoping that I will not harbour in my diocese Papists who have been expelled from Scotland.[1]

Claude encouraged his agent, Robert Algeo, to keep on good terms with the native Irish on his estate, which was in the heartland of Turlough Luineach

---

[33] Abercorn was the eldest son of Lord Claud Hamilton, Lord Paisley, the youngest son of the Duke of Châtelherault, Regent of Scotland for James's mother Mary. Lord Claud had been in great favour with James despite becoming Catholic, but tragically became insane in about 1590. Although the King's adherence to Protestantism was absolute, he had a soft spot, while in Scotland, for a group of Catholic nobles led by Lord Claud and the Earl of Huntly, and manipulated them to weaken the 'overweaning power' of his Protestant Government, which he had no means to influence, supported as they were by the Kirk. (The extraordinary relationship between James and 'the Catholic Earls' in Scotland is covered in more detail in my book, *The Survival of the Crown*, published by the Book Guild in 2014.)

O'Neill's former lordship. He flouted Plantation conditions by leasing extensive areas to local families. This allowed his estates to prosper. The area was not exclusively Catholic as fifty Scottish Protestants settled on Sir William's lands at Eden and Killeny. In 1628, when plantation conditions were relaxed to allow undertakers to lease up to one quarter of their lands to native Irish (see page 172), Sir William still faced a fine for exceeding his quota. As a devoted Royalist, he lost everything in supporting the Crown against Cromwell and 'travelled to the Continent with the exiled Charles II'.[m] He was one of the few Catholics in Ulster to have his estates returned after the Restoration.

The remaining allocation of Scottish undertakers was quickly filled. Most applicants were Reformers, generally the younger sons of minor lairds or merchants from around Edinburgh, who had to be cut back to smaller areas than requested. Under English law, Scots were 'foreigners', who were not entitled to full property rights, but their position was secured by making them denizens, a first step towards naturalisation. It was not until July and August of 1610 that most patents were allocated, but, by the early autumn, forty-five of the fifty-nine Scottish undertakers or their agents had arrived. The land transfer went more smoothly than Chichester had dared to hope, but the settlers were shocked to find their lands ravished with buildings in ruins on arrival. Several sold up and went home. Those who stayed needed enough food to see them through the winter and faced the expense of importing cattle and grain from Britain. They spent the winter building forts and homes, while preparing the land for the following year's crops. With the Scots being familiar with the need for security, their castles were built strongly in typical baronial style, well-provided with gun loops.

James continued to fret over delays, although Chichester assured him that 'great things move slowly'.[n] He remained concerned at the non-arrival of some undertakers and the lack of British tenants. He threatened to forfeit those who were not in occupation by 1 May 1611. Although settlers began to appear, he remained impatient. He appointed Lord (formerly Sir George) Carew as head of a commission to assess the situation. In July 1611, it set out with Chichester from Dublin and established that both English and Scottish undertakers had made a very slow start. Although they had taken possession of their lands, many had returned to Britain without any action to remove the native Irish. Servitors commanding forts had done better, but had enjoyed the Crown's financial support.

There were pockets of progress. As already shown in footnote 32 on page 92, Audley, who had been severely wounded at the battle of Kinsale, became Chief Undertaker in the Barony of Omagh. Although it had been intended that he should allot proportions to subtenants, he retained everything for himself and his family. He also became a servitor at Orior, where he was allocated 500 acres with 2,000 more to be received on the death of Art MacBaron O'Neill, whose grant extended only for life. In all, Audley and his family received close to the 100,000 acres that he had originally requested, but much was 'infertile mountainous land'.[o] He 'threw himself into the enterprise with energy and enthusiasm',[p] and managed estates on behalf of his sons. Davies received two proportions, each of 2,000 acres, which Audley supervised. Yet Audley's lands had insufficient timber for his building needs. Despite his dreams of smelting iron[34] at great profit, he had insufficient wood to make charcoal. By Christmas 1612, he had almost completed his castle at Ballynahatty, but Bodley reported that he

> was much hindered and cast behind by a violent storm of thunder, lightning and tempest, which overthrew part of the said building, slew one of his workmen, and hurt divers others. The same he is now again re-edifying and purposeth to encompass with a bawn of good circuit.[q]

Ten years later, Ballynahatty received praise from the Commissioners. In 1615, James congratulated Audley on having settled English and Scottish tenants with English cattle on 'the most barren and rough land in all the country'.[r] Unfortunately this was not correct; his lands did not appeal to British tenants and, by 1619, only sixty-four colonists remained.

Audley built two further castles on Davies's proportion and the elegant Castle Curlews, with its wonderful views on the slopes of Slieveglass and Bolaght Mountain, although Davies considered it indefensible and in an area unfit for habitation. He started the building of Castlederg[35] on the site of an old O'Neill tower house at the ford across the River Derg. This was completed by Davies at a cost of £3,000 after Audley's death in 1617, aged sixty-six. The land was then let to twenty Irish undertakers, who established 3,000 tenants. Audley's son, Sir Mervyn Touchet, who was created Earl of Castlehaven, proved an inefficient landlord. He speeded up the departure of British settlers by trebling their rents and sold much of the estate to his mother's relatives, the Mervyns. 'He was eventually convicted of homosexuality and of raping his wife, resulting in his execution in 1631.'[s] Sir Richard Fiennes, Lord Saye and Seale, was granted 3,000 acres at Oneilland in County Armagh. Although already an old man, he was hoping to demonstrate his leadership skills. He took up his patent in June 1610, but soon passed it to Sir Anthony Cope, a substantial Oxfordshire landowner. Cope's son built 'a grand cross-shaped house at Castleraw'.[t] 'The Savages, one of the few remaining Old English families in Ulster, built a tower house at Kirkistown in the Ards in 1622.'[u] Castle Caulfeild, built by Sir Toby Caulfeild, 'was fitted with splendid bay windows, rendering it indefensible',[v] but it had the strong fort at Charlemont nearby.

By 1620, Lough Erne was ringed with castles in various styles. Thomas and Sir Edward Blennerhasset, farmers from Norfolk, had acquired 1,000 acres at Tollimakein to add to their proportion at Lurg, and became 'the pre-eminent

---

[34] There was iron ore to be found at the bottom of Slieve Gallion, in the south east of County Londonderry.

[35] It was strong enough to withstand the assault of the rebel commander, Sir Phelim O'Neill, in 1641.

landlords in north Fermanagh'.[w] Thomas encouraged friends to join him, but realised that hard work would be needed to develop the lands' fertility. He claimed:

> Fayre England, she hath more people that she can well sustaine; goodly Ulster for want of people unmanured, her pleasant fields and rich groundes, they remain, if not desolate, worse.[x]

Although he admitted that these were dangerous conquered lands, there were 'fortes and garrisons in paye' and 'many good neighbours'.[y] The two brothers each built a substantial fort for protection. Termon Magrath near Pettigo was another stronghold on Lough Erne. It had been granted by Elizabeth to the Franciscan friar, Mieler Magrath[36], after he converted to Protestantism. He later became Bishop of Clogher and Archbishop of Cashel.

Chichester was responsible for allocating estates to servitors. He did not relish this task, knowing that there was insufficient land to meet demand. Yet forts generally had land allocated to them, and servitors commanding them often obtained outright possession. Chichester seems to have acted fairly, although some grantees were quick to sell up. Many were disappointed with what they were offered, but Chichester had no choice. He hoped that they might become better provided by leasing lands being granted to the Londoners in Coleraine and elsewhere.

'All over Ulster new castles, defensive works and mansions were rising up, providing outward and visible signs of the arrival of a new order.'[z] Castles were in a variety of styles, reflecting each builder's background. These supplemented the network of forts already built for protection. Chichester never forgot the need for security. Joymount, his principal home at Carrickfergus, was close to the defensive wall being built with great industry to secure the town[37]. This Jacobean mansion was strongly built, despite its bay windows, and had 'a good quantitie of grounde for an orcharde'.[aa] In 1611, he rebuilt Belfast Castle to provide him with a second Jacobean mansion[38] on the site of the old Norman fort. This also had bay windows, but was surrounded by a new City, with which

---

[36] He seems to have faced a hostile time. In 1617, a Franciscan reported that he was 'cursed by the Protestants for wasting the revenues and manors of the ancient see of Cashel, and derided by the Catholics who are well acquainted with his drunken habits'.[bb]

[37] The stone for building the wall was being hewn into shape in nearby quarries, with teams of oxen and horses carrying it to the site. Limestone mined at Whitehead, which was used for quoins and facings, had to be brought in by barge. These could be damaged if they did not approach in very calm weather.

[38] This was largely rebuilt by Chichester's heir, his brother Edward, Viscount Chichester. When completed, Sir William Brereton recorded:

> At Belfast my Lord Chichester hath another dainty stately house (which is indeed the glory and beauty of the town also), where he is most resident, and is now building an outer brick wall before the gates. This is not so large and vast as the other, but more convenient and commodious; the very end of the lough toucheth upon his gardens and backside; here are also dainty orchards, gardens and walks planted.[cc]

many members of his family would later be associated. This was populated mainly with Scottish settlers living in 'good tymber houses with chimneys'.[dd] Settlers were fined if they failed to attend church. He built an inn 'with very good Lodginge which is a great comforte to travellers in those partes'.[ee] The Government survey of 1611 reported that his mansion and castle was close to completion and 'there is a strong Bawne almost finished which is flankered with foure half Bulwarkes'.[ff] Although this was initially an earthen rampart, reportedly of 'dubious value',[gg] the new survey stated:

> The foundacion of the wall and bulwarkes to the height of the water table is made of stoane, and the reste, being in alle 12 foote high above the ground, is made with bricke. The Bawne will be compased with a lardge and deep ditche or moate which will always stand full of water. The Castle will defend the Passage over the Foorde at Bealfast between the Upper and Lower Clandeboye, and likewise the Bridge over the Owynvarra [the Blackstaff] between Malon and Bealfast. The work is in so good forwardness that it is lyke to be finished by the mydle of the next Somer.[hh]

James's Commissioners found many 'tenementes inhabited, some of them by such cyvell Irish as doe speak English'.[ii] Yet most residents were English or Scottish. There were already three mills nearby, with timber and materials being gathered for a fourth.

In 1612, Chichester was created Lord Chichester, and, in the following year, Belfast was incorporated and could now provide two members to Parliament in Dublin. As 'Lord of the Castle' he had the right to appoint the Sovereign [Mayor]. By 1622, the ecclesiastical commissioners had rebuilt the Parish Church at the junction between the Farset and Lagan rivers. This rivalled the later St. Columb's Cathedral in Londonderry for size. Although 'plotted out in good forme',[jj] Belfast was never planned so grandly as Londonderry and the layout developed as it grew. Chichester fenced off a park with 'a three myle compasse'[kk] (now known as Oldpark). Colonisation in Antrim and Down proved very successful, with Belfast attracting English, Scottish and Manx settlers. Government officials, who were well-positioned to receive choice areas, preferred to be close to the principal towns. 'The Reporte of the Voluntary Worke Done by Servitors and Other Gentlemen of Qualitie upon Lands Given Them by his Majestie or Purchased by Themselves'[ll] made encouraging reading. Chichester leased out large areas to settlers. These were often grossly undervalued by juries of native Irish, whose decisions were not based on rental values but on the much less onerous 'renters' that had traditionally been paid to superior landlords.[mm] He also raised £1,700 in London to acquire estates in Lower Clandeboye. Sir Moses Hill leased lands at Whitehead, where he built a fortified tower, naming it Castle Chichester. This was 'a fayre tymber house walled with brickes, and a towre slated' surrounded by a strong palisade with a drawbridge. His son, Arthur, later planted the area with Lancashire and Cheshire farmers. Baptist Jones established an estate at Marshallstown, enclosing fields with deep ditches and a strong pale. Captain Hugh Clotworthy leased an area near Massereene Fort, where he built

> fayre tymber houses after the English manner … covered over with good shingle togeather with necessarie houses to keepe his Majesties stores of victualles and munition.[nn]

He was captain of the King's boats on Lough Neagh. These included a barque of thirty tons, another of fourteen tons and others of between ten and eight tons, which delivered military stores across the lough into Tyrone and Armagh. Clotworthy raised £91 5s. 0d. to acquire an estate at Templepatrick and was later a tenant of the Londoners. In Donegal, the servitor, Sir Basil Brooke, established himself as a principal landowner at Burt. He 'repaired and strengthened the fifteenth century O'Donnell stronghold but added a Jacobean manor house wing in the English style next to it.'[oo]

William Cole, the son of a member of the Goldsmiths' Company, was responsible for developing Enniskillen. After a distinguished military career in the Low Countries, he arrived in Ireland to fight under Mountjoy at the Moyry Pass and at Kinsale. He was then appointed as servitor of Maguire's Castle at Enniskillen with control of all vessels on Lough Erne. He progressively amassed land; he was granted the Cornagrade estate nearby and acquired Portora. Enniskillen Castle and bawn were badly damaged during the rebellion of 1610-11 leaving them open to surprise attack. Yet Cole established a work force and was paid £266 13s. 4d. to complete repairs. In 1612, in return for undertaking further maintenance, he was granted lands on Enniskillen Island. In 1614, he received a further £133 6s. 8d. to complete more work on the Castle and became the patron of a project to develop Enniskillen. He was instructed to bring in 'twenty persons being English or Scotch and chiefly artificers and mechanics to make, erect and construct a town in a convenient place'.[pp] It was to include a church and cemetery, a market house, a jail for the county, and a public school with a court and gardens adjoining. It was stipulated that he should

> build and erect edifices and buildings … in streets and squares, in such manner and form as shall best suit its site and situation, and for the defence and decency of the said town.[qq]

There was to be a square at the mid point approached by streets from each side.[39] When incorporated in 1613, Enniskillen was authorised to send two members to Parliament, and Cole became its first provost.

Houses in Enniskillen were generally on one storey with an attic lit by dormer windows above. Cole did not stop with housing for settlers. Bodley reported that he was building two bridges over the lough with 'divers carpenters and other artificers that purpose to settle there'.[rr] He established mills; he fired 300,000 bricks and an equivalent proportion of tiles; he completed a church in 1627 with a tower added ten years later; and he built himself a 'good timber house after the English fashion'[ss] with 'a fair garden'. He progressively amassed

---

[39] This was a fairly standard layout, known as a 'diamond'.

more land. Much was acquired from six native Irish land owners, who had fallen into debt, but some came from another servitor, Peter Mostin. This provided sizeable areas for letting to other settlers. By 1641, about two hundred had arrived, a mix of both Scots and English in accordance with James's wishes, although a few native Irish still remained. He was, by then, receiving rent from fifty households. He proved a model 'planter'; he was later knighted[40], and became a valuable Member of Parliament.

Not every servitor was successful. In 1608, John Leigh replaced his brother, Edmund, as custodian of Omagh Fort, which had adjacent abbey lands. Yet he unwisely bought Fintona, a 2,000 acre proportion at Clogher, from Sir Francis Willoughby. The poor boggy and mountainous heathland on one half was impossible to let on any terms. The remaining 1,000 acres were so remote that he could not attract reasonable rents without better access, and could not find tenants prepared to swear the Oath of Supremacy. With a dearth of woodland, to provide timber to meet his building obligations, he needed to drag it 'about 12 or 14 miles at the nearest over bogs and mountains, and some above 22 miles' over poor tracks.[tt] In 1622, he wrote explaining his difficulties to Sir Toby Caulfeild (now Lord Caulfeild of Charlemont), a member of the commission looking into the plantation.

Leigh was always full of good intentions and went on to become High Sheriff of Tyrone. In 1608, he advised James of the shortage of schools. Within a year, James was calling for at least one Free School in every county 'for the education of Youth in learning and religion'.[uuu] Although Chichester undertook to mark out areas of school lands with 'mears and bounds', little more was done. In 1614, James again called for lands to be allocated for what became known as the Royal Schools, and, in 1615, a Free School was opened in rented premises near Mountjoy Castle in Tyrone. This was followed by a school near Mountnorris in Armagh endowed with seven hundred acres. Others were established in Cavan, Fermanagh and Donegal, but the one in County Donegal was poorly located.

Sir Ralph Bingley, who had helped to put down O'Doherty's rebellion, was an unscrupulous and uncompromising soldier. In 1602, he became servitor at Rathmullan and obtained a lease over its monastic lands, including the island of Inch and the fishing rights over Lough Swilly. In 1603, he acquired Carrigans and the monastic lands of Kilmacrenan. He now held 7,120 statute acres, on which he intended to establish settlers. He later took over two undertaker proportions from grantees, who had either died or wanted to sell, and was accused of using devious means to buy out at least eleven patents from native Irish, who were in a precarious financial position. This resulted in them complaining that he had obtained land from them improperly. Despite Bingley's thirst for acquisition, he suddenly sold off 26,240 acres, some to former military associates and some to Andrew Knox, Bishop of Raphoe, who became an

---

[40] Cole was the ancestor of the Lords Mountflorence and of the later Earls of Enniskillen.

energetic coloniser. On his remaining land at Farsetmore and Drumboe, he erected two 'well seated' fortified houses with bawns and provided housing for tenants. He also developed Ballybofey with twelve thatched houses and cottages 'inhabited for the most part with British',[vv] and, in 1619, obtained a licence to hold fairs and markets there. Pynnar's survey showed that it was inhabited by fifty families, some from Flintshire and Cheshire, but also Scots. With a lust for military adventure, in 1627, Bingley took a force from Ireland to join Buckingham's ill-fated expedition to La Rochelle. When he was killed in action on the Ile de Ré, his widow was left destitute and had to sell his remaining estates to pay his debts.

Although a total of 94,013 acres was allocated to native Irish, leases were often only for the duration of the grantee's life, after which they were reserved for English or Scots. Even the 'deserving' Irish found that they were required to move, and were given only a year to uproot themselves from family homelands to unfamiliar territory. Chichester realised that this would 'disquiet the people',[ww] and there was insufficient land on offer to ensure future peace and stability. He believed that military force would be needed to induce some of them to move. To avoid the cost of having to serve on juries, many native Irish refused to accept the freeholds being offered to them. They preferred to take their chance as tenants at will, hoping to remain at the places of their birth. Davies believed that this would make them more comfortable. Chichester was much less optimistic; he feared that they were only waiting for 'an opportunity to cut their landlords throats; for sure he is, they hate the Scottish deadly'.[xx] Although he told Salisbury that he would endeavour to prevent a revolt, he feared that they were 'infinitely discontented'[xx] and were arming themselves, despite a lack of powder and lead. Irish farmers believed that they had been cheated. Despite promises that the plantation would make them better off than under their chieftains, the land they were offered proved inadequate, and they faced substantial building costs. Despite ingratiating themselves with the settlers, they bided their time 'dangerous and resentful'.[yy] 'The passionate hopes of eventually butchering the undertakers and regaining control of the escheated lands burned brightly.'[zz] Those who took to the woods could rely on food, clothing and shelter from those of their kinsmen in employment. These wood-kerne were a serious threat to settlers and to any Irish who complied with the plantation terms. They struck without warning and vanished without trace. Although the settlers organised themselves into posses, manhunts generally proved pointless.

There was another problem. Insufficient settlers were arriving from Britain to fill the available land. It was partly that Protestants feared being isolated in a Catholic community when the Monarchy was being threatened by Catholic plots attempting to undermine the Reformation. The Gunpowder plot had taken place in 1605, and there were continuing fears of a Spanish invasion, which was likely to gain local support if it landed in Ireland. The settlers did not have the financial substance that Bacon had been advocating. To ensure that they could remain on their ancestral lands, the Irish were blindly offering higher rents than British settlers were prepared to pay. Those settlers who did establish themselves needed Irish labour to farm their land and to undertake their building obligations. Notwithstanding the undertakers' commitments to move the Irish out, most retained them as labourers or tenants paying higher rents. With servitors also in short supply, the native Irish remained *in situ,* putting security severely at risk. In the King's eyes, progress in developing settlements lacked the energy and thoroughness he was demanding. His Government feared that the plantation could be undermined at any time, if Tyrone should return at the head of a Spanish and Papal force. They needed to justify continuing to hold O'Cahan without trial in the Tower, when he had not been found guilty of any crime. This left the legality of forfeiting his lands round Coleraine in doubt and made the settlers' occupation of them 'shaky in law',[aaa] a factor which discouraged undertakers from accepting allocations there.

The shortage of settlers was not just an issue of security. It reduced the Dublin Government's tax revenue leaving it with insufficient income to pay its costs. By 1615, despite hoping for substantial plantation profits, the Irish Government was virtually bankrupt. In 1612, its income was £24,000, while expenditure was £33,000. The Crown had inadequate resources to follow through with its plantation scheme. When Salisbury proposed using the financial muscle of the City of London to colonise the most disturbed parts of County Tyrone occupied by the O'Neills and O'Cahans, 'the King responded with alacrity'.[bbb]

Part 3

The plantation of Londonderry

Chapter 9

Initial plans for a plantation
by the City of London
1609 – 1610

Chichester greatly respected Phillips as a soldier and, in 1607, arranged his appointment as military superintendent of Coleraine. Yet providing it with settlers was proving difficult, as the local O'Neill and O'Cahan clans still expected the return of Tyrone with a foreign invasion force to Lough Swilly or Lough Foyle, where swordsmen awaited him in numbers. Despite Phillips's efforts to expand his settlement, it was clear to Salisbury that this would need a lot more financial resources than a servitor could provide. Although Salisbury considered appointing either Lennox, d'Aubigny or Lord Clifton as Chief Undertakers, none of them was enthusiastic. The lack of settlers made James worry that Ulster's security was in jeopardy. The Government could not afford the cost of a Crown-backed plantation, and it needed a body with deep pockets to foot the huge cost of building and fortifying towns.

James supported Salisbury's idea of coercing the Corporation of London into financing Londoners to settle in the fertile and well-wooded area round Derry and Coleraine, and it now became 'one of his pet projects'.[a] The flight of the Earls and O'Doherty's rebellion had left him recognising that the retention of a Gaelic hierarchy would never make Ireland safe. London had a population of 250,000, and its economic and financial strength had been vital to the Crown during the Nine Years' War. The City had provided Elizabeth with £80,000 in loans and a substantial number of men to fight for her. In return, its merchants had benefitted from valuable contracts to provide military supplies. When Salisbury was asked to promote the scheme with the City, he took Phillips into his confidence. Phillips later recollected him as

> conceiving the Londoners to be the ablest body to undergo so brave and great a work as the plantation of that county, and well knowing the experience I had in those parts was well pleased to grace me with the trust of his thoughts and made me acquainted with his purpose herein, the apprehension whereof breeding in me a most savoury estimation of the design, I forthwith applied to labour it by the fairest and best means I could.[b]

James I and Robert Cecil, Earl of Salisbury The stained glass in Londonderry Guildhall shows Salisbury presenting a scheme for the *men of substance* of the City of London to bring British settlers to County Londonderry.

EARL OF SALISBURY · EXPLAINS · THE · PROJECT · FOR · THE · SETTLEMENT · TO · KING · JAMES I · 1609 · A D ·

A settlement of Londoners would inevitably curtail Phillips's efforts at Coleraine. From the outset, he claimed £2,500 compensation to relinquish his interests. He was requested to prepare a paper identifying 'the county's natural resources, the fortifications required and his calculation that the City would need to find fifty thousand pounds to undertake the project'.[c] Money would be needed to build 'houses, mills, tanneries, shipyards, fortifications and roads'.[d] With Salisbury's help, he produced 'a less ambitious and more tightly written document'.[e] This provided a different concept from the earlier plantation of Munster where huge tracts of farmland were allocated to wealthy English landlords. It was to be a business enterprise focusing on Ulster's commercial advantages. The City Corporation was advised that the country was well-watered, suitable for breeding cattle, growing hemp and flax better than elsewhere, well stocked with game, with excellent sea and river fisheries and containing 'such an abundance of provisions as not only to supply the plantation, but also to assist towards the relief of the London poor.'[f] This land of plenty was 'mostly free from those dismal tracts of bogs that render many parts of Ireland gloomy and unappealing',[g] and it contained a great number of natural harbours. The scenery was (and remains) 'unforgettable, hauntingly lovely, and beyond compare. There is nothing like it in the world: the County of Londonderry must be one of the most enchanting places on earth'.[h] A plantation would also relieve London's unemployment and risk of plague.

The Salmon Leap above Coleraine The view from The Irish Society offices at the Cutt

Emphasis was placed on the need to develop market towns to provide an infrastructure for trade.[i] Derry and Coleraine were both ideally located at the mouths of rivers flowing out of the plantation areas. Derry stood on a hill above a splendid natural harbour. Although the Bann was narrow and shallow, Coleraine was the highest point to where goods could be barged; above it was the rock formation known as the Salmon Leap, where the water fell twelve feet. The creation of these two market centres was at the core of the plan. London offered 'a distinctive civic ideology in the notions of civility by which the barbarous Irish were to be tamed'.[j] As Edmund Spenser recorded:

> Nothing doth sooner cause civility in any country than many market towns by reason that the people repairing often thither for their needs will daily see and learn civil manners ... besides there is nothing doth more stay and strengthen the country ... than many towns.[k]

'The spread of markets was about more than profit, it was the core of forming a new type of society, British in outlook and legal in articulation'.[l] Despite the criticisms that were later levelled against them, the Londoners were the catalyst for delivering a significant mercantile presence.

Merchants from Scotland, Chester and London were soon frequenting the two ports, while as early as 1614-15 a merchant fleet of seven ships accounted for 18.5 per cent of Derry's exports.[m] This made Derry a place of 'supreme strategic significance',[n] and O'Doherty's rebellion reinforced the need for proper fortifications. To ensure that a robust settlement was established, merchants were 'commanded by authority' to go there and 'compelled to remain and set up their trades and corporations'.[o]

Phillips's final document, dated 25 May 1609 and entitled '*Motives and Reasons to Induce the City of London to Undertake the Plantation in the North of Ireland*', was presented to the Lord Mayor. It recommended Derry, which could be made almost impregnable, and Coleraine as the most suitable places for plantation. The Corporation was to be offered the customs at Derry,

Coleraine and Portrush, and other rights. Phillips estimated that most of the £50,000 investment would be needed to build and fortify Derry and Coleraine. He also wanted to see twelve protective forts, but was vague about their location and cost. The document 'indicated that the King would be prepared to grant Charters of Incorporation to both Derry and Coleraine, and to make the City of London the grantee of substantial areas of land to provide their Commons; 'the remaining territories were to be colonised by undertakers selected by the City'.[p] The City was also to be granted Admiralty rights (generally to salvage) along its lengthy coastline and all the fishing in the Foyle and the Lower Bann up to Lough Neagh, with a ninety-nine year lease over the customs within its territories and at Portrush. The scheme would offer work for under-employed Londoners 'to the great service of the King, the strength of his Realm, and the advancement of several Trades', which 'might ease the City of an insupportable burthen of persons ...'[q]

Sir Humphrey Weld of Holdwell was Lord Mayor at the time that the Londoners' Plantation was first mooted and he promoted the scheme among the Livery Companies.
Circle of Abraham van Bylenborch oil on canvas Private Collection

The Lord Mayor of London, Sir Humphrey Weld, approached Sir John Jolles, Master of the Drapers' Company and a former Sheriff, and William Cockayne, the Master Skinner, a recently appointed Sheriff. Both these men had profited from Crown contracts to provision forces in Ireland. When Phillips met them, they seemed to be won over, and were quite probably enthusiastic. At a meeting of the Court of Aldermen 'it was emphasised that His Majesty had offered the City the idea, mindful that it would bring profit and glory to London as well as to the strength of the Realm'.[r] On 1 July, the Lord Mayor called 'the gravest and most substantial members' of the Livery Companies to a conference attended by Phillips, who faced a stream of queries and provided a calculation … that nearly £10,000 could be made in the first year of 'trading', and expressed his astonishment that a proposal involving his handing over of the prospering town of Coleraine was not more gratefully or enthusiastically received.[s]

Although Phillips believed that he had gained support for the project at the meeting, it is clear that it caused considerable disquiet. When the Livery Companies held their own Court Meetings, members showed little enthusiasm, many being conveniently 'absent in the country'.[t] The Companies had already been called on to contribute to the plantation in Virginia, and many complained that they did not have the means also to finance an Irish plantation. Yet it was always intended that Companies should call on their wealthier members to make contributions as a form of tax. A deputation of fifteen aldermen, including Jolles and Cockayne, attended a meeting with the Privy Council, who became 'angry' at their lack of enthusiasm for the project. When several respected citizens were imprisoned and fined, there was a realisation that the will of the Crown could not be thwarted, and, within a week, they were 'induced to enter upon the Irish venture'.[u]

The four 'wise grave and discreet citizens' of London inspecting Londonderry From the stained glass at Londonderry Guildhall.

In an attempt to allay fears, the City agreed to send a deputation of four 'wise grave and discreet citizens'[41] to examine the prospects in Ireland for themselves, and it provided £300 to finance their expedition. Both Phillips and Chichester were employed by the Crown to conduct them. As both owned lands to be acquired, they stood to benefit from the Londoners' involvement. Undertakers elsewhere in Ireland were generally enthusiastic about a proposal which might end rumblings of discontent among the Gaelic Irish in Ulster. Thomas Blennerhasset described it as a new Troy ... offering possibilities as yet undreamed of, and argued that the extirpation of the Irish from Ulster was the best means of securing 'that wilde countrye to the crown of England'.[v]

Chichester was instructed to 'see that [the deputation was] afforded every comfort and all possible assistance' and to 'order the company the agents were to keep'.[w] On 22 August 1609, the four representatives arrived at Carrickfergus and immediately travelled to Limavady to meet Chichester. From there, they visited Lifford before catching up with Phillips at Derry. They were taken to the forest of Loughinsholin and then travelled to Toome, from where they took a boat down the Bann to Coleraine.

Chichester kept them well away from less hospitable areas and from the English surveyors, who were receiving armed protection after the attack on Bartlett. He steered them towards more fertile estates, where they could be entertained in style in recently built houses, and away from more barren and rebellious districts. They saw iron ore at Slieve Gallion and the rivers teeming with salmon and other fish, and were provided with local produce at knock-down prices. They even chartered a ship to carry home samples of salmon, eel, herring, iron ore, raw hides, tallow and pipe staves [to make barrels]. On 28 August 1609, Davies reported to Salisbury: 'We all use our best rhetoric to persuade them to go on with the plantation.' The deputation professed itself impressed and 'found everything better' than Phillips had indicated. Phillips was so confident of 'success that he ordered the felling of ten thousand trees so that the timber would be seasoned by the following spring'.[x]

The City of London visitors were not fooled. They agreed to move forward only if the southern boundary was clarified and if the plantation area was expanded to offer greater security. They also demanded the extensive forests at Glenconkeyne and Killetra in County Tyrone to provide timber for building materials including shipbuilding. All these requests were subsequently granted by the King, who took personal charge of negotiations. By the time the representatives were on their way back to England, during which they were accompanied by Phillips, it was quite clear to them that they were being given no choice, even though the citizens had 'little heart in the scheme'.[y] Yet they were careful to assure Chichester 'that they had been much impressed'.[z] There is no doubt that there was fairly general concern. The City claimed repeatedly

---

[41] The four chosen were John Broad, a Goldsmith, Hugh Hamersley, a Haberdasher, Robert Treswell, a Painter Stainer, and John Rowley, a Draper.

that it had no desire to be involved, but was undertaking the project in deference to the Crown's wishes as 'an endeavour of obedience not of contract'.[aa]

After arriving in England, the four City representatives met with the Common Council on 2 December 1609, which appointed a committee to draw up the terms under which the City was prepared to become involved. A new county to be called Londonderry was to be created, incorporating Coleraine with parts of Antrim, Donegal, and Tyrone. The Londoners were to rebuild Coleraine into a fortified town and to erect a walled city at Derry to be renamed Londonderry to reflect their involvement. There was no mention of the number of settlers to be provided or whether the native Irish were to be moved out (an omission which they were to use in their defence in the Court of Star Chamber in 1635). The Court of Common Council was required to raise the initial tranche of £20,000 (increased from an initial request for £15,000); this included £5,000 to buy out 'private men's interests'[42].[bb] In accordance with its traditional practice, the City turned to the Livery Companies to raise the money and they in turn intended to tax their wealthy members rather than to fund it from their own reserves. It was the twelve 'Great' Livery Companies, who became responsible for raising the money, but they called for contributions from the 'Minor' companies in accordance with traditional practice. All fifty-five Companies were involved, although the twelve Great Companies were to supervise the investment for the remainder.

The Companies all struggled to raise the required funds. The Mercers, while thanking the King for his offer, pointed out that

> they are for the most part men that live by merchandise and therefore are very inexperienced in managing business of that nature and withal want means and ability for the accomplishment thereof. [So] this company are not willing to have a hand or intermeddle in the same.[cc]

The Ironmongers expressed their 'desire with our best means to help the state and commonwealth, but what we would we cannot in respect of weakness'. When it came to attempts to generate subscriptions, members were curiously absent, or unavailable because of dwelling out of the City. Of the forty-six men on the Ironmongers' original subscription list, nine were absent, ten out of the city, and two allegedly 'not of ability'.[dd]

Yet the City found itself committed and signed the Articles of Agreement on 28 January 1610. This required £5,000 to be raised, being the first part of the City's commitment to provide £20,000. When voluntary subscription failed to provide a sufficient sum, the aldermen and the Court of Common Council were forced 'to raise cash by assessing each livery company in accordance to its wealth and standing of its members'.[ee] Within each Company, the Court of Assistants appointed a committee to allocate the charge across the membership in accordance with each member's capability to pay. Members generally

---

[42] These included the amounts payable to Phillips for lands at Coleraine and Toome, and the nine townlands belonging to Sir Randal MacDonnell on the right bank of the Bann River.

dragged their feet, although the Fishmongers, Merchant Taylors and Vintners met the deadline, and defaulters were imprisoned until they paid. These included the wardens of the Mercers' and Clothworkers' Companies and, in June 1610, three reluctant Drapers found themselves behind bars. In July, the wardens of the Salters', Brewers' and Cooks' Companies were locked away. 'The Grocers threatened all defaulters with the loss of the benefit of their freedom[43].'[ff] The Vintners approach the Common Council in an effort to have their levy reduced. When the Ironmongers made a similar approach to the Lord Mayor in the face of their difficulties, it was to no avail, and they had to borrow money and charge their livery four times the normal quarterage. Even the Mercers, the senior Livery Company, was at that time in relative decline, and 'felt much put upon',[gg] appealing without success to the City authorities and to Privy Council. After repeated warnings from the Lord Mayor, the first contribution was raised, but on future calls there was some minor adjustment to allocations between Companies to prevent prisons from overflowing with respected citizens. Levies on the Mercers, Goldsmiths, Skinners, Salters and Ironmongers were reduced and those on the Grocers, Merchant Taylors and Haberdashers were increased, leaving the Drapers, Fishmongers, Vintners, and Clothworkers unchanged. Members of several Companies surrendered their interests back to their Companies, which undertook to meet future contributions from their corporate resources funded by fines on the total membership. By 1613, the Mercers, Grocers, Fishmongers, Goldsmiths and Ironmongers and all the minor Companies were contributing corporately, and the Drapers, Merchant Taylors, and Vintners were in the process of acquiring individuals' interests.

The reluctance of Livery Company members to part with their money did nothing to help the plantation's progress. They

> had little faith in the wisdom of committing their capital to distant, hostile, unstable, unknown, uninteresting, barbarous, Gaelic, Papist Ulster, especially since a large part of the lands to be planted probably belonged to someone else [O'Cahan] (and indeed documentary evidence of title took a remarkably long time to materialise).[hh]

There was great resentment. The problem of delivering funds to Ireland in safety also had to be resolved. Chichester warned Salisbury of 'pirates infesting the north coast of Ulster bent on intercepting the money for the works of the City of Coleraine'.[ii]

---

[43] This would have debarred them from taking on apprentices or engaging in retail trade.

Chapter 10

The formation of The Irish Society to supervise the Londoners' plantation 1610 – 1616

There were immediate complications for the plantation, as the Privy Council failed to put the City of London in legal 'possession of the land'.[a] By an indenture dated 30 April 1610, Phillips was paid £1,000 for all his property in and about Coleraine, although he had asked for £2,500. He was unhappy with this; it seems to have been foisted on him and he wanted to retain some of his interests for himself. He must have complained to Salisbury, as the Privy Council ordered the City to release back to him 2,000 acres in Killetra forest at Loughinsholin providing timber for building work. When he was later granted O'Cahan's old castle at Limavady with 3,000 acres, the Killetra woodland was withdrawn from him and his woodland round the River Moyola near his castle at Toome[44] was reduced to 500 acres. Yet he surrendered his townlands east of the Bann, his rights to hold a market at Coleraine, his ferries, his estates in Derry and his patent to make whiskey in County Coleraine and in the Route. In return, he received a pension of 6s. 8d. per day and was granted the right to hold a weekly market at Toome. In 1611, when his estate at Limavady was converted into a freehold, he developed a settlement there, and even approached the City of London to make it the location for assizes, particularly because of its convenient location between Derry and Coleraine. Yet the judges complained that the Londoners did not have jurisdiction there and called assizes at Derry.

With the City of London's estates amounting to nearly four hundred square miles, the King undertook to provide 'sufficient forces' for the safety of the undertaking. After negotiation, it was agreed that the ownership of Church lands within the estates should be divided so that the City obtained nine advowsons and the bishops retained six. Church liberties within the plantation, from which the Bishops in Ulster received rent, were to be handed over to the sees. About one-tenth of the plantation lands were allocated to 'deserving' Irish freeholders. Natives could also remain on Church lands, Phillips's lands and glebe lands, making about one-third of the total available to them.

---

[44] He acquired the freehold of Toome in June 1611.

At Londonderry, the Londoners had an obligation to build two hundred houses (with space for three hundred more), with a further one hundred at Coleraine (with space for an additional two hundred). A bridge was to be built over the Bann River at Coleraine. Building work in the towns started immediately but in Londonderry there were delays, while problems of title with the local inhabitants were sorted out. Although Londoners were expected to replace the native Irish in the towns, just as elsewhere, there were insufficient arrivals to force all the Irish out, leaving those who did arrive with uncertain security.

To direct their negotiations with the Crown and activities in Ireland including the administration of funds, the Livery Companies set up *'The Society of the Governor and Assistants, London, of the New Plantation in Ulster, within the Realm of Ireland'*, known after 1660 as 'The Honourable the Irish Society'[45] ("The Irish Society" or the "Society"). This received substantial powers and was similar in concept to other 17th Century commercial enterprises such as The East India Company, The Virginia Company and The Newfoundland Company. It operated as a standing committee of the Court of Common Council and was answerable to them. Cockayne became its first Governor, a position which he held for four years. The administration also included a Deputy Governor, five aldermen assistants and twenty-one others drawn mainly from the twelve Great Livery Companies. Yet the Deputy Governor and half of the alderman assistants were replaced each year, causing a lack of continuity.

Early in 1611, the Society began to let the fisheries, the profits of which were to be distributed proportionately to the Livery Companies. Yet the Companies remained apprehensive and there was continuing difficulty in raising money from them. They soon realised that the initial tranche of £20,000 was only 'a drop in the ocean'.[b] Some even tried to sell their investment for the cost of the capital that they had laid out, but only the Haberdashers succeeded (as will be explained).

The Irish Society had soon appointed John Rowley, a member of the Drapers' Company (and one of the original deputation of four City representatives who had visited Ireland), as their Chief Agent to be assisted by Tristram Beresford. Rowley was already a wealthy merchant and had undertaken business dealings with Chichester. He appointed his brother-in-law, William Gage, to supervise a workforce of about one hundred and thirty skilled English artisans to undertake construction at Coleraine and Londonderry, including its Cathedral and fortifications. Gage became an Alderman of Londonderry. On 20 May 1610, they landed with tools and essential materials at Larne, but a dedicated fleet of ships was needed to move men and materials to Londonderry and Coleraine. Local were initially in short supply and money was slow to arrive. Yet Chichester was instructed by the Privy Council 'to render all help and every facility'[c] by supplying food at reasonable prices and making

---

[45] The Irish Society occupied chambers next to the Guildhall in London, but these were destroyed by fire in 1784, when many of its records were greatly damaged.

'labourers available to burn lime, quarry stone and fell trees'.[d] With the logistical problems resolved, the building work moved forward with reasonable speed.

Despite being the most recent of the undertakers arriving in Ireland, the Londoners received initial praise. During the summer of 1611, the Government asked Carew, with his wide experience, to review progress. He reported that they already had some five hundred workers on site. He visited Coleraine and examined Bodley's plans for a six-sided fortification, with earthen dykes and ditches on five sides and with the Bann River on the sixth. (Phillips considered the river bank dangerously exposed, and in need of 'a strong stone wall with convenient flankers'.)[e] There were plans for a 'rampier' fourteen feet thick and twelve foot high with a ditch forty feet wide and three feet deep. When Carew visited

> the ramparts were only about half their proposed height and only two of the projected seven bastions had been anywhere near finished. ... There were to be properly fortified gates on the east and south sides, and a postern gate ... on the north side.[f]

He reported it as a hive of industry despite the problem of man-handling building materials past the waterfall at the Salmon Leap. The Parish Church was repaired and re-roofed (although it was rebuilt by The Irish Society in 1613-14). The Society chose three successive Cambridge graduates as incumbents there.[46] A jetty was built for the ferry to Killowen and there was a quay for unloading goods. A brewery was established and timber-framed houses and tenements with large gardens were being constructed by two hundred and fifty men. There were ample building materials and limestone was provided free of charge by MacDonnell. The bridge across the Bann to Killowen had not been begun, and 'Phillips noted that its want much impoverished the town'.[g] Londonderry was a project in name only, an 'untidy arrangement of buildings' round the old church of St Augustine 'within the massive corset of bastions built by Docwra'.[h] Yet this was only a fraction of the proposed walled area. Carew noted a ship being built next to the water and one hundred and fifty active workers. Building materials were being stockpiled, and Culmore Fort had been allocated to hold stores. There was a quay to receive timber being floated downstream, and eighty-four men cutting it at Glenconkeyne.

In Loughinsholin, timber cutting was being actively progressed by nearly one hundred workers, some of them Irish. A further fifty men with oxen and horses were engaged in moving timber from the woods to the banks of the Bann, where prefabricated sections for ships and house frames were being assembled with numbered parts before transportation by barge down the Bann River. At the Salmon Leap, they had to be moved to Coleraine overland, where they were loaded onto a ship for the sea voyage to Londonderry.

---

[46] It is significant that even at this stage the Londoners were showing signs of siding with the Parliamentarians, and preferred to avoid incumbents from Royalist Oxford.[i]

It did not take long for progress to deteriorate. Carew saw little evidence of British settlers arriving in rural areas and noted native tenants paying rent to the City's agents. When the initial tranche of the Livery Companies' money had been expended, a call was made for a further £10,000, but the Livery Companies were dragging their feet. The Londoners continued to have doubts about the new colony's prospects. They complained at being unclear how their money was being spent and wanted clarification on when they might expect a return. They were told firmly to provide the additional call or pull out and forego what they had already paid. The Brownbakers and the Coopers chose to lose their investment. 'The Bowyers and Fletchers, representing 'decayed' trades, were also excused further levies.'[j]

The delays in raising the second call starved the project of money. Unpaid artisans became drunken[47] and demoralised and the native Irish caused friction by committing atrocities. Workmanship in Coleraine was soon being criticised. In Londonderry, the agents delayed paying wages and deducted the cost of tools from what was due in an effort to prevent pilferage. Several workers went on strike and little building work was started. Native Irish, who faced the demolition of their homes to make way for new buildings, refused to move before receiving compensation. They had to wait until March 1612 for the 1000 marks due on surrendering their properties. Efforts to induce them to profess allegiance to the Protestant church and the Crown were treated by them with contempt and simply added to the irritation. Despite their substantial allocations of land, neither the Bishop nor Dean of Derry did much to develop it. Rowley and Beresford were able to lease significant areas from them at great personal profit.

With 'the history of rebellion and massacre being fresh in the minds of all',[k] the Irish were assured that the Agents of the Society would buy their crops on departure at the current market price. Londoners were given every encouragement to move to Ulster and land was offered to them at four pence per acre, but they had to be there by May Day 1611, the date by when the Native Irish were required to leave. Settlers needed to bring every necessity, including money for their required building works. Although some pioneers were attracted, 'numbers were disappointingly small'. Barnabe Rich, an author, who had seen service as a soldier in Ulster, visited Dublin in 1610. On his return to London, he was commissioned to write a prospectus, which he entitled:

A New Description of Ireland ... no lesse admirable to be perused than credible to be believed; neither unprofitable nor unpleasant to bee read and understood, by those worthy Cittizens of London that be now undertakers in Ireland.

Being designed to encourage settlers, it provided a glowing account of their prospects. Yet he was frank about the difficulties, making clear that Ulster

---

[47] Rowley was told to limit the numbers of taverns and ale houses, which seem to be springing up at every other house.

would only be safe if Papists of any nationality were prohibited from settling there. He recorded:

> I was asked sixteen several times what I thought of the plantation in the north of Ireland, and whether it were possible that those labourers and workmen that are now sent over for the building could save their throats from cutting, or their heads from being taken from their shoulders before the work were finished.[l]

With the expected influx of British settlers failing to materialise, dispossessing the Irish would have caused a total breakdown in agriculture, and they were permitted to remain until May 1612. With an almost complete absence of settlers, the Society entered into tenancy agreements with the Irish to provide it with income. Those settlers, who did arrive, required local labour for their building and farming needs. Yet both the Lord Deputy[48] and the Privy Council were determined that security would only be achieved with British tenants on the land. When Chichester sensed that the Society was unlikely to deliver sufficient settlers, he proposed detaching Loughinsholin from the plantation lands. Yet the Society insisted on retaining this valuable area and agreed 'to carry out the [intended] obligations of the grant without any further procrastination'.[m]

> Nevertheless, The Irish Society, as the representative of the City, was never a zealous agent of colonisation, and the removal of the natives was put off, avoided, ignored or pretended: the Irish inhabitants were not only determined to sit tight, but they were essential to the settlers as providers of food and other goods. What is more, the Irish were careful to pay their rents, to be obliging and friendly to the newcomers, and to offer their services as labourers, handymen, or helpers as required.[n]

Although the Companies were later blamed for 'stealing' land and for driving the natives off their ancestral property, for the most part they were retained.[o] Yet other undertakers were not permitted the same leniency.

In the spring of 1612, Rowley was called to London to assess progress and to account for the money he had expended. While there, the Society complained that they 'had heard that pipe-staves [for the manufacture of barrels] had been made in the woods of Loughinsholin and exported overseas 'contrary to our order and our Articles of Agreement, which is very displeasing to us'.'[p] With one of his tenants, Oliver Nugent, being the worst offender, Rowley was warned that 'if the destruction of the forests continued, he would be held personally responsible'.[q]

> 'Great disorder' in the woods had to be brought to an end. Much 'disorder' had resulted from workmen spending their 'time and substance' in the 'great number of taverns and alehouses'.[r]

---

[48] Chichester even went to the lengths of threatening to seize for the Crown all rents payable by native Irish who remained on the Londoners' lands, but this was not proceeded with.

The cutting of woodland for pipe staves also caused a deterioration in Phillips's relationship with the City. He complained that Rowley had no right to cut for staves in Killetra, which was 'contrary to the intentions of the Crown' and on land that was presumably on or contiguous to his own at Toome Castle. Phillips surmised that Rowley was operating for his own account. When he took action to try to prevent the timber cutting, Beresford wrote to one of his men 'marvelling 'by whose order' employees of the City were being prevented from carrying out 'work for the City's use and behoof''.[s] The Irish Society sent Phillips a letter denouncing him for 'presuming to meddle' in the business of the Society and complaining at his 'intention to domineer over their jurisdiction'.[t] With Rowley still in London, Phillips arrived there to complain that the Society had delayed its grant to provide him with possession of the woodlands as previously agreed and demanded compensation for his loss of rent for the last year and a half. The Society claimed that it would not 'assent to so bare-faced a piece of chicanery',[u] but eventually conceded to his requests, which suggests that he was within his rights.

'Phillips's initial enthusiasm for the Londoners' undertaking [had] completely evaporated and he became the hostile and indefatigable critic of their conduct in Ulster'.[v] He complained at the slow progress of their building work and sought to have them evicted, arguing that undertakers would do better. This made him 'obnoxious to the Society'.[w] It is clear that Salisbury, while supporting Phillips, who was showing a lot of energy at Limavady, thought it wiser to keep him out of harm's way by employing him on missions outside Ireland. Unfortunately for Phillips, Salisbury died a month after his arrival in London, and, with his views not being heeded, lasting antagonism continued between Rowley and himself.

Despite misgivings about Rowley's integrity, The Irish Society reconfirmed him as their Agent, and he 'was assured of the esteem in which he was held'. Yet there were already signs of him being mistrusted and his management was being questioned. Although he had received gold and bills of exchange totalling £2,017 10s. to pay 'arrearages', the Society began to 'marvel much'[x] when Beresford continued to complain of 'the great want of money to pay workmen and for other occasions'. Rowley was given a long list of instructions of matters which needed to be rectified. He was to maintain detailed accounts, to economise and to stick to the Articles of Agreement. He was 'to send 'idle and disordered' workmen back to England'.[y] Several artisans and 'needless' supervisors were to be dismissed. The stipend of Raven, the cartographer, was to be reduced to a reasonable level[49]. He was only to retain one ship's carpenter. The Society's ship, the *Dove* was to be hired as a cargo vessel. Artisans for building the towns were to be encouraged to arrive. The import of items that could be produced locally was discouraged. 'He was to preserve both wild game and the woodlands.'[z] A jetty was to be built by private enterprise at Portrush to

---

[49] It would appear that Raven was infuriated at having his terms of employment reduced, and he later collaborated with Phillips in Phillips's indictment of the Londonderry plantation.

save ships having to journey to Coleraine by river, which was 'dangerous' at all times and hardly passable in winter.[aa] Labourers were to travel without charge on ferries, which were also to be free on market days.

Perhaps it was concerns at Rowley's shortcomings, which caused differing views on how to progress the rural areas in accordance with the terms of the Charter. Most Livery Companies agreed that they should be subdivided so that each of the twelve Great Companies took responsibility for its own proportion. On 29 December 1611, Cockayne, the Governor of The Irish Society in London, met with the King's representatives to begin negotiating a proper agreement, but it was realised that the division of the land would require a much more detailed survey, which would take time.

By July 1612, the new call of £10,000 had been fully subscribed, but the Companies withheld payment until the land was assigned by the Crown. The Government countered by complaining at the slow progress on building works. Yet £4,000 was sent from London so that work could be focused on Coleraine. By August, better progress was being made there, but the money appears to have been used mainly to complete and repair buildings already erected, where leaks and cracks had arisen from using unseasoned timber. Efforts were also being made to attract private enterprise into undertaking some of the building work. Sites were offered on sixty year leases at a quit rent for those prepared to build houses to a standard design with a minimum of four rooms. Although similar terms were to be offered in Derry, construction work there had ceased. When it was able to restart, its houses were built of brick and stone to an agreed plan. Timber was already in short supply and was reserved for joists, door and window frames. Rowley was again criticised for the delays and, in November, was again summoned by The Irish Society to London. He was given precise instructions that tenancy agreements on new houses in Coleraine should run for twenty-one years, and was told to complete a drawbridge and gates, including a prison at one of the gatehouses. It was agreed that a cutting round the Salmon Leap would facilitate the barging of timber without disturbing the salmon run, and he was to encourage 'gentlemen of the county' to cut through two other leaps further up.

The City's agents still made no efforts to remove Irish tenants and labourers, and Beresford sought consent for them to remain until works were further advanced. Chichester was exasperated and considered the Londoners to be the slowest of all undertakers to establish British settlers. With labour for cutting timber in Loughinsholin being supplemented from all over Tyrone, there were now more native Irish than ever before. He sensed problems when he heard that the City's Agents were encouraging Irish labourers to treat judges of the assize with 'scant respect'.[bb] With Chichester sharing Phillips's misgivings over security, Carew recommended building a fort at Desertmartin[50] on the road between Coleraine and Dungannon to make the southern parts of the plantation

---

[50] In 1613 a fort was built and garrisoned by Sir Francis Cooke, although the Bishop of Derry eventually regained possession in 1633.

less vulnerable. As this was to be on land leased to Rowley by the Bishop of Derry, he was due to receive compensation.

At the end of 1612, the King wrote impatiently to Chichester complaining that the plantation's progress was so slow that 'neither the safety of that country nor the planting of religion and civility amongst those rude and barbarous people' had been achieved.[cc] He again called for a 'true and exact survey ... with as much speed' as possible.[dd] He complained that, although the Londoners had 'pretended the expense of great sums of money', 'the outward appearances' were very limited. Chichester was asked to establish whether the City's Agents were abusing their positions.[ee] (Sadly no records of his findings survive.) Yet it caused the King to become aware that the terms of the agreement with the City needed clarification and that the Londoners were stalling because of the Crown's failure to assign proper title to them.

The King's intervention provided an opportunity for City representatives to meet with the Privy Council to resolve various problems of title, which were still being disputed by former landowners. The Irish Society produced a 'catalogue' of evidence that rents due from native Irish tenants were being withheld. Sir Toby Caulfeild, who had held 'huge estates at Kilrea and Agivey long before 1607, and whose land therefore had never been forfeited to the Crown, resisted attempts to hand his properties over'.[ff] Although Chichester had agreed that his estates did not form part of the lands granted to the Livery Companies, in 1612, he was forced to relinquish his interests. A commission finalised the boundaries of the 4,000 acres annexed to Derry and the 3,000 acres attached to Coleraine. Yet fishing rights were being withheld and the manufacture of beer and whiskey was still being exercised by persons, whose rights had been extinguished.[gg] The Society complained that it was being charged rent on 'high, infertile and boggy ground' contrary to undertakings given.[hh] When the Privy Council realised the extent of the problems, it acted leniently. Much aggravation was resolved, when it permitted native Irish still in occupation to remain until Mayday 1615.

On 29 March 1613, a new Charter providing title to the City of London and the Livery Companies was at last ratified. This clarified that County Londonderry comprised County Coleraine with parts of Antrim, Donegal and Tyrone. 18,000 acres was withdrawn from Antrim across the Bann from Coleraine. 12,500 acres was taken from Donegal north west of the Foyle including the City of Londonderry. 171,000 acres of the Barony of Loughinsholin as far as the River Ballinderry was detached from Tyrone, although surveys were still needed to establish the exact boundaries. This increased County Londonderry to more than 500,000 acres. The Charter allocated 52,050 acres to native Irish chieftains, who had remained supportive, but, apart from these, only Phillips with 19,400 acres, and the Church with 116,400 acres (nearly one quarter of the whole area)[51] were permitted to retain

---

51 Church lands included those allocated to the Bishop and Dean of Derry and to the Archbishop of Armagh. These were spread about in parcels all over the County.

native Irish tenants. With legal possession clarified, the Livery Companies paid over all the money being retained allowing the Society to settle its debts. Yet a loophole arose, because the document failed to commit the Londoners to remove the native Irish (although this was the King's firm intention). This was to give rise to future disputes.

As soon as The Irish Society was legally incorporated it had authority to regulate every aspect of the County's Government. It was the legal owner of all the lands and fishing rights[52] and could lease them to users. It could nominate all local officials, including members of Parliament. It obtained customs duties and Admiralty rights. It was exempt from exactions due to the Crown. It arranged for both Londonderry and Coleraine to be constituted as civic corporations with their own structure for providing regulations (although it retained the power of veto or amendment). Each was to be represented by two burgesses in the Irish Parliament. Markets and fairs were permitted. In Londonderry, guilds were to be formed with their own halls for regulating trades. Despite their apparent shortcomings, Rowley became Alderman and the first Mayor of Londonderry and Beresford became Mayor of Coleraine.

The new Charter failed to end disputes with previous owners over the Crown's title to the lands it had granted. At the outset, the City had allocated £5,000 to be provided as compensation. Some old Derry inhabitants still refused to move and presented a list of grievances to the Crown. When Chichester was instructed to resolve them, he reported that no settlers had arrived in Derry apart from workmen. The Londoners responded to complaints at their lack of progress by claiming that they had done more than other undertakers and spent £25,000 rather than the £15,000 to which they were committed. In addition to paying compensation for native Irish houses demolished at Derry, they owed MacDonnell for nine townlands adjacent to Coleraine; the Bishop of Connor was to be paid for its rectory; Chichester was owed for the castle of Culmore, and Captain Edward Doddington[53] for Dungiven; Hamilton and Chichester were due to receive payment for the fishing rights on the Bann and Foyle rivers. By early 1613, everything had at last been settled.

Despite having arranged for a survey so that the estate could be divided into twelve proportions of equal value, Rowley had made no allocation to the Livery Companies, but was now told to 'settle a course for the division of the City's lands'.[ii] The Commissioners recommended that Coleraine and the City of Derry

---

[52] Although the fishing rights had been promised by the Crown, it failed to establish good title to all of them, which caused disputes for many years to come.

[53] Doddington was another servitor, who was being successful in providing British settlers. He had built a large house attached to the remains of O'Cahan's Castle and the old Priory at Dungiven, eight miles south of Limavady. Although it was originally intended that Dungiven should be incorporated as a town, when Londonderry, Coleraine and Limavady gained charters, Doddington's interest in Dungiven was transferred to the Livery Companies. Without it becoming a major centre, the County's defences were irreparably weakened for the future.

with their surrounding lands, together with woods, ferries, fishings and the rights of Admiralty should remain under The Irish Society's control, leaving only the rural areas for division. Twelve 'proportions' varying in size according to the fertility and location of the land were at last established, each separated from the next either by church-owned lands, areas in the possession of 'native Irish gentlemen' or of Phillips. Each proportion was to be fenced and to contain a fortified manor house, English style villages, churches and tree plantations. Settlers were required to adhere to English law, speech, custom and Established [Anglican] Church dogma. The native Irish were to be moved to neighbouring lands allocated either to the Church, Phillips or Irish landlords. Yet without settlers arriving in numbers, there was a security problem, as the native Irish still greatly outnumbered the few, who had found their way there.

On Phillips's eventual return to Ireland, he remained Superintendent of The Irish Society at their special request. At the same time, he set to work with great industry to create Limavady into a thriving and efficient settlement, showing up the Londoners' shortcomings. He had his hands full. He owned 13,100 acres at Limavady running up to the banks of Lough Foyle and 6,300 acres mainly of woodland at Moyola. Although he was still Governor of the old county of Coleraine, he found himself at odds with the City of London's Agents, who failed to provide him with title to the woodlands he had been allocated. As has been seen, this required him to travel to London to obtain recompense and soured his relationship with them for good. At the end of 1614, he was diverted to provide support to Sir John Campbell of Calder to gain control of Islay, which had been promised to Campbell if he would lead a force to put down a MacDonald rebellion. When Chichester was asked to send two hundred troops from Ireland, Phillips was given command and successfully captured Dunyveg Castle after a three day bombardment.

Activity at Limavady remained frenetic. Stone was quarried locally and Phillips delivered thirty tons of shell on horseback from the shores of Lough Foyle for burning to make mortar. He extended O'Cahan's old castle by constructing a circular crenelated tower house with two tiers of ordnance high above the river Roe. This was accessed by a drawbridge. He built a stone residence with farm buildings and a geometrically laid out garden. The whole area was surrounded by a wall, partially crenelated and partially with loopholes offering awesome protection. At Newtown Limavady, about a mile away, he built eighteen English-style houses of stone with thatched roofs, a water mill for sawing timber and a one-and-a-half-storey inn for travellers moving between Derry and Coleraine. This had a stableyard behind. One house was used as a place of worship. One hundred and twenty properly armed English and Scottish settlers were soon in occupation. The new settlement was granted a Charter on 30 March 1617 and obtained a licence to hold a weekly market.

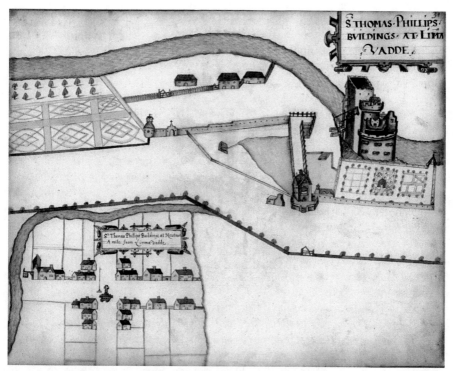

Raven's 1622 map of Sir Thomas Phillips's estate at Limavady shows the substantial progress made by Phillips in comparison to the Livery Companies.

The Livery Companies were well aware that their venture was in need of more capital and they received a demand for a further £10,000, making a total of £40,000. 'There seemed no limit to the capital necessary for the enterprise',[jj] especially as the King was complaining that the fortifications at Derry and Coleraine remained unfinished. After this latest levy, the Companies sent two Commissioners to Ireland to see for themselves what could be done to improve progress. They reported back that there was an immediate need for materials to build the walls. They recommended that a 'town house' should be built to accommodate the garrison and provide a prison, but had no authority to take further action.

By now Rowley's integrity was under close scrutiny. It was reported that the Bishop of Derry had demised eighty-one townlands to him at an annual rent of £65. Having obtained a grant to fell timber on diocesan lands, he cut three thousand trees for sale to Spain as pipe staves on his own account. The Privy Council instructed Chichester to restore the Bishop's rights and declared Rowley's lease forfeit. The King warned Chichester that 'the aims of a Christian Prince were being thwarted by 'Backwardness and Slack Proceeding in the Plantation'',[kk] which was being used 'to improve the fortunes of unscrupulous individuals'.[ll]

The Common Council of the City of London was also concerned to establish how the Companies' money had been spent and, in June 1613, it sent two assistants of The Irish Society to Londonderry, George Smithes and Matthias Springham, as Special Commissioners to assess expenditure and to work on improving progress. They arrived in Dublin in August accompanied by the City's solicitor, Clement Moss. Chichester was instructed to provide every assistance. On reaching Ulster, 'Rowley and Beresford were both indicted for pursuing their own fortunes and personal trading deals to the detriment of the Londoners' collective interests'.[mm] It was found that they were not operating the Society's brewery, but Rowley had his own establishment at Castle Roe.[nn] He was building a water mill of his own only a few miles from that of the Society at Coleraine. He had moved the Saturday market onto land he was leasing from the Bishop at Killowen, and both he and Beresford were despoiling the woods at Loughinsholin to make pipe staves and other commodities, as if supplies of timber were infinite. Beresford, alone, had made forty thousand staves, and 'the value of the woods had been reduced by a vast percentage',[oo] causing a colossal mess. Rowley and Beresford 'had abused their positions to acquire property and capital contrary to the interests of the City of London that they were supposed to uphold'. While involved in all this corrupt and crooked dealing, four hundred workmen at Derry were left in arrears of pay for between seven and twelve weeks and were in debt and demoralised. Food was being provided to them on credit at double its value to be subtracted with commission by the City's Clerk from their wages when paid.[pp] Delay in paying workers was in direct contravention of the instructions given to Rowley while in London in 1612. Smithes and Springhame immediately paid all the workers their arrears and sacked the City's Clerk. They also established a £1,000 fund so that workers were paid at least monthly in future.

There was a litany of further findings. Rowley and Beresford were defrauding the City on 'carting' expenses. Smithes and Springham found that the *Dove* and the *Lark,* used for carrying cargo between Derry and Coleraine had been 'put to unauthorised use'.[qq] The *Dove* was sold and the *Lark* was returned to London. All transport and cartage rates was standardised and rationalised. A new transport contract was agreed to save the City about half of its previous charges. Despite earlier instructions to Rowley to cut out waste, there were still many people on the payroll with nothing to do; these were dismissed. Imported goods in damp and unsound stores were deteriorating. Nails stored at Coleraine had been allowed to rust; butter and cheese had rotted; loaves sold in the towns were found to be three ounces underweight. The Warehouse Clerk was dismissed, when the warehouses were found to be leaking, and arrangements were made for them to be repaired. Fares to cross the Foyle and Bann rivers were outrageous. At Londonderry, the Corporation was given control of the ferry and, at Coleraine, 'it was let to a reliable entrepreneur for twenty-one years'.[rr] The handsome earthen rampart built at Coleraine at a cost of £1,400, should have been of stone. It was already in poor repair and needed a smaller circumference as there were insufficient settlers to defend it. The

Commissioners arranged for Coleraine's muddy streets to be paved. The interior of St Patrick's Parish Church was rendered and limewashed and more pews were provided. The passage round the Salmon Leap should never, in their view, have been begun, but was sufficiently far advanced, after the vast sums already expended, to set money aside to complete it. Most of the one hundred and sixteen houses built at Coleraine at a cost of £10,550, were badly constructed or incomplete, and repairs were costing too much. The new houses were often so small that they had to be amalgamated to accommodate a family. Although they were admired, the effect was lost when old Irish cabins next to them were not removed. Many lay empty as the rents being asked were too high and they were without land. The Commissioners allocated land to each house and offered to let them on twenty-one year repairing leases. This increased total rental income from three hundred to five hundred pounds per annum.

At Londonderry, the thirty houses already completed had a single room with an attic above, and, as in Coleraine, several needed to be combined to accommodate a family. The Commissioners allocated land to both the Bishop and Dean for parish churches and presented each with a gilt communion cup. They re-let the fishery, the Society's principal source of profit, at £866 13s. 4d. per annum for three years, an increase of 44 per cent. With advice from experienced military personnel, they 'trod out' the layout of the fortifications, but delayed construction until sufficient stone and lime had been stockpiled. The Castle of Culmore, which was crucial to Londonderry's defences, was found to be ruinous with its keeper incompetent. Captain John Baker, an Alderman, was now put in command. The 'liberties' allocated to Londonderry were found to be on disappointingly poor land, so they added land at Rossnagalliach, a former nunnery.

The Commissioners found both Rowley and Beresford guilty of negligence and of lining their pockets at the City's expense. Both were found guilty of setting up rival markets, breweries and water mills, and of despoiling the woods of Loughinsholin.[ss] More than half the money contributed by the Livery Companies could not be accounted for. Yet surprisingly, they reconfirmed Rowley as mayor at Londonderry and Beresford at Coleraine and took no further action against them until they returned to London to explain themselves.

The Commissioners now tackled the land allocation between the twelve Great Livery Companies. At the outset, more survey work to clarify land areas was commissioned, as the mapping ordered by The Irish Society had made little progress. More land was allocated to proportions in remote and mountainous regions to compensate for their lack of 'usefulness'. They took into consideration 'resources, access, nearness to towns, defensive possibilities and quality of land'.[tt] This resulted in proportions ranging between 11,000 and 49,000 notional acres. Any shortage of building materials (particularly timber) in an area was to be supplemented from supplies from contiguous lands by arrangement with The Irish Society's Agents. The land was valued and divided into twelve proportions of equal value with assistance from Raven, Doddington and 'other gentlemen'. Although The Irish Society was to retain ownership of the two major towns, it was the Livery Companies who would finance their continuing development. With contributions of £40,000 to The Irish Society having already been spent, there was a further call for £5,000 to be paid by February 1614. Any income generated by the Society, was to be shared among the investing Companies as dividends.[54]

With their job done, Springham remained in Ireland to supervise the agreed changes, while Smithes returned to London to report to the Common Council. At their meeting on 8 November 1613, the Council praised their actions[55]. Rowley was summoned to London to reply to the accusations made against him and was dismissed from the City's service, being ordered to hand over to Springham any money still in his possession. On Springham's return in the following year, he reported that, despite initial opposition from racketeers, the reforms had now been implemented and piecework contracts had greatly speeded construction work.

Dismissing Rowley was easier said than done. He was Mayor of Londonderry and its Member of Parliament. Both he and Beresford had become 'indispensable' and there was a great difficulty in finding anyone more trustworthy to replace them. The Companies continued to rely on them to provide labour, which could easily be switched to other undertakers or servitors. Rowley was appointed Agent for the Drapers, his own livery company, but he died in 1617. Beresford was restored to favour, with Rowley being held responsible for most of the abuses, and now became The Irish Society's Agent. 'He was no model of rectitude',[uu] (and had married Rowley's daughter), but continued in office to amass a great fortune. Like Rowley, Beresford fell out with Phillips, and seems to have continued to exploit woodlands for his personal benefit, even though they were by then on Livery Company proportions. He was no doubt competing with the woodland activities of Phillips, who believed the Companies' Agents were in league with him. He concluded that the plantation, which he had helped to establish, was being ruined in the execution and felt that he would have succeeded a lot better on his own.

Phillips's criticisms of progress reached the ear of the King and, from now on, the Londonderry plantation was closely scrutinised by the Crown. In 1614, Chichester was instructed to arrange yet another survey[56], and, in June 1614, Sir Josias Bodley, Director-General of Fortifications in Ireland, was asked to evaluate the work being carried out. In a 'devastating indictment',[vv] he criticised everything he saw. He began his report:

> Having taken an exacte survey of the works and plantacon performed by the Cittie of London, I cannot find in the one or the other they ever intended his

---

[54] The understanding established at this time seems at odds with the judgement reached in the Skinners' case against The Irish Society in 1845. (see pages 346-7)

[55] Smithes very soon replaced Cockayne as Governor of The Irish Society.

[56] James had been advised by Sir Francis Bacon to monitor progress by conducting regular surveys.

Majesties satisfacc'on and regarded the true end and drifte of his favourable graunte soe that whatsoever they talk of great masses of wealth by them expended, naming what somes they please, yet of anie reall plantacon for fortificacon to the purpose (the onlie meanes of settinge and secureing these partes which they have undertaken) they have little or nothing to say.[ww]

'Apart from workmen and labourers and a few voluntary settlers, the City had not sent over any colonists to either Coleraine or the city of Londonderry.'[xx] Bodley's inspectors criticised the building work in both the towns and the proportions. Although Coleraine now housed three hundred settlers, its houses were 'jerry-built'[yy] with cracks appearing in the walls; very few could withstand the weather. He was also furious to find that the rampart design he had approved at Coleraine had been altered to save money. It needed enlargement; the ditch, 'which was rapidly being filled by mud, refuse, and vegetation',[zz] was too shallow 'and the gates were constructed only of timber cagework',[aaa] when masonry was required. Although Londonderry provided homes for five hundred settlers, Bodley still believed they had inadequate land allocated to them, so that residents were likely to become impoverished. Although 'three hundred pounds had been spent in preparing stone and moving earth, no work had been begun on erecting the walls'.[bbb] Bodley 'could not understand the engineers' design and doubted whether the defences when finished would be any use'.[ccc] The number of settlers was insufficient to man the fortifications at either location and, in Londonderry, the walls that had survived O'Doherty's rebellion were ruinous, making them hopeless to provide defence. It was only Chichester's efforts in colonising and fortifying Inishowen that provided any protection. All this tended to depress confidence and contribute to a general poverty and decidedly unbuoyant economy. Inhabitants of the towns were becoming surly, demoralised, and uncooperative, and could not be expected to remain for long. [ddd] Bodley also reported that, although some levelling and paving of the Londonderry streets had taken place, in neither town had Londoners built 'the number of houses required, nor fortified' them, nor arranged for settlers to be planted.

At the time of Bodley's survey, the proportions had seen almost no expenditure (except a small start by the Salters), and their Agents seemed poorly qualified.

Instead of the eight hundred armed British under-tenants intended by the Crown to be settled, there were none, and the armaments in Londonderry were pathetically few. The natives, on the other hand, were present in numbers, and The Irish Society was under the impression that it had no obligation to remove them.[eee]

Despite it being against the King's wishes, Bodley reported that some companies appeared to have handed over their interests (although, apart from the Haberdashers', this proved to be incorrect). He concluded:

131

I dare confidentlie affirme that … above twentie thousand … poundes[57] [of the City's investment have] gone some other waies then directlie towards their buildings and plantings in this Country.[fff]

The Londoners showed no evidence of having

anie purpose by their endeavour to deserve his Majesties soe Royal and bountiful graunte unto them, as if nothing els hade beene intended by it but to make them gainers.[ggg]

The report made James furious and, on 25 March 1615, he made his attitude clear in his reply to Bodley:

Some few only of our British undertakers, servitors and natives, having as yet proceeded effectually by the accomplishment of such things in all points as are required of them by the articles of the plantation, the rest and by much the greatest part, having either done nothing at all, or so little . . . that the work seems rather to us to be forgotten . . . than any whit to be advanced by them; some having begun to build and not planted, others begun to plant and not built, and all of them retaining the Irish still upon their lands, the avoiding of which was the fundamental reason for the plantation.[hhh]

He told Bodley that he could have converted the lands to the great improvement of the revenues of the Crown, but had preferred to pass them on at 'extreme undervalues' to achieve 'the safety of that country and the civilising of that people'.[iii] He immediately called on the Lord Mayor and Aldermen for information, but they failed to appease him and he remained dissatisfied.

The King gave the Livery Companies until August 1616 to demonstrate better progress and threatened to seize the lands of anyone 'found defective in performing any of the Articles of the Plantation'.[jjj] Bodley was then to undertake a further survey. The King advised Chichester:

My lord, in this service I expect that zeal and uprightness from you that ye will spare no flesh, English nor Scottish, for no private man's worth is able to counterbalance the perpetual safety of a kingdom which this plantation being well accomplished will procure.[kkk]

---

[57] He seems to have his arithmetic wrong, but the point is clear.

Blue Coat Boys from Christ's Hospital arriving as apprentices in Londonderry From the stained glass at Londonderry Guildhall.

BLUE·COAT·BOYS·SENT·FROM·LONDON·TO·BE ✦✦✦ APPRENTICED·IN·DERRY·1615·A·D·✦✦✦

Needless to say, The Irish Society was again short of funds and had borrowed £10,000 to continue its building work. Early in 1615, 'a further £7,500 was levied on the reluctant Companies' making £52,500 in total. By the autumn, they were again out of money and a further £5,000 was called for payment at the beginning of 1616. With everyone stirred into action by the King's letter, the main concern was to complete the Londonderry fortifications, and this was the Society's principal project until 1618.[58] 'The layout and plotting of the wall was carried out by Peter [probably Thomas] Raven'.[lll] He was supervised by Doddington, Captain Panton and Sir John Vaughan, later Mayor of Londonderry. Peter Benson, a tiler and bricklayer from London, was the main contractor. He had tendered to build them in 1614, and appears to have operated efficiently, becoming chief mason of Londonderry[59], responsible for several

---

[58] The guardhouses for the walls were added in 1628.

[59] Although the walls were completed in 1618, at a total cost of £10,757, in 1624, Benson had to petition the King for arrears of £1,157 2s. 10d. This reflects badly on the Society's

further buildings. There was a dearth of labour, and, in March 1616, the Society called on each of the Great Companies to send one or two artisans with their families, tools and baggage to Londonderry and Coleraine, to arrive before the end of May. There was a requirement for men to 'work with iron, glass, candles, dye, cloth, felt and pewter. Fishermen, weavers, manufacturers of felt, hat-makers, locksmiths, tanners, basketmakers and curriers were urgently needed'.[mmm] They were to be 'God-fearing men, unlike the riff-raff and boozers who appear for the most part to have comprised the first consignments dispatched from London'.[nnn] The Society also sent out twelve poor boys from Christ's Hospital as servants or to be apprenticed, as artisans were precluded from taking on Irish apprentices.[ooo] Twelve London boys were 'enticed' away from their London masters to go to Ireland. Ten were employed in Londonderry and the other two in Coleraine.

James may have felt that a more forceful Lord Deputy was needed than Chichester, and in November 1615, he terminated his appointment, although Chichester remained as Ireland's Lord High Treasurer. He had presided over Irish Government for ten years but was now unwell after falling from his horse while travelling to London in the spring of 1614. He retired with his wife, Letitia, who was also frail, to convalesce at Carrickfergus, where he supervised the building work of his home, Joymount, completed in 1618. At the start of the Thirty Years' War in 1620, he had sufficiently recovered to become England's ambassador to the Habsburg Empire and lived on until 1625 continuing to advise on Irish affairs. His brother, Edward, inherited his vast estates and was immediately created Viscount Chichester, perhaps in recognition of Arthur's achievement. Edward made Belfast his principal home and, at the Restoration, was created Earl of Donegall. St John, who was a distinguished soldier, became Lord Deputy. As Master of the Ordnance since 1608, he had already been closely involved in plantation matters, and was an undertaker in County Armagh. He was created Viscount Grandison.

With Bodley due to start another survey in August 1616, the Court of Common Council wanted to send two Commissioners to assess progress, but The Irish Society insisted on sending its Governor, Alderman Peter Proby, with Springham and the City Solicitor, because of their familiarity with the issues. The Londoners' investment of £60,000 was now three times what was originally expected (even if some of it may have gone astray). On their arrival in the spring of 1616, the Commissioners focused on the two towns. They went first to Coleraine, where Beresford was Mayor, in addition to his role as Agent for the Society. His accounts were carefully audited, and despite initial fears that he could not fulfil both appointments satisfactorily, he appears to have 'established a regime that was less corrupt, but progress was still slow'.[ppp] Complaints made against him by the Recorder of Coleraine were found to be false, and this

---

concern for its tradesmen. He eventually became an undertaker, having been granted 1,500 acres of plantation lands at Lifford.

allowed him to consolidate his position as Agent, while laying the foundation of the Waterford family fortune.

Coleraine was showing some improvement. Laying out and building the ramparts were no mean tasks.[qqq] Although it was in constant need of repair, the ditch held water with the aid of dams and sluices, and there was a palisade next to the Bann River, providing some protection when the tide was out. Two large drawbridges were installed during the Commissioners' stay. Although one hundred and sixteen houses had been completed, some had to be combined and could accommodate only sixty-three families. The use of unseasoned timber and hurried construction had resulted in repairs being required, with the timber walls suffering weather damage and the dormers, originally clad with boards, needing slating. Only thirty-five families had taken leases and most of these were not paying rents regularly. Although some artisans associated with the building works were dismissed, Beresford's assistant, John Wray, was retained. It was agreed that timber-framed construction was unsuitable in such a damp climate and future houses should be of stone. Subsidies were offered to those prepared to build their own homes, resulting in eighty being erected by private enterprise. Edmund Hayward, who later built on the Merchant Taylors' proportion, contracted to build nine houses. Further afield, the cutting through the Salmon Leap was considered poor value for the money spent on it, and plans to build a harbour at Portrush were shelved by the Commissioners, who considered it too rocky and exposed. If the citizens wanted a harbour, the Commissioners believed they should build it themselves, but they would offer a contribution of two hundred pounds. Finally, the Commissioners negotiated an undertaking with MacDonnell to assign 2,000 acres on the east side of the Bann River to form part of the town's 'liberties'.

When the Commissioners examined progress on the walls at Londonderry, they reported to the Common Council:

> For the fortification at Derrie we have exactly reviewed the same and find it very commendable and when the same is finished will be very strong and that the walls thereof are well nigh half done ... Also there are two drawbridges finished and one gate was in erecting.[rrr]

They thought it prudent to increase the planned height from sixteen to nineteen feet, making it into a fortress. They employed Raven[60], the surveyor, for a further two years to complete the layout of the fortifications at Culmore[61] and Londonderry. Beresford managed to resolve the problems caused by the late

---

[60] Raven was soon improving the surveys of the Livery Company proportions, probably with assistance from Simon Kingsland. He achieved this very speedily, perhaps by avoiding the remoter areas where he might fall prey to the wood-kerne. This caused some of his maps to be vague.

[61] Even Phillips was impressed with the massive fortifications at Culmore, despite its shortage of ordnance and troops. These were further 're-edified' in the second half of the 17th Century.

payment of workers, and the walls progressed quickly. When finished, they 'were among the greatest building achievements of the Londoners in Ulster'.[sss]

Culmore fort Only the tower remains of the original fortress so crucial to Londonderry's protection from the sea.

Almost all the two hundred and fifteen houses being built by the Society at Londonderry were now complete, and twenty-five were being built privately. The streets were paved and three houses had been combined to provide a town hall, but plans for other civic buildings and jails in both Londonderry and Coleraine had come to nothing. With the church now inadequate to accommodate Londonderry's population, public worship was neglected.[ttt] Plans for a new church building were being prepared and costed. Springham personally financed a free school. The City's deputies offered three hundred acres for its maintenance, but reverted to an annual monetary sum rather than committing land, which could have other needs.[uuu] Culmore Fort was largely rebuilt and was being properly supervised and garrisoned by Baker to provide essential protection on the City's seaward side.[vvv] Arms were provided to both townspeople and workmen, and the Mayor of Londonderry maintained an arsenal. Buoyage with beacons was installed to mark the sea channel. Despite all this apparently satisfactory progress, there had been no increase in settlers to support the market, so that 'trade was sluggish'.[www] Yet leases of the fisheries were renewed at one thousand pounds per annum and both towns were well supplied with salmon.

On 1 October 1616, when the Commissioners reported back to the Court of Common Council, they were able to confirm Chichester's satisfaction with progress at both Coleraine and Londonderry, despite continuing concerns over

Coleraine's defences. Blatant asset stripping of woodlands had been brought under control with corruption being rooted out. The Court of Common Council used this timely moment to authorise a further levy of £2,500 making a total of £60,000.

In November 1616, Bodley was commissioned by the King to undertake his second survey. He remained highly critical, but now focused on performance in the Livery Company proportions. He reported that they had failed to build castles and bawns of any strength; they had not brought in colonists, but retained the native Irish *in situ*. By this time, attacks by wood-kerne were increasingly frequent and ferocious, and he saw the native Irish 'as a great and dangerous threat'.[xxx] He considered that London had 'failed in its duty' to make Londonderry a safe place. This was certainly true. Settlements were being forced to organise armed posses against the wood-kerne. The new fortress at Desertmartin became a base from where to attack them, and during that winter, several were captured and killed.

Based on Bodley's findings, the Privy Council formally accused The Irish Society of breach of contract for failing to implement the Articles of the Plantation. It required answers to its list of faults. These were examined by the Attorney- and Solicitor-Generals, but they held back from a formal charge. Worse was to come. Events in Ulster were causing a significant rift between the City and the Crown. When Parliament took the City's side, the stage was set for an English Civil War. This was followed by the upheavals of the Commonwealth and by Williamite settlements, all of which would have far reaching effects on Ireland and the Ulster plantation.

Chapter 11

The resilience of the native Irish
1610 – 1616

Few gave much thought to the plight of the native Irish, but Sir Toby Caulfeild, Member of Parliament for Armagh, wrote to Chichester in late 1610 warning that they were 'seething with discontent'.[a] It was not just Tyrone's supporters; the 'deserving Irish', who had supported the English against him, were also furious.

> Immediately after the flight of the Earls a proclamation was issued from Dublin Castle promising the Gaelic inhabitants of the north that they would 'not be disturbed in the peaceable possession of their lands so long as they demean themselves as dutiful subjects'. Ten days later Lord Deputy Chichester made a promise to every man of note or good desert so much as he can conveniently stock and manure by himself and his tenants and followers, and so much more as by his conjecture he shall be able so to stock and manure for five years to come.[b]

Yet these promises were not endorsed by the Commissioners for Irish Affairs in London, and many natives of Ulster, who had turned against the rebel Earls, felt that they had been hoodwinked,

> especially those of the counties of Tyrone, Ardmagh and Colerayne, who, having reformed themselves in their habit and course of life beyond others and the common expectation held against them, (for all that were able had put on English apparel, and promised to live in townreeds [villages], and to leave their creaghting [nomadic cattle farming] had assured themselves to better conditions from the King than those they lived in under their former landlords; but now they say they have not land given them … which is very grievous unto them.[c]

Little is recorded about the views of those who actually farmed. 'They were a conquered people, and their illegal presence on lands assigned to under takers … depended on the whim of landlords'.[d] They found themselves facing eviction from their properties at the beginning of winter before the harvest could be gathered in. Caulfeild warned:

> They hold discourse among themselves that if this course had been taken with them in war time, it had had some colour of justice; but having been

pardoned and their lands given them, and having lived under law ever since, and being ready to submit themselves to mercy for any offence they can be charged with since their pardoning, they conclude it to be the greatest cruelty that was ever inflicted upon any people.

Although some 'deserving' Irish had been granted lands after supporting the English against Tyrone and Tyrconnell, only 20 per cent of Ulster's total land area was being made available to them. No recipient was restored to his traditional land, and new grants were generally significantly less than previously enjoyed. There seemed to be no justice in land allocations. Many native Irish, who had supported Tyrone and Tyrconnell received better allocations than those who had remained loyal to the English. It is true that rents due to the Crown were much less than former obligations to provide for and billet troops and to pay tribute in support of a superior landlord, but in terms of wealth creation they now had less land to farm and were worse off, even having to pay higher rents than British settlers. Within the six escheated counties, only two hundred and eighty native Irish obtained plantation land grants, and many of these were only for life, after which the land was to be transferred to servitors. The great majority received nothing.

Not only had the conquered natives lost their lands, but Gaelic culture, language and farming practice was frowned upon. The Irish elite was untrained to carry on any practical trade. Many found it difficult to adapt. Native proprietors became hopelessly indebted, living in constant fear of forcible eviction. 'Surviving members of the Gaelic learned classes wrote principally of the sufferings of their high-born fellow-countrymen.'[e] Niall Óg O'Neill of Killeleagh was a principal loser in County Antrim having previously occupied his extensive lordship on the northern shores of Lough Neagh. Chichester described him as a poor man with many dependents. On his death in 1616 he was found to be heavily in debt, and his son, Sir Henry, was left with lands worth forty pounds per annum. Yet, as a man of culture and learning, Sir Henry proved an astute survivor, emerging relatively unscathed as ancestor of a clan with the present day Lord O'Neill of Shane's Castle at its head. As colonisation spread, servitors and successful undertakers like Hamilton and Montgomery acquired further estates from those Irish who had fallen on hard times. Although there was no violence, the loss of ancestral lands was 'dangerously dislocating'[f] and generated profound feelings of insecurity for surviving Gaelic proprietors.

It was only in the proportions allocated to undertakers that the native Irish were to be completely excluded; elsewhere they could buy land, but those that did so seemed to lose ground. In the 1590s, before any decision was made to plant British colonists on escheated lands, arrangements were made for native Irish to acquire land in County Monaghan. This was known as the 'native plantation' and the objective of the move was to reduce the power of the 'over-mighty lords'. In 1605, the Commission for the Division and Bounding of the Lords' and Gentlemen's Livings started to apply this process more widely. One example was the Magennis lands in the lordship of Iveagh (see page 68). In

February 1607, the Commission divided the lordship into freeholds in a scheme prepared with James's approval by the Solicitor-General, Sir Robert Jacob, and put into effect at assizes at Newry between 1607 and 1610.[g] Of the fifteen freeholds granted, thirteen went to leading members of the Magennis clan, who were required to pay entry fines and had to adapt to a much altered lifestyle. They were obliged to let the lands they had acquired on long leases on which they too received entry fines, but on low rents fixed for many years. They were left in constant need of cash to pay for estate management, capital improvements and ever more rapacious legal fees. To adopt an English style, they needed to provide marriage portions for their daughters and education for their sons to provide careers for them in the army or the legal profession, often by attending the Inns of Court in London.[h] The financial position of Art Roe Magennis, now Lord Iveagh, was soon precarious. Despite the cost involved, he sent his son Hugh to Oxford, but this 'in no way bettered him in those things which we specially desired'.[i] Magennis freeholders, having traditionally paid tributes in kind, were now obliged to pay rents in cash to the King's sheriff and became subject to feudal charges together with recusancy fines for non-attendance at Protestant churches. Most had to mortgage their land. This involved granting the rents to the mortgagor. If these proved insufficient to repay the debt at the end of twenty-one years, the land was lost. On death, land was subdivided to give every son a share. Glassney McAholly Magennis of Clanconnell married four times and had to provide for at least seven children. When money ran out, swathes of lands were sold to eager servitors around Newry, who had ready cash to offer from their pensions and were not averse to gaining possession by unscrupulous methods. Once in their control, the land was planted with Scottish settlers, enabling them to amass great fortunes.[j] By 1641, it is estimated that the Magennises had lost 44 per cent of the land granted in 1607, and much of the remainder was encumbered with debt.[k] The pattern of decline in estates held by natives became prevalent throughout Ulster. Yet there were rare examples of some improving their positions. The O'Haras of Crebilly, close allies of Sir Randal MacDonnell, now Earl of Antrim, were rewarded with four townlands, which became outright grants from the Earl in 1629. They also acquired church lands from Chichester and, by 1630, were one of the more prominent native landowners in eastern Ulster.

With no time being allowed for wounds to heal, religious persecution magnified tensions.

> The Government sought to bring 'civility' to Ulster not only by plantation and law but also by bringing the native inhabitants into the state sponsored church – by persuasion if possible, by force if not.[l]

Many Catholic priests and friars were executed and Catholic churches were destroyed, some by native chiefs anxious to stop them being used as shelter by invading troops, but most by the English, determined to wipe out any vestige of Catholicism. In 1599, Captain Edward Cromwell had set fire to the Church of

Down, destroying 'what were believed to be the relics of Patrick, Brigid and Columba'.[m]

The Catholic faith remained part of the fabric of native Irish society. When the Established Church took possession of all former Catholic parish churches, the Irish, who associated them with local saints, considered that their sanctuaries had been desecrated. 'Traditional church lands were assigned to the [Established] church as soon as King James had begun his reign.'[n] Such land had been farmed on the Catholic Church's behalf by 'erenachs', usually the heads of a local family, who shared the cost of maintaining the church with the priest and paid rent to the bishop for the land's use. Erenachs continued farming the lands and did much to preserve Catholic relics for posterity, but 'their status as subtenants was severely reduced'.[o]

The majority of Irish priests were trained by being apprenticed to local Catholic clergy. Despite their poverty, they gained some knowledge of Latin, which became the language for communicating with the British. Priests often married, although the Jesuits had called on the Earl of Tyrone to promote celibacy. Before the English Reformation, Irish priests from well-to-do families had been sent to Oxford for training and later to Glasgow until the Reformation also took hold in Scotland. Trainee priests were then forced to travel to Salamanca or other seminaries on the Continent, returning 'fired with the spirit of the Counter-Reformation to rebuild the Catholic Church in Ulster'.[p] This caused Catholicism to make a strong recovery while the plantation was being established. In 1609, Davies noted that well-educated Irish priests and scholars were establishing Catholic schools throughout what was to become Londonderry, and they continued to operate through the 17th and 18th Centuries. The Franciscans took the lead, arriving from their base at St Anthony's near Louvain in the Spanish Netherlands, and they subsisted by begging. With monasteries in Ireland no longer available to them, they sought safe houses among the natives and constructed wooden buildings deep in the forests. Chichester described them as 'the very furies and firebrands of the rebellion'.[q] Some were executed, but others remained at large 'like Satan compassing the earth, seducing the people and persuading them to run into rebellion'.[r]

As early as 1604, Archbishop Loftus of Dublin had warned the English Privy Council that he was unable to see 'how, without some moderate course of coactions [force], [the Irish Catholics] can be reclaimed from their idolatry'.[s] James and his Council hoped 'that the 'least civil' natives in the remote parts would be the easiest to win over'.[t] Although Davies, the Attorney-General, agreed, he felt they would need 'suitable preachers to evangelise them'.[u] Yet the Protestant clergy failed to offer the necessary charisma. Bishop George Montgomery proved 'a bitter disappointment' to hopes that he would act as 'a new St Patrick among them'. He focused only on his 'lands and incomes from the three dioceses of Derry, Raphoe and Clogher'.[v] Although Gaelic speaking clergy were needed, Montgomery made no attempt to convert local priests. He brought in nineteen English and Scottish preachers, but, within a year, was writing of 'the great difficulty of reducing this people to civility'.[w]

Montgomery's successors, Brute Babington at Derry and Andrew Knox (fresh from a missionary campaign in the Western Isles) at Raphoe, were energetic in efforts to enforce conformity. Both claimed some progress, particularly Babington, who adopted a persuasive rather than confrontational approach, only to be met by stubbornness. He eventually won over a diocesan chapter to a compromise program of change. This included an oath of allegiance to the King (but not the Oath of Supremacy), a recognition of royal supremacy over the Church, the use of scriptures, and approved liturgy translated into Irish. But the Bishop died unexpectedly in September 1611.[x] Knox lacked Babington's sensitivity, but 'enthusiastically set about destroying religious artefacts',[y] including 'a wooden statue of the Virgin at the chapel of Agivey',[z] recognised as a place of pilgrimage to seek miracle cures. Babington's death soon afterwards was seen by the Irish as 'proof of divine wrath'.[aa] When Knox brought seven Gaelic speaking clergy from Scotland, they faced so much hostility that they were forced to live in the Bishop's residence for protection. Their efforts met with 'deadly hatred'.[bb] Chichester agreed that coercion was required but had 'little assurance of their obedience'.[cc] In Carrickfergus, a short-lived move by local priests to conform, often a result of mixed marriages, was brought to a halt by the Franciscans, and those who converted were side-lined. Elsewhere conversion proved the exception. At Christmas 1614, a Catholic congregation 'dragged a native Irish minister, who had conformed, out of his house in south Tyrone and stabbed him to death.'[dd]

Although the University of Dublin was established to educate the 'uncivil and barbarous' Irish youth for training as Protestant graduates to preach to native Irish in the Established Church, it signally failed in its objective. At its most productive, it provided five graduate clergy per year, leaving the Established Church with an acute shortage of Gaelic-speaking clergymen. The 1622 survey recorded that there were only thirteen graduates of the University of Dublin in the six counties of the plantation. The Established church clergy was left with a 'mediocrity of learning', often drawn from 'unsuitable men, including mechanics and soldiers'.[ee] Clergymen were regularly accused of leading 'lewd lives', and Archbishop James Ussher reported that the poor example set by 'many unworthy ministers gives exceeding much hindrance to the progress of the gospel amongst us'.[ff] Although they held non-conformist beliefs, 'Bishops tolerated Puritan clergy to present a united hostile front to Catholicism.'[gg] After failing to find livings elsewhere, they had flocked to Ulster, where they were not required to adhere to prescribed liturgy and articles of faith. Yet they were treated by the Irish with constant hostility. With settlers remaining thin on the ground, the Protestant clergy focused on their own flock and could not prevent the locality from worshipping as they wished. They shared churches, even though many were roofless. Only when settlers started to appear in greater numbers were churches repaired and new ones built, but the Catholics were left unmolested.

If anything, the quality of the Protestant clergy in Ulster became rather better than elsewhere in Ireland and their parishes provided each incumbent with more generous allocations of land. In successful settlement areas, colonists found themselves well served by clergy 'with a genuine spiritual call to evangelise the natives'.[hh] Yet such were the tensions that they were unlikely to make progress. Conflict was exacerbated by the eagerness of the Established Church to fine and exploit Catholics through the ecclesiastical courts and assizes. Fines included tithes, recusancy fines (for non-attendance at Protestant services) and fees arising from 'rites of passage' (baptisms, confirmations, marriages and funerals). Tithes were collected in kind, but the amounts varied from place to place. Although most clergy were absentees, they began to impose a tithe on milk, despite the vital part it played in the native Irish diet. This caused great hardship in the winter of 1614/15, when many cattle died. Chichester stepped in to insist on 'a milder temper hereafter in tithing'.[ii] Recusancy fines were also considered unfair, as the native Irish did not understand services conducted in English. Native Irish arranging baptisms, marriages and funerals in Catholic churches paid a fee to the priest, but also had to provide a second 'composition' to the local Protestant Church which had not been involved. Fees were even charged for stillborn children. 'Mortuaries' (death duties) were levied at one-fifth of the deceased's property in Derry and one-third in Raphoe. If a beggar died on someone's premises, the householder had to pay 2s. 6d. to the Church. The money raised was substantial, funding the repair of numerous Protestant churches.

To keep the British Government in control, early steps were taken to pack the Irish Parliament with Protestants. Thirty-eight new seats were assigned in Ulster, some for corporations yet to receive their Charters and for plantation towns still being built. This resulted in the old English Lords of the Pale losing their majority. In the spring of 1613, the most prominent of the 'deserving Irish', Sir Turlough MacHenry O'Neill of the Fews, arrived at the Armagh shire house to stand for one of the two county seats with support from a large number of native Irish freeholders. He had been granted 9,900 acres despite being a half-brother of Tyrone, but the term 'deserving' meant nothing. His supporters were prohibited entry to vote, allowing the Protestant candidates, Sir Toby Caulfeild and Sir John Bourchier to be elected.

Natives in the new County Londonderry were considered barbarous by the arriving settlers, alien in language, custom and religion. Their most cherished areas and fisheries were seized and their forests plundered. They lived in daily expectation of expulsion from their native lands. Although Chichester had shown some sympathy, he was now ill and had retired from active involvement. Rebellion was never far below the surface. In April 1615, Phillips stamped on a planned uprising to free both O'Cahan from the Tower of London, and Tyrone's son, Conn na Creaga O'Neill, from Fort Charlemont in County Armagh. The plot was led by Rory O'Cahan (Sir Donell Ballagh O'Cahan's son), who again made overtures for help from Spain, and it involved a number of freeholders, including the MacDonnells, whose loyalty to the Crown was thought to be assured.[ii] The ringleaders had planned to capture Limavady Castle and to kill Phillips, but he was warned of the plot and, after arresting the leaders before their revolt could begin, received instructions from Chichester[62] to arrange their trial and execution at Londonderry. In May 1615, other Tyrone kinsmen led a second conspiracy to surprise and destroy the Londoners' plantation. Yet again, Phillips came to the rescue by arresting the six principal ringleaders for trial and execution at Londonderry, but this highlighted the dangers of 'filling the Country with Irish at whose mercy the few English lie for they may at their pleasure surprise their horses, cut their throats, and possess their arms'.[kk]

Piracy was another problem. When Phillips's barque was carrying provisions from Dublin to Derry, it was seized by Sorley Boy MacDonnell at Larne. MacDonnell sailed it round Scotland, plundering as he went. He eventually arrived at Dunkirk, where Phillips's dispossessed captain was lucky enough to meet an acquaintance and was able to arrange the pirates' arrest. Although Phillips had sent a second ship in hot pursuit, it was held off the Orkneys by a Dutch man-of-war, who thought it was a privateer. It was escorted to The Hague, where the English ambassador was eventually able to arrange its release.

The native Irish in Ulster strongly resented their treatment and rumours abounded that Tyrone would return at the head of a great Spanish and Papal army. Although he continued to press Philip IV to support an invasion, neither Philip in Spain nor the Pope in Rome gave him encouragement. Philip was bound up in negotiating the betrothal of his daughter to James's son, Charles. Yet Catholic priests in Ulster, who must have been aware of Tyrone's invasion hopes, were rumoured to be inciting their congregations, and Chichester concluded that they were ready to take up arms. When 'the Irish Parliament met in 1613, the King expressed his concern that the Gaelic Irish were in 'preparation of arms''[ll] and were concealing weapons.

The Government in Dublin was without the resources to defend the new settlers. Chichester needed to raise a subsidy, but this required parliamentary consent. He resorted to subterfuge by arranging for several purported ringleaders to be arrested and tortured. Under duress, they revealed their plan to seize Londonderry, Coleraine, Lifford, Culmore and Limavady. He then called for Parliament to be prorogued to allow members to hasten north, and pushed them into rushing through a subsidy to pay for Ulster's defence. Without a coherent plan, the rebel force was hopelessly inadequate. The ringleaders were brought to trial and six were convicted of treason. They were dragged through the streets, hanged, disembowelled, beheaded and quartered before being burned. The rebellion, if it was a rebellion, came to nothing. At last, in 1616, Tyrone suffered

---

[62] 'Chichester felt that it was time the Irish understood that any persons involved in further plottings or rebellions ran 'the danger of losing their heads'.'[mm] He also seized any freeholds held by the rebels. Yet he was extremely worried by a rebellion in the Londonderry heartland, reporting to the Privy Council that 'unless the County could be better protected it would fall sooner or later to the Irish'.[nn]

a fever and died unexpectedly in Rome. He was buried with great pomp at San Pietro in Montorio beside his son Hugh and Tyrconnell. The prospect of help for the native Irish from abroad died with him.

Chapter 12

The Livery Companies' poor management of their proportions
1613-1625

Raven's 1622 map of County Londonderry depicting the division into the proportions occupied by the twelve Great Livery Companies. The shortcomings of 17th Century map-making should be noted.
Courtesy of the Drapers' Company

By 1613, when the decision for the Livery Companies to manage their own proportions was taken, they had subscribed a total of £40,000. This placed a notional value on each of the twelve proportions of £3,333 6s. 8d, although the money had mainly been utilised in Londonderry and Coleraine. Agreement of boundaries had been delayed by the death of the Bishop of Derry and by 'the truculence' of Rowley, who at the time of the allocation was still with The Irish Society. Each proportion was projected to provide an income of £150 per annum, but it is clear that neither the King nor the Livery Companies expected an early profit. Each of the twelve Great Companies was to take responsibility for its own area, supported where required by associated Minor Companies[63] in agreed shares. The Merchant Taylors and Grocers both had an interest in a second area, as their investment already made exceeded that of a single proportion. The following contributions had been made (the order of precedence of the twelve Great Companies is shown in brackets):

	£	Rank
Merchant Taylors	4,086	(6/7)
Grocers	3,874	(2)
Haberdashers	3,124	(8)
Drapers	3,072	(3)
Goldsmiths	2,999	(5)
Mercers	2,680	(1)
Fishmongers	2,260	(4)
Clothworkers	2,260	(12)
Vintners	2,080	(11)
Skinners	1,963	(6/7)
Salters	1,954	(9)
Ironmongers	1,514	(10)
	31,866	
The forty-three Minor Companies	8,134	
	£40,000	

Detailed inventories of each proportion were put together, and

> on 17 December 1613, at a Court of Common Council, the City Sword-bearer, with great pomp and ceremony, drew the lots of the twelve proportions of the Londonderry Plantation.[b]

Some were split into more than one area to accommodate lands already allocated to the church or native Irish.

> By the luck of the draw, the Grocers, Fishmongers and Goldsmiths [with lands near Lough Foyle close to Londonderry] got what eventually turned out to be the most fertile and accessible proportions. ... The Drapers and Skinners [with land bordering the Sherrin Mountains to the west] were left with the most inaccessible proportions, with much infertile land.[c]

County Londonderry now amounted to 508,700 notional acres, divided as follows:

---

[63] The Minor Companies were generally not involved in management and appear to have left decisions on 'dividends to their senior partners on a principle of trust'.[a]

	%
The Livery Companies	57.3
The Established Church	22.8
The native Irish	10.2
The Irish Society	5.9
Sir Thomas Philips	3.8
	100.0

When The Irish Society transferred lands to each of the twelve Great Livery Companies, they, in turn, issued shares to their Livery Company associates. Yet there were delays. It took a further two years for the Companies' legal title to be confirmed, and, in some instances conveyancing from the Crown was not completed until 1619. This requires explanation. As corporate bodies, the Companies required a special Royal Licence to obtain their grants. Time taken in its preparation delayed the Letters Patent to transfer title until 1615. Before the Irish Society could prepare the conveyance, each Company was required to allocate its land between its manors, land to be leased to tenants and land to be held by six named freeholders. Each freeholder was to receive a 'balliboe' (or 'townland') of land after paying twice the annual rent due to the Crown. This was defined as 'sixty acres of profitable land' in accordance with traditional Irish measurement and was not a finite area but a measure of its economic worth. (see page 88) In the Goldsmiths' proportion, balliboes varied in size from ninety-seven to six hundred and nine acres. Although the requirement to nominate freeholders in advance had been imposed to provide greater security, the negotiation of the area of each balliboe only delayed matters.[d] In 1616, there were still insufficient freeholders available for jury service, and it was not until 1617 and 1618, that each Company at last established them.

Each proportion was conveyed as a 'Manor' with its own demesne lands in addition to townlands for transfer to freeholders or for lease to tenants. As in England, a Lord of the Manor had the right to hold a Court Baron to dispense justice within his estate. To ensure that commodities were shared fairly between proportions, The Irish Society retained all rights to timber, building materials, game and fishing. Each Lord of the Manor had rights of usage over those on his proportion in return for a small rent payable to the Society. To encourage the building of mills, all corn grown on a Manor was required to be ground locally. Within two years of receiving his grant, the Lord of the Manor was required to build a house with at least six rooms, where he or his agent was to live for the next seven years. The lands were to be enclosed (after making allowance for roads) using hedges, ditches and dykes. Arms with powder and shot were to be kept readily available. Each proportion was bound by the Articles of the Plantation, which included a requirement to install British settlers and to remove all native Irish. The inclusion of a requirement for freeholders was 'an essential element in the attempt to clone English conditions and ensure that the expensive burdens of jury service were met.'[e]

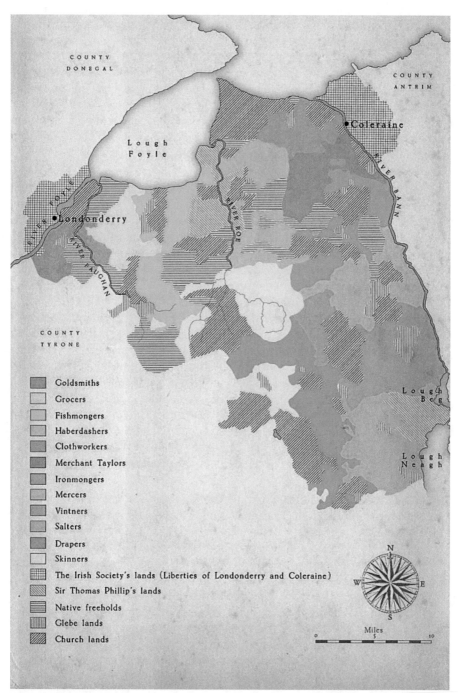

Map of County Londonderry showing the division of land into the proportions taken by each of the twelve Great Livery Companies, with other areas retained for The Irish Society, the Church, Native Irish and Phillips.
Drawn by David Atkinson, Handmade Maps Limited

149

Each Company remained under The Irish Society's supervision and was to continue to contribute to the upkeep of Coleraine and the City of Londonderry. As has been seen, a further £20,000 was contributed to The Irish Society between 1614 and 1616. This was in addition to the money that each Livery Company needed to expend on developing buildings and improving land on its own proportions in accordance with the Articles of Agreement.[f] The Companies were extremely nervous and were reluctant to provide more money than absolutely necessary. This left a shortage of resources, which remained a continuing problem for the plantation throughout its early years.

To mitigate their required expenditure, some Livery Companies leased large parts of their proportions to a single tenant, receiving an entry fine in return. There were doubts whether the new landlord shared the Companies' obligation to evict the native Irish, and this can be seen as a deliberate attempt to circumvent James I's objective. In most respects the Companies' performance in expelling the native Irish was lamentable. Although they were later to deny it, they were well aware that they should be gone by 1 May 1615. Given that this was impracticable, they requested that any native Irish prepared to swear the Oath of Supremacy, to conform to the Established Church and to adopt English customs should be permitted to stay. Although the Privy Council was supportive, James had by then 'fired off an indignant letter to Chichester',[g] after receiving Bodley's highly critical report of 1614. He had 'examined, viewed and reviewed' this and 'found greatly to his 'discontentment the slow progress' of the plantation'.[h] He 'stirred upp' things to great effect.[i] Realising that the King meant business, The Irish Society was galvanised into action. It wrote to the Goldsmiths complaining at their 'great slowness' in development.[j] Each Company was required to repair and reroof derelict churches on its proportion, providing a bible, prayer book and communion cup. It was also to appoint a suitable English parson, subject to approval from both the Bishop and Beresford.[k]

When it came to building work, there was a degree of 'rivalrous emulation' between the Companies and a clear recognition that buildings should be of better quality than those being provided by servitors and other landlords. This encouraged compliance with the building requirements of the Articles of the Plantation, even if the timetable fell behind the King's expectation. In early 1615, the Companies were required to report on the state of their proportions to The Irish Society, who were to provide a full return to the agitated King. He gave them until August 1616 'to make good omissions, poor, or sub-standard works'.[l] At this point Bodley was to undertake another survey (see page 137). By then, Chichester was empowered to seize any lands belonging to undertakers who had failed to comply, and 'bestow them upon some other men more active and worthy'.[m]

Neither The Irish Society nor the Livery Companies did much to overcome the shortage of settlers, despite settlement being the plantation's principal objective. As has been shown, Bodley was extremely critical of this failure with the resultant lack of security, but the Companies' reluctance was understandable. In addition to danger from wood-kerne, 'the seas were infested with Scottish pirates'.[n] With the loyalty of local native freeholders also in doubt, English settlers faced danger and uncertainty. The Companies could not offer them protection in such a remote and hostile location. The threat was brought home by a native Irish rebellion in 1615. Although Phillips was able to stamp on this by executing and forfeiting the ringleaders, it caused a stir. Both The Irish Society and Livery Companies received 'precepts from the Privy Council demanding contributions towards defence: arms were rushed to Londonderry and Coleraine'.[o]

The few settlers who did arrive from London had no experience of farming. They needed farm labour and advice. If the objective was to import English farming methods, the Londoners were not the right people. It was much more straightforward to retain the native Irish on their lands. This would stop immediate unrest at a stroke, and despite inefficient farming methods, the Companies would receive higher rentals than English settlers were obliged to pay. It might not achieve the King's objective, but it was the only realistic way forward. Having just a few settlers was worse than having none. It was different for the Scots. Ireland offered better farming opportunities and a less severe climate than at home. They were already experienced farmers and moved to the less hostile areas in large numbers. Yet it would not help them if the Londonderry plantation remained a pocket of unrest likely to spill over into their areas.

The surveys by Carew in 1611 and by Bodley in 1613 had shown that a great many undertakers blamed an unrealistic timetable for their failure to meet their obligations. Despite his frustration, James had had little alternative but to extend the limits initially to August 1616. Sadly only fragments of Bodley's survey to monitor progress at this time have survived. It cannot have reported what James wanted to hear and there is no doubt that it remained critical of progress. Yet the Companies had, on the face of it, made reasonable progress with building works.

The death of Tyrone in Rome in 1616 heralded a more optimistic outlook. In August 1617, following Bodley's 1616 survey, Grandison extended until 1 May 1618, the time limit for the native Irish to move to the lands of servitors or those of the Church, failing which they were to face 'such penalties as the Lord Deputy should think fit to impose'.[p] Yet again this ultimatum failed to produce the desired result. On 1 October 1818, there was a further proclamation extending the deadline to 1 May 1619 or face a ten shilling fine 'and thereafter at the Lord Deputy's pleasure'. The King was only too aware that the plantation objectives were being foiled. Despite the proclamation to banish priests educated abroad, this too was only partially implemented.[q]

Although England's attention was focused on the start of the Thirty Years' War in Bohemia, the King remained 'thoroughly [if intermittently] provoked' by the lack of progress in Ireland, which Grandison was reporting to him. On receiving wind of this, The Irish Society produced a statement on the plantation, and warned each Company of shortcomings, which needed their immediate attention. On 28 November 1618, the King appointed Captain Nicholas Pynnar as his Commissioner to 'survey and make a return of the proceedings and performance of conditions of the undertakers, Servitors and Natives planted' in the six escheated counties.[r] Pynnar knew the area well, having served as a Captain of Foot under Docwra. In 1611, while a servitor, he appears to have turned down an offer to become an undertaker in County Cavan.[s] Working from December 1618 to March 1619, he produced a comprehensive survey to report on both progress on building work and the arrival of settlers.

Taking the escheated counties as a whole, Pynnar reported a fairly satisfactory improvement in security. He reckoned that there were one hundred and seven castles with bawns, nineteen without bawns, forty-two bawns without castles or houses, and a minimum of 1,897 dwelling houses of stone and timber after the English manner located in villages. Although some were still incomplete, there was a castle or bawn in each Livery Company proportion. The Salters and Skinners had both built two castles with bawns. With the walls at Londonderry being higher than previously claimed, Pynnar reported that the City was

> now encompassed about with a very strong wall, excellently made and neatly wrought; being all of good lime and stone; the circuit whereof is 283 perches and 2/3 at 18 feet to the perch [almost a mile]; besides the four gates which contain 84 feet; and in every place the wall it is 24 feet high, and 6 feet thick. The gates are battlemented ... The bulwarks are all very large and good, being in number nine; besides two half bulwarks; and for four of them there may be four cannons, or other great pieces ... The rampart within the city is 12 feet thick of earth; and all things are very well and substantially done.[t]

Outside the walls, there was a large fosse ten feet deep and thirty feet wide. On the inside, the earthen rampart was banked up to make the walls even stronger, but there was no shelter for troops on watch. It was probably the last walled city to be constructed anywhere in Europe; 'the Londoners had created perhaps 'the most impregnable fortified urban centre in Ireland''.[u] Culmore fort, which provided the City with protection from the sea, was also complete. Londonderry had been made into the ideal place to provide protection during a siege. Yet Coleraine's earthen ramparts were another story. They were disintegrating and unable to support guns; there were insufficient inhabitants to man more than one-sixth of their length, making them indefensible.

Pynnar showed that, taken as a whole, the migration to Ulster had been impressive, comparing favourably with the Spanish colonisation of the Americas undertaken at a similar time. In 1613, Bodley had estimated 2,000 adult British males settled in Ulster as a whole. Pynnar now reported 6,215 adult British males in the escheated counties alone, made up of:

Tyrone	2,469
Donegal	1,106
Cavan	711
Fermanagh	645
Armagh	642
Londonderry	642
	6,215

He believed that these numbers could be an underestimate, and a total of 8,000 was probably more accurate. By 1620, numbers had risen to about 12,000, and, by 1630, to 16,000. With harvests in Scotland starting to fail from 1633, more Scots arrived and, by 1641, it was estimated that there were between 40,000 and 45,000 adult settlers throughout Ulster, of which two-thirds were Scots. On arrival, the English and Scots were settling down amicably together, linked in a common determination to secure themselves from the Irish wood-kerne.

It was not just the weather that encouraged a preponderance of Scottish arrivals. Travelling from Scotland was relatively straightforward, involving a three hour crossing from Portpatrick on a regular ferry service to Donaghadee, which transported both settlers and goods. The journey from southern England was altogether more time-consuming. In 1614, Canning recorded that he left London on 30 September, arriving at Chester two days later. With no ship available, he waited at the little port of Hilbree from 14 to 21 October, when, at last, he boarded the *Bride of Derry*. This arrived at the Foyle after a three day journey, skirting the treacherous headlands of the north coast and finally reaching Coleraine on 26 October.

Pynnar's main concern was the lack of a housing infrastructure and he focused on shortcomings in the Londonderry plantation. He reported that the City of Londonderry contained only ninety-two houses, accommodating one hundred and two families (compared with Proby and Springham, who had counted two hundred and fifteen single room dwellings as houses) and there was a lack of space for the one hundred further dwellings still being projected. This left Londonderry with insufficient residents to defend it. At Coleraine, only three more houses had been built since the previous survey. The areas still undeveloped were 'dismal and filthy, and the shapeless market place was so squalid with piles of dirt and refuse that nobody could cross it'.[v] In the Company proportions, Pynnar counted one hundred and eighteen houses, some timber-framed and some brick, built near the castles as required, but there were others more isolated and difficult to defend. He also noted work being undertaken on building and repairing churches.

By this time many of the Companies had concluded that it was preferable to lease out their estates as a whole. Nine of them leased out their proportions for terms of sixty-one years to a 'Farmer'[64], who took over the entire management,

---

[64] This resulted in Sir Robert McClelland taking over a huge area including the Haberdasher and Clothworker proportions.

'but the Mercers, Drapers and Ironmongers had appointed resident Agents, and so had direct control over developments.'ʷ Yet the Drapers soon appointed their own Farmer, despite being the only Company to have sunk large sums into building works before seeking occupiers, and the Ironmongers let their proportion to their Agent, George Canning. This left the Mercers as the only Company to retain direct control,ˣ although this did not turn out to be a satisfactory decision for them.

The appointment of Farmers infuriated James, who was still seeking an increase in British settlers to improve security. Nearly half of those arriving remained in Antrim and Down. In the escheated counties, the principal area of disappointment was County Londonderry where work on developing the land did not equate to the level of building construction. Pynnar explained:

> The abode and continuance of those inhabitants upon the land is not yet made certain, although I have seen the deeds made unto them. My reason is, that many of the English tenants do not plough upon the lands, neither use husbandry, because I conceive they are fearful to stock themselves with cattle or servants for those labours. Neither do the Irish use tillage, for they are uncertain of their stay upon the lands; so that, by this means, the Irish ploughing nothing … the English very little; and were it not for the Scottish tenants, which do plough in many places in the country, those parts may starve.ʸ

He recorded that, of the 642 adult male settlers arriving in County Londonderry, about 500 were on the Livery Company proportions,[65] compared to the original target of 912 to be achieved within three years of the grant. This left it 'grossly underpopulated with British Settlers'. Six of the Livery Companies (Fishmongers, Goldsmiths, Skinners, Merchant Taylors, Haberdashers and Vintners) accounted for 402 adult male settlers (not far short of their projected requirement), but, on the other six Company proportions, the bulk of the population remained Irish, 'with hardly a British man to be found'.ᶻ Pynnar reported these Companies' assertion that their patents were silent on any obligation to plant British settlers. They argued that when long leases were granted to Farmers, any obligation disappeared. In reality, they all recognised that 'it was less trouble and more profitable to let to Irish tenants,'ᵃᵃ who were prepared to pay better rents (or offer services in lieu) to farm their cattle, but would not grow crops while in fear of eviction. If the Irish left, the few remaining English would be forced to sell, as they lacked labour and would be open to robbery. The Mercers had a worse problem. They had let forty-six townlands to native Irish, but some were the most dangerous of the O'Donnells. The few settlers who did arrive found their position precarious. The Companies

---

[65] Numbers progressively improved. From 500 British male settlers in 1619, the numbers rose to 617 in 1622 and to 947 in 1628. In 1630 the muster role showed 894, which equates to at least 1,000 settlers. (Dr Ian Archer *London-Derry Connections: The early years, 1613 – 1640*, p. 5)

failed to recognise the urgency to confirm title to tenancies even though tenants were putting up buildings. Some tenants 'showed ominous signs of abandoning the Plantation and returning to England'.[bb]

Apart from the walls at Londonderry, Pynnar's survey offered the King little comfort on the Londoners' progress. When he took time to focus on Irish matters, a failure to attract sufficient settlers and to remove the natives was high on his list of criticisms. He suspected that this 'was due to the 'covetousness' of the merchants'.[cc] This is very hard to refute. He was furious and determined to 'take that advantage of those that have soe grossly failed, as eyther in lawe or policy of state hee may justly doe'.[dd] The Companies were trying to exploit a loophole to avoid having to force out the native Irish, but, in doing so, completely ignored the King's objectives. He 'doubled Crown rents and imposed fines on those who had failed to abide by the Articles of Association'.[ee] He also appointed Edward Wray, one of the Grooms of his Bedchamber, to collect fines and forfeitures from native Irish still occupying British undertakers' lands. Wray paid £100 in advance for the right to collect fines for the next seven years. At last, James was beginning to accept that the complete eviction of the Irish was not feasible.

In 1620, the Privy Council told The Irish Society 'that his Majesty considered the City of London to be in breach of covenant with the Crown'.[ff] The Solicitor-General started to develop the Crown's case by preparing an inventory of the Companies' faults. To protect their position, The Irish Society called on the Companies to provide details of their progress. These included lists of castles, bawns, houses, places of worship and other structures being built, with details of their condition, lists of tenants and freeholders, details of arms supplied and distributed for defence, income and expense from rents, and details of lettings. The returns received were vague and it was apparent that, where proportions were let to Farmers, some Companies had no idea how many subtenants there were. Yet expenditure still exceeded income. The King warned Grandison that he was considering the seizure of their estates, but would offer new Patents if he received double the existing rents and fines for failing to honour contracts.[gg] The City again explained the difficulties that would be caused by dispossessing the native Irish, and the Privy Council at last conceded that any, who took the Oath of Allegiance and conformed as Protestants, would be acceptable as tenants on 25 per cent of the Londoners' lands.[hh] The Companies were given until 1 May 1622 to remove them from other areas and were prohibited from retaining Irish servants. The Companies accepted these terms, including the doubling of their rents. After taking into account lands allocated to native Irish freeholders, and lands held by Phillips and the Church, more than half of County Londonderry was available to those native Irish prepared to conform. They made no great move to do so, but a few did join the Established Church. The revised terms were to be confirmed under new Patents, but the Privy Council postponed implementing them until a survey had been undertaken to establish the state of Ireland as a whole. Its objective was not aimed just at the situation in County Londonderry, but at financial difficulties in Dublin.

Although it had been expected that the plantations would greatly improve Irish Government revenues, between 1604 and 1619, it had required subsidies averaging £47,170 annually from an English exchequer already close to insolvency. English Government debt amounted to about £500,000, and was increasing by £50,000 annually. In 1611, Salisbury had tried to mitigate the shortfall of plantation income by selling a new order of hereditary knighthood, a baronetcy[66], at £1,095 for each grant. Although James limited this to families already bearing arms, £90,000 was raised. Each baronet was obliged to maintain thirty soldiers in Ireland for three years. After Salisbury's death in 1612, James realised that he could raise more money by this means and, when he took personal control of Government, he started to sell peerages. Following the sudden death of his beloved son, Prince Henry, in 1612, James sought companionship from younger attractive men. When the glamorous George Villiers arrived at Court in 1614, the ailing King lavished honours on him, appointing him Viscount Villiers in 1616, rising to Duke of Buckingham in 1623.

Buckingham acquired extensive properties both for himself and his family in Ireland, but his involvement in Irish politics only added to its financial difficulties. The English Lord Treasurer, Lionel Cranfield, Earl of Middlesex, detested Buckingham and was determined to understand what was going on. In March 1622, Middlesex persuaded James to order another searching enquiry, while Buckingham did what he could to cloud 'the questionable activities of his agents, relatives and hangers-on'.[ii] It was not just the plantations that were under scrutiny. The Commissioners spent much time in Dublin examining the Established Church, Government revenues and the Courts of Justice. Despite the delaying tactics of Buckingham's agents, the survey had made good progress by the autumn, and Phillips offered himself in an unpaid capacity as one of two Commissioners, the other being Richard Hadsor, to examine the Londonderry plantation.

Having adeptly avoided being sucked into war in Europe, James hoped to cement his alliance with Spain by proposing a marriage between his son Charles and the Infanta Maria. In 1623, Charles and Buckingham set out incognito to Madrid in a ludicrous mission to secure her hand. With the prospect of a Spanish marriage, Grandison was considered to have been over-zealous in promoting religious conformity in Ireland and was forced to resign. He was replaced in 1622 by Buckingham's protégé, Henry Cary, 1st Viscount Falkland. Although the Spanish marriage negotiations dragged on, it was unfortunate that Falkland chose this time to issue a proclamation requiring all Catholic priests to leave Ireland within forty days. Although the Privy Council ordered him to suspend

---

[66] The proceeds of such sales were designated to maintain English power in Ulster. Hence the coat of arms borne by Baronets contains a bloody red hand, the armorial ensign of the O'Neills and of Ulster.[ji]

it, the Spanish heard of it. The Infanta's brother, Philip IV, who had succeeded to the Spanish throne in 1620, put up impossible marriage terms. These included a requirement for Parliament to ratify complete toleration for Catholics, and for any child of the marriage to be raised as a Papist. Inevitably, negotiations were ended, but the snub led to war, only worsening the English Government's financial position.

The O'Neill Coat of Arms From the stained glass at Londonderry Guildhall. The bloody red hand became the armorial ensign of Ulster and is in the coat of arms borne by the order of Baronetcy.

Financial difficulties were exacerbated by a downturn in trade and a succession of bad harvests. Irish corn was in such short supply that, on 23 November 1622, the Government prohibited its export. With Ulster particularly hard hit, the Commissioners undertaking the survey had to carry food with them. Natives still outnumbered settlers on every Company proportion[67] and incursions by wood-kerne were discouraging new arrivals. The land areas granted were found to have been much greater than previously assumed using notional acres. With settlers thinner on the ground than anticipated, security was even worse. Undertakers did not have the resources to finance additional fortresses, housing and infrastructure required for the increased tenantry, and even more native Irish were needed to farm the larger than anticipated area. Later surveys did not point out this problem, and, if James's advisers were aware of it, they did nothing to resolve it. Without enough British settlers, the Irish remained where they were. Some Companies even rented out land to Catholic

---

[67] 'This was confirmed by a census of natives on undertakers' estates completed by Easter 1624.'pp

priests, finding them 'good farmers and prompt payers'.[kk] An incensed Phillips sent a list of them, including four on the Fishmongers' proportion and others on Grocers' lands, to London. He also reported nine 'mass houses' (Catholic chapels) on Company lands.

It was clear that the King's plan to evict the native Irish was unenforceable and the planters lacked the military strength to achieve it, even if they had wanted it. This discouraged further settlement despite attractive offers being made. Yet those who arrived found the natives making desperate efforts to avoid being driven out. 'Local people acted as guides and helped to erect dwellings to enable English and Scots to survive the first winter.'[ll] The new arrivals were not generally experienced farmers; many were discharged soldiers and others were either unemployed or under-employed, leading, perhaps unfairly, to comments that they were 'the scum of both nations'.[mm] [68] Even if Irish ploughs were pulled on the 'garron's tail',[69] the Irish played a crucial part in working the lands and helping with the 'harvest at a time when British settlers had either not arrived or were thin on the ground'.[nn] The continued use of Irish farming methods explains the small amount of corn being planted by comparison to Down and Antrim, where Scottish farmers were ploughing assiduously. Very few settlers brought cattle with them, and most stock was acquired locally. Although 'Irish butter matured in raskins and sunk in bogs was not much to their taste', the settlers were grateful for it.[oo] The Irish were also employed in felling timber, quarrying stone, building fortifications and digging bawns.

The King was also concerned at the 'bewildering frequency'[π] with which townlands were changing hands. Vendors generally sold to neighbours, causing estates to become larger than was thought prudent, spreading settlers even more thinly. Yet plantations elsewhere in the escheated counties were progressing well despite frequent changes of ownership. Pynnar reported one hundred and ninety-three settlers at Lifford, compared to the one hundred and fifty stipulated, even though many original grantees had sold up. Although colonists were expected to live in towns and villages for their security, those who were farming found this inconvenient. New arrivals sought out less isolated areas with more fertile lands accessible to markets, and they tended not to remain on the lands initially allocated to them. This resulted in settlers congregating in fertile valleys near coasts and navigable rivers, including the areas to the south and west of Lough Neagh, the Foyle basin round Londonderry and Strabane, the Lower Bann River to the north coast, Upper and Lower Lough Erne and the middle of County Cavan. Less accessible areas remained underpopulated and insecure. This pattern was similar to Down and Antrim, where the most densely populated

---

[68] There were similar problems in Virginia, where, in 1620, there were complaints of 'a great scarcity, or none at all' of 'husbandmen truly bred'. Many arrivals were vagrants, who had arrived in London to escape the effects of the Poor Law. Some were convicted criminals and stowaways who deserted to become pirates.[qq]

[69] The Irish had a custom of attaching their ploughs to the tails of their horses rather than using traces. This caused the deaths of innumerable animals.

areas included the Lagan Valley, north and east Down, the Lecale and Ards peninsulas, south Antrim, Ballymena and the Bush Valley. These were the areas, which before the plantation had been densely populated by native Irish.[ss]

In July 1617, Phillips had laid a statement of the plantation's deficiencies before Government, including the problem of granting leases to Farmers highlighted by Pynnar. On several occasions he offered to help the Companies and there is evidence, initially at least, that they thought well of him. The Goldsmiths wrote:

> Sir, the Companie of Gouldsmiths have been well informed of your good affecc'on on the plantac'on and are desirous to make themselves beholden unto you for your advice and direcc'on.[tt]

In February 1622, he was entertained to dinner by the Mercers, who sought his opinion on the state of their proportion and the character of their Agent.[uu] Yet, by then, he was already planning a new attack on the management of the Londonderry plantation.

Collectively the Companies had invested £22,000 on building work in their proportions, and in the twenty-one years from 1613 to 1634 averaged a rental income of £1,785 per annum, a total of £37,500. During this time, farming methods improved. While the native Irish continued to rear stock, by the 1620s, Ulster was also contributing 18 per cent of Ireland's grain exports. This was thanks to the industry of Scottish settlers. 'The infrastructure of markets and fairs signalled the growing commercialisation of society'.[vv] The Companies invested a further £2,000 (making £62,000 in all) on building work in Londonderry and Coleraine on The Irish Society's behalf. Yet their dividends, which they only received between 1620 and 1626, amounted in total to only £5,940. During the 1620s, the Society was earning income of £650 per annum from rentals in Londonderry and £410 in Coleraine; the fisheries yielded £1,000 and the customs at Derry and Coleraine provided a further £700 per annum. After paying an annual rent of £205 due to the Crown, it should have been generating more than £2,500 per annum, although rental arrears were high.

Phillips used his role as Commissioner to continue his vendetta. He was forced to sell his estates at Moyola after spending vast amounts of his own money to provide a survey of the Londoners' lands. It was extremely thorough and included coloured picture-maps prepared by Raven 'to drive home the comprehensive indictment contained in the report'.[ww]

Raven was still 'ill-disposed' towards the Londoners following his earlier salary reduction. Although the report revealed better progress in meeting the requisite number of settlers, it showed that neither the undertakers nor their tenants had adhered to the plantation objectives as set out in their Patents, principally in failing to remove the native Irish. Phillips did not mince his words:

> Your Majesty's pleasure often signified by letter and published by proclamations for the performance of the conditions of the plantation, yet now in so long a space after the time limited for building and planting, there

is a general defect in a greater or lesser measure … which is likely to increase if some speedy course be not taken for reformation thereof.[xx]

He pointed out:

the many defects and omissions in the Londoners' plantation, a place principally designed by Your Majesty for the future and continual settlement of the whole province of Ulster, which I have not manifested out of malice to the Londoners as they unjustly charge me, but out of zeal for Your Majesty's service and the safety of the commonwealth.[yy]

The defects included:

the non-residence of undertakers, many of whom 'live in England or Scotland or remote from their proportions';

the retention of a 'great store of Irish families upon their lands, which is the cause the British can get no reasonable bargains';

reluctance to give British tenants formal leases, preferring verbal arrangements giving the landlords ability to rack-rent;

tenants being cheated by unscrupulous middlemen and kept in the dark about the Articles of the Plantation;

the almost complete absence of freeholders;

failure to complete building works within time limits, inadequate defensive works, particularly bawns built of sods, which are 'ruinous and decaying already' often without houses in them or gates;

failure to keep tenants in villages or towns but to let them live 'scattered and dispersed in woods and coverts, subject to the malice of any kern to rob, kill and burn them in their houses';

failure of colonists to maintain 'in their houses a convenient store of arms'; and 'selling of grants without permission, leading to the creation of over-large, unmanageable estates'.[zz]

This last was seen as a principal cause of the failure to perform the conditions of the plantation, as it 'allowed the chief freeholders' obligations to be extinguished'.[aaa] Phillips commented more specifically on Londonderry saying:

1. The City is well fortified but in need of three hundred more houses to accommodate sufficient settlers to provide it with protection.
2. Apart from the semi-annual fair, there are no food shops for residents.
3. The fortifications are short of cannon with platforms and munitions.
4. Guard and sentinel houses need to be placed on the battlements.
5. The wharf requires a stone quay, as the wooden one needs constant repair.
6. The bog next to the town should be cleared to provide space for mills.
7. Only forty freeholders occupy the City's 4,000 acres of 'liberties', with the remainder being kept by the City for its own use. Although land should have been allocated to support a Free School, this could not be identified.

Phillips was also critical of the Londoners' failure to improve the church, which could only accommodate half of Londonderry's citizens. He wanted the town hall fortified to act as a citadel and he provided a drawing of what he proposed. He wanted a ditch filled with water round the walls to provide added security. He believed that the profits generated from fisheries and customs should easily be able to finance such improvements.

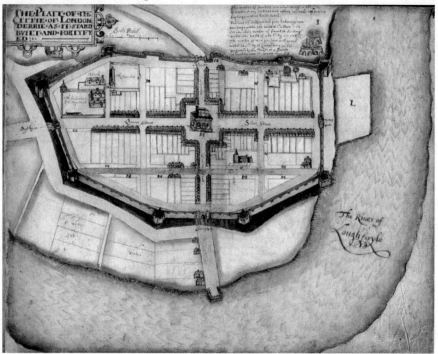

Raven's map of Londonderry in 1622 shows Phillips's scheme for a fortified town hall at the diamond. It was never built.
Courtesy of the Drapers' Company

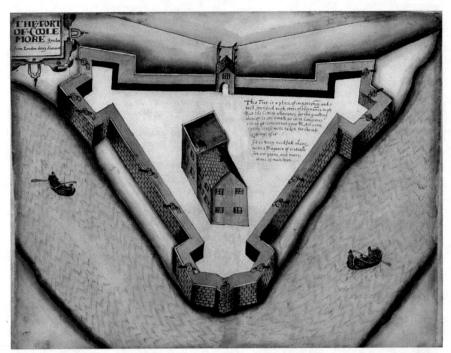

Raven's drawing of the fort at Culmore in 1622 with three bastions, each housing three guns. Everything except for the central tower has now disappeared.
Courtesy of the Drapers' Company

Phillips found the fort at Culmore well-built with its three bastions, each housing three guns manned by local residents. Yet The Irish Society had not provided sufficient victuals, ordnance and ammunition. He reported gaping holes in the earthen ramparts at Coleraine, but the ditch surrounding it was eight feet deep and full of water. There were six large and two small bastions, but the two small gates only had timber-framed guard houses over them. Both Phillips and Hadsor considered them disgraceful and recommended rebuilding in stone. There was a market place and the two main streets were paved. Out of seventy houses built by the Society, eighteen were of stone, and fifty-two timber-framed. Although it had counted them as one hundred and twenty-five single room dwellings, many had been amalgamated for family use. There were a further twenty-one privately built stone houses, each of which had received a Society grant of twenty pounds. There were also five unsubsidised houses and fifty-seven thatched cottages and 'cabins', some being used by the garrison. The total population amounted to one hundred and forty-five families, providing only one hundred armed men, still insufficient to cover the ramparts, with a further twenty-four families based outside the town. The Commissioners confirmed Pynnar's findings, that there had been very little building since 1616. Between Londonderry, Culmore and Coleraine, only two hundred and seventy British men were armed from among the two hundred and sixty-seven families settled

162

there.[bbb] Phillips and Hadsor recommended building ramparts faced with stone to fortify the river side of Coleraine. They wanted to see a citadel built in the market place and a bridge constructed over the Bann. They recommended spending £2,500 to remove the sand bar at the river mouth to make it safe for shipping. As at Londonderry, they wanted more freeholds on the lands allocated to the town.[ccc] Attention must have been paid to some of Phillips's suggestions, as the Society refaced the walls in stone and built a citadel, which was demolished in the 1660s.

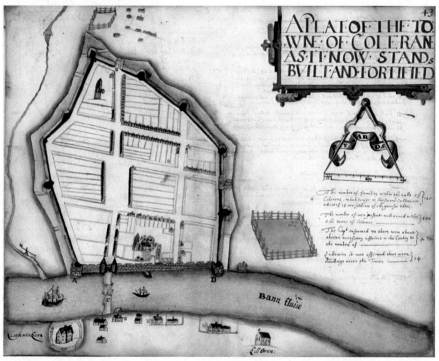

Raven's map of Coleraine in 1622 shows the earthen bawn protected by a ditch to landward and a wooden palisade along the banks of the Bann. The bridge with its lifting section had not at that time been built.
Courtesy of the Drapers' Company

In Phillips's view, the proportions were doing no better, despite his conviction that the Livery Companies were generating a lot of rental income. Although their records show this to have been untrue, they certainly turned a blind eye to timber exploitation and failed to protect their forests as a great natural resource. The fundamental problem was that the Irish were paying higher rents than the 4d. per acre being asked of settlers as an inducement to allow them to remain. Yet the Irish did not provide good husbandry. Although freeholders were offered plots of one hundred acres, only about sixty were granted, often in poor mountainous areas. Very few freeholders were resident and some never visited or made efforts to improve their land. Without them, there was still a shortage of men to undertake jury service, and juries had to be filled by poorer settlers 'to their ruin'. Those failing to attend were fined, even though they had neither the time nor means to travel to the courts. This drove many settlers to leave and those remaining were in a sorry state.

Phillips and Hadsor also highlighted shortcomings in construction work, noting:

> The Mannor houses and villages adioyninge thereto are scittuated in … pleasante and commodious places neere the Rivers, but not soe fit for the safety of the Cuntry, soe that it is very requisite that [the whole area] bee forthwith strengthened by erecting severall forts and villages in the heart of the Cuntry neere the Mountaines, and that sufficient Brittish bee planted there to secure that Cuntry … which the Londoners ought willingly to yield unto in respect of the ample benefit already accrewed and daily accrewinge unto them.[ddd]

They complained that there were only one hundred and thirty-one stone and timber-framed houses, mainly grouped in villages, and one hundred and nine small 'cabins'. Some houses were too isolated to defend and many of the bawns were poorly constructed.[70]

The proportions could muster three hundred and eighty-six armed men, which, when added to those in the towns, provided only six hundred men for protection. Phillips counted 2,324 native Irishmen, many with access to arms, in addition to wood-kerne, who could strike at any time with no realistic means of apprehending them. He provided a frightening indictment of the Londoners' failure to protect their settlers after more than a decade of involvement. Phillips and Hadsor wanted to see more British settlers, particularly freeholders, 'who would be zealous in pursuing the aims of the plantation' by acting as jurors and sheriffs. They recommended 'at least one further village on the remoter areas of each Proportion', particularly in Loughinsholin, then the most lawless part of Ulster.[eee]

The Commissioners were also critical of servitors and Irish landlords. Although servitors had no obligation to plant, some of their bawns had 'no houses, people or gates'.[fff] Many of their tenants would 'not take the oath of supremacy' and 'lived dispersed so as a few kerns may easily take victuals from them by force, if they give it not willingly'.[ggg] Irish landlords also faced criticism of their bawns and continued to 'take Irish exactions as before' and to plough 'by the tails of their garrons and not after the manner of the English Pale'.[hhh]

The Commissioners made constructive suggestions for improvement and commented on Phillips's success at Limavady. They concluded that new patents should be issued, and that the Irish should be offered more land on twenty-one

---

[70] Phillips was particularly critical of the Ironmongers where the houses were generally isolated and their bawn, which had no flankers, was only built on three sides and could not be defended. The Mercers' proportion was full of the 'wickedest' Irish. In both proportions, the settlers 'lived in daily fear of their lives'.[kkk]

year leases (as previously recommended), if they agreed to live in villages, attended Established Church services, dressed in English fashion, and adopted English agricultural methods. Parts of their lands were to be enclosed with fences, hedges, ditches and dykes, and their children were to be trained in a respectable trade. More bridges were to be built, passes cut and communications generally improved. A highway was to be constructed along the Bann River to Lough Neagh.[iii] Providing adequate numbers of armed men in each proportion to defend castles, manor houses and bawns was essential. Posses of men were to be 'in permanent readiness to track down and capture criminals'. Although staves were required for cooperage, woods needed to be preserved. Income should be reinvested to assist local commerce, rather than being returned to London. Phillips again promoted Limavady as a central location for assizes, and he wanted to see a county jail. The Commissioners recommended that, if the Londoners failed to apply these remedies, the plantation should be forfeited.[iii]

Although the report was presented to the Commission of Inquiry of 1622, it had no immediate effect. Phillips spent much time and energy writing critical letters to both London and Dublin. In 1623, the Mayor, Commonalty and Citizens of Londonderry wrote a letter backing Phillips and commenting on the poor state of the Church. Although Springham's school was supported by The Irish Society, income from land allocated by the King to pay for teachers' salaries and upkeep was being diverted elsewhere, so that poor children were prevented from attendance. Only 1,500 of the 4,000 acres allocated to the 'liberties' of Londonderry, had been granted by the Society to fund civic activities and these were proving insufficient. The Society even denied that the remaining 2,500 acres were intended for the City's use. After allocating six acres to each house, it retained the remainder, offering leases at high rents and only for short periods. Confidence was so low that trade was being restricted and, without a bank, remained almost non-existent. There was a need for inhabitants to buy licences to export linen yarn. The lessees of the fisheries were failing to supply the local market.

'Phillips's survey was so thorough and so damning that he gradually acquired the ear of the Government.'[lll] 'Beresford had tried to argue that there was no need for any inquisition, as the City was not bound by the Articles of the Plantation, but only by the Charter of Londonderry and its own Articles of Agreement with the Crown',[mmm] a view which the Crown had repeatedly rebutted. Nevertheless undertakers were required to submit authenticated lists of natives residing on their lands with the types of tenancies granted. These showed that of the 600 or so townlands in the proportions (excluding Church or servitors' lands), 305 were let to 863 Irish tenants[71], and 301 were planted with settlers. When his information reached London in April 1624, Phillips suggestions were, at last, embodied in a program of reform, known as the

---

[71] Phillips's Survey had counted more than one thousand native Irish in the Livery Company proportions, and Curl contends that the Companies deliberately understated the numbers to prevent embarrassment.

Twenty-Three Articles, which James approved. Phillips became overseer of the plantation at a salary of two hundred pounds per annum. The Privy Council called on The Irish Society most urgently to implement changes largely based on Phillips's findings.

Many of the recommendations were taken up in rectifying the 'serious defects in the fortifications, armaments, and manning'[nnn] of the County, particularly against wood-kerne. At Londonderry, there was a call to provide platforms, sheds and ordnance on the fortifications with guard houses and sentry boxes[72]. 'Fort Culmore was to be maintained, garrisoned and supplied with ordnance and munitions.'[ooo] At Coleraine, the gates were to be rebuilt using masonry with guardhouses to accommodate sufficient men to man the ramparts. Given the cost of facing the ramparts in stone, it was proposed that a citadel should be centrally located to house troops and munitions.[ppp] As a precaution against wood-kerne, trees and undergrowth were to be removed on each side of the Bann within two hundred yards of the walls. There were to be victuals stored at each location sufficient to withstand a four-month siege. Two new castles were to be built by the Society, one at the foot of Slieve Gallion, and the other between Dungiven and Londonderry. In country areas, 'castles and bawns were to be protected, guarded day and night, and stocked with arms'.[rrr]

The remaining Articles related mainly to the requirement to build up the settler population to provide greater security. At Londonderry, those buildings unsuitable either as accommodation or shops were not to be included in future counts of houses, but The Irish Society was to establish two hundred houses suitable for occupation by tradesmen and skilled craftsmen. 'If occupants could not be found, then the Crown would 'grant commissions and warrants to impress and transport them'.'[sss] Once these were built and occupied, three hundred more were to be erected at the rate of fifty per annum with their own curtilage and garden. Rents were to equate to 5 per cent of the building cost. The City of Londonderry's land was to be 'set to men able to labour, stock, and manure it for the good and profit of the tenants'.[ttt] Produce was to be taken to markets used by tradesmen and artisans. Some lands were to be sold as freeholds and some provided on long leases, so that they were occupied for longer periods, and rents charged were to reflect the land's quality. Two hundred additional houses with their own lands were to be built in Coleraine at the rate of fifty per year for tradesmen and skilled craftsmen.[uuu] Each proportion was to have a minimum of six British freeholders with at least one townland and ten British leaseholders with a life interest at one shilling per acre. Irish tenants prepared to conform were also permitted, and deeds allocating land to them were to be prepared immediately.[vvv]

There were also recommendations for the benefit of the community. Londonderry urgently needed a new church. A limestone quay was to replace the existing wooden structure. At Coleraine, the Bann was only to be crossed by

---

[72] Falkland had reported that there were 'great defects of munition and arms, whereby the people of the Plantation [were] in great danger of a 'Sodain Massacre''.[qqq]

recognised ferries, but more were needed. If neither The Irish Society nor the Crown would foot the cost of a bridge, private entrepreneurs were to be encouraged, and could charge tolls in perpetuity. A bridge was also needed over the River Roe at Limavady. Timber from Loughinsholin could be used to fuel the ironworks at Slieve Gallion.

The Irish Society retaliated with its own list of grievances against the Crown. 'It claimed that it had carried out all the requirements, and objected to what it considered were new demands,'[www] which were 'outrageous'. It agreed to build a new church in Londonderry, and to encourage tradesmen and craftsmen to settle. Although it felt it had met its obligation under the Charter for house building, it agreed to rebuild the gates at Coleraine, 'but a citadel was out of the question'.[xxx] Security was a matter for the Crown, as was the building of two new castles, which were not part of the original agreement. While it would co-operate to allow these building works to be undertaken, 'it was not the duty of the City to provide troops and arms for State purposes'.[yyy] It had only ever become involved 'out of respect for the King's wishes'.[zzz]

Phillips was determined to have his survey taken seriously. From now on, the plantation was under rigorous examination. Rents were sequestrated on two occasions. When Charles I became King, Phillips sent him his written evidence backed by Raven's maps to support a charge that the City of London had misconducted and mismanaged its plantation. The Irish Society would need to defend itself; the mounting costs of litigation and sequestrations would result in it suffering expenditure estimated at £3,200. Dividends to the Livery Companies were stopped; the Society was never a good investment for them. Yet the Londoners sensed that the new Monarch might compromise if offered money to assist him to meet his obligations under the terms of his marriage settlement. It was hoped that this might relieve pressure on the Irish Society to remove the native Irish and settle British tenants in County Londonderry.[aaaa]

Chapter 13

Charles I takes action against the Livery Companies 1625-1635

During the last years of his reign, James's authority was tarnished by his affection for Buckingham. On his death in March 1625, his son, Charles I, succeeded to the throne, but only made matters worse for those involved in the Ulster plantation, particularly for the City of London. On his accession, there was every expectation that he would make a fine ruler, but he quickly squandered his reserves of goodwill. Having fallen out with the English Parliament, he was determined to rule as an absolute Monarch. Yet he needed Parliament to enable him to raise taxes.

Charles I shared none of his father's enthusiasm for the plantation and listened to Phillips's pleas for the charters to the London Livery Companies to be revoked. *Sir Anthony van Dyck (1599-1641) (workshop of) oil on canvas, Private Collection, © Philip Mould Ltd, London, Bridgeman Images*

It is difficult to be critical of Phillips. Almost all his comments on the City of London's poor performance in Ulster were justified and his proposals to remedy shortcomings were entirely appropriate. The Livery Companies had been forced to undertake an investment that they did not want, but, instead of accepting that they should do the job in accordance with the Crown's wishes, they tried to cut corners. The Irish Society failed to supervise their Agents adequately, and the likelihood is that the Companies were defrauded of at least £20,000. This left them jaundiced against the whole project. When their frauds were uncovered, both Rowley and Beresford were considered indispensable and were permitted to return to Ireland, with Beresford being retained as Agent. With the notable exception of the fortifications at Londonderry, the building works at both Londonderry and Coleraine remained sub-standard, and neither town offered security or a market environment to support the locality. In the proportions, the Livery Companies had done no better. They had failed to attract settlers in the numbers demanded, preferring the simpler and more lucrative option of letting to the native Irish. The Crown expected British settlers to employ British farm labourers to work their land. Although the native Irish were required to move from their ancestral lands, they were being offered alternative locations nearby; there was plenty of room for everyone. By failing to honour the Articles of the Plantation, the Londoners failed to provide security for those who arrived, and failed to introduce English farming methods to boost the local economy. It was a sorry tale.

The problem of security started to come home to roost. 'In 1623 there were some serious outbreaks of robbery, terrorism and concerted attacks on settlers by the wood-kerne.'[a] Despite malicious rumours that Phillips had organised them, 'he quickly set up posses of armed men in each proportion to round up all suspicious persons'.[b] Stricter security regulations were imposed. Landholders were only permitted to accept as tenants those for whom they were prepared to be answerable. Phillips organised a network of support for mutual protection. Yet some Agents objected to his interference and became deliberately obstructive. Falkland sent him to London to report his problems.

Charles I took advantage of the situation. On 2 September 1625, the Privy Council reported the City's failure to implement the Twenty-Three Articles and 'ordered that the requirements to strengthen Londonderry, Culmore and Coleraine, and the castles of the Companies should be executed at once'.[c] These included the clearance of undergrowth on the sides of the Bann River at Coleraine. The King called for Phillips's appointment as overseer to be implemented. He shared none of his father's enthusiasm for the plantation and began listening to Phillips's pleas for the Company charters to be revoked; he called in the old Patents for replacement with new ones.

The Privy Council set up a new Commission, which included the elderly Chichester and Sir Richard Weston, the Chancellor of the Exchequer, to instruct the City to put Phillips's proposals into effect. With the Londoners still dragging their feet, the Council sequestered all rents falling due in Londonderry. This was ostensibly to enable Phillips, after his return from London in December 1625, to fund the additional cost of defence arrangements in accordance with the Articles of the Plantation. Yet it appears to have been an effort to divert the rents for the Crown's use. The King was using every expedient in his desperate search for money. In September 1625, the Treaty of Southampton, with the Dutch, led to war with Spain. In the following month, a military expedition to Cadiz ended in defeat for the British fleet, after which it was put about that a Spanish invasion of Ireland was imminent. Beresford was not taken in. On 16 December 1625, he wrote to Phillips regretting that he would be

> unable to hand over any money to the sequestrators, and suggested that if the panic over the invasion had any basis in reason, the State itself would have provided The Irish Society with funds to secure Culmore and Londonderry.[d]

He had received wind of the sequestration order before it reached Dublin and moved fast to collect the rents and transfer them to The Irish Society in London before it was put into effect. The City of London made strong representations to the Privy Council, which took the City's side. When the Londoners undertook to carry out the requested remedial works, the Council set aside the order. Beresford had at last started to serve The Irish Society well.

On 16 February 1626, Falkland wrote to Beresford calling for copies of the rent-rolls to be sent to Dublin and telling him in no way to interfere with the next sequestration due in May. He argued that the cost of defence should be borne by those receiving the benefit. He told him that, for the previous sixteen years, the Crown had borne this cost in Londonderry, which would not have been necessary if the Londoners had 'planted with British, as they were bound by their contract'.[e]

> The Irish Society was to 'take some speedy course', and was to carry out its obligations, for it had failed most signally to serve either God or the King. … It was essential to get things moving in the spring.[f]

The Society responded that the troops had provided them with no benefit and had 'created intolerable burdens of upkeep on a small county' all at the Society's expense.[g]

With The Irish Society refusing to hand over its income, Phillips stood down, complaining that he had been 'prevented from collecting the sequestrated rents by the 'insatiable covetousness' of The Irish Society'.[h] Although this deprived him of his salary, he did not consider it his job 'to meddle with the City's moneys'. Yet he was determined 'to secure the Plantation from certain ruin' and, in May 1626, petitioned the King to 'attend most urgently to the building of forts and to the safety of the Plantation'.[i] The Crown consulted the Attorney-General and the Solicitor-General, who concluded that The Irish Society had failed to build the agreed number of houses in Londonderry, had not 'laid' sufficient lands to the new city, had not fortified [Londonderry and Coleraine] to required standards, and had not armed or manned Fort Culmore so that it would be secure.[j]

'The Crown insisted that by the original contract the City of London was obliged to plant County Londonderry with British tenants.'[k] It considered that the 'Plantation was in such parlous state that it had to be reformed on the lines of the Twenty-Three Articles as it was a danger to the whole Kingdom'.[l] Yet it conceded that the Charter of Londonderry taken on its own without reference to the Articles of the Plantation was prejudicial to the Crown's interests. The City argued that the Articles of the Plantation were of no concern to them as they had only agreed to take on the Plantation if released from onerous conditions that were applied to other undertakers: the City was only bound by the Charter of Londonderry and by the specific Articles of Agreement that applied only to the Londonderry Plantation, and not to anywhere else.[m] With the City insisting that it had honoured its agreements, it began to gain support for its view that it was acting within its rights. Yet, the Crown was determined that it was not, as the natives continued to live where they should not,[73] and there were many other clear breaches of the general Articles. Most importantly, it had failed to provide reasonable security to protect settlers from the increasingly hostile native Irish.

Up to this point, Charles had placed all his faith in Buckingham's advice, but with the war against Spain going from bad to worse, Buckingham was assassinated while attempting to quell a mariners' mutiny at Portsmouth. Left to rule alone, Charles was in desperate need of money. Yet, in 1627, he embarked on war with France. In November, his naval expedition to support the Huguenots at La Rochelle ended in another humiliating failure. This bought time for the City of London. The Crown was reminded that in times of war it needed the City's goodwill and was dependent on it for finance. The Irish Society argued that the sequestration order had deprived it of its rightful rents and had provided no benefits for the County of Londonderry. In July 1627, the order was quashed and the implementation of the Twenty-Three Articles was suspended.

In his thirst for finance, the King also turned to the old English Catholics in Ireland, approaching the Irish Parliament for substantial and regular 'bounties' to support an army of 5,000 foot and 500 horse. In return, he offered them various 'graces'. These included religious toleration, the right to hold Government posts and hope of regaining legal title to their estates. The native Irish were to be relieved of the requirement to attend the Established Church. Planters in Ulster concluded that 'it might be politic to back the graces being offered to Irish Catholics and pay their fines 'to sweep away the danger of forfeiture''.[n] In January 1628, a deputation of leading Irish landlords, including some from Ulster, arrived in London. It was agreed that 'in return for three successive annual subsidies of forty thousand pounds, English money, to be used principally to support the army, [the Fifty-One] Graces would be conceded [by the King]'.[o] If this had been honoured, it would have ended 'the careful policy of segregated settlement in Ulster' allowing undertakers' title to be confirmed without having to comply with the plantation conditions. Charles's offer caused consternation in Dublin and, in April 1627, the Establishment rejected it. 'War

---

[73] In 1626, there were 922 British and 2,474 Irish males in County Londonderry.

with Spain and France prompted a fresh drive for religious conformity, antagonising the Old English Lords'.[p] Catholics now faced heavy recusancy fines. In a remarkably short time, the new King had managed to fall out with France and Spain; he had breached faith with the papacy; he had demonstrated his incompetence to the Huguenots; he was treated with suspicion by all sides in Ireland; and, was rapidly acquiring a reputation for sacrificing principles in return for money.[q]

In August 1627, after negotiating for his pension arrears to be settled, Phillips provided assistance to another group of Commissioners tasked with gathering more evidence for what became known as 'The Great Enquiry' into the London plantation. The Commissioners included Falkland, the Lord Deputy, James Ussher, Archbishop of Armagh, George Downham, Bishop of Derry, Sir William Ryves, Irish Attorney-General, Sir Edward Bolton, Irish Solicitor-General, Vaughan and some others. In early 1628, they reported to the King that measures to improve the defences as required by the 1624 Articles, had not been carried out. The King immediately sequestrated all rents falling due in the following May. Yet Phillips complained that Beresford remained obstructive to both the enquiry and the sequestration.

The City of Londonderry was involved in a flurry of activity. A petition to the Crown ostensibly sent by its British citizens, complained that their lives had been made intolerable by 'the encumbrances of Patents and burdens placed on their lands by the impositions of the Government'.[r] It called for the sequestration order to be revoked, and for the great benefits enshrined in the Articles of Agreement to be restored.[s] It also complained that, having been 'first induced to leave' their native countries to settle in the 'remote and unpleasant northern parts of Ireland within the City of London's Plantation', settlers were finding life sufficiently grim without making it even more difficult. The petition blamed Phillips's hostility to the City of London for creating a 'lack of confidence and discontentment, and for ruining the economy'. Yet a second petition was sent by the citizens to Falkland. This condemned the first 'as a wicked fabrication cooked up by The Irish Society's Agents',[t] and stated that the petitioners had always supported Phillips. The signatories seem to have been representative of a good cross-section of both British and Irish opinion in the City.

In the summer of 1628, the Commissioners reached some sort of compromise with The Irish Society. In return for fines and an increase in their rents, British undertakers could retain Irish tenants on one quarter of their lands. Yet again, this was subject to them adhering to British dress, speech and farming practice, but they were no longer required to conform in religion. Both The Irish Society and the Livery Companies petitioned for the sequestration order on their rents to be lifted, claiming that, although County Londonderry was once the most barbarous part of Ireland, their efforts had made it the 'best civilised'. They complained that

172

the Crown's interference was unfair, for many privileges granted by the Crown had been eroded or withdrawn, the fishing-rights had been intruded upon, and the tenants were unduly burdened by having to maintain troops.[u]

Despite having spent £100,000 on developing the plantation, they were now prepared to provide a further £4,000 to build a cathedral. The foundation stone for St Columb's was laid in 1628, and Vaughan supervised William Parratt's building work. (Parratt became Mayor of Coleraine in 1642.) When completed in 1633, it had cost the Society £3,800, largely provided by the Livery Companies. It was built in a Gothic Survival style with a six-bay nave and lean-to aisles; its southern porch was crowned by a wooden tower clad in lead sent from London; its wooden roof was also leaded. In the words of James Stevens Curl, it was 'a reassuringly familiar type of building that would remind settlers of home' and was 'by far the most distinguished architectural work on the Londoners' Plantation'.[v] It was both Parish Church and Cathedral, seating one thousand people. In 1634, it was granted in perpetuity to the Bishop of Derry. Charles I provided bells at a cost of £500 (but probably after borrowing the money from the City of London). The desired effect was achieved. In July 1628, the sequestration order was withdrawn on condition that The Irish Society honoured its obligations.

Phillips believed too soft a line was being taken with the Londoners 'who had allegedly shown their contempt for the whole process by entertaining the Commissioners to a performance of *Much Ado About Nothing*'.[w] In May 1629, the Commissioner's report to the King set out the plantation's history and substantiated most of Phillips's criticisms. It was again accompanied by maps, which can be independently verified as accurate. These showed that many of the fortified manor houses were still incomplete. The number of settlers from London was also disappointing[74], and most were poorly armed. It reported only one hundred and eleven houses in Londonderry (ignoring ninety barns with lofts above, which were not considered as housing) and eighty in Coleraine.[75] This demonstrates that the deadline for completing the building work had been ignored. There were deficiencies in 'fortifications, able-bodied men, arms, the quays, and other buildings: Londonderry was not geared to withstand a siege' with so many discontented Irish around.[x] Victualling and armaments remained inadequate everywhere. The Commissioners caught Beresford out for claiming wages for two wardens at Culmore, who turned out to be his cook and butler. They also claimed that, if the original offer to British tenants of land at four pence per acre had been implemented there would have been 'plenty of British settlers, no natives in huge numbers, no Popery, and no problem'.[y]

---

[74] 'There were found to be 1,412 able British men on the City's Plantation, and 2,293 Irish',[cc] 'but, of course, these figures did not include the Irish on lands outside the Londoners' holdings.'[dd]

[75] Beresford later published his rent-rolls, which showed two hundred and sixty-five houses in Londonderry, but Moody has established that these included houses which The Irish Society had not built.[ee]

Despite the compromise reached in the previous year, Phillips called for all natives failing to conform in religion, speech and dress to be removed from both temporal *and* church lands.[z] With settlers in the proportions receiving much larger areas than stipulated in the Articles of the Plantation, they were too thin on the ground to provide security. The Society was 'the victim of individual greed' with its woodlands continuing to suffer from unauthorised cutting in Loughinsholin.[aa] Inadequate tracks and a shortage of bridges made communication difficult. Land measurement was in a 'chronic muddle' caused by confusion between balliboes, Irish acres (7,840 sq. yards), English acres (4,840 sq. yards), plantation acres (one-sixtieth of a balliboe – see page 88), and other difficulties.[bb]

The Commissioners also made recommendations. There was an urgent need to provide more houses for British settlers, charged out at lower rents. Companies should reassume direct possession of their proportions, planting them with more British tenants and any native Irish who could be relied upon. With trade at a virtual standstill, there was a need to increase the population, giving them access to money and banking facilities, and to reduce the number of tap houses available to them. Customs duties were set at a level to deter overseas trade.[ff]

With Phillips becoming older, he was convinced that the Companies were compounding their iniquities by making 'gigantic profits'.[gg] Included in his collection of documents presented to the King in 1629, he provided a calculation that from 1609 to 1629, they had generated £160,000 from their presence in Ulster. This involved some blatant 'creative accounting' and according to Moody, who studied it in detail, was 'shear fantasy'.[hh] Phillips claimed that the Companies had generated income of £98,665 against expenditure of £68,730, but the income included '£10,000 made from the spoliation of the woods',[ii] none of which had been earned by the Companies, and his expenditure ignored the cost of 'the Cutts at the Salmon Leap' at Coleraine. Quite incorrectly, he then added a number of items to his calculation about £30,000 of net profit, which were not profits at all. These included the Companies' original investment of £60,000, his estimate of £30,000, being the Crown's cost of maintaining soldiers in Ulster over the period, and a further £42,585 as his calculation of income generated by the Companies and their Farmers on the proportions, which was a double count. His allegations were 'clearly nonsense' and 'are not only wildly dishonest: they are malicious and fraudulent'.[jj] Phillips never had access to the accounts of either The Irish Society or the Livery Company proportions, which would have demonstrated that their collective income never exceeded £2,000 per annum.[76] Yet, 'blinded by prejudice',[kk] he 'urged King Charles to 'cast … his princely eye upon the important and material things contained' in his report,

---

[76] Moody estimated that 'the Livery Companies collectively could have generated a maximum of £37,500 in income in the twenty-one years from 1613 to 1634, but the actual figure was about £15,500. Against this they faced expenditure of £56,000, leaving them with a net loss of £40,500.'[oo]

to 'revoke the Londoners' Patent' and to reassume the plantation 'into royal hands''.[ll]

It was not just Phillips. The Livery Companies also found that the Dublin Establishment was turned against them. The Dublin Government persuaded the King that 'the Londoners involvement ran counter to the principles of aristocratic society, for it rested on an extraordinary degree of collective decision taking'.[mm] [77] These views were shared by the Privy Council, who believed that management by committee 'could not promise any great hope of advancing public service'![nn] Other servitors, including Viscount (Edward) Chichester, supported Phillips's views. As Canning, the Ironmongers' Company Agent, realised, all this concerted criticism was prejudicial. He warned the Company that the judges at Derry might be biased:

> I verily suppose that the servitors who are the chiefest in that Court at the Derry would gladly yield advantage to any gentleman against any of the city's agents.[qq]

The evidence submitted to The Great Enquiry was of great importance. Phillips prefaced his Collection with 'a statement reviewing the long history of charges against the Londoners in which they were accused of deception, neglect of obligations, greed, and cynicism'.[rr] He claimed that he was 'only driven by the highest motives to secure the realm'.[ss] With the King already calling on the Companies for taxes to fund his wars with France and Spain, he followed Phillips's advice by seeking to expropriate their Londonderry estates. In 1630, the Attorney-General examined the report of The Great Enquiry and interrogated The Irish Society. After seeking the Privy Council's advice, he recommended legal action against the Londoners. At the instigation of Sir John Coke, the Secretary of State, the Crown charged the Companies in the Court of Star Chamber, a tribunal without jury whose membership was limited to Privy Councillors. With Phillips continuing to provide evidence, the City was 'charged with having obtained a grant of exorbitant rights and privileges and of violating the Articles of Agreement'.[tt] It was claimed that it 'had obtained the grants and rights by disreputable means; that the Articles of Agreement had been wilfully violated; and that the plantation was ruined to the peril of the Realm'.[uu]

It took four years to prepare the evidence. The Irish Society called on each Company to provide details of income and expenditure, population, buildings, and letting arrangements. Raven provided advice on the terrain and the problems of measurement. Phillips, 'whose diligence, fidelity, and circumspection, we [the King] are well assured of',[vv] headed a commission containing representatives of both the City and the Crown to examine witnesses in Ireland. Among its findings, the extent of Roman-Catholic observance in the proportions was noted, with priests accepted as tenants by six Companies. Phillips reported that, even now, witnesses were being intimidated by Beresford. Aged over

---

[77] It is in these attitudes that the beginnings of the schism between the City of London and the Royalist cause can be identified; they were 'a milestone on the high road to Civil War'.[pp]

seventy, Phillips was exhausted both physically and financially, but he 'pushed doggedly' on.[ww] On his return to London in 1632, he was obliged to reside in increasing financial embarrassment until the hearing. In the following year, he appealed to the King for financial support, and the Government bought out his pension entitlement for five hundred pounds.

In 1633, the City realised it was in trouble and tried to reach a settlement with the Crown. Its offer to hand over Culmore, its Admiralty rights and to provide £20,000 for the Royal coffers was rejected, despite it having provided the King with a staggering £200,000 in loans to finance his disastrous military exploits in Europe. The Irish Society made a special call of £100 on each of the twelve Great Companies, ostensibly to support the building of the Cathedral in Londonderry, but in practice for their defence. Early in 1635, a further call was needed, as the collective costs of the Cathedral and litigation had topped £7,000. The Companies paid immediately, despite difficulties being caused by most tenants, who were now withholding their rents.

At last, in February 1635, 'the eyes of all men' focused on the trial in the Court of Star Chamber. The Privy Council, three Royal judges and City representatives sat for thirteen days to hear the vast amounts of evidence submitted. Despite the Society and the Companies presenting their accounts to the Court, Phillips's calculation of their outrageous profits prevailed. It was clear that the King wanted any excuse to lay his hands on plantation rentals for the impoverished privy purse. The Companies successfully addressed much of the prosecution's case; a claim that they had obtained their Charter by subterfuge[78] was shown to be specious; although the woods may have been despoiled, this was the fault of Farmers, not of themselves; they had put up more buildings in Londonderry and Coleraine than required; the fortifications at Coleraine only looked inadequate in comparison to Londonderry, where the brief had been significantly exceeded. Yet, when it came to the removal of the native Irish, the Crown's ministers pressed home their advantage. The Companies' record could not be defended, and it 'gave their critics the crucial lever to secure their humiliation'.[xx]

Although undertakers elsewhere in Ulster had paid fines to mitigate their failure to remove the natives, the Livery Companies had not done so. They continued to argue that they were not bound by the Articles of the Plantation, which, they claimed, had been superseded by later agreements between the City and the Crown, which made no mention of this obligation. This was disingenuous to say the least, as the Companies acted through the 1610s as though they considered themselves bound, and it was only in 1623 that they began to argue otherwise.[yy] Eventually, the Attorney-General demonstrated to the Court's satisfaction that the Londoners knew that they were bound by the Articles and had failed to honour them. The City was sentenced to a fine of

---

[78] The terms were significantly amended by negotiation between the initial offer of the Charter and the version that was signed 'many things being inserted which are not in the warrant'.[aaa]

£70,000 with its Patent over all the Irish property being forfeited. Although The Irish Society was in effect a committee of the Court of Common Council and had signed the original Charter, the Mayor and Corporation of London refused to assist the Livery Companies in their difficulties, claiming that it 'had merely lent its influence to the venture for the purpose of raising money'.[zz]

Without Phillips, the Crown would never have succeeded in its case. Although he was promised £5,000 for his part in providing the evidence, this was to be paid out of the rents of the forfeited lands. The full amount was never settled, even though Thomas Wentworth, the new Lord Deputy, considered it well deserved. Phillips did not consider £5,000 to be adequate recompense for his earlier outlay. 'No doubt he had hoped to be treated with generosity and respect',[bbb] but 'found his claims to compensation regarded as an unpleasant liability'.[ccc] Although he was probably motivated by jealousy caused by his disagreements with Beresford, 'in his own eyes he became an instrument of providence for the exposure and punishment of a great crime against the state'.[ddd] He recorded that 'the policie of the Londoners hath more troubled me than all other my adventures or undertakings'.[eee] He never acted dishonourably (even though misguided on the plantation's profitability). Initially, he saw the outcome as a personal victory to vindicate all his diligent work in monitoring the City's performance, and was considered 'brave, honest, persevering and methodical'.[fff] He wrote to Wentworth's former chaplain, John Bramhall, Bishop of Derry:

> By the assistance of my gracious sovereign, I have after 25 years' employment in this business accomplished my long and tedious labour against the great citty of London.[ggg]

Bramhall, who had been instructed to obtain several large parcels of The Irish Society's land for the Crown, responded: 'To surprise that great and rich city after so long a siege was a work worthy of yourself.'[hhh] Phillips's criticisms of the Londoners' failure to provide new settlers was coloured by his abhorrence of the native Irish, who he saw as 'a people sunk in barbarism, whom the English had a divine right to expropriate and rule.' 'He saw himself as a pioneer of civilisation in a land of savages … Nothing but constant vigilance could save the British colony from eventual disaster.'[iii] As early as 1628, he was warning the Government that 'it is fered that they will Rise upon a Sudden and Cutt the Throts of the poore dispersed Brittish'.[jjj] Within five years 'the blundering policies of Charles I'[kkk] made his prophesy come true. When he died at his home in Hammersmith in August 1636, Phillips left a successful settlement at Newtown-Limavady with eighteen good English houses occupied by one hundred and twenty well-armed English and Scottish tenants.

Curl sees Beresford as a hero, despite his earlier shortcomings. He proved 'a shrewd and formidable adversary' for Phillips, and, in the battle over sequestration, he served the City of London well. Rumours of him having his hand in the till may explain Phillips's antipathy towards him and his hostility towards the Londoners. Certainly he amassed a huge fortune, particularly as a timber merchant and manufacturer of pipe staves, and there is no doubt that he had an eye to the main chance. In his defence, he was fully committed to Ulster and was one of the few colonists to reinvest large sums in its real estate. His many interests included the Haberdashers' proportion where he became a joint proprietor, the Skinners' proportion, where, in 1627, he became joint Farmer, and lands at Coleraine. He also leased areas of church lands, stocking them with cattle. The outcome of the trial deprived him of these interests and he 'was dealt with very roughly by the receivers of rents appointed by the Crown'. This made him the Crown's implacable enemy.[111]

Chapter 14

Confrontation with Wentworth as Ireland's Lord Deputy 1632-1641

Thomas Wentworth, Earl of Strafford (1593-1641) As Lord Deputy, he was blamed for inciting the Court of Star Chamber case and for raising Irish taxes to support the King in the Civil War. The Long Parliament demanded his execution.
After Sir Anthony van Dyck (1599-1641) Sherborne Park Estate © National Trust Images No. 1008464

In January 1632, Charles had appointed Thomas Wentworth as Lord Deputy of Ireland. On his arrival in the following year, Wentworth supported the King's determination to maintain the Crown's supreme power over both Church and State. He proved 'arrogant, overbearing and insensitive'[a] and backed Charles's decision to take the Livery Companies to court. It has been suggested that the King reached an accommodation with certain of his Irish supporters, probably including Wentworth and Chichester, who were prepared to give evidence against The Irish Society, but this seems unlikely. Yet Wentworth was jubilant at the successful outcome. For some time, he had had his eyes on the customs revenue of Londonderry and Coleraine, 'a feather not fit to be worn in the round cap of a citizen of London', to supplement the Irish Exchequer.[b] In March 1635, the Companies were called upon to surrender their estates, and proceedings to collect the fine of £70,000 were begun. They used every delaying tactic in hope of being able to mitigate the fine. Even Wentworth warned the King that the Londoners had laid out 'great sums upon the plantation, and it were … very strict in their case … if the uttermost advantage were taken'.[c] Yet he advised the King to retain the Londonderry estates, push up rents and raise money from customs and other sources of revenue.

In an effort to obtain redress, the Livery Companies appealed directly to the King. During 1636, The Irish Society remained in existence and elected new officers. In May, the Crown was offered £100,000 to discharge the fine, restore the Ulster plantation (released from all plantation conditions), repay all arrears of rent due to the City and grant a formal pardon.[d] The King's advisers demanded £120,000 coupled with a request to pay £5,000 to Phillips and to surrender the Castle of Culmore and the rights of fishing, which Chichester was thought to have his eyes on. When the Companies turned this down, negotiations dragged on until in 1637. Surrender would leave the Companies facing great losses. The Irish Society sought approval to handle negotiations on their behalf, and, once agreed, it offered to surrender the estates to the King but with the fine reduced to £10,000. After further negotiation, the proceedings at the Star Chamber were reopened and The Irish Society agreed to surrender its Charter 'without acknowledging [its] fault'[e] and to pay a fine of £12,000, 'which the Queen happened to stand in need of at the time'.[f] In 1638, the Letters Patent were passed to the King, and the fifty-five Companies raised the amount due and handed their deeds and records to the Attorney-General. The City had lost an estimated £120,000, making it a principal cause of its estrangement from the King, whose interest was only in the money, not in civilising Ireland.

The surrender had the effect of voiding settlers' titles. In July 1638, a petition, signed by five hundred of them (including Beresford), was sent to the King asking him to secure them in the possession of their lands. They were told that, when they came to dispose of them, 'the King would have regard for those of them who had carried out their obligations'.[g] For those settlers remaining, the escheated counties were a lonely place. 'The baying of the wolf at the moon must have sent a chill down the spine of many a colonist.'[h] The threat from wood-kerne was real enough, but the main problem was the smouldering resentment of the native Irish working and farming on the settlers' behalf. Many settlers decided to leave.

Having dithered on what to do with the lands that he had acquired, the King handed over control to Wentworth and the Irish Government. His objective was to soak both the native Irish and the settlers for everything that he could take, regardless of wider issues.[i] On his master's behalf, Wentworth squeezed out everything he could. His former chaplain, Bramhall, now Bishop of Derry, became sequestrator and was given charge of the fisheries. Following the findings of a Commission set up in 1639, all castles, manors and tenements were seized and new lease terms were negotiated. Rents in the towns were doubled with 'indecent haste',[j] and in the twelve proportions they were tripled. The Government called in the leases of some of the greater landowners, including those of Sir John Clotworthy, principal tenant on the Drapers' Company lands. As the brother-in-law of the key Parliamentarian, John Pym, Clotworthy was a dangerous protagonist. The tenants were now far worse off than they had been under the Livery Companies. There was an immediate failure of confidence, of business and trade, resulting in a decline in rent collections.

Not for the only time, Wentworth adopted punitive tactics to collect rents, thereby uniting tenants in their plight. With Charles alienating everyone in Britain by asserting the Crown's supremacy in both spiritual and temporal affairs, Wentworth attempted to enforce conformity in Ireland as a means of raising money. In July 1634, after calling the Irish Parliament, he threatened to enforce recusancy fines from those failing to attend Established Church services, if subsidies to the Crown 'be not freely and thankfully given'. With every expectation that the 'graces' would be implemented, the Irish Parliament voted generous payments to the King for the next four years.[k] Despite them, Charles failed to offer toleration to the Catholics. He reneged on the Crown's promise to provide Irish landlords with secure legal title to their estates, even though they had been in their possession for centuries. He used pretended defects of title to claim further lands for the Crown. When he denied Catholics the right to hold public office, he alienated Irish aristocrats everywhere; they had made a poor investment in funding the King. Even Wentworth was caught out. Although he expected to use some of the money raised to support the Irish Exchequer, the King wanted it all in London.

> The Irish Parliament drew up a remonstrance against Wentworth, noting the extreme and cruel usage … towards the inhabitants of the City and County of Londonderry, by means whereof the worthy plantation … is almost destroyed, and the said inhabitants reduced to great poverty, and many of them forced to forsake the country … to the great weakening of the Kingdome.[l]

Wentworth also turned on the Presbyterians. Up to this time, the Established Church had tolerated a wide range of Protestant beliefs. Without having their own kirks in Ireland, Scottish Presbyterians had happily joined the Established Church, so long as it followed Puritan dogma with plain forms of worship and sombre dress. Yet the High Church liturgy now being promoted by the King was an anathema. In Ulster, Bramhall and Henry Leslie, Bishop of Down and Connor, were instructed by Wentworth to enforce conformity. In 1636, Leslie called a diocesan meeting of clergy at Belfast, where he castigated Presbyterian Ministers for not being ordained. They in turn criticised some of the forms of worship prescribed in the Book of Common Prayer as popish. When he called for them to adhere to Anglican liturgy, some of them refused. By depriving them of office and financial support, he forced them to leave Ireland.[79] Presbyterians in Scotland were in similar conflict over High Church doctrine, making support for the covenant a bond of union between them. When Wentworth insisted on all Scots in Ulster over the age of sixteen taking 'The Black Oath' (an 'oath of abjuration of their abominable covenant'),[m] Clotworthy, who had lands in Antrim, saw his action as the final straw.

With Scotland up in arms, the King travelled north to restore his authority. Wentworth raised an Irish army to help him. While they awaited transshipment across the North Channel, nine thousand soldiers were billeted on tenanted lands at Carrickfergus. With Ulster's crops having failed, there was insufficient food to go round. Chichester wrote:

> The poor people … are so much impoverished that they can no longer subsist, and the plantation which was here begun and brought to some perfection is now much ruined as there is little hope to recover it.[o]

When five hundred troops were moved to billets in Londonderry, where the population was about one thousand, food prices were driven to ruinous levels.

Having reached Berwick, Charles realised that he had insufficient forces to challenge the Scots. In June 1639, he was forced to agree a pacification, which left the Presbyterians north of the border in control. Wentworth's troops never left Carrickfergus, but were used to enforce religious conformity in Ulster. This pushed more diehard Presbyterians back to Scotland, leaving the remainder to swear the 'Black Oath' on their knees. In January 1640, Wentworth was created Earl of Strafford by a grateful king and continued his heavy-handed money-raising to support the Royal coffers. In April, faced with so much hostility at home, Charles withdrew him from Ireland to address his more pressing domestic needs.

Despite his uncompromising approach, Strafford had proved an effective administrator, streamlining the process of Irish Government by removing inefficient officials. He had also benefitted the Irish economy by improving agricultural methods. By the time of the City of London's removal, colonisation had raised agricultural output to a level where Ulster as a whole was starting to prosper. It was still heavily dependent on grazing cattle, but there was now more cultivation in areas settled by Scots. With its access to cheap labour, Irish woollen manufacture could compete favourably with England. In 1632, to avoid a price war, Wentworth encouraged the Irish to manufacture linen with a view to discouraging Irish production of woollen cloth. Flax had been grown and spun

---

[79] In the autumn of 1636, a group of Presbyterians set out for New England on the 150 ton *Eagle Wing*. After leaving Belfast Lough on 9 September with one hundred and fifty passengers, they were driven by contrary winds onto the Scottish coast, where they had to repair a leak. They then sailed out into the Atlantic reaching nearly to the Newfoundland Banks, where they faced strong contrary winds and rain. Having broken their rudder, they hove to to repair it, but the ship began leaking so badly that they could hold out no longer. They turned back, reaching Belfast Lough on 3 November.[n]

into thread in Ireland since ancient times. The manufacturing process, which had probably originated in Egypt, was brought to Ireland by the Celts in about 500 BC. By the 16th Century, peasants were kept warm by wearing linen shirts often containing up to fourteen yards of cloth. These were dyed yellow with saffron, although Henry VIII complained at both their colour and length (to little noticeable impact!). Between 1621 and 1640, exports of linen yarn, which was produced mainly in northern Antrim, doubled, but Wentworth realised that production methods were antiquated. 'Bandle linen' cloth for clothing was too narrow to succeed in the export market. He arranged for the import of high quality flax seed, which was sold to farmers at cost, and he brought in the latest Dutch equipment with European technicians to provide advice. He arranged for better looms to be manufactured and initiated production methods, which saved having to knot threads. The older peasant women, manufacturing linen on a cottage industry basis, resisted his 'new-fangled' methods, but, in determined fashion, he fined those who persisted with old ways and had their yarn seized by officials. This left many women 'now starving that were able to live'.[p]

In 1640, Strafford's friend, the Anglo-Irish Protestant James Butler, 12th Earl of Ormonde, took command of the Establishment's forces to deal with sporadic outbreaks of Catholic rebellion. Ormonde had become one of the principal land owners of southern Ireland after marrying Elizabeth Preston, daughter and heir of the Earl of Desmond, thereby uniting the hitherto rival Ormonde and Desmond clans. Ormonde, who was to succeed Wentworth as Lord Deputy, continued to encourage the flax industry with help from Presbyterian immigrants. It was Scots and Quakers from across the North Channel, who developed Irish linen manufacture to an exportable standard. 'The majority [of Scottish settlers] set parts of their farms aside for the growing of flax' to tide them over in hard times. It could be sold to generate cash, or be processed, spun and woven into linen.[q]

In the same period, exports of cattle and horses rose tenfold and fourfold respectively. In 1637, while undertaking a survey of Customs in Ulster, General Monck was 'very glad to see such a store of shipping in the Derry and the good increase of boats and barques in all the ports by the way'.[r] Yet the Ulster economy was thrown into crisis by the expropriation of the Londoners' estates. This was exacerbated by failed harvests caused by bad weather in both 1638 and 1639. Yet the principal problem was political. Wentworth's imposition of religious conformity on Scottish Presbyterians and Puritans caused many to flee back across the North Channel. 'Lord Conway's agent in Antrim warned his employer that summer [1639] that rents would be late, because the Scots tenants were leaving.'[s] On their return to Scotland, many joined the growing insurgency against Charles; civil war only added to the dislocation of trade.

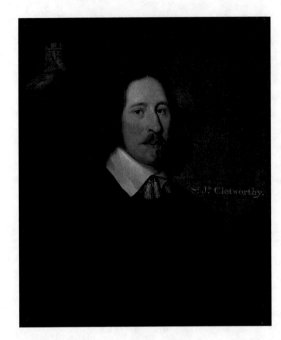

Sir John Clotworthy, Viscount Massereene As the Drapers' principal tenant, his lands were expropriated by the Court of Star Chamber. Despite having been Strafford's main protagonist in the Long Parliament, Charles II later restored his estates.
Artist unknown after 1648 oil on canvas © National Portrait Gallery London, NPG No. 2110

The Londoners had always blamed Wentworth for the King's action to expropriate their estates and his growing prominence in London only magnified their hostility to the Crown. Despite this, some London citizens continued to contribute to the impoverished Royal Exchequer, but limited the amounts offered by claiming that the forfeiture in Londonderry had 'consumed their stocks'.[t] In 1639, the City refused to finance the King in his war against Scotland. On 28 August 1640, when his army was defeated at Newcastle-upon-Tyne, the City of London refused to provide the £120,000 he needed to come to terms. In a last ditch effort to raise money, the King was forced into calling Parliament despite its opposition to him. When the Long Parliament assembled on 3 November 1640, Clotworthy led the charge with a long petition on behalf of Presbyterians and Puritans in Ireland. He demanded that 'this unlawful hierarchicall government with all their appendices may bee utterly extirpate'.[u] Clotworthy was now Strafford's parliamentary opponent and would later orchestrate the case against him.

When Pym called for Strafford's impeachment as 'the greatest enemy to this country and the greatest promoter of tyranny that any age has produced',[v] Clotworthy seconded him. On 3 January 1641, when the King heard of their denunciation, he had no means to protect his protégé. On 12 May, Strafford was executed.

With the Long Parliament still in session, the City lobbied against the Star Chamber verdict, declaring it 'illegal and irregular'. Although The Irish Society was by then in abeyance, the City demanded a parliamentary bill to provide redress. In August 1641, Parliament found the action of the Star Chamber to have been *ultra vires* and ordered the King to reinstate the City to its Londonderry estates. The King was prepared to make concessions, particularly as there was a hint that the City might provide him with a loan, if their estates were restored. When he returned from Scotland in late 1641, he reported to Parliament that he was much troubled by the judgement that had taken away the City's charter in Ulster. On 25 November, in a 'superbly choreographed royal entry' he declared:

> One thing I have thought of as a particular affection to you which is to give back to you freely that part of Londonderry which heretofore was evicted from you.

He also restored the large estates of Beresford, Clotworthy and others. These were promises, as he admitted, that he was in no position to fulfil. Ulster was in the throes of a major rebellion, which was causing colonists to be slaughtered. It would take many years for Oliver Cromwell to implement the King's wishes.[w] Unfortunately for the King, as Clarendon reported:

> The Londoners imputed his concessions to the 'power of Parliament and remembered how it had been taken from them rather than by whom it was restored'.[x]

With opposition to the King continuing to grow, the City swung its considerable financial might behind Parliament, playing a major part in the King's removal and subsequent execution.

Chapter 15

The Great Rebellion 1641-1643

Revolt in Ireland had been bubbling up on several fronts. Strafford had brought in *émigré* Irish colonels, Catholic veterans from the European wars, to train his Royalist troops. With the cost of maintaining his army running at £1,000 per day, the men were put on half pay, and, following his departure from Ireland, the army was disbanded. With the colonels being out of work, they contemplated a Catholic rebellion to capitalise on the Crown's difficulties and to advance a Counter-Reformation, but this plan fizzled out.

The man, who galvanised the Gaelic lords into rebellion was Rory O'More, an Irish army officer from Longford. He convinced the Gaelic Irish chieftains in Ulster that if they rebelled, they would gain support from the Catholic Old English in the Pale, who, after Charles's failure to provide his 'Graces', would take no more. O'More hoped to recruit military personnel from Wentworth's army before it was disbanded. He also approached Sir Phelim O'Neill, one of a group of Gaelic members of Parliament from Ulster, looking to take advantage of the lull in Ireland caused by the English Parliament's stand against the King. As one of the 'deserving Irish', Sir Phelim had done well under Stuart rule. He had converted to Protestantism and, after having been educated in the English manner, spent three years at Lincoln's Inn. He had attracted British settlers to his 4,500 acre estates in Armagh and Tyrone. He purchased a knighthood in 1627 and became a member of the Irish Parliament. Yet, like many other 'deserving' Irish, he failed to manage his estates efficiently and was £13,066 in debt. Although he was pleased to see the departure of the hated Strafford, he now had to deal with 'Lord Justices', who were deputising until a new Lord Deputy was appointed, and they continued Strafford's hard line anti-Catholic approach. Discontented members of the Irish Parliament witnessed the success of extra-parliamentary action in Scotland, but feared that the Scottish success would cause 'a ferocious Puritan crackdown on the Catholic majority in Ireland'.[a]

When Sir Phelim turned to the Papacy for help, he was recognised by the Pope as Prince of Ulster. He was inaugurated as The Great O'Neill at Tullahogue and was appointed Lord General of the Catholic Army. Yet his focus was only on rebellion by Ulstermen in Ulster with the objective of taking the walled city of Londonderry. He and his Gaelic colleagues needed the native Irish peasantry to rise up in support. On 4 November 1641, he produced a forged commission under the Great Seal of Scotland detached from a land patent. This purported to confirm the King's authority for 'all Catholics of the Romish party both English and Irish' to 'seize the goods, estates and persons of all the English Protestants'.[b] On seeing it, many hesitant Catholics took up arms against the settlers.

O'More planned a two prong attack. While the colonels were making a surprise attack on Dublin Castle, scheduled for 23 October, the Ulstermen would raise the north in attacks made only on English settlers to demonstrate their opposition to the English Government. Scots were not to be molested, unless they proved hostile.[c] In October 1641, news arrived in London from Carrickfergus that unrest had broken out in Ulster. Sir Phelim 'set the rebellion in motion, plunging the whole island into a state of perpetual warfare for more than twelve years'.[d] It was particularly ferocious. His first objective was to capture every fort garrisoned with English troops. The English were caught completely unawares, and authority in Ulster collapsed. On 22 October, Sir Phelim invited himself to dinner at Charlemont with its commander, Sir Toby (now Lord) Caulfeild, who knew him well. Once inside, the rebels seized the fort, imprisoning Caulfeild and his garrison. Similar ruses were used to take Dungannon, and Castle Caulfeild. Other clans focused on forts on their traditional lands. The O'Hagans took Moneymore, and murdered any settlers in the locality; Tandragee fell to the O'Hanlons; Cavan was taken by the O'Reillys; Mountjoy[80] was captured by the O'Quinns; Fermanagh fell to the Maguires; and Sir Conn Magennis led a successful assault on Newry and Lurgan, which surrendered in flames on the following day. Within two days a large part of Ulster was in rebel hands. On 4 November, Sir Phelim was acclaimed Commander-in-Chief of all Irish troops in Ulster.

The rebellion spread south. After Dundalk fell on 21 November, the insurgents besieged and captured Drogheda. On 29 November, they defeated Government forces at Julianstown. The Lords Justices in Dublin called the Catholic Old English of the Pale to arms, but, after years of religious persecution and threats to expropriate their lands, they were in two minds where their sympathies lay. On reaching the walls of Drogheda on 3 December, they made the momentous decision to join the rebels. In Ulster, the rebellion devolved into a wholesale butchery of Protestant settlers.[e] The Londonderry plantation was in mortal danger.[f] The early surrender of Moneymore had caused consternation, and refugees reaching Coleraine franticly strengthened its defences, so that it managed to withstand a siege of one hundred days until relieved from Londonderry. Two hundred and fifty men were sent to defend the fort at Garvagh, but, on 13 December, its garrison was wiped out with its commander,

---

[80] At Mountjoy, the rebels ransacked the adjacent school and robbed the schoolmaster and his wife, who took their family and hid in the woods for ten weeks, until the master and one of his children died from hunger and cold. The school was left abandoned until the Restoration in 1662.

William Canning, son of the Ironmongers' Agent, being killed. This sparked off further atrocities around Coleraine with many settlers' properties being burned. Even Strabane fell to the rebels.

Settlers fled, some to the fortified towns, while others hid in the mountains, where they starved to death.[g] Although Sir Phelim brought 9,000 men from mid-Ulster to break Lisburn's defences, the garrison under Sir Arthur Tyringham managed to hold out, despite rebel attempts to force open the gates by charging at them with one hundred head of cattle. Taking both Belfast and Carrickfergus was of huge strategic importance, and the rebels made three attacks on 8, 22 and 28 November, but, when Hamilton and Montgomery sent veteran Lowland Scots troops as reinforcements, each was repulsed, on the last occasion causing the rebels to suffer great loss.[h]

Early in 1642, Paul Canning, eldest son of the Ironmongers' Agent, was besieged at Agivey by Manus Roe O'Cahan. By this time, Archibald Stewart, the Earl of Antrim's Agent, had garrisoned a regiment of the Earl's tenants at Portna. Among these was a company of Catholic Highland Scots, a company of Irish and a force of English musketeers. When Stewart called on them to relieve Agivey, neither the Highland Scots nor the Irish were prepared to fight the O'Cahans. A troop of the English musketeers was detached and, with the help of other troops from the eastern side of the Bann, they relieved Canning and his garrison, although Agivey later fell to the rebels. Meanwhile the Irish and Highland Scots contingents at Portna butchered the remaining English musketeers with help from some of the O'Cahans. With so much blood lust, the Catholic MacDonnells were spoiling to join the rebellion. Although Alastair MacDonnell led a force of Catholics and Protestants ostensibly to protect Portna, he persuaded the Catholics under his command to turn on the Protestants, killing sixty of them. To avenge this, a group of Protestants massacred Catholic tenants at Templepatrick and Islandmagee.

These were not the only appalling atrocities. Manus Roe O'Cahan imprisoned at least one hundred men, women and children in the church at Loughgall, where many were tortured by strangling and half-hanging. He then forced them to the bridge over the Bann at Porterdown. After being stripped naked, they were pushed into the river, where many died. Any trying to swim were shot in the water. On several occasions, Protestant settlers were herded into houses and burned to death. At Tully Castle on Lower Lough Erne, fifteen men with sixty women and children held out for several days but on Christmas Eve, Lady Hume surrendered, expecting the women and children to be spared. Yet, apart from her, they were all stripped and imprisoned in the vaults. On the following morning, she and her family were moved to a nearby barn before being transferred to Monea Castle, but the rest were taken into the bawn and murdered.

The natives fought with great savagery to gain control of Loughinsholin. Within a fortnight, the Gaelic chieftains could no longer control them. The distinction between English and Scots was forgotten as they 'threw themselves with merciless ferocity on the settlers'.[i] They were seething both from hunger caused by failed harvests and wild rumours of a Puritan plot to annihilate them. Their progress was so rapid that more people surrendered to them than they could handle. In Cavan, prisoners were robbed and stripped before being 'turned naked, without respect of age or sex, upon the wild, barren mountains, in the cold air, exposed to all the severity of the winter'.[j] If released, many made for Dublin, but often died of exposure before getting there. Caulfeild and Francis Blennerhasset were shot dead.[k]

It was not just the Irish. Sir James Montgomery, commanding a Presbyterian force in South Down, wrote that he could not contain his men, for they:

> had seen … their houses burned, their wives and children murdered. So they were like robbed bears and tygers, and could not be satisfied with all the revenge they took … being full of revenge … most partys killed many, and giving no quarter.[l]

Many Scottish settlers returned home, with more than five hundred taking shelter on the Isle of Bute and four thousand more facing starvation around Ayr and Irvine. The Scottish Privy Council were obliged to order a food collection and urgently called on London to send a relief force to Ulster.

When the rebels reached Fermanagh, a wealthy Dublin merchant, Arthur Champion, a Justice of the Peace and Member of Parliament, and three of his companions were stabbed to death by his tenants, and several other landowners in Fermanagh were arrested and killed. Yet Sir William Cole made the island town of Enniskillen impregnable.[m] Elsewhere the insurgents swept all before them. Only Belfast, Carrickfergus, Enniskillen, Coleraine, Limavady and Londonderry were able to hold out in Ulster. Both Londonderry and Coleraine became grossly over-crowded. At Coleraine, the parish church and churchyard were filled 'with little Hutts, pestered and packed with poore people'.[n] There were 3,000 women and children in need of sustenance, and food was running out. Many deaths were caused by disease, and several refugees huddling inside the parish church were killed when it was struck by lightning. The Mercers' Company Agent mustered five hundred unarmed men and raised two companies of foot. When Alexander Stewart led out a sortie against the rebels, his men were routed. At last, in May 1642, provisions arrived from London.

Although Sir Phelim had targeted Londonderry, now the principal place of refuge for settlers, he moved slowly and lost his element of surprise. Although the settlers were heavily outnumbered, they held back the insurgents on a line south from Londonderry through Strabane and Newtown Stewart to Augher. Sir Phelim failed to gain support from insurgents in Donegal who were expending their energy in seeking plunder. Yet he was able to station one thousand troops between Limavady and Coleraine to prevent British troops arriving from the east.

At Limavady, Phillips's sons, Dudley, aged thirty-one, and Thomas, defended their father's settlement. Although the two castles held out, the insurgents burned Newtown Limavady, butchering any settlers' families in the vicinity. In 1642, the brothers were able to send word to Dublin that one thousand men, women and children were sheltering with them in the castles. If they sallied out for food, the Irish were waiting and caused several losses. The authorities sent the brothers commissions to take command and provided weapons, ammunition, money and food. When Coleraine was relieved, the brothers joined the 'Lagan Army', made up of settlers in Londonderry, who had formed into four regiments and were supported by Presbyterians who had fought under Monro (see page 191). They made ferocious counter-attacks to secure the City's western approaches before relieving Limavady and Ballykelly. They also took part in the rout of the insurgents at Dungiven, where Manus O'Cahan was holding many British men, women and children prisoner. Further south, Sir Ralph Gore prevented Donegal Castle, Ballyshannon and Castle Murray from falling into rebel hands. The Livery Companies played a considerable part in defending Londonderry, sending four ships to provision those being besieged. Each Great Company provided two pieces of ordnance to supplement the twenty pieces already there.

Most of the settlements in the proportions were abandoned. The insurgents razed houses to the ground, slaughtering any occupants, who showed resistance. John Starkey, headmaster of the school at Mountnorris in Armagh was drowned with his family in the river Blackwater. There have been wildly exaggerated reports of the numbers of settlers killed, but it is estimated that between 527 and 1,259 died in Armagh out of a total of more than 3,000 British settlers. This would equate to 12,000 deaths in the whole of Ulster.

Sir Phelim called on Tyrone's nephew, Eoghan Roe O'Neill, to return to Ulster from the Continent. As a veteran commander of one of Philip IV's regiments, Eoghan Roe had distinguished himself at the siege of Arras in 1640 and was the acknowledged leader of the Irish in exile. After receiving pressure from Pope Urban VIII, the Spanish released him with Papal money to 'stiffen the ranks of the Ulster Irish'.[o] He was promised French help by Cardinal Richelieu and by Roman-Catholic families exiled from England. With Charles I facing opposition both in Scotland and from his own Parliament, it seemed a good opportunity to bring a Catholic expeditionary force into Ulster. At the end of July 1642, Eoghan Roe landed at Doe Castle in Donegal after sailing round the north of Scotland from Dunkirk. He found Ulster 'like a desert'. Despite all the promises, no troops arrived from either France or Flanders. France and Spain were now at war and neither was prepared to risk upsetting the English. On 29 August, the Assembly at Clones in County Monaghan placed the Ulster army under Eoghan Roe's command, but he was depressed by the quality of its men and their lack of equipment. Despite his misgivings, he was persuaded to engage the Londonderry settlers. On 13 June 1643, his raw recruits, who were outnumbered two to one, were comprehensively routed at Clones by the Lagan Army. He retired into Connaught to train a force of native Irish Ulstermen in modern fighting methods.[p]

When Charles I failed to send assistance to the Ulster settlers, Parliament and the City of London turned on him, and civil war in England was now inevitable. It was the Scottish covenanters, who came to the settlers' aid. On 15 April 1642, Major-General Robert Monro landed a Scots army of 2,500 men at Carrickfergus. Yet Parliament discouraged Monro from setting out to relieve Londonderry, as the English settlers there were unlikely to welcome a Covenanter army any more than the Irish insurgents, so he went south in pursuit of rebels in Down. As a hardened veteran of the Thirty Years' War, Monro slaughtered everyone he caught. On 1 May, he relieved Newry, shooting and hanging sixty men, but stopped short of allowing his men to throw the women in the river for use as target practice, despite several being killed.[q] When he returned north, the rebels hid in the woods, but he slaughtered any native Irish he found and seized their cattle. When he recovered Mountjoy and Dungannon, the Ulster rebels were ready to capitulate, and both Down and Antrim were cleared of insurgents. Yet, until the end of 1642, much of County Londonderry remained in danger, and both Londonderry and Coleraine were in ruins.

In the rest of Ireland, the rebels did rather better. In 1641, Ormonde's cousin, Richard Butler, 3rd Viscount Mountgarret, led a rebellion in the south, which, by 1642, had established control almost everywhere other than Dublin. They were well organised and, in October, were joined by Old English Catholics from the Pale. They raised regular troops to replace their militia and formed a Government, known as the Catholic Confederation, at Kilkenny in the south east. On 22 March, the Roman-Catholic bishops and priests of Armagh met at Kells, where they declared the Catholic war to be just and excommunicated any Catholics still supporting the Protestant settlers. In May and June, their action was confirmed by a nationwide meeting of Catholics at Kilkenny. Yet they also confirmed their loyalty to the King.

Although rebellion broke out in Dublin, the authorities were warned by Sir John Clotworthy's manager, Owen O'Connelly, of a plan to take the Castle. O'Connelly was a newly converted Protestant and he gathered as much information from the conspirators as he could, before defecting to warn Lord Justice Parsons. Although Parsons did not know whether to believe the story, he placed the castle on a high state of alert, resulting in the leading conspirators being seized and imprisoned. Ormonde remained in Dublin, where the King sent reinforcements to him from England and Scotland. He now mounted several expeditions to clear the Pale of Catholic resistance. The Lords Justices were initially suspicious of his loyalty given his close kinship with so many Confederation leaders, but, on 5 March 1642, he proved himself by lifting the siege of Drogheda and, in April, relieved Royalist garrisons at Naas, Athy and Maryborough. After returning to Dublin, he defeated Mountgarret's numerically superior forces at Kilrush. This gained him plaudits from Charles I and a monetary reward from the English Parliament. Yet the Catholic Confederation still controlled two-thirds of Ireland[81], and Ormonde had no expectation of further reinforcements. Despite an indecisive victory after making a sortie to New Ross, south east of Kilkenny, his situation was difficult.

With his desperate need for troops to support the Royalist cause in England, Charles needed to withdraw Royalist forces from Ireland.[82] This required a complete *volte face*. He instructed Ormonde to treat with the Catholic Confederation with whom he was fighting and to enlist their support for the Stuart cause. In September 1643, the King agreed a one year 'Cessation of Arms' with the Irish Catholics in return for limited toleration. The Catholics considered that Charles offered better prospects of religious freedom than Parliament's Puritans. With both Ormonde and the Protestant Establishment continuing to mistrust them, their view proved misplaced.

Cromwell's New Model Army was by this time winning the war in England on Parliament's behalf, but it took a radical line. It believed that 'the King should face justice for his crimes against the people'.[r] It undertook a military coup known as 'Colonel Pride's Purge', which surrounded the House of Commons and expelled all members refusing to accede to its non-conformist demands. In the face of a threatened vote by the resultant 'Rump' Parliament to exterminate Catholicism in Ireland, the Irish lords and gentry within the Catholic Confederation lost their nerve and intervened with the Ulster Catholic wood-kerne to stop any further slaughter in Londonderry. With peace there restored, the Livery Companies were able to return to reclaim their lands. They granted new leases and collected rents, but legal title was not regained until after Charles had lost his head.

As a Protestant, Ormonde faced a dilemma and his newly-established Irish Catholic allies varied in the extent of their support for Charles I. The Lords of the Pale, English by descent, remained zealously loyal to the Crown, particularly with the Stuarts harbouring Catholic sympathies; the Ulster Irish were still determined to recover their lands expropriated by the plantations and to expel the settlers; the men of Connaught and Leinster sought approval of the 'Graces'; and those in the south west and other Gaelic Irish, such as Eoghan Roe O'Neill, wanted an independent country under a Catholic sovereign appointed by the Pope. In October 1645, the Papal Nuncio, Archbishop Giovanni Battista Rinuccini, arrived from Italy to represent the newly elected Pope Innocent X. He came with arms, 20,000 pounds of gunpowder and 200,000 silver dollars, heralding calls for Irish independence.

With little common ground and much squabbling between the rival factions of Catholic Royalists, they failed to make common cause with the Protestant Royalists behind the King, but those, who supported the Stuarts, grouped

---

[81] The Confederation's Supreme Council acted as a Government, appointing generals, issuing writs and minting its own coinage.

[82] When 4,000 Royalist troops were withdrawn to England, half came from Cork City where its Protestant residents promptly sided with the Parliamentarians.

themselves behind Ormonde. Had they been able to work together, they would undoubtedly have regained Royalist control in Ireland. They were thwarted by 'fatal hesitation, conflicting aims and wasting disputes'. Loyalties became almost unfathomable, with generals and their men changing between Royalists and Parliamentarians with bewildering frequency.[s] Monro's Scottish troops in Ulster, who had backing from Montgomery and Hamilton, were initially Royalist, then Parliamentarian, and then Royalist again.[t]

Part 4

The individual Livery Companies on their proportions (1) 1613-1641

Chapter 16

Mercers

The Mercers are recognised as the senior of the twelve Great Livery Companies in accordance with an order of precedence laid down by the Court of Aldermen of the City of London in 1515. There were forty-eight Companies then in existence, and those formed after 1515 are ranked after them in seniority of creation.[a] As has been seen on page 147, the Mercers were not the most prominent Livery Company at the time of the plantation, but their senior ranking has never been questioned. In the Middle Ages, they supervised the London trade in 'silks, wools, cloths and velvets',[b] but like all Livery Companies continue to administer substantial charitable funds, often the benefactions of wealthy burgers held in trust for purposes laid down by each donor.

The Mercers were among the most reluctant participants in the plantation. They were in relative decline at the time, and their Liverymen felt that, as 'a guild of men who lived by merchandise' they 'lacked the means and ability' to become involved.[c] Despite appeals to the Privy Council, it refused to intervene on their behalf and, when two of their wardens were imprisoned, they concluded that there was no option but to stump up what was requested. It was the Company rather than individual members, which made the initial investment, supported by specified contributions from a number of the minor companies to meet the required £3,333 6s. 8d. When further calls were demanded, members became increasingly concerned at the extent of its commitment. Calls were allocated as follows:

	Contributions to 1611			Contributions 1611-1616			Total to 1616		
	£	s	d	£	s	d	£	s	d
Mercers	2,680	0	0	1,240	0	0	3,920	0	0
Innholders	200	0	0	100	0	0	300	0	0
Cooks	200	0	0	100	0	0	300	0	0
Embroiderers	153	0	0	80	0	0	233	0	0
Masons	100	0	0	50	0	0	150	0	0
Cash payment		6	8					6	8
	£3,333	6	8	£1,570	0	0	£4,903	6	8

On 17 December 1613, the Mercers drew Lot 8, an area of 21,600 acres, known as Movanagher. It was mainly in the Barony of Loughinsholin but partly in Coleraine to the north and west. Given its relatively remote location, it was one of the larger proportions, divided into two parts, which were both on the west side of the Bann River. There was a long riverside strip that included the settlement of Movanagher and a larger area to the west, stretching to the foothills of the Sperrins[83]. The two areas were separated by lands allocated to the Ironmongers, by glebe lands and by a native Irish freehold already well populated with O'Neills and O'Cahans. Their proportion was occupied by native Irish including the notoriously unreliable O'Donnells, who willingly gave succour to wood-kerne. This made it vulnerable and indefensible.[d]

In 1613, when the Mercers took possession, they found that there was much fertile land, particularly along the banks of the Bann, but there were also many small lakes and large areas of bog. As a large part was in the forest of Glenconkeyne, it was well supplied with wood and there was more woodland in the Bann valley. The small settlement of Movanagher was at the point of embarkation for timber being moved down river to Coleraine. There were delays to the granting of the title caused by complex land ownership problems; the Grange lands of the Manor of Kilrea had been granted to Sir Toby Caulfeild in 1604 and 1607, and needed to be reacquired from him for transfer to the Mercers. It was not until 17 October 1618 that the conveyance was at last finalised, and, during the five year delay, the woodlands suffered extensive clearance. At this time, the Innholders chose not to become further involved; they allowed their interest to lapse, and forewent the £300 they had already paid. The Irish Society valued the proportion at £5,000 9s. 3d. and required the Mercers to provide a further £97 2s. 7d. to make up the shortfall from the £4,903 6s. 8d. already contributed.

The Company appointed a Committee for Irish Affairs, responsible to its Court for its activities in Ulster.[e] There does not seem to have been a formal agreement with its associated Minor Companies. The Mercers were established as legal owners to manage the proportion on their behalf. Like the Drapers and Ironmongers, the Mercers appointed an agent, choosing Richard Vernon[84] to become their 'Agent Attorney'. From the outset, he seems to have been more interested in personal gain than the proportion's welfare. On 18 October 1618, as soon as the land was conveyed, six freeholders were identified and were granted estates by The Irish Society as required by the Articles of the Plantation. One of these was Vernon himself, but there is evidence that the land allocated

---

[83] The Sperrins are a range of hills that run north-south through the middle of County Londonderry.

[84] Vernon's early involvement is not clear. The Ironmongers' Agent, George Canning referred to an agent named 'Warner', who seems to have overseen the building of the Castle and its bawn. It may be that Warner was the original Agent Attorney, who was replaced by Vernon in about 1618, or Canning may have got his name wrong.

to other freeholders was very poor. There were no buildings on the estate other than a few traditional cabins occupied by native Irish farmers.

The Company retained the right to cut timber on freehold lands for building and repair work. This was in addition to The Irish Society's rights to fell timber, to hunt, fish and ride, and to remove stone, slate, sand, gravel and other minerals. Freeholders were required to pay a quit-rent to The Irish Society, to swear the Oath of Allegiance, to maintain arms for their defence, to attend jury service and to grind their corn at the Mercers' mill. The design of buildings was dictated by covenants. Freeholders were also restricted from leasing to native Irish. British tenants were to be offered security of tenure and to pay reasonable rents in accordance with the Articles of the Plantation. Such were the restrictions imposed by the conditions that many freeholders left, although the Company made no immediate effort to replace them. Nor did it appoint a Farmer as its middleman, and was the only Livery Company not to do so. The natives must have become more confident of avoiding eviction, but they remained implacably hostile. When a native freehold at Bovedy, adjacent to the Mercers' lands was forfeited after the rebellion of 1615 (and granted to Beresford's son-in-law, George Carey, the Recorder of Londonderry), the Mercers made no corresponding move to dispossess natives on their lands, but this did not stop their gangs becoming involved in continuing atrocities. At Lislea near Kilrea, nine terrorists broke into the house of a settler, John Brown, who was sitting with his wife and his neighbour, Williams. After tying up the men, the gang devoured their food and drink. When Brown's two servants, who had gone to Movanagher that morning, returned, they were hacked and stabbed in many places, although one, amazingly, survived. Having slaughtered Williams and Brown, the gang left Mrs. Brown and the seriously wounded servant as the only two alive.

Although there was plenty of timber for building, the only stone of good quality was black basalt (whinstone). Local limestone was poor, but there was clay for brickmaking at Movanagher and Carnroe. There was also valuable salmon and eel-fishing at Kilrea, noted for quality and flavour, with a fish salting activity nearby. The demand for casks and boxes to pack the fish became a principal cause of the spoliation of the woodlands. Vernon supervised the building of tenements to house workers at the sawpits, carpenters' shops and water mill at Movanagher; an Anglican parish school was also opened. Workers arrived from Coleraine to prefabricate building frames. This confluence of workers persuaded the Mercers to make Movanagher their principal settlement to be protected by a castle and bawn. Despite the merits of its proximity to the fisheries and an ancient ford[85] crossing the Bann River, it was not well-organised defensively. The surrounding land was covered in small mounds and deep woods, making it ideal for guerrilla warfare. Unlike the settlements on the Drapers' and Vintners' lands, Movanagher 'lacked coherent shape and form,

---

[85] The ford was used to bring in building materials, particularly bricks and lime from County Antrim.

and consisted of a small hamlet made up of several isolated buildings, a castle and a bawn'.[f] Its fortifications did not command a wide area and were unimpressive and insecure. The lime used in constructing the walls was so poor that much of the initial building work collapsed. In 1618, Pynnar noted that it did not conform to plantation building requirements, but, by then, its castle was 'not inferior' to any other. It had dormer windows in its attic floor with a slate roof and brick chimneys. Although basalt was used for building the rubble walls, openings were faced with brick and limestone. The bawn was one hundred and twenty feet square, with brick battlements and four flankers, all of 'good stone and lime'. Yet, being at the extreme eastern end of the proportion, the whole of the western part was left unprotected. In 1622, Phillips recommended rebuilding it more centrally.

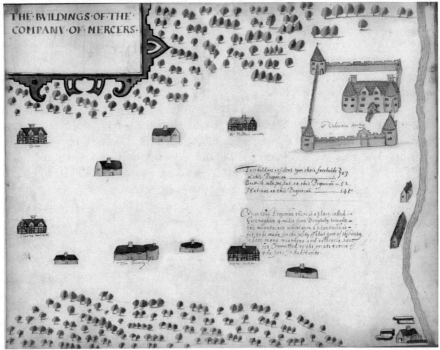

Raven's 1622 drawing of the Mercers' castle and bawn at Movenagher, which was surrounded by a settlement of four timber framed houses and other lesser structures. *Courtesy of the Drapers' Company*

The Agents were always short of money to pay for building works at Movanagher. Like the castle, most structures were built of basalt rubble, dressed with brick or limestone. Yet the main contractor was Benson, who had already built the walls of Londonderry and the Ironmongers' castle at Agivey. During the building programme, it must have become a hive of activity, despite its isolation. Benson completed four large timber-framed houses on two storeys, but, with slate in short supply, three were thatched and the fourth was roofed with shingles. In the absence of settlers, they were let to 'poor men', who took in Irish under-tenants. There were already five Irish beehive style houses with central chimneys and thatched roofs. There was no church, but a further five substantial stone-built houses with thatched roofs were built in a clearing and another three by the river.[86] The occupiers of simpler structures in the woods were molested by wood-kerne.

Phillips's and Hadsor's survey of 1622 reported that the timbers of some houses were already rotting, and they were being used as cattle sheds after lying unoccupied for six years. It recorded only three remaining freeholders. Overall there were fifty-two British settlers and one hundred and forty-five native Irish. Phillips estimated the expenditure on building works at £1,438, but complained that settlers were unarmed and their isolated homesteads could be attacked with impunity. At a remote place called Greenaghan, he reported: 'many murthers and robberies have bin Committed to the great terror of the poore Inhabitants'.[g] Despite this, settlers were starting to arrive, and houses became more fully occupied.

Four townlands were allocated as demesne lands for the castle. The objective was to allow the Agent Attorney sufficient income to provide hospitality and defence. Other townlands were let as single lots to British tenants for periods of twenty-one years or a number of lives. By 1615, almost half the land had been let in this way. Although head tenants were expected to sublet to British settlers, in practice the Irish remained. There was no shortage of natives prepared to pay higher rents to stay on their traditional lands. Yet, without security of tenure, they lacked the confidence to invest in a farming infrastructure, and their poor farming methods quickly reduced them to a subsistence lifestyle with every prospect of penury if crops failed.

Vernon's management as Agent Attorney was not distinguished by efficiency or good relations with tenants.[h] Although he completed Movanagher's fortifications and settlement, the workmanship was variable. The mill was 'jerry-built', damaging the grain that tenants were being obliged to grind there. His rent collection was so inefficient, that one freeholder, Thomas Church, complained.[i] Vernon seems to have leased out townlands at an under value to his friends, who then relinquished them back to him, so that he benefited from the better rates. Although the townland of Claragh was part of the Castle's desmene, it somehow became his freehold. The Irish Society failed to pay attention to the way freeholds were granted (or more likely Rowley and Beresford were in on his scam). Vernon also seems to have sold timber and lime contrary to the Articles of the Plantation. Not content with defrauding the Mercers, his 'instillation of a taproom at the castle for the sale of whiskey was not likely to raise the tone of the neighbourhood nor the esteem of the Company'.[j] The Mercers were left with a large annual deficit, and Vernon failed

---

[86] Despite a profusion of contemporary maps, there is some doubt how many houses were built and where they were situated. There is evidence of a second settlement, similar to Movanagher at Tamlaght-Vow near Carnroe.

to attract settlers or to induce those already there to stay. He was also a confidant of Phillips and may well have fed him with information to the Mercers' detriment. Yet when they asked Phillips what was going on, he did not defend Vernon, reporting that the work carried out did not account for the moneys he claimed to have disbursed and his rental returns reported less than the actual sums collected. It was a clear case of embezzlement.[k]

When Vernon was at last dismissed in 1621, he was replaced by Church, who continued to live in the large house[87] he had built on his freehold at Landmore. This left the Castle, which contained arms for its protection, unoccupied. When Phillips conducted his survey, Valentine Hartopp was living there. Phillips considered Hartopp a 'needy and grasping adventurer'.[l] Until 1621, he had been the Merchant Taylors' Farmer, but had assigned his lease after falling into arrears. He also tried to gain control of the Drapers' lands.

Phillips's criticisms caused the Mercers to make improvements. Church's home was repaired and re-roofed. Lands were leased out, generally for twenty-one years, to provide better security of tenure. Several under-tenants, facing financial difficulties after poor harvests, were given time to pay. Expenditure on buildings rose to £3,000. By 1623, thirty townlands had been let to native Irish and eighteen to British settlers, but rental income was under £170 (although Phillips calculated a much higher figure, which may be explained by rack-renting [the charging of exhorbitant rents] to the native Irish).[m] Although, in 1622, Phillips reported one hundred and forty-five native Irish on the proportion, in the following year, official sources showed only one hundred and three, but this may have been an understatement caused by the difficulty of counting in the woods.

Following the sequestration of rents as a result of the Star Chamber trial in 1635, the Company avoided handing over rental moneys already collected, which Church sent direct to them in London. It remained in touch with him until 1639, hoping for 'some good composition ere long with His Majesty about the lands'.[n] When this failed to materialise, morale fell to a low ebb and many tenants, doubtful of their security of tenure, refused to pay rents to the Crown.

During the 1641 rebellion, Movanagher was abandoned and all the buildings within the proportion were destroyed. Church retreated to Coleraine, although he seems to have returned to the proportion at a later date. Despite losing their estates, the Mercers provided guns to defend Londonderry.

---

[87] Church's house appears to have been the largest timber-framed construction in the County of Londonderry, being forty-six feet by twenty-one feet on plan. Houses were usually one and a half storeys high.

Chapter 17

Grocers

The Grocers were originally incorporated in 1345 when they were known as 'Pepperers', which denotes their spice trading origins. In 1515, they were named second in order of precedence among the twelve Great Livery Companies. Sir Humphrey Weld, Lord Mayor when the plantation was first mooted, was a member of the Company and he addressed a meeting with them to describe the proposed scheme and to request contributions. Forty-six members offered to invest, but only seven of them named what they would be prepared to offer. In March 1610, the Company called on members to pay up, but there must have been a lack of enthusiasm, as, by June, the Wardens received powers to imprison defaulters. This seems to have achieved the desired objective and, by February 1611, the Company was in a position to accept lands in Ulster. To meet its first instalment, it appropriated funds from one of its bequests, (a frequent expedient among Companies in extremity) but, in July 1612, the Court advised members that they would be responsible for future calls. Nevertheless, when the scale of the required investment became apparent, it was agreed that the Company itself would meet future levies from its common stock and would receive any future profits. Earlier contributions made by individuals were eventually repaid to them.

As has been explained, the investment required by the Grocers exceeded that of a single proportion, so it also acquired a share in the Vintners' estates, which will be discussed in the chapter on that Company. At the time of the land allocation, they had already contributed £3,874 to the Irish Society. With the total required for each proportion amounting to £3,333 6s. 8d., the Grocers' money was allocated as follows:

	Contributions to 1611			Contributions 1611-1616			Total to 1616		
	£	s.	d	£	s.	d	£	s	d
Grocers' proportion	3,333	6	8	1,666	13	4	5,000	0	0
Vintners' proportion	540	13	4	333	6	8	874	0	0
	£3,874	0	0	£2,000	0	0	£5,874	0	0

When lots were drawn at the Guildhall, the Grocers' Company received Lot 2, amounting to 15,900 acres on the east bank of the Foyle north east of Londonderry. The proportion was divided into two parts, a larger division around the settlement of Muff, five miles from Londonderry, and a much smaller area on the banks of the Foyle opposite Culmore fort. The two areas were separated by the freehold of Captain Manus O'Cahan. The proportion was bounded by the Fishmongers to the east, the Goldsmiths to the west and the Skinners to the south. There was a large population of native Irish. Despite being well-located, the land quality was only average.

In May 1615, the Grocers subcontracted their obligations under the Charter by leasing the whole proportion to Edward Rone of Essex, conditional on him agreeing to build a castle, bawn and twelve houses by September 1618. In view of his building obligations, a relatively low rental of £116 13s. 4d. was agreed. Unfortunately, Rone died in January 1618, leaving his executors headed by Robert Goodwin[88] to continue the building works he had begun.[a] Muff, with its central location, was chosen as the site for the castle, which became known as 'Grocers' Hall', built in the corner of a bawn with four flankers. One of these was incorporated into the castle's structure, which was on two storeys with three gabled dormers. The walls of the bawn had 'rudimentary crenellations' and were initially only five feet high. The circular flankers had conical roofs and the one incorporated into the castle had 'fanciful upperwork'.[b] By 1622, in response to The Irish Society's questionaire, the Company reported that it had

> builded a faire, stout, and substantial Castle, with a faire tower upon it of 12 feet high above the ground, well coped, and strongly builded like the wall of a town of war, with loop-holes and spaces in the top of the wall for ordnance or other pieces of defence.[c]

An old church, about half a mile from Muff, was in ruins and the Company considered it too small. It agreed to build a new structure, sixty feet by twenty feet, 'for the ornamentation of the town and the convenience of its inhabitants'.[d] This decision was prompted by Goodwin, who pointed out the Fishmongers' church at Walworth and the Drapers 'chapel of ease' at Moneymore. It contributed £150 towards its cost and it remained the parish church until 1821. The 1622 questionaire described it as a 'FAIRE CHURCH', to which the Dean of Derry was nominated as Rector.

On 12 February 1617, the Company described its progress on house building by producing *'A View of the Proportion of the Country Lands allotted to the Right Worshipfull the Company of Grocers of London'*. This showed that a stone house was being built at Muff, which was by then half-slated. Its walls were

---

[88] Goodwin was a member of the Drapers' Company. He became an employee of The Irish Society and was the first Town Clerk and Chamberlain of the City of Londonderry. He was involved in a number of negotiations to facilitate agreements on behalf of the Livery Companies.

36 feet in length, 20 feet in breadth, having a flanker or outlet of stone of 12 feet square; the walls are 14 feet high. The shafts of the chimneys, the door-cases, windows and coigns, both within and without the house, are made of free stone. This house contained a kitchen, hall, buttery, and three lodging chambers, and hath four chimneys.[e]

Progress was also being made on a second house built in similar manner and on 'two other houses conjoined', where the walls were already ten feet high with materials on site for their completion. At Cregan a substantial stone-built house of one storey was having its roof slated. There was another at Gortney and substantial ones at Belud and 'the Mornceys'. There were plans for one more at Edenreaghmore and a mill was under construction at Maydown.

By 1619, the bawn of the castle and eight houses were complete although four of these were outside Muff. In October 1618, the Company forced a large number of native Irish to leave as required by the 'Articles of the Plantation', even though this left a shortage of labour and caused a delay in construction work.[89] A further hold up arose when a ship carrying structural frames manufactured in Coleraine was wrecked *en route*. In 1619, Rone's brother-in-law, Robert Harrington stepped in to take a fifty-seven year lease over the proportion, having already leased glebelands from the church. By 1622, with Goodwin's help, he had met the proportion's building requirements. The Grocers' records indicate that their contribution was only £60 (mainly to provide materials for the new church), but they had also reinvested £100 from their total of £850 rents received.[90] Like the Goldsmiths, the Grocers had found tenants to undertake much of the building work at their own expense, but with both proportions being on the opposite side of the Foyle to Londonderry they offered desirable locations. By 1623, the The Irish Society returns show that they had already earned £2,800 in rents and were calling on Harrington to remit money to London, having spent only £200 on construction on the proportion. This was less money than any other Company except the Goldsmiths.

Most settlers lived near Muff, but there is conflicting evidence on how many there were. In 1618, Goodwin reported nine English and nine Irish tenants 'all on an equal footing'.[f] Yet in 1622, Phillips recorded one freeholder, thirty-four British settlers (twenty-two of whom were armed) and seventy-five native Irish. Phillips wanted to see more settlements:

> further into the Cuntry and brittish sent over which would prevent many robberies and murthers daily Comitted by the Irish to the greate terror of the few pore brittish already settled.[g]

---

[89] This is the only significant exodus of native Irish reported on any of the Livery Company estates. Curl has concluded that it may have been short-lived, being followed by a stealthy return. A 'Mass-House' remained on the proportion throughout the early years of the plantation.[h]

[90] In addition to this, the Company received £21 6s. 8d. in rent from Captain Manus O'Cahan. His payments were collected on behalf of The Irish Society and were duly paid over to them.[i]

His records show six 'English' houses in Muff, one of which was timber-framed, and five, which were slated. Raven's map also shows an Irish cabin, and there was a small house by the river, which may have been a mill or an inn. Phillips's statistics conflict with the Companies' response to the 1622 questionaire. This reported six freeholders (including Robert Goodwin) all resident on the proportion, and thirty-four substantial 'English' houses, inhabited by British tenants. It is probable that some of these were in more inaccessible areas, which Phillips did not visit.[j]

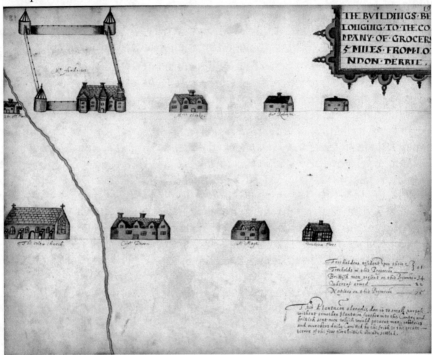

Raven's 1622 drawing of the Grocers' castle and bawn at Muff surrounded by the settlement along the main street of what is now Eglinton.
Courtesy of the Drapers' Company

After receiving Phillips's survey, the English Government increased its military presence by billeting soldiers on settlers. This caused Harrington, who had hitherto been punctilious in his payments to the Company, to face financial difficulties. The Government did not make life easy. In 1628, it extracted £1,500 to pay for military services, and, between 1625 and 1630, the Crown sequestrated rents on two occasions. Settlers were also fined for retaining native Irish on their lands, placing a further strain on both Harrington's and the settlers' resources.

When the Court of Star Chamber verdict resulted in the estates being forfeited, the Crown tried to force up rents. Many settlers simply packed up and went home, while others were ruined. Although this left the proportion derelict, there was still a store of arms in readiness against attack. In 1641, it came into its own when the castle was besieged by the MacDonnells. The remaining settlers managed to hold out during the winter until troops from Londonderry arrived to relieve them. At some later point, the castle fell into Royalist hands, as it was severely damaged by the Parliamentarians. Although its ruins survived until the 1820s, these were then deemed 'inconvenient'.

Chapter 18

Drapers

The Drapers' Company remains the third Livery Company in order of seniority in the City of London. It was incorporated by Royal Charter in 1439, although this superseded an earlier one dated 1364. It was a reluctant participant in the plantation and, in its struggle to gather contributions, committed several members to jail and had to threaten others. Those who had already been assessed were warned to meet future calls or surrender their initial investment. Realising that there was no choice in the matter, in February 1611, the Company signified its willingness to accept land in Ulster. It was supported by the Tallow-Chandlers and made the following contributions:

	Contributions to 1611			Contributions 1611-1616			Total to 1616		
	£	s	d	£	s	d	£	s	d
Drapers	3,072	0	0	1,536	0	0	4,608	0	0
Tallow-Chandlers	260	0	0	120	0	0	380	0	0
Cash payment	1	6	8				1	6	8
	£3,333	6	8	£1,656	0	0	£4,989	6	8

In 1618, the Drapers bought out the Tallow-Chandlers' interests for £374 11s. 0d. leaving them as the sole investor in the proportion.

The Drapers drew Lot 11, which amounted to 38,800 acres of remote woods and mountains of Loughinsholin containing 'huge tracts of bleak and mountainous lands'.[a] They named it the Manor of Drapers. As a consequence of its inhospitable location, it was one of the largest proportions, but its infertile farmland presented formidable problems and its remoteness made it extremely dangerous for settlers. It was divided into three principal districts: Moneymore, Brackaslievegallion and Ballinascreen (with Dunlogan). Moneymore was to the south, bordering with County Tyrone to the south and west. The village of Moneymore was on its northern boundary. The southern part of Brackaslievegallion was only a mile north of Moneymore with land rising from the south and east towards its border at the summit of Slievegallion in the west. Yet the soil was sufficiently deep to be cultivated along the contours. Ballinascreen, two mile further north west contained its parish church near the village of The Cross (or Moyheelan). Its land lay in two parcels rising from the River Moyola to its boundary at the tops of the Sperrins to the north and west. To the north, it abutted the lands of the Skinners, Mercers, Vintners and Salters. With its three divisions being separated from each other by Irish freeholds and church lands, they were difficult to defend.

The Drapers set up a committee to supervise their investment and, from the outset, appointed an Agent, realising that it would be difficult to find a Farmer to occupy the inhospitable terrain and concluding that they would need to bear the cost of establishing fortified villages themselves. Surprisingly, they chose Rowley, despite him being discredited by The Irish Society, but he was a member of their Company and seems to have acted entirely properly on their behalf. Robert Russell was sent from London to assist him. By 1615, they had outlaid £3,200 on building works at Moneymore. Despite its location on the main highway from Coleraine to Dublin, involvement in building work was dangerous. Rowley told the Company that his men were working 'as it were with the Sworde in one hande and the Axe in thother'.[b] Russell was full of eccentric ideas. He spent a large sum in piping a stream for half a mile to provide water to the village, providing him with a monopoly over its supply. This left the Agents short of funds for housebuilding. In 1615, Rowley built a water mill with mill race and water wheel. This 'up-to-date' mechanism transmitted the drive to the grinding stones using a trundle-wheel (a wheel with dowel-like teeth which engaged the cogs of the vertically mounted lantern pinion).[c] The wheel was reinforced with 'many iron plates and nails' made by the Moneymore blacksmith. William Bignall, the miller, needed twelve hundred feet of planks and boards to build sluices and floodgates. It was so robust that it remained operational for many years.

To meet the proportion's security obligations Rowley began work on the castle and bawn, incorporating a chapel into the structure with its own access. In 1616, he arranged for George Birkett, a bricklayer from London, to build the bawn walls and, in the following year, employed James Bodkin on the castle. It was probably designed by Antonie Lipsett, a mason who had also tendered for building work in Londonderry. Both Birkett[91] and Bodkin occupied houses in the settlement.[92] Other contractors built stone houses dressed with local limestone.

The difficulty in moving materials to site delayed progress, although timber was available locally and there were several sawpits on the estate. In the absence of slate, Humphrey Barlo, with lands on the Fishmongers' proportion, delivered 40,000 laths to make shingles, and Richard Jennings shingled two houses and the bawn gatehouse. In the absence of slate, shingles were preferred for roofing

[91] Birkett later became a surveyor and was responsible for the repair of the parish church at Stewartstown.
[92] Both Birkett and Bodkin were granted fifteen acres of land away from their houses on eighty-year leases. They were required to plant the land with trees to make an enclosure. They were also obliged to arm themselves and to pave the street in front of their houses.

dormers, as it was difficult to make the roof valleys watertight with thatch. By 1620, the growing scarcity of good oak, meant that most houses were being constructed of stone. 'The denuding of the woods was rapid, inexorable, and contrary to all the intentions of the Plantation.'[93d] Glass and lead to make windows had to be imported from London along with more sophisticated door furniture and locks. Despite these problems, by the beginning of 1617, twelve houses had been built, and Moneymore had become an important staging post on the main road.

On Rowley's death in 1617, Russell became Agent; but the quality of the building work deteriorated and a bawn wall collapsed. When he ran short of money, he opened a brewery.

His brewhouse project depended on paying his workers' wages in barrels of beer and maintaining three taphouses which seemed to reduce the villagers to a state of permanent inebriation.[e] Morale became so low that, in 1618, a deputation of the workforce went to London to complain to the Company. Although drunkenness was rife, the brewery's profits enabled Russell to purchase the mill and smithy. With his monopoly over piped water, he charged the villagers a high rent to access it, but diverted large amounts to the brewery, which was producing more beer than the settlement's needs. This prevented other residents from brewing in competition with him.[f] With four of the new houses being converted to alehouses, the native Irish flocked to Moneymore, causing drunken revelries which degenerated into brawls.

When Pynnar conducted his survey in early 1619, he noted a strong bawn of stone and lyme 100 feet square, 15 feet high, with two flankers.

> There is a Castle within the bawn of the same wideness, being battlemented, the which has also two flankers, and nearly finished. Right before the Castle there are built twelve houses whereof six are lime and stone, very good, and six timber, inhabited with English families; and this the best work I have seen for a building; a Water Mill, and a Malt-house also. A quarter of a mile from the town there is made a conduit head, which bringeth water to all places in the bawn and town in pipes.[g]

Pynnar's plan shows a ditch dug on the outside of the bawn. He also reported a good store of arms in the castle. Yet the Company's inventory of arms shows '6 bows with arrows, 2 'Musketts', 20 swords, 6 daggers, 20 girdles (body armour), and bullets', hardly sufficient to provide protection, despite a barrel of powder being available. Despite his assurances, both the castle and bawn were unsound and unfinished. His surveys were not always as thorough as they should have been.

Soon after this, Goodwin undertook a survey for Harrington, the Grocers' Farmer, who was looking to become the Drapers' Agent. Goodwin believed the

---

[93] Following Phillips's Survey the woodlands were further reduced, mainly to generate income from the sale of timber or for iron smelting. Reducing the forests was also seen as a means of preventing guerrilla warfare. By 1640, little woodland was left.

settlement should have been more centrally located in the proportion, a view with which Phillips was to concur. Phillips wanted a new one at the foot of Slievegallion, where Tyrone had made his last stand. He believed that it could be protected by Sir Will Windsor with his company of foot at Desertmartin.

Slievegallion This significant landmark on the Drapers' proportion commands fine views over the proportions. It was the location of Tyrone's final stand.

He also believed that security would be improved with compact settlements of British settlers rather than scattered hamlets. Goodwin complained that the bawn was without a gate and that the mortar in its unfinished walls crumbled to the touch. One wall of the castle bulged outwards and the roof of neither castle nor chapel was weatherproof. There were no interior fittings, and he believed that the money expended had been wasted. Russell blamed Birkett, as he 'was a bricklayer not a mason, and the Company admonished him for idleness and drunkeness when his 'business should have byn performed''.[h] The conduit carrying piped water was also collapsing and needed to be relaid. According to Pynnar, none of the land was tenanted, 'as the Agent can make none, neither will they have estates till such time as the land can be improved to the utmost'. Yet Goodwin agreed with Pynnar that the new houses were excellent, as was the mill with its mill-race near the castle.

Following Goodwin's inspection, Harrington did not immediately accept appointment as Agent. Sir Thomas Roper became Farmer and contracted to meet all future building costs. This gave the Drapers some hope of recouping their outlay. In its somewhat fanciful returns made to The Irish Society, the Company reported that the Castle and its chapel were 'nearly finished'; the church near the settlement at Desertmartin with its garrisoned fortress was deemed in good repair. It also reported twelve completed houses, of which eight were occupied by British tenants and three remained uninhabited. There were ten further cottages, with a mill, brewhouse and smithy all complete and working. By the end of 1621, four more houses were reported as completed.

These reports painted a rosier picture than was justified. In 1622, Phillips revealed that all was not well. He recorded only sixteen 'Brittish men present on this Proporćon meanly armed', one of whom was a clergyman, and one hundred and eighty-six natives. Out of a total of sixty townlands, sixteen were occupied by British settlers and forty-four by natives. Although the castle with its bawn was nearly finished, Raven's map recorded:

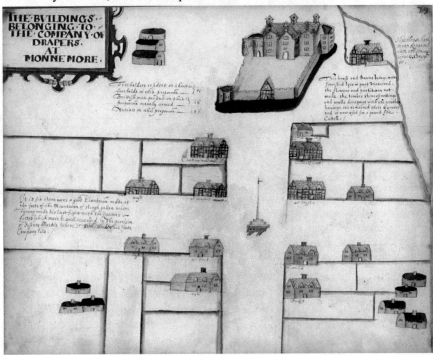

Raven's 1922 drawing of the Drapers' castle and bawn at Moneymore This was on the site of Gibson's 1820 school buildings (now the Moneymore Orange Hall) with the principal buildings of the settlement along what is now the High Street.
Courtesy of the Drapers' Company

It lyes in part uncovered, the flowers (guttering) and partitions not made, the timber thereof rottinge and walls decaying with the weather having soe remained theis 6 yeares and is now used for a pound for Cattell.

He makes clear that even the roof of the castle was shingled rather than slated, and house chimneys were brick rather than stone. In 1623, Richard Parr was paid to fell oak trees for shingles to finish the castle. The use of oak was not ideal, as shingles made from it needed to be relaid after a year because of shrinkage.

Roper never lived on the proportion, and when he failed to pay his rent as Farmer after three years, the Company repossessed its lands. By then, the castle and bawn had deteriorated further. In October 1622, Harrington at last became Agent with Goodwin being retained as Steward of the Manor, empowered to hold Courts Baron. In 1623, the Company's records show that it was involved in substantial expenditure on building works. Having paid out only £50 between 1615 and 1618, £1,750 was expended from 1618 to 1628. Yet the tenants were unsettled by wood-kerne, so that rents could not be raised to help in defraying building costs.

In 1628, when Peter Barker became Farmer, Harrington ceased to be Agent. Barker, who was a drover from County Antrim, acquired a sixty year lease, after paying an entry fine of £500 and agreeing an annual rental of £200. After spending all his resources maintaining Moneymore, he was unable to pay his rent. He faced interminable disputes with other freeholders, particularly Rowley's brother William, who had also applied to become Farmer. Yet he made progress. In 1630, the response to The Irish Society's questionnaire showed that Moneymore was in good repair with its streets paved, as was the road towards Desertmartin. Yet problems with wood-kerne continued. With the church near Desertmartin being a mile outside Moyheelan, a decision was taken not to repair it as the settlement would be left unprotected during services. The chapel in the castle at Moneymore was preferred.

On Barker's death in 1631, Sir John Clotwothy was granted a lease for sixty-one years from 1 November 1631. When the Company was dispossessed by the Court of Star Chamber, Clotworthy claimed the proportion for himself, but, when the Star Chamber verdict was reversed in 1641, Clotworthy's claim was deemed illegal by the House of Commons. Not that it made much difference. Most of Moneymore, except for the bawn and a part of the castle, had been destroyed in the rebellion.

Chapter 19

Fishmongers

The Fishmongers are recognised as the fourth senior of the twelve Great Livery Companies. The original Company, the Stock-fishmongers, received its charter in 1272, although there is evidence of an earlier charter well before this. It amalgamated with the Salt-fishmongers in 1536.

Although the Company lost its monopoly of the fish trade in the 15th Century, its officials can still examine all fish coming into London, and have powers to 'survey wither the same be wholesome for Man's Body, and fit to be sold, seizing that which fails the test'.[a] The Company retained statutory powers relating to the condition of freshwater and sea fisheries, including shellfish. It is 'concerned to improve the condition of rivers and seas, and concerns itself with pollution, conservation, and the setting of standards for fishing'.[b]

The Fishmongers were 'less than enthusiastic' participants in the plantation, and their Court meeting reported: 'it would be very foolish to entermeddle in this busynesse, for it will be exceedingly chargeable'.[c] Yet they raised the money required among their liverymen without too much difficulty. In 1610, most contributors surrendered their interests to the Company after paying the first two levies, leaving the Company to meet all future contributions out of its common purse.[d] When the offer of land in Ulster was first received, the Fishmongers declined it, but on finding other companies accepting, they agreed to take a proportion provided that everyone else did so.

At the drawing of lots on 17 December 1613, the Fishmongers were lucky enough to draw Lot 3, an attractive proportion on the shores of Lough Foyle. It was not only accessible, but contained some of the best land in the County of Londonderry, although there were tracts of mountainous lands with bogs and poor thin soil about twelve miles further inland. Its 24,100 acres were in two blocks, one round Greysteel on Lough Foyle, and the other a narrow tongue from Lough Foyle around Ballykelly as far as Foreglen and Feeny further east. There were four distinct divisions split into forty-eight townlands, with the 'lush' valley at Drumcovit near Banagher to the south. The proportion was named the Manor of Walworth after Sir William Walworth, a distinguished member of the Company, who had been Lord Mayor in 1374 and 1380.

The Company was joined by several minor companies, and, at the time of the conveyance on 24 October 1618, their contributions to the Irish Society had been:

	Contributions to 1611			Contributions 1611-1616			Total to 1616		
	£	s	d	£	s	d	£	s	d
Fishmongers	2,260	0	0	1,130	0	0	3,390	0	0
Leathersellers	950	0	0	500	0	0	1,450	0	0
Plaisterers	40	0	0	20	0	0	60	0	0
Glaziers	32	0	0	16	0	0	48	0	0
Basketmakers	32	0	0	16	0	0	48	0	0
Musicians	20	0	0	10	0	0	30	0	0
Cash payment		(13	4)					(13	4)
	£3,333	6	8	£1,692	0	0	£5,025	6	8

Yet several changes took place. In 1614, the Musicians sold out to the Fishmongers. Although the Leathersellers bought out the Plaisterers, they too sold out in 1617 to the Fishmongers, at two-thirds of the value of what they had paid. This left only the Glaziers and Basketmakers as associates.

On receiving their grant, the Fishmongers employed Alexander Fookes, a fish buyer from Rye, as Agent at 3s. 4d. per day. Despite early questions about his integrity, Fookes acted efficiently. He chose a site for the principal settlement at Ballykelly (derived fron *Baile Uí Cheallaigh* – or Kelly's town) about ten miles from Londonderry. Despite its lack of formal structure, he built a fortified house there, completed in 1616, which became known as Walworth. The house was fifty feet square with sixteen rooms, all enclosed in a bawn one hundred and twenty-five feet square and twelve feet high built of stone and lime, with four robust flankers and an ornamental gateway.

By 1617, the Fishmongers had spent three thousand pounds and were worrying how to achieve an adequate return. Raven, the cartographer, offered an annual rental of 4½d. per acre, but the Company turned this down on the excuse that they did not know what to charge. On 10 February 1617, it granted a lease for sixty years from 25 March 1617 to James Higgins (or Higgons), a merchant from London Bridge close to the Fishmongers' Hall. Higgins paid an entry fine of £400 and agreed a rental of £167 per annum. Apart from occasional visits, he remained an absentee.

With its proximity to Londonderry, the lands attracted British tenants, and by the time of Pynnar's survey in 1619, he reported six British freeholders and twenty-eight leaseholders occupying 3,210 acres. They could muster forty able-bodied men among them. He noted the excellent house surrounded by a strong bawn at Ballykelly. It was now T-shaped with three gable bays facing to the front and on three storeys. This was occupied by Higgins, when in Ireland, and his associate George Downinge. Pynnar noted a second settlement north of the castle surrounding a church. This had no side aisles but there was a two-bay chancel and four-bay nave.

The ruins of Walworth Old Church All that remains of the church used by the Fishmongers' settlement near their former castle and bawn at New Walworth House.

He also reported three timber-framed[94] and four substantial stone-built 'English' houses with dormers and brick chimneys near the castle. There were a further four cottages and several Irish cabins, with more outside the settlement. These numbers do not seem sufficient to accommodate the thirty-four settler families reported, but some may have been elsewhere. Upstream from Ballykelly, Higgins and Downinge erected a large stone mill house with its mill powered by water delivered down a long and deep water course. Higgins also embarked on the major task of enclosing the land with rails, for which Downinge delivered 50,000 lath nails from London.

Phillips's survey in 1622 recorded that there were no freeholders and only twenty-three settler families, although there were 'arms ready for as many more'.[e] He also reported two hundred and forty-five native Irish. In Raven's accompanying maps, seven substantial 'English style' houses are depicted, four of which appear to have been of stone (although it is possible that they were rendered).

There is no report of a great exodus of native Irish, but both Phillips and Raven were biased towards painting a less than glowing account of progress. There had certainly been some freeholders, as the Fishmongers were

---

[94] The timber-framed houses appear to have been harled to make them weatherproof. This makes it difficult to differentiate between timber-framed and stone built houses on the various maps.

'displeased' at them being allocated lands near the castle and bawn, as they had hoped that they would be placed further inland, but 'the prudent settlers wanted the best land at Ballykelly near the safety of the castle and bawn, and not the worst land in the hostile territory so far from the sea'.[f] It is just possible that the Fishmongers' requests for them to move further inland caused some freeholders to leave. Yet, in July 1623, a third survey thought to be by Thomas Croddin, whose name is associated with surveys in Essex and Leicestershire, shows the castle and bawn and many more houses than reported by Raven. It is thus probable that Phillips and Raven understated the numbers.

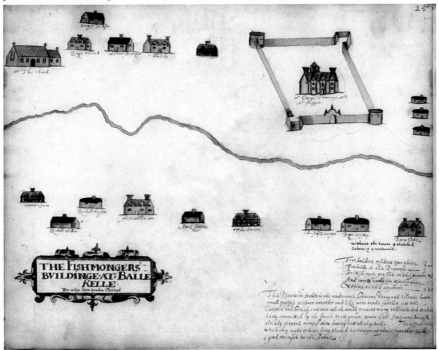

Raven's 1622 drawing of the Fishmongers' castle and bawn at Walworth This is on the site of New Walworth House at Ballykelly. To the left is Walworth Old Church with a range of settlement houses placed randomly on each side of a stream.
Courtesy of the Drapers' Company

The Commissioners principal concern was for security. As so often, Phillips considered Ballykelly to be an unsuitable location for the principal settlement. He described it as standing

in the roade waie between Derry and Colrane but to small purpose without another such like were made further into the Cuntrie and british sent over which would prevent many robberies and stealths daily committed by the Irish, to the great terror of the few poore British already planted many have lost all they had. The 6 freeholders which they ought to have been planted in a conveynient place together withe a good strength to the Cuntrie.[g]

217

More settlers would be needed to protect the small number of British arrivals 'who are daily spoiled'.[h]

Between 1617 and 1631, annual rental income grew from £167 to £215. In 1619, Higgins assigned a third of his interest to Willam Angel and a second third to John Halsey. In 1626, Angel and Halsey sub-let to Christopher Freeman and surrendered their leases. In 1632, Freeman renewed his lease over his two parts and Higgins renewed his remaining one part. Samuel Lewis[i] states that, from 1628, Freeman leased to the Hamiltons and Beresfords, but the Fishmongers' records do not confirm this, and 'Lewis cannot always be relied upon for any factual consistency'.[j] The *Civil Survey* of 1654-6 shows 'the beneficiaries of the wills of Higgins and Freeman … still very much in control'.[k]

By 1630, nearly one hundred British male settlers were in residence, mainly English, but also Scots. The Company made no attempt to evict the native Irish, despite persistent Government threats. When the Lord Deputy issued a warrant for their removal, they complained that without them no settlers would be able to pay his rent, causing great loss to every Company. They preferred to settle the fines imposed. English tenants were totally dependent on the Irish to farm their land, and with Foreglen and Feeny being so remote, the natives were left to farm there almost undisturbed.

Little remains of Ballykelly's original settlement except for three flankers of the original bawn. These are in an excellent state of preservation in the garden of New Walworth House, as are the 'romantic' ruins of the old church including its 17th Century chancel arch.

A flanker of the castle and bawn at the Manor of Walworth situated in the garden of New Walworth House.

Chapter 20

Goldsmiths

The records of the Goldsmiths' Company date back to 1180, but it received its Charter of Incorporation in 1327. It was responsible for 'inspecting, trying, and regulating gold and silver wares throughout the Kingdom, and had powers to punish those who dealt or worked in adulterated precious metals'.[a] It continues to administer the assay offices for hallmarking gold and silver and encourages modern craftsmanship. It is fifth in order of precedence of the twelve Great Livery Companies.

The Goldsmiths' Company was always a reluctant participator in the plantation. With many members failing to pay their contributions, the Court of Assistants rented out property in an effort to defray the cost of the levy and borrowed to pay the remainder. It made no further calls on individuals. In February 1611, the Company agreed to accept an estate in Ireland to offset its contributions to the Irish Society. It was supported by a number of the Minor Companies, who shared in their contributions[95] as follows:

	Contributions to 1611			Contributions 1611-1616			Total to 1616		
	£	s	d	£	s	d	£	s	d
Goldsmiths	2,999	0	0	1,460	0	0	4,459	0	0
Cordwainers	250	0	0	120	0	0	370	0	0
Painter-stainers	44	0	0	22	0	0	66	0	0
Armourers	40	0	0	20	0	0	60	0	0
Cash payment		6	8					6	8
	£3,333	6	8	£1,622	0	0	£4,955	6	8

On 17 December 1613, when the lots at the Guildhall were drawn, the Goldsmiths' Company received Lot 1. This was an area of 11,050 well-located acres of 'lush' but unwooded land on the south bank of the Foyle. It was only one-and-a-half miles across the river from the City of Londonderry and its garrison. The proportion surrounded three sides of the freehold of Captain Manus O'Cahan, which divided it into two parts and made it impossible to

---

[95] The Goldsmiths were able to negotiate a small rebate on the collective requirement to provide £5,000. (See page 116)

defend. To the west were lands allocated to Strabane and to the east were the Grocers' and Skinners' proportions.

After accepting its lands, the Company tried to assert that it was not bound by the Articles of the Plantation, 'but was quickly disabused of this vain opinion'.[b] Agents arriving in Ulster to report on its condition must have been impressed, as a Farmer[96] was soon appointed to take control. In 1615, John Freeman arrived from Essex, having been granted a thirty year lease, but there were already several British settlers on the land before the Goldsmiths' arrival. When The Irish Society called for a progress update, the Goldsmiths reported five English style houses already built and occupied by British, but did not admit that these were in place before its involvement, or that the occupants had sub-let to native Irish. They confirmed that a large part of the proportion was allocated as a freehold [but in fact a lease to Freeman] 'for the benefit of the County of Londonderry'.[c] They confirmed Freeman's plans to build a castle with a bawn and twelve other substantial English-style houses, each costing £30, in a settlement named somewhat unoriginally, New Buildings. Six English families were expected to be settled by Michaelmas.

When Freeman was told to increase the rents charged to established settlers, several of whom were influential, he became unpopular locally. He was soon in financial difficulties, finding that he could not build the twelve houses as required for the sum allocated. He had also received a consignment of poor quality timber from Coleraine and a ship was lost (probably the one also carrying roof frames to the Grocers' proportion). He went to London to renegotiate his contract, and the Goldsmiths agreed to reduce the number of houses required to six. By 1617, six houses of one-and-a-half storeys had been completed, and the parish church at Clondermot on lands belonging to the Dean of Londonderry had been re-roofed and slated, but Freeman had not begun constructing the castle and bawn.

By an indenture dated 10 September 1617, the Company's title was at last handed over. Beresford, with assistance from Goodwin, was designated by The Irish Society to take possession of the land for delivery to Freeman. It was allocated as a single manor and renamed the Manor of Goldsmiths' Hall. This was divided into forty-four townlands of which thirty-six were demesne lands and eight were for allocation to freeholders. On 9 September, Freeman was also granted three of the freeholds, but the Society retained the right to cut timber and to extract minerals in accordance with agreed practice. His obligations were to pay a modest annual rent, to grind corn at the Society's mills and to subdivide his land with fences or ditches. He was also to maintain a store of arms and was not to let land to anyone who would not swear the Oath of Allegiance and Supremacy. Within two years, he was to build a substantial six room manor house, which he was to occupy for seven years.

---

[96] The right to appoint a Farmer was denied to Companies with landlocked or 'dangerous' proportions, but only the Mercers did not do so.

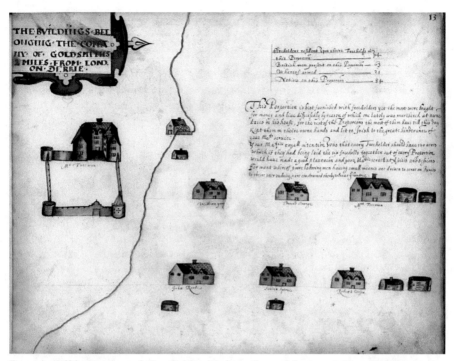

Raven's 1622 drawing of the Goldsmiths' castle and bawn at New Buildings near Clondermot Parish Church but the site is now completely built over.
Courtesy of the Drapers' Company

Although Freeman received a £300 contribution from the Company towards the cost of building the manor, in 1619, Pynnar reported only the bawn as being complete. By then it had three flankers and crenelated walls with cruciform loopholes. Although the manor remained unfinished, its walls filled the remaining corner of the bawn. He also reported six new timber-framed houses, six freeholders and twenty-four leaseholders. Among these thirty families, there were ninety men. Pynnar's report was confirmed in 1620 by the Goldsmiths' return to The Irish Society, which recorded six freeholders and about one hundred men. Phillips's survey of 1622 showed only one additional house, but there was a mill by a little river and the manor was finished. This was 'a two-storey house[97] with two gables and with two projecting wings joined by a wall, so there was an inner court within the bawn'.[d] It was fifty-eight feet by twenty-two feet and contained eighteen rooms. Phillips counted only four resident freeholders, eighty-four men, of whom twenty-one were armed, and eighty-four native Irish, but these may have been those living in the main settlement. Raven's accompanying map showed six stone-built houses in addition to six Irish cabins and a small rectangular cottage all laid out in two neat rows. With

---

[97] Raven's plan of 1622 indicates that there were three storeys in the middle section with attic space in the roof above lit by dormers, but this may be a draftsman's error.

timber having to be shipped from Coleraine, it was found preferable to build in local stone and slate. Yet New Buildings was never a complete settlement; it had no church or community buildings.

By 1622, Freeman had contributed £426 13s. 4d. for building work in addition to the Company's £544 15s. 8d. He was undoubtedly conscientious, but was overwhelmed by costs. The Company had done well to agree terms obliging him to meet a large share of the building costs. Its expenditure up to 1634 was only £693, by when it had generated income of £1,758. Appointing a Farmer from the outset proved beneficial, but poor Freeman must have suffered from having only a thirty-year lease.

Although the Company claimed to have covenanted with lessees to plant only with British tenants, in 1628 the Commissioners found one hundred and four British and one hundred and four native Irish on the proportion. The settlers were by no means secure. This is borne out by the fact that very little of the original settlement survives, and in all probability it was destroyed in the 1641 rebellion.

Chapter 21

Merchant Taylors

The Merchant Taylors' Company vies with the Skinners to be the sixth Livery Company in order of precedence. They have traditionally changed their ranking between six and seven half way through the year of office of each Master. Although the Company received its Charter in 1503, it had existed before that as Taylors and Linen Armourers. Its Patron is St. John the Baptist. Despite ranking at only six or seven among the twelve Great Livery Companies, it was the largest contributor to the plantation of Londonderry.

Although Merchant Taylors' records show that some members refused to contribute to the plantation costs, there was a 'healthy interest' in the project, and collecting money for the initial investment proved relatively painless.[a] Although it was less enthusiastic about taking control of a proportion, unlike any other Company, it paid its second instalment due in 1612 in good time. From 1613, levies were paid from the Company's common stock, but individual members could continue to contribute if they wished, but, if not, they were obliged to surrender their interests to the Company. By the end of that year, all individual interests had been taken over. Given the wealth of its members, the Company was required to raise the colossal sum of £6,186.

At the drawing of lots at the Guildhall on 17 December 1613, the Company acquired Lot 6 with the balance of their required investment being included in the Clothworkers' proportion. The money was allocated as follows:

	Contributions to 1611			Contributions 1611-1616			Total to 1616		
	£	s	d	£	s	d	£	s	d
Merchant Taylors' proportion	3,333	6	8	1,666	13	4	5,000	0	0
Clothworkers' proportion	752	13	4	433	6	8	1,186	0	0
	£4,086	0	0	£2,100	0	0	£6,186	0	0

Lot 6 consisted of 18,700 acres made up of forty-four townlands in the Barony of Coleraine, extending for four miles up the Bann River towards Garvagh. It was bounded by the Aghadowey River adjacent to both the Ironmongers and the freehold of Manus McCowy Ballagh O'Cahan and extended to the

Haberdashers' proportion to the west and to the Clothworkers in the north, where its boundary was the Macosquin River. The proportion was compact and conveniently close to Coleraine, being named the Manor of St John the Baptist. Although two-thirds of its land was bog, moor or rocky high ground, the soil was generally light arable. There had been an earlier Cistercian Abbey dating from 1172 at Macosquin on the highway between Londonderry and Coleraine, and this was chosen as the site for the settlement. It was in 'attractive, gentle, and pleasant country, with the added benefit of the River Macosquin running through it'.[b]

As the largest investor among the Livery Companies, the Merchant Taylors were determined to be the best. 'From the beginning, [they] were excellent landlords, and decided to allocate their freeholds on good land near the castle and bawn for the protection of their tenants.'[c] They were determined that 'no other company shall go before us either in good husbandry as well managing these affairs'.[d]

On 18 July 1617, the Company appointed Valentine Hartopp as their Farmer with a lease for fifty-one years from 1 November 1617, for which he paid an entry fine of £500 with an annual rental of £150 with a requirement to provide arms for defence. In 1618, *The Grace of God* from Dublin brought 'a vast arsenal of muskets, callivers, touch boxes, swords, daggers, belts, and other weapons for delivery to Mr. Hartopp'.[e] Although Hartopp showed great reluctance to remove the native Irish, the Company firmly pointed out that this was part of his agreement with them. He was soon in arrears with rental payments and failed to meet his other obligations. The Company appointed the ubiquitous Goodwin to become Steward of the Manor of St. John the Baptist in an effort to bring him back on track. In 1621, Hartopp resigned to become involved on the Mercers' proportion and assigned his lease to his son-in-law, Ralph Wall. Although Wall paid Hartopp's arrears, he had to be continuously chased by the Company for his rent. After being threatened with eviction on two occasions, in 1628, he was issued with a Bill of Complaints to recover overdue rent of £500. He was jailed in 1629, but, after paying some of what was due, was permitted to return. Yet the quarrel continued and, in 1633, he was again £500 in arrears.

Like the Drapers, the Merchant Taylors met the entire cost of development themselves, spending large sums on Macosquin. Given their unsatisfactory relationship with both Hartopp and Wall, they had little choice. They did better with George Costerdyne, who was sent from London to supervise the building works. On 1 February 1614, he was appointed Agent on an annual salary of £40 and was made responsible for improving security. There were already plans to build 'a bawne with a strong stone house or castle … at Macosquin at a spot most fitted for defence and safest for the inhabitants against any rebellion'. He also wanted a second protective bawn 'near some part of the Mountaine and to have four or five houses about it',[98] but it was never built.[f]

The first survey of both the Merchant Taylors' and Clothworkers' proportions was prepared by Simon Kingsland in 1613. Given the Merchant Taylors' involvement with the Clothworkers, it is clear that they joined forces to map the two estates. The plans for laying out Macosquin date from about 1615 and were probably prepared by Lipsett, who had worked on the Drapers' castle and tendered for work at Londonderry. Spaces were allocated for twelve houses, each with its own garden, and the plan showed a proposed church and castle set into a bawn with four flankers. The castle was drawn as a house with a formal garden with its bawn accessed from the main street. Merchant Taylors' records show that they originally intended to build ten houses with plans for ten more at a later stage. Costerdyne organised a labour force and kept meticulous notes of materials used. Stone was supplied from a local quarry and a limekiln was built. Canning, the Ironmongers' Agent, supplied bricks for the chimney stacks. These were barged from Agivey along the Bann and Macosquin Rivers. Wood for the roofing beams, doors and window frames came from Movanagher. More complex artefacts, including glass and iron casements, were sent from London. Everything smacked of quality. The carpenter, William Parratt, who later worked on Londonderry Cathedral and Dunluce Castle, became Mayor of Coleraine in 1642.

Raven's 1616 map of the Clothworkers' proportion depicts the Merchant Taylor settlement at Macosquin, with its castle, bawn, a church and six houses. By the time of Pynnar's survey in 1619, there were six freeholders and eighteen leaseholders, comprising twenty-nine families, providing forty men. Although, in 1620, the Company advised the Irish Society that the estate was tenanted entirely with British, this cannot have been true. It also claimed that the bawn had been completed by a tenant, although it was still unfinished in 1622. A tenant had reportedly built a tannery, but there is no further mention of one. The 1620 return reported six freeholders, including Costerdyne, and eight stone-built houses. Yet two years later, Phillips found only two resident freeholders, and six houses of stone. By then, he was reporting eighteen leaseholders and thirty-six men, of which twenty-nine were armed, but one hundred and twenty-four native Irish.

In the suspect return to the Irish Society of 1620, the Company reported that the 'castle' had been completed before any lands were let. By this time, expenditure on buildings had been £1,524 18s. 3d. and, from December 1615 to August 1616, Costerdyne spent a further £461 19s. 4d. The 'castle' was a three-storey house, and Lipsett was probably involved in its design. The attic area was lit by windows at both gable ends and in two gabled dormers. The porch was reached by a flight of steps with canted window bays to three storeys on each

---

[98] Phillips agreed with Costerdyne. Raven's map of 1622 recorded: 'It were fit another Plantaćon were made towards the Mountaines upon this proporćon for the safety of the inhabitants therof.'

side. Although it was not designed for security, its ornamental crenelated parapet linked to square 'bartizans' (battlemented turrets) at each end. In 1622, Raven's drawings show that the bawn was still incomplete. Although four walls had been built to surround the castle, space was left at each corner for the four flankers, which had not been begun. The six English-style stone-built houses were on two storeys with the upper floor lit through gables in the slated roofs. Their dimensions were generally thirty-six by eighteen feet, but one was a couple of feet wider. Despite their good workmanship, two were still unoccupied. There were also three simpler houses, all of which were thatched, and a watermill. The parish church had a bellcote above its west door. The nave consisted of four stone-built bays and was eighty feet by thirty-two feet with a substantial timber roof covered in slate. It was on the site of the old abbey church, but was about half its size, and fragments of the mediaeval abbey stonework still survive. Much of the remaining stone was reused in the new settlement. The tithes in both Camus and Macosquin were 'blended', allowing a minister to be appointed in 1617. Costerdyne provided 'a Bible, books, a Communion-cup, a 'Flaggon', a cushion, cloth, and bells to embellish the building, duly invoicing the Company'.[g] Despite this, he seems to have lived outside the settlement at his house at 'Craham'.

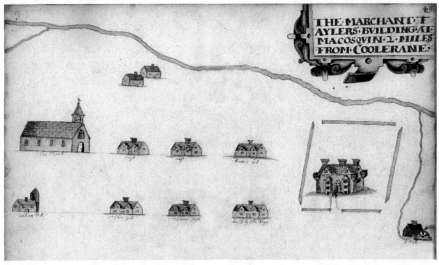

Raven's 1622 drawing of the Merchant Taylors' castle and bawn at Macosquin This shows the unfinished bawn without flankers, but the former abbey church formed the site of the Parish Church of Camus-juxta-Bann.
Courtesy of the Drapers' Company

By 1626, rental income had amounted to £2,160 17s. 3d., but the Company had spent £1,836 18s. 6d. on building works, leaving a surplus of only £323 18s. 9d. on its huge investment. In 1628, settler numbers started to improve. The Commissioners counted twenty-seven British men and one hundred and sixty-nine natives, and the 1630 Muster Roll showed forty-eight British men. The estates were confiscated after the Star Chamber verdict, and everything was left in ruins after the 1641 rebellion and the War of the Three Kingdoms. Yet Wall continued to cause trouble in his continuing efforts to collect rents as Farmer.

Chapter 22

Skinners

The Skinners' Company was incorporated in 1327. It retained 'considerable powers to control the fur trade and could take action against misconduct or to prevent sharp practice'.[a] Furs were of huge importance. They were anciently of very high value and were marks of rank and distinction. The Company shared with the Merchant Taylors the claim to be ranked number six in the order of precedence of the twelve Great Livery Companies.

When the plans for the plantation of Londonderry were first discussed, the Court of Assistants of the Skinners' Company informed the Corporation of the City of London that it would be unable to take part. Despite the prospect of profits, the investment would be very great and the Company would have difficulty raising the money. Its members showed such reluctance that special efforts were needed to extract the money from its 'elusive brethren', and the Company's common stock had to be tapped to raise the funds required.[b] This reluctance continued when it came to accepting land in Ulster. The difficulty of raising money from individual members resulted in several being brought 'into custody where they languished until their assessed shares were paid up'.[c] By 1613 the Skinners and the Clothworkers were the only major Companies still raising funds by individual assessment, and even the Skinners had had to find a quarter of their total contribution by milking the common stock of the Company.[d]

The Company's Court of Assistants decreed that any member failing to pay his contribution would need to surrender his earlier investment for the benefit of those who had paid, if he wished to avoid further demands. Even so, 'unwilling participants had to be coerced by threats of further fines, imprisonment, or other unpleasantnesses'.[e] The Company eventually raised the required £2,903 and needed considerable support from among the Minor Companies. The contribution was shared as follows:

	Contributions to 1611			Contributions 1611-1616			Total to 1616		
	£	s	d	£	s	d	£	s	d
Skinners	1,963	0	0	940	0	0	2,903	0	0
Stationers	520	0	0	280	0	0	800	0	0
White-bakers	480	0	0	240	0	0	720	0	0
Girdlers	370	0	0	200	0	0	570	0	0
Cash payment		6	8					6	8
	£3,333	6	8	£1,660	0	0	£4,993	6	8

When the draw took place on 17 December 1613, the Skinners were unlucky to receive Lot 12, a huge but landlocked proportion of 49,000 acres in the southern and most mountainous part of the County of Londonderry bordering with Tyrone. Its northern boundary abutted the Goldsmiths', Grocers', Fishmongers', Haberdashers', Ironmongers', Vintners', and Drapers' proportions. Given its poor location, it was the largest, containing seventy townlands, but about 24,000 acres were mountain, moor and bog-land. Yet there was fertile land near Dungiven, its only settlement of note. The proportion consisted of a patchwork of isolated parcels of land. An area with Crossalt (later Brackfield) at its centre was wedged between native freeholds. The largest division surrounded Dungiven and its castle, but four smaller areas were cut off from the rest. When the proportion was conveyed to the Company on 22 March 1618, it was named the Manor of Pellipar (Pelliparius was the mediaeval Latin name for a dresser of hides).

With the whole area having previously been an O'Cahan stronghold, the natives were belligerent and it was horribly exposed. After O'Cahan's submission in 1602, he had allied with the British against Tyrone, allowing them to garrison one hundred and fifty troops under Captain (later Sir) Edward Doddington at Dungiven Castle, one of a network of forts designed to combat the O'Neills, and it provided a measure of control in the Sperrins. Doddington had first come to prominence as a Captain of Foot in Munster and had been Constable of Killybegs Castle in Donegal before moving to Dungiven. The Castle was securely positioned, with the River Roe to its south and west and high ground further west providing 'considerable strength'.[f] After O'Cahan had been arrested by Phillips, the whole area became more settled. Doddington's garrison could be reduced to fourteen men and he was granted the lands surrounding the Castle. He spent £300 of his own money and received a grant of £200 from the Crown to refurbish the garrison's old tower house. He built a house and outbuildings for himself, even creating a formal garden. He also re-roofed the chancel of the 12th Century Augustinian priory, although the nave remained open to the elements.

The ruins of the priory and its churchyard, Dungiven Sir Edward Doddington converted the old priory and the remains of O'Cahan's castle into a garrison fort, which he adapted to become the Skinners' initial castle and bawn.

Doddington must have been disappointed in 1610 to have his entire estate allocated to The Irish Society. Yet it was obliged to buy him out, and he was permitted to remain at Dungiven. He quickly gained influence with the Skinners, not least because his wife, Anne, was Beresford's sister. They concluded that the retention of a servitor in such dangerous territory would be prudent and he was appointed as their Farmer. In May 1616, he was granted a lease over the proportion for fifty-eight and a half years at an annual rental of £112. By July, he was already actively involved in designing and adapting the old tower house to conform to plantation standards and was probably assisted by Peter Benson. He established a cobbled bawn, seventy-six feet by forty-six feet, within the old Priory's structure. He re-roofed the nave of the Priory church with oak beams and slate.[99] Thus the original Priory, having been converted into an O'Cahan stronghold, was adapted into a castle and bawn for the Skinners, with its earlier square tower house becoming a flanker.

---

[99] The Priory Church was used for Protestant services until the 18th Century.

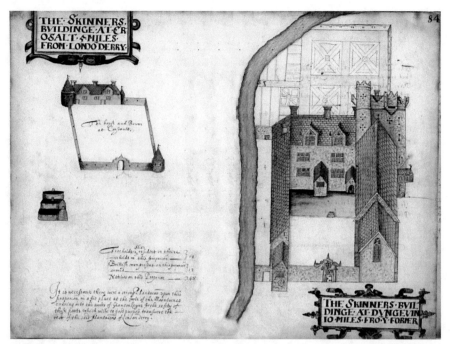

Raven's 1622 drawing of the Skinners' castle joined to the priory at Dungiven This was converted by Skeffington from the original O'Cahan tower house to protect the settlement at Dungiven. The Crossalt castle and bawn is shown to the left.
Courtesy of the Drapers' Company

Doddington must have had his hands full; he was also directing work on the fortifications at Londonderry being built by Benson, was a burgess of Limavady and he fulfilled aldermanic duties at Coleraine. He was also associated with the Ironmongers for a short period to supervise Benson, who was building Agivey castle on their behalf. He leased land from the Archbishop of Armagh 'to replant and edify the 'decayed cyttie'.[g] The tomb commemorating his first wife in Coleraine Parish Church records that he was the first person to build there in 'the English style'.

Aerial view of the ruins of Crossalt (later Brackfield) bawn All that remains of the Skinners' second castle and bawn.
Photo by Abarta Audioguides

Given their lack of security, the Skinners were required to build a second castle and bawn at Crossalt only five miles from Londonderry. This was also designed by Doddington and the bawn soon had walls fourteen feet high and a 'modest house of one-and-a-half storeys with chimneys'. Sadly Doddington died in 1618, but he had made a considerable contribution. Raven's map of 1622 shows Crossalt with 'two circular flankers with conical roofs, a gate with a gable above it, [and] a small turret beside the house'.[h][100] Raven recorded only three 'poor houses of the Irish type' at Crossalt, but Phillips mentioned two villages with twelve houses each, and it is not at all clear why Raven omitted them. He also omitted the twelve houses at Dungiven, but they may not have been in the 'English' style in such a remote location.

By 1619, the two castles with their bawns were complete, and Pynnar noted seven freeholders, eight leaseholders, twenty-seven families and eighty men. In 1622, Phillips's count showed twelve British men being armed. He claimed that there was only one British freeholder resident, but there were three hundred and eighty-four Irish and one native freeholder. He believed that it was

---

[100] A substantial part of the ruined bawn still exists, including a gable of the house, parts of both flankers and the entrance gate.

232

necessarie there were a strong Plantaćon upon this proporćon in a fit place at the foote of the Mountains entering into the woods of Glenconkeyne for the safety of those parts.[i]

This population imbalance failed to improve. In 1628, the Commissioners recorded twenty-three British and three hundred and sixty-one Irish, which was probably an understatement.

Dungiven continued to be occupied by Doddington's widow. She later married Sir Francis Cooke and, on 1 May 1627, was granted a forty-seven-and-a-half year lease over the Castle, which was managed on her behalf by Beresford and his son-in-law, George Carey, Recorder of Londonderry (he died in 1640). She lost three-quarters of her estate after the Livery Company's forfeiture in 1637, when she was accused of failing to bring any British settlers onto the Skinners' lands, and she seems to have been 'a great fosterer of Papists'.[j]

The 1641 rebellion destroyed the settlement completely. Although the castle fell to Manus O'Cahan, it was still standing in 1656, by when Lady Cooke had regained possession.

Chapter 23

Haberdashers

The Haberdashers are eighth in seniority among the twelve Great Livery Companies, having received their charter in 1448. Their trade selling ribbons, beads, purses, gloves, pins, caps and toys had originally been supervised by the Mercers' Company. In 1502 it was joined by the hatmakers' fraternity, although the two trades remained segregated.

The Haberdashers were 'less than enthusiastic about accepting land in Ulster'.[a] By the spring of 1611, the Company had raised only £1,124 towards the cost of the first three levies, and chose to forego what had already been contributed and to pull out of the venture if anyone would take over its responsibility. Two members of the Company, William Freeman and Adrian Moore, stepped forward and, in April 1611, the Haberdashers agreed to relinquish their interest to them, if they would meet all future obligations including the next levy of £400, which was already due. This resulted in the Company being only loosely connected with the plantation. By the time of the drawing of lots, it had nominally contributed £3,124, but £2,000 of this had been provided by Freeman and Moore. Yet the proportion was shared with a group of associated Minor Companies, allocated as follows:

	Contributions to 1611			Contributions 1611-1616			Total to 1616		
	£	s	d	£	s	d	£	s	d
Haberdashers	3,124	0	0	1,600	0	0	4,724	0	0
Wax-chandlers	80	0	0	40	0	0	120	0	0
Turners	68	0	0	34	0	0	102	0	0
Founders	60	0	0	30	0	0	90	0	0
Cash payment	1	6	8				1	6	8
	£3,333	6	8	£1,704	0	0	£5,037	6	8

On 17 December 1613, at the Guildhall, the Haberdashers drew Lot 4, an area of 23,100 acres in Loughinsholin, south west of Coleraine. The proportion was named the 'Manor of Freemore' after its principal investors. It lay in three distinct divisions separated by church lands and various O'Cahan and O'Mullan freeholds, making its southern parts particularly vulnerable, although there were Skinners' lands on its southern boundary. The northern division contained an old Norman fort on a steep-sided site at Ballycastle above a bend in the River Roe; the roofless church at Aghanloo was nearby. Although Ballycastle was a defensible location, it was not well positioned to protect the proportion as a

whole. The estate's western boundary was the River Roe, with the Clothworkers to the north east, and the Merchant Taylors (with a small division of the Ironmongers) to the east. It was bleak and generally unwooded, but contained 'good rich farmland' sheltered by massive rocky hills terminating at Binevenagh. As this was the best land in County Londonderry, it attracted large numbers of settlers.

On 15 April 1617, the proportion was duly conveyed in the name of the Haberdashers' Company. This caused legal problems for the future. Moore was a City of London Alderman, and he leased several properties in Coleraine as part of a further speculation, but the two 'adventurers' seem to have become stretched financially. In 1614, Beresford joined in with them, and became their Agent. When William Towerson and William Stone were also taken into the partnership, the Haberdashers were not advised. On Moore's death, his interests were taken over by his son, another Adrian, who seems to have suffered from bouts of insanity, and the Haberdashers seem to have acted as his trustee. Although he sold his one-third interest to Sir John Culpeper, when the Haberdashers received wind of the transaction, they were doubtful whether Culpeper could claim title to his share. When Towerson also died, his stake was transferred to Beresford, who thereby claimed a one-sixth interest. On Freeman's death, his brother Ralph inherited his one-third share, while Stone's one-sixth interest went to his son, John. Their combined claims completely ignored the entitlement of the associated Minor Companies, resulting in disputes over ownership. In 1631, proceedings were taken against the Haberdashers' Company in the Court of Chancery. After further litigation in 1632, the Haberdashers conveyed a one-sixteenth interest to the associated Companies. In the final analysis, Ralph Freeman received one-third, Beresford one-sixth and John Stone one-sixth. The remaining third, less the part allocated to the Associated Companies, was held by the Haberdashers in trust for Adrian Moore. The Associated Companies now kept a much closer watch on everything, and were careful to claim any dividends they were due. These were received by the Haberdashers, for reallocation in the proportions agreed.

When Beresford became involved in 1614, he took over the practical management of the estate. He had to resist demands from Freeman and Moore to save money by building 'small and inferior' houses and proposing earthen bawns rather than a castle, as he knew they would be unacceptable to the Crown.[b] To delegate the management of the estate, and no doubt to gain entry fines to defray some of his outlay, Beresford quickly appointed twelve freeholders. In 1615, he also arranged contracts for each leaseholder to build a good house with a chimney and a loft to hold arms for three men; to keep a fit horse; to enclose the land in stages; to support the Company's mill; to serve at the Court Leet and Court Baron; to remove the natives when their permission to remain expired; and to plant their lands with British tenants.

He undertook to provide the natives with long leases in adjacent townlands, but, during the period that their grant was delayed, 'the tenants lacked security of tenure'.[c] On 6 August 1616, the King stepped in to persuade the partners to appoint a Farmer, recommending Sir Robert McClelland,[101] who was Gentleman of the Bedchamber to both James I and Charles I, and had been an undertaker in Donegal since 1610. His family were hereditary sheriffs of Galloway, and he could attract his Galloway kinsmen to join him. The partners granted him a fifty-one year lease from 1 May 1617. The terms required him to pay £1,000 by Christmas Day 1616, being three years' rent in advance, and thereafter at £350. 10s. 0d. per annum. He also became the Clothworkers' Farmer. In 1619, Pynnar recorded that there were only six freeholders, but, by then, there were twenty-one leaseholder families, providing eighty able-bodied men. By 1622, there were one hundred armed settlers and one hundred and twenty-five native Irish. This was a better balance than elsewhere, and, by 1630, there were one hundred and twenty-seven British settlers, the highest number on any proportion.

McClelland chose the 'hauntingly lovely'[d] location at Ballycastle in its elevated position overlooking the Roe River to build a castle and bawn, which became his residence. The castle of Freemore, completed by 1622, was symmetrical with two storeys over a basement. Its roof was slated and the upper floor was lit by windows in gables 'set behind crenelated canted bays'.[e] It was surrounded by a square bawn with a flanker at each corner and an entrance gate surmounted by a Dutch gable. The flankers were not roofed, but the castle was strongly built and well supplied with arms. There were three nearby cottages with gables and two Irish cabins, all of which appear to have been thatched. By 1623, the partnership had expended £1,124 on the castle and a water mill, including survey fees and Beresford's charges. The church was in need of restoration, but was eventually re-roofed by McClelland.

When Phillips surveyed the estate in 1622, his principal concern yet again was security. Despite plenty of able-bodied settlers, he reported that they had

> susteyned greate losses by the wood kerne and theeves soe it is very requisite for theire better safety another Plantaċon were made further towards the Mountaines.

He proposed Artikelly, a mile from the mountains, despite its 'unimpressive street' of Irish cabins and a few gabled cottages. With five freeholders living there, it housed one hundred armed British settlers and one hundred and twenty-five native Irish. For once, his advice was taken, and a castle and bawn were built. When besieged in 1641, many settlers 'sought the protection of its stout

---

[101] McClelland was made a baronet by Charles I and, in 1633, became Lord Kirkcudbright. He was well connected. After the death of his first wife, Agnes Campbell of Loudoun, he married Montgomery's daughter, Mary, who came with rich holdings in County Down. On her death in 1636, he married Rowley's widow, Mary Gage, who had previously been married to Chichester's nephew, Sir George Trevelyan. Mary Gage was Beresford's mother-in-law. All this helped to consolidate McClelland's fortune.

walls'.[f] The defenders held on grimly, despite being half-naked and starving, and suffering many casualties.

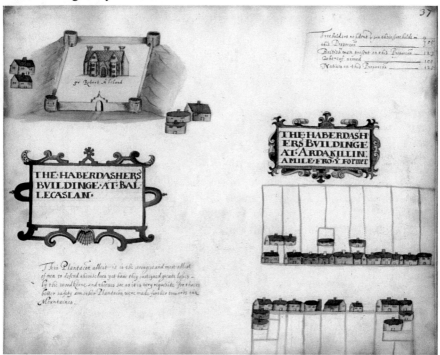

Raven's 1622 drawing of the Haberdashers' castle and bawn at Ballycastle The castle of Freemore was built by the partnership of Freeman and Moore with Beresford supervising the building work, but it was converted by McClelland to become his home.
Courtesy of the Drapers' Company

When the church at Ballycastle was damaged in the 1641 rebellion, it fell into decay. Yet McClelland continued to live at the castle between extensive visits to England and Scotland. After spending enormous sums raising forces in Scotland, he was often unable to pay his rents as Farmer. In 1630, he negotiated a reduction to £200 per annum, in recompense for having provided his own troops. On his death in 1639, his estates were heavily encumbered. Ballycastle passed to his son-in-law, Sir Robert Maxwell of Orchardtoun, but eventually fell to the Irish in 1650.

Chapter 24

Salters

The Salters' Company received its first licence to operate as a Livery Company in 1394, but had been in existence for several centuries before that. The licence was renewed in 1467 and 1510 and a Charter of Incorporation was granted in 1559, but its Royal Charter was only granted by James I in 1607. The Company was involved in providing salt and other chemicals used in the preservation of food, particularly fish. It is ninth in order of precedence among the twelve Great Livery Companies.

The Salters' Company was clearly unenthusiastic about investing in the Londonderry plantation, as the Court of Aldermen of the City of London was obliged to commit the wardens of the Salters', Brewers' and Cooks' Company 'for failure to deliver the money due'. Yet they eventually met their obligations in full and, by February 1611, were able to confirm that they would accept lands in Ulster. They were associated with five Minor Companies and contributions were as follows:

	Contributions to 1611			Contributions 1611-1616			Total to 1616		
	£	s	d	£	s	d	£	s	d
Salters	1,954	0	0	960	0	0	2,914	0	0
Dyers	580	0	0	320	0	0	900	0	0
Sadlers	390	0	0	200	0	0	590	0	0
Cutlers	225	0	0	120	0	0	345	0	0
Joiners	164	0	0	82	0	0	246	0	0
Woolmen	20	0	0	10	0	0	30	0	0
Cash payment		6	8					6	8
	£3,333	6	8	£1,692	0	0	£5,025	6	8

At the meeting held at the Guildhall on 17 December 1613, the Salters drew Lot 10, consisting of an area of 23,250 well-wooded acres of Loughinsholin in the southern part of the County of Londonderry. The estate was in two separate divisions. The larger part was bounded to the east by Lough Neagh and lands belonging to Phillips at Toome. To the south it bordered with County Tyrone, a small part of the Drapers' and some church lands. To the west it again linked up with Drapers and the church lands of Desertmartin, and to the north it joined with the Vintners. The smaller division on the west shore of Lough Beg, was sandwiched between Phillips's and Vintners' lands. In all it amounted to fifty-five townlands. Once the woods were cleared, the land was suitable both for growing crops and for pasture.

The Company selected Baptist Jones as its Chief Agent to be assisted by William Smith. Jones, who was the son of the Archbishop of Dublin, arrived from Chester in 1614 accompanied by twenty English craftsmen. He considered Smith simple and ignorant. Although Smith proposed manufacturing soap from wood ash and making Spanish oil (probably an essential oil), neither of these plans came to fruition. With the estate containing more woods and less farmland than other proportions, low rents were to be expected, but Jones took advantage of the ample supplies of timber by manufacturing pipe and barrel staves, in an effort to finance the Company's ambitious building programme. By 1615, The Irish Society required him to testify that the timber being cut was for house building on the proportion. The first structures soon appeared when Thomas Starkey, a carpenter, built three timber-framed houses for £60. Other buildings were erected by the Redferne and Starkey families, who also worked for the Drapers at Moneymore. The Company appointed Hugh Sayer as Farmer, but he did not last long, and Jones contracted with Joyes (Josias) Everard, a Dutch mason, to build the walls of two castles and their bawns, providing him with tools. Everard had previously supervised the building of fortifications under Bodley and, in about 1604, had worked on Fort Mountjoy. The locations chosen for the two castles were Magherafelt towards the west and a new site named Salterstown on the shores of Lough Neagh. Everard, John and Ellis Redferne all occupied houses built at Magherafelt.

In about 1616, as quickly as it had started, building work at Magherafelt stopped. Timber framework of houses was left incomplete and the castle had only one storey. It is not clear why this happened, but William Finch and his partners had replaced Sayer as Farmer at an annual rental of £160. From now on all attention was focused on Salterstown. On 10 February 1618, the proportion was named the Manor of Sal and was at last conveyed to the Company on 12 February 1619.

By 1622, Phillips's survey recorded one freeholder[102], four leaseholders and sixteen 'reputed leaseholders' (presumably without formal lease agreements). They could muster twenty-seven able-bodied men compared to one hundred and twenty-eight native Irish. The settlers must have been spread across the two locations. Raven's plan of 1622 shows Magherafelt with its unfinished castle and bawn and eight houses (two of which remained unoccupied) and two unfinished timber frames. The houses were all built of timber on one-and-a-half storeys with shingle roofs, dormer windows and brick chimneys. A timber-

---

[102] The Freeholder was Sir William Windsor, who lived in a modest stone built house outside the two settlements. He had commanded a Company of Foot at Coleraine and later took charge of the garrison at Desertmartin. He was one of several 'worthies', who, in 1621, formed into the 'Mayor, Constable, and Society of Merchants of the City of Londonderry'.

framed watermill was nearby. The unfinished castle and bawn were built of stone and lime. Phillips noted:

> Although begun by the Company of Salters and builded to the first story, hath soe remained theis 6 yeares, the timber rottinge and decayinge, being now used for a pound for Cattell.[a]

It was never completed.

Salterstown castle near the shore of Lough Neagh The remains of the castle and bawn, now incorporated into farm buildings, provide a robust but haunted sensation.

By 1622, Salterstown was altogether larger than Magherafelt. The stone and lime bawn was already completed and had two circular flankers with conical roofs in diagonal corners. The 'castle', which was occupied by Finch, was in a third corner and was on one-and-a-half storeys with its attic lit by dormers and a window in the gable end. Massive stone ruins can still be seen, but these may be of a later building, as, in 1622, Phillips considered the castle 'poor'. At that time there were ten large timber-framed houses with shingle roofs and four poor thatched cottages at Salterstown, all completed, and a timber frame erected for a further large house.

Both in Magherafelt and Salterstown, houses were positioned in long wide streets leading from the castle, each with their own plot of ground. There was little building work elsewhere, except the roofless church of Ballyscullion on an island in Lough Beg and a roofless structure at Ballytemple in the south east. With the lands being so remote, Phillips called for an additional castle and bawn at Ballymoghan to protect Killetra between Magherafelt and Moneymore and

240

recommended building highways through the woods to improve access to Lough Neagh.

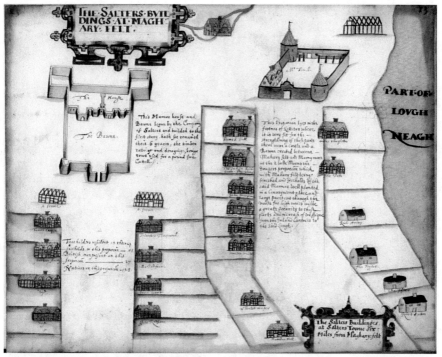

Raven's 1622 drawing of the Salters' castles and bawns at Magherafelt and Salterstown
To the left is the unfinished castle at Magherafelt. Very little of the settlement at Salterstown near Loch Neagh has survived, but the stark ruins of the castle and bawn can still be seen.
Courtesy of the Drapers' Company

In about 1622, Jones was replaced by a new Agent, whose name has not been recorded. On 1 May 1627, Ralph Whistler signed a fifty-one year lease at £100 per annum and became Farmer, after paying an entry fine of £400. He seems to have manufactured pipe staves in contravention of the Articles of the Plantation. Yet his family[103] remained at Salterstown until the mid 18th Century. Despite significant sales of timber, the Salters's income from 1613 to 1634 totalled only £2,940, but they expended £2,600 on building works.

In the rebellion of 1641, both settlements were burned and plundered, but it was Magherafelt, perhaps surprisingly, that recovered. Salterstown was almost completely abandoned, although the remains of its castle and bawn can still be seen.

---

[103] They were the ancestors of James McNeill Whistler, the American artist.

Chapter 25

Ironmongers

The Ironmongers' Company received its Royal Charter in 1463, but had been in existence well before that, having previously been referred to as Ferroners. It was responsible for supervising the manufacture of and trade in iron artefacts. It is tenth in the order of precedence of the twelve Great Livery Companies. As its crest it has 'two scaly lizards erect'. [104]

The arms of the Ironmongers' Company From the stained glass at Londonderry Guildhall

When efforts to establish the plantation in Londonderry were begun, the Ironmongers' Company claimed that it did not have the means to participate, and it was, by quite a long way, the least wealthy of the twelve Great Companies.

---

[104] The Company considers these to be salamanders, an animal thought to have been born in fire (like iron), but a lizard was the closest heraldic equivalent.

When the Corporation of London insisted, a list of contributors was drawn up, but about half the members remained conveniently out of town or were reluctant to pay. When pressure was applied, individual liverymen, widows and yeomen were assessed for payment, but the Company had to augment their contributions by borrowing. Although the first levy was paid, the second proved more difficult, and the third had to be met out of the Company's common stock. From the outset, it considered itself as the investor, but no repayment was made to individual contributors. By February 1611, it was able to confirm that, with support from its associated Minor Companies, it would accept land in Ulster. With its six associates, contributions were made as follows:

	Contributions to 1611			Contributions 1611-1616			Total to 1616		
	£	s	d	£	s	d	£	s	d
Ironmongers	1,514	0	0	716	0	0	2,230	0	0
Brewers	500	0	0	200	0	0	700	0	0
Scriveners	370	0	0	200	0	0	570	0	0
Coopers	280	0	0	140	0	0	420	0	0
Pewterers	240	0	0	120	0	0	360	0	0
Barber Surgeons	230	0	0	120	0	0	350	0	0
Carpenters	200	0	0	100	0	0	300	0	0
Cash receipt		(13	4)					(13	4)
	£3,333	6	8	£1,596	0	0	£4,929	6	8

On grounds of poverty, the Ironmongers seem to have negotiated a discount on their later contributions, but were obliged to take over the very small interests of the Bowyers and Fletchers, who were associated with the Clothworkers and had been excused further investment after the first levy.

On 17 December 1613, the Ironmongers drew Lot 7, an area of 19,450 acres, upstream from Coleraine on the west bank of the Lower Bann. The proportion was fragmented into several areas, separated by church lands and native freeholds. One parcel at Killure and Ballywilliam was entirely surrounded by Merchant Taylors' lands. Although a land swap was mooted, this came to nothing. Another large area was surrounded by native Irish freeholds, making it completely indefensible. As Curl points out, 'It was a dotty arrangement.'[a] The lands was divided into about fifty-two townlands, all heavily populated with native Irish. There were two larger divisions, a long strip, which included Agivey, stretching from the west bank of the Bann, and a rectangular area further west, bounded by the Mercers to the south, the Skinners to the west and church lands to the north and east. Most of the area was traditionally hostile to the English, leaving it dangerously exposed. It was also bisected by three large rivers, the Agivey, Aghadowey and Macosquin all of which flowed into the Bann. This made communication across the proportion difficult.

Canning family tree

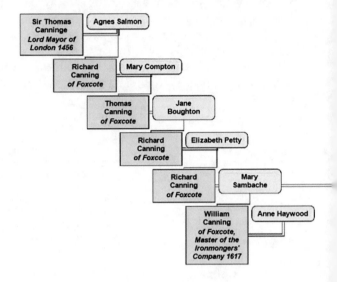

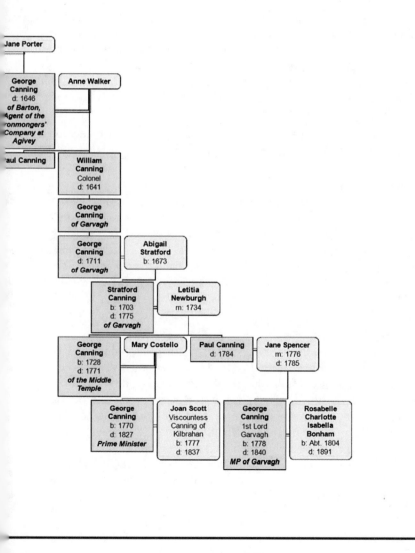

The Company's particularly good early records provide a detailed insight into progress, and these are supported by the letters and other documents of George Canning, soon to become Agent, which were collected together in the 17th Century by Richard Hunter, the Ironmongers' Clerk. These provide a wealth of information on the proportion's development. Before Canning's arrival, Sir Edward Doddington, servitor at Dungiven and the Skinners' initial Farmer, took temporary charge. With its fragmented lay out, consideration was given to dividing up the proportion among each of the associated Companies, but this was quickly dismissed, as the provision of security in each area would have been very difficult. With the Ironmongers being left to manage the whole estate, it was renamed the Manor of Lizard. It was uncharted territory, and Simon Kingsland was commissioned to provide a map, which he completed quickly, but fairly inaccurately.

The Company was lucky in its choice of George Canning as Agent. His brother William was a member of its Court and was to become Master in 1617. The brothers were great-great-grandsons of Sir Thomas Canninge, who had been Lord Mayor of London in 1456. The Lord Mayor had acquired Foxcote in Warwickshire, and George was brought up there in some style. As the sixth son of his family, he was looking for an opportunity to establish himself and applied to become Agent at a salary of £100 per annum. He was

> a country gentleman of the type most needed to make the Plantation a success. He was consciencious, persevering, and capable, with a real interest in the little colony of which he was the centre. He was a reasonable landlord and a scrupulous tenant.[b]

In reality, he was a rarity among Agents, compared to the likes of Hartopp, Baptist Jones and Roper. Such men 'seem to have been more interested in making a quick profit than in securing the safety of the Plantation'.[c] On arrival in Ireland in 1614, Canning proved able and energetic. He received very precise instructions with regard to 'fencing of lands, establishing boundaries, letting land, collecting rents, and keeping accounts'.[d] He arrived from Warwickshire with several bricklayers and carpenters, who were to form a nucleus of building workers on the settlement. The first job was to provide shelter, and one of them, Tristram Robbins, repaired several Irish cabins.

To achieve a secure foothold for a settlement, a castle and bawn were needed, and Canning quickly identified a suitable site at Agivey, opposite the lands of an ancient church at Mullaghmore. It was surrounded by pasture and woodland and was on the side of the Aghadowey River flowing into the Bann about three miles away. This enabled barges of two or three tons to deliver materials. Yet building materials were difficult to source. Lieutenant Thomas Perkins from Lifford in Donegal was appointed to search for natural materials available locally. It was soon apparent that there was a shortage of building stone, but he reported favourably on the quality of the land. He recommended using local clay for bricks and suggested surrounding door and window openings with oak rather than stone. Yet the prices he offered proved too high, and he was dismissed. Canning reported enthusiastically on

> the goodness of the soil, the levelness of the land about it, and the portableness of the rivers which will help much for transportation of material in time of building and yield great relief to the castle in time of trouble or rebellion.[e]

Agivey churchyard at Mullaghmore The church shown on the early maps of the Ironmongers' proportion was destroyed during the rebellion of 1641, but the churchyard retains many more recent gravestones.

'The Company wanted buildings that would stand it in good credit,'[f] but Canning tried to balance quality with economy. He stressed that their building works would

> be performed with as little expense of money (the remoteness of the materials considered) as any of the twelve proportions and as well to the content of those that shall have view of the plantation.[g]

He used the small amounts of stone available but it proved too soft for making quoins for the corners of buildings. Although there was better stone on the Fishmongers' proportion, transportation costs proved too high. He collected slate and timber, but little of the timber was suitable for building and none could be used to manufacture shingles. Local bricks and lime also proved to be of poor quality, and, in the absence of reliable local suppliers, he turned to Coleraine, from where lime could be delivered. Having signed a contract for timber, slate, limestone and lath, they could not be delivered because of 'the extremity of the weather … the waters so extreme with the abundance of snow that it was impossible to pass anything on the bar [at Coleraine]'.[h] Although iron (including nails) could be delivered for £1 from London to Coleraine, it cost a further five shillings to bring it by river to Athgeave, as it needed to be unloaded for transportation past the Salmon Leap, and another five shillings to move it by horse and cart the short distance from the river to the settlement.

At last progress was made. Slate was delivered from New Buildings on the Goldsmiths' proportion. With clay available locally, a brick works was planned for the manufacture of bricks and tiles, but initially they had to be sent from London. With the Mercers having plenty of wood on offer at Movanagher further up the Bann, Canning decided to build in 'half timber', despite the transportation difficulties. His carpenters from Warwickshire were soon at work on framework for houses. They built a stable for horses, a sawpit with a roof over it and completed the brick kiln. Canning was urged to bring over artisans from London to support the building work with the hope that they could be encouraged to stay. Yet, without consulting the Company, he employed two carpenters in Coleraine, seeking out those, who had experience of other plantation building work. He offered them accommodation on thirty-one year leases, conditional on them accepting only British under-tenants and expelling the local Irish. To build the walls, a plate (a horizontal timber supporting the structure) was placed on a stone plinth. Walls were constructed using five or six inch timbers with a five inch gap between each. This was then 'nogged' with cleft oak driven between the uprights and plastered, making the walls extremely strong. Houses were generally thirty-two by sixteen feet on one-and-a-half storeys. Each one required 'above 26 tones of squared tymber besides boards' and was either slated or shingled.[i] Wattles or noggings attached to exterior walls supported a wet type of stucco, sometimes roughcast and mostly made of clay. Lime plaster was mixed with hair to render laths on the interior. Chimney stacks were built of brick and often contained a bread oven. Casement windows were hung on iron hinges secured with bolts. In 1615, the newly completed roofs were blown off in a storm. Canning admitted ruefully that low lying Irish dwellings covered with turf and straw and bound with ropes remained unscathed.

During 1615, Canning granted fifteen leases over townlands on thirty-one year terms to British settlers. Within a year of their arrival, they were expected to build two houses and to assist in church repairs. He gave strict instructions on how to build 'including houses of brick, stone or timber after the English manner enclos[ing] a garden and orchard'.[j] Boundaries were to be marked and, within three years, farmland was to be hedged. Farming was to be in the English style, growing crops in permanent enclosures. Creaghting (nomadic farming of roaming cattle) was prohibited. Any native Irish on the lands were to be evicted after a suitable period of notice. By December 1615, Canning had arranged leases with English and Scots committed to building a total of twenty houses. He was nervous that they might not honour their terms and, in May 1616, reported a few having begun work, but 'others have done little yet and one or two I fear will give me the slip'.[k]

Canning recognised the danger of evicting the Irish and wanted settlements to have at least six houses. Yet, when letting on the Company's behalf, his constant need for income forced him into six-monthly lease arrangements with locals. He urged the Company to call on the Government to allow those who attended church and took the Oath of Supremacy to stay. Without them he realised that there would be economic collapse and a huge loss of income. Yet the Company responded that this could not be achieved, and would only result in them being fined.

Canning was always cavalier over security. On the surface, he seemed to be making good progress in removing the native Irish. From 1614 to 1616, lettings of townlands to British settlers increased from thirteen to thirty-three, while townlands let to Irish tenants decreased from thirty-seven to nineteen. Yet one hundred and nineteen out of one hundred and twenty-seven under-tenants were Irish, despite the embargo on British tenants sub-letting to them. They often paid rack-renting terms, making already hostile natives ever more impoverished and seething with anger. The Company seems to have been oblivious and instructed Canning to allocate less good land to them. This was short-sighted and would lead to disaster in 1641.

One of the big issues for Canning was to decide the form of the castle and bawn. The Ironmongers' Committee asked William Brock to make proposals, and he prepared a model, although this has not survived. Brock travelled to Ireland, and provided a plan for a castle with strong walls accessed by a drawbridge over a surrounding ditch. This would have avoided the need for a bawn. His offer to build it for £415 was turned down, and he received a rather measly four pounds for his trouble. With timber being unsuitable for the castle walls, Canning decided to use stone on the lower levels with brick above. By the end of 1615, he had stockpiled enough materials, but needed good bricklayers. He wanted to hire Benson, who was still working on the castle and bawn at Movanagher and had worked on the walls of Londonderry. He was a respected employer with a reputation for paying workmen promptly to assure loyal service. This was not the norm elsewhere.

Although Agivey was an ideal place for delivery of materials, the subsoil was boggy and the castle foundations needed to be piled. They took eight months to dig and the piling operation lasted forty-two days. By the end of 1616, they had completed a castle of fifty by thirty feet on two and a half storeys with a slate roof. Its walls were four feet thick and thirty-one feet high, with a circular flanker topped by a weather vane at each corner. Brick chimneys were placed in the gable ends and there were two further gables, one-and-a-half storeys high, to the front. To save money, there were no interior fittings not even stairs.

Canning was very satisfied with the castle. He claimed it was the best house built on any of the plantations, although others had been costlier. The brickmaker was now instructed to produce 300,000 bricks for the bawn walls. In 1617, with his standing as Agent having become well-established, he was permitted to become Farmer and negotiated a lucrative forty-one year tenancy over the Manor of Lizard from 1 November 1617, payable at £150 per annum from 1 November 1619. His lease included the castle, five houses and nine townlands. He was soon building bridges, erecting a mill, repairing, furnishing and glazing the church, and constructing its bellcote with four bells. Being at last properly settled, he arranged 'to have my wife and family out of Warwickshire, for me thinks it is uncomfortable living as I do'.[1]

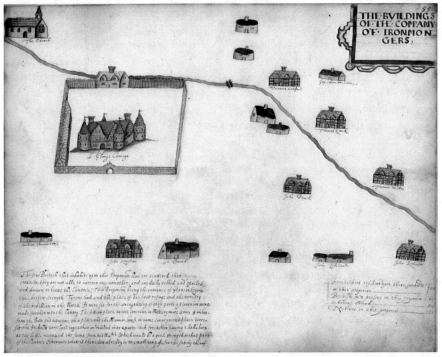

Raven's 1622 drawing of the Ironmongers' castle and bawn at Agivey built on a site chosen by George Canning opposite the chapel at Mullaghmore. The drawing shows a number of timber framed houses and Irish cabins nearby.
Courtesy of the Drapers' Company

By 1616, Agivey consisted of six small timber-framed houses, three of which were slated, one covered with straw for want of slates, and two, which would need to remain uncovered until spring. Canning saw it as 'a great town in this country'.[m] With thirteen further houses built by tenants elsewhere in the proportion, he considered it 'a good plantation'. Granting leases to the native Irish had its rewards. Between 1613 and 1634, the proportion generated income of £2,940, against £1,500 expended on buildings, arms and legal expenses.

In 1619, Pynnar pronounced himself impressed with the castle, but was concerned that the bawn wall had only three sides (with the side nearest the river still unbuilt) and was without flankers. In 1622, Raven's map recorded six English-style houses at Agivey with another eight scattered throughout the proportion.

250

The bawn was accessed through a gateway surmounted by a Dutch gable, and there was a line of outbuildings on its east side. As these had chimneys, they may have been occupied. Phillips noted that the walls on three sides of the bawn had 'no strength', and there was only a timber stockade along the river, with a second house at its centre[105]. This was similar to other timber-framed buildings in the settlement, but may have been rendered. A small bridge, which crossed the river, provided access to the church at Mullaghmore. This was a simple hall with a bellcote at one end.

As expected, Phillips complained at the lack of security and criticised the proportion's fragmented divisions, which made it indefensible. He added:

> The few British that inhabit on this Proporċon live soe scattered that upon occasion they are not able to succour one another, and are daily robbed and spoiled and driven to leave the Cuntrie. This Proporċon being the entrance to Glenconkeyne the chiefest strength Tyrone had and the place of his last refuge and the nurcery of the rebellion in the North. It were fit for the strengthening of these parts a plantaċon were made further into the Cuntry. … Otherwise what is there don already is to small purpose for the safety thereof.[n]

The safety of the estate was already irretrievably jeopardised. Violence from wood-kerne interfered with the building work, particularly that which was near the woods. With workers being stripped of their clothes and having their tools stolen, Canning had difficulty persuading them to remain. In 1616, after a more concerted outbreak of violence, Canning made an urgent request for arms to be delivered from London. His letters are full of lurid accounts of violence:

> I pray God in his mercy spare us from these bloody minded villains and put into their minds which are in authority to take some speedy course to cut them off, else I fear it will be to overthrow of the whole plantation.[o]

Meeting the Company's building obligations proved less difficult than finding settlers willing to take on tenancies. Canning did not turn anyone away 'who will condescend to indifferent conditions'.[p] He found that English and Scots already in Ireland had entered into leases elsewhere on favourable terms[106]. When he tried to recruit from England, he complained that new English settlers would not pay the rents he was asking, and those Scots, who would pay, would not build to the designated quality. When settlers started to build, they were left with insufficient money to pay their rents, causing arrears to mount. Yet the 1630 Muster Rolls show that some of Canning's original craftsmen had settled as tenants. The Company tried to avoid its obligation to settle freeholders,

---

[105] It is likely that Canning and his family occupied this house as the castle, without internal fittings, which would have been pretty Spartan.

[106] Leases were generally granted for thirty-one years or 'three lives'. This extended the lease to the last death of three nominated individuals. As leases were on a fixed rental basis, the long terms tended to favour the tenants and cause difficulties for landlords in periods of inflation.

instructing Canning to limit them to a single townland in remoter locations. Canning replied:

> Most men here do think that the freeholders that shall be on the companies' lands are worthy to pay little or no rent for it, in regard to the continual charge and trouble which they shall be subject to for attendance at assizes and sessions.[q]

When the Company at last accepted his view, six freeholders were identified.

In 1619, Pynnar reported fifty-six British male settlers, more than in any other Company, and it appeared that the Articles were being complied with. Yet native Irish remained as subtenants. Pynnar noted: 'Here is an infinite number of Irish upon the land which give such rents that the English cannot get land.' With the Irish prepared to pay more, British tenants always preferred to sub-let to them, and this left occupancy unchanged. In 1622, Phillips counted one resident freeholder, three leaseholders and twenty-three 'reputed' leaseholders (without leasehold agreements). He also reported sixty-five able-bodied British men, of which fifty were armed, but there were still one hundred and thirty-one native Irish and two native freeholders.

Nothing remains of Canning's settlement; it was completely destroyed in the Great Rebellion of 1641. By then, of course, the Ironmongers' interest had been expropriated by the Crown. After the rebellion, there were not twenty trees fit for building left standing. Even the church had gone although there is a graveyard with more modern graves. Although Canning escaped to Londonderry, living on until in 1646, his eldest son, Paul, held Agivey for a short period until relieved by English troops. (See page 188) It soon fell to Manus O'Cahan and any remaining settlers were butchered. Canning's second son William was killed with many others in a doomed attempt to defend Garvagh, a castle within Manus's native freehold a few miles further north. With Manus having played a leading part in the rebellion, the Cromwellians forfeited Garvagh in 1649, and Paul Canning was permitted to acquire it. He established his own settlement there, initially with six houses. Garvagh became the Canning family estate, from which their later title takes its name. Yet Agivey was never rebuilt.

Chapter 26

Vintners

The Vintners were formed as a Livery Company in the 12th Century and received their Royal Charter in 1364. They held a right to import all wines from Gascony (Bordeaux) and to sell them without licence, but, in 1553, they lost this monopoly, except in London and up the Great North Road. Their remaining rights only lapsed in 2006. The Vintners are eleventh in seniority among the twelve Great Livery Companies.

Initial demand to fund the plantation in Ulster did not cause a great stir in the Company, but, in July 1610, two Assistants (members of the Court) approached the Court of Common Council of the City of London seeking to reduce the Company's contribution. By February 1611, it had indicated its willingness to accept Ulster lands and a special committee was established to manage the property when allocated. By the end of that year, it needed to draw on funds from its Common Stock to supplement individual contributions by members. Levies on the membership were soon abandoned and the Company agreed to meet the contributions of any defaulters wishing to surrender their interests. In 1613, individuals who had paid all six of their instalments were also permitted to surrender their interests to the Company. Yet some retained a personal involvement for some time.

With the Grocers' contribution having exceeded the cost of a single proportion, the excess was allocated to the Vintners. Support was also received from eight Minor Companies. The required contribution was allocated as follows:

	Contributions to 1611			Contributions 1611-1616			Total to 1616		
	£	s	d	£	s	d	£	s	d
Vintners	2,080	0	0	1,040	0	0	3,120	0	0
Overplus from Grocers	540	13	4	333	6	8	874	0	0
Woodmongers	200	0	0	120	0	0	320	0	0
Weavers	100	0	0	50	0	0	150	0	0
Plumbers	80	0	0	40	0	0	120	0	0
Poulterers	80	0	0	40	0	0	120	0	0
Tilers and Bricklayers	80	0	0	40	0	0	120	0	0
Blacksmiths	64	0	0	32	0	0	96	0	0
Fruiterers	64	0	0	32	0	0	96	0	0
Curriers	44	0	0	22	0	0	66	0	0
Cash payment		13	4					13	4
	£3,333	6	8	£1,749	6	8	£5,082	13	4

At the meeting in the Guildhall on 17 December 1613, the Vintners drew Lot 9, an area of 32,600 well-wooded acres in Loughinsholin with forty-nine and a half townlands. It was split into two main divisions. The larger contained the river valleys of the Claudy and Moyola with an area of glebe lands at its centre. It was bounded by the Bann to the east, the Mercers across the River Claudy to the north, church lands to the west, with the Salters and Phillips's properties at Toome to the south. The smaller division had the Mercers to the south, the Skinners and Drapers to the west and church lands to the east. Between these two was a further small division bisected by the River Claudy. The soil was generally good with very little bogland.

The Vintners employed Henry Jackson as Agent, and he arrived in Ireland in 1614, sending back his first report at the end of that year. He chose Bellaghy near Lough Beg in the eastern part of the proportion for the main settlement, and it was renamed Vintnerstown. In 1615, having received more funds, he was instructed to proceed with housebuilding. With progress being slow, the committee employed Rowley as Farmer. Despite him being under a shadow after falling out with The Irish Society, he had access to a labour force, and, on 9 May 1616, an agreement was signed. In October, Goodwin[107] was instructed to cut roads and to clear areas of woodland to open up land for agriculture with help from William Cottesmore and John Raye. Goodwin is known to have played a significant role in the building design, specification and supervision of Vintnerstown, but Jackson seems to have designed other buildings and was paid for his contribution. Little is known of what was done, but, by 1619, most houses had been completed. It was unfortunate that Thomas Egerton, their master carpenter, returned to London that autumn.

After Rowley's death in 1617, the Company signed a new fifty-seven year lease on 16 April 1619 with his former partner, Baptist Jones at an annual rental of £120. Jones, who was the Salters' Agent was required to retain armed men

---

[107] Goodwin was involved in building work at Muff for the Grocers between 1616 and 1619 and became Steward of the Clothworkers' proportion in 1617.

with 'corselets, pikes, and muskets, with ample powder and shot'. [108a] He was expressly forbidden from assigning or leasing land to native Irish or any others, who had not signed the Oath of Allegiance. Yet many natives remained where they were. Jones was soon making pipe-staves, despite it being in direct contravention of his agreement.

The Manor of Vintners was conveyed on 22 October 1618, when each approved freeholder received a townland at £2 per annum. Jones acquired one for himself. In the following year, Pynnar reported seventy-six British men on the proportion, but substantial expenditure was still needed to provide security. With the land dangerously exposed to wood-kerne from the surrounding woodlands, Jones went to London to request rental concessions. Raven's map of 1622 shows Vintnerstown with fifteen timber-framed houses, each with brick gables in regular rows down the sides of a main street with its own generous plot of land. There was a market cross and stocks at its centre. In 1622, there was a timber-framed mill, one house still unfinished, another unoccupied, seven Irish cabins and three humble cottages. Quite unusually the new buildings had tiled roofs, but existing cabins and cottages remained thatched. A huge castle, which Jones occupied, was at the end of the street. It had a crenellated bawn of brick and lime with two circular flankers in diagonal corners, each with an ornamented roof. The Carew manuscripts say that the walls were protected by an earthen rampart, a unique feature within the twelve proportions. There were two buildings inside the bawn walls in addition to a guard house.

One of the flankers of the Vintners' castle and bawn, Bellaghy The original structure has been much altered and was for a period, the castle occupied by Sir Baptist Jones.

---

[108] As with many other Companies, the Vintners delegated responsibility for defending the proportion on the Farmer, freeholders and tenants.

While Jones was in London in 1618, he raised a loan of £500 from Elizabeth Feltham by mortgaging his lease as Farmer; this was guaranteed by the Company. The ostensible purpose was to enable him to build a new parish church at Ballyscullion next to Vinterstown. The Company also subscribed funds and permitted Jones to retain a year's rent towards its cost and to have it consecrated. In 1621, the church was still incomplete, and although Jones was knighted, work seems to have been delayed by his financial problems. The Vintners agreed to renegotiate the terms of his lease, but, in November 1622, he was put under pressure to settle his debts. Having only ever paid one rental instalment, the Company took legal steps to recover what it was owed. He had already fallen out with the Salters over the running of their proportion and was described as a 'needy and grasping adventurer'.[b]

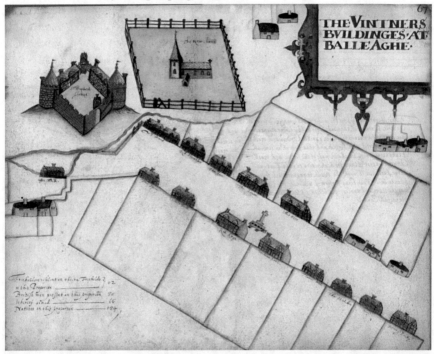

Raven's 1622 drawing of the Vintners' castle and bawn at Vintnerstown (Bellaghy) The Vintners' imposing castle next to the Parish church of Ballyscullion has been much rebuilt, but it remains a robust structure. Its settlement was neatly laid out on each side of its main street.
Courtesy of the Drapers' Company

Despite Jones's difficulties, Raven's map of 1622 shows the new church with a four-bay nave standing in its own enclosure. When finished, it was sixty by twenty-five feet, with walls sixteen feet high and four bricks thick. It had a tiled roof, a tower with a spire at its western end and a porch to the south. It was glazed and had a pulpit and seating. By then, Phillips recorded that there were two resident freeholders, nine leaseholders, four more leaseholders without formal leases, providing a total of eighty male settlers, of whom sixty-six were armed, but there were still one hundred and eighty-four native Irish. Phillips pointed out the risks, as the proportion lay within

> Glenconkeyne, a very vast country, by reason of the woods, bogs, and bordering mountains, so as it is fitted there should be a great care had in the well planting thereof with British; and that from these several plantations there be choice made of the fittest and most convenient places for highways to be laid out, and large [passes] cut through the woods to answer each several plantation.[c]

On Jones's death in 1623, the Company sent Henry Conway to Ireland to resolve the financial muddle and Goodwin was given power of attorney to recover amounts due. By 1624, nothing had been recovered and £300 of rent was still in arrears. Conway made it more complicated for the Vintners by marrying Jones's widow and was granted a new lease as Farmer for fifty-one years from 1625, if he would pay off Jones's debt. Yet he failed to do so and, by 1634, owed the Company £394. From 1613 to 1634, the Company's income was £1,926 against building expenditure of £1,457, leaving only a small return on its investment. Conway's arrears remained unpaid, but eventually, without advising the Vintners, he sold out to Clotworthy, who was to prove no better.

By 1624, twenty-and-a-half townlands were planted with British settlers and twenty-nine let to native Irish. In 1628, there were seventy-three British men and two hundred and seven natives. In 1631, the Muster Roll counted one hundred and two British men, but they were hopelessly outnumbered. With so many native Irish about, it is easy to understand that Vintnerstown was destroyed in the 1641 rebellion. The foundations and one flanker of the castle with a section of the bawn's crumbling brickwork are all that remain.

Chapter 27

Clothworkers

The Clothworkers' Company is twelfth in order of precedence of the twelve Great Livery Companies, associated with the craft of finishing woven cloth. It arises out of the amalgamation of the Fullers and the Shearmen, both of whom had been branches of the Weavers' Company. The Fullers were incorporated in 1480 and the Shearmen in 1508, and the combined Company succeeded to the rank of the Shearmen. It received its Royal charter in 1528.

In July 1609, the Company called a special meeting to discuss the Londonderry plantation project. Many members were fined for being unaccountably absent. In 1610, the Wardens were called before the Lord Mayor to explain why both of their first two instalments were in arrears, and, on the following day, 'members who had not contributed were threatened with imprisonment unless they disgorged the necessary funds'.[a] In July, two Wardens were jailed for several months, while one member, having resisted arrest in the street, barricaded himself into his house. It was self-evident that the Company remained among the most reluctant of contributors. There was so much difficulty in raising the £200 assessed on one member that it was forced to contribute from its common stock. Although it offered its interest to anyone, who would repay its outlay, unlike the Haberdashers, it could find no takers. In desperation, it agreed to allow members to surrender their interests to the Company, but they could continue paying personally if they wished. In September 1611, the common stock was tapped to meet the next precept, but it was still the intention that future demands should be met by individual subscription, and the precept of 1613 was met by 'zealous extraction of cash from members'.[b] In 1616, when a third quota was called, the Company gave up trying to collect from individuals and paid from its common stock. In 1618, it agreed to repay contributions made by individual members over two years.

In addition to the Company's contribution, allocations also came from the Merchant Taylors' surplus over what was required for its own proportion and from five Minor Company associates. The total was shared as follows:

	Contributions to 1611			Contributions 1611-1616			Total to 1616		
	£	s	d	£	s	d	£	s	d
Clothworkers	2,260	0	0	1,130	0	0	3,390	0	0
Merchant Taylors' overplus	752	13	4	433	6	8	1,186	0	0
Butchers	150	0	0	80	0	0	230	0	0
Brown-bakers	90	0	0	40	0	0	130	0	0
Upholders	44	0	0	22	0	0	66	0	0
Bowyers	20	0	0	10	0	0	30	0	0
Fletchers	20	0	0	10	0	0	30	0	0
Cash receipt	(3	6	8)				(3	6	8)
	£3,333	6	8	£1,725	6	8	£5,058	13	4

After providing their first instalment, both the Bowyers and Fletchers were exempted from further contributions and, in 1618, the Ironmongers took on their interests, settling their arrears.

On 17 December 1613, the Clothworkers drew Lot 5, amounting to 13,450 acres in forty-nine and a half townlands on the west side of the Bann opposite Coleraine, extending north to the sea. There were two large areas of church lands at Dunboe and the Grange pushing into it and causing security problems. To the north west were other glebe and church lands and a native freehold belonging to Richard McAveny O'Cahan. The Haberdashers were to the south west, and the Merchant Taylors to the south. The church lands of Killowen ran along the Bann to the east.

In 1613, the Clothworkers combined with the Merchant Taylors to commission a survey of their two proportions by Simon Kingsland. It was agreed that both the Merchant Taylors and the associated Minor Companies should be repesented on the Clothworkers' management committee, which also held regular meetings with the Merchant Taylors' committee to discuss respective issues. The first Agent, Nicholas Elcock[109], who had become a freeman in 1603, had reached Coleraine by 1615. The committee made the logical decision to build the 'Castle or stone house' on the ruins of an O'Cahan fort at Killowen, opposite Coleraine. Although Elcock supervised the building work, Rowland Aynsworthe, who had become a freeman of the Clothworkers in 1598 arrived to monitor progress, as there were some concerns over Elcock's financial dealings. Aynsworthe reported that work on the castle was well advanced, and, in 1616, Elcock received money from London to pay for 'Musketts' and other arms.[c] Raven's plan of the Clothworkers' estate, made at this time, showed the castle and a rudimentary settlement of cabins at Articlave about two-and-a-half miles from the mouth of the Bann. Although building work had begun there, with nails and other ironmongery arriving from London, it was 'an unprepossessing place' with one English-style house in clay and stone, but this was thatched and 'was a poor thing of cagework'.[d] Aynsworthe also

---

[109] In the 1616 disturbances, Elcock was captured by Revelyn McCollo MacDonnell, and was held ransomed for £100, Yet, some Irishmen well-disposed towards the Clothworkers rescued him. MacDonnell was later captured by Irish troops under Sir Francis Cooke of Desertmartin, and his severed head was put on display in Coleraine.

reported the ruinous state of the parish church on church lands at Dunboe further west, and the building committee offered to fund a 'reasonable proportion of the cost of repair'.

The ruins of the pre-plantation church at Dunboe In 1620, the Company contributed to the cost of repair of the church, although it was not on its proportion.

In 1618, the Company appointed Sir Robert McClelland as Farmer at £250 per annum for fifty-one years from 1 May 1618. He paid £600 8s. 4d. in advance to meet the first three years' rent. This charge proved too high for him to make a profit and, in 1626, it was reduced to £150 annually. In 1616, he had also become Farmer of the Haberdashers' adjacent proportion. He successfully attracted Scottish settlers as subtenants, but did not adopt English buildings styles, preferring more rudimentary Scottish bothies. He was already resident at Ballycastle on the Haberdashers' proportion, but provided weapons for the Clothworkers' protection. In 1618, he paid for the delivery of materials to both Killowen and Articlave to allow building activity to be accelerated as soon as he became Farmer.

Aynsworthe made a second visit in 1620 to supervise the works on Dunboe Church, including a new roof of timber and slate, a new floor, and two new windows. These were carried out in 1621 at a cost of £112 14s. 0d. Despite being repaired twice, the its location was inconvenient and a new site was found at Articlave, where there were already twenty-one cottages spread out on either side of the road. There were also two more substantial houses of clay and stone and a cage work dwelling roofed with thatch. A second new church with a spire is shown at Killowen on Raven's 1616 map, but it must have collapsed, as, in 1618, McClelland offered to build a new one, which is shown on Raven's 1622 map without a spire.

Another reason for Aynsworthe's second visit was the Company's renewed suspicion of Elcock's 'unreasonable' charges. By 1620, its income had reached only £1,469 7s. 7d.against expenses of £1,445. 16s. 11d., leaving a negligible surplus. When Elcock's Power of Attorney was 'annihilated', Aynsworthe was tasked with sorting out the mess.[e] In 1621, the ubiquitous Goodwin was appointed as steward to live at the castle at Killowen, now known as the Manor House, and he seems to have taken over Elcock's executive duties. In addition to acting as steward collecting rents for several companies, he also collected the customs for The Irish Society at Londonderry.

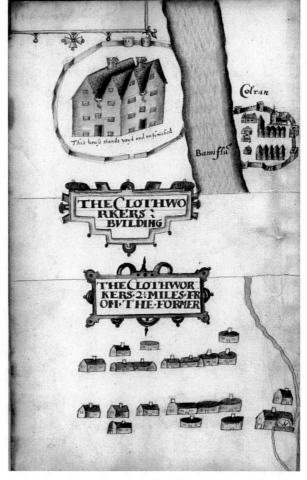

Raven's 1622 drawing of the Clothworkers' castle and bawn at Killowen
The site of the castle was close to the Clothworkers' Arms Hotel across the river Bann from Coleraine. It was 'voyd and unfinished' in 1622.
Courtesy of the Drapers' Company

By 1622, Raven's map was showing a 'huddle of [twenty-one] single-storey cottages', some with gable ends and some being cabins. Although the mill was the largest building, even this was a humble structure. It included some detail of the Manor House on the banks of the Bann at Killowen 'set within a loose girdle of walls'.[f] It was built of stone but still unfinished and unoccupied, and reportedly in a poor state of repair. There was a basement, two storeys and an attic; its two steeply pitch roofs with a valley between had gables to the front. Its surrounding bawn wall did not echo other proportions and may have been the outer wall of the original castle. Phillips quickly criticised its lack of preparedness for attack, despite the location's strategic importance. It also showed a 'huddle of [twenty-one] single-storey cottages', some with gable ends and some being cabins. Like Articlave, the Killowen settlement, which was built on church land adjacent to the proportion, had little structure, but its houses, spaced along the Bann, included three one-and-a-half storey dwellings in an English style. Despite regular meetings with the Merchant Taylors, neither settlement bore similarity to Macosquin, whose orderly layout of English-style houses was planned on sound architectural principles.

In 1622, Phillips reported one freeholder and eighty-six British men on the proportion, of which seventy-five were armed. There were only fifty-one native Irish, and the proximity to Coleraine may have discouraged them from staying. By 1628, there were one hundred and six settlers bolstered by an influx of Scots, and one hundred and seven native Irish. Yet the 1630 Muster Rolls showed only sixty-five colonists. The Manor House at Killowen, opposite Coleraine, must have been repaired, as, in 1637, it was being occupied by William Barraby, Mayor of Coleraine, who farmed four hundred acres. Yet the whole settlement was wiped out in 1641.

Part 5

Control by Parliamentary forces
1642 – 1660

Chapter 28

The war of the Three Kingdoms
1642-1649

With so much skirmishing throughout Britain and Ireland, it was inevitable that the fighting would develop into a civil war. On 22 August 1642, Parliamentary forces marched against Charles I's cavaliers. In Ireland, it became known as the War of the Three Kingdoms. To bring what seemed to be a Royalist uprising in Ireland under control, the English Parliament raised loans of £10 million under the Adventurers' Act,[110] to be repaid out of lands to be confiscated from Irish Catholic rebels. Parliamentary soldiers, who agreed to fight in Ireland, were promised allotments of land in lieu of wages. There were soon 37,000 of them, and, under the Act, an initial two and a half million acres was promised as security for loans. To honour its terms, Parliament needed to bring Ireland under its rule, but the extent of its offer under the Adventurers' Act was going to cause future problems.

After intercepting Charles's instructions to him, the Protestant community in both Britain and Ireland vehemently opposed Ormonde's truce with the Catholics. It was horrified at him arranging a deal with 'malignants' and 'idolatrous butchers' of this 'popish party'.[a] Ormonde was in a difficult position, as almost all Ireland was in Catholic hands. Only the Dublin Pale, areas round Cork City, Londonderry and Belfast with a few small outlying garrisons remained Protestant. The King was also instructing him to keep Monro's Scottish Covenanter army in the north fully occupied to prevent it returning to reinforce the Parliamentary cause in Britain. On 25 September, 1643, the English Parliament came to a Solemn League and Covenant with the Scots. This proved a watershed in the Civil War in Britain. In Ireland, it had the effect of transferring all Scottish troops in Ulster, including Monro's Covenanters, into supporting the Parliamentarians. They now opposed Ormonde, who, as a consequence, lost control in Ulster.

---

[110] Under the 1642 Act, anyone, who provided £200 was promised 1000 acres in Ireland. Under the Doubling Ordinance of 1643, people were promised double the land previously allocated if they invested a further 25 per cent. By 1653, 11 million acres of Ireland had been expropriated from Catholic rebels for allocation to Parliamentary supporters.

In November 1643, Ormonde was created a Marquess and was appointed Lord Lieutenant (rather than Lord Deputy), a position, which had remained unoccupied since Wentworth's departure two years earlier. Yet again, he was asked to deliver troops to support the Royalist cause in England. He had to persuade Irish Catholics of the merit of fighting for an English Crown, which had so recently usurped their lands to provide plantations for English settlers. Even though Ormonde had many friends among the Catholic leaders, his negotiations were tortuous, but, in 1644, he assisted Randal MacDonnell, 1st Marquess of Antrim, in mounting a large Irish Confederation expedition to Scotland[111]. This was led by Alisdair MacColla, who joined the Marquess of Montrose in supporting the Scottish Royalist cause. They inflicted a series of stunning defeats on the Covenanting Scots, until finally being routed at Selkirk in 1645.

Despite this modicum of Irish support, Charles was not satisfied. In 1645, he sent Edward Somerset, 2nd Marquess of Worcester, to Ireland, where, on 25 August, he signed a treaty with the Irish Catholic Confederation in Kilkenny without airing any of the terms with Ormonde or the Irish Protestant community beforehand. They were furious, and, when Charles realised he was pushing them into backing the Parliamentarians, he was forced to repudiate the new agreement. On 28 March 1646, Ormonde met with the Catholics to conclude new terms on the King's behalf, which granted a number of concessions. Yet the Nuncio persuaded their General Assembly to reject them and to arrest those Catholics, who had agreed to them.

In May 1644, Monro occupied Belfast for the Parliamentarians and received fresh reinforcements from Scotland. Yet Eoghan Roe O'Neill believed that his Irish forces were now in a position to challenge him. When Monro left Antrim to meet him with 6,000 men and six field guns drawn by oxen, Eoghan Roe, with an equal number of men but no guns, attacked him from the rear at Benburb on the River Blackwater. Despite receiving a pounding from Monro's cannon, he called to his men:

> Let your manhood be seen by your push of pike! Your word is *Sancta Maria,* and so in the name of the Father, Son, and Holy Ghost advance! –and give not fire until you are within pike-length![b]

With this, the Irish pushed the Scots back into the river and slaughtered them. 'Monro escaped only after he had cast away his coat, hat and wig. Between a third and a half of the Scots were killed, the Irish sustaining only trifling losses.'[c] When the news reached Rome, the Pope attended a *Te Deum* to thank God for

---

[111] It is probable that Viscount Chichester supported this expedition, although he died in England in 1648. All the Chichester family property was confiscated by the Commonwealth in 1644, and it was not until 1656 that it was restored to his son, Arthur, who had been created Earl of Donegall by Ormonde in 1647. By this time, Donegall was greatly in debt, presumably from supporting the Royalist cause. He recovered possession of his estates after returning to Belfast in August 1660. This was confirmed by Royal Charter in 1668. In his absence, Belfast had grown significantly.

this Irish triumph. It caused Monro to complain: 'For ought I can understand, the Lord of Hosts had a controversie with us to rub shame in our faces.'[d] Yet, despite having the north at his mercy, Eoghan Roe turned south to help the Nuncio in taking control of the Confederation at Kilkenny.

In Britain, the Royalists' military position went from bad to worse. Two months after Benburb, the King was defeated at Marston Moor and, in 1646, was captured at Newark. Although an Irish peace was proclaimed in Dublin and at Kilkenny, the Nuncio, who felt that its terms failed to give Roman-Catholicism sufficient prominence, rejected it and the war continued. Ormonde's Royalist forces were divided, and he feared that he could not hold Dublin against Irish Catholics now seeking independence from Britain. With Protestant Royalists openly declaring their dislike for their Catholic allies, they in turn refused to support Royalists of English descent. Ormonde preferred to negotiate with the English Long Parliament, rather than to hand Dublin over to the Irish Confederation. On 19 June 1647, he signed a treaty ceding Dublin to the English Parliamentarians on terms protecting both Protestant Royalists and those 'innocent' Catholics, who had not joined the Confederation's rebellion. Two months later, the Parliamentary commander, Lieutenant-General Michael Jones, arrived from England with 5,000 men, and Ormonde handed over Dublin to him with the command of his remaining 3,000 Royalist troops. Jones, who was of Welsh descent, had been brought up in Ireland and had previously served under Ormonde in Ulster before establishing his reputation by joining the Parliamentary forces in England.

Ormonde now sailed for England, where, during August and October, he attended Charles at Hampton Court Palace. In March 1648, to avoid being arrested in England, he travelled to Paris to join Charles I's wife, Queen Henrietta Maria, and their son, Charles, Prince of Wales, to develop a plan to consolidate Royalist support in Ireland, which was on the brink of becoming a second front in the English Civil War.

With Jones's Parliamentary forces being equipped with up-to-date artillery, the Catholic Confederation was soon on the back foot. After persuading Ormonde's 3,000 Protestant Royalist troops in Dublin to support him, Jones led out his combined force to face the Confederation. After relieving a siege at Trim, he crushed a powerful Catholic force from Leinster at Dungans Hill in County Meath leaving 3,000 dead. Another 4,000 Irish died at Knocknanuss Hill in County Cork.[e] These were body blows to the Confederation, but, after returning to Dublin, Jones's men were suffering from disease, and he was pinned down over the winter of 1647-48.

At the end of 1647, the Irish Confederation linked with the Presbyterian Scots, until so recently their bitter enemies, and with Ormonde's former Royalist allies to provide a Royalist axis in support of their captured King.[f] Charles was calling on Scottish Royalists to assist him in England, but, in May 1648, a Scottish Royalist army was defeated by Cromwell at Preston. The King's invitation to 'foreigners' was seen by Parliament as the treasonable grounds they needed to justify his execution, allowing the legal process against him to be open and transparent. His execution in 1649 brought the Civil War in Britain to a close.

In Ireland, the King's death came as a great shock, not only to Catholics, but to Scottish Presbyterians who had not only fought under Monro, but made up the main part of the Lagan army, which had defended Londonderry against the Catholic Confederation. In April 1648, when Sir Charles Coote, commanding the Londonderry garrison, declared his support for the Parliamentarians, the Lagan army, for so long its protector, laid siege to the City, joined by Montgomery and Scottish Covenanters from County Down. Yet the Parliamentarians kept Londonderry well supplied by sea. One of the besieged recorded:

> After three months' siege there is not one sick or feeble body among us, and now in better condition than the first day of the siege: our greatest want is and will be firing [firewood], there being no other firing than old houses, and trees got out of orchards; for we suppose provisions will be plentifully sent us by the parliament.[g]

Quite bizarrely, it was Eoghan Roe O'Neill who came to Londonderry's rescue after seeking a temporary alliance with the Parliamentarians. Both sides, for entirely different reasons, wanted to be rid of the Stuart Kings. On 8 August 1649, he drove off the Royalist besiegers, both Catholic and Covenanter, allowing Coote to open its gates to entertain him, even though his father had been killed in action seven years earlier by the native Irish.

Ireland had now become the battle ground, not for Catholics against Protestants, nor for British against native Irish, but for the continuing campaign between Royalist supporters of the Stuarts and their Parliamentary opponents. The local inhabitants were the cannon fodder in between.

Chapter 29

Ireland under Parliamentary control 1649-1660

Although the Civil War in England had been brought to an end by Charles I's execution, Ireland continued in turmoil, not helped by regular outbreaks of smallpox and dysentery afflicting all sides. Both the Irish Establishment and Irish Catholics clung to hopes of the Crown's revival, if the Stuarts in exile could gain assistance from Catholic France. Yet the two groups were fatally divided and could not work together. With the Peace of Westphalia ending the Thirty Years' War in October 1648, a Counter-Reformation in Ireland led by Continental Catholic powers was no longer probable.

Royalists in Ireland realised that their only hope was to set aside their religious differences. After expelling the Nuncio, the Catholic Confederation became much more amenable to compromise, particularly after their reverses at the hands of Jones. In September 1648, Ormonde returned and, in the following January, concluded a peace, which united all Catholics behind the Royalist cause. With Jones still hemmed into Dublin, the rest of Ireland remained under their control, particularly because, after Charles I's execution in January 1649, Ormonde brought in English Royalist troops from France and continued to have the support of Scottish Presbyterians horrified at the King's execution. Having declared Charles II as King of Ireland, Ormonde was made a Knight of the Garter by the Royalist Government in exile.

To regain control of the English Parliament after Charles I's execution, moderate Puritans recognised the need to break the power of Cromwell's New Model Army. Parliament disbanded some of its units and, in 1649, moved 'the more radical regiments out of the way by sending them to Ireland',[a] where Royalist opposition was growing. The army knew it was being marginalised and Cromwell's continued support for his men caused mistrust for him in Parliament. In August 1649, he was appointed Lord Lieutenant of Ireland and took command of the Parliamentary campaign to restore control. He set out with 12,000 of his more bigoted but seasoned 'Ironsides' from the New Model Army, who saw their campaign as a crusade. Realising that Cromwell would need the port of Dublin for disembarkation, Ormonde attempted a pre-emptive strike to prevent a landing. When he deployed his Royalist troops at Rathmines, Jones made a surprise sortie from Dublin and crushingly defeated him. With Admiral

Robert Blake blockading the remaining Royalist fleet under Prince Rupert of the Rhine at Kinsale, Cromwell crossed the Irish Sea on thirty-five ships unmolested and, on 15 August 1649, landed both men and equipment unopposed. Two days later, his son-in-law, Henry Ireton, landed a further seventy-seven ships.

Oliver Cromwell After the victory of his New Model Army in Britain, in 1649, he brought it to Dublin, where he adopted brutal tactics against the resurgent Catholics before returning to England as Protector.
After Samuel Cooper oil in canvas, feigned oval 1656 © National Portrait Gallery, London, NPG 514

On arrival, Cromwell promised civil liberty to those who would remain at peace, but the Irish were in no mood to listen. In July 1649, an outbreak of plague had added to the ravages of 'starvation, war, burned harvests and a ruined economy'.[b] From the outset, Cromwell's clear objective was to avenge the 1641 massacre in Ulster. He told the Irish:

> You, unprovoked, put the English to the most unheard of and most barbarous massacre without respect of sex or age, that ever the sun beheld, and at a time when Ireland was in perfect peace.[c]

After gaining control of the ports on Ireland's east coast[112] to protect his supply lines, he systematically captured the line of fortified towns across the country, which Ormonde was trying to hold. On 11 September, Jones took the first of these, the Royalist stronghold of Drogheda, after a short siege, during which he desolated the surrounding countryside. Cromwell was taking no prisoners. He forbade his men 'to spare any that were in arms in the town'[d] and sealed Jones's victory by massacring the garrison of 3,000 Royalist and Catholic Confederation troops including any civilians, who refused his offer of quarter. He reported back

---

[112] Monck had taken Carrickfergus for the Parliamentarians in September 1648, although he was obliged to withdraw shortly afterwards.

to Parliament: 'This is a righteous judgement of God upon these barbarous wretches, who have imbrued their hand in so much innocent blood.'[e] Following this, he sent five thousand men north under Colonel Robert Venables, a veteran of Naseby, to regain eastern Ulster. Venables took Newry and Belfast, and besieged Carrickfergus before turning west to relieve the Livery Company settlers, who were again under siege in Londonderry. With the siege lifted, Coote, who had relieved Coleraine in the autumn, sped south east to join Venables at Lisburn, where, in December 1649, they mounted a joint attack at Lisnagarvey outside Lisburn on Covenanter troops mustered by Montgomery and Hamilton at Newtownards and Comber. One thousand Covenanters were cut to pieces in a relentless cavalry pursuit. When their commander, General Tam Dalyell, capitulated, Carrickfergus was forced to surrender.

When Eoghan Roe O'Neill died in November 1649, Bishop Heber MacMahon of Clogher was elected to command Ulster's Catholic resistance. In December, a Synod of Roman-Catholic Bishops at Clonmacnoise appealed for Catholics to unite behind the King. Cromwell called this the 'undeceiving of deluded and seduced people'.[f] In the following spring, the Catholics had an early success when MacMahon took Ballycastle and Dungiven, where the inhabitants were put to the sword, but Royalist resistance started to collapse, in the face of superior organisation by the Parliamentary troops, and Limavady remained under the control of the Phillips brothers. Scottish settlers soon 'realised that their best interests were served by supporting Venables'.[g] On 21 June 1650, Parliamentarians under Coote with support from English settlers routed an army of 6,000 Ulster Catholic Royalists at Scarrifhollis on Lough Swilly, with two thousand prisoners being executed. MacMahon was hanged after being captured at Enniskillen and his head was affixed to one of the gates of Londonderry. On 14 August 1650, Charlemont, the last fort held by the Confederation in Ulster, was surrendered by Sir Phelim O'Neill. Although he escaped to an island hideout in Tyrone, he was betrayed in February 1653. At his trial, he at last admitted the forgery of the Royal Commission in 1641 and inevitably faced a traitors' death. Although sporadic guerrilla fighting continued, in April 1653, the Parliamentarians made a successful assault on Lough Oughter, where Rory O'More was last seen attempting to swim away near Inishbofin on the Galway coast.

With Venables and Coote being left to settle Ulster, Cromwell turned south and, in October, secured Wexford, where he executed a further two thousand defenders, including Catholic clergy, who came out to surrender carrying their crucifixes. Although he made further progress, he failed to gain immediate control of Waterford and Duncannon. During the winter of 1649, his army rested at Cork and Youghal, where, yet again, many of his men died of typhoid and dysentery. Tragically, one of these was Jones. In the spring, Cromwell eliminated pockets of Royalist resistance at Kilkenny and other places, but lost 2,000 men after facing stiff resistance while besieging Clonmel. Yet opposition to him was disintegrating. He could now sit back and watch while the divided Royalists tore themselves to pieces.

In May 1650, Ormonde's Cork garrison mutinied. Until 1648, it had fought on the Parliamentary side, so its desertion to Cromwell was little surprise. This left Cork and most of Munster under Parliamentary control. Ormonde's forces were pushed back behind the Shannon River either into Connaught or the peninsula of Kerry further south. When Cromwell offered Protestant Royalists generous terms if they surrendered, many either capitulated or joined him. With Irish Catholics left on the back foot, the Stuarts again let them down. Charles II repudiated the Stuart alliance with the Catholic Confederation, preferring to link with the Covenanters, who were supporting him in Scotland. Ormonde was left with just a few diehard English Royalists, and opposition to Cromwell was now completely undermined.

In mid-1650, with his job as good as done, Cromwell returned to England to deal with the threat of a new Scottish-Royalist alliance, and Ireton took over command of the Parliamentary forces in Ireland. In October, he crossed the Shannon to defeat a small Catholic Confederation force at Meelick Island. Ormonde was already discredited after a string of defeats and, in late 1650, the Catholics ousted him from command. After spending most of his personal fortune supporting the Royalist cause, he was acutely short of funds, but rejoined Charles II as a key member of his Court-in-Exile in France. In his absence, he was repudiated in Jamestown by a Catholic synod, which also excommunicated his remaining Protestant followers.

Ormonde was replaced as commander of the Confederation forces by Ulick Burke of Clanricarde. Although his troops were penned in west of the Shannon, Burke was determined to defend the cities of Limerick and Galway with their modern walls. Without heavy guns to mount an assault, Ireton blockaded Limerick, while Coote surrounded Galway. When a Catholic force from Kerry attempted to relieve the two cities, it was intercepted and routed at Knocknaclashy. A combination of hunger and disease eventually forced both cities to surrender, although thousands of Parliamentarians also died from plague. These included Ireton, who died at Limerick in 1651. Although the Catholic surrender removed the last Royalist army in Ireland, guerrilla attacks by as many as 30,000 Irish men in arms continued to threaten Parliamentary supply convoys for a further two years. Parliamentary troops retaliated against these 'heathen' Irish Catholics, by destroying food crops and evicting anyone thought to be assisting the guerrillas.

Cromwell had become a hated figure, although some of his army's reported brutality may have been exaggerated in the telling. He had always relied on locals for food and other supplies for his men. On first arriving in Dublin, he had pronounced:

I do hereby warn … all Officers, Soldiers and others under my command not to do any wrong or violence toward Country People or any persons whotsoever, unless they be actually in arms or office with the enemy … as they shall answer to the contrary at their utmost peril.

Ireton is known to have court-martialled one of his Parliamentary Colonels, Daniel Axtell, for atrocities committed by his soldiers at Meelick Island. Yet there is no doubt that Cromwell exercised 'the utmost severity' on those who tried to resist him, particularly after the seige of Drogheda.

In 1652, the Parliamentarians brought the war to an end by granting terms, which allowed Irish troops to travel abroad to join foreign armies not at war with England. In April 1652, when the Catholic Confederation's army surrendered in County Cavan, a handful of English Puritan soldiers had become the masters of Ireland. Irish Catholics saw them as 'merciless butchers' and 'the scum of England, a generation of mechanic bagmen who had come to power by conquest'.[h] Under the Act of Settlement of 1652, the English Parliament approved the execution of 80,000 adult males[113] including any remaining leaders of the Catholic rebellion of 1641. To meet its obligations under the Adventurers Act, it passed a new wave of Penal Laws authorising further confiscations of Catholic-owned lands, even from those who had not been involved in the wars. Only the very few, who were able to prove 'constant good affection' to the Parliamentary cause, kept their estates intact,[j] although Protestant Royalists and Catholics prepared to adopt the Anglican faith were permitted to pay fines to avoid confiscation.

The war had caused widespread famine, worsened by outbreaks of bubonic plague. Although this decimated the native Irish population, it eased land confiscations. 'Dr. William Petty, the Army's Physician-General, estimated that 504,000 native Irish and 112,000 colonists and English troops perished between 1641 and 1652.'[k] He also estimated that 100,000 Irish men, women and children, including prisoners of war, were forcibly transported to colonies in the West Indies and North America as 'indentured labourers' (slaves). A further 54,000 enlisted with the armies of France, Spain and the Holy Roman Empire.[l] The collective effect was to reduce the Irish population by as much as 40 per cent (although there are other wildly differing estimates). Much of Ireland was left without 'a living creature, either man, beast, or bird, they being either all dead or had quit those desolate places'.[m] 'Packs of wolves became numerous and audacious, even invading the streets of Dublin.'[n] Military commanders had to organise hunts to kill them. Despite the depredation, low level guerrilla attacks and lawlessness by peasant brigands continued until the Restoration.

With the military conflict over, many members of the New Model Army, facing the prospect of religious persecution on return to England, chose to remain in Ireland. The war there had cost £3,500,000, with British soldiers, particularly the New Model Army, being owed about half of this in back pay, which Cromwell promised to settle in land in accordance with the Adventurers' Act. In 1654, the Privy Council also urged him to restore The Irish Society's

---

[113] After two years two hundred had been rounded up and executed, but the thirst for revenge had at last been slaked.[i]

rights in County Londonderry, but Letters Patent were only issued by Parliament in 1658.

Except in County Antrim, there were very few Catholic freeholders left in Ulster after the confiscations of the previous fifty years, but those remaining now lost their entire estates. They were promised alternative lands wherever Parliament might decide, but this was generally in Counties Mayo and Galway. Almost all the O'Donnells ended up in County Mayo. Despite being promised two-thirds of the area they were relinquishing, they were rarely offered more than one-third. Regardless of origin, other native landowners were consigned 'to hell or Connaught'[114] or, in the case of vagrants, to America. Even in Connaught, efforts were made to stop new arrivals from moving into walled towns or from practicing their religion. 'Priests found in the exercise of their religious duties were hanged without ceremony',[o] although some were sent to the West Indies. The Marquess of Antrim had not joined the Covenanter rebellion, but he was a staunch Catholic and Royalist, having served Charles II overseas, and his vast estates were confiscated by the Commonwealth without recompense. Despite continued Catholic hostility, the Cromwellians remained a powerful force, and they pioneered, on a 'magnificent scale',[p] a plantation in Leinster and Munster. Soldiers and others who had funded Parliamentary loans under the Adventurers' Act received land allocations drawn by lot. In the north, plantations of pre-war Protestant settlers were extended over almost the whole of Ulster. In County Fermanagh the principal beneficiary of the land seizure was Henry Brooke, after his distinguished service on the Parliamentarians' behalf. He acquired 10,000 acres at Magherastephana, and, in 1707, his son, also Henry, received a patent to convert it into the manor of Brookeborough.[115] Sir John Cole gained more than 4,000 acres at Clanawley to form his family's Florence Court estate. The effect on land ownership was dramatic. Before the wars, Irish Catholics had owned 60 per cent of Irish land, but Commonwealth confiscations reduced this to 8 per cent. Even after the Restoration, when Catholic Royalists received some compensation, they still controlled only 20 per cent.

For the many British settlers in Ulster, particularly the Royalist Covenanters, it was not immediately apparent that their future was secure. Having routed their army, Venables demanded that their ministers should swear allegiance to the Commonwealth. The majority refused to do so and fled back to Scotland. Others left their homes in country apparel to conduct services in barns or in fields and glens, where they were hunted down and imprisoned at Carrickfergus to await transportation back to Scotland. By the end of 1651, there were only six ministers remaining in Ulster. Eventually, it was proposed that Covenanters in Antrim and Down should relinquish one fifth of their estates. Other Protestant proprietors, who failed to swear allegiance to the Commonwealth, were to be treated similarly. On 24 April 1653, Venables

---

remained in Ulster, where they were expected to work for the new plantation landowners.
[115] Brooke, now Lord Brookeborough, set about rebuilding Banbridge in brick on a cruciform plan, making it one of the most elegant towns in the north.

approached Lieutenant-General Charles Fleetwood,[116] the newly appointed Commander-in-Chief, with a plan to transport Presbyterians to towns in the south. Recalcitrant Presbyterian ministers were advised to accompany their congregations to County Tipperary. Even Montgomery was included in the list of transportees. Fleetwood confirmed to Venables that those, who had been listed, would be moved by 1 November 1653 with their families to follow by 16 April 1654. This was easier said than done. When leading members of the Government met Venables to work out how to implement the move, it was quickly concluded that forcing such determined colonists to give up their land 'might be well nigh impossible'.[q] A softer line was considered desirable. On 9 July 1655, Cromwell's son, Henry, became Major-General of the Parliamentary army in Ireland, after easing his brother-in-law Fleetwood aside, and he became, in effect, supreme governor. As a rigid Anabaptist, Fleetwood had been found too unyielding by other Protestants and Henry Cromwell was easier going. The Government started to fine offenders twice the annual value of their estates, but very few paid. It resorted to transporting 'popular men ... of whose dutiful and peaceful demeanours [it] had no assurance'.[r] These were jailed at Carrickfergus with other malcontents, including any ministers, who refused to swear the Black Oath, and those suspected of a part in the massacre at Islandmagee in January 1642.[s]

In County Down, Colonel Arthur Hill of Hillsborough headed a Commission of the Revenue to seize lands forfeited from the Irish. The Magennises lost all their ancestral estates and were transported to Connaught. Much of it was transferred to beneficiaries under the Adventurers' Act. In Donegal, almost every Catholic was forfeited, including about twenty Gaelic nobles, although the MacSweeneys retained theirs by becoming Protestant. Anyone involved in the rebellion of 1641 was sentenced to death if caught. Turlough O'Boyle had not joined the rebellion, but had supported the Nuncio and Eoghan Roe O'Neill as a representative of the Confederation at Kilkenny; he was the largest landowner to be forfeited.

Before the land in the twenty-two counties involved could be allocated to the Cromwellians, William Petty received instructions to map everything being made available. 'In lieu of their back pay, 33,419 soldiers got what were called 'debentures' – pieces of paper entitling them to Irish land.'[t] Only about 12,000 of them chose to farm. As they were widely spread out, some 'went native' very quickly,[u] ignoring an ordinance forbidding them from marrying Irish women. They often became Catholic and allowed their children to be brought up speaking Gaelic rather than English. Some congregated in towns such as Cork, Youghal and Bandon, where they established ministers to their liking. Others remained in Dublin, joining two of the more freethinking congregations originally set up by English Presbyterian settlers in Elizabethan times. These were already calling for freedom to express their more radical religious views

---

[116] Fleetwood was Cromwell's son-in-law, having married his daughter, Bridget, Ireton's widow. He had taken over command of the Cromwellian army in Ireland on Ireton's death.

and the Dublin 'Cromwellians' found themselves on common ground with Scottish Presbyterians. The remainder sold their debentures, usually at great loss, often to Scottish land speculators, who had previously colonised Ulster. These were soon importing a fresh influx of Scots tenants eager to restore the lands to full production.

In Ulster, an estimated 80,000 Presbyterian arrivals during the 1650s challenged the Established Church, causing a profound change in its religious make-up. Efforts to suppress nonconformists were forgotten, and, when Henry Cromwell arranged for their glebes and tithes to be fully restored,[v] seventy Presbyterian ministers returned to give the 'poor church ... a new sunshine of Liberty'.[w] By 1660, Ulster's population was between 217,000 and 260,000 with nearly half being made up of settlers. With them continuing to seek out fertile and accessible areas, the Irish were pushed onto poorer land, although the English still relied on them for farm labour. In 1659, County Londonderry contained 4,428 English and Scots and 5,306 Irish. By the 1660s, there were 1,770 British households and only 1,000 Irish. Yet, with Charles II starting to call for both Presbyterians and Cromwellians to adhere to religious conformity, arrivals from Scotland started to dwindle.

Being reduced in numbers, the native Irish in Ulster were in an infinitely weaker position than before the Great Rebellion. By 1650, there were already large numbers of Scots in County Londonderry, so the process of reconstruction could begin. Yet, in 1652, when Charles II was crowned King of Scotland at Scone, the Parliamentarians put an embargo on Scottish shipping to Ireland. This did not stop the Scots in County Londonderry continuing to farm, but most of the remaining English settlers moved to the towns or left altogether. By 1653, plague and famine in Londonderry was at last brought under control, but the proportions were like a desert. Almost every building, other than the castle at Limavady, was destroyed. It had taken the Great Rebellion to force the Londoners to take security seriously. Adequate arms had now been shipped for the defence of Londonderry.[x] The array of cannon on the walls, each supplied by the Livery Companies, included the celebrated 'Roaring Meg' provided by the Fishmongers.

Roaring Meg This monstrous cannon on the walls of Londonderry was provided by the Fishmongers' Company. All the Companies sent similar pieces to protect the settlers during the 1641 rebellion.

With a new survey being completed with Cromwellian efficiency, the Privy Council gave instructions for The Irish Society to be restored to all its former rights. Cromwell signed the Letters Patent on 24 March 1656, but it took two more years for the Livery Companies' conveyances to be finalised.

Cromwell's New Model Army, with all its religious fanaticism, had crushed the Irish to avenge their atrocities in the Great Rebellion. The City of London, alienated by their treatment at the hands of the Stuart Kings, had financed them. Yet Roman-Catholicism was embedded in the Irish psyche. It remained the bulwark against the English, despite all the forces thrown against it.

Part 6

The Restoration
1660 – 1691

Chapter 30

The restoration of Charles II and Ormonde's return to influence 1660-1685

On Cromwell's death in 1658, his son Richard became Protector in England, but his lack of military experience lost him the backing of the New Model Army. Without military support, the non-conformists forming the Rump Parliament needed to demonstrate their legitimacy. It became clear that the election of a new Parliament or a return to the position prior to Pride's Purge would 'produce a majority in favour of some kind of restoration of the monarchy'.[a] The Royalists persuaded General Monck to march south from Scotland with his Parliamentary army to back Charles II's restoration. On 14 May 1660, he was proclaimed King in Dublin, having been proclaimed King of England a few days earlier. This was greeted with great enthusiasm by Irish Catholics, who hoped to see the Cromwellian land settlement overturned.

The New Model Army realised that Charles's return would lose them Parliament's support. When his restoration became inevitable, they approached him to highlight their role in settling Ireland for the Crown, and Charles undertook to support 'the Protestant interest'.[b] In August 1660, Parliament passed an Act of Free and General Pardon, Indemnity and Oblivion, but one section 'specifically excluded all persons involved in the Irish rebellion from any acts of clemency'.[c] The restoration also threatened the newly restored Londoners in County Londonderry. Although their return had been approved by Cromwell in a Charter of 1657, Charles did not recognise any Commonwealth actions. When a City deputation met him in October 1660, he pronounced that his Majesty would perform what his father had promised, and more, and that his Majesty would deny the City nothing; that his Majesty found they dealt honestly with him, and his Majesty would deny them nothing.[d]

James Butler, 12ᵗʰ Earl and 1ˢᵗ Duke of Ormonde (c. 1610-88) in Garter Robes As the principal Irish landowner and a Protestant, he backed the Crown, succeeding Strafford as Lord Lieutenant. After Charles I's execution, he left for Paris, but was re-appointed at the Restoration.
Sir Peter Lely (1618-80) oil on canvas 1678 Kedleston Hall, © Matthew Hollow, National Trust Images No. 173501

On 10 April 1662, Charles II provided a new Charter, repeating most of James I's original. Apart from rights to the customs of poundage and tonnage at Londonderry and Coleraine, which were given up against a payment of £6,000, the new arrangements left the original terms unchanged. Supervision of Londonderry was given 'for ever ... [to] six and twenty discreet citizens of London'.[e] Charles was also determined to do what he could for those prominent men, Catholic as well as Protestant, who had stood by him during his years in exile. Soldiers and 'adventurers' were to keep the lands granted to them, but 'innocent papists' and other named individuals, who had served the King with special fidelity, were to be given preferential treatment. Ormonde, who accompanied Charles on his return to England from France, received a number of lucrative appointments including that of Lord High Steward of England. He was also raised to the Earldom of Brecknock in the peerage of England and, on 30 March 1661, became Duke of Ormonde in the peerage of Ireland. At the same time, his huge Irish estates were restored and he received grants, which went some way towards reimbursing his earlier expenditure on behalf of the Royalist cause. In November, he was reinstated as Lord Lieutenant of Ireland and immediately pleaded with Charles to redress some of the injustices of Cromwell's Act of Settlement of 1652. In 1662, a new Act was passed by the Irish Parliament, which required all new settlers to give up a portion of the lands they had been allocated to the 'Old English' and 'innocent Catholics', as determined by Commissioners. Settlers were to be compensated with equal amounts of land elsewhere in Ireland. Unfortunately, the Court of Claims set up in 1662 to resolve matters identified far too many 'innocent' Catholics, leaving insufficient land available to provide compensation. As a result, very few Catholics recovered their estates, but there were continuing attempts to resolve the issue for the rest of the decade.[f]

There was another difficulty. The expropriated lands had been occupied just as much by Church of Ireland and Protestant Establishment colleagues as by Cromwellians. The Crown was sufficiently pragmatic to recognise that its interest would best be served by continuing to bar Catholics from public office or from sitting in Parliament. The King also left 'the property of nearly the entire country in the hands of "the Protestant and English interest"'.[g]

In 1665, in an effort to provide a workable solution to the compensation difficulty, Ormonde steered an Act of Explanation through Parliament. This required Cromwellian settlers (with some named exceptions) to give up one-third of their lands received under the 1652 Act of Settlement. This was made complicated because the original grantees had often resold what was allocated to them. Although a 'favoured minority'[117] of Catholics, generally Old English Royalists including Ormonde, but also the Marquess of Antrim[118] in Ulster,

---

[117] Even James, Duke of York (later James II) received 95,000 acres of Irish lands.
[118] There was no one who had provided 'constant good affection' to the Crown, and Antrim was known to have entered into deals with agents of the Commonwealth and was also thought to have provided support for the insurgents in the 1641 rebellion in Ulster. After

received back much of their pre-war estates, most recovered little or nothing and, yet again, felt that the Stuart Monarchy had betrayed them. Although Charles personally lobbied for the restoration of Arthur Magennis, 3rd Viscount Iveagh, other local landlords raised sufficient objections to prevent it and he was fobbed off with a pension.[i] No one was satisfied and grievances continued. Moreover, those, who retained lands expropriated from Catholics believed, and they believed justly, that is ever the Catholics and native Irish recovered political ascendancy, they would immediately demand the restoration of the forfeited estates; they lived therefore in a state of continual alarm and excitement, and they were forced to place themselves completely under the control of England, in order to have British aid in protecting the property which they had acquired. … They felt like a garrison in a conquered country.[j]

Ormonde now focused on turning Ireland into a peaceful community by cracking down on religious dissent and political militancy. John Bramhall returned as Archbishop of Armagh and Primate of the Church of Ireland. He insisted on adherence to the Thirty-Nine Articles, the articles of faith of the Church of England.

> In January 1661 the Lords Justices forbade all meetings of 'Papists, Presbyterians, Independents, and Anabaptists and other fanatical persons' as unlawful assemblies. These included Presbyterian congregational church sessions, which not only enforced church discipline, excommunicating if necessary, but also had functions similar to those of a court of petty sessions.[k]

Bramhall's approach was always likely to give rise to major conflict in Ulster, where massive new investment would be needed to rebuild the settlements and to make good other damage caused by the rebels, and some had to be abandoned. By 1662, George Phillips was the proprietor of Limavady Castle, but it had been severely damaged. Although he built a new home at Newtown Limavady, he fell into financial difficulties and, in 1672, was obliged to mortgage his property. In 1668, the greater part of the City of Londonderry was destroyed by fire. Although the Livery Companies in London were suffering from the after-effects of the Plague in 1665 and the Great Fire in 1666, The Irish Society provided resources for rebuilding. In 1669, the King granted a charter to empower Erasmus Smith[119], a member of the Grocers' Company, to

---

the death of his wife, Katherine (widow of the Duke of Buckingham) in 1549, the Marquess had remarried Rose, daughter of the Protestant Henry O'Neill of Killeleagh, and she had inherited her father's estates at Toome. Despite Antrim's enormous debts, he made his way to London, where the King ordered his arrest and he was committed to the Tower for nearly a year until May 1661. He only survived by subterfuge. He denied raising an army for use in England at the behest of Charles I. On 10 March 1663, Charles II declared him 'innocent of any malice or rebellious purpose towards the Crown'. Despite having to face a public hearing, he was eventually restored on 1665. Yet Pepys recorded in his diary that the 'king hath done himself all imaginable wrong in that business of my Lord of Antrim in Ireland'.[h]

[119] The Erasmus Smith Foundation continues to support Schools in Ireland.

erect Grammar schools in Ireland, allowing County Londonderry to receive a share of his munificence. The Society also granted two hundred tons of timber free of charge to build a new bridge across the Bann at Coleraine, linking it to Killowen and the Clothworkers' proportion on the other side. The bridge, completed in 1673, had a drawbridge at its centre to allow taller ships to pass upstream. It was built by Captain William Jackson, The Irish Society's Wood-Ranger, who had a personal interest as, in 1663, he became the Clothworkers' Farmer. As Wood-Ranger, he was well-positioned to source the most suitable timber for the job, but, in 1672, he was dismissed after using large quantities of the Society's timber to make pipe staves and other commodities for his own account. Depredation of the woodland was a serious problem; it was not just needed for house and bridge building, to make pipe staves, or in the tanning process. Large quantities were being used to construct ships and for fuel at the newly established ironworks on the Vintners' and Salters' proportions. The shortage became so acute that, in 1685, the Irish Society introduced a clause into its new leases to limit further damage.

The Londoners' faced an unexpected challenge to their lands through their own bad management and carelessness. The Bishops of Derry had started to claim rights to church lands held by the Companies. Once having made appointments to livings on Companies' lands for a first time, the Bishops claimed precedent on the next occasion. The Companies took the diocese to court and, although the Bishops claims were rejected, the Companies suffered expensive legal costs.

In June 1666, with Charles being a Catholic at heart[120], the Roman-Catholic bishops and clergy met in Dublin to pledge allegiance to him. At about the same time, Ormonde was able to purge the Cromwellian army, reducing its numbers from 15,000 to 6,000. In desperation, the Cromwellians instigated two rebellions, one led by Colonel Thomas Blood[121], in attempts to take Dublin Castle and kidnap Ormonde, but failed in both. This resulted in the executions of a Presbyterian minister and three military officers. There was also a mutiny among the troops in Carrickfergus.

Ormonde tried to deal with the 'Dissenters' in Ulster[122]. Large numbers of radical Presbyterian ministers had arrived from Scotland as refugees, after being

---

[120] In 1670, Charles II signed the secret Treaty of Dover with the French. Under this, he agreed to declare his adherence to the Roman-Catholic faith on receipt of a French subsidy, but this was never paid.

[121] Blood was a Cromwellian soldier, who was ruined by the partial restoration of Irish lands to 'innocent Papists'. He is better known for his later kidnap of Ormonde in St James's Street in London and for his attempt to steal the Crown jewels.

[122] Religious conflict in Ireland, particularly in Northern Ireland, is a subject on its own, but it is important to understand the political consequences of new theological thinking among Presbyterians. Pioneering Presbyterian theologians in both Scotland and England were beginning to question long held Christian doctrines which lacked a biblical foundation. The word "Dissenter" has sometimes meant those on the extremes of religious radicalism, but

disenfranchised for supporting the republican cause at home, and they had little sympathy for a return to Monarchy. Dr Robert Mossom, the Anglican Bishop of Derry reported that 'fractious preachers run out of Scotland like wild boars hunted out of the forest and throw their foam of seditious doctrine among the people'.[q] When they were joined by more than 50,000 uncompromising Scottish Presbyterian extremists, they acted 'as a stimulus to an independence of mind that already existed.'[r] When Jeremy Taylor was appointed Bishop of Down and Connor, he 'lost no time in dealing with those ministers who refused to acknowledge the rule of episcopacy'.[s] Sixty-one dissenting ministers were turned out of their livings and either 'had to flee or only continue their ministry by preaching in barns, houses and even open fields'.[t] Only seven or eight

---

initially it referred to "those who could not accept the king's or the bishop's authority over their religious consciences". They espoused freedom of thought and "believed that a man can find his way to God through scripture and required no priest . . ."[l] They firmly opposed a church hierarchy of bishops as imposed by Anglicans and Catholics. Although collectively known as Dissenters, they were not a unified grouping with a single set of beliefs. Some, who baptised their converts as adults, became known as Baptists and those who 'trembled in the fear of the lord'[m] became Quakers, whose egalitarian principles forbade them from raising their hats. Others were particularly concerned about belief in the Trinity. Although Father, Son and Holy Spirit are mentioned in the Bible, there is no reference to them being embodied in one being. Thus some Dissenters, who became known as Unitarians, held that there was just one heavenly God, with Jesus being the great teacher or master, but the son of man and not of God. They also questioned those sections of the bible which appeared doubtful in scientific terms. These doubts were not limited to the creation, where the book of Genesis was being recognised as implausible more than two hundred years before Charles Darwin, but the miracles of Jesus were also doubted, reinforcing a growing view that he was not a deity. Such Unitarian philosophies were, of course, heretical in the eyes of the Established Church, whether Anglican or Presbyterian, but a dogma which presented Jesus as the son of man, suited republicans, looking for a theology to justify claims that earthly kings lacked scriptural validity. Unitarianism was thus a dangerous philosophy to espouse; it was not only heretical but treasonable. Dissenters, both Scottish and English, backed the English Parliament during the English Civil War, and used their beliefs to justify Parliament's action against the King. 'The Presbyterian majority in Parliament was made up of moderate puritans, who sought to replace the Anglican established church with a Presbyterian Church establishment',[n] in which authority resided with the synod and presbyteries, not with bishops. Had these moderates received backing from the Stuart Monarchy, Parliament would have supported the Crown. In 1643, a group of moderate divines produced the "Westminster Confession of Faith", based on Calvinist principles, to which all Protestants were expected to subscribe. This was resisted by both episcopal Anglicans and by the soldiers of Cromwell's New Model Army, who were fighting and winning the Civil War on Parliament's behalf. Cromwell's army was drawn largely from East Anglia, where religious 'Independency' was stronger and where authority resided with congregations, who claimed their right to choose their own ministers. 'Their most frequent and vehement disputes were for liberty of conscience as they called it ... that every man might not only hold but preach and do in matters of religion what he pleased.'[o] The New Model Army strongly rejected any form of church establishment and believed from the outset that 'the King should face justice for his crimes against the people'.[p]

conformed. Although Ulster Presbyterians had played no part in the Cromwellian rebellion in Dublin, and had been persecuted by Venables, Ormonde used this as his excuse to imprison all Presbyterian ministers in Ulster. The Bishop of Derry now complained at having insufficient space to hold all his prisoners securely. Dissenters among them, not unreasonably, resented Ormonde's stance, claiming that they were being treated more harshly than Catholics, who were still pressing their claims to be restored to their estates.

Charles II had no sympathy with radical Presbyterians and Independents. He blamed them for having started the Civil War, branding them as guilty of 'overthrowing a protestant church and murdering a protestant king'.[u] Once firmly back in power, the Established Church 'insisted that Non-Conformist views were heretical. Dissenters were banned from civil and military office'.[v] In England, Chancellor Edward Hyde [later Earl of Clarendon] introduced the Clarendon Code, designed to suppress religious dissent. This required ministers to subscribe to the Book of Common Prayer, and banned Non-Conformist ministers from coming within five miles of a town where they had served.[w]

Although this only applied in England and Scotland, Ormonde adopted a similarly oppressive policy in Ireland. The Act of Uniformity of 1662 made it obligatory for ministers to be consecrated by a bishop. This resulted in 2,000 ministers throughout Britain and Ireland being ejected from their livings, although many of their congregations stood by them.

Politicians, who supported the King, now became Tories (a term which had originally applied to Irish outlaws). Initially, they supported James, Duke of York, as heir to his brother, Charles II, but, when his conversion to Catholicism became clear, their loyalties focused on support for the Crown and the Established Church. Those believing that the Crown was answerable to the people became Whigs and included Dissenters to a man. 'Those opposing episcopacy and the Established Church were by definition also the enemies of monarchy.'[x] Opposing camps were deeply divided, but, as so often, those who wrote the history were on the winning side.

Royal propagandists transformed Charles I from a "Man of Blood" into an Anglican saint. 30 January, the anniversary of his death, was designated a church holiday and Tory churchmen used it to praise passive obedience, to condemn rebellion and to attack religious dissent.[y]

Yet, until the end of the 18th Century, Dissenters in Belfast saw 30 January as a day for celebration.

Following the Civil War, much of Ireland lay in ruins. Many Irish Royalist strongholds had been destroyed by Parliamentary forces. The destruction of buildings, crops and livestock during the Commonwealth caused great depression in Ulster. For much of the 1660s, returning settlers struggled to restore their farmlands. The colossal losses suffered in London resulting from the Great Plague in 1665 and the Great Fire, which destroyed many Companies' Halls in 1666, meant that there was a general shortage of cash to provide assistance in Ireland. The Establishment's persecution of Presbyterian clergy delayed the arrival of Scottish settlers and caused friction between English and Scots. With insufficient labour, lands remained destitute and farm production declined. Some relief came when The Irish Society appointed Colonel Gorges as their Agent to replace Beresford. Gorges invested large amounts of his personal fortune to help impoverished settlers. In 1668, he became Farmer on the Merchant Taylors' proportion for a period of sixty-one years; he was also the Goldsmiths' Farmer and leased the Society's fisheries. In addition to his house in Londonderry, he maintained a property named Summer-seat (Somerset) near Coleraine. Yet, as Agent for The Irish Society, he was not considered a success.

Despite a modicum of new investment, recovery took time. Rebuilding work on the proportions consisted of patching up what was left after the Great Rebellion. In 1670, Mossom, Bishop of Derry, made a representation to the Companies in London, blaming the poor state of Ulster's churches on the extreme poverty of the inhabitants, who were not even able to pay their rents. Very few of the churches were habitable and services often took place in ale houses. Yet the restoration of the Londoners to their lands increased confidence and 'the County of Londonderry entered a time of slow but sure improvement'.[z] The re-establishment of the Beresfords and other entrepreneurs on their lands also provided 'a degree of continuity'.[aa]

It was Ormonde's determination to return Ireland to economic normality, which prompted his efforts to end religious unrest. Following Bramhall's death in 1663, he started to take a more moderate line but the hoped for improvement was slow to materialise. In 1667, he challenged the English Government after it passed the Importation Act to prohibit Ireland's principal export of cattle being landed in Britain.[123] This had been promoted by the maverick George Villiers, 2nd Duke of Buckingham, in an effort to protect British farmers. It pressaged an economic catastrophe for Ireland where its cattle were left unsold. In Antrim, a shortage of feed caused a great many cattle to die, and tenants had insufficient corn to sow or to make bread. 'Rural poverty and hardship [became] endemic'.[bb] Ormonde retaliated by barring the import of English and Scottish goods into Ireland until the Act was eventually reversed. The economic situation was made even worse by a contraction in trade caused by the Dutch Wars of 1672-74. By 1674-75, there was widespread famine, exacerbated by absenteeism among landlords.

Ormonde's efforts to protect the Irish lost him favour in England. Although he had removed Irish Catholics from any remaining authority, he was criticised for the mildness of his approach and was attacked by the 'irresponsible' element at Court led by Buckingham.

---

[123] In County Londonderry, this resulted in a remarkable growth in the tanning industry, but the large quantities of bark, which were required led to a further depredation of the woodlands.

George Villiers, 2ⁿᵈ Duke of Buckingham deceitfully thwarted Ormonde's efforts to promote Irish trade by seeking protection for British farming prices. He was later implicated in the attack on Ormonde in London.
Sir Peter Lely c. 1675 oil on canvas
© National Portrait Gallery NPG No. 279

He remained aloof, saying: 'However ill I may stand at court I am resolved to lye well in the chronicle.' Buckingham threatened him with impeachment, and, in March 1669, he was dismissed as Lord Lieutenant and from the committee for Irish affairs. He retired to his estates at Carrick on Suir in South Tipperary, where, in 1670, he established a woollen industry. He did not complain at his removal, but it was a token gesture. His son, Thomas Butler, Earl of Ossery, became Lord Lieutenant in his place, while other friends and relations, over whom he had influence, retained their posts. As a mark of the respect in which he was more generally held, he was appointed Chancellor of Oxford University.

Hostility to Ormonde continued to surface. In 1670, Blood, (see page 285) a well-known hired assassin, had attempted to arrest him in London while he was being driven up St. James's Street. Blood's fellow conspirators dragged Ormonde from his coach and took him on horseback along Piccadilly, intent on hanging him at Tyburn, but he overcame the horseman to whom he was bound and managed to escape. In the King's presence, Ossery accused Buckingham of instigating the attack and threatened him with instant death if any further violence should happen to his father. Yet the King seems to have been implicated, as Blood was subsequently pardoned. Despite this, Ormonde continued to act on the King's behalf. He defended the Act of Settlement of 1662 in the English Parliament and visited Ireland in 1673.

In 1671, Richard Talbot (later Viscount and then Earl of Tyrconnell)[124] presented a petition to the King on behalf of the Irish nobility and gentry. This resulted in the English Parliament protesting to the King about growing Popery and the 'insolencies of the papists' in Ireland.[cc] The King showed Talbot some sympathy and appointed a commission under Prince Rupert of the Rhine to examine the Irish land settlement. In the following year, he made a 'Declaration of Indulgence' relaxing the Penal Laws faced by both nonconformists and Roman-Catholics. He also authorised the grant of a regular stipend, the *'Regium Donum',* for non-conformist ministers, even though they were not restored to their livings.[dd] This encouraged Scots to return in great numbers,[125] particularly after a Covenanter uprising at Bothwell Bridge in Scotland was suppressed in 1679. Despite their welcome arrival, the economic problems still took time to resolve.

The King's more moderate religious approach suffered a blow when the English Parliament declared his Declaration of Indulgence illegal. In 1673, it passed the Test Act requiring all office-holders to take the sacrament in accordance with the rights of the Established Church. Roman-Catholic bishops and priests were banished and their religious houses and schools were closed. The King retaliated and, in 1675, established a commission to hear grievances from Catholics, who had been transplanted to Connaught.

During the final ten years to Charles's reign, an almost imperceptible improvement in the Irish economy became a sustained recovery. In 1676, The Irish Society even paid a dividend to its Livery Company investors. In 1679, a quay was built at Coleraine for exporting timber (although this was contrary to plantation agreements) and for building ships. By the mid 1680s, there was a boom in exports of beef, pork, Irish linen, hides and leather. Imports into Londonderry included wine, vinegar, sugar, indigo, cotton and salt.[ff] With timber in short supply, the gentry imported coal from Scotland, but their tenants burned peat, which needed to be cut and then dried.

Large numbers of settlers arrived from north west England. Many Quakers settled up the Lagan Valley into Armagh and spread out from there. They had soon turned Oneilland into 'the Granary of Ulster'.[gg] With settlers being required to plant apple trees, a thriving cider business was developed, and linen production continued to expand. Trade benefitted, in 1681, from the expiry of the Navigation Act, allowing goods to be shipped direct between Ireland and the British colonies in America. In the Ards Peninsula it was found that crops of winter grain and summer barley were greatly improved by a mulch of seaweed.[hh] Even the exceptionally cold winter of 1683-84, which ruined the crops of many Ulster farmers, did not halt the recovery.

---

[124] Talbot had suffered an impoverished upbringing as the sixteenth child of a family of Catholic gentry from Kildare, and was one of the few Catholic survivors of Cromwell's siege at Drogheda.

[125] The departure of so many tenants to Ireland in 1678 made the Scottish Privy Council greatly concerned that Scottish lands were being left destitute.[ee]

Lands were everywhere improved, and rents advanced to nearly double what they had been a few years before. The Kingdom abounded with money, trade flourished, even to the envy of neighbours ... Gentlemen's seats were built or building ...[ii]

Yet prosperity

depended on support from the Government in London, on the permanence of land settlements, on the rule and observance of Law, and on the narrow band of political and bureaucratic powers held by the Protestant ruling classes.[jj]

By this time, only 4 per cent of Ulster was in the ownership of native Irish, and 'the few Irish we have amongst us are very much reclaimed from their barbarous customs, the most of them speaking English'.[kk] The great majority of people at Kilroot were 'presbiterians and Scotch, not one natural Irish in the parish, nor Papist'.[ll] A steady flow of English and Scots continued to arrive, despite the competing attraction of the British colonies in America.[126] Although the Papists also enjoyed economic success,

this fragile structure was endangered by the resentment of those who had lost lands, power and public office, and who, as devout Roman-Catholics, could only deplore the anti-Papist trends.[mm]

Ormonde had done much to promote learning and the professions, establishing the Irish College of Physicians. He insisted on appointing men with legal training as judges, choosing those with a record of loyalty to the Crown. When he tried to appoint those with Gaelic or Roman-Catholic leanings, he was accused of favouring old friends, some of whom were too old to be effective, but Elrington Ball has remarked: 'Those whom Ormonde loved, he loved to the end.'

In 1672, Ossery was replaced as Lord Lieutenant by Arthur Capell, 1st Earl of Essex. In his efforts to restore the authority of the Established Church, he limited the political power of both Dissenters and Catholics, entirely against the King's objective. He also took steps to remove corruption in the Irish Exchequer not realising that it was feeding Charles II's almost limitless thirst for money. Charles would not condone his meddling and, in 1677, Essex was recalled, allowing Ormonde to be restored once more. Ormonde now placed both the Revenue and army on a proper footing, but 'the mildness and moderation' of his anti-Catholic measures again came in for question, particularly because of a

---

126 There were significant differences between Ireland and the American colonies. Ireland was far closer to home and was well endowed with secure harbours. It was not subject to a climate with continental extremes. Being far less densely populated, America offered far greater areas of land. Although the native Irish had resisted British settlers, they provided them with a valued source of labour. In America, Indians almost completely disappeared from colonial districts in an effort to escape the scourge of European diseases. Yet both Ireland and America were considered promising areas for investment.

threatened Counter-Reformation in England. The Catholicism of James, Duke of York, heir to the throne, was now fully recognised.

Oliver Plunkett, Archbishop of Armagh As the saintly Primate of Ireland, he was executed for his completely unfounded part in a 'Popish Plot' to raise a Catholic invasion force against Charles II. He was beatified in 1920. *Garrett Morphey, Edward Lutterell 1681 oil on canvas © National Portrait Gallery, London NPG No. 262*

In 1678, Titus Oates created an entirely fictitious story of a Popish plot to launch a Catholic invasion on England. With the backing of several other senior English noblemen, Ashley Cooper, 1st Earl of Shaftsbury accused Ormonde of being involved, but Ossery defended his father 'with great spirit'. Then the Roman-Catholic Primate of Ireland, Oliver Plunkett, the saintly Archishop of Armagh, was accused of conspiring to raise a foreign Catholic invasion force against the King. This seems to have been a story fabricated by Essex, who was angling to resume the Lord Lieutenancy by discrediting Ormonde. Although Ormonde defended himself, he was cautious of providing open support for Plunkett, but wrote privately that 'no schoolboy would have trusted them [the informers] to rob an orchard'. Plunkett[127] was brought to London, where, on spurious evidence, he was found guilty of treason. In 1681, he was hung, drawn and quartered at Tyburn. This was followed by renewed calls for the removal of Roman-Catholic bishops and priests in Ireland and for their religious houses and schools to be closed down. This forced Catholic services and schools underground.

With Ormonde still having to defend himself, he wrote an open letter explaining his actions during the Civil War. Charles backed him and, on 29 November 1682, he was summoned from Ireland to be granted the English title

---

[127] Plunkett was beatified by Pope Benedict XV in 1920, and canonised by Pope Paul VI in 1975.

of Duke of Ormonde. Although he returned to Ireland in June 1684, there were further intrigues, and he was recalled four months later. Laurence Hyde[128], Earl of Rochester, was appointed to replace him as Lord Lieutenant. Yet he never took up office as Charles died within a few months. Ormonde's final task as Lord Lieutenant in Dublin was to proclaim James II as King. He then retired to England, where he attempted to block James's efforts to promote Catholicism. Although he remained nominally Lord Lieutenant, he stayed in England until his death in 1688, when he was buried in Westminster Abbey.

---

[128] Laurence Hyde was the second son of the Earl of Clarendon; he had been created Earl of Rochester two years before his appointment. His elder sister had married James, Duke of York, although she died in 1671.

Chapter 31

The Ulstermen's support for
William of Orange
1585-1591

With Charles II having no legitimate heir, the Whigs awoke to the reality of his brother, James, Duke of York, becoming King. James had become a confirmed Catholic after his second marriage in 1673 to Mary of Modena. The prospect of a return to Papal authority and the oppression of "Bloody" Mary's reign appalled Irish Protestants, who had lived through the Great Rebellion in 1641-42. James was equally unacceptable in England. In 1679, the Whig majority in Parliament passed an Exclusion Bill to prevent his succession, but Charles, who avowed his own Catholicism on his deathbed, dissolved Parliament to prevent it from passing into law. Whig extremists attempted to assassinate James as he returned from Newmarket races, but the Rye House Plot, as it was known, failed because a fire at the King's house forced the Royal party to leave earlier than expected. When the plot was exposed, some of the principal conspirators, including Richard Rumbold, the ringleader, and the Duke of Monmouth, an illegitimate son of Charles II, escaped abroad. Yet, two senior Whig leaders, Algernon Sidney and William, Lord Russell, were executed after being convicted by the foul-mouthed and often drunken Judge Jeffreys.

Sidney had been a key figure in developing Dissenting principles. He had supported Cromwell and, for a short period in 1646, had acted as Governor of Dublin, although he fell out with him over the execution of Charles I. In his *"Discourses Concerning Government"* published after his death, he 'was one of the first writers in early modern history to question hereditary kingship and suggest that a free people should choose its government'.[a] He expounded the dictum: 'Where liberty is, there is my country'. He died proclaiming his loyalty and lifelong commitment to 'The Good Old Cause' (complete religious toleration and the Catholic right to vote) and was later recognised as the Whig's foremost martyr and a secular saint. Thomas Jefferson, the architect of the American Revolution, acknowledged his Discourses as 'a rich treasure of republican principles'.[b]

Despite the prospect of a Catholic Monarch for the first time since "Bloody" Mary, Whigs 'shed no tears'[c] on Charles II's death. He had restored episcopacy and 'reneged on promises of religious toleration' made at his restoration and was considered to have 'presided over the persecution of dissenters'.[d]

James II The prospect of another Catholic monarch was abhorrent to the English Parliament, who offered the throne to his son-in-law, William of Orange. Yet he gained Catholic Irish support in return for promised concessions. *Sir Godfrey Kneller 1684, oil on canvas © National Portrait Gallery, London NPG No. 666*

James's accession renewed Irish Catholic hopes for an end to their repression and for the restoration of their ancestral lands. Irish Protestants were plunged 'into a state of profound anxiety' that Government policy would change.[e] The Revocation of the Edict of Nantes in October 1685 caused further shock waves when 400,000 industrious French Huguenots were forced to seek asylum all over Protestant Europe. The Irish economy also suffered a loss of confidence, made worse by an Act of Parliament, which restored the prohibition of direct trade between Ireland and the American colonies.

After the Irish Catholics' flirtation with Spain, even James recognised that Protestant colonists were 'the guarantors of English power'.[f] Seeing the advantage of retaining 'the English interest', he turned down initial Catholic demands for fairer treatment. He even appointed his brother-in-law, the Protestant, Henry Hyde, 2nd Earl of Clarendon, as Lord Lieutenant. Yet with

Protestants controlling 80 per cent of Irish land, James was determined to water down their ascendancy. He issued a warrant for Roman-Catholic archbishops and bishops to be paid and he placed Talbot, who became Earl of Tyrconnell, in joint command of the Irish army with another Roman-Catholic, Justin MacCarthy, who became Lord Mountcashel.

Richard Talbot, Earl and Duke of Tyrconnell Having survived the siege of Drogheda, he became joint commander of the Irish Catholic army and later Lord Deputy. He was James's principal agent for promoting the Jacobite cause in Ireland.
Unknown artist, England, 17ᵗʰ century, British oil on canvas, Photo © National Gallery of Ireland NGI.4167

The Irish Protestants were dismayed, and, in 1687, Tyrconnell replaced Clarendon as Lord Deputy to become 'James's principal agent in promoting the revival of Catholic fortunes in Ireland'.[g] The 'process of appointing Roman-Catholic Irishmen to positions of power throughout the Kingdom gained momentum'.[h] Tyrconnell purged the Irish Army of its remaining Cromwellians[129] and replaced them with Catholics; he ensured that the Irish House of Commons was overwhelmingly composed of Catholics;[i] Catholic sheriffs were appointed in each county; and banned religious orders were permitted to return from the Continent. He also amended the land settlement by returning about half of what had been acquired by Protestants to its former Catholic proprietors.

By placing Irish Catholics in positions of authority, James could claim to be supporting the majority population, but his promotion of Catholics in England was seen as the manoeuvring of a tyrant. With Jesuit guidance, he was encouraged to appoint to office those with whom he had been in exile in France, aligning himself with Louis XIV, par excellence an absolutist Monarch. 'The rich and well-established Catholics of England, and even the Pope thought

---

[129] Many of their officers gained commissions with William of Orange in the Netherlands.

James's links to the Jesuits and Louis ill-advised.'[j] The court of Rome recommended that 'if he joined with the interest opposed to France, he would have the hearts of the people'.[k]

Many Dissenters left Britain to plot a rebellion in Holland. This was to be led by Monmouth, who was influenced to promote religious toleration for all. He arrived in England with eighty-two supporters, fully expecting the populace to flock to him. Although many did so, he was comprehensively defeated at Sedgemoor, where he was captured. On 15 July 1685, his executioner needed five attempts to sever his head and even then finished the job with a knife. On James's instruction, Judge Jeffreys chaired the "bloody" assizes, imposing the death penalty on more than one thousand of Monmouth's Dissenter supporters. Of these, two hundred and fifty, including two women, were beheaded and quartered with the remainder being sent as slaves to the West Indies.

William III (1650-1702) of Orange
As James II's Protestant son-in-law, Parliament offered him the English throne. After landing at Torbay, James fled to France to seek 'Jacobite' support to challenge him on Irish soil.
Sir Godfrey Kneller (1646-1723) (Attr. to) oil on canvas, Bank of England, London, Photo © Heini Schneebeli, Bridgeman Images

With James making one tactical error after another, even Tory bishops would no longer tolerate his Jesuit leanings. The birth of a male heir (Charles Edward, the Old Pretender) in June 1688 seemed to assure a Roman-Catholic succession. A week after the birth, a Royal Warrant reserved teaching posts in all British schools for Jesuits. This convinced Protestants of all persuasions that James should be removed from the Crown. Tories combined with Whigs to look for an alternative. They fixed on his eldest daughter, the Protestant Mary, who was married to William, Prince of Orange, leader of the Dutch and a grandson[130]

---

[130] William was the son of Charles I's eldest daughter Mary, the Princess Royal. He was thus a first cousin of his wife.

of Charles I. William was a good choice; he had already established a strategic alliance to thwart French aggression on the Continent, during which an opportunist Turkish incursion had reached the gates of Vienna. His allies included the Holy Roman Empire, many German States, Poland, Savoy, Spain and most importantly the Pope, who had been outraged at the French revocation of the Edict of Nantes in 1685. With William being invited to lead an invasion of England, James called for Tyrconnell to bring his Catholic army from Ireland to support him. This caused outrage.

On 5 November 1688, William landed with an imposing Dutch army at Torbay ready to face the Jacobites (from *Jacobus* the Latin for James), who had French support. 'After fatal vacillation',[1] James fled to France before Christmas, abandoning his kingdom without a fight. The 'Glorious Revolution' was won without a battle on English soil. In February 1689, William and his wife Mary were declared joint sovereigns of England, Scotland and Ireland. Although the French declared war on the Dutch, Tyrconnell's army in England was disbanded, but he still retained significant forces in Ireland.

Although Irish Protestants supported William, Tyrconnell continued to hold Ireland for the Jacobites, despite an acute shortage of money, supported by an army of 40,000 mainly Irish Catholics, who were continuing to press their land claims. On 12 March 1689, James landed a well-equipped Jacobite force led by French officers at Kinsale and was also backed by Tory members of the Established Church. Yet, he soon doubted their loyalty and disbanded several of their regiments, despite the imminent arrival of William and his Orangemen. Dissenters in Dublin had little hope of mercy from James's Catholic troops. This was not just a war for England to retain control of Ireland, but to prevent it from becoming a second front for a French attack on England. As one member of the English Parliament concluded: 'If Ireland be lost, England will follow.'

Just as in 1641, the City of London settlers faced the spectre of a rising by the native Irish. Although they threw their weight behind King William, they had little prospect of success. Realising the strategic importance of Londonderry with its almost impregnable fortifications, Tyrconnell sent William Stewart, 1st Viscount Mountjoy with his Royalist Regiment of Foot to establish control. Being Protestant, Mountjoy and his mainly Protestant force of 7,000 men were welcomed there; this caused Tyrconnell to become concerned at their loyalty and he instructed them to withdraw to Dublin. He intended to replace them with 1,200 Catholic Jacobite troops of the King's 6th Regiment of Foot led by the aging Alexander MacDonnell, 3rd Earl of Antrim. When Coleraine refused to provision them, they were billeted at Limavady, where George Phillips, a staunch Williamite, had to entertain Antrim and his family. He[131] sent a warning to the Londonderry authorities, giving time for thirteen apprentice boys (of which four were from Christ's Hospital) to take matters into their own hands.

---

[131] Phillips was in severe financial difficulties as a result of the destruction of his properties. He died in 1696, when his son, William, succeeded to Limavady, but William sold the property to William Conolly (see page 313) for £1,800.

While Antrim led his fearsome bare-legged 'Redshanks' from the Scottish Highlands across the Foyle River by ferry, the boys, on 7 December 1688, closed the gates of Londonderry in their faces. Any Roman-Catholics left in the City departed, while the remaining citizens prepared to defend the walls. With James still being seen as the legitimate English King, Hopkins, the Bishop of Derry, believed that he owed unconditional allegiance to his divinely appointed Monarch and prudently withdrew from the City.

The apprentice boys closing the gates of Londonderry against the Jacobites From the stained glass at Londonderry Guildhall.

THE·SHUTTING·OF·THE·GATES·7·DECEMBER·688·A.D

A compromise was needed. Tyrconnell arranged for two companies of Mountjoy's men to return to Londonderry under the command of Lieutenant-Colonel Robert Lundy, a Scottish Episcopalian. With Mountjoy and his remaining men returning to Dublin, he was sent on a diplomatic mission to France, but Tyrconnell secretly arranged for the French to detain him in the Bastille, where he remained until 1692. Lundy was granted a Williamite commission and was appointed Governor of Londonderry, where he took steps to improve the defences against an impending Jacobite attack. His small garrison was supplemented by six companies raised by the citizens, who had heard that William was sending troops and supplies.

The settlers' prospects were not good. On the advice of his French military experts, James II moved his expeditionary force from Kinsale to Cork, where he was greeted by Tyrconnell with a huge Irish army. Tyrconnell had granted commissions to Irish Catholics to raise troops at their own expense to support the Jacobite cause. Even Catholic priests recruited men and Tyrconnell had been able to establish control over the whole of southern Ireland. James rewarded Tyrconnell with a dukedom. Yet their combined forces, living off the land, placed a great strain on the rural economy. They moved on to a rapturous greeting in Dublin before continuing north.

In early 1689, Hugh Montgomery, 2nd Earl of Mount Alexander (grandson of Viscount Montgomery of the Ards), tried to organise resistance among Protestant Ulstermen, but his army was shattered at 'the break of Dromore' in County Down and an assault on the Catholic garrison at Carrickfergus failed completely. The Jacobites soon controlled the whole of Ulster except for the island town of Enniskillen and the walled city of Londonderry.[m] About 30,000 Protestants sought sanctuary in Londonderry with its garrison of 7,000 men, knowing that Ulster's fate depended on them holding out.[n] They arrived with their cattle and as much food as they could carry. If Londonderry fell, Ireland would become the base for James to make an assault on England to recover his throne. A message reached The Irish Society in London, and they sent agents to Scotland to buy arms. The *Deliverance,* under escort from a naval frigate was able to land arms, ammunition and cash at Londonderry.

The settlers showed great determination. The Rev. George Walker[132], Rector of Donaghmore, nearby, raised his own regiment and took personal command of it. On learning of the imminent arrival of James's formidable force, Walker entered the City, and warned Lundy that he needed to face the enemy in battle before it gathered in strength. Yet Lundy was very unsure of success and there were doubts over his loyalty. He had already advised that Coleraine should be abandoned as it could not be defended, but, on 27 March, Sir Tristram Beresford (Beresford's grandson) attacked the Jacobite forces and inflicted considerable loss. With James's army having already crossed the Bann, Walker proposed making a stand at the Finn Water. Although Lundy stationed forces there, they were pushed back and he shamefully escaped back into the City, shutting the gates against his own troops, who were also seeking refuge.[133] Yet Walker managed to break into the City and prevented Lundy and its Governors from surrendering immediately.

---

[132] Walker had been born in County Tyrone, the son of a farming family from Yorkshire.

[133] There has been much debate on Lundy's motives. It has been suggested that he retained Jacobite sympathies and wanted to see Londonderry fall, but he later denied this and made no later attempt to rejoin the Jacobite army. It is clear that he did not believe that Londonderry could be held against such a powerful force and was concerned that it was not provisioned for a siege. Yet he showed great cowardice, and *Lundyism* has 'become synonymous with betrayal and deceit'; his effigy is burned each year at the anniversary of the shutting of Londonderry's gates.

The Rev. George Walker He galvanised the citizens of Londonderry to make a stand against the Jacobites, having raised his own regiment. After the relief of Londonderry, he was killed at the battle of the Boyne.
Artist unknown early 18ᵗʰ Century? oil on canvas © National Portrait Gallery, London NPG No. 2038

When two English regiments arrived in Lough Foyle by sea to support the garrison and bring provisions for their relief, Lundy advised their Colonels to leave their men on board, but to bring some fellow officers for a consultation. On their arrival, he claimed that Londonderry was only provisioned for ten days, and he needed all unnecessary personnel to be removed. The officers joined a council of war with other senior citizens and, in the light of Lundy's representations, agreed that it could not be defended. With the Jacobites making a slow advance, the British officers agreed to withdraw their ships with two regiments of Williamite troops, who had been intended to supplement the garrison, taking the Governors with them. The inhabitants were thus to be left to come to terms, as best they could.

Furious at their betrayal, the citizens killed one of the Governors as he attempted to escape. At this point, the popular Colonel Adam Murray, a Scottish settler from the Skinners' proportion, arrived at the gates with local reinforcements. Although Lundy ordered him to retire, he insisted on entering, and was fêted by the inhabitants. When he called on them to defend themselves, they went to the walls, where they fired on James's army of 20,000 men, who had devastated what remained of the Livery Company proportions in their wake. When the King approached the walls to demand entry as their Monarch, the defenders shot at his entourage, killing several of his men. Although the City Governors sent a deputation to apologise for their citizens' headstrong actions, they had lost authority. Lundy resigned and hid in his house.

The garrison immediately appointed two new Governors, the 'gallant' Rev. Walker and Major Henry Baker, after Murray had turned down the position. By appointing two, if either one fell, the City would not be left without command. They supplemented the garrison with townspeople and fugitive arrivals formed into eight well-organised regiments, each responsible for its own area; military personnel now totalled 7,020 men and 341 officers. The principal problem was to provision the 30,000 fugitive arrivals. Eighteen Anglican clergymen and seven non-conformist teachers provided inspiration from the pulpit (despite inevitable disagreement on dogma!) with the motto, 'No Surrender'. Those wishing to leave were permitted to join the ships still anchored in the bay, and, with the connivance of the new Governors, Lundy went with them, disguising himself by bending under a load of matchwood.

The besieging army lacked the artillery for a full-scale assault, and if the defenders had had to face a well-equipped European force, the walls would hardly have survived. Although James remained with Tyrconnell during an eleven day bombardment, it failed to achieve a breach, and he began to fear that 'the unpopularity of such an act would destroy his chances of restoration in England'.[o] Yet Jacobite mortars lobbed bombs with high trajectories from across the Foyle River, and these crashed through the roofs of houses with deadly effect. The defenders responded with their twenty artillery pieces supplied by the Livery Companies including the Fishmongers' 'Roaring Meg'. With James full of criticism of Tyrconnell's Irish troops, he retired to Dublin. Despite his impatience, he gave instructions for 'a slow siege, so as to inure the Irish forces to fatigue and discipline, and to teach them the arts of war'.[p]

It was famine, which proved the inhabitants' real enemy, with pestilence breaking out as a result of their poor diet. As hunger grew, disease also took its toll, and some crept away, only to provide a constant flow of intelligence to those outside. Yet the besiegers were also suffering from inadequate shelter in very wet conditions. Walker arranged random sallies 'in a manner unauthorised by military rules',[q] and his irregular tactics disrupted the besiegers with considerable success. On 30 April 1689, Murray led his cavalry to attack the Jacobites at Pennyburn. Although he was forced to retreat, he led the Jacobite cavalry, which pursued him, into an ambush manned by his infantry, where the French commander, the Marquis de Maumont was killed. On 6 May, he made a successful attack to recover Windmill Hill outside the walls, which had been captured on the previous day by the Jacobites, but a month later, he was driven back in a second battle there. The fact that Enniskillen was holding for the Protestants from south Ulster and north Connaught was crucial for Londonderry's defence. They were able to mount 'aggressive expeditions' against the besiegers, 'seriously weakening the effectiveness of [their] operations'.[r] In May, they routed a Jacobite force at Belleek in County Fermanagh.

On 28 June, the besiegers brought two pieces of artillery to bear on the Butcher's Gate and managed to dig a mine into a cellar under one of the bastions.

Their attack was only repulsed after a fierce struggle, during which Walker rose magnificently to the occasion. He had very few horses, no forage, no engineers to give advice, no fireworks or hand grenades and his guns were not properly mounted. Among the besiegers, there appears to have been acrimony between French officers and Jacobite commanders, with both Richard Hamilton and John Drummond, 1st Earl of Melfort, seemingly being 'inefficient and lacking in backbone'.[s]

The citizens faced great frustration when thirty ships commanded by Admiral George Rooke[134] arrived in Lough Foyle carrying troops under Major-General Percy Kirke with arms, ammunition and provisions. Yet the besiegers were in such strength that neither Kirke nor Rooke was prepared to hazard their men in a relief attempt, although an early attack might have provided an element of surprise. The besiegers had placed batteries on each side of the lough as it narrowed towards the City and had constructed a boom across the narrows near Culmore Fort. This was made of strong timber strengthened with thick cables joined by iron chains. When the warship *Greyhound* attempted to approach the City, it ran aground and was badly damaged by fire from Culmore, forcing it to return to England to make repairs. In light of this, Kirke concluded that he should make no futher attempt to break the boom. He sent intelligence to the City that he would take provisions to Enniskillen, but would return with a stronger force to relieve Londonderry.

With supplies of meat from cattle, sheep and horses rapidly disappearing, 'dogs, cats, rats and mice began to appear in the butchers' shops'.[t] The inhabitants even ate hides and tallow. From the pulpit, Walker continued to assure his congregation that the Almighty would grant them deliverance. With 30,000 people still within the walls, 10,000 were permitted to leave when James offered protection to any who would acknowledge his authority. Those who remained suffered a progressive decline from disease and starvation. One fatality was Baker, who was succeeded as Governor by John Mitchelburn, another officer. Even though the defenders were almost too weak to support arms, the Governors threatened anyone contemplating surrender with death. When the besiegers shouted dreadful menaces at them, their resolution only hardened. The French General, the Lithuanian Conrad von Rosen, threatened that, if they failed to submit by 1 July, Protestants in the surrounding areas would be rounded up and brought to perish under the walls. When captive Protestant settlers arrived, they beseeched the defenders not to submit. The garrison retaliated by raising a gallows in the besiegers' view and threatcned to execute all Jacobite prisoners unless the Protestants were freed. It also sent messages to Dublin and the Bishop of Meath, which persuaded James to free the Protestant prisoners. Those, who had managed to survive without sustenance or shelter for three days, were permitted to go. The besiegers were little better off; the devastated countryside could barely sustain them.

---

[134] Rooke was a potent force in the Royal Navy. He went on to capture Gibraltar in 1704.

The Mountjoy breaking the boom at Culmore Fort to gain access to Londonderry
From the stained glass at Londonderry Guildhall.

With conditions in Londonderry 'beggaring description',[u] tentative negotiations were begun with the besiegers, who offered them security and religious toleration. Yet allowing the City to fall would be a disaster for William and he immediately ordered his naval force to make a relief attempt. On 26 July, four ships were spotted sailing towards the town. Kirke had returned. The frigate *Dartmouth*, commanded by Captain John Leake, was escorting three armed merchant ships, the *Mountjoy* of 135 tons, the *Phoenix* and a cutter, the *Jerusalem*. A second frigate, the *Swallow*, remained out of range, but its long boat was being towed by one of the other vessels. At about 1900 on 28 July, the little flotilla made course for Londonderry.

> The Dartmouth came under fire from Culmore, but didn't [return] fire until the other ships were getting close. When the Dartmouth fired, the other ships sailed past in the cover of the Dartmouth's cannonade. The other ships were heavily fired upon as they moved towards the boom. The Mountjoy, being the larger ship, sailed into the boom "and broke the iron part thereof" while the crew of the longboat "cut the wooden part of the boom" with axes. However the Mountjoy rebounded from the collision and her stern was stuck

in the mud on the west bank. The Irish were yelling with triumph as they prepared to board the Mountjoy.[v]

Plaque commemorating Baker and Browning, Londonderry Cathedral This plaque records the heroism of Baker and Browning during the siege of Londonderry.

Captain Michael Browning of the Mountjoy, who was on deck encouraging his men, was shot through the head by a musket ball and died immediately. The inhabitants of Londonderry could see everything that was going on and their spirits sank as hopes of relief seemed dashed.

> In an attempt to halt the Irish advance, the Mountjoy fired three guns loaded with partridge shot. Their attempt succeeded [in] killing several of the Irish and causing the rest to flee. The recoil of those three shots had set the Mountjoy off the mud, into deeper water, where she re-floated. Led by the Phoenix she passed through the broken remains of the boom and continued on her way to the City.[w]

By 2200, they were tied up at the quayside, from where Browning's body was carried to the Cathedral. The siege, which had lasted one hundred and five days, was over.

15,000 colonists are estimated to have died. Of nearly 7,500 men forming the Londonderry regiments, only 4,300 lived to see the ships' arrival, and of these 1,000 were incapable of service. By the evening of 31 July, the Jacobites were burning their encampments and marching off. They had lost 8,000 men and retired in disorder to Strabane. After receiving sustenance, the residents of Londonderry were determined to chase the enemy, and some lost their lives by adventuring against its rearguard. Protestant troops from Enniskillen destroyed a Jacobite force under Mountcashel at Newtownbutler. Yet the Jacobites wreaked havoc as they went, destroying Limavady and burning and looting any other remaining settlements in their path. 'There were rural revolts among the peasantry, and anarchy was rampant'.[x] The roads were in a terrible state with bridges impassible. Virtually no livestock survived, and any grain was reserved to victual Danish troops, who were terrorising the area.

The City of Londonderry was seriously damaged. The spire of the Cathedral had been demolished before the siege, with its lead being used to make bullets. The roof of the nave, which provided a platform for cannon, required considerable repair. Very few houses remained standing. Yet its defiance had given King William time and provided a 'much-needed tonic for Williamite and Protestant morale',[y] with Walker being fêted as a hero. His published account provided admirable propaganda. Although he was promised the bishopric of Derry, he had died at the Boyne before he could receive it. 'Lord Shrewsbury[135], on King William's behalf, wrote of "the eminent and extraordinary services" of the Governor and inhabitants' which he put down to divine assistance.[z] Yet adulation for Walker annoyed the Presbyterians, who felt that their contribution had been ignored and the garrison's survivors were never paid for their heroism. When Mitchelburn went to London to plead for compensation for Londonderry's destitute citizen army, he was thrown in the Fleet prison for debt, despite William's promises of 'recompense' for services and sufferings. It took more than a century for a monument to be placed over his grave in Old Glendermot burial ground.

It has been argued that William was slow to send his forces to Ireland to challenge the Jacobites, but he faced the threat of war with France. Irish Roman-Catholics still believed that they had a good opportunity to recover lost ground. 'They supported the legitimate King of Ireland, they were in control of the [Jacobite] army and of State machinery, and they had French support'.[aa] Although the French had become increasingly frustrated by James's incompetence, both English and Scottish Royalist troops were fighting along side them. William was still uncertain of the Scottish reaction to his arrival, until John Graham of Claverhouse, Viscount Dundee, raised the Scottish Highlanders in support of the Jacobites. If the Scots were to prove an effective fighting force, William would have his hands full. Dundee inspired his Scottish troops to a great victory at Killicrankie, cutting a Williamite force to pieces, but he was killed and no other Scottish Jacobite leader had the charisma to rouse the clans to follow up on his victory. The Highlanders' advance was brought under control at the Battle of Dunkeld, and William could turn his attention to Ireland.

---

[135] Charles Talbot, 12th Earl and later Duke of Shrewsbury, who was to become Lord Lieutenant of Ireland.

Old Glendermot burial ground This rural location south east of the Foyle River surprising contains the tombs of Mitchelburn and Murray, two of the heroes of the siege of Londonderry.

The Protestants in Ireland viewed the rapid increase of Roman-Catholic influence and power with dismay, and knew their position under an Irish Roman-Catholic Parliament and State would be very weak, if not untenable.[bb] Inevitably, they looked to William and Mary as their rightful sovereigns and William knew that he had to send them belated support. On 13 August 1689, despite having deployed the bulk of the English army to face the French in the Netherlands, he sent the seventy-three-year-old Protestant Frederick-Armand, Duke of Schomberg, with an Irish expeditionary force to Ballyholme Bay. This was made up almost entirely of Protestants, mainly inexperienced Irish, who had taken refuge in England, supported by hardened Dutch and Huguenot troops. This balanced opposing sides, each having large armies under professional soldiers displaying 'courage and verve'.[cc] English and French warships fought out a naval engagement off Cork without any clear result. Although Schomberg recovered Carrickfergus after a punishing bombardment, 'the next ten months were spent in inconclusive campaigning',[dd] particularly because his transport and provisions failed to arrive. With his Irish troops lacking basic hygiene, disease killed many thousands of his men.

Frederick-Armand, Count of Schomberg, 1ˢᵗ Duke of Schomberg (1615-90) He took command of William III's forces against the Jacobites in Ireland, but he lacked the military strength to act decisively. He was killed at the battle of the Boyne.
Jacques Delaroche (17ᵗʰ -18ᵗʰ Century) oil on canvas 1720 Château de Versailles Photo © Gérard Blot, RMN Paris

Although Tyrconnell worked wonders in reorganising the Jacobite army, James 'subsided into an apathetic lethargy'.ᵉᵉ He led the Jacobites north, forcing Schomberg to retire to Lisburn, but failed to press home his advantage and retired to spend the winter of 1689-90 in Dublin. In March 1690, William disembarked a further 7,000 Danish mercenaries at Belfast Lough to assist Schomberg. During April and May, English, German and Dutch troops, well supplied with guns and ammunition, also landed in Ireland in great numbers, allowing Schomberg to capture Charlemont. Yet William realised that he had to come himself, and the very threat of his arrival caused mass Jacobite desertions. His fleet of about three hundred vessels crossed the Irish Sea, escorted by a squadron of warships under the command of Sir Cloudesley Shovell. On 14 June 1690, he landed a further 36,000 men at Carrickfergus, made up of English, Dutch, Danes, French Huguenots and Germans, all members of the Grand Alliance against France formed at the Treaty of Vienna. In an effort to contain the 'overweening ambition' of the French King, even Pope Innocent XI provided all the financial and diplomatic support he could muster.

The eyes of Europe were now focused on the war in Ireland between William and the Jacobites. One of William's first acts was to raise the *Regium Donum,* the stipend paid to Presbyterian ministers, to £1,200. This secured loyalty for him from both English and Scottish nonconformists, who resented having been treated as inferior citizens by the Established Church. The settlers, particularly those from Enniskillen,[136] joined William's army as skirmishers. The combined Williamite army advanced south to a position on the left bank of the River Boyne.

With Irish Catholics continuing to pressing their land claims, James curried favour with his Irish troops by rushing a repeal of the Act of Settlement through the Irish Parliament, but 'no provision was made to remunerate the Protestant occupants for the improvements and outlay that they had made'.[ff] The Act was accompanied by an Act of Attainder making it treasonable to join William, but the combination of the two had the effect of persuading Presbyterians to join him in droves. Although the Acts had again abolished the Livery Companies' ownership of their proportions, they could not be implemented so long as the military campaigns continued. It had never been the King's intention to restore Ireland to its original Gaelic ownership, and the legislation went far further than he intended. It turned Ireland into an independent self-governing Kingdom with a Roman-Catholic dynasty as its head. He recognised, only too late, the effect on British public opinion of disinheriting the settlers and removing the future influence of the English Parliament in Ireland. Irish Tories and the Established Church were in a dilemma. If they accepted that kings were above the law and that subjects should be passively obedient, they had to accept legislation that they considered outrageous. The English were furious and William and Mary gained not only popular support, but the powerful backing of the City of London.

In March 1690, 7,000 additional French troops landed at Cork under the Compte de Lauzun to replace Mountcashel's Irish Regiments, which were recalled by Louis XIV to France. The Irish were found to be far more effective when fighting under French officers on the Continent, where there was no opportunity to run for home. De Lauzun replaced de Rosen as the French Commander-in-Chief, but proved far less willing to engage in combat. Although Tyrconnell retained a substantial Irish Catholic force, many of his men lacked military experience. Although he considered coming to terms with William, he broke off negotiations after being advised that James's party 'had every chance of recovering England'.[hh] In June 1690, Jacobite confidence was greatly boosted when a French squadron badly mauled a combined Anglo-Dutch fleet off Beachy Head.[ii]

On 1 July, James lined out his army of 23,500 men to face William's force of 36,000 at the Boyne River. Both sides were well-organised, but James's infantry was made up largely of native Irish pressed into service. He had acted against the advice of his French military officers, who recommended approaching William's army from the west. William sent his right wing westward in a feint to entice some of the Jacobites away from his proposed line of attack across the river. Both James and the French fell for his manoeuvre and

---

[136] They were described by an army chaplain as 'half-naked with sabres pistols hanging from their belts ... like a horde of Tartars'.[gg]

moved the bulk of their forces to cover them. Tyrconnell with only one-third of the Jacobite force was left to face the full might of William's advance. When the Williamites crossed the Boyne at Oldbridge spearheaded by Schomberg's men, they faced a ferocious attack from the Jacobite cavalry led by Patrick Sarsfield, during which both Schomberg and the Rev. Walker were killed. The outcome looked a close run thing until William with the forces from Enniskillen broke Tyrconnell's men in a flanking manoeuvre. Further upstream, the French led a rearguard action, which allowed most of the Jacobite forces to retire in good order. Yet the result was decisive, and many inexperienced Irish troops abandoned their equipment as they retreated. James left almost immediately, fearing that his involvement in the conflict would prejudice his dwindling popularity in England. On 4 July, he re-embarked for France at Kinsale and was never to return. This 'was a severe blow to Louis XIV's pretensions to European hegenomy',[jj] and the victory at the Boyne was greeted with 'delirious joy'[kk] not only in England, but in the central European heartland of the Holy Roman Empire and by the Papacy in Rome. William advanced to Dublin and, on 6 July, he demanded the Jacobites' unconditional surrender. Tyrconnell and the French commanders were only too ready to conclude terms, but Sarsfield was determined to fight on.

By deserting Ireland, James had devastated his cause and sacrificed his Irish Catholic and French forces. 'The Catholic Irish suffered for their loyalty to a dynasty that regarded [them] as, at most, expendable pawns in a game, the objective of which was to rule Britain.'[ll] Once refreshed and re-equipped, the Williamites marched west. William occupied a prefabricated house designed by Sir Christopher Wren, with no shortage of comforts 'for him to lye in, in the field'. According to Narcissus Luttrell, this could be 'taken into peices and carried on two waggons', and might be 'quickly fixt up'.[mm] With William controlling Dublin and most of eastern Ireland, Sarsfield regrouped the Jacobite forces at Limerick, and it was here and at Athlone that he made his stand.

In July, the Williamites failed in an attempt to take Athlone, but, at the beginning of August, William besieged Limerick. Both he and his Dutch General, Baron von Ginkel[137], underestimated the Irish determination to continue the fight. Sarsfield's cavalry dealt a crushing blow by destroying a Williamite convoy of heavy guns, ammunition carts and baggage, which left William short of equipment. Although he breached the walls of Limerick, its defenders 'fought bravely and effectively',[oo] resisting all attempts to storm the breach, helped by lightening strikes from Sarsfield's cavalry.[pp] By the end of August, William had had enough; he raised the siege and returned to England.

---

[137] Von Ginkel was 'a dour general noted for his caution, who resented being dragged away from the Netherlands to take part in some obscure skirmishes in a sodden and uncivilised island far from where the main action was'.[nn]

Patrick Sarsfield, Earl of Lucan (Jacobite) (d. 1693) He proved a brilliant Jacobite cavalry commander at the battle of the Boyne and in the subsequent Irish campaign. He later joined Louis XIV on the Continent, but was killed at Landen in 1693. *Irish school oil on canvas 17th Century, Private Collection ©️ Bridgeman Images*

On 23 September, John Churchill, Earl (and later Duke) of Marlborough was sent by William with fresh troops to tidy up the campaign. Despite having been closely associated with James, Churchill had joined William when he landed in England. When Cork and Kinsale surrendered to the Williamites, the Jacobites' main link with France was severed. Realising that he could do no more to assist the Irish, Louis XIV[138] recalled his French army, taking Tyrconnell with it. The Jacobites, who were left under the command of James's twenty-year-old illegitimate son, James Fitzjames, Duke of Berwick,[139] became 'uncertain and confused'[qq] Yet they soldiered on, fighting 'doggedly behind the Shannon River for another year'.[rr] During the winter of 1690-91, Sarsfield continued to raid Williamite positions, 'aided by guerrillas who stole, intercepted dispatches, and attacked persons and property'.[ss] He was rewarded with the Jacobite Earldom of Lucan.

---

[138] Louis had always treated the French campaign in Ireland as a nuisance to limit the deployment of British troops on the Continent, and he never provided the Irish Jacobites with a sufficient force to achieve a decisive advantage.[vv]

[139] Berwick was James's son by Arabella Churchill, the sister of John Churchill, Earl (and later Duke) of Marlborough. He soon found himself up against his illustrious uncle, but survived to become one of Louis XIV's greatest Marshals.

Godert de Ginkel (1630-1703) 1ˢᵗ Earl of Athlone with the taking of Athlone, County Westmeath As commander of the Williamite forces after the Boyne, he achieved a decisive victory at Aughrim Hill, the bloodiest battle in Irish history. This led to the Jacobite withdrawal from Ireland.
Godfrey Kneller, German, 1646-1723 oil on canvas Photo ©National Gallery of Ireland NGI.486

Despite Marlborough's arrival, von Ginkel remained in overall command of William's forces, convinced that he could stabilise Ireland by buying off the Irish Jacobites. Yet Tyrconnell persuaded Louis XIV to send him with more assistance, and, in January 1691, he returned to Limerick. In May, the able French General Saint-Ruth arrived to take command of the Jacobite forces, but the principal French objective was to divert Williamite resources from the Netherlands. In June, Von Ginkel stormed Athlone, offering a pardon and security of property to Jacobites who would surrender or change sides. This had little effect.

Although he had failed to come to Athlone's rescue, Saint-Ruth tried to restore his reputation in the defence of Aughrim Hill, nearby. The two opposing armies each had about 20,000 men. On 12 July 1691, an Irish advance drove the Williamites back over marshy terrain and almost took von Ginkel's artillery. When victory looked almost certain, Saint-Ruth was decapitated by a cannonball, and, without him, the Irish could not be rallied even by Sarfield's cavalry. 'Von Ginkel's Dragoons moved forward in a concerted charge, cutting down the demoralised Irish troops'.[tt] It was the bloodiest battle in Ireland's history;[uu] many of the 7,000 dead were members of leading Roman-Catholic Irish families. It was Aughrim not the Boyne that proved the decisive battle. Ulster Protestants celebrated the end of the war with bonfires and would do so annually thereafter.

Although the French second-in-command, d'Usson, attempted to hold Galway, he had no support from its burghers, who surrendered to Von Ginkel on 21 July. In August, Tyrconnell died in Limerick and the siege was resumed eleven days later. In September, Sligo surrendered, but Von Ginkel was looking for a speedy settlement so that his troops could be diverted back to Europe. He offered generous terms to the Jacobites and, on 3 October 1691, signed the Treaty of Limerick, which allowed Irish Jacobite forces to retire to France. Those willing to swear the Oath of Allegiance to William and Mary were to be permitted to keep their estates. On 20 October, a French fleet arrived in the Shannon estuary and three months later, Sarfield and the remaining Jacobite army sailed from Ireland to form the core of the 'the Wild Geese', the crack Irish regiments in the French army.[140ww]

The Irish Parliament considered Von Ginkel's terms too lenient. It withdrew the repeal of the Act of Settlement, and forced the Irish to recognise English title to areas previously settled. Under a succession of Penal Laws, the Irish Catholics were excluded from holding public office or from sitting in the Irish House of Commons. Among the Irish, only Protestants gained restoration. Roman-Catholics considered that this breached the terms of the Treaty of Limerick. 'Roman-Catholics were to become second class citizens in the country they regarded as their own'.[xx] Very few Ulster Catholics had much land to lose, but, the authorities had no evidence against the Scottish Earl of Antrim, and he was restored to his estates. His grandson, the 5th Earl, was brought up as a Protestant and took his seat in the House of Lords.

'Nine-tenths of Ireland now belonged to the English Interest', and 500,000 acres of expropriated land were made available for sale. There were few buyers and half the land was granted at a knockdown price to a consortium with the unlikely name of the 'Company for Making Hollow Sword-Blades in England'. Its speculation achieved significant profits when it sold out six years later. William Conolly, the son of a family of Irish innkeepers, became the richest man in Ireland by land-jobbing, later becoming Speaker of the Irish House of Commons.

Catholics continued to farm as tenants, but were gradually eased off more fertile lowland areas. It was their resentment at losing their most fertile land, as much as the Penal Laws, which fostered conflict with their Protestant neighbours. Cultivating upland areas involved 'unremitting labour' to burn off the whin and heather and to prise out rocks and stumps.[yy] In west Donegal, 'thin acid soil had to be painstakingly enriched with seaweed and sweetened with shell sand'.[zz] The land's variable quality led to the planting of potatoes, which could tolerate poorer soil and eliminate scurvy by adding vitamin C to the Irish diet. In an attempt to alleviate food shortages among Catholic communities, who continued to graze cattle to the exclusion of arable crops, those farming more than one hundred acres were required to plough at least 5 per cent of it. Yet the real problem was landlords' absenteeism. So long as they lived abroad, their income from rents no longer circulated through the local economy. To encourage them to live on their estates 'and to contribute to the economic and

---

[140] If they ever returned, those who had served in the French or Spanish armies were barred from holding Irish property.

cultural life of Ireland',[aaa] non-residents were levied with a tax of four shillings in the pound.

The Glorious Revolution was now secure and, under the Protestant Ascendancy, Ireland would enjoy the longest period of peace in its history. The Livery Companies could begin the slow process of rebuilding Londonderry and its surrounding settlements for a third time. Yet Protestant landowners remained nervous of the prospect of the Irish recovering control. Roman-Catholicism had not been stifled.

Part 7

Domination of Irish Government by the Protestant Ascendancy 1691 – 1800

Chapter 32

The Protestant Ascendancy's assertion of authority 1691 – 1715

The Establishment in Ireland now joined with Presbyterians and Whigs in England to acknowledge William as King and to seek James's deposition. Although Dissenters loyal to The Good Old Cause would have preferred to avoid another Monarchy, they supported William in the hope that he would respect Parliament, restore liberties and show tolerance. When he enacted the Act of Toleration in 1689, they believed that, at last, they had found an English King in sympathy with them.

'For Tories, the Glorious Revolution was an act of God; for Whigs, it was an act of the people.'[a] 'Did civil and religious authority reside in the person of kings and bishops, or did civil authority reside in the people and religious authority in a man's conscience?'[b] This great debate between Tories and Whigs over the role of Monarchy would continue for the next century. Tories believed that 'the Established Church and its convocation of bishops were the only legitimate source of religious authority and that anyone who refused to accept this was a blasphemer, a heretic or worse'.[c] 'Any attack on the privileges of the Established Church was seen as an attack on the State as well.'[d]

From 1692 until its abolition by the Act of Union of 1800, the Irish Parliament consisted only of Protestant landowners. When it met for six months every two years, it focused only on protecting its Protestant interest by enacting a progression of Penal Laws. In 1695, the English Parliament passed an Act (7 William III. Cap. 4) prohibiting Roman-Catholics from sending their children abroad for their education or from teaching in Irish schools. Two other Acts (7 William III, Cap. 5 and 7 William III, Cap. 21) quickly followed; the first prohibited Catholics from keeping arms or horses valued at five pounds or more. The second attempted to suppress armed robbery by forcing both Roman-Catholics and Protestants to pay collectively for crimes committed by their co-religionists.[e] In 1697, the Irish Parliament passed the Banishment Act which required all Jesuits, monks, Catholic bishops and other clergy to leave Ireland by 1 May 1698. In 1699, Papists were banned from the legal profession, and a Commission of Inquiry was set up to look into the administration of forfeited estates, resulting in trustees being appointed to arrange their disposal. In 1704, further legislation prohibited Catholics from buying land or from acting as guardians. This kept them out of Parliament, as landownership was a prerequisite for holding a parliamentary seat.

It might be assumed that the Penal Laws were imposed out of high-minded religious conscience, but 'they were designed solely to maintain the wealth and influence'[f] of those enacting them. Religion was merely 'a convenient cry to secure the prejudices of the English people in support',[g] and the restrictions were enforced far more rigorously than legislation prohibiting Catholic worship. Apart from requiring Catholics to pay tithes to an alien church, no real efforts were made to prevent them from practicing their religion.

With the great majority of the Irish remaining Catholic, the Establishment felt insecure, particularly as 'France remained strong and hostile'.[h] The Papacy only added to their concerns by delegating the appointment of Irish Catholic Bishops to James, who was now in exile in France. This left the Roman-Catholic Church in Ireland 'avowedly Jacobite'.[i] On William's death on 8 March 1702 (and James having died in the year before), Louis XIV recognised 'James III and VIII' ('The Old Pretender') as King. All Irish office holders, lawyers and schoolmasters 'were required by Act of Parliament to take an Oath of Abjuration recognising Queen Anne as their rightful Sovereign and disowning the Stuart Pretender'.[j]

Meanwhile, on 3 November 1692, Parliament had passed an Act (4 William & Mary. Cap. 2) 'for the encouragement of Protestant strangers to settle in the Kingdom of Ireland'.[k] This allowed them to 'worship in the form to which they had been accustomed'.[l] Presbyterian Scots started to appear in Ulster in large numbers before the end of the Williamite war. Many had followed the army to purchase booty scavenged by the military. Yet, it was a natural disaster at home which triggered their mass exodus from Scotland. In 1693, the volcano of Hekla in Iceland erupted and, for seven years, spewed huge amounts of volcanic dust into the atmosphere, causing a mini-ice age. Scandinavia faced a terrible famine and Scottish harvests failed in each year. It was reported that 200,000 starving Scots were begging for sustenance from door to door, with an estimated one-in-five dying.[m] With Ireland escaping the worst effects of the dust cloud, many Scottish survivors, particularly from lowland areas in the south-west, headed for Ulster.

Claims that 50,000 Scots arrived in Ireland between 1689 and 1715 may be exaggerated,[n] but their departure from their traditional tenancies caused great difficulties at home. They were motivated by the availability of exceptionally cheap land, and their arrival forced out the Catholics. The Scots came with large numbers of cattle and adopted more intensive farming methods. By the time that Scotland's climate had started to recover, allowing the flow of immigrants to Ireland to decline, Scottish Presbyterians outnumbered Catholics in Ulster. With the 1689 Act of Toleration providing Dissenters with a period of relative freedom, Ulster recovered rapidly from its recent severe loss of life, which had borne no comparison to the bloodletting of the 1640s. A period of unbroken peace lasted from 1691 until the outbreak of the United Irish rebellion in 1798, and with peace came prosperity.

Despite being surrounded only by an earthen 'rampier', Belfast's fortifications were never put to the test and it had escaped the destruction faced by so many towns in 1641 and thereafter. The Scottish arrivals made it 'the most dynamic centre of trade in Ulster and, possibly, the fastest growing town in Ireland'.° It was dominated by Belfast Castle, with its elaborate formal gardens, from where the Earl of Donegall did much to encourage the new arrivals. They were permitted to become freemen, allowing them to benefit from lower property rates, reduced customs, tolls, fines and court fees. Up to then, freemen had been legally obliged to take an Oath of Supremacy to conform to the Church of Ireland, but with his strong Puritan sympathies, Donegall made no attempt to enforce this on Presbyterians. Thanks to his efforts, Belfast grew in importance and he promoted maritime navigational skills by funding a mathematics fellowship at Trinity College, Dublin.

By the 1660s, about 3 per cent of Irish customs duties were being raised in Belfast. In 1673, the Sovereign (or Mayor), 'Black' George Macartney led a petition, which successfully arranged for the customs house to be moved from Carrickfergus and to extend stone quays to receive more ships at Belfast. The devastation caused by Schomberg's bombardment in 1689 eclipsed Carrickfergus, and it never again matched its rival, which now became the principal port for exporting Ulster's agricultural produce. This included not only salt beef and butter, but hides, tallow, corn, linen, furs and salted herring. The export of barrel staves was cut back to ensure that there was a sufficient supply for local needs, but, with its lack of coal mines, Ireland depended on English and Scottish supplies, which arrived at Dublin and Belfast. Very soon comparable quantities of cargo were being collected for the return journey. A new bridge across the Lagan linked Belfast to Lisburn and was for many years the longest in the British Isles. By 1706, Belfast's population had reached 5,000, almost exclusively made up of colonists. This compared to 62,000 in Dublin and 17,500 in Cork.

The increase in the Presbyterian population did not please the Irish Establishment. It was not just Catholics who faced discrimination. Although Dissenters had kept their heads down to avoid charges of heresy and treason, the relative freedom provided to them by the Act of Toleration of 1689 did not extend to Unitarians (see footnote 122 on pages 285-6), and, by 1702, Queen Anne's Tory Government was campaigning against them. The Penal Laws now attacked all brands of non-conformists, both Scottish and Cromwellian, with their traditional hostility to the appointment of bishops and eagerness 'to establish the Presbyterian form of Church Government'. The Tory Government in London imposed the Westminster Confession of Faith on all new ministers. Although Calvinist in tone, it reasserted the doctrine of the Trinity, which was opposed by Unitarians. This was followed by The Test Act of 1704, which 'made it necessary for all persons holding public appointments to take Communion in the Established Church within three months of their assuming office.'[p] Some non-conformists overcame their religious scruples and adhered to the Test so that they could sit in Parliament 'ready to embrace every opportunity to weaken the episcopal establishment'.[q] Yet the Act was extended so that Dissenters were also required to swear an Oath of Allegiance to the Crown. Presbyterians saw this as a denial of the rights they had won during the Glorious Revolution. The majority of aldermen and burgesses in Londonderry and Belfast were Presbyterian and the Test Act resulted in their dismissal. No Presbyterians could legally conduct a school; in many instances land would not be let to Presbyterian tenants and, if magistrates so wished, church services could be declared illegal and the building of churches prohibited.[r]

Despite the Penal Laws, the Kirk remained well-attended and its elders insisted on its congregations studying the bible each day for guidance, with ministers laying great emphasis on reading skills. Ulster was soon the most literate corner of Ireland. Congregations were formed into presbyteries to maintain discipline and these supervised every area with regular visitations, co-ordinated by annual meetings of the Ulster Synod. The Church of Ireland remained highly suspicious; William King, Archbishop of Dublin, reported:

> They are a people embodied under their lay leaders, presbyteries and synods … and will be just so far the King's subjects as their lay elders and presbyteries will allow them.[s]

He was determined to curb their 'arrogant pretensions'.

Faced with the requirements of the Test Act and Catholic Irish discontent, many Presbyterians left for America. With their ability to read, they were better able than Catholics to learn of the opportunities being offered by emigration, and America offered attractive prospects for Protestants of every persuasion. Close bonds developed between Ireland and the American colonies, which had been begun at a similar time and had attracted a similar number of initial settlers. Americans shared with Irish settlers a sense of frustration at the way they were being treated. It was not only freedom of religious thought, but controls of trade designed to protect English business and farm prices. In 1718, five ships left Londonderry filled with emigrants bound for New Hampshire, and a further wave of emigration occurred in 1729.

The Presbyterian clergy was blamed for inciting its congregations to depart. Yet members of the Church of Ireland also left in considerable numbers. Most emigrants headed for Delaware, Philadelphia, New York or Boston. North and South Carolina made great efforts to attract them, particularly because of the growing fear of insurrections by slaves, if the European population was not strengthened. Settlers arrived in family groups and became known as the Scotch-Irish. It was hoped that their skills in clearing the Ulster hinterland could be put to good use in the American 'back country', and they were successful in pushing hostile natives ever westward. The new arrivals, who represented about one-sixth of the total colonial population, were 'implacable enemies of British rule, and were one of the most significant factors in the success of the American Revolution'.[t] It took the fighting in America to stop the flood of departures from Ulster but, by 1779, between 100,000 and 200,000 Scotch-Irish are thought to have arrived;[141] the flow started again as soon as peace was declared in 1783. It was former Ulster tenants, who formed the principal part of the 'body which brought about the the surrender of the British army at Saratoga'.

The departure of settlers caused great concern in Dublin. The Catholic Irish did not leave in the same numbers; they were still tied to the land of their ancestors and had difficulty in raising the cost of the fare. Although Presbyterians still outnumbered both Catholics and Anglicans in Ulster,[u] there were fears of an upsurge in the Catholic population 'being a breeding people'.[v] The security for those settlers that remained was weakened, but Dissenters started to creep back to their meeting houses despite lingering taunts of them being regicides. The more radical soon started to express their republican ideals.

---

[141] When the Tithe of Agistment [a rate on land used for pasturage] was repealed shortly before the start of the American revolutionary wars, it had the effect of making pasturage far more profitable than tillage. This resulted in Landlords consolidating their farms and expelling tenants involved in arable farming. Most of these were Presbyterian, as the Catholics were rarely more than agricultural labourers, and it resulted in the wholesale emigration of Irish Protestant farmers, mainly from Ulster, to America, where 'they supplied the United States with a body of brave determined soldiers ... [with] ... a thorough detestation of the supremacy of England'[w]

Chapter 33

Efforts to control
the Protestant Ascendancy
1715-1800

On the death of Queen Anne in 1714, the aging Ormonde appeared at the Old Pretender's Court in France. Although there was a Jacobite rising in Scotland, it soon failed and there was no similar response by the Irish, 'wearied of the apathetic indecisiveness and uninspiring generalship of the Stuarts'. George I, the first of the Hanoverian Kings, ascended the English throne, without any serious opposition.

Although efforts were made by the English to alleviate the plight of Irish Catholics, these were sabotaged by the Irish Parliament. By 1728, Catholics were not permitted to vote and were again prohibited from bearing arms, inheriting property, or practising their religion. The legislation went on and on.

> They were debarred from the professions [except medicine] ... Such abuse of power naturally encouraged the practice of every kind of evasive deception by the Catholics, and fostered the abominable system of proselytising and informing among the Protestants.[a]

A child of a Catholic of any age, on conforming to the Protestant faith might file a bill against his father ... [to obtain] one-third of the father's goods and personal chattels.[b] When a Catholic died, his estate was divided between his children, but any child prepared to conform could receive everything. In 1746, new legislation (19 George II. Cap. 13) declared null and void any marriages celebrated by a Catholic priest, where one or both of the participants were Protestant. Despite these punitive regulations, the Established 'Church gained only a few indifferent members, whilst the sovereign lost the affections of some millions of subjects'.[c] Irish Catholics lost heart. Regiments of foreign troops, which had been left in Ireland to maintain order, were disbanded. The Jacobite rebellion of 1745 caused little impact for the demoralised Roman-Catholics who had no powers to act, and less inclination to sacrifice anything more on the altar of Stuart fortunes. Jacobite collapse at Culloden was unreservedly hailed by the Ascendancy in Ireland.[d] At the same time, Anglican doctrine was promoted. In 1746, legislation was passed to provide grants for charter schools and to encourage 'English Protestant Schools'.[e]

When George III became King, he extended the limitations imposed on Catholics. They

were debarred from holding any office in the state, civil or military, above that of constable, parish overseer, or any like inferior appointment. They could not endow any school or college; they could not contract marriage with Protestants, without subjecting the priest who solemnised such marriage to the penalty of death, if unfortunately discovered; any justice of the peace, even without information, might enter their houses day or night to search for arms; they could obtain no degrees in the University of Dublin; they, with all the inhabitants of this realm, were charged to attend divine service, according to the established religion ...[f]

The Dissenters were little better off. Their ministers were required to swear the Oath of Abjuration to the Crown, but some refused to do so, not wishing to be bound to the heirs of the House of Hanover. This laid them 'open to a charge of Jacobitism, with which they had no sympathy at all.'[g] 'It was [their] dislike of prelacy which made the great body of the [Irish Presbyterians] hostile to a union with England.'[h] They looked back nostalgically to 'the pious, glorious and immortal memory of William III'. This became a pledge towards revolutionary principles, as successive English Monarchs chipped away at the freedoms granted by the Act of Toleration. Presbyterians now found themselves politically isolated, hostile to both 'the population of Ireland and the power of England'.[i] It led to them embracing republicanism, particularly in the security of Ulster, where they dominated the population. They were conscious of their own strength. In the rest of Ireland, the Protestants, thinly scattered over a wide surface, were obliged to rest their hopes of defence on the British Government, and were therefore led to cling to the Established Church as a bond of connection with England.[j]

It was the Presbyterians' republican beliefs that would instigate the failed rebellions of 1798 and 1803, in which a union with disenchanted Catholics to form an Irish republic was promoted. While Scots, who fought in the Scottish rebellions of 1715 and 1745 are remembered as local heroes, Irish rebels have only been seen as traitors. Their plans were doomed from the outset, but their objectives, in the face of the utmost provocation, may have been misguided, but were entirely honourable.

It was not until 1763 that agrarian Presbyterians in Ulster began outbreaks of 'Oakboy' (or 'Heart of Oak') disturbances, followed by sundry rioting elsewhere. These started as complaints over tax levels imposed by both the Established Church and State. Yet their lack of violence hardly troubled the Protestant Ascendancy. Between 1769 and 1772, the 'Hearts of Steel' riots required legislation to suppress them. The Mendicity Act of 1772 established work houses (or houses of industry) to take in itinerants and offer them occupations. In 1784, outrages by sectarian gangs, known as Defenders

(Catholic) and Peep o' Day Boys (Protestant), were begun and, by 1791, Defender outrages had become commonplace in southern Ulster. It was at this time that the Society of United Irishmen ("the United Irish") was founded in Belfast, linking extremist Presbyterians and Catholics in their search for religious toleration and relief from tithes to fund the Established Church. Catholic recruits were often drawn from the ranks of the Defenders, but received no sympathy from the Catholic hierarchy in Dublin.

In 1778, in the light of an undercurrent of disturbances, efforts to ameliorate some of the injustices of the Penal Laws were begun. The Catholic Relief Act allowed Catholics to aquire 999 years leases and to inherit in the same way as Protestants. This was promoted by the Protestant Henry Grattan, a prominent and eloquent member of the Whig party. In 1780, the Protestant Dissenter Relief Act repealed the Test Act of 1704. These concessions were followed by further legislation to relieve the plight of both Catholics and Dissenters. Yet it stopped short of offering full Catholic emancipation, which, it was feared, would pass control of the Irish Parliament to the Catholics, with the risk that they would seek to restore their ancestral lands. This concern was brought into greater focus in 1783, when the British Parliament recognised the exclusive right of the Irish Parliament to legislate for Ireland, even though it was made up entirely of Protestants. This was a response to criticisms of its controls to protect English trade. With England embarking on war with France, the reliefs were a recognition of Ireland's vulnerability if British forces there had to be withdrawn to the Continent. This was a particular concern when Dissenters were showing sympathy for republican views being espoused by the French Jacobins (republican revolutionaries – and not to be confused with Jacobites). Fears of a French invasion of Ireland led to the formation of the Londonderry Association to defend the County. Volunteer Corps were also set up and these were joined by members of the Catholic hierarchy, who, in 1793, were permitted to hold civil and military office and to sit for University degrees. The Catholic hierarchy had no sympathy for Jacobins or for their plans to launch an Irish invasion. To nip any threat in the bud, the British Government approved new legislation (35 George III, Cap. 21) to establish Roman-Catholic seminaries, resulting in the opening of the Royal College of St Patrick at Maynooth in County Kildare. Yet full Catholic emancipation remained a stumbling block.

Sectarian unrest continued. On 21 September 1795, a pitched battle at Loughall between Peep a' Day Boys and Defenders led to the formation of the Orange Order, an exclusively Protestant Masonic-style society devoted to the memory of William III, which paraded in strength in the following year. The Order grew rapidly in south and west Ulster, recruiting some landed gentry and penetrating both the Yeomanry (part-time local forces raised to combat the threat caused by war with France and from the United Irish and Defenders). The English Tory Government became so paranoiac about Dissenter sympathies for Jacobinism in both England and Ireland that William Pitt (the younger), the Tory Prime Minister, called on the Whigs to form a coalition Government. The Whig leader, Charles James Fox, who had strong Dissenter and Jacobin sympathies, was forced to resign when his colleagues failed to support him, and William Henry Cavendish-Bentinck, 3rd Duke of Portland, assumed the leadership of the Whigs and joined the coalition. Portland needed support from the influential William, 4th Earl Fitzwilliam, who agreed to back the coalition, despite mistrusting Pitt, if he were appointed Lord Lieutenant of Ireland. Although this was agreed, there was some confusion over the level of his authority.

William, 4th Earl Fitzwilliam Pitt's coalition government appointed him as Lord Lieutenant, but he exceeded his authority by offering full emancipation to Catholics and Presbyterians. His withdrawal caused great distress.
William Poole (fl. 1804-38) Sheffield Galleries and Museums Trust, UK ©
Bridgeman Images

Fitzwilliam's arrival in Dublin was welcomed by both Irish Catholics and Dissenters. He concluded that the Catholic Irish should be granted full emancipation, believing that they could be persuaded to follow English Government policy. He also believed that this would help to control outbreaks of sectarian violence, which did not seem politically motivated. Catholics were certainly unlikely to ally with the Protestant Jacobins in France. To gain Catholic backing, Fitzwilliam was encouraged by the Irish Whigs to remove the two most hated members of the Protestant Ascendancy, the Rt. Hon. John Beresford[142] and John FitzGibbon, later Earl of Clare, the Irish Attorney-General. Beresford was the First Commissioner of the Revenue for Ireland and was thought to be using his position to line his own pocket. Yet he was a close ally of Pitt and a member of the English Privy Council. When Fitzwilliam dismissed him, believing that he had Pitt's authority to do so, Beresford travelled to London to complain. Pitt denied Fitzwilliam's authority to act as he had and, when Portland supported Pitt, Fitzwilliam was forced to resign. It is one of the great tragedies for Ireland that FitzWilliam was not permitted to follow through with his plan.

---

[142] Beresford was the great-great-grandson of The Irish Society agent and an uncle of the 1st Marquess of Waterford.

It would seem that Pitt and Portland had concluded that the better solution was for Ireland to seek parliamentary Union with England, which would allow Catholics to be emancipated without granting them a parliamentary majority.

Without Fitzwilliam in authority, the United Irish held clandestine meetings to support a French invasion designed to create an Irish republic in which all men were free and equal. When their rebellion began in Leinster in May 1798, it was disorganised and quickly degenerated into a sectarian massacre. Many Protestants were brutally murdered and all the fine talk of liberty and fraternity 'dissipated in an orgy of settling old scores'.[k] In Ulster the rebels were led by the charismatic idealist Henry Joy McCracken, but were quickly defeated by Government troops. He had failed to gain the support of Belfast's Presbyterian hierarchy, which, with The Irish Society, contributed to the cost of restoring order. Although murders and other outrages took place in County Londonderry, it did not suffer greatly. The promised support from France was too little and came too late. When a French force landed in County Mayo in August 1798, it routed Government troops at Castlebar, but in the following month was forced into surrender by General Charles Cornwallis in County Longford. A second French force was routed by the British Navy in Lough Swilly, when another United Irish leader, Theobald Wolfe Tone, was arrested.

With the threat of a French invasion out of the way, thoughts returned to the union of British and Irish Parliaments. Its approval required a majority vote in the Irish Parliament dominated as it was by the Protestant ascendancy. It had the support of Grattan and the Irish Whigs, but Pitt found himself having to bribe 'place sitters' among the Irish Tories, who remained fearful of the threat of republicanism, to push the Union through. Irish Catholics of course backed it, realising that they could be fully emancipated, even if they did not gain control in Parliament. They also saw it as the means of breaking the corrupt stranglehold of the Protestants. Yet they did not have a vote. Although the Orange Order opposed the Union, it had little support. The last session of the Irish Parliament took place on 15 January 1800, and the Act of Union was passed on 1 August. Yet, even in the British Parliament, George III was persuaded that Catholic emancipation would contravene the terms of his Coronation oath and Pitt was forced to resign. It took many years for Catholic objectives to be realised.

Chapter 34

The Londonderry plantations under William and the Hanoverians
1691 – 1800

After all its heroics in 1689, Londonderry was promised a grant of £10,000 from the English Government, but this was never paid. With the Jacobite danger abated, little interest was paid to the settlers who had defended it so bravely. 'Most of the houses in Derry were demolished by the military operations of the enemy during the late siege'.[a] Many of Londonderry's more prominent merchants, who had done so much, were bankrupted when they received no recompense. Even Aldermen were obliged to petition The Irish Society and Livery Companies for help. The Society raised money to pay the 'citizen-army' which had defended it. It also levied one hundred pounds from each of the twelve Great Livery Companies to send immediate relief to the City and to encourage those who had fled to rebuild their property.[b] In 1690 a survey of the damage was prepared by Captain Francis Neville, and funds began to be raised for 'the building of a court house, and other accommodations'. The Society abated rents and its wood-rangers supplied sixty tons of timber from nearby forests 'towards rebuilding the Market House, repairing the gates, and other public buildings'.[c] A further 'one hundred and twenty tons of timber, and forty thousand laths, were allowed for building the town house of Derry'[143]. A

---

[143] All over Ulster, timber was in short supply; it was needed for building, charcoal burning and export. Much of it was cut as a means of making quick profits and to open up more land for grazing and cultivation. Little attempt was made to preserve woodland by coppicing. Iron founding used two and a half tons of charcoal in making one bar of iron. Bark was stripped from living oak trees as part of the process of tanning leather, but this eventually destroyed the trees. The Livery Company management of its woodlands was not immune from criticism. In 1734 a new woodland survey was ordered, but the Surveyor, Archibald Stewart, (former agent of the Earl of Antrim) proved inefficient. When his maps were found to be inaccurate, he was 'directed' to prepare a new set, which were presented in 1738. Middlemen supervising the woods had been involved in a massive asset stripping exercise with the collusion of the wood-rangers. The Society ordered any remaining timber to be cut down and they then restored the cutting rights to the Livery Companies in the hope of better

deputation arrived from London to 'view the wastes and ruins by the siege' both at Londonderry and Coleraine.[e] Beresford (the grandson) had sustained personal losses of about £4,000. By 1706, there were 2,848 inhabitants in Londonderry. Although trade and commerce was still languishing, sentiment was slowly starting to improve. The school founded by Matthias Springhame in 1616 was again filled with settlers' children. In 1710, the local economy benefited from the first Irish Banking Act.

In the proportions, settlements were also slow to recover. Most land was devastated and there were ongoing arguments between individual Livery Companies. The Irish Society had to arbitrate over disputes, and it withheld payments due to protagonists until matters were settled. Coleraine had faced 'an orgy of destruction' during the Jacobite retreat.[f] Some of its tenements remained ruinous for many years, but a Free School was established in 1705 to teach children to read, write and comprehend accounts. It soon faced difficulties caused by 'the mismanagement and incapacity of the master, and the gross negligence of the [Coleraine] Corporation'.[g] In 1739, it fell into misuse and was not revived until the following year when it reverted to The Irish Society's control. Between 1717 and 1720, St Patrick's Church received a new spire.[h] In 1735, The Irish Society contributed £200 towards the cost of a new Market House and, in February 1741, provided thirty-five tons of timber and a further £700 towards its building costs.

In 1689, Newry had been burned to the ground by Jacobites under Berwick, but as soon as peace was declared, Nicholas Bagenal threw himself into rebuilding it. It recovered quickly, particularly when leases were granted in perpetuity. The rebuilding of Armagh only started after 1704, but things slowly improved. Towns such as Augher, Dungannon and Strabane, which had been ransacked in 1641, were again badly damaged by the Jacobites, but not so extensively. The village round Dunluce Castle disappeared completely, and Tully Castle remained derelict.

Rebuilding was hampered by the shortage of timber. In 1699, an Act of Parliament required landholders and leaseholders to plant and conserve trees, and The Irish Society continued to scrutinise replanting. Yet thefts of wood continued and some proportions appointed wood-rangers to preserve and improve trees. The Vintners' proportion, which was let to Viscount Massereene (Sir John Clotworthy), faced continuing problems. The Society also preserved the fisheries, backed by a survey undertaken by Thomas Neville. It took an Act of Parliament to resolve a long running dispute with the Bishopric of Derry over fishing rights on the Foyle and Bann rivers. This required the Bishopric to pay £250 per annum to continue fishing. Other disputes with the Bishop involved

---

success in conserving woodland for the future. Yet 'by 1803 County Londonderry was [still] "the worst wooded county in the King's dominions"'[d]

title to valuable advowsons, which appear to have reverted to him by default[144], losing the Londoners 'an important right of patronage and presentation'.[i]

Between 1717 and 1720, the Drapers built a new market house at Moneymore and the Salters repaired Magherafelt church. With political stability re-established, the Williamite victory had lulled landlords into a sense of false security. Although London settlers in County Londonderry should have flourished in an environment hostile to both Catholics and Presbyterians, the Presbyterians remained dominant. Middlemen leasing Livery Company lands were unable to increase rents, even though they remained low by English standards.[j] On arrival in 1718, the new Bishop of Derry, William Nicholson, found 'dismal marks of hunger and want' on the faces of the people.[k] Famine was everywhere.

In 1720, many London liverymen were ruined when the South Sea Bubble burst[145], and their Companies were temporarily unable to continue financial support. The effect spun off in Ulster, where Companies looked for any means to generate cash. They received lucrative entry fines on letting proportions to middlemen on long leases without stipulating required duties between landlord and tenant. This resulted in appalling abuses by unscrupulous middlemen, who milked estates for everything they could take. When leases expired, many Presbyterian tenants and undertakers, already seething at the requirement to pay tithes to the Established Church simply emigrated. So universal was the departure from the Bann Valley in particular that a new settlement called Londonderry was founded North Carolina.

During the 18th Century, Protestant emigration and Catholic fecundity resulted in Ulster returning to a majority Catholic population. Rivalry between evenly balanced Protestant and Catholic groups caused dangerous volatility. With the 1641 rebellion still within living memory, the departure of Protestant settlers increased the sense of isolation for those who remained. It was not until the 19th Century that Roman-Catholics started to leave for America in numbers to escape the potato famines, but, even then, some stayed 'to continue their remorseless dream of recovering their lands'.[l]

There were numerous other factors which contributed to delays in improving the economy and to the Scottish exodus to America. In 1720, farming was suffering from disease among cattle and harvest failure. The Irish Society

---

[144] Slade was later very critical of the Earl-Bishop of Derry, who derived an annual income of £15,000, which he spent in Italy and France and left buildings unfinished at Downhill and Ballyscullion.[m]

[145] The South Sea Company, was a Government sponsored venture formed in 1711 to establish a trade (mainly in slaves) with Spanish America. The first voyage brought only limited profits, but when George I was appointed Governor of the Company, there was new confidence and the stock rose to dizzy heights and then collapsed, bringing down the value of Bank of England stocks with it. Three Government ministers were later found guilty of corruption, but the Company survived, making modest profits, particularly from whaling in Greenland, until 1853.[n]

was unable to let its fishings, and had to manage them itself. Although the price of salmon at Lough Foyle fell to a derisory twelve pounds per ton, a better price was obtained in London. The fishings were still unlet in 1724. In a continuing effort to find new markets, the Society, in 1739, started to send casks of salted fish to Venice and Leghorn, but, in July, the cargo vessel foundered with the loss of all lives. In 1726, one of a series of harvest failures 'obliged The Irish Society and other bodies to raise subscriptions for purchasing corn for the poor'.[o] In 1739, a wet summer again reduced the grain harvest, and cut turf would not dry. In the exceptionally cold winter that followed, famine caused many deaths and much distress, which the Society again tried to alleviate with grants of money. It was so cold that mill wheels became frozen, lamps were snuffed out in the Dublin streets, winter sown grain crops failed, potatoes became inedible after becoming frozen in their clamps and large numbers of cattle and sheep were killed. 'The Year of the Great Frost' was followed, in 1740, by a year of storms and drought, which destroyed newly sown crops and caused acute food shortages. With people dying of starvation and disease, dogs ate the dead in the fields 'for want of people to bury them'.[p]

Violence broke out in Drogheda, where a ship loaded with oatmeal destined for Scotland was boarded by starving local citizens, who removed the sails and the rudder to retain the cargo in Ireland. In May 1740, rioters in Dublin, where food prices had soared, broke into bakers' shops to obtain bread. The Lord Mayor, Samuel Cooke, looked for ways to stop hoarding and bring down prices. Archbishop Boulter launched a feeding program at his own expense, and Bishop Berkeley recorded:

> I have seen the labourer endeavouring to work at his spade, but fainting for want of food, and forced to quit it. I have seen the aged father eating grass like a beast and in the anguish of his soul wishing for his dissolution. I have seen the helpless orphan exposed on the dunghill, and none to take him in for fear of infection; and I have seen the hungry infant sucking at the breast of the already expired parent.[q]

War in Europe exacerbated the problem, with Spanish privateers attacking vessels carrying grain destined for Irish ports. In the following winter, chunks of ice floating down the River Liffey at Dublin overturned smaller vessels. Yet at last the weather improved and, with prices starting to fall, hoarding ceased and food prices returned to normal. It is estimated that 400,000 died, causing the Irish population to fall by 20 per cent, a greater proportion than those dying during the six years of the Great Famine of the 1840s. Although the whole of Europe was affected, only Norway faced a similar level of depredation to Ireland. It was the poorer Catholics in Ulster, who were hit the hardest.

In 1744, both potato and oat crops again failed after a wet and cold summer, so more relief was provided.

Matters became so bad that most of the Companies rid themselves of direct involvement in their estates by letting them to individuals for a term of "lives"[146].[r]

In 1730, the Goldsmiths had agreed to sell the Manor of Goldsmith's Hall to Henry Petty, Earl of Shelburne for £14,100. In 1737, the Vintners sold their proportion for £15,000. The Irish Society successfully resisted a proposal to build major ports at Rathmullan and Ballycastle, which would have competed with Londonderry and Coleraine.

Although many Livery Companies tried to encourage linen production in agricultural communities, Protestant tenants remained so disillusioned that emigration reached 'epidemic proportions'. Those that stayed behind in Ulster took advantage of opportunities offered by linen manufacture. Coleraine approached The Irish Society for help in establishing its own industry. Gradually the ravages of war were made good. More accurate surveys of the land allowed bogs to be drained, and those farmers adopting more sophisticated methods started to prosper. In addition to flax, they grew barley and oats, and raised cattle, horses, sheep and pigs. Roads were improved and bridges erected. (In 1730, The Irish Society contributed £500 towards the cost of a stone bridge across the Bann at Coleraine.) In the 1750s, there were moves to make the Bann navigable,[s] and the navigation from Belfast to Lisburn was opened in 1763.[147] In 1769, at the initiative of the Earl-Bishop of Derry (see page 332), who contributed £1,000 to the cost, there were plans for a new wooden bridge, manufactured in America, to cross the Foyle at Londonderry. Work began in 1789, and it was completed two years later at a total cost estimated at £10,000. It had a lifting section to enable boats to pass through it. Mail coaches started running in 1790 so that differing means of communication slowly began to flourish. This made the 18th Century a time of economic and social growth, with 'the building of large numbers of public edifices and fine houses'.[t]

In the 1750s, The Irish Society made determined efforts to establish values for all land and buildings in the Londonderry plantations.[u] Roads were repaired and built, with street lighting being installed. In 1766, it began to grant leases in perpetuity, if lessees would carry out building works and other improvements. Tenancy agreements were changed so that, on expiry, tenants were recompensed for work undertaken. This greatly encouraged tenants to make improvements. These arrangements quickly spread throughout Ulster, but did not become the practice elsewhere for another one hundred years. This resulted in 'superior prosperity and tranquillity in Ulster compared to the rest of Ireland'.[v]

---

[146] Such lettings lasted for the period of the longest living of (normally) three nominated individuals. Some Companies nominated George III, as a child, to be one of their 'lives', so that direct control of their estates was not restored to them until 1820.

[147] In 1826, there was a scheme by Richard Owen to make the Bann navigable from Lough Neagh to Coleraine.

Frederick Augustus Hervey, Bishop of Derry (1730-1803) and 4th Earl of Bristol at Ickworth, Suffolk The flamboyant Earl-Bishop 'carried out his episcopal duties with the minimum of conviction and the maximum of style', but cultivated 'a spirit of toleration'. He funded a programme of fine church building.
Attr. To Hugh Douglas Hamilton (1736-1808) © Angelo Hornak, National Trust Images No. 13013

The Irish Society's efforts had their parallel in the Church. In 1768, Frederick Hervey became Bishop of Derry, and succeeded as Earl of Bristol in 1779. The 'Earl-Bishop' 'carried out his episcopal duties with the minimum of conviction and the maximum of style' and, 'when sectarian jealousies ran high, did much by his example to soften their asperities and to cultivate a spirit of toleration'[w] by showing sympathy for both Catholic and Dissenter emancipation. His arrival encouraged 'a magnificent sequence of church-building, landscape improvements, and the creation of fine houses'.[x] In 1783, in his capacity as the Colonel of the Londonderry Volunteers, he attended their Grand Convention in Dublin, accompanied by a troop of dragoons. He proceeded from Londonderry

> with all the pomp and ceremony of a Royal progress. Dressed entirely in purple, with diamond knee and shoe buckles, with white gloves fringed with gold lace, and fastened with long tassels, he entered Dublin seated in an open landau, drawn by six horses, caparisoned with purple trappings, and passed slowly through the principal streets to the Royal Exchange.[y]

Chapter 35

The development of the Irish linen industry 1691-1800

With the Irish economy starting to flourish after Charles II's restoration, the English Parliament imposed controls to prevent competition with English manufacturers. Charles assented to a series of Acts prohibiting the export of Irish woollen goods to either England or her colonies. Both native Irish and settlers were 'jealous of the supremacy claimed by the English Parliament, and of the restrictions imposed upon their trade by the English people'.[a] They directed their woollen exports to France and Spain, where they competed favourably with goods of English manufacture. Yet this contravened English Navigation Laws. The initial Navigation Ordinance of 1651, passed by Cromwell's Protectorate, restricted the shipment of goods from Britain's colonies, including Ireland, to British ships. This Ordinance was replaced in 1660 by the English Navigation Act, under which Ireland, along with other colonies, received some trading rights, but, in the first instance, all goods had to be shipped on an English vessel to England, where they were unloaded, inspected and duty was charged. They were then reloaded onto a second English vessel for delivery to their final destination, adding substantially to the cost and speed of delivery. This not only depressed colonial trade, but it deprived Irish and all other colonial ports of duties. It also pushed up prices of Irish goods when it was already beset with restrictions.[b] This unfair arrangement, which also applied in America, became a principal cause of the American Revolution.

During William III's reign, English woollen manufacturers started to complain at Irish competition and asked him to apply laws to prohibit its woollen industry. Although this request was outrageous, it was supported by the English House of Commons, and William agreed to 'do all that in me lies to discourage the woollen manufacture in Ireland'. Yet he undertook to promote the manufacture of Irish linen, while supporting woollen goods manufacture in England. In 1696, the English Parliament passed an Act (7 and 8 William II. Cap. 39) 'to encourage the linen manufacture in Ireland, and to permit the export of plain Irish linen to England free of duty'.[c] As an initial step to discourage its woollen industry the Irish Parliament placed a duty on exported Irish woollen goods, but this proved insufficient to allow English manufacturers to compete. In 1699, the English Parliament placed an embargo on all goods containing wool being exported from Ireland except to England and Wales, where a licence was needed from the Commissioners of the Revenue, who imposed duties at a level to ensure their total prohibition. The Irish Government had no means of redressing this injustice and tensions continued.[d]

In 1704, the House of Lords received a complaint 'that the Application of the People of Ireland to the Linen Manufacture was not a matter of choice, but was pursuant to the Desires of the People of England'. William's solution was to encourage 'Huguenot families to settle in Ireland ... to develop the linen industry'.[e] It now became the principal activity of the Belfast locality, particularly in Lisburn outside Belfast. In 1698, he invited Louis Crommelin, a successful linen weaver from Cambrai (hence cambric), to come to Ireland.

Louis Crommelin (1652-1727) As William III's instigation, he led an influx of Huguenots to Lisburn near Belfast to develop the Irish linen industry. Many of the regulations that he formulated are still in place to this day.
Artist unknown 17th century oil on canvas (c. 1690-95) © National Museums Northern Ireland BELUM.U25

Crommelin had already become well-established as a banker and merchant in Holland before the Revocation of the Edict of Nantes. On arriving in Ireland, he attracted other Huguenots to join him, and his family was to remain influential in the Lagan Valley for generations. In 1700, he received Government subsidies to promote linen production and he transformed the quality of Irish weaving. He was appointed by the Irish Government to extend his skills over a wide area, and almost the entire industry was placed under Huguenot control. Even though Lisburn was badly damaged by a disastrous fire in 1707, it was rebuilt within a year. In 1711, Crommelin was made responsible for forming the Board of Trustees of the Linen Manufacturers of Ireland, which sets standards for the industry to this day, even framing regulations to prevent the pollution of rivers from the bleaching of flax.

Flax spinning became a constant occupation for women among Ulster's farming families, providing a significant source of income for their hard-pressed agricultural households. With their cheaper labour cost and the skill to spin finer yarns by hand, this Irish cottage industry continued to compete successfully with flax spinners elsewhere. It was well placed to service the local weaving activity, which also continued mainly on a cottage industry basis. 'In the early decades of the eighteenth century the domestic weaving of linen became the main economic activity of eastern Ulster,'[f] and accounted for a quarter of all Irish exports. By 1727, County Londonderry was also producing flax in some quantity. Linen was a major component in the manufacture of clothing, fabrics and commercial goods, such as sailcloth. Although there was no import duty levied on linen goods being sent to England or, after 1704, to British colonies in America, they still had to pass through an English port and be shipped on English vessels. From Belfast, goods were moved initially to Chester although eventually Liverpool became the entrepôt. The Irish complained that the cost of English freight left margins on their linen products unacceptably low. This led to calls for the Irish Government to be independent of English control. English interference with shipping arrangements enfuriated settlers in Ireland. It was a principal factor in the decision for many to leave for America. Emigration reached a peak in 1728-29, placing the maintenance of the linen industry in jeopardy.

There was also a flourishing trade in flaxseed. This encouraged growers and weavers to buy seed supplied by Dutch merchants from the Baltic. In 1731, with flax already being grown successfully in America, the English Parliament permitted the import of American flaxseed to Ireland. With labour costs already one-third higher than in Ireland, Americans preferred to sell it as cattle feed, as vegetable oil or for use in paints and varnishes, rather than become involved in the laborious process of linen manufacture. By 1751, 69,000 bushels of flaxseed were arriving in Ireland from Philadelphia alone, and finished linen goods were being exported to America in return. With linen goods occupying less cargo space than imported seed, emigrants filled the ships for the return journey.

With the establishment of cotton plantations in the southern states of America, there was a huge surge in low-cost cotton arrivals to Europe. Cotton weaving became well-established in Lancashire, but hand spinning was labour intensive, and much raw cotton was sent from Lancashire to Ireland to be spun into yarn and returned for weaving. Cotton spinning in Ireland was undertaken on a cottage industry basis by farmers involved in linen manufacture. This often left Lancashire weavers with a temporary shortage of cotton yarn during the flax harvest, when spinners were in the fields. Yet spinners needed to avoid their hands becoming roughened by heavy farm work and some areas started to focus entirely on spinning and weaving. This reduced farming activity to an area large enough to grow flax and provide a patch of grass to maintain a cow. A 'linen triangle' developed between Dungannon, Lisburn and Armagh, where spinners and weavers needed to buy their foodstuffs from elsewhere. In 1753, approval was granted for the Lagan to be made navigable from Belfast to Lough Neagh. There were even hopes of creating a canal to allow ships to travel from Belfast to Coleraine, providing renewed prosperity for County Londonderry.

When Newry also became involved in linen production, drapers started to buy cloth prior to bleaching, and they invested in 'greens' 'where, with the aid of water power, they finished the cloth to the high standard required by the English and overseas markets'.[g] 'By the end of the 18th Century the production of linen was a major industry and a source of prosperity.'[h] When Catholics also started spinning and weaving, trade rivalries developed into sectarian rivalries. There was much friction caused by the preferable locations, which had been granted to settlers. 'Memories of seventeenth-century dispossession and massacre remained stubbornly alive'.[i] Sectarian riots involved gangs of hooligans, both Protestant and Catholic, committing night time atrocities in the name of religion.

So long as cotton spinning benefitted the Irish economy, cotton was not seen as a threat to linen production. Yet, in 1767, James Hargreaves in Lancashire developed the Spinning Jenny, which spun cotton mechanically. It transformed the availability of cotton yarn and greatly reduced the production cost of cloth. This 'brought widespread distress in rural Ireland, followed by the inevitable epidemics'.[j] Although a domestic cotton weaving industry had been developed in Belfast, there was little coal and no iron to justify mechanisation. One effect of the Act of Union was to remove the tariffs which protected Irish cotton goods, leaving Irish cotton mills unable to compete with mechanised imports. This caused Irish cotton cloth production to decline, particularly when, in 1827, one of the major Belfast cotton mills was destroyed by fire.

It was not just Ireland's cotton cloth production which suffered. Linen, everywhere, was suddenly facing price competition from cotton. Spinners now had to compete with imported yarn spun mechanically in America, the Netherlands and Riga, and their own remained unsold. To improve yarn production, the Irish Linen Board tried to introduce spinning with both hands, which had long been practiced in Scotland. Female spinners arrived from Scotland to teach the technique to the Irish, increasing their wage from four pence to six pence per day.[k] Yet the downturn in demand following the end of the wars in Europe finished off yarn production as a cottage industry, and looms moved to factory production.

English linen weavers had made concerted efforts to replicate the Spinning Jenny for flax, but it was a much more delicate spinning process. Although several machines were developed in both England and Continental Europe, they caused yarn breakages, and could not spin the finer qualities. With each new machine being a development of earlier versions, an argument developed over patent rights. The Irish were not initially involved in trying to resolve the problem, but, in the second half of the 18th Century, a few water-driven mills experimented in mechanised spinning. Even in 1824, when a mechanical wet spinning process for flax was successfully developed by James Kay in Lancashire, hand-spinning continued in Ireland, but it was soon realised that machine spinning was becoming cheaper and was providing better quality yarn. Irish loom operators started to send Irish flax to England for spinning before it was returned for weaving, causing hand-spinning at last to fall into decline.

Part 8

Ireland after 1800

Chapter 36

The Londonderry plantations
1800 - 1850

During the fifty years to 1841, the population of County Londonderry increased by about 100,000 to 222,174, despite large amounts of emigration, principally by Presbyterians. Those families remaining, especially the Catholics, found themselves having to divide their holdings among their children making them progressively smaller and less viable. Yet they brought larger landowners parliamentary votes. With landlords, up to this point at least, spending very little money on reclaiming bog- and slob- (saltmarsh) lands, tenants began living from hand to mouth. The only safety valve was emigration. Large numbers of Presbyterians, in particular, left for America, blaming absentee English landlords, with much justification, for their plight. Being determined to maintain their historic connection to their lands, native Irish stayed, but lived in increased penury with the potato being the only crop able to provide them with subsistence. It took the Great Famine of 1846-47 to make them realise that emigration was their only survival option.

The burgeoning population had a disastrous effect on the availability of timber. During the 18th Century, asset stripping had caused woodlands on the proportions almost to disappear. In 1802, The Irish Society arranged a new timber survey and Robert Slade, the General Agent and Secretary of the Society from 1789 to 1831, prepared a report and valuation. The narrative of his visit to County Londonderry is 'replete with valuable information, relative to the Society's property in Ulster'.[a] He reported that Londonderry had a thriving market in linen manufactured on a cottage industry basis, resulting in a high density of housing development. This meant that the gardens allocated to each house within the walls to provide produce had been built over.

Robert Slade, General Agent and Secretary, The Irish Society 1789 to 1831 His 1802 narrative was very critical of the Livery Companies' management of their proportions.
John Opie, 1806 oil on canvas
Courtesy of The Irish Society

Slade was very critical of the proportions. He considered that their original purpose had been completely lost. Rural poverty could be explained by the complete absence of landlords and their under-tenants. He complained that this was 'a grievance which greatly prevails in Ireland' but particularly in City Companies. Poor management of estates was causing 'poverty, ignorance and laziness of the "lower order of the people", who toiled "for a miserable subsistence", and saw "the fruits of their labour carried off … by an agent of their landlord, to be spent in a foreign country".'[b] He went on to explain:

> The want of example, assistance and consolation from the resident land owners deprives the inhabitants of all inducement … Each family lives by itself in a little cabin without a chimney, with a clay floor, and a bed of straw or rags. A group of nearly naked figures are often seen at the doors, consisting of the wives and children. The husband finds the means by working at his loom, to pay an extravagant price for four or five acres of land, on which a cow is kept for the family, and some potatoes and flax are grown. This, with a turf fire, kindled in the corner of their cabin, round which the family crouch, with some oatmeal for stir-about, constitutes all the wants, and whiskey the luxury, of the Irish peasant; who, never looking beyond it, has no temptation to enterprize or exertion.[c]

The peasants' lifestyle was miserable. After planting potatoes in the spring, their families left their homes to become vagrant beggars over the summer, returning only to harvest them and cut turf to see them through the winter. Poverty caused inevitable unrest. Although Grattan and others introduced more

Catholic Relief bills into the British House of Commons, they were defeated. In 1803, a second United Irish rebellion was nipped in the bud. This was followed, in 1813, by a succession of sectarian riots in Belfast caused by an influx of Roman-Catholics attempting to escape rural poverty.

Slade noted that rentals charged to Irish under-tenant farmers were far higher than the value of what they could produce from the soil and it was only their profits from linen manufacture that allowed them to be paid.[d] If the linen trade should slump, destitution would follow, as the cow or the pig would have to be sold to pay the rent. If the potato crop failed, as it did on several occasions, the cow and the pig had to be eaten. When the rent could not be paid, eviction would follow.

It was not only Slade who voiced criticisms. In 1802 the 'wise and humane' Rev. George Vaughan Sampson published his *Statistical Survey of the County of Londonderry, with Observations on the Means of Improvement; Drawn up for the Consideration, and under the Direction of The Dublin Society.* Sampson had been Rector of Aghanloo since 1794 and was a supporter of the United Irish.[148] His massive tome 'deals with the geology, agriculture, industry and social conditions of the inhabitants'.[e] He reported that much of the land had become infertile and ridges of bare basalt protruded through the topsoil. Yet there were better areas at the Grove, Garvagh, Aghadowey and Camus, and a reasonably fertile stretch from Coleraine to Port Stewart and at Ballykelly. (Slade commented that the most fertile land was round Limavady, which must have benefitted the Phillipses.) Oats and barley were the main crops, but wheat could also be grown in some areas. Potatoes could survive in more mountainous districts, and flax production was widespread, grown from seed imported from Riga, the Netherlands and America. Farmers reared cattle, horses, sheep, goats, pigs, hens, ducks, geese and turkeys. Cattle were fed with turnips in winter, while clover and grass seed were sown to provide pasture in summer. The land was fertilised with compost, manure, lime, ground shells, peat ash, and seaweed. By 1814, wandering flocks of sheep had been prohibited, causing their numbers to diminish, and farmers turned to tillage within enclosed areas. Fields were enclosed with thorn hedges planted on dykes excavated from ditches.

Sampson painted a picture of impending disaster, explaining that 'the poor lived in dens of indescribable wretchedness, without hope or incentive'.[f] He saw absentee landlords as a curse, uninterested in their lands or their tenants other than to squeeze as much cash out of them as possible, so that the County, once so well-wooded, was stripped of its trees. Poorer dwellings were built of stone bonded with mud and rarely had more than two rooms separated by a flimsy partition. (Better quality houses were built of stone or brick bonded with mortar and were on two storeys.) Thatch was the principal roof covering and, in the absence of stone, walls were created from mud bonded with straw. Roofs were

---

[148] Sampson's brother, William, was a friend of Theobald Wolfe Tone, and William's daughter, Catherine Anne, married Tone's son, William Theobald Tone, who had had a distinguished career in the French army.

supported with curved timbers. He recommended that Landlords should provide more soundly built cottages, but little work on these was begun until the middle of the 19ᵗʰ Century. He went on:

Holdings were far too small to support the families living on them, as, if any part of the system (making linen, growing potatoes for food etc.) broke down, rents could not be paid, and eviction and starvation would follow.

He considered that farms of four acres or less could not possibly be economic and that twenty-one year leases were inadequate. Any tenant who improved his land found it being auctioned to the highest bidder when the lease ended. He advocated a more realistic allocation of land and the provision of adequate drainage.

He noted that enormous areas of slob- and bog-land could be reclaimed for use and in any case the bogs ought to be better managed or they would be ruined as a resource.

He wanted seed to be sold to tenants at cost, better breeding methods adopted for livestock, and orchards of fruit trees planted within the cultivated land. A rationalisation of the transportation system and of weights and measures was needed, and he recommended using the decimal system as standard (demonstrating the United Irish admiration for all things French).

Something needed to be done, and Sampson recommended that

cash collected from tenants should be ploughed back into the estates to improve them, build houses and other structures, and transform the economy, rather than be squandered on dissipations in London or Bath. ... He concluded that a huge transformation and much effort was needed to bring prosperity, civilisation, peace and other benefits to a land ruined by a century of exploitation and neglect.ᵍ

He then provided a list of further recommendations designed to achieve:

a stop to the excessive sub-divisions of farms and the process of rack-renting; the reduction of all rents to reasonable levels; the resumption of proportions under the direct control of the Companies; the planting of boglands and the establishment of nurseries for trees;[149] programmes of draining and enclosing lands by means of fences and hedges to improve and protect it; a scheme of reclamation of slob-lands by the banks of Lough Foyle; planting of all thin soil with rape to provide food for sheep and to produce oil; the amalgamation of small farms to form establishments of 20 to 200 acres apiece; the creation of small townships on each proportion to facilitate trade; reclamation of all wastelands; a programme of building of model farm-houses; encouragement of the industrious to stay put rather than to emigrate, and the encouragement of the surplus population to emigrate;

---

[149] Sampson's recommendations on tree planting pre-dated the work by the Forestry Commission and were far more creative than their later proposals. He wanted to experiment to find trees suitable for land that was otherwise useless for agriculture.

the building of mills; improvement of all roads, bridges, and infrastructure; and the establishment of model schools in decent buildings, with properly trained schoolteachers, books, and other equipment provided and paid for by the Companies.[h]

This was a 'faultless' list of proposals, and when the war with France was ended, The Irish Society woke up to Sampson's criticisms and heeded his recommendations.[i]

In 1812, a Bill had been introduced into Parliament for the building of a new Court House in Londonderry as the first had been destroyed in the siege; a handsome new building was completed in 1817. This was the first in a massive programme of public building works. In 1814, the Society sent a large deputation from London to survey Ulster property and to re-establish the precise rights of both the Companies and itself. It also discussed:

the building of schools (the Irish Endowed Schools Act (53 George III. Cap. 107) had been passed in 1813, providing for permanent commissioners to direct Royal schools and supervise others), the relationship with the Corporations of Londonderry and Coleraine, the drainage of the slob-lands, the future of the bogs, and the ownership of lands.[j]

It re-asserted its rights to areas of land that had fallen into abeyance and it leased out unlet property, including bog-lands and slob-lands, under terms which confirmed proper principles for their management. 'Specifications and elevations of all future houses proposed to be built in Coleraine or Londonderry were to be submitted to the Society for approval.'[k]

It was more than just structural improvement. 'A new religious zeal and a concern for Good Works were to temper the material advances of the Victorian epoch.'[l]

The London Companies developed their estates in the new climate after the Union. The 19th Century was, after all, the age of caring and of kindness, when, inspired by the Evangelical Conscience, society in Britain began to realise that all was not well with the labouring classes, and, that in order to improve health and morals, it was necessary to provide decent housing at reasonable rates.[m]

They established 'an era of great reform' to make good the years of neglect, including the replanting of trees and hedges, and land reclamation. Many towns and villages were rebuilt, notably Moneymore, Moyheelan (Draperstown), Kilrea and Eglinton. The Fishmongers, Grocers and Salters mounted impressive school building programmes and 'the provision of dispensaries further indicated that the age of philanthropy had replaced the exploitation, absenteeism and neglect of the 18th Century'.[n] It came to be realised that 'a properly managed estate could not only be more profitable, but could contribute to the improvement of the moral welfare of the nation'.[o] This was long overdue. The Irish Society granted Sampson three hundred guineas for the painstaking records and advice he had provided.

In 1816, thanks to Sampson's persuasive efforts, an Act of Parliament (56 George III. Cap. 88) encouraged Irish landlords to repossess their lands. Several Companies took back direct control of their estates, managing them through their agents rather than letting them to Farmers. In 1826, an Act restricting the subletting of lands and tenements helped to induce landlords to keep their estates in hand. This ended 'the somewhat detached way in which the Londonderry Plantation had been run during the previous century'.[p] On regaining control, some Companies

> built model farms, schools, churches (for all denominations), exemplary dwellings, mills and other structures, and began a major programme of improvement on the land (including draining, planting with trees and thorns, and reclaiming slob-lands).[q]

County Londonderry was transformed by the establishment of neat towns and villages, proper countryside management and the development of trade.

> The coming of the railways was encouraged and assisted, and improvements were carried out to harbours and wharves. Roads were built and repaired, bridges were constructed (including the very important bridges over the Foyle connecting Waterside with the City [of Londonderry], and over the Bann, connecting Killowen with Coleraine), and massive encouragement was given to the farming community in all manner of ways. The Irish Society supported education with the building of schools, encouraged higher education in Londonderry and concerned itself with the appearance of its estates in a way uncommon in Ulster.[r]

The Agricultural Improvement Society, formed in 1841, encouraged better farming methods. Commissions were set up to manage drainage schemes. There were new regulations to conserve fisheries. County Londonderry was now much better placed to cope with natural disasters. In January 1839, a 'Great Wind' caused extensive damage and several church spires were brought down, but resources were in place to repair them. It was only in County Londonderry that potato blight did not cause the insuperable problems, which swept through the rest of Ireland. A principal factor was that its farmers were still growing flax, as a much needed source of income from its use in linen manufacture, and flax required a rotation of crops. Unlike in the rest of Ireland, potato crops were rotated and not replanted continuously in the same soil, greatly reducing the impact of the blight. The problem for Londonderry was the huge influx of destitute poor. They arrived

> from their miserable smallholdings in County Donegal, [and] had to be supported, housed and given food, all of which strained the resources of the county and its inhabitants.[s]

By 1830, the Livery Companies' income from their proportions had improved and, for some years, The Irish Society distributed dividends to them, in addition to making charitable donations within the locality. In 1832, the

Skinners' Company[150] took The Irish Society to Court over the right of the Companies to be furnished with the annual accounts of the Society, based on a suspicion that the Society was failing to hand over a fair share of its profits. The real test was to establish whether The Irish Society was a trustee for public [charitable] purposes, or a trustee for the Livery Companies, who had funded its investment. The case started in the Court of Chancery in 1835 and, after ten years of expensive legal argument, eventually went to the House of Lords, where, on 8 August 1845, the Lord Chancellor, Lord Lyndhurst, and Lord Campbell found that the proportions, which had been owned and funded by the Livery Companies, were

> under the paramount jurisdiction of The Irish Society, and liable to contributions if necessary, in common with the indivisible estates in the Society's hands, towards the general expense of maintaining public works and edifices; supporting the civil Government of the city of Derry and town of Coleraine …

They concluded that the Society had complete discretion to utilise its surpluses for the public good, before any distribution to the Livery Companies. As its income was never likely to satisfy all public needs, the Companies have been excluded since then from further dividends, but have not been called upon to make further contributions.

During the second half of the 19th Century, philanthropy was to become progressively less impressive, marked by growing political uncertainty and the aftermath of the famines. This was to be a period of gradual disengagement by the Livery Companies from their involvement in Ulster. Although legislation was designed to help both landlords and tenants, widespread mistrust and disillusionment was festering.[u]

---

[150] The Skinners were particularly riled by The Irish Society over its criticisms of the way that they had managed their estates, 'and there was clearly bad blood between the two bodies'. They were among the worst offenders in failing to adopt the improvements recommended by Sampson.[t]

Chapter 37

Problems in Ireland outside Ulster
1800 - 1900

To gain a measure of the Livery Companies' achievement in the first part of the 19th Century, it is relevant to compare their progress with problems elsewhere in Ireland.

Following the Union, Grattan increased his calls to grant Catholic rights, and the Catholic Daniel O'Connell became a new force calling for change. In 1823, O'Connell set up a pressure group, the Catholic Association, to seek reform of electoral rights, of the Church of Ireland, of tenants' rights and economic development.[a] His Association was funded by a Catholic 'Rent', which he collected in conjunction with the Catholic Church. In July 1828, despite being a Catholic, he was elected as Member of Parliament for Clare. On arrival in London, he was eventually permitted to take his seat despite refusing to swear the Oath of Supremacy. In 1829, thanks to his efforts, the Roman-Catholic Relief Act (10 George IV. Cap. 7) approved a new Oath of Allegiance, which permitted Roman-Catholics to enter Parliament, to belong to Corporations and to be eligible for senior military and civil positions.

Catholic emancipation seemed to herald a new era for the Irish, with Roman-Catholic Bishops expressing their thanks to the British Government and calling on priests to avoid future political activity. The Livery Companies in Londonderry helped to provide their native Irish tenants with more appropriate places of worship. Yet Roman-Catholic bishops opposed education systems that were non-sectarian 'on the grounds that they endangered the faith and morals of Roman-Catholic students',[b] even though this reinforced segregation between differing faiths.

Emancipation was not enough. Ever since the Union in 1800, there had been agitation for its repeal. Calls for Home Rule were led by O'Connell, who held a series of 'Monster Meetings' in southern Ireland. A principal grievance was the requirement for Catholics and Presbyterians to pay tithes to fund the Established Church, which they did not attend, and the Church's extravagance only made matters worse. The Church Temporalities (Ireland) Act of 1833 (3 and 4 William IV. Cap. 37) suppressed ten bishoprics and appointed ecclesiastical commissioners with powers to divide livings and to build and repair churches.[c]

Yet local Anglican clergy depended on tithes for their income, and non-payment caused them huge financial difficulty. Some were forced to sell their future rights for a fee to 'tithe farmers'. The Irish Tithe Arrears Act of 1833 (3 and 4 William IV. Cap. 100) advanced £1,000,000 to relieve clergy unable to collect them from Catholics and Presbyterians. In 1838, tithes were converted into rental charges, which had the effect of reducing amounts due.

The British Government made considerable efforts to promote economic improvement. Wars with France and America had increased demand for linen and other goods, bringing an appreciable rise in prosperity. In 1824, duty on goods moved between England and Ireland was abolished. Excise licences were brought into line with those of Britain. The merging of British and Irish currencies under the Currency Act (6 George IV. Cap. 79) of 1825 also facilitated trade. The first steamship travelled from Dublin to London in 1815 and the completion, in 1826, of the road bridge across the Menai Strait opened up access to Holyhead and a ferry service to Dublin. During the 1830s, the Irish railway system was also developed. In 1824, Thomas Colby was directed by the Board of Ordnance to provide the first Ordnance Survey maps of Ireland. He started in County Londonderry where new maps were published in May 1833.

Efforts at improvement did not extend to agriculture. With legislation having imposed restrictions on industrial manufacture in Ireland, it remained an essentially agricultural economy, reliant on farm produce to feed its growing population despite its uncertain climate. Other than in Ulster, landlords did not cooperate with tenants to develop their land. It was not until 1845 that a Royal Commission recommended bringing the rest of Ireland into line by providing tenants with compensation for improvements to land they were vacating. The Irish peasantry had traditionally been cattle farmers, and, with the English propensity for eating beef, much of their produce was destined for England. As land confiscations had increased in the 17th Century, the more fertile grazing pastures were transferred to English and Scottish settlers, leaving the natives as tenants on poorer soil, often covered in a layer of peat, which needed to be cut out before crops could be planted. A shortage of farmland resulted in great competition for tenancies, forcing up rents to levels that were not affordable. As Sampson noted, this caused tenancies to be broken down into ever smaller plots.

Smaller tenancies could only subsist by growing potatoes, a vegetable brought in as a garden crop in the 17th Century. The potato provided larger yields per acre than any other crop and it was suited to both the soil and the climate. By the early 18th Century, it had already become the staple diet of the poor and was used as fodder for cattle. It could support life without any other supplement and 'was the thin partition between famine and the millions of the Irish people.'[d] Yet peasants still needed to supplement their income by making seasonal trips to England and Scotland to provide cheap labour at harvest time. Even larger tenancies faced acute difficulty in generating sufficient income to pay rents, often resulting in them being settled in wheat, oats and livestock, while the farmer was left to subsist on his potato crop. If this was abundant, the landlord received the surplus, 'returning nothing to the soil. [He absorbed] its whole produce minus the potatoes strictly necessary to keep the inhabitants from dying of famine'.[e]

A successful potato crop had always been dependent on reasonable weather, and it failed in many seasons before the famine. The unprecedented cold spell of 1739 and 1740, which is estimated to have caused the death of 20 per cent of the Irish population has already been discussed on page 330. In 1816, a major famine reinforced the urgent need to reform the agricultural economy. This was followed by a typhus epidemic in the autumn. It was so virulent that, in 1818, the establishment of hospitals and dispensaries was authorised under the Fever Hospitals Act (58 George II. Cap. 47). In 1817, Parliament passed the Poor Employment Act (57 George III. Cap. 34) to empower the authorities to employ the destitute to undertake public works. This was to be financed by a mortgage on the rates. In 1822, 'half-starved' wretches appeared in Galway from fifty miles away, with 100,000 subsisting on charity in County Clare and a further 122,000 in County Cork despite a successful grain crop in both 1821 and 1822.

A succession of Government committees reported on the parlous state of Irish agriculture. In 1819, a lack of employment was highlighted. In 1824, a Government report stated: 'A very considerable proportion of the population, variously estimated at a fourth and a fifth of the whole, is considered to be out of employment.'[f] This was blamed on a shortage of capital, caused by Landlord absenteeism and the consumption of tenants' capital on farm improvement. In 1823, rack-renting was denounced. In 1829, a Bill was tabled to arrange for bogs to be drained and waste lands to be reclaimed. In 1830, a Select Committee recorded:

> The situation of the ejected tenantry, or those, who are obliged to give up their small holdings in order to promote the consolidation of farms, is necessarily most deplorable. ... They have increased the stock of labour, they have rendered the habitations of those who have received them more crowded, they have given occasion to the dissemination of disease, they have been obliged to resort to theft and all manner of vice and iniquity to procure subsistence; but what is perhaps the most painful of all, a vast number of them have perished of want.[g]

Rural overpopulation had to be halted, and farms needed to be of a size to allow the poor to be fed and prosperity to increase. A policy of assisted emigration was adopted to remove the surplus rural population. Ship captains found that transferring passengers was a lucrative business and they provided commissions to Livery Companies' and other landlords' agents to provide them with emigrants. Yet numbers continued to grow. The 1831 census recorded a population of 7,767,401, but, ten years later, it was 8,175,124. The increase caused both disease and food shortages. With poor public hygiene, fever epidemics became rife and famine continued. In 1832, an outbreak of cholera in Belfast spread rapidly into County Londonderry, particularly to Limavady.

Window[151] and hearth taxes were abolished to allow homes to be properly ventilated and warmed. With three million people dependent on the potato for sustenance, senior Irish figures called on the British Government to authorise new public works such as railways to provide employment and a Select Committee provided £50,000 to allow the destitute to build roads. In 1831, The Public Works (Ireland) Act reorganised the Board of Works and laid the foundations for major schemes including piers and harbours. In 1838, the Poor Law in England was extended to Ireland by the Poor Relief (Ireland) Act (1 and 2 Victoria. Cap. 56), and Robert Peel set up a commission to augment the relief effort.

There is no doubt that a significant cause of the poverty was absenteeism among landlords, often proprietors of substantial areas. (Lord Lucan's estates amounted to more than 60,000 acres.) Unlike in Scotland, they fostered no hereditary loyalty or bond of kinship with their tenants and being 'separated from the tenant by creed, race and caste aggravated all the evils of the system'.[h] 'Behind [their failure to act] there stood at least a century of extravagance.'[i] The Irish squire was 'a spendthrift, a gambler, often a drunkard', and was often suffering from the sins of the father.[j] He spent his money on his Dublin town house, generally built on a more lavish scale than the counterparts of English landlords in London. Although he had expected the Irish Government to remain in Dublin, following the Act of Union, he had been obliged to build a new residence in London. He fell into debt and pawned his Irish estates to money lenders, whose only interest was to collect the rents, when due. He was still in debt at the time of the Great Famine. With tenants 'brooding over their discontent in sullen indignation', Ireland, according to the Earl of Clare, was a hostile place for landlords to live. They preferred to milk their estates from afar. Rarely, if ever, did they visit their properties, which were managed by 'middlemen', often described as 'land sharks' or 'bloodsuckers', who took long leases and sublet in small parcels to subsistence farmers. Rents were high and, as the population grew, inferior land was leased out in ever smaller plots providing insufficient areas for pasture. 'Industry and enterprise were extinguished, and a peasantry created, which was one of the most destitute in Europe'.[k]

There were calls for the relationship between landlord and tenant to be settled on 'rational and useful principles' as 'no language could describe the poverty'.[l] In November 1830, the Irish Solicitor-General 'described the houses of the tenantry as such as the lower animals in England would scarcely, and as a matter of fact did not, endure'.[m] Even the Duke of Wellington denounced absentee landlordism, and, in 1831, Lord Stanley reported 'a crisis of awful distress in Mayo' resulting in a subscription being called among landlords, which had raised the small sum of £60 from two of them, when the total annual rental they received was £10,400. The ejection of tenants, who failed to pay rents

---

[151] This was before window tax was abolished in England.

caused inevitable disturbance. Although this was blamed on their poor relationship with their landlord, measures to relieve their lot came to nothing.

The Poor Law Inquiry of 1835 reported 2,235,000 people out of work and in distress for thirty weeks in a year. The Poor Relief (Ireland) Act of 1838 established Boards of Guardians to administer workhouses with responsibility to the Poor Law Commission. These were funded by a rate on landlords, who were required to make a contribution for each tenant paying less than four pounds annually in rent. Landlords with large numbers of small tenancies faced crippling bills. They immediately evicted smaller tenants, amalgamating plots to lift them over the four pound rental threshold. Although tenants received small sums to induce them to leave, they were 'cheated into believing the workhouse would take them in'.[n]

Sir Robert Peel, Bart. (1788-1850) As Chief Secretary in Dublin in 1812, he was well aware that the rapid increase in the rural population was causing unrest. Yet, as Prime Minister, he was slow to react to the potato famine.
William B. Essex oil on canvas © Palace of Westminster Collection, WOA 2066

It can be no surprise that an undercurrent of unrest persisted.

Unprotected by the law from robbery, and face to face with starvation, the tenants formed secret and murderous organisations, and assassination and eviction accompanied each other in almost arithmetical proportion.[o]

It was unrest that had attracted the British Government's attention, not its cause. As early as 1800, immediately after the Union, Parliament had passed a Coercion Act, which empowered military tribunals to try those accused of being involved in violence. In 1812, Peel became Chief Secretary in Dublin, 'an office [according to Cates Dictionary of General Biography], which he held with much advantage to the country till 1818'. Yet T. P. O'Connor cynically saw the 'advantage' as 'the preparation of the famine'.[p] There can be no doubt that Peel believed that the only way to bring unrest under control was to reduce the number of agricultural tenants. He formed a constabulary, the 'Peelers' and abolished trial by jury. He established martial law, under which 'no act shall be questioned in a court of law'.[q] In 1817, he permitted landlords to hold their own tribunals, after forming themselves into a body of 'justices' accompanied by a Sergeant-at-Arms or a Queen's Counsel. These could impose sentences of up to one year's imprisonment or seven year's transportation with no right of appeal. In 1822, the Irish Constabulary Act (3 George IV. Cap. 103) required local magistrates to establish and direct a police force in every county, regulated by central Government. In 1826 and 1827, new laws facilitated the eviction of tenants. To reduce agitation, political meetings for 'seditious purposes' were suppressed. In most years from 1802 to 1834, Habeas Corpus (the right to trial) was suspended, and, although there were regular Acts relating to coercion, eviction, insurrection and importation of arms, eight attempts to gain approval for relief bills were dropped.

Despite the food shortages, there was no anticipation of disaster in 1845. Yet, 'there never was an event [the Irish famine of 1845-48] in human history, which could have been more clearly foreseen, or that was more frequently foretold.'[r] In 1844, Benjamin Disraeli described Ireland as 'a starving population, an absentee aristocracy, and an alien church, and in addition the weakest executive in the world'.[s] The British Government set up numerous commissions, which

> without exception professed disaster; Ireland was on the verge of starvation, her population rapidly increasing, three-quarters of her labourers unemployed, housing conditions appalling and the standard of living unbelievably low.[t]

By 1845, 24 per cent of plots outside County Londonderry were between one and five acres, and a further 40 per cent between five and fifteen acres. With an estimated 500,000 evictions, the poor houses were overwhelmed. Although soup kitchens were opened, paid from local rates, the Poor Laws forbade anyone holding as much as one quarter of an acre of land from receiving relief. This caused 200,000 tenants to hand their meagre holdings back to their landlords. Yet the difficulties were 'borne with patient endurance' in the face of 'greater sufferings' than anywhere else in Europe. In February 1845, William Courtenay, 10th Earl of Devon chaired a commission, which made clear

> that the famine was inevitable without land reform; and that its advent could fail to be foreseen only by invincibly ignorant Ministers and Parliaments.[u]

The report continued:

> It would be impossible adequately to describe the privations which [the Irish peasantry] habitually and silently endure … in many districts their only food is the potato, their only beverage water … their cabins are seldom protected against the weather … a bed or a blanket is a rare luxury … and nearly in all, their pig and a manure heap constitute their only property.[v]

It cited the evidence of a well-known engineer, Alexander Nimmo:

353

I have seen a great deal of the peasantry, ... I conceive [them] to be in the lowest possible state of existence; their cabins are in the most miserable condition, and their food is potatoes, with water, very often without anything else, frequently without salt, and I have frequently had occasion to meet persons who begged me on their knees, for the love of God, to give them some promise of employment, that from the credit, they might get the means of supporting themselves for a few months until I could employ them.[w]

Despite all the signals, the arrival of potato blight *(Phytophthora Infestans)* from America in about 1844 was devastating. It spread rapidly through Europe, and there was no known cure. It reached Ireland in September 1845 causing about 40 per cent of the cultivated acreage to be lost, rising to 75 per cent in the following year. A crop could be sound one day and rotten the next. Even potatoes already harvested rotted in their pits (clamps). By 1847, there was such a shortage of seed potatoes that few could be planted. Although Irish Members of Parliament and commentators called for food exports to be banned, they were powerless without support from the British Government. O'Connell, speaking at the Dublin Corporation, warned of wholesale starvation and· complained at the export of wheat and oats, both of which crops were abundant. He was a loan voice in calling for the Corn Laws to be suspended to allow imports from other countries. Yet no remedial steps were taken. 'The Irish land system [approved by Parliament] necessitated the export of food from a starving nation.'[x]

Peel, now Tory Prime Minister, was preoccupied with a serious political struggle to retain office. He seemed to believe that initial reports of hardship were exaggerated. When, at last, he realised the danger, he was impotent to provide assistance. Although he proposed opening the Irish ports to free trade, his colleagues would not agree. To do so would conflict with the Corn Laws, which, since 1815, had protected the price of English grain by setting a duty on imports. He found himself at odds with most Tory Members of Parliament, who, being landowners, benefitted from protection. With his personal fortune based on mill owning, Peel had support from other factory owners, who complained that the Corn Laws kept bread prices artificially high. With bread forming the British workers' staple food, factory owners had to offer higher wages to attract employees, thus making their production less competitive. Despite worrying that it would act as a disincentive to local relief efforts, Peel purchased £100,000 worth of maize from America. When it arrived in Ireland in November, it needed milling, but no local equipment was able to undertake the double milling process required. Without a lot of cooking, it was indigestible and caused bowel complaints. With its yellow colour, it was soon known as 'Peel's brimstone'.

Peel made the potato famine a major plank in his call to repeal the Corn Laws. Yet protectionists and landlords united to dismiss his bill, claiming that distress caused by the famine was 'unreal and exaggerated'.[y] On 3 November 1845, the Evening Mail reported: 'The potato crop of this year far exceeded an average one.' Some days later it stated: 'The apprehensions of a famine are unfounded, and are merely made the pretence for withholding the payment of rent.' And yet again: 'There was a sufficiency and abundance of sound potatoes in the country for the wants of the people.'[z] Lord George Bentinck claimed: 'The potato famine was a gross delusion – a more gross delusion had never been practised upon any country by any Government.'[aa]

It was Disraeli who led opposition to the repeal of the Corn Laws on behalf of the landed classes. With most Members of Parliament being landowners, they benefitted from the protection for British produce, which the laws provided. Despite their concerted opposition, Peel had parliamentary backing from O'Connell and Lord John Russell, the leader of the Whigs. Such was the realisation of the famine's horrendous impact that, in early 1846, Peel carried the repeal through Parliament, despite having backing from less than one-third of his Tory party colleagues.

Although duties on imported corn were now removed, Ireland was on its knees. The Poor Employment Ireland Act of 1846 yet again encouraged public works to provide employment, with Treasury loans being floated to pay for them. In fairness to Peel, he was well aware that repeal of the Corn Laws would not of itself resolve the Irish problem. He recognised that the farming population had grown to a level which the land could not sustain, and small farmers had become totally reliant on the potato for food. With the British Government discouraging industrialisation in Ireland, fearing that cheaper Irish labour would make it overly competitive, there was no Irish industrial revolution to offer urban employment to surplus agricultural workers. The Highlands of Scotland faced a similar problem, causing landlords to clear out their tenants and utilise their poorer land for grazing sheep. The Highland clearances in Scotland resulted in the wholesale emigration of their Gaelic-speaking peasantry to America, Canada and Australasia. Peel saw emigration as the best solution, but without landlords in occupation in Ireland, he had no mechanism to bring it into effect.

Despite the famine, landlords continued to dispossess their tenants. At Ballinglass one landlord turned out two hundred and seventy people, taking the roofs off their sixty homes. With nowhere to go, the ousted tenants hid in ditches, but were again driven out. The roads were full of the homeless, starving and dying, and no emigration plan was properly formulated. In the face of horrendous provocation, tenants became involved in murdering several landlords. Although evicted tenants were encouraged to turn to the workhouses, these became the objects of 'dread and loathing' having become a refuge for 'the rustic victims of vice and the outcasts of the towns'. Entrance to the workhouse meant 'social ruin' and 'moral degradation', so that people preferred to die rather than enter 'those hated walls'. When at last they had no choice, they were full. At Westport, three thousand people needing relief arrived in a single day, but its workhouse could accommodate only one thousand and was already full beyond capacity.

With unrest growing, Peel tabled a Coercion Bill[152] to allow the arrest without trial of people causing disturbance. If passed, it would have empowered the Lord Lieutenant to proclaim a curfew. 'No person could with safety visit a public house, or a tea or coffee shop, or the house of a friend'.[bb] The penalty was transportation. Although the Bill would have given the Lord Lieutenant authority to tax any proclaimed district to pay for additional police and magistrates to maintain order, the landlords were to be exempted from payment, but even the poorest tenants were to be subject to it. Peel might have expected that protectionist support would give his Bill an easy ride, but, after the abolition of the Corn Laws, protectionists wanted him removed from office. They combined with the Whigs and O'Connell to oppose it. In June 1846, when his Bill failed, Peel resigned.

The Tory party was split; the Peelite faction, including William Gladstone, joined the Whigs in an attempt to form a new Government under the Whig leader, Lord John Russell. During his three month interregnum, it became clear that the 1846 Irish potato crop was again going to fail. What had been great hardship during the winter of 1845 was now a catastrophe. The hoarding of foodstuffs had the effect of forcing up prices. Famine advanced 'with giant strides'[cc] Russell's Government should have placed an embargo on Irish food exports to Britain (a relief measure imposed, despite the lobbying of merchants, after the earlier crop failure in 1782-83). This would have reduced prices in Ireland, although tenant farmers had no money to buy anything. According to Cecil Woodham-Smith, Ireland continued to be a net exporter of food throughout the famine, and livestock exports actually increased. Cattle and sheep were escorted to the ports from even the most famine stricken areas under armed guard. Russell then blindly halted Government food and relief efforts. Although grain exports sent to Britain were eventually returned to Ireland, unscrupulous Irish merchants retained the cargo on arrival, hoping for yet higher prices, and refused to release it even when offered a generous price, until it eventually rotted in store.

Russell's feeble attempts to alleviate the plight of the starving Irish proved inadequate and counter-productive. He was wedded to the concept of free trade, which had led to his support for the abolition of the Corn Laws, and he was determined not to interfere with the regular operation of merchants by supplementing grain imports. After the Achill potato crop failed, a deputation with money to purchase food from Government stores went to Sir R. Routh, head of its Commissary Department. On arrival, they were turned away as 'nothing was more essential to the welfare of the country than strict adherence to free trade'.[dd]

Relief organisation proved a shambles. The charities did not know what was required. Some sent books, believing that they would be helpful. Although Peel's Government had employed 100,000 relief workers to handle distribution,

---

[152] When a Perpetual Crimes Act, introduced by Arthur Balfour, then Minister for Ireland, was passed in 1887, it resulted in hundreds being arrested and imprisoned without trial.

Russell dismissed them, and this only added to the numbers out of work. Peel had allocated £100,000 to employ destitute people in Government works, expecting them to become involved in extending railways and roads or in bog clearance. Russell's Government called on Sir Charles Trevelyan to supervise the relief projects, but he limited the amounts advanced, believing that 'the judgement of God [had] sent the calamity to teach the Irish a lesson'. Outside County Londonderry, efforts to use the money on useful works 'met with flat refusal, and a lecture on political economy'.[ee] Russell was determined that nothing should interfere with private enterprise, and devoted the money exclusively to 'unproductive works', building new monuments, roads to nowhere, digging holes and then filling them up again. 'Miles of grass grown earthworks throughout the country now make their course and commemorate for posterity one of the gigantic blunders of the famine time.'[ff] With no income being generated, no means were provided to defray costs.

The Labour Rate Act turned famine relief into an orgy of red tape, with everything needing approval. Independent initiative was stifled.

> Over the whole Island, for the next few months, was a scene of confused and wasteful attempts at relief … striving to understand the voluminous directions, schedules, and specifications, under which alone [donors] could vote their own money to relieve the poor at their own doors.

Ten thousand officials, often corruptly appointed, were involved in 'the maddening preliminaries of vexatious and imbecile official delays'. When projects were ready to begin, the starving people were 'too wasted and emaciated to work and those that did fainted away or died on the roadside'.[gg]

People became distraught as the effects of the famine only worsened. The few remaining dogs ceased to bark. Merriment disappeared and children looked like old men and women, 'with parents willingly dying the slow death of starvation to save a small store of food for' them. By the end of August, calamity was universal. People 'grasped on everything that promised sustenance; they plucked turnips from the fields; many were glad to live for weeks on a single meal of cabbage a day'.[hh] 'In some cases they feasted on the dead bodies of horses and asses and dogs',[ii] and 'there is at least one horrible story of a mother eating the limbs of her dead child'.[jj] 'Seaweed was greedily devoured, so also were diseased cattle'.[kk] 'Corpses lay strewn by the side of once frequented roads'.[ll] The dead and dying lay together in their cabins. There were no funerals, and bodies lay for days unburied allowing ravenous dogs to make a meal of the corpses. When disease broke out among the starving populus, the Irish Public Health Act of 1846 enabled the Lord Lieutenant to appoint a Central Board of Health with powers to direct the Poor Law Guardians to provide fever hospitals, dispensaries, medicines and food.[mm]

In October 1846, Peel was returned to office, but valuable time had been lost. Even now, efforts to bring the famine to an end proved totally inadequate. O'Connell complained with justification that, if the Act of Union were repealed, a Government in Dublin would be better able to deal with the crisis. The English

Government's objective was to stop riot and assassination. The Nation reported: 'The only notice vouchsafed to this country is a hint that more gaols, more transportations and more gibbets might be useful to us.'[nn] Clarendon[153], the Lord Lieutenant, feared another outbreak of rebellion, and called more troops to Ireland. At least he understood the hardship. He reported:

> It is quite true that Landlords in England would not like to be shot like hares and partridges ... but neither does any landlord in England turn out fifty persons at once and burn their houses over their heads, giving them no provision for the future.[oo]

Earl Grey later admitted: 'Ireland would never have got into its present state if the landlords, as a body, had done their duty to the population under them ...'[pp]

The Press did not let the British Government off lightly. On 13 February 1847, The Illustrated London News reported: 'There was no laws it would not pass at [Irish Landlords'] request and no abuse it would not defend for them'. According to the Times, on 24 March 1847, the Government had caused 'a mass poverty, disaffection and degradation without parallel in the world. It allowed proprietors to suck the very life-blood of that wretched race'. There were views that the British Government's principal objective was to reduce the Irish peasant population. Although potato crops had failed all over Europe, it was only in Ireland that this led to famine. If the Government had taken prompt action to prevent Irish exports and to provide humane assistance, the hardship could have been averted.

There was the whimper of an uprising in 1848 initiated by Thomas Francis Meagher and William Smith O'Brien, joint leaders of a group calling themselves the Young Irelanders, who became progressively more militant. Although they advocated force to help dispossessed tenants, the peasantry was too starved and demoralised to offer them meaningful support. When the rebels failed, in an almost bloodless affray near Ballingarry, County Tipperary, to capture a party of police holed up at the house of a widow, whose children they were holding hostage, it was over. Despite a plea for clemency signed by 70,000 Irish and 10,000 English, O'Brien, Meagher and their fellow ringleaders were sentenced to death for treason, but this was commuted to transportation to Van Diemen's Land (Tasmania). Meagher escaped and went to America, where he became a Brigadier-General commanding Irish troops during the American Civil War. In 1854, O'Brien was permitted to return to Belgium and, two years later, was granted an unconditional pardon, which allowed him to return to Ireland, but he was never involved in further agitation.

In 1848, there was another general failure of the potato crop, and there was more blight in 1849. The continuing reduction of the Irish population seemed the only remedy. Agitators were transported; families were still being evicted from small holdings; outrage and murder continued. 'Ireland was once more in a state of chronic disorder and economic disaster.'[qq] A series of cold and wet

---

[153] George William Hyde, 4th Earl of Clarendon.

seasons in 1860, 1861 and 1862, followed by severe drought in 1863 and 1864, continued the 'disastrous agricultural depression'.ʳ Further remedial legislation was enacted. Towns with more than 1,500 residents were required to elect commissioners for their supervision. In 1858, a new Act facilitated the sale and transfer of land.ˢˢ

The Irish were too proud to ask for charity and too bitter to seek it from Britain, but British fund raisers called for money and arranged its distribution, resulting in probably unfair criticism that 'it took the profit of it'. Massive amounts were raised; Queen Victoria contributed £2,000; Irish soldiers and civil servants in India sent £14,000; The British Relief Association raised £200,000. Money came from as far afield as Turkey and from American Indians. Dispensaries were again established on a wide scale. These were based on pioneering efforts by the Drapers' and Fishmongers' Companies. Yet bureaucracy seems to have slowed the release of food supplies, which arrived too late to prevent the deaths of about a million people, although just as many died from disease as from starvation. The Society for Improving the Condition of the Labouring Classes inspired relief work and called for better quality housing. This resulted in the Land Improvement Act of 1860, which authorised loans to erect new dwellings for the labouring classes.

Paupers in work houses were granted assistance to emigrate. Husbands, who went first, sent back money to enable other members of the family to join them. The census of 1861 showed that the Irish population had fallen 11.5 per cent to 5,798,967 over the previous ten years, and is estimated to have fallen by between 20 and 25 per cent as a direct result of the famine. Emigration took place on a massive scale with a million leaving for a new life abroad so that the Gaelic language almost disappeared. In the United States, the 1860 census showed that its Irish-born population amounted to 1,611,304, about 40 per cent of its foreign-born total. Toronto, which was then a township of 20,000 people, was engulfed by 38,000 Irish famine victims. One-fifth of those who journeyed to Canada in 'coffin ships' died in transit. By 1850, about 25 per cent of the populations of New York, Boston, Philadelphia and Baltimore were Irish. There were similar proportions in Glasgow and Liverpool and the principal cities of Eastern Canada. In Ireland, the population fell from 8 million in 1845 to 4.4 million in 1911. During the 18ᵗʰ Century it had been mainly Protestants emigrating to America (resulting in many presidents of the United States being of Ulster stock). While Protestants continued to move to Canada, Catholics went in their thousands to the United States and the growing cities of Britain, particularly London, Liverpool, Manchester and Glasgow. It was only later in the 19ᵗʰ Century that emigration to Australia and New Zealand began to increase.

Calls for Irish nationalism became progressively more vocal, and anti-Unionist Members of Parliament were a perennial thorn in the side of successive Governments. A secret organisation, later known as the Irish Republican Brotherhood, was founded in 1858, and in the following year the Fenian Brotherhood was founded in the United States. These marked the beginnings of modern Irish Nationalism, which called for a complete break with Monarchy and with Britain. When the Fenians became involved in rebellions on both sides of the Atlantic, they were denounced by the Roman-Catholic Archbishop of Dublin and were condemned by Pope Pius IX. Yet, in 1867, a group of priests in Limerick issued a declaration calling for repeal of the Union. In 1869, the Supreme Council of the Irish Republican Brotherhood adopted the 'Constitution of the Irish Republic', giving birth, in the following year, to the Home Rule movement.

'Fenian outrages throughout this period, and a deteriorating relationship between Roman-Catholics and Protestants led to sectarian rioting and murders.'[tt] Unlike the republican rebellions in 1798 and 1803, agitation was now almost exclusively Roman-Catholic and became associated with 'the ideal of reviving Gaelic culture', romantic, backward-looking and deeply conservative.[uu] This had no appeal for Presbyterians, and growing fanaticism alienated the Anglo-Irish, despite their desire to preserve the Irish language, culture and antiquities.

With pro-Fenian sentiments being openly voiced in Ireland, Gladstone, in 1869, started to carry major enactments through Parliament 'to weaken and finally dismantle the fabric of the Protestant Ascendancy'.[vv] The first of these, the Irish Church Act (32 and 33 Victoria. Cap. 42), disestablished and partly disendowed the Anglican Church of Ireland. It provided for a Synod to govern it with a Representative Church Body to administer its finances. Capital sums were to be paid to the Presbyterian and Roman-Catholic Churches in place of the *Regium Donum* and the Maynooth College grant. It permitted the sale of Church lands to its tenants and vested ruined churches in a Commission of Public Works to preserve them as national monuments. Gladstone's Liberal party was, of course, courting the growing number of Irish anti-Union Members of Parliament by providing legislation to appease Nationalist opinion. Yet it failed to satisfy Irish activists.

The Landlord and Tenant (Ireland) Act of 1870 (33 and 34 Victoria. Cap. 46) was so poorly drafted that it had the effect of making tillage uneconomical. Returning land to pasture only increased rural poverty. There was another wave of emigration to the United States, Australia and New Zealand and the ever-expanding cities of Victorian Britain. At the General Election of 1874, sixty Home-Rule members, led by Charles Stewart Parnell, were returned to Parliament. When the National Land League was formed in 1879 to protect tenants' rights, Parnell became its president. During the 1880s, Home Rule politicians campaigned, not only for self-government, but against English landlords. Yet Irish Protestants allied themselves with the landlords to uphold property rights by setting up the Orange Emergency Committee and the Property Defence Association against the Land League, which was made up mainly of Roman-Catholic tenant farmers. The scene was set for bitter conflict and would end the London Livery Companies' involvement in Ulster.

There were three successive years of poor harvests starting in 1874, culminating in a major economic and agricultural crisis in 1879. Gladstone continued his efforts to relieve the distress. In 1881, his Land Law (Ireland) Act (44 and 45 Victoria. Cap. 49) proposed a system of fair rents, the freedom for tenants to sell their occupancy rights, and fixed tenancy rights. Rules were made to prevent squatters from being intimidated, despite them occupying land from which tenants had been evicted. Tenants' rights in Ulster were represented by a Land Committee and local authorities were empowered to borrow to build dwellings for agricultural labourers. In 1885 the Purchase of Land (Ireland) Act (48 and 49 Victoria. Cap. 73) weakened the landlords' position irretrievably by arranging for Government money to be advanced to tenants to purchase their holdings with annual repayments being less than their former rents. Home Rule now gained support from Roman-Catholic bishops, as it 'alone can satisfy the wants, the wishes, as well as the legitimate aspirations, of the Irish people'.[ww]

When the 1886 election provided Irish Nationalists with eighty-six seats in Parliament, Gladstone had to side with them to retain his Liberal majority, causing the Liberals to be split between Unionists and Home-Rulers. This was a major cause of their decline. When Ulster Conservatives came out firmly against Home Rule, nearly one hundred Liberal Unionists joined the Conservatives to bring Gladstone down and to form a new Government with a large majority.

Chapter 38

The seeds of growing unrest in Belfast
1800 – 20th Century

By the beginning of the 19th Century, Belfast's population was expanding rapidly. The dredging of the Lagan estuary enabled ships to dock at all tides and allowed shipbuilding to begin. By 1901, Belfast was the United Kingdom's third most important port after London and Liverpool. Yet great changes were taking place in linen production which remained Belfast's principal activity. Irish flax farmers had failed to maintain good practice in growing flaxseed. Flax grown in Belgium and north-western Germany was now superior. Irish flax growing survived for a time only because of local demand and inducements paid by English flax spinners desperate for supplies to meet English loom workers' requirements. Yet flax growing progressively declined until almost all flaxseed was imported.

With cotton spinning in Belfast becoming uncompetitive, the mills diversified into mechanised flax spinning. In 1830, a flax spinning operation with 8,000 spindles was opened, putting most remaining local hand spinners out of business. By 1850, mechanised flax spinning in Belfast had overtaken cotton spinning in importance. Yet linen weaving continued as a cottage industry. With the wholesale exodus caused by the Great Famine, Belfast's industrial spinners needed alternative outlets for their yarn. There was a rapid move towards factory operated power looms. While this assisted industrial producers, it undermined the rural economy for those who remained.

Demand for factory produced linen benefited from a disruption to cotton imports during the American Civil War. This allowed Belfast manufacturers to enjoy great prosperity, which continued until the end of the First World War, when linen was even used as a covering for aircraft wings. Belfast was affectionately known as Linenopolis, and overtook Lancashire as the world's largest producer. Not only did it boast the world's biggest linen mill, but ropeworks, a tobacco factory, shipyard, dry dock and many other industrial activities. With business burgeoning, people arrived from rural areas in large numbers. Although Belfast landlords continued to evict Catholic tenants hoping to replace them with more compatible Protestants, many of the new arrivals were

Catholic and old antagonisms remained 'etched into their folk memory'.[a] Sectarian battles moved from the countryside to the Belfast streets. A clear demarcation developed between Protestant and Catholic areas, and religious hatred had ample opportunity to fester among the low-paid majority eking out a wretched existence in 'brutalising conditions'.[b] There seemed no way to end the violence. In 1849, fifty Catholic 'Ribbonmen' died in a conflict with Orangemen.

As the Rev. George Hill reported in 1877:

> The dragon's teeth, so plentifully, and if so deliberately sown in the Ulster Plantation, have, indeed, sprung up at times with more than usually abundant growth, yielding their ghastly harvests of blood and death on almost every plain, and by almost every river side, and in almost every glen of our northern province.[c]

Confrontation was exacerbated by a new drive from English Evangelicals to convert Irish Catholics to Protestantism. 'By 1816 there were twenty-one Methodist missionaries' in Ireland,[d] and Catholics felt deep resentment at the religious tracts and bibles being distributed. The Catholic Church made similar efforts at renewal, with thirty thousand Catholics hearing confession in Belfast. Adults, who had missed the opportunity as children, were now being confirmed in large numbers. Catholic churches and even cathedrals sprung up. It was religion not language that was now the mark of distinction. With so much inter-marriage between native Irish and British settlers, no ethnic divide remained, and many Irish names were anglicised. Yet sectarian strife was endemic.

Part 9

The individual Livery Companies on their
proportions (2) and those of
The Honourable The Irish Society
in Londonderry and Coleraine
1641 – 20th Century

Chapter 39

Mercers

There was almost nothing left of the Mercers' proportion after the rebellion in 1641, and, in 1649, the remains of the castle at Movanagher were levelled by Parliamentary troops[154]. It had proved a poor site for a settlement and all its buildings were destroyed.

With the Irish Society being restored to its estates on 24 March 1656, in the following year, the Mercers regained their lands under Letters Patent and a Deed of Conveyance from the Society. Many of the native Irish in remoter and less fertile areas had already resettled; not even Cromwell's might had been able to shift them entirely. English Protestants resumed their exclusive occupation of the better townlands and teachers were re-employed in the schools. The Company at last followed other Companies in 'farming' out its estate to a middleman. Gervaise Rose took a forty-one year lease at £300 from 1 November 1558 after paying an entry fine of £500 and an annual rent of £300. His arrival relieved the Company of direct control, saving it much time, trouble and expense, but it pushed up rents. This was

> the inevitable outcome of the financial losses caused by the destruction of the first Plantation, the constant drain on resources, and the catastrophes of the Fire of London, the financial disaster of 1699[155], and the South Sea Bubble.[a]

Rose focused on the proportion's 'agricultural possibilities, including the woodlands'.[b] Some trees had survived, and attempts were made to develop iron smelting using charcoal; this continued until about 1710 to the great detriment of the remaining woodlands, which also suffered from the use of bark for tanning. Movanagher remained a 'market of sorts', but the centre of gravity moved towards the church at Kilrea on higher ground, where the Company established its principal town. With its central location, it was the natural place for its market.

By 1688, Rose had transferred his lease to the Jacksons of Coleraine, who began to develop Kilrea. Its Protestant residents rallied to the Williamite cause,

---

[154] A part of one of the circular flankers and a short length of the bawn wall still survive, but in a poor state of preservation.
[155] This was a failed scheme by the Scots to colonise Darien, on the Isthmus of Panama.

and, although the Jacksons tried to consolidate a line of defence along the Bann, this was broken by Jacobite troops. Settlers fled to Londonderry and Coleraine with many leaving Ulster altogether. Even though the Williamite victory provided those that remained with security, the proportion was left severely denuded. With rents falling, a new wave of Scottish settlers arrived, but found themselves competing for tenancies with the native Irish. This forced prices up again and threatened standards of living.[c] Although native farmers were determined to stay, they were allocated the poorer land, which reduced them to a subsistence existence.

It was the establishment of the linen industry by the Huguenots, which provided farmers with an important secondary source of income. With spinning and weaving being undertaken in every dwelling, the brown linen cloth being manufactured was sold in the markets to bleachers, who had developed 'greens' on the Ironmongers' lands at Aghadowey, but, by the 1740s, the Mercers also had their own bleach-greens and a water-powered linen mill.

Following the financial difficulties caused by the South Sea Bubble, the Mercers were not alone in trying to generate cash from their investment. In 1714, John McMullan took over the head lease at a reduced annual rental of £450 for forty-one years, after paying an entry fine of £6,000. The lease terms also required him to build a manor house and good houses on each townland, to plant trees, to enclose waste lands and to encourage the linen industry. He was soon short of money and had to sub-let to Protestant undertakers for thirty-nine years on similar terms. As a result of rack-renting, subtenants were left 'in a state of permanent poverty and insecurity'.[d] Although McMullan achieved some house building, land reclamation and tree planting, it was not on a 'spectacular' scale and he remained short of cash. Faced with an embargo on letting to Roman-Catholics, some undertakers entered into partnership with native Irish to avoid breaking the letter of the law. On McMullan's death in 1716, only two years after becoming the lessee, it was found that he had borrowed heavily against his leasehold to finance other ventures. His 'tangle of legal and financial problems' left several lenders in severe financial straits. James Wilson was in such difficulty that he took over the lease in an effort to recoup his outlay, but McMullan had creamed off the entry fines paid by undertakers, leaving Wilson with only small amounts of rent due, which his subtenants struggled to pay. Within three years, the Mercers were owed well over £1,000 and faced growing arrears, despite frantic efforts by Wilson to recover what he was owed. His problems were made only more difficult by a slump in linen prices. Although he asked the Company to apply to The Irish Society for a new timber quota to repair and reconstruct buildings, little work was undertaken. Subtenants made little attempt to improve their land and were charged higher rents if they did so, but some income was generated from a water-powered corn mill developed at Kilrea.

When the leases of Presbyterian subtenants expired, many left for America, but reasonable numbers remained in lowland areas, particularly round Kilrea, leaving Roman-Catholics with the poorer soil. In an attempt to retain his Protestant subtenants, Wilson petitioned the Mercers for leases to be extended for lives, but they would not agree. By the 1730s, most had left, and the native Irish were so determined to retain their ancestral lands that they outbid new Presbyterian arrivals, regardless of the consequences. They

> became first of all impoverished almost beyond endurance by rack-renting and subsistence farming, and then even more implacable enemies of British Government.[e]

Although a survey was carried out in 1714, with a second map being produced in 1722 by one Newe, neither proved accurate. A further survey by Thomas Brown, undertaken in 1740, established the proportion as 19,667 acres, but it was still run down.

> Enclosure had been neglected, the woodlands were in a dreadful state, buildings were in a poor state of repair, roads were terrible, and there was widespread rack-renting and emigration.[f]

The Mercers (and they were not alone) had made no real attempt to ensure the success of their investment. They badly needed good management. No interest was taken in welfare. Rents were never ploughed back into land improvement or infrastructure. Tenants had no means of fertilising the soil and were left with no choice but to overwork it. If they carried out improvements, they were charged higher rents. Unlike in England, agents were not versed in all aspects of advanced agriculture. They were rent-collectors attempting to skim a living for themselves.

On the expiry of the Wilsons' lease in 1751, the proportion reverted to the Company. After so much financial loss, the Mercers wanted to avoid further problems and obtained an Act of Parliament to grant a lease for a period of up to eighty years to be offered by competitive tender. It was taken up by Alexander Stewart of Newtown, County Down for a huge entry fine of £16,500 and an annual rental of £450 for the lives of himself and two of his children (which resulted in it continuing until 1831). Stewart had ample resources, having, in 1737, married Mary Cowan, heiress to a fortune made in the East India Company. He also had extensive estates in County Down and his elder son, Robert, become Lord Londonderry in 1789, rising to Viscount Castlereagh in 1795 and Marquess of Londonderry[156] in 1816. Although a handsome rectory was built in the 1770s, there is little building work or other improvement to show for the Stewarts' tenure, and they remained absentee landlords. 'Rack-renting reached appalling heights of exploitation,'[g] and the proportion's settlers had strong sympathies for the United Irish, but, Castlereagh, despite being of Dissenting stock, strongly opposed the 1798 rebellion and was closely

---

[156] Robert's son, also Robert, served as Foreign Secretary in the British Government, and was largely responsible for the political settlement at the Congress of Vienna both before and after the Battle of Waterloo.

associated with efforts to put it down. He is reputed to have secreted a guillotine at Lisnagrot near Kilrea, which was tried on some hapless dogs.

On Slade's visit in 1802 he showed his disapproval by singling out the proportion's very poor condition and lack of housing, painting 'a dismal picture of poverty and seediness'.[h] He complained at the lack of timber caused by the Stewarts felling of many acres of ash and sycamore near Kilrea,[157] and reported that the innkeeper at Kilrea was very scathing of their absenteeism. Slade quickly realised

> the reasons for the poverty and ignorance of those who toiled for a miserable subsistence. Exploitation, frightful housing, disease, indescribable filth and poverty, dreadful food, and whiskey drinking (mostly of illicit spirits) were ruining the population, while the money was leaving the country to be spent in England.[i]

It was thanks to Sampson's recommendations for improvement that 'the climate for responsibility changed, and a new sense of caring and social awareness developed',[j] so that the Mercers began to work on reform. They started donating money to relieve poverty and for education. In 1829, a water pump was provided at Kilrea.

Castlereagh's one contribution was to establish a 'precise definition of the boundaries', which identified an additional 1,000 acres for the known estate.[k] The survey was arranged through W. Armstrong, the Mercers' legal agent in Dublin. Yet the Stewarts' efforts stopped there. Armstrong wrote to the Company in 1814 that they were raising their 'rental to the highest pitch'. Improvements were discouraged and with smallholders' tenure remaining uncertain, 'rural demoralisation was rife'. Tenants could not afford to repair their cabins and the absence of trees made the landscape 'dreary'. Armstrong warned that unless remedial steps were taken immediately to encourage agriculture, planting and improvement, the Company would find itself with worthless, exhausted lands and utterly demoralised and hopeless tenant-farmers.[l]

In 1821, with tenants continuing to be charged higher rents if they made improvements, Alexander Clark of Upperlands wrote to the Company in London that he would cease further remedial work unless his tenure was assured.[m] The Company sent Robert M. Barnard to Ireland to report on what was going on. He 'waxed lyrical' about Clark's estate where trees and hedges had been planted, and there were fine new buildings and a mill. The Company assured Clark of 'sympathetic consideration' when it regained possession from the Stewarts. Barnard blamed the short leases being offered by the Stewarts for the proportion's lack of industry of any consequence, other than Clark's linen establishment. He found conditions elsewhere to be appalling. When Sampson

---

[157] John Claudius Beresford wrote: 'The County of Londonderry was the worst wooded county in the King's dominions thanks to the asset-stripping of unscrupulous tenants like Stewart who were taking advantage of the turpitude of 18th Century landlords.'[n]

called for major tree planting schemes, the Company encouraged Clark and other tenants to plant, and Sampson was invited to proceed with a conservation scheme for timber growing. In 1824, the Company set up a register of trees and provided £20 for them to be marked. Although Castlereagh, now Marquess of Londonderry, objected, Clark and others complied. By 1825, Sampson's survey had recorded 23,001 trees and, on his recommendation, John Kennedy of Tamlaght was appointed the proportion's permanent timber agent.

Barnard also

> urged that education should be improved so that 'children now in a state of brute ignorance and more resembling the offspring of savages than inhabitants of a civilised state will be instructed in their duty to God and to Man.°

With support from the Mercers, Sampson built two schoolhouses at Carhill and Swatragh. In 1829, the Company assisted in the repair of the Presbyterian Church at Kilrea, but, so long as the Stewarts held the lease, its hands were tied.

At last, in 1831, Alexander Stewart (Londonderry's brother) died, and their era as landlords was ended. After a meeting with their associated Minor Companies, the Mercers sent a deputation on a tour of inspection to re-establish control. From the outset it was recognised that areas allocated to each farm needed to be increased to make them viable, and Kilrea, which was already a significant settlement, needed to be 'reformed'.[158] Although the Stewarts had generated annual rental income of £9,205. 17s. 6d., there were arrears of £20,057. The Company bought these out for £12,000 and appointed John Henderson of Kilrea as Seneschal, building a counting house and offices to administer the estate and prepare monthly returns. William Henry Holmes of Lewisham, a member of the Mercers' Court, was appointed Agent at a salary of £700, but he was required to provide a bond of £2,000 as surety. He was instructed to be unbiased in religious matters and to establish a good relationship with the tenantry. Each farm was to be visited twice per year to ensure that buildings were kept in proper repair. By making himself approachable, he immediately improved morale. He considered himself 'reasonably independent and was unbound by considerations of personal gain'.ᵖ He became Chief Magistrate of the Manorial Court, and having leased land himself, qualified as a Grand Juror.

A period of great activity was begun. 'From that time on the Company did everything in its power to improve the estate and the lot of tenants,'�q exercising complete control over developments. It ploughed back £4,000 of its total annual income of about £10,000, and made great strides in agricultural management and forestry. To allow farms to be amalgamated, 'attention was given to a policy of assisted emigration to thin out the overpopulated countryside.'ʳ 'A crash-programme' of land-drainage, reclamation and conservation of bog-lands was

---

[158] According to Barnard, it needed to be reformed 'not indifferently, but altogether, for a worse Town in every respect is not to be found in the North of Ireland'.ˢ

begun. Trees and hedgerows were planted. Methods of livestock breeding were improved and hardier strains of seeds were developed.[t] With Sampson having recommended the building of an Agricultural School at Templemoyle on the Grocers' proportion, young farmers were trained in modern techniques. In 1835, the Mercers established a Model Farm, again as recommended by Sampson, and several model cottages were built, with the first pair being completed in 1839. With outbreaks of cholera and typhoid prevalent, houses were limewashed inside as a precaution, and unsound and unhygienic buildings were demolished.

A new survey was commissioned 'to define and record the accurate boundaries and extent of the two Divisions of the proportion, and to iron out disputes and ownership problems'.[u] This involved a full examination of deeds and records, and discussions with neighbours, including the Skinners and Ironmongers. 'The Company 'gained' much land as a result.'[v] Natural resources were developed; a new lime quarry was opened and stone was extracted near Movanagher. Brick clay was available at Movanagher and Claragh.

The Mercers' Arms, Kilrea Once 'one of the chief ornaments of the town', this former inn sits unloved next to the modern town hall, which is on the site of the former market house in one corner of the Diamond.

Kilrea was strategically positioned at the junction of roads from Maghera, Garvagh and Limavady. To improve transportation, plans were made to build better roads with reduced gradients. In 1783, a new bridge had linked Kilrea with Antrim and Belfast, providing access to the linen industry. A 'convenient and ornamental' Market House was built, surmounted by a weathervane, and Kilrea superseded Movanagher in importance. It had 235 houses for its population of 1,215, boasting representatives of every trade. The former Agent's House, near the Market House, became a 'well-managed' inn, *The Mercers' Arms* ('one of the chief ornaments of the town'), and there were three 'eating houses'.

The Mercers' former Agent's House, Kilrea Despite proposals to provide the Agent with a more modest dwelling, the Company insisted on 'something more grand in keeping with his status'. William Barnes's design, which cost £4000, is now a golf club.

A Town pump provided water, and the streets were paved and had lighting. In September 1832, an accountant was employed, and Holmes submitted plans for a new Agent's House. Although this was originally a modest design, the Company insisted 'on something much more grand in keeping with his status as Agent'.[w] This resulted in a classical building on two storeys with five sash-window bays, a plain triangular pediment and slated roof, set in its own parkland with a lake, outbuildings and servants' quarters. It ultimately cost £4,000 and is now a golf club. The Company provided all public buildings and, in an effort to encourage private individuals to build substantial homes, it granted forty-one year leases on favourable terms. Buildings were required to conform in height and shape so that 'a coherent architectural scheme' was achieved.[x] Many were thatched initially and strict control was enforced over middens. Loans were provided to make improvements. To raise the tone, the 'style' and 'class' of each house was expected to be appropriate for its projected occupier and 'villas' were built to attract 'gentlemen of independent property'. The building of 'inferior houses' was prohibited[159], and poor dwellings and sheds were demolished to make way for new development.

---

[159] Cottages 'with only one 'sleeping room' were rejected on moral grounds as incest was becoming a scandalous problem by the 1840s'.[y]

Villa at Kilrea designed by William Barnes This was one of several properties just outside the town centre designed to attract 'gentlemen of independent property'.

Between 1831 and 1890, the Mercers built four schools, with two being at Kilrea, and it rebuilt three more. They provided an annual allowance of £400 towards running costs. There were also ten Roman-Catholic Schools, but not all these were supported by the Company. Yet it did support the Kilrea Deaf and Dumb School founded in 1835 with a grant of £20. By 1837, it is estimated that one thousand children were receiving free education. This progressively became the responsibility of the State, which converted the Mercers' buildings to 'National Schools'. Yet the Company continued to maintain the fabric which resulted in them spending £20,000 up to 1905. It then provided an endowment managed by Trustees for their future maintenance.

Churches were also built, and the Company assisted in repairs to other places of worship. In 1836, with 'an ecumenical concern for fairness',[z] it made a donation to re-thatch the Roman-Catholic church at Craigavole and, in 1837, provided land for the new Roman-Catholic church of St John the Baptist at Swatragh. Both the Company and The Irish Society contributed to the building cost of the Presbyterian meeting house with a burial ground in Kilrea. In the following year another Presbyterian church was needed when its 'Second Presbyterian Congregation' seceded from the original group. In 1840, several alternative drawings were prepared for the Parish Church of St Patrick in Kilrea, before a Romanesque Revival design with a stone spire was eventually chosen. When completed in 1843, it could accommodate between six and seven hundred people. The contractor was John Little and Sons of the Minories in London,[160] which later built the new school at Movanagher. In 1852, the Company contributed to a new Anglican Church in an early English Gothic style at

---

[160] English contractors were sometimes preferred as they could often undercut Irish tenders.

Swatragh, and supported the building programmes of other religious denominations.

The First Presbyterian Church, Kilrea William Barnes's design of 1837 caused 'the Anglicans to do something to overshadow the splendours of the large meeting-house'.

St Patrick's Parish Church, Kilrea In 1839, George Smith, the Mercers' Surveyor, provided designs for the Parish Church. These were adapted by William Barnes, and in 1842, the town clock was incorporated into the tower.

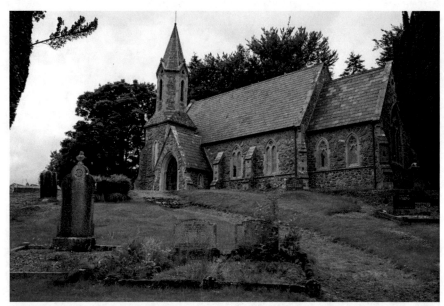

The Parish Church of Killela, Swatragh This early gothic style church was erected in 1852 to designs by Joseph Welland

The former Estate Office, Kilrea This building opposite the Parish Church was also designed by William Barnes in 1843 and completed in 1849.

The inn at Swatragh The deputation of 1847 considered this to be in an 'excellent position'. It remains a busy public house.

The Company established dispensaries at Kilrea and Swatragh. A Doctor's house at Swatragh was built during the 1830s, but was converted to an inn in 1845. Money was set aside for a lending library, and clothing was provided for the poor. A new police barracks was completed in 1835. In 1842, a town clock was designed, but this was ultimately incorporated into the tower of the Parish Church. In 1844, it contributed to the cost of St. Mary's Catholic Church at Drumagarner. So considerable were the improvements that tenants wrote to the Company expressing their satisfaction. They were particularly appreciative of the removal of old feudal exactions, such as bog-fees and leet-money.

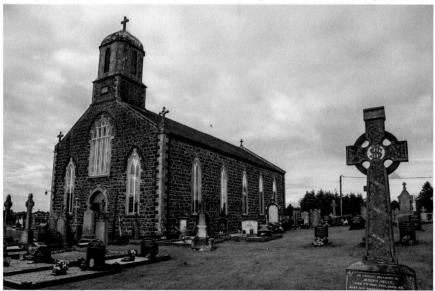

St Mary's Roman Catholic Church, Drumagarner In 1844, the Mercers contributed to the cost of this church, constructed of basalt with freestone dressings.

377

Contributions were made to the Derry Central Railway, drainage schemes, roadworks and other communication improvements.[aa] A report was commissioned for improving the navigation on the Bann round the falls at Portna[161] and to provide water power, but the Company was reluctant to become involved, despite the opportunity to provide a link to the Lagan valley. It may have realised that the railway would make the navigation redundant (as it did), but a new wharf was built near Kilrea with new buildings and machinery for the corn mill and grain market.

When Holmes resigned as Agent in 1844, he was succeeded by George Bicknell of Bloomsbury. After Holmes's considerable achievements, things took a sudden turn for the worse. It is clear that Bicknell was slow to grasp the impact of the potato famine. In 1847, when a massive influx of itinerants brought in disease, Bicknell authorised work on a new fever hospital at Kilrea. When a deputation arrived from London to review progress, it was horrified to find it sited in the town centre next to the church. One member, James Sutton, who kept a diary of his findings, accused Bicknell of being 'offhand' when told to demolish it, but the deputation insisted on all further work being stopped 'pending the pleasure of the Court'.[cc] Bicknell became offensive, questioning their authority, and refused. This annoyed them even more. Having warned him about his behaviour, the deputation told him 'in no uncertain terms that the character of the building was highly objectionable'.[dd] It believed that a new house recently completed outside the town centre would be suitable. It is clear that James Turnbull, the long-standing surveyor, took the deputation's side. When rebuilding was agreed, he was instructed to undertake the work.

The deputation spotted other shortcomings. After walking through the 'back parts' of Kilrea, where several new houses had been constructed, it found 'drainage middens' and hygiene 'poorly ordered'. Sutton was disgusted at the 'misery, dirt and degrading filth' behind new houses and considered the whole town 'unfit for habitation'. Both Kilrea and Swatragh were in a disgraceful state, and a programme for cleaning them 'was an immediate concern'. Houses were overcrowded and 'foetid'. Sutton gave

> distressing descriptions of crippled women with many children, rural poverty, destitution, and general sickness. In front of the houses, more often than not, were 'stagnant pools of fermenting water': the stench can be imagined. Examination of the town, the Market-House, and the flax-market

---

[161] A principal difficulty for the navigation system was that Lough Neagh at the headwater of the Bann regularly flooded surrounding farmland, so that water needed to be stablised at summer levels by drainage schemes along the river's entire length to the Salmon Leap and from there along the tidal stretch to the sea.[bb] This met with resistance from the Mercers, even though it provided employment for labourers left destitute by the famine. Although the construction work provided them with much needed income, native Irish on the Mercers' lands, although unaffected by the famine, neglected their holdings for the better wages being offered to 'navvies'. Despite being lukewarm, the Company did contribute to a steamer to ply the navigation to the coast.

revealed filthy stores and appalling attention to public health: the stands for the linen market were used as privies, and the girls of the school (situated in the upper part of the Market-House) used the underside of the staircase as a communal privy: the place was a mass of faeces and urine, and it was no wonder 'fever' stalked the streets of Kilrea.[ee]

The south side of one street in Kilrea needed to be demolished and rebuilt, and essential repairs to the Market House were required.

The deputation was similarly critical of sanitary arrangements in the townlands, where streams were being polluted. It was also critical of farming methods, finding that tenant farmers were 'uninterested in weeding' or thinning turnips as they grew.[ff] Other than Clark's estate at Upperton, farms were 'all wretched' and yielded only half of what should be expected. 'The policy of encouraging emigration had failed as there were still far too many people on land that could not support them.'[gg] Farms still had to be subdivided between families with pieces being sold off, when they needed to be amalgamated, and a comprehensive scheme of land reclamation, drainage and tree planting was still required. There was also an urgent need to provide employment.

The deputation faced another problem. On visiting the site of a proposed Presbyterian meeting house at Bovedy, two miles west of Kilrea, it was surprised to find two 'unfinished barns' about two hundred feet apart. Two Scottish farmers had seceded from the minister with half the congregation, causing great animosity. The deputation was surrounded by 'a number of primitive Scotchmen', whose features 'betokened much fire and religious fury'.[hh] The minister seemed to have absconded to America with the money raised to build their meeting house. The deputation agreed that it should not advance money, but the minister was removed from his living. Perhaps surprisingly, both meeting houses were ultimately completed.

Matters improved when Bicknell was replaced by Robert Holbeche Dolling, followed by a succession of more efficient Agents. Emigration allowed the population on the estate to fall from 10,737 in 1841 to 7,013 in 1871, and improving yields made farms much more viable. Yet, during the 1880s, poor harvests and the consequent failure to pay rents resulted in several evictions. Even so, the estate remained intact until 1903, when the Wyndham Act 'supported the principle of owner occupiers'. The Mercers offered generous terms, and most of the estate was sold to its tenants by 1909, generating the enormous sum of £211,796. The few remaining properties were granted to tenants on perpetual ground rent leases, which they generally took up. In 1906, the Company provided £500 per annum as a 'Sustentation Fund' to maintain churches, clergy, ministers and schoolteachers. Rents from the Kilrea Hotel (the former Mercers' Arms) were transferred to trustees for the estate's benefit and to meet other minor liabilities. Even in 1963, small amounts of rent were still being collected, despite tenants' resentment at having to pay a distant landlord in London. At that time, the Mercers severed their links completely, transferring their remaining income and obligations to The Irish Society. Yet it has continued distributing money on a charitable basis to promote the welfare of the local populace at the behest of a Local Advisory Committee.

Chapter 40

Grocers

When the Grocers' lands were restored in 1657, Harrington, the leaseholder, returned to collect arrears, but found that no rents had been paid for many years. Perhaps surprisingly, the Company appointed Beresford as their Agent, but Harrington, who had arrived first, claimed that the arrears were due to him. Beresford found those tenants remaining to be united behind Harrington, even though 'the land was gone to waste, houses were ruinous, and tenants were 'unsettled'.[a]

> Beresford advised the Company either to settle Harrington again in the land, buy him out, or evict him by a legal action for failure to pay. He felt that buying him out would be the best way, as he owed so much there was no possibility of recovering the rents due since before the rebellion.[b]

He offered to replace Harrington as lessee for a term of sixty-one years, paying all Harrington's arrears (in addition to all collection fees) and would contribute to the cost of buying out his lease. The Grocers postponed an immediate decision on this apparently generous offer, and ultimately turned it down.

The Grocers faced their own difficulties.

> Being greatly embarrassed in their circumstances, on account of the forced loans, which had never been repaid, and of the losses incurred by the Great Fire of London, they came to the determination of raising a sum of money to relieve their immediate wants, by granting a long lease of their Irish estate for a fine in hand, and at a trifling rent. Advertisements for tenders were circulated, and the result was that they demised the lands to Mr. George Finch, for a period of 31 years from Allhallowtide 1676, at a rent of £10, and a fine of £3,600.[c]

Finch did not have an easy time. Being on the opposite side of the Foyle River to Londonderry, the proportion was completely destroyed by the Jacobites during the siege. It was not just the depredation caused by the Williamite war. The Company was suffering from the effects of the South Sea Bubble and other financial calamities. Finch had to soldier on without their help, but he died in about 1700, when his widow requested a seven year extension 'to save what she could'.[d] This was granted to their nephew, also George Finch, who obtained an extension of fifty-three years to 1760, but, in 1708, he assigned his interests to

Conolly, (see page 313), reputedly, the wealthiest man in Ireland. Conolly was already Agent and later farmer of the Vintner's proportion, and used his position to further his political career. On his death in 1729, the lease of the Grocers' estate was vested in his nephew, William, whose son, Thomas Conolly, purchased the Vintners' proportion in 1737 (see page 469). In 1760, Thomas paid a fine of £15,500 to extend the Grocers' lease for a further sixty years and three lives at £600 per annum.

In 1805, The Irish Society's law agent, David Babington, obtained a demise of the remainder of the Conolly lease at a fine of £2,750 and a rental of £2,100 per annum fully expecting it to be renewed on expiry. Yet, in 1820 (on the death of the third life – George III), when Babington applied for renewal, he suffered a 'severe blow' when this was turned down by the Company. According to the *Report of the Deputation* of The Irish Society in 1836, Babington had 'spent a great deal of money in improving, draining, and subdividing his land, and built a good mansion thereon'.[e] This was the new 'Grocers' Hall' (later Foyle Park) at Fallowlea. He had also built houses and converted buildings at Templemoyle nearby.[162] He introduced the practice of providing fertiliser by burning poor quality limestone with peat. Yet he was unpopular with the tenants, and 'the populace as a whole was in a wretched state'.[f] A deputation sent by the Grocers in 1822 noted that other proportions were in better condition. They were unimpressed with Babington, and, after some 'wrangling', the Company bought 'Grocers' Hall' and its grounds for £7,000, which The Irish Society considered a 'liberal price', but it 'by no means repaid Babington's expenses'.[g]

By 1820, the fortunes of the Grocers' Company and the City of London were much recovered and the Grocers resumed direct control. They had been goaded into action by Sampson's criticisms. (see pages 343-5) The Company resolved to do all in its power to ameliorate the condition of the occupiers of the soil, by enabling them, without reference to the more or less quality of land they rented, to hold immediately from the Company.[i]

---

[162] Sampson was surprisingly full of praise for Babington. He strongly approved of his improvements at 'Grocers' Hall', and commented that the 'value and efficacy of resident and patriotic gentry can no where be better exemplified'. He referred to the

> extensive plantations, so judiciously planned ... as to confer ornament without detracting from utility; the substitution of well shaped, and well cultivated fields, in place of everything which could degrade and deform a neglected country ... Mr. Babington's zeal is by no means confined to the improvements of his own demesne: every where through the whole estate over which he presides, cottages, rising in place of hovels, limestone quarries opening where no limestone was thought to exist, excellent public roads multiplying where scarce a swampy private path could be found, wastes reclaiming into good soils, where good soils were formerly in a state of waste; a general system of order, of industry, and neatness ... Such has been the improvement ... that to one who has not been a witness to the intensity of labour and expense, it might almost seem like the creation of enchantment.[h]

The lands were quickly enclosed. Rebuilding began at Muff 'with every attention to the wants and comforts of the tenants'; schools[163] and hospitals were built and 'munificently aided' by the Company.[j] In the space of a few years, the Grocers transformed their estate into 'a thriving ornament of County Londonderry'.[k] Heath believed that the 'condition of the peasantry' would be held as an 'inducement to the possessors of the lands in other parts of Ireland to follow so noble an example'.[l]

On regaining direct control, the Company sent its Surveyor, Richard Fowler of Lincoln, to undertake a complete survey of the proportion and to make recommendations for new buildings and repairs which needed attention. All these would require the Company's approval. On arrival, he also acted as Agent for two years to agree new tenancies until, in 1822, Richard Warner, was appointed. When a deputation was sent to review his survey and recommendations, it noted that he had managed the lettings with good judgment and had encouraged good husbandry among 'a feckless and ignorant tenantry'.[m] It found his survey to be accurate, showing that the proportion was already well-developed with settlements at Muff, Edenreaghmore and Fallowlea. Fowler accompanied the deputation on its tour and may have designed some of the proposed buildings. It counted 282 tenants' and 409 cottars' houses, all 'in the most wretched state of dilapidation'.[n] The great majority of the inhabitants had been 'highly Rack Rented during Mr. Babington's occupation; and some reduced to a State of Beggary'. Just as elsewhere, peasants had an 'enthusiastic attachment to the residence' of their fathers, and would 'submit to any privation rather than quit'.[o] Yet the land was generally 'cropped out'. Most tenancies were under fifty acres and some as small as ten acres, but mountain areas provided common grazing at a nominal rent. Most 'cottars' spun and wove flax to make linen, and whole families were involved in cultivation. The deputation called for sub-letting to be stopped, seeing middlemen as the 'Bane and Curse of the Country', and the Company prohibited it. It reduced rents by 20-25 per cent to remove the worst effects of rack-renting. It also provided spinning wheels and loans to purchase looms and other equipment. It was so 'horrified by the appalling state of the Proportion'[p] that it determined to carry out a

> crash-programme of new building and repairs. Muff was considered of paramount importance and required particular attention as it consisted of 'long ranges of low straggling buildings, each only one storey high'.[q]

Only six houses in Muff were deemed capable of repair. Plans were made to rebuild 'Grocers' Hall', and a four acre site was allocated for a new Agent's house with sufficient room to house a visiting deputation. Meanwhile Warner had to live at the Inn, which also became the deputation's headquarters. The old one-storey Sessions House in Muff had only three rooms and 'lacked the dignity required'; a new one, suitable for the reception of magistrates, was to be built

---

[163] In 1810, two acres of land near the Church at Muff was given for a school to be built by the governors of Erasmus Smith's Charity (see pages 284-5). This was completed in 1814.

adjacent to a small market house and dispensary. A Senechal and Bailiff[164] were appointed to swear and summon juries. A 'decent public house' was established on the site of the whiskey shop. Plans for a new school were also prepared, and a second dispensary was to be built at Cumber.

Faughanvale Parish Church of St. Canice, Eglinton The ruins of the original plantation church can be seen in the foreground.

John Bowden of Dublin, who was commissioned to design the new parish church of St Canice, provided a 'pleasing late-Georgian Gothic hall with a pretty tower at one end'.[r] Work on it began before the departure of the deputation, who reported that it would be a 'handsome structure' and 'ornament' to the village. It was completed in 1823. Although a curate was appointed, he occupied 'ruinous' rooms in the Castle. This was considered 'inconvenient, wretched and worn out', and the deputation agreed to its demolition.[s] This was undertaken in 1824, with the materials being reused to build the Glebe House on its site. The Fishmongers joined with the Grocers to pay for this, as the parish lay partly in the Fishmongers' proportion.[165] The Company provided thirty acres to the Board of First Fruits (the committee of the Church of Ireland responsible for church building) for £500. Although its first loyalty was to the Established Church, it wanted to be unbiased in religious and Irish matters, and provided donations to both Prebyterian and Catholic communities and to support their clergy. With tithes being 'a frightful source of difference between a Clergyman

---

[164] The bailiff was also the keeper of the woods.
[165] The Company also contributed to the maintenance of the church at Clondermot on the Goldsmiths' proportion as its parish extended onto Grocers' lands.

and his parishioners', the deputation proposed including them in the rent collection. Although the estate included some 'very respectable and responsible' Roman-Catholics, generally they were 'the least reliable tenants', and Protestants, as specified in the plantation requirements, were preferred.[t]

The former Rectory, Eglinton designed by Edward Farrell of Londonderry.

The Company delivered stone, lime, slate and timber for the building programme to each townland to enable tenants to carry out their own repairs. A new lime quarry was opened at Dungallion and slate was delivered from Gorticross to replace thatched roofs. It established excellent 'flag-quarries' producing the heavy slates used in the construction of the church and the Rectory'. These 'helped to create sound buildings at reasonable costs'.[u] Although stone was plentiful, a depot had to be built on the banks of the Foyle to land timber brought direct from the Baltic (for preference) or from Canada, and later from London. Fowler prepared plans for land drainage near to the Foyle and on swampy ground in mountainous areas, and he arranged for slob-lands to be embanked. Road building projects received grants from the Grand Jury of the County as confirmed by the Judge of Assize. The Company's Agent became a freeholder so that he could sit on the Grand Jury. Yet a plan to build a canal from the Foyle to Lough Erne, which would have crossed the estate, was not encouraged and came to nothing.

The former Court & Market House (right) with the Manor House (left), Eglinton The Manor house was the former agent's accommodation having originally been an inn.

The deputation's recommendations were followed by a decade of construction activity. Muff was rebuilt in a 'decent, reticent, simplified' classical style, much being designed by the respected Joseph Gwilt and Michael Angelo Nicholson. The Glebe House, together with Castle Farm, the inn[166] and several houses were completed in 1825, followed by the Sessions House in 1826. Its original design was amended by James Bridger, a Warden of the Drapers' Company, who spent some time in Moneymore and also worked on buildings for the Fishmongers. The quality of its masonry work is exceptional, making it 'one of the most distinguished buildings on the whole of the Londonderry Proportions'.[v] A Police Barracks was built behind it, and there were shops with allotments behind to house a blacksmith, butcher, baker, cooper, tailor and shoemaker. These were let at moderate rents to encourage trade 'and raise the tone of the neighbourhood'.[w] Six further houses were built at Muff and others for the bailiff and the muleteer at Templemoyle Mill. Single storey buildings provided accommodation for twelve widows. The main drainage canal linking Muff to the sea was completed in 1827. This necessitated a bridge over it to link the town to the main road. The canal allowed shell to be delivered from the banks of the Foyle. All over the proportion, farmbuildings were erected using lime and bricks, and the land was improved by planting and fencing with thorn quicks.

To follow Sampson's recommendations and improve husbandry, the Company sponsored the formation of the North-West of Ireland Agricultural Society. In 1827, 'many gentlemen', who had become patrons, contributed £3,000 towards the cost of building an agricultural 'seminary' on Babington's old estate at Templemoyle, opposite Grocers' Hall at Fallowlea in the centre of the proportion. Grocers' Hall had already been converted into a Classical

---

[166] Even now the inn required improvements for letting, and as it was still being occupied by the Agent, it was decided to leave it unlet until these had been made.

School[167] for the sons of farmers and now became associated with the seminary. Templemoyle Seminary was 'handsome and solid', providing training in all departments of agriculture, while Grocers' Hall housed the residential area with dormitories. The Company provided one hundred and forty acres for experiments in practical farming. It had a well-maintained plantation, and kitchen gardens round the house for growing herbs and flowers. It achieved massive advances in agricultural methods, with students excelling at land surveying. It initially accommodated both masters and one hundred pupils (each of whom paid £10 per annum), but, in 1827, it was extended to accommodate 'day scholars' and a corn mill and store were built at Muff Glen. With the Irish Society also contributing to Templemoyle's maintenance, students came from all over County Londonderry, regardless of religious persuasion.

Templemoyle mill and corn store, Muff Glen built in 1827 to handle to produce from the Templemoyle Seminary.

In 1827, when a second deputation visited Muff to examine progress and the further plans for development prepared by Warner and Fowler, it was agreed that the works should be completed as soon as possible. The most important issue was to convert the former inn into a house for the Agent. The schoolhouse proposed in 1823 had still not been built, but it was completed in 1831 with a house for a schoolmaster.[168] This was almost identical to the one built on the

---

[167] It taught Latin, Greek and Hebrew, in addition to reading, writing and arithmetic. Thackeray reported that pupils studied scientific agriculture, carpentry, masonry, elementary engineering and other useful pursuits, comparing it favourably with Eton and Harrow.[x]

[168] It still has a plaque showing the Grocers' Company camel insignia.

Fishmongers' proportion. The parish church was already in need of repair as a result of poor workmanship and a bell was required. A manse was built for the Presbyterian minister at Faughanvale, and a subsidy was provided to complete the Roman-Catholic Church at Mullabuoy. Warner, as Agent, received much credit for the improvements at Muff. The Irish Society reported that 'from being a wretched little hamlet, [it] is now a pretty neat town'.[y] It was unfortunate that, in 1834, Warner faced a 'disagreement' with the Company and had to be 'removed' after accounting discrepancies were found. Gwilt, who was now the Company's Surveyor, was sent to Ireland 'to remove all documents from Warner's hands'.[z] [169] Warner refused to meet him and Gwilt was appointed as acting Agent, although he was soon replaced by John Wiggins, who had managed the impovements at Lord Headley's estate in southern Ireland.

Camel motif in the wall of the school at Lower Gortnessy This emblem of the Grocers' Company has been restored above the door of the modern School.

The Company believed that leaving the town unfinished had a 'bad moral Effect with Reference to English Controul'.[aa] Wiggins was instructed 'to remove the uninhabited cabins that disfigured Muff, and to carry out new works'. The Company joined with the Fishmongers 'to embank and reclaim the slob-lands on the banks of Lough Foyle'. Wiggins's son, Henry, undertook another major survey, which provided a very full account of the proportion, bringing him much praise for his thoroughness. He was appointed to superintend all new building work and repairs, including the alterations to the inn to provide the Agent's residence. A carpenter's house with yard and stores was also built. It was a surprisingly distinguished pedimented building, (now a shop) and may have been designed by Henry. In 1838, The Irish Society considered the Grocers's estate to be the best managed of all the proportions, other than the Drapers'. Muff was 'neat and clean' with an 'excellent church, market house and other buildings'.[bb]

---

[169] A part of the difficulty seems to have been Warner's expenditure on new buildings. The deputation of 1840 noted that, 'costly as they no doubt were', they appeared 'substantial and ornamental'.[cc]

The former Carpenter's House, Eglinton This surprisingly distinguished pedimented building is now the village store.

The Presbyterian Church at Lower Gortnessy This stripped down classical hall was built in 1841 with a subscription from the Grocers.

In 1840, a new deputation noted that hedges were growing and woodland plantations were thriving. !n 1841, a Presbyterian Church was complete at Lower Gortnessy, which had received a contribution from the Company. Schools were well-attended and compared favourably with Erasmus Smith's academies. William Makepeace Thackeray, who visited in 1842, was so impressed on learning that Muff had been established by the Grocers' Company of London that it should cause cockneys to exclaim: 'Well done our side!' In 1840, Henry Wiggins's achievements were recognised when he was appointed

Joint Agent with his father. The deputation recommended the formation of a building fund to repair and erect new structures. In 1845, a new estate map was prepared and houses were progressively re-roofed with slate. With the Wigginses' keen support, the Templemoyle Seminary was granted a new twenty-one year lease.

In 1857, improvements were made to the parish church, but the Company was starting to cut back on its 'liberality'. Its lack of enthusiasm was undoubtedly coloured by the outcome of the Skinners' case against The Irish Society. With total receipts of only £4,288 16s. 7d. from 1821 to 1834, the proportion was proving a poor investment, and Ireland's political instability was beginning to tell. It had been badly affected during the famine years, when it reduced rents by 10 per cent to alleviate distress. With many families abandoning their holdings, the population fell.[170] Wiggins Sr. was instructed to explore the possibility of selling, and in 1862, Thomas McClure of Belfast offered £120,000, but this was turned down. Distress had also put a strain on Templemoyle. It struggled on until 1866, when it was closed down. The Company repossessed the buildings, which, in 1869, were partially demolished, but Grocers' Hall and the mill survived. The site was bought by Edward Herrick Allingham, whose family still own it, although Grocers' Hall (now Foyle Park) was sold separately. The Wigginses soldiered on, draining slob-lands and building a new school at Lower Cumber; Henry remained as Agent almost until the Company's involvement ended.

By 1869 Muff[171] had been renamed Eglinton. By then, problems were increasing, and the Grocers must have regretted not selling to McClure. By 1872, they had started piecemeal disposals to 'sound yeomen', hoping to create a much needed rural middle class, but political uncertainty left few buyers. By this time, there were widespread rumours that the Livery Companies' titles to their proportions was flawed, and that they held them as trustees. It took the case between the Irish Attorney-General and The Irish Society (see page 502) to establish that the Companies owned them outright. Sales at last speeded up, and, in 1877, James Davidson of Glasgow bought most of Eglinton for £41,500. With the rest of the estate being sold in several parcels, the Company stopped its contributions to building repairs. Despite its heritage of fine buildings, poor planning regulation in the meantime has allowed many to be demolished, resulting in the loss of much of Eglinton's graceful charm.

---

[170] There is no record of Muff being overrun by starving peasants as happened on the Mercers' proportion, but the Wiggins may have been better organised to cope with them.
[171] It was renamed after the popular 13th Earl of Eglinton and Winton, who had been Lord Lieutenant of Ireland. With a second town called Muff on the borders of Donegal and Londonderry, there was a problem with mail delivery.

Chapter 41

Drapers

When the Manor of Drapers was reconstituted by The Irish Society on 30 May 1663, Clotworthy, who had, by this time, been created Viscount Massereene, tried to purchase the proportion, but the Company decided on retaining it.[172] Yet it granted a new lease to his niece, Mary Clotworthy, and her husband the Hon. Robert Fitzgerald (brother of the 17th Earl of Kildare). In 1676, Fitzgerald and his wife sold their interest to Captain George Dawson of Moylelough, but he was left destitute by the events prior to the siege of Londonderry, when Moneymore was badly damaged. Most tenants deserted their holdings, and only a few returned. In 1690, a Mr. Muckeridge (or Mogridge) prepared a report on the condition of the proportions. It provided the following description of the Drapers' estate:

> Monimore towne consists of about 34 howses and families, the Castle and Mill. The castle has been a handsome structure, but demolished for the greatest part in the 41 War, the Bawne or Court Square are handsomely built and two flankers on the front thereof towards the Towne outstood the fury and malice of the then and now late enemy. Within this court was built a long range of houses and the flankers made upp, which was a convenient habitaćon for a Gentleman's family; this and a double Corne Mill close to it was burnt down by the enemy Anno 1689; the rest of the proporćon escapt the Flames and one Mill of the two is rebuilt. Butt the Towne and all the houses which are planted in the proporćon are ruinous and greatly decaied for want of repaires. There were att first 12 handsome houses laid out and built in the towne of two Stories each and each had ten or 15 acres of land nigh the Towne for conveniency. Other houses were of little consideraćon, and small rent. If I am rightly informed the town yeiled about [£80] per ann. And the Mills Thirty, but what estimate to make now I cannot tell for the houses are so ruinous and the people so poor that much if anything this yeare cannot be expected of them: and this briefly as to the Towne.[a]

---

[172] Up to 1679, individual members of the Company held personal stakes in the proportion, but at this point, these were all transferred back to the Company.

It was a dire situation. Most farmland and buildings were derelict. Although there was plenty of corn ('if the Armies fall not downe upon them'), other produce and stock were insufficient to sustain the locality. Although some poor Scots had arrived, they were 'not likely to stock or plant in haste'. Muckeridge hoped that, if peace were restored, thousands of Scottish settlers would arrive to improve things.

Although Dawson was re-established as chief tenant, rebuilding work was slow and painful. 'Papists' were distressingly numerous and tenants needed protection from 'Popish Priests'. Young Roman-Catholics needed to be cured of 'the twin habits of idleness and sloth (not to mention the Demon Drink), to which the native Irish were apparently addicted'.[b] In 1721, a site for a new Parish Church was granted at Ballinascreen, and £50 was donated for English Protestant Schools. In 1730, William Sarrat prepared a 'Map and Survey of the Tennaments and Parks of the Toun of Monymore in the Mannor of Drapers in the County of Londonderry'.

Ballinascreen Parish Church, Draperstown This handsome church was built in 1760, with its octagonal spire added at the behest of the Earl-Bishop of Derry in 1792 with support from Sir William Rowley and the Drapers.

The Dawsons' lease was extended on two further occasions. In 1725, Arabella Dawson had married Captain William Rowley (no relation of John Rowley, the former Agent) and, in 1729, Rowley extended the lease for a further thirty years from 1751 to 1781. In 1756, Rowley, who was by then an Admiral and had been knighted, again extended it for sixty-one years or three lives if longer. The rental income must have been good, as he agreed an entry fine of £6,732 and an annual rental of £600. Although he began to build a 'handsome' new rectory in 1762, progress was slow, and, by 1792, neither the spire of Ballyscullion church (to which the Company had contributed £100)[173] nor the rectory was complete.[174] On Rowley's death in 1768, the lease passed to his son, Sir Joshua, who sought a further extension in 1789. Yet the Drapers, in common with most other Companies, had by then resolved to take the management back in hand as soon as the lease expired. During the 1798 rebellion, a corps of Drapers' Yeomanry was raised to provide protection, but the proportion was little affected. Although the Rowleys made several further attempts up to 1809 to have the lease extended, these were all rejected and the lease expired with the death of their last life in 1816.

Ballyscullion Parish Church, Bellaghy This was built in 1794 and its octagonal spire was added to conform to the wishes of the Earl -Bishop of Derry, and could be seen from his palace on the shores of Lough Beg.

The Drapers' decision to bring the estate back in hand was strengthened by Sampson's criticisms of poor management and the hardships that tenants were facing. It was now almost devoid of trees and there were few hedges. Those that there were marked boundaries and were of little use for containing cattle. With an acute shortage of timber, there were no gates, and, without the natural shelter

[173] The Drapers provided the money to the Earl of Bristol, then Bishop of Derry, who was anxious to be able to look out on the spires of churches from his handsome property begun in 1787 at Ballyscullion on Lough Beg. The Earl-Bishop was pleased to have the spire completed without him having to pay for it himself.

[174] The incumbent persuaded the Company to accept a transfer of Glebe lands eight miles from the church in exchange for a tenancy adjacent to it granted by the Rowleys.

provided by trees, the country was 'bleak and unattractive'. The deputation sent to Ireland to plan for the future was determined to adopt Sampson's recommendations.

In fairness, the Rowleys had made notable improvements, and had reclaimed much mountainous land for cultivation. They had not let to middlemen, and had enjoyed a gross annual income of £9,871 6s. 11d. From this, had to be deducted Agency and management costs. The tenants were responsible for any building and repair work and paid rates and taxes (collected to pay for items of communal interest such as the upkeep of roads, bridges, public buildings, assizes and sessions). The Rowleys received no income from the Court as these went to their Agent, John Miller, who, as Seneschal (Judicial Officer), was entitled to all fees. Despite them being absentees, Miller managed the estate 'meritoriously'. He received one shilling in the pound on all rents collected, together with a fee for each lease granted or renewed. He also earned ten guineas for every attendance at Assizes in addition to Court fees.

The Drapers' deputation made proposals of lasting importance and benefit, resulting in Moneymore becoming the capital that other Companies aspired to emulate. 'Modern methods of draining, valuing, surveying and building were introduced',[c] with buildings being designed by professional architects. A new survey was urgently needed, 'so that arrangements with new tenants could be drawn up by 1819',[d] as those available were 'not always to be relied upon for accuracy as to quantity'.[e] Charles Stewart was appointed Land Surveyor and, by the time of the deputation's arrival, he had already provided accurate plans, although the survey was not fully completed until 1819 (and published in 1825). When finished, he was praised for its thoroughness despite the poor weather he had had to endure and it remained in use until the 1840s. By then, an 'Ordnance Survey' of the proportion had been begun, showing the revised layouts of Moneymore and Moyheelan (later renamed Draperstown) and the extent of more recent tree planting, but it was not completed until 1857-58.

When the Rowleys' lease expired, Miller became the Company's Agent at a salary of £150 Irish. He was permitted to remain in the Mansion House free of rent with his expenses borne by the Company. He was also granted the freehold of Fair-hill and the customs and tolls of the Fair at Moneymore. He remained as Agent until his death at a great age in about 1873. Although his son, John Rowley Miller, later became joint agent with his father, he predeceased him in 1862 aged fifty-four.

By 1819, Moneymore consisted of 'upwards of 100 houses and a grist-mill'.[f] Yet 'houses' were mainly small cabins; it was only the Mansion House, occupied by Miller, and another occupied by the curate[175] of the Parish of Desertlin 'that could answer to the description of a gentleman's dwelling'. There were sixty-eight different tenancies among the cabins' occupants, providing a

---

[175] With the Rector being over ninety, he was unable to discharge his duties, but a curate, 'a gentleman of private fortune' carried out his work 'admirably'.

total income of £571 6s. 9d., with the mill being let for £114 13s. 11d. A monthly fair sold cattle and linen, but the market was no longer operational. The deputation reported:

> The town is built in general of rough stone, white-washed; it is paved for the greatest part, and has a neat appearance. It is not wholly free from a great nuisance, prevailing in most towns and villages in Ireland, namely, a dung-heap in front of every house: by the vigilance, however, of Mr. Miller, the Agent of Sir William Rowley, there are fewer in proportion than in other places in that country.[g]

There were two or three public houses, but no inn or stabling for travellers, which caused inconvenience, as monthly fairs were attended by up to one thousand weavers. (Linen valued at £2,500 was sold at each fair held in the open street.) Vendors crowded into the private homes of shop-keepers on the night beforehand. Perhaps surprisingly, the brewery failed, even though this preceded the influence of the temperance movement. Although there was a plan to demolish its buildings, they were later used as a distillery, which discouraged illegal distillation and provided an outlet for local corn with employment for several people.[h]

The Moneymore division contained 5,072 acres of cultivated land with a further 1,212 acres of turf bog and rough pasture. It was divided between 277 tenants (an average of 18.3 acres of cultivated land per tenancy), generally the descendants of Presbyterian Scottish settlers. The rent roll totalled £3,384 9s. 6d. (an average of 13s. 6d. per acre). Several farms showed signs of affluence, with most tenants undertaking commercial activities, in addition to agriculture. Two of the principal farmers ran tanning businesses. Although the Presbyterian minister farmed, his meeting house was in poor repair. The few Catholics, who were 'principally of the lower class', utilised a small chapel outside the town, and there was 'a respectable [but not so numerous] congregation belonging to the establishment of the Church of England and Ireland'. The Methodist minister was a stocking weaver from Leicester of 'excellent character'. He ingratiated himself on the locality by opening a Sunday-school under the curate's direction, which was the only free school available to the poor. Perhaps surprisingly, the clergy 'as well as the laity of the different persuasions' lived 'in the same charity with each other as if their tenets were the same'.[i] Despite the lack of schools, an ability to read and write was 'pretty widely extended'.

Brackaslievegallion amounted to 4,438 acres of cultivated land divided into 355 holdings (an average of 12.5 acres each) and a further 4,760 acres of mountains and bog. There was no town, 'not even any cluster of houses which deserves the name of a village'. There were a few 'respectable farm houses … occupied by men of comparative wealth and substance',[j] and a large population of mainly Catholic Irish peasants, living in cabins spread all over the division, served by a small Catholic chapel.

Ballinascreen contained the village of Moyheelan (later Draperstown) with the Ballinascreen Parish Church nearby. It consisted of 4,251 acres of cultivated land let into 315 holdings (averaging 13.5 acres) and 6,312 acres of mountain and bog. The residents were mainly descendants of Catholic Scots, who had settled before the Reformation. Although they looked distinctive, their farming methods were similar to those of the native Irish. The division contained a mill, and tenants were obliged to use a Company mill for grinding their corn. An informal monthly market took place 'without regular authority'. In addition to the three divisions, seven tracts of freehold land were held by 'free tenants', who paid modest 'quit-rents'.

Much of the Drapers' difficulty can be put down to tenant poverty, particularly among the native Irish. The land holdings of peasant farmers had become progressively smaller and cabins were rarely watertight, being little more than mud huts covered with straw. Chimneys consisted of holes in roofs or, more often, smoke escaped through door openings. Livestock, which sometimes included a horse, was separated from the living quarters by a partition. There were few barns where cattle could be cared for and fed. Furniture and clothing was generally poor and sometimes 'miserable in the extreme', particularly in the Brackaslievegallion division. Some of the hardship seems to have been caused by 'slovenly habits', and the practice of passing down cast-off clothes did not help health and hygiene. Peasants grew only oats, potatoes and flax, but without a consistent rotation of crops, the potato crop failed in 1816, causing huge hardship. The Company contributed ten guineas towards a soup-shop 'to meet the extreme distress occasioned by the want of provisions'.[k][176] Peasants were reduced to subsistence farming and only rarely were there surplus crops to sell. It was by growing flax, which was spun and often woven before being taken to market, and by selling pigs that they paid their rent. The deputation could see plenty of scope for improving farming methods.

A census at this time counted 1,791 families providing a total population of 10,740 on the Drapers' estates. There were 534 Established Church members, 4,347 Presbyterians and 5,859 Roman-Catholics. 2,419 children, principally from Roman-Catholic families were considered too poor to educate. It was recognised that Roman-Catholic poverty arose because of their 'deprivation of property', and the Company was concerned that Catholic land ownership was still being discouraged by Government. The 1819 deputation was 'not a little surprised at the size of the rents commanded for 'miserable huts''.[l] Arrears were not just caused by the poor harvests of 1816 and 1817. Although 305 tenants were in arrears at Ballinascreen, 'threats of eviction brought in £500 almost at once'.[m] The deputation explored the feasibility of providing each family with a 'substantially built' house of at least four hundred square feet, and Bridger provided a model design costed at £50 each. 'The Company was advised to build

---

[176] In 1816, there had been a very wet summer and only a limited amount of turf could be dried. Crops of oats and potatoes failed, and linen prices were extremely low. Many cattle died of starvation. The Company felt obliged to purchase seed to lend to the 'poor tenantry'. Clergy of all persuasions were tasked with distributing it.

about seventy small houses to replace those in a ruinous or insanitary state,'[n] to be progressed as funds permitted. The offer was 'cheerfully accepted', but was only made to tenants, who cleared their rental arrears. In 1820, rents were set at affordable levels and new letting conditions prevented tenants from dividing their holdings or from building new dwellings on them for workers or other family members.

The Drapers concluded that more freeholders were needed to assist in public business such as jury service. To attract gentry to settle, they made great efforts to preserve game. Yet the main concern was to improve the lot of the peasant farmers. There was no point in replacing them, but they needed to inculcate a desire among them to better themselves. A proper rotation of crops was needed. They stopped the requirement for corn to be ground at the Company's mill. Like the Grocers, they delivered spinning wheels from Scotland, providing them free to the poorest families.

The 1818 deputation concluded that the Company's investment in the estate was far too small. It proposed that 'about half the yearly income should be used to invest in building, plantations, and drainage'. This 'enlightened thinking ... in introducing long-needed reforms'[o] was followed by other Companies. It was to herald a major construction programme, which allowed money to circulate through the community. A 'scutching-mill', erected at Annahavil to improve the quality of dressed flax, became operational in 1820. The Company encouraged apprenticeships, by building houses for craftsmen in and near the towns. It fitted out young women with 'decent clothing'. It planted trees to provide building material, fuel and shelter, but strong walls and fences were needed to provide protection from wandering cattle and sheep.

New schools were planned at Moneymore, Lecumpher and Moyheelan (Draperstown) open to 'children of parents of any religious tenet'. Religious instruction was not 'to be given to any child inconsistent with the beliefs of the parents'.[p] Yet

> the Priests thundered against them so that all the Roman-Catholic children [were] withdrawn, but 'so strong was the desire for instruction' that 'threats of excommunication became disregarded ... in less than six months the children had all come back'. And in due course Roman-Catholic parents and a Priest were admitted to the governing body.[q]

The school at Moneymore was opened in 1818 on the site of the old castle and bawn, the foundations of which can still be seen behind it at the southern end of the main street. This required older dwellings to be removed and their occupiers rehoused. It was thought necessary to expend a small amount to make schools 'ornamental to the town, which will have a tendency to introduce and make habits of cleanliness and order fashionable'.[r] In 1820, a school was positioned between Brackaslievegallion and Ballinascreen to service both localities, and four other school locations were identified.

The school buildings, Moneymore These symmetrical 1820 buildings designed by Jesse Gibson are situated on the site of the old castle and bawn at the end of the High Street. They now house the Moneymore Orange Hall.

Cranny Free School and schoolteacher's house 1818-20 This now derelict school is one of several designed in rural areas by Jesse Gibson.

Although the poor were dependent on the County infirmary in Londonderry for medical aid and the Company continued to pay it ten guineas per annum, it was too far for emergencies and care provided by the dispensary at Cookstown was rudimentary. This led to calls for the Company to subscribe to an existing dispensary or to establish a new one. It advertised for a 'person fitly qualified', offering one hundred guineas per annum and a house at Moneymore rent and tax free. It was to have 'proper rooms for seeing patients and compounding the medicines'. The Company realised that it would have to foot the bill and plans were prepared in London to incorporate it into the proposed new Market House. The 1818 deputation reported that the building works were in 'as forward a state as could be expected' and were 'nearly covered in before the deputation left',[s] with the help of a new Clerk of Works, George Bridger,[177] who had been sent from London. A projected annual cost of £300 was allowed for a similar dispensary at Draperstown.[t] Clergy of all denominations were asked to support both the schools and the dispensary. They were also asked to encourage 'social meetings' to bring 'persons of all persuasions and different ranks of life, into honourable contact with each other'.[u]

Jesse Gibson, The Drapers' Company Surveyor (detail) by Charles Thompson, 1822 He designed most buildings of consequence at Moneymore and Draperstown between 1818 and 1822.
Courtesy of the Drapers' Company

Most buildings of consequence built between 1818 and 1822 were designed in London by Jesse Gibson, the Drapers' Company Surveyor, supported on the ground by Bridger, who later became the estate's Surveyor. Between them, they were largely responsible for the appearance and planning of Moneymore and Draperstown. The local gentry 'much admired the substantial manner in which [buildings] were erected'.[v] The 1818 deputation had decided that all doors, windows and other joinery should be undertaken in London by a joiner 'equal to such a job' under Gibson's watchful eye, as no one could be found closer than Belfast or Dublin. To ensure that the workmanship became a model for future works, the London joiner sent over a foreman to supervise local plasterers, painters and other artisans to complete the finishing.

---

[177] Bridger was the son of James Bridger, who had been responsible for the final designs of the Session-House, built on behalf of the Grocers at Muff.

Being located on the direct route between Dublin and both Londonderry and Coleraine,[178] its plans for an inn, public stables and a Market House at Moneymore were well received. Building an inn was seen as speculative, as there had not previously been one in the town, but a three-year lease was granted to a Mr. Henry of Cookstown. It had already opened by 1819, when the deputation found it 'beneficial', with 'comfortable' accommodation at 'reasonable' charges. When repairs were needed in 1827, the landlord was offered £100 'to be expended in building two additional rooms for servants and a granary', which were 'much required',[x] and he renewed his lease for a further seven years. Its design 'did credit to Mr. Gibson' and the workmanship showed that Bridger was 'a master of his business'. By 1819, all the new buildings were 'in a considerable state of progress', and Bridger submitted a general layout of Moneymore for consideraton.

View down the High Steet, Moneymore This shows the former Drapers' Arms, Market House, and dispensary to the left and the grand entrance to the corn store on the right. The Manor House can just be seen in the distance.

In 1822, William Joseph Booth replaced Gibson as the Drapers' Company Surveyor. He had become a freeman of the Company in 1816, and his father, John, a distinguished London surveyor, became Master in 1821. Booth was then aged about twenty-six, but had travelled in Greece and Italy and was already an accomplished draughtsman having exhibited at the Royal Academy. He visited the proportion in 1827 and made 'beautiful drawings in pencil with sepia

---

[178] Without an inn, a brothel had flourished in cabins on the outskirts of Moneymore 'where lodgers of suspicious character were entertained'.[w] It was decided to clear this site to make way for the new Presbyterian Meeting House.

watercolour ... of selected sites' to show the run-down state of some of the buildings.[y] There are eight of these at Drapers' Hall. He was responsible for the design and improvement of many buildings at both Moneymore and Draperstown, and those that were not his designs he approved. At Draperstown, he was also responsible for the lay-out and made proposals to enclose The Fairhill, the triangular green where the fair was held. He kept a close eye on workmanship and sought advice on any concerns from James Turnbull, the Fishmongers' Clerk of Works.

The Parish Church of Ballinascreen, Draperstown One of a set of sepia wash drawings made by W. J. Booth in 1827 now held by the Drapers' Company.
Courtesy of the Drapers' Company

Although the 1819 deputation had believed that the diocese of Londonderry was well able to fund the maintenance of Moneymore's parish church, it assisted the Presbyterians, particularly as they were obliged to pay the Established Church's tithes and rates. It provided a site and made 'a handsome contribution for building an entirely new meeting-house' so long as the plans were approved by the Company and the old meeting house site reverted to it.[z] Although the congregation raised only £300 towards its cost, the Company contributed the balance of £1,000. Great care was taken in its positioning, and the result was a fine edifice 'that dignifies that part of Moneymore'.[aa] Booth was later able to report that the workmanship 'both external and internal [did] credit to the builder, Mr. George Bridger'.[bb] Booth later added a stucco front to it. Unfortunately its congregation elected a Mr. Barnett to its pulpit, and he proved to be 'a ranter who inveighed against other sects, but especially against the

Established Church'.[cc] The Company sought his resignation and withheld its annual 'present' to him. One group of Presbyterians seceded from the remainder, and the Company provided a plot for a second meeting house. Booth exercised close control over the classical design of this small structure, which was not completed and paid for until 1839.

The Market House, Moneymore The design by Jesse Gibson was topped by a later cupola by Booth.

It was not just Presbyterians, who caused ripples. Some Roman-Catholic priests attempted 'to prevent their flock from reading the Scriptures'. The Company stopped its 'usual donation' to two priests, allocating it for the fabric of their chapels. The Master and Wardens had greater moral difficulty over providing Catholic support, but

considering the good character of the Rev. Mr. Mackle, the priest of Moneymore, they would not be in dissonance from any obligation which the Company may be considered to be under, specially to support the Protestant against the Catholic religion, and therefore they ordered that the sum of ten guineas should be presented to him annually, subject to the pleasure of the Court.[dd]

Similar grants were made to other Catholic priests serving the community. With 'the Roman-Catholic chapels at both Moneymore and Gortahurk [being] in poor condition, the Agent was instructed to repair them'.[ee] Two Alms-Houses were also endowed and one guinea was given to a poor widow.

First Presbyterian Meeting House, Moneymore Bridger's workmanship was much praised by Booth in 1834

By 1827, the estate's appearance had already greatly improved. The tenantry were generally living in harmony with each other, the tree plantations were thriving, giving an air of optimism for the future. The paving of Moneymore High Street had been added and schools were well-attended. Good use was being made of the dispensaries. Although a drought in 1826 had caused another crop failure, bog-land was being reclaimed 'much to the comfort and cleanliness of the town' and a new street was created.[ff] Both linen and cattle markets were well-attended. Tenants were encouraged to maintain their hedgerows and the Company provided 'quicks' (hawthorn plants) to improve enclosures. A 'rundale farming' system was adopted. This involved dividing larger areas of land into mathematically arranged strips to create 'ladder-farms', with each tenant farming his own non-contiguous strips. This was designed to even out land quality between tenants, and it revolutionised field patterns. Although the Drapers pioneered it, many other Companies followed their lead.

The Norman-style Parish Church of St. John, Moneymore This imposing building on an equally imposing site was designed by Booth in 1830. It was completed in 1832 at a cost to the Drapers of £6,000.

It was realised that a new Parish Church was needed at Moneymore to replace the existing one which was small and falling down, and a 'new one would tend to encourage the residence of a superior class of society'.[gg] Booth proposed building it on the site of a dilapidated house and garden just off the High Street. After Grecian and Gothic style designs had been rejected (because of the expense of the ornamentation required), he proposed a Norman style, using Tewkesbury Abbey as an exemplar. The work was undertaken by James Boyd of Belfast supervised by the new Clerk of Works, George Cuthbert, at a cost to the Company of £6,000. By 1831, the roof had been slated, and work to the level of the bell floor was complete. Yet Cuthbert fell out with Boyd over delays, and Boyd refused to tender for the boundary walls to be built round the churchyard, despite being offered payment in instalments. When Cuthbert complained of Boyd's 'inattention', Booth shared his concerns. Yet matters improved. In 1832, the new deputation attended the consecration of St. John's Church by the Bishop of Down. Booth's design and his 'sound judgement' over its location was much respected. (Although it suffered a disastrous fire in 1889, it was restored and reopened in 1891.) Cuthbert also supervised the building of six houses near the mill at Moneymore, followed by two more. These were built in 'a substantial manner'. The first six were completed in 1830, with two others shortly after. Booth added two rooms over the dispensary at Moneymore 'to make the elevation rather more ornamental'.[hh]

The Market House, Draperstown was completed to Booth's design in 1841, but the Potato Famine soon took its toll. To improve morale in 1846 the Drapers contributed £10 towards a clock tower.

Presbyterian Meeting House, Draperstown The Drapers contributed £1,000 to its building cost.

The main objective of the 1832 deputation was to consider Booth's detailed plans for Draperstown, which included the erection of a Market House, an inn and other buildings. All these had already been approved in principal by the Court. The deputation was later able to conclude that its situation 'was admirably calculated to render it a market town of first rate importance in that part of Ireland'.[ii] To finance the project, in 1833, the Company raised a loan of £20,000 from Bancroft's Trust Fund (one of its charities), so that work at both Moneymore and Draperstown could begin. Booth's final drawings for Draperstown were completed in 1834, but a corn store, dispensary and another dwelling were later added and the contract was eventually finalised at £2,560 19s. 10d. By 1836, the inn, surgeon's house and dispensary had been roofed. Booth designed fittings for the inn's interior, which were also undertaken. He also provided designs for houses, which could be varied internally, so long as exterior elevations remained unchanged. His plans for 'handsome structures with their pedimented gables' became the model for better buildings of all types.[jj] These included the Presbyterian Meeting House at Draperstown built in 1843.

In 1832, a fall in linen prices and a general uncertainty in agriculture had caused great hardship on the proportion. Matters were made worse by a 'ferocious' cholera epidemic, which 'attacked high and low'. Miller immediately limewashed house interiors and tended 'to matters of elementary hygiene'. Tenants were given free limestone from local quarries. They demanded rent reductions and assaulted bailiffs trying to collect arrears. The deputation responded by abolishing tolls to attend the Moneymore Fair. It was 'highly pleased with the state and general appearance of the town', which compared favourably with other towns through which it passed. Its members congratulated the Court on its 'complete and entire success' over the previous fifteen years. The new roads and bridges built by the Company had already provided considerable benefits. Four 'handsome' new houses on the Circular Road greatly improved the town and did 'credit to the Architect and Builder'.[kk] These were another attempt 'to attract persons to reside in the town who would raise its tone and provide a middle class'.[179] 'The schools seemed to be prospering, and the deputation was impressed by the appearance and conduct of the children.'[ll] It admired 'the classical and grammar school established for the sons of such of the tenantry as could afford to pay [its master's] 'extremely moderate charge''.[mm] When it visited Blackhill School outside Draperstown, it believed that 'it would be situated to the much greater convenience of the majority of the children' if it were moved into the town, but this does not seem to have been acted upon. It was noted that the Agent's house in Moneymore was, by then, in 'a state so frail' that it required urgent action. In 1834, Booth provided designs to convert Torrens House into the Manor House to provide offices and accommodation for the Agent, and this work was completed in 1835. Old cabins also needed to be 'speedily removed' for replacement by new cottages, with street paving to be extended with open areas being planted.

---

[179] These were sentiments shared by many of the other Livery Companies.

The Manor House, Moneymore In 1834, Booth submitted plans to convert the former Torrens House into a fitting residence for the Drapers' Agent.

The rear façade of the entrance to the corn store, Moneymore The view taken of Booth's imposing 1835 design looking back towards the High Street.

In 1835, Bridger proposed building a new corn-store and Market House at Moneymore. He was again asked to provide plans, which included a public scale opposite *The Drapers' Arms*. He proposed the conversion of the existing Market House nearby into 'four convenient shops with dwelling houses over them' facing the street. Once the Court had approved his plans, they were sent to Miller. It is apparent that the contractors were becoming overstretched by the level of building activity, and completion was delayed until 1839. A communal threshing barn, which was also proposed, was not completed until 1843. Despite this, Miller reported that 'the whole pile of buildings is extremely well executed', and the Court found 'the several buildings ... plain and simple in their character, solid in their construction, and well adapted to their object'.[nn] In 1836, with the Belfast Bank adding to confidence by opening a branch in Moneymore, Booth produced designs for yet more houses, including a smithy, near the Market House. The Company also enlarged the Parish Church of St. Comgall at Desertmartin, and Booth may have designed its rectory with its whitewashed stableblock on one side.

The Parish Church of St Comgall, Desertmartin This pretty church was designed by Booth and enlarged at the Drapers' expense in 1836.

When the wheels at the mill at Moneymore, built in 1785, had fallen into disrepair, the deputation asked the Company to rebuild the mill race, wheel and pond to provide a more powerful mechanism. The new wheel was to be eighteen feet in diameter with a cast-iron shaft, although work did not begin until after 1836. Local labour was also employed in improving roads[180], benefiting both the look and well-being of the proportion. One hundred acres of trees were planted at Brackaslievegallion, including oak, chestnut, ash, beech, sycamore, fir and larch. A second plantation was positioned on high ground overlooking Moneymore. (By 1839, there were three hundred and forty acres of woodland 'of great beauty and value' to the 'delight and admiration of the neighbouring

---

[180] The Drapers' efforts to relieve unemployment by undertaking public works, such as roads, predated Government projects during the Potato Famine of 1846 and 1847. The cost to build roads, including hedging and ditching, was estimated at £86 13s. 4d. per mile.

gentry'.)[oo] These were managed by foresters brought in from Scotland. With the turf bog being rapidly stripped of peat, and timber remaining in short supply, it was recognised that finding coal would be of huge value. Captain John Richardson was commissioned to prepare a report and he drilled a bore hole to three hundred feet between Desertmartin and Slievegallion, but without success.[181]

The Irish Society's deputation in 1836 was impressed by the 'inducements for all classes of society to locate upon [the Drapers'] estate'.[pp] Tenants of 'moderate property', were able to take houses at below 'reimbursing rents'; they found Moneymore a delightful place to retire, and they spent their incomes for the 'great advantage' of the locality. The Society described Moneymore as 'quite an English Town, most beautifully laid out and managed'.[qq] The proportion 'was an example to all',[rr] with small woodland plantations 'agreeably diversifying the approach'.

The Parochial Sunday School, Moneymore Booth positioned the Sunday school, which he designed in 1834, close to the Parish Church. It is now used as Assembly Rooms.

Matters did not always go entirely to plan. Booth complained that the Company was not always answering his letters as quickly as he hoped and was altering his plans quite arbitrarily. Even his 'best workmen' were 'addicted to

[181] It was not until 1857 that coal was found at Cullion. Although it was probably not an economic working, it was adequate for David Allen, the Blacksmith and tool maker at Moneymore, to operate his forge. A gasometer was established at the mill at Cloughog, presumably using coal gas to provide power.

the sad habit of drinking', which may have delayed the completion of building work at Draperstown until 1838. The spire of its church had to be rebuilt after being destroyed in the Great Wind of 1839. Yet the 1839 deputation applauded the removal of dung heaps in front of doorways, allowing them to enjoy 'an air of English comfort'.[ss]

In 1840, work began on a schoolhouse for infants on the site of the old Presbyterian meeting house at Moneymore. Eventually the Company supported seven schools on the proportion. These included a Parochial Sunday School next to the Parish Church at Moneymore.

Tudor-Gothic cottages, Draperstown Two of a range of cottages designed by Booth and completed in 1843.

A police barracks was also built. By then Moneymore was transformed, and its array of handsome buildings made it the finest settlement on any of the proportions. Draperstown was also very satisfactory, but the proportion's boundary with a native freehold ran down its southern side cutting off the triangular green from the lower town. It was feared that this could limit future development, but sites were found for a further eight houses and building work continued apace. In 1843, paired cottages designed by Booth replaced a row of old mud cabins.

It was not just the towns which were developed during the 1830s. The Company encouraged the building of new farmsteads 'in entirely English fashion' as models for future development, as those built by tenants were generally 'mean and ill-arranged'.[tt] Despite loan offers being made to tenants, the 'model' designs 'do not appear to have sired many progeny'.[uu] In 1853, Robert Forster, the Company's surveyor, was still complaining that a lack of orderliness in the arrangement of farm offices added to the 'slovenly appearance of things'. Efforts were made to increase the areas of each farm by encouraging tenants to take on adjacent plots as they became available and to demolish superfluous dwellings. Yet this happened infrequently and provided no better buildings.

The proportion was not spared the calamities of the Great Famine, and it proved a watershed in the Drapers' fortunes. The failure of the potato crop reduced farm revenues by one-third, and the Company distributed five pounds to all its most destitute tenants and often forgave rents, but this laid it open to exploitation.[vv] In 1849, when tenants again would not pay rents, Miller began the desperate process of evicting them. Although this did not please the Company in London, he felt that some evictions were needed *'pour encourager les autres'*. Between 1845 and 1850, town building work was almost forgotten. The focus was on employing the destitute in building roads, walls and hedges. By 1853, the Company had built fifty-three miles of 'hard road', which were then transferred to the County for maintenance out of the County 'Cess', but it continued to repair minor roads at 'considerable outlay'. Between 1847 and 1853, it contributed £8,000 to a scheme to drain 2,200 acres of bogland. 366 acres of plantations were established, mostly at the Company's expense, as it did not want to adopt Sampson's recommendation for tenants to register trees they had planted. This would have entitled them to compensation for their value, if they sold up. Although the woodlands flourished, they would take a long time to reach maturity, and, by 1856, were still of 'little value', despite hopes that they would eventually repay the considerable outlay. Up to 1850, the Company had paid £18,964 4s. 8d. on tree planting with a further £4,127 10s. on the Forester's salary. Six years later, the five hundred acres of woodland not only provided employment, but 'attracted the admiration of the whole county'.[ww]

The Company seems to have faced almost insuperable problems in its efforts to help the 'labouring poor'. Although their residences were 'well arranged', they were 'slow to adopt' improvements, and dung heaps in back streets became 'rapidly out of order' unless continuously watched. Forster proposed a 'standing expenditure' to keep the town clean, to be paid in part by the inhabitants'. The Society for Improving the Condition of the Labouring Classes recommended the creation of cheap allotments to provide poorer tenants with food and a source of income. Areas reserved as parks in Moneymore were allocated for this purpose. An agriculturalist, Richard Pattleson, advised on draining, planting and managing cultivated land, and the blacksmith, David Allen manufactured agricultural implements. Yet progress on betterment was slow.

Eventually optimism started to return. The Dublin, Armagh, and Coleraine Junction Railway ran a branch line into the proportion, which became operational in 1853. This encouraged the Company to continue making improvements despite its falling revenue. To boost morale, it contributed ten pounds towards the cost of a new clock on Draperstown's Market House. Forster noted that tenants were at last rotating their crops. In 1853, although there was still some potato blight, the crop was generally good and abundant. Land had been improved. English breeds of cattle and pigs were superseding 'inferior'

Irish stock. Farmers started to buy manure and seed on a cooperative basis. Carts and implements were improved. By this time, most tenants were planting between two and ten acres of flax, and were using the Company's scutching mill at Annahavil for processing. Although Forster's brief was to revalue farms with a view to increasing rents, tenants, who had undertaken their own improvements were not charged more. Yet, where the Company had paid, as with land drainage schemes, increases were applied. This called for 'local professional judgment'.[xx] Forster admired the 'excellent, good and airy' school buildings, but proposed that better teachers should be attracted with higher salaries, to be paid for out of a small weekly levy on children attending. Yet the Company was satisfied that salaries were adequate, as the teachers' housing was provided free of rent.

Forster reported that Moneymore was 'well built and pleasantly situated', being accessed by well-maintained roads. It was 'ornamented by several handsome buildings' and occupied by about one thousand residents. It bore 'such an air of neatness and good arrangement, so seldom seen in an Irish town, as to make [it] strikingly attractive', with good shops and 'eight or ten private houses' for the 'better class of independent families'. There was also a dispensary and a surgeon. It was clean, picturesque and tidy, and its inhabitants were 'happy and comfortable'. The Company could be rightly proud of Booth's achievement. Yet the inn was run down 'and not so well sustained as could be desired' and much repainting of the markets was needed.[yy]

It came to be realised that the Market House in Moneymore was built on too large a scale. Cookstown, only twelve miles to the south west, absorbed most of the local trade. This left the stone-built storehouses at Moneymore, built at considerable expense and originally designed to store corn, flax and linen, only partially used and in need of repair. By 1856, following the repeal of the Corn Laws,[182] they had become 'nearly unproductive'. Efforts were made to convert them 'to a beneficial account' such as a barracks for the Derry Militia, but, in 1865, advertisements to let 'this excellent pile of buildings, erected at great cost to the Company' were still being placed in Belfast newspapers, and they were still unlet in 1871. (They are now converted into flats.)

Draperstown proved to be more 'favourably situated' as a market town than Moneymore, and it also had a dispensary and surgeon. The market at The Fair-hill handled one thousand head of cattle, two hundred horses, one hundred and fifty sheep, one hundred pigs and two thousand pieces of linen each month. By 1856, the Company supported a plan for a pork market. Although the grist mill at Cloughog was grinding more oats than wheat, there were plans to use its waterpower for spinning linen yarn mechanically. By 1856, it employed one hundred and thirty people, and, with the Company's assistance, its managers,

---

[182] The Corn Laws were repealed, in part at least, to mitigate the problems caused by the Irish Famine. In this way protection for British and Irish growers was removed and cheaper foreign imports started undercutting local prices to the great distress of farmers.

Glasgow and Wood, repaired the weir and sluices and built a handsome dwelling house. Yet the business failed before 1869.

Draperstown's growing prosperity attracted new arrivals and, by 1856, many houses were being built privately. Yet its inn was 'a very uninviting place, dirty and untidy', and had become a drinking den. The Company hoped to improve the town's layout as leases fell in. In 1862, the holder of the adjacent townland of Cahore was 'stimulated' to develop his part of the town, and 'nearly rebuilt the whole ... setting the houses back [from the green], and giving it a most respectable appearance'.[zz]

In 1856, the Drapers' Clerk paid a visit. By then, the Randalstown-Cookstown railway, being built through the proportion, was in a 'very foreward state, and was expected to open about the middle of October'.[aaa] There was to be a station near Moneymore on the road to Draperstown. (By 1877, there was a direct railway line from Moneymore to Dublin.) The Clerk much admired Moneymore, which was still expanding. There were plans to build new houses on the site of the old Manor House, but a shortage of funds delayed their completion until 1865. Following the Company's substantial contributions to local clergy and the fabric of churches, he was pleased to find them well-attended. He commissioned a new survey, which was undertaken by Charles Pollock, a local man, who had done similar work for the Salters. Yet rural poverty shocked him. Many dwellings were disappointingly 'wretched', after 'so much had been done to 'introduce better habits' among the tenantry'.[bbb] Men wore cast-off clothes, although the women were better attired and 'strong and healthy'.[ccc] Yet again, the small size of individual farm holdings was to blame. Although emigration had reduced the locality from 10,740 in 1818, to 10,591 in 1841, and 7,978 in 1851, those left behind still suffered, and, if a crop failed, they were reduced to penury. It was worst in Brackaslievegallion and in Ballinascreen, as Scottish Presbyterians in the Moneymore division were 'beginning to appreciate the comforts of a different mode of living' having built and slated their own houses with Company support. There were signs of economic improvement, which would continue unless some 'political movement prejudicial' to Ireland developed. Within a generation, all these efforts were undermined by 'the political expediencies of the day'.[ddd]

In 1862, the Drapers' Arms at Moneymore was made more comfortable for the deputation's official visit. It was further improved in 1877. By then, Draperstown had overtaken Moneymore as the 'foremost among the market towns' of County Londonderry. Tenants considered themselves 'blessed' by the Company's efficient and benevolent management. There is no doubt that the Company,

> having been the first to take the management of its Irish property back into its own hands, had set an example that was followed by the other Companies, to the great benefit of that part of Ireland.[eee]

As a mark of enthusiastic respect, the visiting deputation was fêted with 'illuminations, bonfires, and other matters of a similar kind'.[fff]

Between 1867 and 1871, there was a shortage of accommodation in Moneymore. It became necessary to curtail the practice of taking in lodgers and underletting, which left the town dirty and overcrowded. New cottages to designs laid down by Booth were being built at a cost of £100 each. Yet many cottier's houses had become 'unfit for human habitation'. The 1867 deputation was disappointed to find such hovels still existing, when model houses had been built as exemplars. It agreed to build a number of 'decent cottages' at a cost of £60 each, and it sought the clergy's cooperation 'to improve the condition of the labouring poor'.[ggg] Work began on cleaning, painting and altering the seating arrangements of the Parish Church; several town houses, including the Police Station, were painted and repaired. At Draperstown, the Company contributed to the cost of improving and enriching the Ballinascreen Parish Church.

The 1872 deputation considered building a concert hall suitable for lectures on Moneymore High Street. With Booth having died, most architectural work was being done locally, and, in 1873, 'Mr. Fetherstone of Belfast' was appointed Architect. After having lain empty for a decade, the flax mill at Cloughog was purchased by Browne of Belfast and was reopened. The 1873 deputation instructed Fetherstone to extend the Manor House (still known as Torrens House), to accommodate future deputations. When this was completed, the 1875 deputation found it 'a very suitable and comfortable residence for members of the Court'.[hhh] By 1877, a wine cellar had been completed and was 'well adapted for its purpose'![iii] A new porch was added in 1879. The new Bailiff, Joseph Allen, who attended the 1875 deputation, had been trained as an architect, and was considered 'thoroughly competent to design dwelling-houses and farm buildings, and to superintend their erection'.[jjj] His houses were much admired and, as an 'intelligent and zealous officer', he was retitled Surveyor of the Company's Irish Estate.[kkk]

Moneymore was still showing little evidence of prosperity. 'The almost entire want of trade or business' was still 'observable' and house rents remained 'stationary'.[lll] Several houses were dilapidated, and one was pulled down and rebuilt at a cost of £350 for letting to a grocer at £14 10s. 0d. per annum (not a promising yield). Although a running programme of house repairs was agreed, it was noted, in 1877, that few inhabitants took an interest in maintaining or cleaning their properties and keeping their gardens orderly. Despite the Company's efforts to maintain building quality, 'there was no longer any overall arbiter of taste in the appearance of towns and villages'.[mmm] Farming practices were still causing problems. Weeds needed clearing, and the Moneymore Farming Society (to which the Company was contributing £25 per annum) was doing little to promote better methods. Yet, new bulls, purchased in 1871, were improving the quality of cattle. The corn stores remained partially empty and were proving difficult to let, except in very small units.

In 1875, all but one of the Company's schools, accommodating a total of 438 pupils, became 'non-vested' schools under the National Board of Education, which had been established in 1831. This ensured that they would receive better books and materials, and more thorough inspection, despite the inspector's previous favourable reports. By 1877, 589 children on the estate were attending school. The Company continued to supervise The Classical School in Moneymore, whose headmaster was a graduate of Trinity College, Dublin. This was fee paying and, in 1877, it was moved to the Sunday School House, which was enclosed with new railings. In 1878, it was renamed Moneymore Male Intermediate School and the former school house was converted into Assembly Rooms. Huge efforts were needed to find employment for children to minimise 'the common Irish problem' of them having to emigrate.

A new survey, which was conducted to enable the estate to be revalued, was found to be full of errors. Its objective was to reassess land values for letting purposes, as the Company was concerned that it was undercharging on its better land and overcharging on poorer tenancies. Despite the politically motivated clamour against 'landlordism' faced by all Companies, the Drapers' rents were considered fair, and the Company was thought 'considerate and liberal'. By 1877, farms were prospering again after good harvests, but moves to increase rents met with strong politically motivated resistance, 'because the profits on farms were very uncertain'.[nnn] It was claimed, quite unfairly, that the tenants' labour and capital had provided the improvements. Tenants demanded that their leases should be extended from twenty-one to thirty-one years to provide them with more incentive. It was not just a problem of rents. Religious and political animosity led to many Roman-Catholic children being withdrawn from schools.

After Miller's death in about 1873, Walter Trevor Stannus replaced him as agent. He seems to have become so traumatised by local hostility that rent collections fell into arrears. The 1880 deputation criticised many aspects of his performance, and he was sacked in the following year with the Manor House and its furniture being surrendered back to the Company. He was criticised for failing to familiarise himself with either the estate or its tenants, and held another agency contrary to the conditions of his contract. He had allowed overcrowding in cottages to become out of hand, and had taken decisions about the schools without the Company being consulted. To cap it all he had sacked the Under-Bailiff for the Moneymore division without reference. Yet he had done much to repair or demolish old cottages in Moneymore and had administered a scheme providing prizes for cottages maintained 'in the neatest condition'. When the deputation asked Allen to take over, he considered the role unsafe and to be a demotion from his position as Surveyor. It decided to amalgamate the roles of Surveyor and Forester, resulting in Allen being sacked as well.

The writing was now on the wall for the large estates. Irish Nationalists were on the warpath against landlords, especially English landlords. The deputation refused requests to make a contribution to the Emergency Committee of the Grand Orange Lodge and the Property Defence Association of Ireland as it considered them inflammatory and the Lodge was taking measures to protect itself against the Irish Land League. The Company now 'adopted a policy of gradual withdrawal of grants to educational, religious and charitable bodies'.[ooo]

The Drapers had first considered selling up in 1872, and, in 1881, the deputation recommended that tenants should be allowed to purchase their holdings. In 1882, Sir William Fitzwilliam Conyngham became Agent, but, despite him threatening to evict defaulters, arrears only increased. The Land Acts caused an administrative nightmare and a general lack of confidence manifested itself in squalor, failure and decay. Moneymore remained dirty and overcrowded; its allotments were appropriated by tenants and changed hands illegally. The 1884 deputation found business at a standstill, with many houses left vacant. In 1885, the tenants in Brackaslievegallion and Ballinascreen petitioned to have their rents cut in half. With the Company being inundated with calls for rent reductions, it became 'noticeably penny-pinching'. It stopped further contributions to the dispensary or other charitable grants. There was so much hatred that Company servants feared for their lives.

> In only a few years the tactics of the tenantry (who had been treated by the Company with an open-handed generosity unparalleled anywhere in the British Isles) had alienated the Company.[PPP]

In 1885, the Company offered to sell to its tenants at eighteen years purchase of their annual rent so long as all arrears were paid in cash; this was later reduced to seventeen years' purchase. These transactions were to be financed by Government loans. In 1888, the Recorder of Londonderry set the rents for tenants in Brackaslievegallion and Ballinascreen in accordance with the Land Act of 1887, which tended to reduce them. The tenants in the Moneymore Division, who were mainly Scottish Presbyterian, agreed to purchase on the terms offered, but in Brackaslievegallion and Ballinascreen tenants would not pay more than fourteen years' purchase based on the new judicial rents. The Company was accused of failing to adopt prescribed rental terms in arriving at valuations for sale. Although prices had to comply with the 1870 laws, the legislation's poor drafting caused delays. The Company was able to demonstrate that these were the result of bureaucratic red tape. A further problem arose when the Land Purchase Commissioners refused to sanction sales on the terms previously agreed by the Company with its tenants. This was generally because large rental arrears were added to the purchase price. To gain acceptance of this, the Agent granted a receipt for the arrears, but, if the sale was broken off, they remained unpaid. When the Company pressed for payment, the tenant produced his receipt. This resulted in the Agent being discharged with the Manor House at Moneymore being sold. Arguments gave rise to questions in the House of Commons and acrimonious correspondence in *The Times*.

In 1889, the Company resorted to wholesale evictions, but would sell to those who were prepared to buy. It was able to demonstrate that evictions only took place where tenants resisted all attempts to obtain payment of their rents. Yet it was attacked in the Irish Press; the *Morning News and Examiner* of Belfast described the Companies as 'London Guzzlers in a Fix'. In 1890, it was accused of deliberately delaying sales, of evicting tenants and of adding interest to arrears. When the legal tangle was eventually resolved, no one was entirely satisfied. By 1891, many of the Moneymore tenants had received Government loans to purchase their properties. Although others had signed purchase agreements, some properties remained unsold. It took until 1900 for the disposal of the greater part of the estate to be finalised, by which time the proceeds had realised £161,252 7s. 11d., a not inconsiderable sum. The remainder was entrusted to the Manor of Drapers' Charity with £2,500 to provide an endowment. By 1906, almost all connection had been severed. It had not been a happy time, and the Company was left with 'a mixture of bemused regret, exasperated relief, and a certain amount of righteous indignation'.[qqq]

The Drapers have provided a legacy of late Georgian elegance at Moneymore and Draperstown, but many of the buildings designed by Booth and others have been insensitively altered. The former Market House in Draperstown has become a library. Yet Draperstown remains the finest example of Livery Company architecture in County Londonderry. The Company's 'experiments in enlightened 19th-century philanthropy'[rrr] designed to raise local standards, now go unrecognised.

Chapter 42

Fishmongers

Like so many Companies, the Fishmongers were reluctant to take personal control of their estates after the Restoration. When their original leases to Higgins and Freeman fell in, they decided to re-let and found the Beresford family to be willing takers. Burdened as it was with its own financial problems, the Company 'did not want to know about their Irish estates, and raised as much money as possible by charging large 'fines' and rents to restore its depleted capital'.[a] Yet letting to middlemen pushed rents upwards, leaving many tenants in penury with no incentive to make improvements; any which were made were used to justify increasing rents on renewal of the short-term leases granted. This led to a massive exodus of mainly Presbyterian farmers to the American colonies.

New Walworth House This was built by Jane née Beresford and her husband, Lt. General Frederick Hamilton, from whom it passed to other members of the Beresford family. It still has a magnificent garden.

With the Beresfords in charge, Jane Hamilton (née Beresford) [183] with her husband, Lt. General Frederick Hamilton, built New Walworth House. This was positioned on the site of the original castle and bawn, and one of the flankers was demolished to make way for it, leaving the bawn as a yard attached to the house. On Jane's death at Walworth in 1716, her husband placed an imposing Grinling Gibbons style marble monument to her memory in Tamlaghtfinlagan Parish Church. The lease then passed through the Beresford family to Jane's great nephew, the Rt. Hon. John Beresford, PC, born in 1738, he 'built a handsome house [Walworth House] on the banks of Lough Foyle, and planted a considerable number of oak, ash and other timber trees'.[b] On his visit in 1802, Slade was impressed by Walworth's woodlands and its prospect of Londonderry. On John Beresford's death in 1805 his sixth son, Henry Barré Beresford, inherited the remainder of the lease, which was due to expire on the death of George III.

Tamlaghtfinlagan Parish Church, Ballykelly With its distinctive octagonal tower, this was another church built at the behest of the Earl-Bishop in 1791-95, being paid for jointly by him and John Beresford. It is recognised as his finest church creation.

---

[183] The likelihood is that the proportion was first let to Tristram Beresford, Agent of The Irish Society. By this time he had become a Baronet and lived until 1673. His interest will have passed to his son Sir Randal Beresford, 2nd Bart. Sir Randal passed it on to his daughter Jane, who married Lt. General Frederick Hamilton, and they resided at New Walworth. (Hamilton was quite remotely connected to the Hamiltons of Arran.) It is apparent that Jane had no surviving children and on her death in 1716, the lease passed to her nephew, Sir Marcus Beresford, 4th Bart., who later became 3rd Earl of Tyrone in right of his wife, Catherine Poer. He passed the lease to his second son, the Rt. Hon. John Beresford, PC, who built Walworth House, probably in about 1790.

Tamlaghtfinlagan Parish Church was one of several built at the behest of the Earl-Bishop of Derry with its 'felicitous' octagonal steeple. It is recognised as his finest in its 'simplified Gothic so favoured by the Established Church of the 18th century'.[c] It was constructed between 1791 and 1795 at the joint expense of the Earl-Bishop and John Beresford. It replaced an earlier building, and Jane Hamilton's monument was transferred to the new structure. On Slade's visit, he considered it 'by far the handsomest building of the kind in the north of Ireland'.[d] In 1851, the Company added a chancel, vestry and gallery, and, in 1859, a three-bay north aisle was built.

Henry Barré Beresford held the lease over the Fishmongers' proportion at its expiry and assisted them in re-establishing control.
Private Collection, Courtesy of The Follies Trust

Following Sampson's criticisms made in 1802, most Companies had concluded that they should take a closer interest in their estates. In 1809, the Fishmongers sent a deputation on a four week visit to consider taking back control on the lease expiry. It based itself discreetly at Newtown Limavady and made a point of visiting Sampson at Garvagh. Although Barré Beresford, now aged twenty-five, was doing much to make improvements, the proportion was full of humble dwellings despite its handsome parish churches at Banagher and Ballykelly and several fine Georgian houses. He 'embarked on a scheme' for Ballykelly, building a school in 1812 and a sunday-school in 1819. In 1818, John Given, a carpenter and architect, built another at Sistrakeel.

On George III's death in 1820, Beresford provided detailed accounts in his efforts to gain renewal, but the Company was determined to reassert control. John David Towse, Clerk of the Company from 1809 to 1839, was closely involved in planning this and he joined a deputation, which visited Ireland in 1820. Its findings were fully recorded in a diary maintained by another member, the Unitarian, John Towgood. Others were William Sturch, a liberal writer on theological matters, and his son, and Thomas Bodley, Prime Warden from 1824 to 1826. This was a group that was 'liberal, humane, and advanced in its outlook',[e] representing a Company, which, at the time, was

> closely associated with progressive, liberal forces, and with the Evangelical movement within and without the Church of England, and so its members were particularly concerned with reform, with education, with universal literacy, and with the revival of devout Christian observances.[f]

Travelling to Ireland was still a major undertaking, and the party went overland to Holyhead, taking a ferry across the Menai Strait. Although a new steam 'Packet' was available, they would not risk this new-fangled mode of transport, and preferred to sail to Howth outside Dublin, which took twenty-one hours. (The steam Packet was fifteen hours quicker!) After waiting for an hour to clear customs, they were struck by the number of wretched beggars appealing for charity. The mansions of the gentry and 'good farm-houses' contrasted with 'the most wretched and squalid appearance of the poor'. Yet their initial impressions of Ireland were favourable and they toured Dublin, which they found 'fine and beautiful'. They set out for Ulster via Drogheda and Dundalk, but the landscape seemed 'very dreary' as they waited at Newtownhamilton for post-horses. They travelled on through Armagh, Dungannon and Cookstown to Moneymore, where they stayed at the 'excellent' *Drapers' Arms*. Moneymore made such an impression on them that it became their model for Ballykelly. Although Miller, the Drapers' Agent, was suffering from gout, they inspected the buildings and were 'gratified' at the school children's educational standards, despite their 'very ragged' appearance. They were particularly impressed to see Roman-Catholics intermingling with Protestants in the same school (although segregation became the norm later in the 19th Century).

As the deputation travelled north, the countryside became progressively more fertile, and it found the King's Arms at Newtown Limavady 'clean and comfortable'. Beresford's invitation for them to stay at Walworth House was declined, probably because he was still pressing for a lease renewal. Yet he assisted the deputation at working breakfasts before joining each day's thorough tour of inspection and providing picnic lunches. The deputation found travel on the poor roads and terrain difficult and even dangerous, but it was handsomely entertained at Walworth House by Beresford's English wife, Eliza, née Baily, and admired its farm buildings, farm and woodlands, which extended to about 300 acres and were in a 'high state of preservation and cultivation'. The woodlands needed careful husbandry, 'especially as Ireland was denuded of trees to a remarkable degree'.[g] The house itself was riddled with dry rot, and Beresford asked for assistance to restore it, as, without extensive repair, it would need to be demolished. He was later granted a new lease at £330 per annum, but only after a detailed structural survey, and the Company contributed to the major reconstruction costs. Although he was a candidate to become Agent, he preferred the opportunity to undertake this role for his cousin the Marquess of Waterford.

The deputation visited Sampson's 'excellent house' at Garvagh to discuss terms for future agreements with tenants and to establish his ideas on estate improvement generally, including tree planting and the rebuilding of Ballykelly. Sampson's advice was helpful and he accepted an invitation to become Agent (and was later succeeded by his son, Arthur). The deputation soon realised that, despite the 'neat farms' of the peasantry, their large families 'extended the poverty', and made their lifestyle extremely precarious.[h] Towgood described them as 'ragged and tattered', but, despite being 'wretched and shabby', they were 'shrewd and abundantly civil'. He described a typical cabin with smoke issuing through the doorway from a peat fire, round which children were dressed in rags. A large pig would have the run of the smoke-filled house, while its piglets lay by the fire with the children. So long as there was a demand for linen yarn, the younger women would be spinning flax. Grandparents would be sitting with a baby in a corner with a dog, while a goose hatched eggs under a dresser. A heap of potatoes would be in one corner of the earthen floor and a pile of peat in another. A second room contained wretched beds. On rare occasions, there would be a loom worked by a man making linen cloth to augment the family's income. Yet, in 1820, the market for linen had become depressed following the end of the French wars. Potatoes on small holdings provided the household's staple food, supplemented with eggs and milk products. Pigs were sold to pay the rent, but, if the potato crop failed, the pig had to be eaten and rents could not be met.

The deputation visited the 'neat and handsome' church at Tamlaghtfinlagan near Ballykelly, meeting Sir Henry Hervey Aston Bruce, its respected Rector (who inherited Downhill from his cousin, the Earl-Bishop of Derry), but very few of the nearby cabins appeared tolerable. It decided to close the Charter school, housed in a large building near the church, and to establish a new one nearby. This would allow the fertile area round the old building to be opened up for improvement. As a temporary expedient, it could be used as an infirmary. The Company soon had plans for other schools around the proportion and for a new dispensary or even infirmary at Ballykelly.

When moving further afield, the Deputation was not always able to return to Limavady by nightfall and it arranged to stay at private houses on its way. On one occasion it stayed with the Hunters at Drumcovit House where it was entertained to a 'tolerable Concert' by their extensive and musical family. Meetings with tenants were not so congenial. It was inundated with petitions and complaints, all 'urged with great vehemence and fluency', in which 'national prejudices' and superstitions were vented, and there was much 'cursing and praying against each other' by tenants.[i]

Drumcovit House, Feeny This beautiful property was visited by the Fishmongers' deputation of 1820, when it was occupied by the musical Hunter family.

The northern shores of Lough Foyle were bordered by 1,500 acres of malodorous 'slob-lands' (salt marsh), which were covered by the sea at high water. The deputation hoped that, by constructing an embankment along its entire length, the land could be reclaimed at moderate expense, making it of considerable value. 'Great tracts of bog [were inspected] in which ... quantities of wood were found'. Bog-land was so extensive that guides were needed to show the way. On one occasion Beresford went in 'up to the middle' and had to be pulled out by a horse. Reclamation plans allowed for a canal to be built linking Ballykelly to Lough Foyle as a means of encouraging trade. Sampson, the Beresfords and other locals were involved in these discussions, and work on reclaiming the first one hundred acres began almost immediately.

The deputation was soon familiar with 'the geography and condition' of the proportion. Sampson appointed John McLaughlin to undertake a survey to establish its size, standardising measures in accordance with English custom. This showed that there were totals of 9,000 acres of arable land and 10,000 acres of mountains and bog valued at £7,635 17s. 6d. The better land was enclosed with good hedges and stone walls. The proportion contained 1,002 families comprising 3,239 Presbyterians, 1,682 Roman-Catholics and 334 members of the Establish Church. Many were desperately poor, and reliant on casual relief, particularly around Glack, a wilder area mainly inhabited by Roman-Catholics reduced to penury by the falling demand for linen yarn. Yet the children at the school recently erected nearby were 'performing well', despite being dirty and dishevelled. 584 'householders and cottars' were unable to pay for medical aid. With no Poor Law in Ireland, the deputation realised that the Company needed to take responsibility for all largesse. It noted a cluster of thirty people with their possessions piled onto handcarts making its way to a ship for America. The depression in the linen industry made such convoys all too familiar, and printed notices were affixed to several cabins with details of ships leaving for the New World. Although the rural poor left in large numbers, many failed to survive the conditions on overcrowded vessels.

The deputation visited Londonderry, admiring the 'Gentlemen's seats' in pleasant countryside on the south shore of Lough Foyle and the bridge crossing the Foyle river. It inspected the large cannon on the walls, particularly 'Roaring Meg' presented by the Company in the 17th Century. It visited the diocesan school, which the Company had supported, but, as it was no longer flourishing, they decided to bring their grants to an end.

On 10 May 1820, the deputation set off for home from Limavady, after stopping at the Earl-Bishop's property at Downhill to see his magnificent collection of paintings and sculpture. It journeyed on through Coleraine, Bushmills and Dunluce (which was much admired), Ballycastle, Glenarm, Larne and Carrickfergus. It passed many 'handsome and well-built villas' on the road to Belfast. After spending the night at the 'capital' *Donegall Arms,* it caught the ferry from Donaghadee to Portpatrick, from where it returned to London by road. It had completed a journey of 1,500 miles.

Despite the change in their landlord, the subtenants all agreed to remain with the Fishmongers, but some needed 'benevolent protection'. The Company reasserted its right to fix rents and, following the land's revaluation, offered twenty-one year leases, which were ultimately accepted. It was noted that the 'Irish are led by the heart' while the 'Scotch are led by the head'. Rents to Roman-Catholic tenants were reduced from levels set 'too high' in 1799. It now followed the Drapers' example at Moneymore, by embarking on a long and prudent policy of careful reconstruction in which Sampson and his son were to play such an important part. Land was to be reclaimed, good stone for building was to be stock-piled, slates were to be obtained from Londonderry and from New Buildings, roads were to be improved and repaired, and financial help was to be given to existing institutions.[j]

'A substantial programme of building, modernisation, planting and philanthropy' was begun.[k] In addition to the Sampsons, Richard Suter, the Company's Surveyor from 1822 until his retirement in 1867, played an important part. After having been responsible for a number of significant buildings in London, he became the proportion's principal architect. He designed the new Presbyterian meeting houses at Ballykelly and Banagher, the Agent's House, the Model Farm at Ballykelly, the schools and the dispensary.

Ballykelly Presbyterian Church This was designed by Richard Suter and built in 1826-27.

Plots were too small to enable many tenants to subsist. As leases fell in, the Company had to insist on smaller holdings being amalgamated. It would only offer new leases in parcels of twenty or thirty acres at a time 'in the interests of common humanity and sense'.[1] Although this made evictions inevitable, the long-running reduction in the size of small holdings was reversed, so that subsistence farming was brought to an end and productivity improved. The Fishmongers joined a group of more progressive landlords offering former tenants financial assistance to emigrate. Many were sent to Canada. Those leaving were generally Presbyterians, as the Roman-Catholic Irish were still determined to hang on. The resultant relative increase in Catholics exacerbated racial and religious tension.

The Company now started to show great munificence. When the Presbyterian minister asked to renew the leases on the mid-18th Century meeting houses at Banagher and Ballykelly, it called for a building survey, which found both to be in poor repair and inadequate for the congregation's needs. It then called on Suter in London to oversee plans to rebuild them. Suter also prepared drawings to convert the Charter-School into an infirmary, and Sampson designed a lime kiln to provide mortar for construction work. With much of the cottar population of Ballykelly having emigrated to Canada, cottages and cabins could be removed, making space for public buildings and better dwellings. Sampson commissioned the Irishman, David McBlain, (who had undertaken work for the Earl-Bishop at Downhill) to provide a series of building designs. In March 1821, his magnificent drawings of classical buildings were sent on to London. In addition to 'a general Plan of the House and Offices', they included a market house with storage and a clock tower, an inn, an agency house, an agent's house, a school house and tradesmen's houses. Most of the deputation's members had joined the London Committee to oversee the proportion, which also included the Fishmongers' Prime Warden. They rejected McBlain's designs, which seem to have 'ruffled the feathers' of Suter.[184] He was able to persuade them to allow him to design the buildings, although cost may have been a factor. Only the designs for the lime kiln by Sampson, and the infirmary by Suter were accepted.

In 1822, a new deputation visited Ireland, again stopping at Moneymore to see Miller and Bridger to discuss the Drapers' developments. Like other Companies, the Fishmongers continued to seek their advice over several years, and Miller was both 'helpful and informative'.[m] In the same year, Towse, the Fishmongers' Clerk, arrived to appoint a new Rector at Tamlaghtfinlagan following Bruce's death. He seems to have opposed the appointment of James Hamilton, but, despite his reservations, Hamilton was presented to the living.

Church Hill, Ballykelly This model farm, built at the behest of the Sampsons, was designed by Richard Suter in 1823. It is now used as Local Government offices.

When Suter had completed plans for an infirmary, he was asked to design a new model farm at Church Hill, Ballykelly, for John Campbell, the tenant of the old Charter-School. This exemplary structure is still standing. Although the intention was to enable the damp and squalid old Charter-School to be pulled down, Campbell asked to remain where he was, probably because he considered the new building too large for his needs, but he was induced to go. Plans for an infirmary on the old Charter-School site came to nothing. A new one, which Suter also designed, was later built on the site of a 'wretched' mud cabin in Bridge Street in the town. The building work, which cost £2,000, was overseen by James Turnbull, who had been appointed Clerk of Works by Arthur Sampson (and was later Surveyor for the Mercers). When completed in 1829, it was on two storeys with a garret and five window bays. According to Ordnance Survey memoirs, it had a pretty garden 'in a high state of cultivation', but

[184] Suter is known to have 'felt his position rather keenly' when the young Henry Roberts won the competition to design the superb new Fishmongers' Hall in London.[n]

'architecturally it was considered too thick and clumsy' (but by that time Gothic design was the fashion). In 1850, Lewis's Topographical Dictionary noted 'an excellent dispensary, with a very good house for a resident surgeon'.

Being such a devout group, the Fishmongers were always likely to make schools a priority. In 1821, plans were prepared locally to provide a school for 500 children on the south side of the main street of Ballykelly. Yet, in 1822, Suter amended them to make it similar to that adopted by Gibson at Moneymore. The building work, which cost £1,200, was again supervised by Turnbull, but was on such a scale that it did not begin until 1828 and took two years to complete. The teacher was housed in a central block, with classrooms on each side constructed in brick with stone dressings.

From 1822, Suter was intimately involved in design work. He oversaw the plans for a new neo-classical meeting house at Banagher drawn up by James Bridger of Moneymore and costed at £2,200. After several alternative designs were provided for the Agent's House at Ballykelly, a 'commodious' double-fronted property was approved in 1824, combining 'the various ideas being floated',° but work was delayed for two years. A site occupied by Drummond House was preferred and it was completed in late 1827. A porch was added in 1832 and gates in 1833, both designed by Turnbull. Sampson never lived there; as a clergyman, he became obliged by Act of Parliament to reside at his rectory at Garvagh. He was already an old man and, on his death in 1827, there was a huge attendance at his funeral, and the Company erected a tablet to his memory in Tamlaghtfinlagan Church.

Beresford Family tree

			Sir Tristram Beresford 1st Bart. of Coleraine		Anne Rowley

	Sir Randal Beresford 2nd Bart. of Coleraine b: Abt. 1635 d: 1681	Catherine Annesley m: 1663 d: 1701		Susan Beresford

Sir Tristram Beresford 3rd Bart of Coleraine b: 1669 d: 1701	Nicola Sophia Hamilton b: Abt. 1667 m: 1687 d: 1713	Jane Beresford d: 1716	Frederick Hamilton Lt. General d: 1732 *of Walworth*	William Jackson

	Sir Marcus Beresford 1st Earl of Tyrone (in right of wife) b: 1694 d: 1763	Catherine Power d. of James Power, 3rd Earl of Tyrone Baroness la Poer m: 1717 d: 1769

George de la Poer Beresford 1st Marquess of Waterford b: 1735 d: 1810	Elizabeth Monck m: 1769	John Beresford b: 1738 d: 1805 *Advocate*	Barbara Montgomerie m: 1777 d: 1788

	Henry Barre Beresford b: 1784 d: 1837 *Land Agent, of Learmont*	Eliza Baily m: 1812 d: 1831

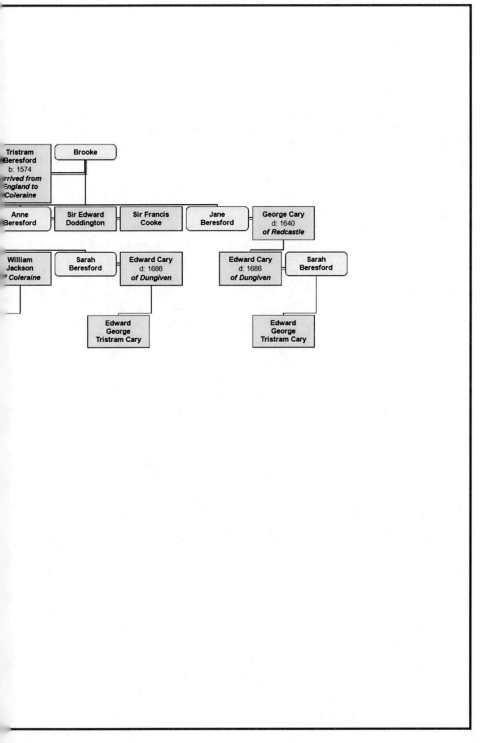

Tristram Beresford
b: 1574
Arrived from England to Coleraine

Brooke

Anne Beresford

Sir Edward Doddington

Sir Francis Cooke

Jane Beresford

George Cary
d: 1640
of Redcastle

William Jackson
Coleraine

Sarah Beresford

Edward Cary
d: 1686
of Dungiven

Edward Cary
d: 1686
of Dungiven

Sarah Beresford

Edward George Tristram Cary

Edward George Tristram Cary

429

In 1824, Sampson's son, Arthur became Agent, and Turnbull started to oversee all building work, including a second lime kiln to facilitate construction at Banagher. Quarries were opened and a brickwork established at Ballykelly River. In 1823, George Given prepared designs to improve New Walworth House, on the site of the old castle, which included new windows, new interior, new roof and new farmyard buildings. The work was supervised by Suter, who also designed a new meeting house[185] for Ballykelly. Its site was chosen in 1823, and the design was eventually approved two years later. When completed in 1827, the 'superlative quality' of its masonry was much admired, but it had cost £4,000.[p] In 1827, plans for a lodge for its sexton were also agreed. The smaller Banagher meeting house was completed in 1825 and is 'architecturally of great distinction'.[q] Suter also designed Ballykelly mill, built in 1825, and in 1826 he proposed a course for supplying water.

In 1827, the new deputation visited the Grocers' proportion to admire Muff. It also instructed Suter to provide designs to enlarge Ballykelly's Roman-Catholic Church. He provided plans for four 'tradesmen's houses' and a terrace of four others on Ballykelly's main street. When completed by the Bridgers, their exemplary design and finish set standards for future development. Turnbull produced plans and oversaw the building work of other small houses, in which he may have been financially involved. Although the Company wanted more freeholds, it could not find purchasers willing to pay the extra cost or to accept the commitment for jury service.

In 1829, Suter's plans for a dispensary at Mulderg at a cost of £1,030 were approved. In that April, the Company also gave instructions for him to design schools at Tirglassan and Mulderg. By then, a scale model of Ballykelly at Fishmongers' Hall was kept updated as new buildings were completed. It was made by Stephen Salter, a well-known architectural model maker of the day, but it has not survived.

The 1833 deputation much admired the new Agent's House and considered the Ballykelly schools 'highly ornamental'. Although Suter may have been responsible for improving its bridge, he now ceased to be involved in design work, but may have continued overseeing plans. It was Turnbull, who now styled himself as Architect, designing new schools for Dumbrock and Killycorr, Greysteel and Gortilie, where he also built a house for the schoolmaster. Despite their simplicity, each was properly designed and they demonstrate the Company's continued commitment to education. He was also commended for his plans for a house with a shop.

In 1838, Sampson commissioned an Engineer, John Macneill, to drain the slob-lands in a concerted effort at reclamation. Although the canal was never successful commercially, its walls helped to redeem a small area. Macneill undertook a survey to provide costs for an embankment which would not interfere with land owned by other parties or with the navigation. Discussions

---

[185] The designs for both meeting house, were exhibited at the Royal Academy in 1827.

rolled on, but were 'bedevilled' by The Irish Society's claims to the waters of the Foyle and the Bann. Eventually some reclamation was agreed and areas were 'drained, planted and fenced with thorn quicks'.[r]

Sampson's Tower, Farlow Wood Built by public subscription in c. 1860 to the memory of Arthur Sampson, who died in 1859. The monument is now derelict.

Later building work on the proportion moved away from Suter's 'robust Classicism'; a Tudor-Gothic design was preferred when a house for the Agriculturalist was built. Although building work continued on a smaller scale in the 1840s, 1850s and even 1870s, the Company was becoming anxious about the political changes heralded by the Great Famine. Yet, in 1846, when the priest at Ballykelly requested assistance to rebuild the Roman-Catholic chapel, Sampson was authorised to arrange plans for a new building at Oghill at a cost not to exceed £1,200. This was designed by Given, who had established his credentials with the Roman-Catholic clergy. Sampson erected a stained glass window at his own expense 'as a mark of respect to the Catholic tenantry'. In the following year, the priest wrote to thank the Company for its grant. The 1847 deputation admired the 'beautiful new district church at Carrick', to which the Company had also subscribed. The deputation of 1850 reviewed its progress, but, by then, the interior was still incomplete. Despite their staunchly evangelical make up, the deputation members attended Mass there. In 1852, the priest wrote to thank the Company for their 'liberality' and for their 'efforts in education'.[s] In 1848, the Company had also approved the building of a Presbyterian manse at Ballykelly at a cost not to exceed £500. Sampson may have been personally involved in the design, and it was completed in 1850.

The work of administering the proportion was growing, and Sampson was becoming older. George Craig of Drumcovit was appointed as sub-Agent to manage the southern area. Yet Sampson continued to be held in the highest esteem. He died at Drummond House in the early 1860s, at which time a tower[186] was erected by public subscription to the memory of their 'liberal and enlightened' Agent, who had not only held office for thirty-four years, but had been a Justice of the Peace. The Company placed a tablet in Tamlaghtfinlagan Parish Church, but he was buried next to his father at Aghanloo.

The Parish Church of Aghanloo with the rugged escarpment of Binevenagh behind This was the church where George Sampson was rector and the place of his burial.

The deputation of 1865 was concerned with 'schools, repairs and the building of several new houses', mainly farmhouses for tenants.[t] There had, by then, been numerous changes and, in 1870, Nolan & Co. of Londonderry was commissioned to undertake a new survey. The Company was continuing to erect new farmhouses and to repair buildings and, in 1871, it made a grant towards the cost of the Town Hall at Limavady.

Despite this later activity, the political situation was becoming progressively more difficult. The Company's 'open-handed beneficence was to vanish entirely when the activities of the Land League, Nationalists, and religious bigots became insufferable'.[u] Grants to educational, charitable, religious, and other

---

[186] This tower, surrounded by woodland, is now completely derelict.

bodies were progressively withdrawn. The problems started in the towns. Just as in Moneymore, allotments were illegally appropriated by tenants and sold. By 1875, the National Board of Education was required to take over the management of non-vested schools. Feelings were inflamed against 'landlordism' and the Irish Land League was involved in outrages. Home Rule politics caused vicious campaigns to be mounted against Company servants.

With the situation deteriorating, the Company offered to sell holdings to its tenants. Transactions had to be carried out in accordance with the terms of the Irish Lands Acts, which greatly weakened the landlords' position. They were required to sell on the basis of a number of years' purchase, but faced unremitting and 'wholly inappropriate abuse' in Irish newspapers.[v] Despite their benevolence, the continued involvement of Livery Companies in Ulster was a political issue. Unfounded rumours that they were not the legal owners provided an excuse for tenants not to pay rents. In 1882, Gage, the new Agent, became exasperated and described the tenants as 'an awful lot of ungrateful blackguards',[w] while complaining that the activities of the Royal Commission looking into land ownership was unsettling them. This was the exasperation of a devoted servant of the Company

> who had laboured with 'zeal and ability' for upwards of twenty years to discharge his duties; who had 'rendered considerable services to the cause of education irrespective of religious and political differences'; who had 'consistently endeavoured to improve the condition of the poor'; and who had 'promoted the welfare of all classes' connected with the Company's property.[x]

Land sales proceeded with the same difficulties faced by other Companies; tenants 'behaved just as dishonourably by withholding rents, assaulting servants of the Company, and procrastinating as much as possible'.[w] The cumbersome bureaucracy caused by having to sell through the Land Commission caused 'uncertainty, delay, and financial difficulties for many'.[z] Yet, by 1900, most of the proportion was sold, well ahead of some other Companies and the Fishmongers had received £100,560 7s. 10d. Curl, ever the architectural historian, has lamented:

> The breaking up of the estates has not encouraged a homogeneity of architecture, nor any attempt to recreate the pleasing compositions that were so earnestly sought by the designers and Agents employed by the Company.[aa]

Chapter 43

Goldsmiths

Like so many of the other Companies, having recovered possession at the Restoration, the Goldsmiths leased out their estate and took little further interest. In 1665, the Manor was granted for fifteen years to John Gorges of Poundisford, Somerset, who paid a 'fine' of £300 and an annual rental of £100. Some of the Minor Companies soon pulled out; in 1677, the Painter-Stainers were paid £43 for their interest, and, in 1680 the Cordwainers received £150. This left the Armourers as the only Minor Company still involved.

From 1719, William Warren leased the Manor for ten years at an annual rental of £200. In 1722, Humphrey Hetherington, the Company Clerk, made a visit. Although he kept a journal, Curl has found it 'infuriatingly uninformative about buildings'.[a] Yet Hetherington was generally unimpressed. In 1728, the Goldsmiths and Armourers agreed that if The Irish Society raised no objection (and it did not), they would sell their interests. Captain James McCullock of Westminster arrived to survey the Manor on behalf of the prospective purchasers, Henry Petty, Earl of Shelburne and his two associates, George Tomkins and Robert McCausland of Limavady. A price of £14,100 was agreed with a continuing annual rental of £200. The Company retained Clondermot Rectory[187] and its advowsons, the fishing rents, and the townlands of Gobnascale and Ballydoyle, which were probably freeholds. Although the purchasers paid their deposit of £4,700, on 7 September 1729, the day of the signing of the conveyance, they defaulted. The Company briefed Counsel, and an action to force Shelburne and his colleagues to complete was heard in the Court of Chancery. Shelburne claimed to be acting as a trustee for James McCullock and Edward Riggs. Although they were added as parties to the suit, the Lord Chancellor dismissed Shelburne's claim and ordered him to pay the remaining moneys plus costs, so that the claim against McCullock and Riggs was dismissed. In March 1730, Shelburne completed his purchase, and the Company invested part of its proceeds in South Sea Annuity Stock with disastrous consequences.

---

[187] Clondermot Church was not on the proportion. It is a handsome building on lands that belonged to the Dean of Derry.

The Goldsmiths did not completely sever their connections with Ulster. In 1807, the Clergy of Derry thanked The Irish Society for a generous donation to improve the Free School, to which the Goldsmiths had contributed. It continued to support other beneficial causes, including the schools at Ardmore and Lismacarroll. It also seems to have supported the Skinners' litigation with The Irish Society over the Companies' rights to receive accounts and dividends. Yet it would not contribute to proposals by the Ironmongers to form an Ulster Association to promote the general welfare of all proportions and to defend their interests.

By 1740, Shelburne had sold out to Brabazon Ponsonby, 1st Earl of Bessborough. In due course, the estate was let in perpetuity to the Ponsonby family. When a deputation of The Irish Society visited in 1836, it found that the Ponsonbys were making no effort to take advantage of its excellent soil and proximity to Londonderry. This was blamed on the tenants' uncertainty over their landlord's identity. They may have had a point. By then, a lease over half of the estate had been taken by Lesley Alexander, and he took on the remainder in the 1840s. Yet the freehold belonged to grandchildren of Bessborough's second son, John. One grandson, Sir William Ponsonby, left his interest to his nephews, who divided it into legacies, but his brother George sold his share to Alexander, who continued to acquire other interests as they became available. Meanwhile, the estate remained very under-developed.

> There was slate and limestone, some timber on the freeholds, three Presbyterian meeting houses, one church, one 'Roman-Catholic Chapel', six schoolhouses (principally supported by Protestant subscribers), one dispensary, and one charitable local society.[b]

Very little construction work took place after the Williamite wars. New Buildings was the only significant settlement and, apart from a much altered Methodist Church, little of its historic fabric survives. With its lack of architectural interest, it compared unfavourably with the adjoining Grocers' and Fishmongers' proportions.

Chapter 44

Merchant Taylors

In 1659-60, the Merchant Taylors were involved in voluminous correspondence with Michael Beresford, Tristram's brother, who they had appointed as Agent, in an effort to collect rents due from Wall's tenants. In 1667, John Gorges, who had signed a lease over the Goldsmith's proportion two years earlier, took a lease over Cranagh, but he soon fell into into arrears. Problems in collecting rent continued, and, by 1680 the Williamite Wars caused further disruption. The Merchant Taylors saw their estate as a bottomless pit into which resources had to be poured.

With the Company wanting to sell, in 1720, the Clothworkers offered them £2,700, but they declined this as derisory and continued to retain their significant stake in the Clothworkers' proportion. Nine years' later, they sold the entire proportion to William Richardson for £20,640. Two years earlier, he had acquired the Manor House for £20 6s. 0d. and an annual rent of £150. The Company had also conveyed the living of Camus to him, although its title to the advowsons was in doubt, with the Bishop of Derry having claimed the gift of the living by default, even though it had originally been granted to The Irish Society. This caused an argument, which continued for two hundred years and 'acrimony was never far from the surface'.[a] Modern research has confirmed that, although The Irish Society had been granted the advowsons under the 1662 Charter of Charles II, when it failed to make an appointment to a parish, the Bishop of Derry assumed patronage through lapse. Meanwhile, the Merchant Taylors had been presenting plate and cushions displaying the Company's Arms, thinking that they controlled it. In the end, the Bishop seems to have won the argument.

After obtaining the proportion in perpetuity, the Richardsons erected a mansion at Summer-seat, later Somerset, and began the planting of 'handsome' woodlands, for which they were warmly commended by Sampson. The Merchant Taylors took no further interest, but retained their share in the Clothworkers' proportion. In 1840, when the Clothworkers recovered direct control of their estates, the two Companies set up a Joint Board for its management. This heralded an era of rebuilding and improvement there until its disposal in the 1870s. The Company's involvement will be be discussed in more detail in the Clothworkers' chapter (pages 471-83).

Macosquin Rectory This 18th Century building in reticent style is on the site of the old castle.

The Parish Church of Camus-juxta-Bann, Macosquin built on the site of the old abbey.
Courtesy of John Campbell

Little remains of the buildings erected at Macosquin, although the shape of the village and the castle can still be seen (Macosquin Rectory, built in the 18th Century, is now on its site) and the parish church remains on the site of the old abbey.

Chapter 45

Skinners

The old church on the site of the abbey at Dungiven was still standing in 1656, and Lady Cooke was firmly back in control of the Castle, which, by then, had a water mill nearby. In 1672, the indenture from the Skinners' Company to Dame Ann Cooke and Edward Cary[188] describes the manor house as a 'late dissolved Abbey, Monastery, or religious house of Dungevin'. Like so many Companies at this time, the Skinners had no ambition to revert to personal management. In 1696, it was demised to Cary's son, another Edward, and in 1742, Henry Carey, probably his son or grandson, obtained a new lease at £500 per annum after paying an entry fine of £5,637. The Rt. Hon Henry Carey held the last of these leases, which expired in 1803. For some time, the church continued to be used for services, but by the end of the 18th Century both chancel and nave had again lost their roofs and had been derelict for some time, but 'part of the tower-house and a fragment of the round tower above the roof survived'.[a] In 1711, a new parish church was built near Dungiven, and it seems that timbers from the old abbey were used in the new structure. The centre of Dungiven migrated round it, and the old castle was abandoned, but a new one was built more strategically opposite the new church.[189] It too is thought to have been constructed from materials taken from the ruined abbey.

---

[188] Edward Cary was the son of George Cary, who had assisted Lady Cooke, until his death in 1640. Edward, who was Lady Cooke's nephew (and presumably heir) married his cousin, Sarah Beresford, who was Tristram's daughter and a niece of Lady Cooke. He died in 1686, and was succeeded by his son, also Edward. (See family tree pp.428-9)

[189] Moody has pointed out that many of the sites of Livery Company villages were 'chosen on grounds of immediate utility'. Being on the perimeter of the proportion, they were generally useless to pacify the dangerous and lawless interior.[b] This was a factor in the disastrous outcome of the rebellion of 1641. Yet Dungiven Castle came in for much praise as it was effectively sited to protect 'one of the worst areas from the British point of view'.[c] This did not make it a convenient location for a settlement, resulting in its subsequent removal.

Ogilby family tree

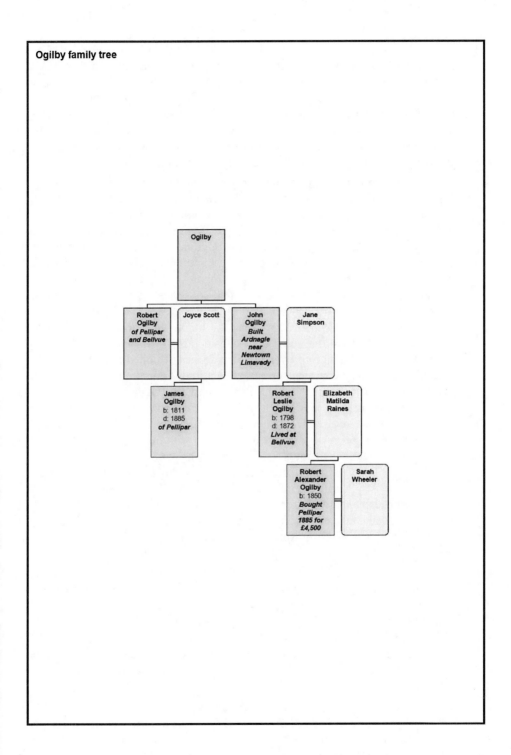

A survey of Dungiven undertaken in 1792 by David and Robert McCool shows that it contained fifty-eight tenaments in poor condition, but there was a new inn kept by Cornelius McDougal and houses, which belonged to James and John Boyle. The 'castle' occupied by 'Mr. Cary' was in 'very indifferent condition'. In 1802, Slade complained that Carey had 'not come forward as he ought with the Company'.[d] This is one of several hints of the suffering being faced by the native Irish on the Skinners' estates. The Company's records make no mention of this or even of the effect of the later potato famines.

In 1794, Robert Ogilby[190] paid Carey £10,000 to purchase the remainder of his lease, which was due to expire in 1803, and he was granted a new sixty-one year lease by the Skinners on expiry at an annual rental of £1,500, after paying a further £25,000 to the Company. On Slade's visit in 1802, he reported that the proportion was let on long lease to 'Mr. Ogilvie, a linen-factor, resident in Dublin'.[e] Slade was concerned that such a high entry 'fine' and rental would push 'up rents to the detriment of the proportion',[f] and, as Ogilby had no residence in Londonderry, he was unable to serve there as a juryman or magistrate. He was also concerned that there were 'no timber-trees of any consequence on the Skinners' proportion'.[g] Initially, Sampson was similarly negative, but, by 1814, he noted that 'considerable retail trade'[h] at Dungiven made it capable of great improvement. Residences exhibited 'an air of comfort and neatness'[i] suggesting that 'no other town in this county has received more useful improvement from the hand of its proprietor [Ogilby]'.[j] The town was clearly benefitting from the linen trade, and there is evidence of bleach-greens being operational locally. The tenements in the old streets were in 'thorough repair'[k] and there were new streets of buildings with others planned. Sampson also noted 'plantations of forests skirting the town and gardens'.[l] Yet progress must have ground to a halt, no doubt caused by the downturn in flax spinning as a cottage industry. Ogilby family records show that, in 1834, Ogilby paid for twelve poor residents to emigrate to America, but this is the only reference to any interest being taken in tenant welfare by either the Ogilbys or the Company, and they were severely criticised by The Irish Society.

For a time, the Ogilbys seem to have continued building properties at Dungiven. The Parish Church, which still dominates the high ground at the top of the town near the 'new' castle, was rebuilt in 1816-17 on the site of the 1711 building. It had cost £1,460, of which £1,200 was provided by the Church of Ireland's Board of First Fruits. Its graveyard contains Gothic memorials to the Ogilbys. By 1830, Robert Ogilby had begun to build 'a handsome castilated mansion of stone', having partially demolished the 'new' castle. This remained unfinished on his death in 1839, but provided 'a very striking and ornamental

---

[190] Robert and his brother John Ogilby were linen factors in Dublin. While Robert built Pellipar House, John built Ardnagle near Newtown Limavady. Yet they seem to have focused on Pellipar, and may have been joint owners as the occupation of Pellipar House switched between their respective descendants.

feature in the landscape'.[m] Its fine symmetrical front still overlooks the Roe Valley.

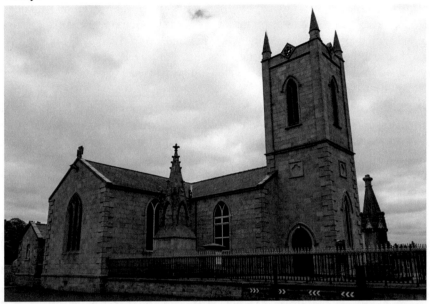

The Parish Church, Dungiven was rebuilt in 1816-17 on the site of the earlier building of 1711, paid for principally by The Board of First Fruits (the Church). There are two monuments to the Ogilby family in the graveyard.

The incomplete 'castle' built by the Ogilby family at Dungiven in 1838-39 is on the site of the Skinners' second castle. It is positioned opposite the church, but was never finished.

One storey of the earlier castle was also standing in 1838, as Ogilby had spent large sums in restoring it. Yet he lived at Pellipar House, which the family also built (and altered), while, by 1838, his brother John lived at Killkattan House nearby and acted as agent for the western side of the estate. This was also a substantial property, five windows wide and on two storeys. Bellvue, yet another smaller house on the estate was also built by Robert, and it was later occupied by John's son, Robert Leslie Ogilby, who had become Agent for his uncle.

None of this extravagant building work benefitted the locality, and criticisms by The Irish Society only riled the Skinners' Company. As reported in more detail on pages 346-7, in 1832, the Company took the Society to Court over the right of the Livery Companies to be furnished with the annual accounts of the Society, based on a suspicion that the Society was failing to hand over a fair share of its profits. Other Livery Companies lent financial support to the Skinners' argument that they were entitled to their share. The case start in the Court of Chancery in 1835 and, after ten years of expensive legal argument, eventually went to the House of Lords, where, on 8 August 1845, the Lord Chancellor, Lord Lyndhurst, and Lord Campbell found against the Skinners. Their judgement concluded that the Society had complete discretion to utilise its surpluses for the public good and for the general purposes of the Plantation, before any distribution to the Companies. As its income was never likely to satisfy all public needs, the Companies have been excluded from further dividends. It was perhaps unfortunate that, up to this point, the Skinners and Ogilbys had been among the least munificent of landlords.

In 1836, with the Court case still in process, The Irish Society sent a new deputation to examine the Skinners' proportion, and the Ogilby regime again came under fire. It reported:

> Considering its value, and its vast extent, there has been less done towards the improvement of this proportion, or the comforts and amelioration of the occupiers of the property than on any of the estates of the twelve proprietors.[n]

It saw Dungiven as 'long, straggling and uninteresting',[o] an opinion that is still true. On Robert Ogilby's death in 1839, Robert Leslie Ogilby moved to live at Pellipar House. At last, the family started to make economic improvements. By 1850, Dungiven consisted of one long street with two short intersections. Its houses were mainly thatched and on one storey, but there were a few two storey dwellings with slate roofs. It had a Parish Church, a Court House where Petty Sessions were held, police barracks, a market house with storage for corn for its monthly fair, and an inn providing a change for post horses. There were by then 1,016 inhabitants, presumably mainly native Irish. Although the bleach-greens were no longer used, the land around Dungiven was 'fertile, beautiful and cultivated',[p] with the lowlands under tillage, and more mountainous regions providing plenty of wild game and pasture for large numbers of livestock. The lease, which was still under Robert Leslie Ogilby's control, was due to expire on his death.

In 1853, realising that the time was coming for them to take back control, the Skinners sent a deputation to visit the proportion. Following Robert's death in 1872, further deputations were sent in 1873, 1874 and 1876 and the Ogilby's Agent, J. Clark was retained as the Company's Agent. The Ogilbys were permitted to retain the tenancy of Pellipar House with four hundred acres and Robert Sr.'s son, James, moved in. The Skinners found the estate properties considerably run down and brought a substantial claim for dilapidations against the Trustees of the Ogilby estates. The Trustees countered by claiming that a field, which had long been considered as part of the Pellipar House estate, should be the property of the Ogilbys. When this was submitted to arbitration at the *Skinners' Arms Hotel* in Dungiven, the Trustees were awarded £900 in recompense for the field. The action for dilapidations dragged on, with the Company claiming £3,000 alone for the castellated house, which Robert Sr. had built, but, in the end, it accepted £4,000 to settle all its claims.

With their financial issues resolved, the Skinners at last started to follow the 'evangelical examples' of other Companies by promoting charitable undertakings. They spent a great deal of money and began a forestry scheme. After much debate, they borrowed substantially to finance the building of the Limavady and Dungiven Railway and the Magherafelt to Draperstown Railway 'in the belief the opening of these lines would be for benefit of the estate and tenants thereof'.[9]

Holy Trinity Church, Lower Cumber Originally built in the 1790s, it suffered a 'subtle metamorphosis' when a new chancel was added in 1874 with a contribution from the Skinners.

In 1873, Burnell, the Company's Surveyor, joined a deputation, which visited the proportion to draw up plans for new schools at Tirgoland, Fincarn, Gortnaskey, Straw, Strawmore and Glenlough. These were visited by later deputations after their completion. Older school structures were either repaired, enlarged or demolished. The Company was prepared to support all religious denominations. In 1874, it improved the stipends of Presbyterian ministers and contributed towards the building of a new chancel at Lower Cumber Parish Church.

A generous grant was also given for the Priest's house in Dungiven. Alterations were made to the Court House. New building leases were granted at Dungiven, and the Company followed the Salters' lead by paving streets and providing modern gaslighting and a new sewerage scheme. A new plan of Dungiven was prepared to enable progress to be monitored and to show that new designs followed a 'comprehensive scheme' which Burnell had provided. In 1876, he laid out four centrally located plots to make it 'more handsome and coherent as an architectural entity'.[r] All plans and elevations were to be submitted to London for the Company's and Burnell's approval, but a local Architect and Surveyor, David McConaghy did most of the design work, including plans for the manse at Upper Cumber built in 1879. Other buildings were soon rising up. Thatched roofs were to be removed and tenants were encouraged to replace them with 'non-combustible' slates.

In 1874, a new survey of the proportion was commissioned and the deputation prepared an elaborate report illustrated with maps of each division. Schemes for land reclamation and ambitious plans for afforestation were proposed. Burnell drew up a plan for completing the unfinished castellated mansion as a new home for the Agent and a headquarters for future deputations as the existing Agent's house (probably Bellvue) was considered 'insignificant'.[s] Yet the mansion had lain incomplete for many years, and the plans were never implemented. In 1880, a disastrous fire destroyed part of Pellipar House. With James Ogilby still being its tenant, Clark was asked to assess the damage, and repairs were quickly put in hand. When James died in 1885, his cousin and heir, Robert Leslie's son, Robert Alexander Ogilby, bought the freehold for £4,500.

Agitation against the payment of rents reached the proportion for the first time in about 1880. Much time was wasted in tenants seeking rent reductions, arbitrations and 'other tiresome and familiar matters that must have wearied the most patient of Londoners'.[t] Rent reductions required under the Land Act of 1881 were agreed, with so called 'fair' rents being fixed for the majority of holdings.[j] When Clark retired as Agent in 1881, there were one hundred and fifty applicants to take on his role, and the Company replaced him with the 'energetically youthful' twenty-three-year-old George Lawrence Young at an annual salary of £600 with provision of a house. He was required to provide a bond of £5,000 as security. By now, political unrest was causing enormous difficulty. Clark had already received threatening letters and Company servants were being subjected to verbal and physical abuse. Young inherited arrears of rent of £7,500, but failed to improve collections. The Company eventually purchased 'Mrs. Ogilby's House' to provide him with a residence, but he resigned in 1889 to become Agent for Lord O'Neill, who seems to have offered a better salary (and probably less hostile surroundings). The Skinners now realised that the 'new relation of the Company' to the tenants 'would not be attended with prevalent cordiality or good feeling'.[u]

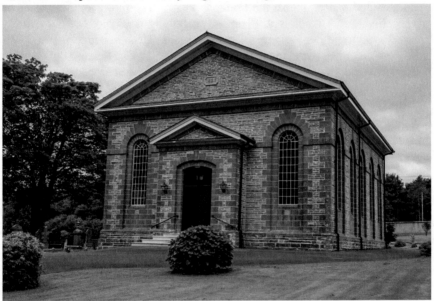

The Presbyterian Church, Banagher was completed in 1825 to designs by Richard Suter (with not inconsiderable advice from Bridger) at a cost of £2,200.

Despite political uncertainty, the Skinners continued their new-found munificence. In 1883, £500 was given to the Presbyterians at Brackfield towards the rebuilding of their church. Two new houses were built in Dungiven. A contribution was made towards the rebuilding of the Parish Church at Ballinascreen in the Drapers' proportion and, in 1891, further funds were given for the rebuilding of its reredos. In 1884 a new Police Barracks was completed at Dungiven. In 1888, the Company gave a generous grant towards the cost of a new Roman-Catholic Church at Banagher on the Fishmongers' proportion, and a grant was later made for Banagher's Presbyterian Church and Manse. In 1889, it helped with alterations to Dungiven Parish Church.

All this generosity belies growing concern for the Skinners' future in Ireland. In 1886, they set up a Committee to consider selling the estate under the provisions of the Land Act of 1885. In 1875, the Company had bought out the Stationers' interest, followed, in 1877, by the Bakers'. Between them they received the handsome sum of £76,301. 4s. 9d. The Girdlers sold in 1887, but agreed to accept their share of the value of the estate when realised. In 1888, the break up of the estate was begun, with leaseholds being conveyed to tenants. By 1890, disposal of most of the better property had been achieved. In 1892, new maps were prepared to clarify land areas and to try to avoid the 'usual difficulties', which incurred 'tiresome and unnecessary litigation'. Great problems arose in the Ballinascreen division, where the Company finally resorted to eviction with police help after years of refusal by tenants either to pay rent or to enter into negotiation to purchase. The reporting in the Press was again heavily loaded against the Londoners. Yet, by 1900, with the assistance of The Irish Land Commission, almost everything was sold, but not entirely cleared up for a further few years. The total proceeds amounted to £199,057 2s. 5d. After expenses, the Company received £159,104 15s. 6d. and the Girdlers £20,504 11s. 8d. (a rather less good outcome than for the Stationers and Bakers).

After their departure, the Skinners continued to receive letters reminding them that their 'customary donations' were due, and they continued grants to schools, churches and parcels for the poor until about 1916, by when they had 'begun to resent in no small measure such presumption'.[v] Since then, Dungiven has faced a 'rash of inappropriate alterations',[w] leaving very little evidence of the Skinners' heritage. Pellipar House and the unfinished castellated mansion still stand, but these were built by the Ogilbys, who had been the main beneficiaries of the estate.

Chapter 46

Haberdashers

At the Restoration in 1660, new grants of the Manor of Freemore were made to the Haberdashers' Company, who passed them on to the investing partners. Adrian Moore Junior died in 1656, when his interest was conveyed to his widow. The *Civil Survey* of 1654-56 shows that Sir Robert Maxwell, Colonel Tristram Beresford, George Phillips and Daniel McManus O'Mullen (a converted Irish Protestant) were among the partners, but, by 1657, Sir Randal Beresford (Tristram's son) held the major share and, in 1674, Lady Beresford, his wife, took this over for £1,200. From now on the Beresfords were the chief landlords. By 1686, most of the remaining interests had passed to them, but part of Moore's and Freeman's original shares remained with the Jackson, Upton and Carey families.

The Beresfords were now well-established, and, in 1800, the estate devolved to Henry Beresford, 2nd Marquess of Waterford. By the time of the visit of The Irish Society deputation in 1836, the proportion was vested, almost entirely, in the Marquess of Waterford, who had been employing his cousin, Barré Beresford, as his Agent since the expiry of his lease over the Fishmongers' proportion in 1820. By then the Beresfords owned and ran all the native Irish schools on the proportion after paying 13s. 4d. to The Irish Society. Under Barré Beresford's leadership the estate was greatly improved, 'so that the inhabitants enjoyed a state of comfort unknown before'.[a] New roads were built and building materials were provided to tenants free of charge. New slate roofs replaced thatch, and mean cabins were superseded. 'Planting of trees and hedgerows was carried out on a considerable scale', and by 1836 the estate was generating £9,000 per annum in rents. Many churches and schools were built at the estate's expense, and schoolmasters received financial support. The Irish Society noted ('somewhat sniffily') that the Marquess focused his benefactions on 'promoting domestic comforts of the tenantry' rather than establishing 'public institutions'. This meant that, apart from Artikelly, which remains only a hamlet of small houses, the proportion had no towns or even villages. Although some larger houses and churches were constructed, there is nothing that can be attributed to Freeman and Moore, who took over the Haberdashers' responsibilities. What remained of Ballycastle after 1641 was probably destroyed in the Williamite Wars.

Chapter 47

Salters

It was not until the Cromwellian defeat of the Royalists that a gradual recovery of the Salters' lands was made possible. The re-establishment of The Irish Society on 10 April 1662, enabled the Manor of Sal to be returned on 3 June 1663. Yet the Salters made no rush to invest. Although a church was built at Magherafelt in 1664, to replace an earlier 15th Century building, the trouble was not over. Not much is known of the town's appearance during the Williamite Wars, but the church at the bottom of Broad Street provided quarters for Jacobite troops. With the settlement being plundered, many inhabitants escaped to Londonderry, but the church survived and, with its churchyard being the only burial ground in Magherafelt, all denominations were interred there. It needed substantial reconstruction from 1717 to 1720, when The Irish Society supplied timbers, and a north aisle was added. In 1755, the tower began to collapse, resulting in its timber spire being taken down for strengthening. Its timbers were sold in 1757, but, in 1758, a collection was raised to replace it; the new tower was completed in 1771, with the spire being added in 1793. The roof seems to have been shingled initially, but was slated in 1779. In 1798 a new floor and seating were added. A Rectory had been built in about 1737, but has been much altered since.

On 8 June 1699, Gabriel Whistler was granted a ninety-nine year lease over the proportion at an annual rent of £100. In 1745, this was passed to Thomas Bateson for the remaining fifty-three years until 1798 at £500 per annum. It was then renewed by the Batesons for a further term until 1853. During the late 18th Century, Robert Stewart, who had recently become Lord Londonderry (and became Marquess of Londonderry in 1816) joined Sir Robert Bateson Bart. as a partner in the lease. In 1831, when it still had twenty-two years to run, the partners approached the Salters seeking a renewal, but the Company had decided to follow other livery companies by bringing its estate back in hand on expiry.

It would appear that the Salters' conscience had been pricked by Sampson's criticisms. From now on, as tenants' leases expired, they resumed possession to enable them to make improvements and offer renewals on better terms. They were soon contributing to civic improvements at Magherafelt. In 1804, with County help, they funded the building of a Courthouse near the old church. They also provided money for 'charitable and ecclesiastical purposes'. To encourage more commercial activity, the Company planned new market buildings. In 1810, it built a new Market House in the town centre with an arcaded ground floor. 'A 'neat' cupola containing the town-clock dignified the northern side.'[a] [191] In 1836, the Committee responsible for the Irish Estate started to meet monthly and was determined 'to stop all waste and abuses'.[b] With an up-to-date survey of the proportion being urgently needed, Ordnance Survey maps were procured and, in 1837, these were tinted by George Edward Valintine, the Company Surveyor. Although a Linen Hall had been built in 1820, in 1837, the Company joined with Bateson and Londonderry to construct a new one.[192] In 1838, when two members of the Company visited, they arranged a donation towards the building of a Presbyterian Meeting House at Kilrea on the Mercers' proportion, and dispensed largesse within the Manor of Sal with 'remarkable liberality'. Yet, until the lease expired in 1853, the Company could not assert control, but it monitored the events leading to the Skinner's case against The Irish Society, which involved lengthy discussion and meetings, not to mention horrendous expense.

At the time of the lease's expiry, the detailed plan of Magherafelt showed 'a very modest urban fabric',[c] with large areas of its parks divided into allotments. Yet the Company recognised the substantial achievements made by the Batesons and Londonderrys. To curtail the depletion of the estate's timber resources, they had planted four thousand trees in one year alone, and, during the 1830s, extensive planting continued.[d] Linen production was a major activity and, by 1846, the year of the famine, the principal manufacturer was employing large numbers in the locality. Weekly linen markets and sales of agricultural produce generated 'remarkable' business. The monthly fairs selling cattle were the largest on the west side of Lough Neagh.

While they were reasserting control, the Salters continued to undertake most of the estate's supervision on behalf of its Minor Company partners, but remained in close contact with them, sharing out profits promptly and providing them with copies of all important documents. In 1838, they discussed the possibility of dividing the estate among them, but this was not felt to be practicable. In 1849, with the date for them to take back full control fast approaching, a new deputation was instructed to visit all buildings and townlands. Andrew Spotswood, the Batesons' and Londonderrys' Agent, assisted by providing a rent roll showing the areas occupied by each tenant. Given the shortage of 'suitable' dwellings in Magherafelt, Valintine was instructed to provide designs for two streets of new houses near the town centre. Although he had intended to travel with them, he died suddenly shortly before their departure. The new Surveyor, Robert Garland, was tasked with completing the plans, including a detailed one of Magherafelt, and he visited the proportion in 1850. These show the substantial increase in the building work since 1837.

---

[191] When the Market House was demolished in 1879-80, the town-clock, which had been paid for by public subscription, was sold, despite 'protests and uproar in the local Press'.[e]
[192] The old site was used to provide a Brideswell [jail].

On 20 May 1853, the lease reverted to the Company. Stewart Gordon, the County Surveyor (and Surveyor to The Irish Society) was commissioned to prepare a schedule of dilapidations, and the outgoing landlords agreed to accept 10s. in the £1 for the purchase of their rent arrears. Charles Pollock undertook a detailed survey and valuation at a cost of £770, which was eventually finalised after Garland had provided advice. 'Members of the Company travelled to Ireland out of personal interest to view the estates.'[f] They generally stopped to consult Miller on progress at the Drapers' proportion. He informed them that the Bateson and Londonderry families had always been excellent Landlords, and Andrew Spotswood was an 'upright' man. To avoid squandering a valuable resource, they asked Miller to advise on one of their quarries. He found it being worked incompetently and reported that wastes from the deplorable lime kilns were rendering the surrounding lands useless.

As soon as it recovered control, the extent of the Company's benevolence was extraordinary. It stuck to its task of improving the proportion with 'evangelical zeal'. Spotswood was retained as Agent at a salary of £500 per annum, but he proved a bigoted anti-Catholic, colouring the views of members of the Company 'rather strongly' against some tenants.[g] His own application to take a tenancy was turned down.

In 1854, a new deputation travelled from London on the London North Western Railway to Fleetwood (north of Blackpool) to catch the steamer to Belfast. On arrival, it inspected Mulholland's 'noble' linen manufactory and the Botanic Gardens. It then took the train to Randalstown, where Spotswood met its members in a coach-and-four for the fifteen mile journey to Magherafelt. On its arrival, there was 'a considerable muster of the inhabitants, by whom the party was welcomed with very cordial cheering'.[h] On its way, it had passed the intended route of the railway to Cookstown, which would facilitate future visits. It later discussed the location of a new station at Magherafelt, fully recognising that the railway's arrival augured well for the future.

From the outset, the Salters realised that they faced significant expenditure, resulting in them raising a loan. In 1854, £10,000 was set aside for immediate improvements, which Spotswood was instructed to organise, and, over the next ten years, the Company spent £29,299 6s. 0d., no mean sum. It ordered sets of cast-iron coats of arms from London to be erected on school and other buildings, many of which still survive. It wanted to encourage house building nearer the new Parish Church, and arranged the construction of villas costing £200 each to 'raise the tone'.[i] Dwellings seemed to go up everywhere, but these resulted in rents being raised. In January 1856, tenants prepared a memorial in protest.

When the deputation attended the Parish Church on its first Sunday, it listened to an excellent sermon and was 'struck by the becoming and devotional manner in which the service was performed'.[j] Yet the church was 'in a very dilapidated state' with the tower again in danger of collapse, and the deputation noted that £1,000 voted by the Ecclesiastical Commissioners was 'not premature'. Although the spire had already been taken down, the Rector persuaded the Company that a new church was needed. The deputation halted the repair work, leaving the old church 'unroofed', and it was left to become derelict. It was agreed that 'arrangements should be made for erecting a new Church with all convenient dispatch',[k] notwithstanding the need for the Company to make a large contribution.

The Parish Church of St. Swithin, Magherafelt In 1856, the Salters contributed £4,000 towards the cost of Joseph Welland's 'elegant and appropriate' design with its 'remarkably rich interior'.

On the following day, the deputation set out with Spotswood to examine other local churches, visiting Moneymore, and Cookstown, 'as being the neighbouring and therefore rival towns to Magherafelt'.[l] It did not consider Moneymore's church to be 'an eligible model' for Magherafelt, probably because Gothic Revival design was then the fashion, rather than Booth's 'somewhat clumsy Norman style'.[m] It preferred the Parish Church at Ballinderry standing on glebe lands, which intersected the proportion. This had been designed by the Ecclesiastical Commissioners' Architect. It also admired Tamlaghtfinlagan Parish Church on the Fishmongers' proportion. On returning to Magherafelt, it discussed the new church's location with the Rector, as the old one was 'too low and the churchyard very confined',[n] and it selected a site on the east side of the town. Although the Company agreed to meet the structural cost, the Rector was to organise a subscription to pay for its internal fittings. Designs by Joseph Welland, the Ecclesiastical Commissioners' Architect, were found to be 'elegant and appropriate' and the Company remitted £4,000 towards the cost. St Swithin,[193] Magherafelt, was begun in October 1855 and consecrated in April 1858. It is an 'ambitious structure' in Decorated Gothic style built of basalt with freestone dressings, with 'a remarkably rich interior'.° Its tower is capped by a spire at its west end. Its west window contains the arms of the Salters, the Batesons and Ralph Whistler, whose 17th Century monument had been moved from the old church.

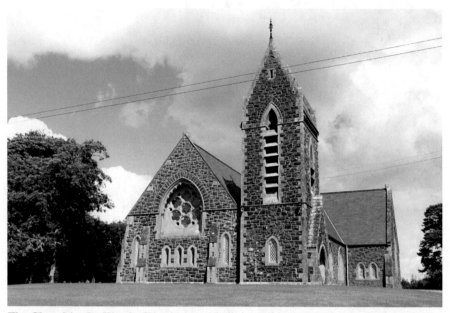

The Chapel in the Woods, Woodschapel built in Gothic style on a site presented by the Salters, who provided £1,000 towards its cost. Building began in 1863, when the Master laid the foundation stone. It was completed in 1867. © Garry McMurray

The deputation also visited Artrea to see the dilapidated Chapel in the Woods, which had a pew reserved for the Company's use, and its adjacent school house. It promised £200 towards the cost of rebuilding and to provide a residence for the curate. When the estimates were eventually completed in 1860, the cost was calculated at £2,700 and the Salters increased their grant to £1,000. The plans were approved in 1861, and Alderman Gibbons, the Master Salter, laid the foundation stone. In 1864, when only half-completed, its new tower collapsed onto the rest of the building, but work had restarted by 1866, and it was consecrated in 1870. The Company continued to provide annual grants until 1887. In 1864, a site for a new Parish Church at Ballyeglish was selected, with subscriptions being promised by the Drapers and Ecclesiastical Commissioners in addition to the Salters. In the following year, plans for this 'dignified, simple

---

[193] Salters' Hall was in St Swithin's Lane in London.

452

and refined' church were approved, using stone from the Drapers' estate. It was consecrated in 1868.[p]

The Church of St Matthias, Ballyeglish Curl regrets that the 'dignified, simple and refined interior' designed by the Ecclesiastical Architects in 1868 has been 'obliterated by ill-advised paintwork'.

The Presbyterian Meeting House built in 1735 was 'not merely dilapidated' but could 'also be termed in ruins'.[q] The Company resigned itself to funding at least half of the £2,500 projected rebuilding cost and to provide a manse; its much respected Minister was granted £20 per annum. In 1855, John Young of Belfast provided designs, which were approved by the Company, but its Gothic Revival Style, so dependent for its success on a rich interior, sits uncomfortably with Nonconformist liturgy. When completed, two years later, the costs had escalated to £3,050 10s. 0d., but Young provided designs for the manse built at a further cost of £600 on the opposite side of the road. The Company baulked at so much additional cost, and the manse was unfortunately burned down on the eve of its completion. Yet a new manse in Saltersland was completed in 1858, and a site for another was granted at the Loup. In 1861, a fine Roman-Catholic church was built at the Loup. The raising of money was organised by Father Patrick Quinn, who, despite having fallen out with Spotswood, proved another effective fund-raiser.

The Presbyterian Church, Magherafelt
Although designed by John Young and completed in 1857, Curl has complained that Gothic Revival style and Nonconformist religion are not happy bedfellows.

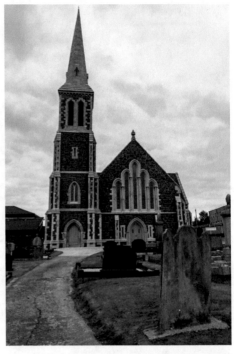

The Roman-Catholic Church of St Patrick at the Loup The fund-raising for this fine church was arranged by Father Patrick Quinn, who had fallen out with the Salters' Agent, Andrew Spotswood.

The Union Road Presbyterian Church, Magherafelt designed in 1866 for a seceding Congregation of Presbyterians by Boyd and Batt of Belfast has a strangely theatrical front.

The Roman-Catholic Church of Our Lady of the Assumption, Magherafelt O'Neill and Byrne's design to bring the Catholics into line with other local churches was approved by the Company in 1878. Many Protestants contributed to the cost and the Company provided £1,000.

£25 was given towards the building of Lecumpher Presbyterian church, which was not on the proportion, but used by some of the tenants. The Company also assisted the Wesleyans in rebuilding their Methodist Chapel, but insisted on all drawings being submitted for approval.[r] In 1864, dissent among the Presbyterians in Magherafelt resulted in a seceding Congregation being formed. Between 1864 and 1868, it plagued the Company for financial help to build a new Meeting House. Eventually a site was provided and a design for a building with a somewhat theatrical front was approved, costed at £1,585 10s. 0d. A manse for its Minister was erected in 1882.

The Company provided £20 annually to Father John Quinn, Magherafelt's Roman-Catholic Priest, who was greatly admired. A 'Mass-House' had been built in 1792 at Milltown about a mile from Magherafelt, but was considerably re-edified in 1831 under Quinn's auspices. The 1849 deputation noted that it was again in a poor state and assisted in its repair. Quinn had been in the vanguard of those fighting against the Penal Laws, which had forced Catholic observances (including marriages and funerals) into people's homes.[s] He now sought to restore Catholic Churches to the 'centre of worship and for the administration of the sacraments'. He proposed the building of a fine new Roman-Catholic church in Magherafelt, but little progress was made under his successor, Father Campbell, who died in 1867. Spotswood wrote: 'It will be very unpleasant if we get an agitator to succeed him'. Luckily the 'excellent' Father Patrick Donnelly took over and led a project to build a 'handsome, scholarly and rich' church accommodating one thousand people. Designs, prepared by O'Neill and Byrne, were approved by the Company, which, in 1871, allotted a site and provided £1,000 to the total of £16,000 required. Many Protestants contributed, and the foundation stone was laid in 1878. It was 'obviously intended to put the Roman-Catholic community on a parallel footing architecturally with the Anglicans and Presbyterians' and was dedicated by Primate Archbishop Daniel McGettigan in September 1882. It remains 'among the best architectural glories of County Londonderry'.[t] Donnelly's remains are interred near the altar.

After examination, it was clear that the 'inferior character' of the schools would involve a rebuilding programme. They needed better ventilation, as 'malodorous children' made 'the atmosphere … unpleasant and apparantly injurious to health'.[u] Spotswood advised on priorities and Young prepared a model design for school houses with adjacent teachers' accommodation. New schools were built at Ballyronan and Killyboggin and the one at Coolshinney was rebuilt. In 1859, drawings for a new Roman-Catholic School were also prepared.

The Salters' Coat of Arms
This cast iron insignia is positioned above the entrance of the rebuilt Rainey Endowed School in Magherafelt.

In 1707, a charity founded by Mr. Hugh Rainey, a local iron smelter, had been set up in Magherafelt to educate and apprentice poor boys, being funded by rents from a twenty acre farm. Its buildings were now in poor repair and the Company was determined to rebuild them if the Trustee (The Archbishop of Armagh) would agree. It resumed direct ownership of the site with its garden, and, after dismissing plans for rebuilding on the farm which provided its funding, in 1861, it instructed Young to prepare plans to include accommodation on its existing site at a cost not to exceed £700. It was approved in 1863 and was completed in the same year. In 1844, the Company had also contributed to the rebuilding of a boys' school in Magherafelt. In 1856, a new school for girls with teachers' accommodation was established near the new church next to the parochial schools. Its plans had initially been considered 'too ornamental' and Spotswood was asked to provide something simpler at a cost of £400. Yet this was an unrealistic sum, and Young eventually provided a design with a frontage in 'blackstone', which cost £800 when completed in 1858. The *ensemble* created a 'pretty, symmetrical composition, in a reticent late gothic style'.[v]

The Company made plans to replace all the principal buildings in the centre of Magherafelt. Spotswood's offices were considered unsuitable, and the dispensary, tucked away in the Court House, was 'inconvenient'. The Market House was 'out of repair' and 'not very ornamental',[w] so a new Market House 'of more pretension' combining an Agent's office, rent room, interview room, dispensary and scales was designed. There was to be an assembly room on the upper floor, surmounted by a clock tower and vane 'ornamental to the town'. It was never built, but further drawings to improve the old Market House for use as a Town Hall were later prepared by Young. He also made a design for a

Classical new Market House with 'capacious' grain stores on its east side 'similar to those at Moneymore'. The grain stores were eventually built on a much reduced plan. Consideration was given to moving the cattle-market to provide room for more housing, particularly as Spotswood had been instructed to acquire three cottages to enable the flax and pig market to be extended. The new flax stores, designed by Collier, eventually cost £920 after an earlier design estimated at £1,750 had been rejected. These could be converted into cottages if desired.[x] They seem to have been in active use, as cast-iron columns supported the centre of the first floor and, in 1867, iron stanchions were added to the wall piers.

A separate Agent's office with the Company's arms on it was designed by Young. This was similar to that built for the Mercers in Kilrea and was completed in 1855 at a cost of £980. The medical officer, Dr. Vesey, needed a site for his residence near the new church, and the Company provided £300 towards its cost. It was already roofed by September 1855, when Vesey's annual salary was agreed. In 1857, the construction of a new Italianate dispensary near the town centre was begun. This was designed by Robert Young, the Agriculturalist (confusingly), who had already provided several agricultural buildings. It cost £375 on completion in 1859 and proved such a benefit that, in 1864, tenders were received for a second one at Ballyronan. A new Police Station was also required. All this development led to the need for new fresh water and sewage systems, which were designed by Collier in 1859.

When the hotel at Magherafelt failed to satisfy the 1854 deputation's 'approbation',[y] it was decided to extend the Agent's residence to house future visitors. It was not until 1860 that Garland was instructed to draw up plans and £3,000 was set aside. His 'strangely archaic' Jacobean design was forwarded to Ireland, but the costings proved higher than in London (a familiar conundrum particularly as Irish labour was cheaper). Members of the Company preferred the Agent's house recently built by the Ironmongers, and Garland based his new design on this. The contract was costed at £2,480, although outbuildings added £475. A 'fine' early Victorian style building was completed in 1862, but ultimately cost £4,305 15s. 7d. To Spotswood's disapproval, in 1890, it became a convent for the Sisters of the Holy Family, who had recently been entrusted with the education of Magherafelt's Roman-Catholic children.

In 1867, the Company provided sites for a new sessions house and brideswell (jail), and, in 1871, it agreed to contribute one-third of the cost of a new court house. Although drawings were prepared in Ireland, Collier made 'slight' amendments in London. In 1872, tenders were invited and the building ultimately cost about £5,000. It was soon hearing a number of cases of infanticide perpetrated by poor young girls, with 'the usual assortment of drunken violent brawls, murders and other familiar crimes'.[z]

Court House, Magherafelt built in 1871 to designs by Turner and Williamson.

The Company's records make little reference to rural poverty, which afflicted all companies. It may well be that Spotswood sought to shelter it from these problems, but it must have been aware of rent arrears, just like the other Companies. There is no evidence of mass emigration, but it must have been taking place, although efforts to develop commercial activity around Magherafelt will have provided some local employment. Yet, on other proportions, the influx of a starving peasantry from elsewhere caused great difficulties and the Salters, being further south, probably faced the brunt of it. There is also little information about rural improvements, but a drainage system for clearing the bog-land was developed by Gordon, The Irish Society Surveyor, to extend an earlier attempt by Young, the Agriculturalist. New mill dams were also constructed and others were embanked and repaired. Roads were improved and more trees planted.

The Salters were justifiably proud of Magherafelt, which was 'thriving and prosperous',[aa] and it commissioned a comprehensive photographic record to attract investment and settlers. In 1865, The Irish Society commended it on its efforts and a general air of confidence was encouraging tenants to make 'creditable' improvements to their homes, so that any remaining tenements could be removed. Streets were paved and the Company contributed £300 to build a gas works, so that, during the 1870s, gas was piped to the streets and houses to provide lighting.[bb]

In 1867, Spotswood retired as Agent and was succeeded by Sir Henry Cartwright on a salary of £600, after he provided a bond of £6,000 as security. There were already early signs of unrest, with the Catholic Church starting to fulminate against 'landlordism'. Spotswood had not been good at dealing with it, but Cartwright was more moderate and fair-minded.

It is interesting to speculate what caused the Salters' strong motivation to take back control in 1853. It was not a concern for the plight of the rural tenantry apparently and they were not critical of the former landlords, even retaining Spotswood, despite acknowledging his bigotry. Their focus was on developing Magherafelt as a commercial centre and in improving rental income by attracting better class residents to their fine houses and beautiful churches. In this, they were probably more successful than any of the other Livery Companies.

It was not until 1874 that the Royal Agricultural Society provided plans for a pair of model cottages to be built by the Company in Magherafelt. The cottages were intended as 'exemplars' for new buildings to be constructed throughout the rural parts of the proportion, in the belief that change could be achieved by example. This was too little, too late. The Company was already selling the freeholds of its residential properties in Magherafelt to encourage individuals to make their own improvements. The 1880s 'saw a gradual and reluctant resignation on the part of the Salters to the prospect of selling the Proportion'.[cc] By 1897, it was being sold on terms similar to those forced on other Companies. The total proceeds of sale before expenses but net of the share applicable to their remaining Minor Company partners totalled £174,934 17s. 8d. This was a significant sum, and it demonstrates the benefit of their investment in property during the previous forty years after the proportion had been restored to the Company's control. Even in the 1930s, it was still being asked for donations for local charitable needs, but only rarely did it make a contribution.

Chapter 48

Ironmongers

In 1654, Paul Canning wrote a report to the Ironmongers from Garvagh outlining the proportion's fate.

> The castle, Manor House and 'all other buildings whatsoever' together with the church, the mill at Culcrow, and bridges, had been 'totally demolished and destroyed.[a]

No tenants would accept new leases, unless freed from rent and taxes for at least a year, with an 'easy rent' for a further five years. No more than twenty trees suitable for building were left standing. Having sold his English estates in 1630, George Canning had reinvested everything in Londonderry. The family 'had lost everything, including many 'dear friends''.[b] Yet more damage was inflicted during the Williamite Wars, when Agivey formed a part of the Williamite defence line at the Bann, until its troops were forced to retreat into Londonderry. In 1690, William's Danish and German mercenaries, who settled in the area, spread terror among a locality still fearful of a new Viking invasion.

In 1658, the Cromwellians granted the Company fresh Letters Patent and provided a new conveyance over the proportion. Paul Canning was granted a new forty-one year lease at £270 per annum after paying an entry 'fine' of £500. In 1662, Charles II issued further Letters Patent to confirm the Company's restoration to all its former lands. Canning, who was unmarried, assigned his interest to his nephew George, son of his brother William. George's son, another George, obtained a further twenty-one year extension in 1705 at a rental of £250 per annum after paying a 'fine' of £1,900. Yet, on expiry in 1726, the Company did not extend the lease to George's son, Stratford Canning,[194] and, in 1729, it repurchased from him the tithes at Agivey for £1,155. This ended the family's Ironmonger connection, but it retained Garvagh, which it continued to expand well into the 18th Century. (See Canning family tree, pages 244-5)

The Company had no inclination to take the lease back in hand and, in 1725, after arranging a survey conducted by John Sloane, it granted a new forty-one

---

[194] Stratford Canning was the grandfather by his eldest son, George, of George Canning, the Prime Minister who died in office in 1827, and by his second son, Paul, of George, 1st Lord Garvagh of Garvagh. (See family tree, pages 244-5)

year lease to Leckey, Macky (or Mackie), Conningham, and Craighead. In 1765, before the lease's expiry, the Company again arranged a survey undertaken by James Crow and Thomas Marsh. When the lease ended in 1767, it conducted an auction for its renewal, which was won by William Alexander. Yet Alexander failed to pay the full entry 'fine' of £21,000 and it was re-let for sixty-one years and three lives to Josias Du Pré, 'a gentleman who had acquired a fortune in the Civil Service of the East India Company'.[c] Du Pré was Alexander's extremely wealthy brother-in-law, who seems to have stepped in to help him out. Although he paid the entry 'fine' and an annual rental of £600, there is no record that he visited the proportion. Slade was later very critical of this, saying: 'The Irishman who cultivates his soil might with justice observe that he derives no protection by such a line of conduct.'[d] Du Pré's lease ran until 1828 and three lives. He named these as his wife's son, Josias Du Pré Porcher (who became a Member of Parliament), his wife's nephew, Nathaniel Alexander (later Archbishop of Armagh) and himself. The lease duly expired on the death of the third life, Nathaniel Alexander, in 1840. Well before this, in 1813, Du Pré's son, James, had sold the remainder of the lease to the Beresford and Hill families, but they provided no discernible improvement for the tenants.

The Parish Church of St. Gaury, Aghadowey After the little church at Agivey was destroyed in the 1641 rebellion, Aghadowey Parish Church on church lands just outside the Ironmongers' proportion was adopted by its Protestant settlers.

During the period of these leaseholds, very little building work took place, but Slade saw the proportion as 'desirably situated'. A Roman-Catholic Church was built at Mullaghinch in 1760, but, by 1853, was very dilapidated.[195] The Anglican church at Agivey was ruined in the 1641 rebellion, although it continued to be used as a cemetery until the 19th Century. In 1797, the 'pretty Georgian-style' Parish Church of St Gaurie was built at Aghadowey by the Earl-Bishop of Derry, although its spire collapsed in 1828, but it stands on church land adjacent to the proportion. A chancel, designed by Joseph Welland, was built in the 1850s and was no doubt provided by the Ecclesiastical Commissioners. By 1812, there was also a Dissenters' Meeting House at Killeague.

While he was still Agent for The Irish Society, Slade became the Master Ironmonger in 1803. This caused a revival of the Company's interest in its Irish Estates, resulting in several visits. In 1812, Archibald Hamilton of Dublin was commissioned to provide *'A General View of the Leading Circumstances Connected with each Townland on the Manor of Lizard in the County of Londonderry in Ireland; the Estate of the Worshipful Company of Ironmongers of London, 1812'* (not a title likely to fill its readers with great enthusiasm!). He noted that 'Agivey was capable of improvement', hardly a surprising conclusion, as there were only a few dwellings constructed of stone or brick with thatched roofs and no remaining cabins. He was very critical of the landlords, and James Du Pré sold out in the following year. Yet Hamilton also noted 'the admirable situations and good land on the estate'.[e] In 1823, the *Reports of the visits of Mr. William Parnell ... and of Mr. Robert Westwood* [both members of the Company] ... *to the Manor of Lizard* 'give a depressing picture' of high rents and subsistance living. At this time the rent roll totalled £4,826 11s. 11d., but arrears were £2,356 9s. 9d. The land was being over-worked, but without security of tenure, there was no incentive for tenants to make improvements. The inhabitants lived in penury on several 'forty shilling freeholds', wholly dependent on their potato crop. A twenty acre farm was considered large. Without a village or town on the proportion, the nearest inn was at Garvagh. Sampson's calls to create a town at the heart of the proportion had gone unheeded.

After building several schools at his own expense, Sampson encouraged the Company to show its benevolence. The inhabitants greeted Parnell and Westwood warmly, hoping that the Company would seek to regain direct control like other Companies. It is clear that the Minor Companies associated with the Ironmongers were also concerned that enough was not being done. In 1833, the Barber Surgeons commissioned Adam Murray to make a visit from London and to undertake a general survey and report. He noted the locality's subsistence lifestyle and described typical houses as being on one storey, built of stone or brick and thatched. Although structurally sound, they were generally very dirty.

---

[195] It was not until 1898, when the Company's interest in the proportion was in the course of being sold, that a new Roman-Catholic Church, dedicated to *Our Lady of the Assumption*, was rebuilt on the site of the derelict 1760 church.

Although the lease held by the Hills and Beresfords continued, during the 1820s, the Company started to arrange some tree planting. In 1830, Robert Sibley, another London Surveyor, prepared a general map of the proportion showing that a crash programme of tree planting was still needed. It also showed significant areas of bog-land. In 1832, the Company appointed a full-time Agent, Edward Oseland on a salary of £400 per annum. Oseland 'introduced tenants to the rules of elementary hygiene and of good husbandry'[f] and encouraged them to repair and glaze their houses. Slate started to replace thatch. Although Oseland achieved much, the reports of the Company's 1836 and 1838 deputations describe it as neglected and 'down-at-heel'.[g] Bog-land was being used to provide bleach greens, but improper exploitation resulted in wastage. Although there was no shortage of peat, limestone, chalkstone and ironstone for soil improvement, poor agricultural practices left the land exhausted, so that tenants needed guidance.

On the expiry of the lease in 1840, the Ironmongers were at last able to take back control and commissioned Sibley to prepare a second map, which 'showed Townlands, roads, buildings, and other details to a high degree of accuracy'.[h] They quickly 'established standards of development control, maintenance, management and cleanliness that incurred the wrath of the tenantry'.[i] These made Oseland unpopular locally, despite his worth. Given their large number of associated Minor Companies, there was some difficulty in persuading tenants of his authority.

The 1841 deputation found that several houses were still ruinous, but it was impressed with experiments to drain mountainous boggy land being undertaken by Henry Anderson, Agent for a nearby landlord, Sir Robert Ferguson. On the back of Anderson's experiments, the Company started to promote land drainage. Yet 'his innovations met with considerable resistance'.[j] Anderson persisted, and, in two years, he was growing oats on land he had reclaimed. This encouraged the Company to develop his ideas. In 1846, finding most houses still to be very poor, the deputation offered loans to encourage the erection of better farm buildings. It also acquired land at Ruskey to provide a house for the Agent. When the famine struck, the poor were employed on general improvement works, including lime-washing of cottages. In 1849, a cholera epidemic took its toll, but the Company organised soup kitchens and other relief, and provided soap to improve hygiene. By amalgamating farms and encouraging emigration, rural poverty was gradually overcome. In 1847, it established a brick and tile works at Agivey, 'partly to make land drainage universal and cheap, and partly to help the local economy'.[k] [196] When Oseland died in 1849, Anderson was appointed Agent at £400 per annum. Bog bailiffs and an Agriculturalist, John Selfridge, were also appointed. Selfridge proved to be quite an architect, providing designs for a new tile kiln and a house for one of the tenants.

---

[196] Twelve years later it was attacked by an arsonist.

In 1853, the arrival of a railway from Castledawson heralded a new era. The deputation arriving from London was escorted by Anderson to each townland. 'The Londoners were impressed by the goodwill, contentment and improvements evident on all sides.'[l] There were twelve rudimentary schools on the estate, and the deputation agreed to install wooden floors in them, as the children were suffering from cold and damp in winter. The Company also repaired 'chapels'. Yet the tenants' poor maintenance of their homes remained a problem. Anderson was told to refuse any applications for assistance from tenants until their houses were put in order and properly cleansed.[m] He progressively introduced better standards of hygiene and agricultural methods, but there was still a long way to go and the 'nettle of how to encourage tenants to improve farms was never really grasped'.[n] The old problem of improvements allowing the landlord to increase rents on renewal left tenants without incentive to do anything.

Lizard Manor built in 1861 as a home for the Ironmongers' Agent Henry Anderson Sr., but he died before its completion.

In 1854, John Bouse and Company of Dublin prepared a new map of the estate, but the Ironmongers appear to have become despondent about progress and, with the great Famine over, they stopped grants for road building. In 1859, Anderson arranged for his son (also Henry) to become joint Agent with him, despite him having an addiction to gambling. Anderson Sr. wrote to the Company that he had suffered 'very serious losses to pay for his son' and had been 'obliged' to sell his house and estates.[o] He pointed out that the Ironmongers' was the only proportion not to provide a 'substantial residence' for its Agent. The Company acted quickly, appointing John Mullins, the District Surveyor of Streatham and Brixton, to prepare plans. After being sent to Ireland,

Anderson Sr.'s revisions were accepted. Lizard Manor was erected in 1861 with offices being added in 1864. Sadly Anderson Sr. never saw its completion, as he died in Edinburgh in 1860, but a fine memorial to him was placed in Aghadowey churchyard. Following his death, a deputation arrived from London, but with building work still in progress, its members stayed at the *Clothworkers' Arms* at Coleraine. After interviewing tenants, they 'noted the improved morale of all the population',[p] and Anderson Jr. was appointed sole Agent.

Memorial to Henry Anderson Sr. at Aghadowey churchyard As the Ironmongers' Agent, he was a pioneer in land drainage, despite local resistance, but it resulted in 'goodwill, contentment and improvements evident on all sides'.

The 1863 deputation was the first to stay at the new Manor House, where it was 'civilly received' by Mr. and Mrs. Anderson, who were in the process of laying out gardens. The house was much admired and was considered a great credit to the builder and Anderson's taste. Anderson Jr. had also erected substantial farm buildings at his own expense and was seen to be encouraging improvements throughout the proportion. 'New roads, public works and agricultural experiment were being implemented',[q] and the tile works at Aghadowey were producing agricultural drains in addition to building materials and floor tiles, all of which were in great demand.

In 1873, a deficiency of over £10,000 was found in the estate's accounts and Anderson Jr. was found to be seriously in debt. Although he apologised and admitted having lived well beyond his means after spending far too much on his farm, which had not proved successful, this would hardly have accounted for the extent of his losses. There was also concern for his health, but the nature of his condition is not recorded.[197] He was unable to repay the missing sum and was declared bankrupt. The Company took over his chattels with an estimated value of £1,500, and seems to have recovered £7,000 from the proceeds of four life assurance policies, which had been provided as surety. Among the chattels acquired were two magnificent salvers with the Ironmongers' coat of arms, which had been provided to the Andersons by the tenants as a house-warming present on their occupation of Lizard Manor. These salvers which now take pride of place at Ironmongers' Hall, are engraved on the back with the names of all the tenants on the estate. This gift suggests that concerns about the Company's management as landlords was political rather than real. Anderson Jr. was replaced as Agent by a connection of the Du Pré family, Captain Edmond Robert Francis Stronge, previously Agent for the Clothworkers, who remained in office until the end of the Company's involvement.

In 1874, all schools, except at Killure and Ballywilliam, remained under the Company's control, but housing in remoter hilly areas was still poorly maintained. The deputation was pleased to note the continuing success of the tile works, which was providing bricks and tiles in large quantities to support the rebuilding programme. In 1876, its boiler exploded, allegedly through the engineer's carelessness, killing eight men. The Company made generous provision for their dependants, but the site was abandoned, and a new factory established elsewhere.

By 1880, improvement in Aghadowey's agriculture was being demonstrated at an annual horticultural exhibition held at Lizard Manor, but rumours that the Company was planning to sell its proportion 'cast a cloud on proceedings'.[r] Like other Companies, its position was greatly worsened by the Land Acts and it had to apply to the Court of Chancery to establish the claims of some of its associated Minor Companies. Although they made proposals to the other twelve Great Companies for the formation of an 'Ulster Association' to promote their general welfare and defend their interests, this came to nothing. In 1884, the Company and its associates signed a deed agreeing to sell their estates, and, in 1889, the long process began. Each associated Company seems to have been involved in selling parts of the estate, but the proceeds were pooled and shared proportionately. Most of the land had been sold by 1896, but the total was not finalised until 1903. By this time, the sale had generated £56,160, which included the proceeds of Anderson's life assurance policies.[s] Expenses associated with the sale amounted to £2,740 1s. 8d.[t] With the Company having a 45.2 per cent stake in the proportion, this suggests that it recovered £24,145 net of expenses.

---

[197] There seems to have been some sympathy for Anderson as the Company was continuing to pay him a small annuity until well into the 20th Century.

Unlike many other Companies, the Ironmongers have left no proud legacy of handsome towns and houses (other than Lizard Manor). It was never minded to devote large amounts of its capital to building works, but it focused its attention on improving the lot of its tenants. In this, it seems to have been moderately successful, thanks to the industry of its Agents. Whatever the concerns of its associated Minor Companies, in the final analysis, they provided the Company with a magnificent monteith and two ornamental silver 'pilgim' bottles in recognition of the work done on their behalf. These remain some of the Company's most treasured possessions.

Chapter 49

Vintners

When Lawrence Cox was appointed Agent in 1658, he realised that Sir John Clotworthy was stripping the woodland. Clotworthy remained the Company Farmer despite having 'acquired [his lease over] the proportion illegally and [being] less than satisfactory in terms of the future welfare of the Company's assets'.[a] It is clear that his political influence in assisting in Charles II's restoration was too important to ignore and it gained for him the Viscountcy of Massereene. In 1669, he was succeeded as Viscount by his son-in-law, Sir John Skeffington, who renewed the tenancy in 1673 (although the Company's seal was not affixed until 1679) by taking a sixty-one year lease at an annual rental of £200, and after paying an entry fine of £2,000. When he died in 1695, his son, Clotworthy Skeffington, 3rd Viscount Massereene took over the lease, but fell into arrears of rent. By then, the Company had appointed William Conolly, later Speaker of the Irish House of Commons, as Agent, and much litigation arose, when he seized possession of the estate from Massereene. On Massereene's death in 1714, Conolly became chief tenant, 'and built up a sound financial and social base to further his political career'.[b] In 1729, he tried to negotiate the purchase of the estate for £6,000 and a continuing rent of £200 'with two fat bucks', but he died before these terms could be agreed. When Sloane was commissioned to undertake a survey, Conolly's nephew, also William, was obliged to increase the offer to £15,000. Although an agreement was signed, completion was delayed until 1737, at which time, Thomas Conolly, William Jr's son, obtained the proportion in perpetuity, and the Vintners and their associates[198] ceased to be involved. Eventually it was demised to four tenants-in-common, the Marquess of Lothian, the Earl of Strafford, the Earl of Clancarty, and Colonel Conolly, all distant connections of Thomas Conolly by marriage. They did little to improve the lot of the inhabitants but built some 'cleanly neat houses' at Bellaghy, where their Agent resided in the 'Manor House' (not a building of great architectural distinction). The Irish Society regretted that there were 'no public institutions of any kind'. Perhaps the proportion was lucky to avoid a visit from Slade. Unfortunately the Vintners'

---

[198] When the Woodmongers were dissolved as a Livery Company in 1668, the Vintners bought out their interest. In 1740 they also acquired the Weavers' share.

building records have not survived, and, as they 'lost interest in their lands at an early stage, there is a scarcity of material'.[c]

In 1785, the Earl-Bishop of Derry took it upon himself to re-edify Bellaghy Castle on the site of the old Vintners' bawn. This was renamed Ballyscullion House, and it became the model for Ickworth in Suffolk. Ballyscullion House was never completed and it was dismantled in 1813. Its portico 'now graces the front of the church of St. George in Belfast's High Street'. In 1794, the Earl-Bishop built a new Parish Church at Bellaghy to replace the remains of the one built by Baptist Jones. Like so many of his church designs, it was given an octagonal spire. Only the tower and spire now remain in their original form as the body of the church underwent substantial alterations in the 1860s.

Chapter 50

Clothworkers

When the Manor was re-created in 1663, McClelland's lease was demised to Captain William Jackson, who received the advowson of Dunboe a year later. He was granted a new fifty-one year lease to 1720 at £100 per annum after paying a 'fine' of £1,000. Meanwhile some of the associated Minor Companies were bought out. In 1675, the Clothworkers paid the Butchers £130 for their interest, and, in 1680, the Upholders sold for £40. In 1727, a Declaration of Trust confirmed that the Clothworkers and Merchant Taylors would manage the investment on the remaining Minor Companies' behalf.

St. Paul's Parish Church of Dunboe, Articlave The church was moved from near Downhill in 1691. It was repaired and altered in the 1830s with the help of a substantial Clothworkers' grant.

By 1666, the old Parish Church at Dunboe was again in poor repair, and plans were made to build a new one more conveniently located at Articlave. In

1670, Jackson made over one Irish acre from his freehold at Lower Articlave[199] to the Bishop of Derry and his successors as a site for a new church and a house for the minister. The church, which was completed in 1691, is a 'pretty building of the utmost simplicity' with a tower at its west end.[a] It was repaired and altered in the 1830s with the help of a substantial Clothworkers' grant. Only a few rubble walls in an overgrown graveyard mark what remains of the original pre-plantation structure at Dunboe. In 1785, the Earl-Bishop of Derry built his imposing home, Downhill,[200] next to the original Dunboe Church. On his death, Downhill was passed to his cousin, The Rev. Sir Henry Hervey Aston Bruce, 1st Bart, but the house collapsed and Bruce's son built an Italianate mansion on a site nearby.

The gates of Downhill These imposing gates with the ruins in the background are all that remain of the Earl-Bishop's masterpiece.

Although some damage arose during the Williamite Wars, the 18th Century saw a gradual return to prosperity for the proportion. With the Company out of sight in London, some rack-renting seems to have occurred, but, on the expiry of Jackson's lease in 1720, it was renewed by Richard Jackson for a further fifty-one years to 1771 at £100 per annum after he had paid a 'fine' of £5,750. It is apparent that this took some negotiation as the new lease was not signed until 1729. In 1770 a further lease was granted for another sixty-one years and three lives to Richard Jackson and G. Crompe at £600 per annum after they agreed to pay a colossal 'fine' of £28,900. On Slade's visit in 1802, he was aware of the

---

[199] This had previously been acquired by his predessessors and himself from the Clothworkers.
[200] Downhill was the model for Ickworth in Suffolk.[e]

enormous entry fine paid by Richard Jackson. This had caused rents to be raised to a level that forced 'almost total emigration' to America by tenants 'seething with indignation'. Yet Slade covered himself by saying: 'Mr. Jackson was considered as a man of the greatest honour and integrity, and that his memory is highly respected by all who knew him.'[b]

In 1804, this was transferred to George Jackson and J. K. Harryngton, who were both absentee landlords, but, in 1831, Lesley Alexander acquired their interest when the lease was close to expiry. In fact, it continued until the death of the third life, Sir George Jackson in 1840, but the Company had great difficulty in recovering control. Jackson and Harryngton had been in severe financial difficulties and this may have contributed to the Company's decision not to extend the lease. The Irish Society was aware that all was not well. By 1820, both the Clothworkers and Merchant Taylors, having listened to Sampson, were aware of the subtenants' problems. Even larger tenant farmers faced difficulties.[c] The Companies realised that they would need to take charge, if the proportion was to be managed on 'sound principles'. Oseland, who was to become the Ironmongers' Agent in 1832, wrote to the Clothworkers advocating road building, tree planting and a massive programme of housebuilding as 'imperative improvements' and long overdue. He was no doubt hopeful of employment.

By the time of the lease expiry in 1840, Alexander had expended large sums of money for very little return during his nine year tenure, but the Companies were determined to stick to their plan to recover control. It did not help him that the Clothworkers' Surveyor, Edward Driver, who arrived from London to conduct a new survey, estimated dilapidations at £5,000. After much negotiation, Alexander agreed to pay £1,250 and to waive all rent arrears. After reaching this accommodation, a deputation of Clothworkers and Merchant Taylors arrived to review the estate. They set up a new Board of Management, in which the Clothworkers retained a majority of one. Driver's 1840 survey superseded one arranged by Alexander in 1837 and was considered a 'thorough job'. It 'established a sound basis for the assessment of new rents'.[d] Although the tenants called for the new rent calculations to be reduced, 'the Companies refused as they had taken sound professional advice'.[e] No underletting or subdivision was to be permitted, and all new building work required the Companies' approval in writing, thus providing them with control over design. In 1834, Driver had shown that there were 1,855 Anglicans, 2,668 Roman-Catholics, 10,688 Presbyterians and 36 Dissenters on the proportion. The high number of Presbyterians was no doubt a legacy of McClelland's ability to attract Scottish settlers in the 17th Century. The total rent roll was £6,100 5s. 4d.

An Irish Estate Office was set up at premises in Killowen, with Charles J. Knox being appointed Agent. The Manor House on the site of the old castle, then known as Jackson Hall, had been let to a Mrs. Maxwell for life. It took some 'financial inducement' to persuade her to move to make it the Clothworkers' headquarters. The first major projects involved land drainage, including the embankment of slob-lands by the shore and embanking the Bann on the Killowen side so that it could be developed for building. Both these projects received The Irish Society's consent. Sampson's advice was heeded;

> implements to facilitate the drainage of wet lands were to be provided by the Company, and flax-seed, clover, and grass-seed of good quality were also made available to tenants at cost, or even free where appropriate.[f]

New roads were proposed and money was set aside for planting trees, which Knox was to supervise. Controls over hunting game were imposed. New regulations protected topsoil and boglands as there was evidence that land was being worked out, and 'subjected to erosion through lack of enclosure'.

The Parish Church of Formoyle This 'simple' but 'dignified' Gothic style church in its remote setting was built in 1841 to the design of a Clothworker freeman, Herbert Williams.

In 1841, the Companies were approached by the Archdeacon of Derry, Thomas Bewley Monsell, to provide a site for a new parish church and school house at Formoyle in a remote mountainous region further south. His extremely 'ill-tempered' approach provoked 'acrimonious' replies, but land was eventually granted. The Church was designed by a Clothworker freeman, Herbert Williams, in a 'simple' but 'dignified' Gothic style, and was completed at the Companies' expense in 1844.[g] Angell (see below) described it as being 'built on the horns of the moon'.[h] It was the first Parish Church actually situated on the estate, although those at Articlave and Killowen were both very close (and easier to access). Money was also provided for the adjacent school, and the incumbent was given assistance to build a Glebe House with a small annual grant for upkeep. This was completed in time for the visit of the 1849 deputation, which included Samuel Angell,[201] the Clothworkers' Surveyor appointed in 1824, who was to become closely involved with the development of the estate. By then, there were 'good plantations of young trees' round Formoyle, which were being expanded and developed.[i][202] (Nearly 100,000 trees were planted at Dartress and Ballywildrick alone.)

The former Clothworkers' Arms Hotel Built to replace Davock's Hotel in 1844, it formed the focal point of Angell's scheme for Waterside at Killowen across the bridge from Coleraine.

With the Companies having regained possession of the proportion, Knox's and Driver's first project was to develop Killowen, which was renamed Waterside. Driver proposed the building of a new bridge across the Bann to link it to Coleraine. Although this had caused earlier contention, pressure from both The Irish Society and the Companies resulted in a design by Stewart Gordon, the County Surveyor, being approved in a spirit of optimism for an 'age of expansion in Ireland'.[j] It was a major undertaking; the road had to be raised and widened on the Killowen side, resulting in the demolition of *Davock's Hotel* and other buildings belonging to the Companies. The contractor was also required to embank the slob-land so that it could be reclaimed for development. In 1843, the rebuilding project, which included a new hotel, was agreed. Driver advised

[201] Angell was also surveyor to the Sadlers' Company, and in 1831 became a London District Surveyor with his work being exhibited at the Royal Academy. He had previously designed the Company's new Hall.
[202] Yet even by 1870, the trees at Formoyle had a long way to go.

them to avoid the 'errors of ornament and decoration committed at Moneymore and Draperstown', which were overly ostentatious.[k]

Angell was appointed to design Waterside's first phase, and he shared Driver's view that the buildings needed 'more business and less show'. As at the Ironmongers, a tileworks was established to provide bricks, but its primary purpose was to manufacture agricultural drains. Designs for a new hotel next to the bridge were soon agreed, and building began in 1844. When completed two years later, the *Clothworkers' Arms* was a 'plain and dignified pile' with stabling at the rear.[l] In 1847, the demolition of poor housing in Captain Street, Waterside, made way for sites so that individuals could build houses, which were required to conform to an overall pattern. By 1849, two houses had already been built, but Angell's scheme was not completed until the following year. Much of the area round the *Clothworkers' Arms* remained vacant for some while, and the deputation was anxious that building work should begin as soon as possible to 'raise the tone and appearance of Waterside',[m] as the contrast between the new hotel and the existing 'mean' housing was 'painful'.[n] Angell took great care over each design. He amended plans drawn up by a local architect 'to provide better accommodation and more serene and refined elevations'.[o] He 'stressed the importance of balance and symmetry of scale' on each side of the road at the bridge, so that 'the entrance to the Clothworkers' estate would be dignified and in the best taste'.[p] He designed the Corner House, completed in 1850, as a large building opposite the *Clothworkers' Arms* to provide 'balanced, plain, classical elevations'.[q] A further three houses were erected on the south side of Waterside to add to Angell's facade, and the Companies contributed £500 towards the £924 cost. All this building work was completed in 1853 under Gordon's supervision. By 1860, the new deputation was able to report that Waterside presented a 'respectible and business-like appearance'.[r] The new gardens, laid out on the south side, received much praise. The demolition of more 'unsavoury' houses was agreed, and the Surveyor was asked to provide plans to replace them with shops and housing.

There were calls for 'places of worship, decent housing, for schools, roads and improvements to land'.[s] In 1845, Driver designed a new road to Articlave and others followed, particularly when road building offered employment to those left destitute by the potato famine. In 1849, the Companies contributed to the cost of improving the Bann's navigation channel to the sea. A proposed railway line and station were also discussed. In 1852, the careful design of the frontage of Waterside nearly came to nothing when the track of the Londonderry and Coleraine Railway was scheduled to pass in front of the *Clothworkers' Arms* at street level. Despite the Companies' strong resistance, this route was still being discussed in 1853, but was eventually moved back from the river.

There were numerous grants for charitable purposes. These included plans for a school house at Glenahorry-Ballyhacket, a grant of twenty guineas for Ballinascreen Parish Church on the Drapers' proportion, money to repair the Presbyterian Meeting House at Dunboe, subscriptions to the Articlave Reading

Society, subsidies for students to attend the Agricultural College at Templemoyle and a grant to complete the splendid Roman-Catholic Perpendicular Gothic church at Waterside. The 1844 deputation reported that the new school built by the Companies at Ballinteer was 'well arranged'. Although there was no requirement under the Poor Law to establish a dispensary, they supported the existing one at Articlave. With other Companies, they contributed £25 towards the cost of rebuilding Coleraine Parish Church and, in 1860, its stained-glass, emblazoned with the arms of both the Clothworkers and The Irish Society, which they funded jointly, was much admired. Small donations were also made to schools and distressed tenants. So great was the munificence, that the Merchant Taylors began worrying about expense. In 1844, they started negotiations to sell their interest, but it came to nothing.

The 18th Century Manor House[203] on the site of the old castle was 'spruced up' to provide a suitable residence for the Agent (but was let to a Captain Rich for a short period). A stone plaque depicting the Clothworkers' motto, which originated from the castle rebuilt after 1641, was set into its walls. When completed in 1850, it was divided into two residences, with one becoming the Agent's house and offices, and the other intended for future deputations. The 1849 deputation stayed at the *Clothworkers' Arms,* which they found 'clean and well-managed' under Mr. Davock's continuing management, but its custom had declined since the *Causeway Hotel* had been opened in County Antrim.

In 1846, a Government Model School in a Tudor style was designed by George Wilkinson, architect to the Poor Law Commissioners. By 1849, this had almost been completed at a cost of £3,000. It was similar to other model schools built at the time, and the 1860 deputation much admired its prominent location. In 1850-51, attempts were made to persuade the Companies to support the building of Magee College on their estate, but, in the end, a site in Londonderry, where much of the money had been raised, was preferred. Yet the Coleraine Court House and brideswell (jail) designed by Gordon and approved by the Grand Jury in 1852 was located in Waterside. This 'dignified and imposing' building with its Doric portico was completed by 1860. (It is now a restaurant.)

In 1853, the Companies supported the building of an Academical Institution on the site originally proposed for Magee College, and plans in a 'severe Classical style' by Isaac Farrell of Dublin were sent to London for approval. Although a large site for this 'substantial' building was identified, it was delayed by the Crimean War, but was completed at a cost of £4,000 in 1860 when the Master Clothworker attended its inauguration. It was expected to 'raise the tone of the youth in the area',[t] and the Companies agreed to provide a scholarship. Sites for new villas were laid out near the school and the college.

---

[203] The Manor was demolished in 1970 to make way for the County Hall.

The Court House and Bridewell, Killowen Built to designs by Stewart Gordon in 1852, this is now a restaurant.

Coleraine Academical Institution, Killowen This was designed by Isaac Farrell of Dublin on a site granted by the Clothworkers. It was inaugurated in 1860 with the Master being present. The Company endowed a Scholarship.

Sir Henry Hervey Bruce 3rd Bart From his home at Downhill, he supported the Clothworkers in building a parish church at Castlerock and in 1870 acquired the whole of their estate for £150,000.
Sir William Charles Ross, watercolour on ivory, Private Collection; Photo © Christie's Images, Bridgeman Images

The arrival of the railway led the 1849 deputation to realise that Castlerock, near Dunboe, offered an ideal location for a north coast holiday resort. When its members visited the site, Sir Henry Hervey Bruce 3rd Bart. placed his pew in Dunboe Parish Church at Articlave at their disposal, and 'Lady Bruce provided excellent luncheons at Downhill on more than one occasion'.[u] After seeing its potential, 'Angell was instructed to draw up a development plan so that any building proposal could fit in with an overall scheme'.[v] He had already designed a house there for Edward Greer in the previous year, and this was erected in 1849-50. (It is now called Cliff House.) He made similar plans for Love's Hotel, which was started in the 1850s, but completed ten years later,[204] and designed two other houses there. In 1849, he also built a stone bathing lodge with cubicles nestling in the rocks. His final scheme for the layout of 'salubrious' residences was approved in 1853.[w] By 1860, eight of them had been built, and plans were set in motion to add a church and hotel. Much of Castlerock's building work was undertaken by William Warke, who was also a principal tenant.

---

[204] This was re-edified by Porter as the *Castlerock Hotel* in 1869-70.

The bathing lodge, Castlerock This was designed by Angell in 1884 as part of the plan by the Company to create a north coast resort.

The deputation of 1860, which had included both Angell and his successor as the Clothworkers' Surveyor, Henry William Porter, faced a rather easier journey to Ireland than that of the Fishmongers in 1820. It left London on 19 July, catching the night-steamer from Holyhead to Dublin. It then took the train to Coleraine arriving at the *Clothworkers' Arms* following a two-day journey from London. The deputation visited many of the schools (as did succeeding deputations) and was pleased to attend a service at Formoyle Parish Church. It was delighted with everything it saw. With Porter having taken over most of Angell's duties, he again visited the proportion in 1863 when there were moves to rebuild Killowen Parish Church on its existing site in a 'simplified Decorated style' to designs by J. G. Ferguson. In 1870, £500 was provided and it was completed in 1875, finished in 'unprepossessing basalt with sandstone dressings'.[x] It does not stand comparison to the more imposing Perpendicular Gothic Roman-Catholic church of St John on the hill behind, to which Ferguson added a bellcote, chancel, robing room and side porch. Despite all the continuing building work at Waterside and Castlerock, the Company's brick and tile yard with its 'inexhaustible supply of clay' was meeting demand for all its major works.

St. John's Parish Church, Killowen By comparison to the nearby Roman Catholic Church, this is a somewhat unimposing structure. It was built to designs by J. G. Ferguson from 1860-75 on the site of the previous parish church.

St. John's Roman-Catholic Church, Killowen This splendid perpendicular gothic church was designed in 1834 by one of the Kirkpatrick family and was built with Clothworker support.

In 1866, the deputation found itself negotiating with the Bishop of Derry, the Archdeacon and Bruce at Downhill to build the proposed Parish Church at Castlerock to serve the growing population of holiday visitors. Porter prepared plans in an Early English Gothic style, and Christ Church was constructed with a fine 'rich and glowing' interior and 'exceptional' furnishings.[y] Despite it being outside the Companies' estate, they contributed generously to the £2,100 cost, for which the Church Commissioners provided £1,400. Yet the deputation was shocked to find men and women bathing 'promiscuously', and, for the sake of decency, it advocated the purchase of bathing machines. It also provided rustic seats and shelter in forested areas so that tourists could enjoy their natural beauty. A viewing platform at Ballyhacket provided 'a breathtaking and unforgettable vista'[z] long before the National Parks movement encouraged such facilities. In 1868, a site was chosen for a new Presbyterian Church at Castlerock, and, again, a 'liberal donation' was provided. Although this had been designed locally, Porter made substantial alterations. The 1870 deputation much admired its newly completed Gothic Hall and allocated a site for a manse. A tower was added in 1885.

Christ Church, Castlerock This early English gothic-style church was designed by Frederick William Porter in 1866 to accommodate the growing population of holiday makers.

In 1869-70, coastguard cottages were also built. By this time, Knox had died and the company appointed Captain Edmond Robert Francis Stronge (he later became Agent to the Ironmongers), to replace him as Agent. Stronge found the records in a mess and was disappointed to find the Agent's House next to the railway station, rendering 'it undesireable as a residence'.[aa] Yet, in 1868, he moved in and continued to manage the proportion in a 'businesslike' manner.[bb] He took a keen interest in Castlerock, and organised the planting of Bent grass

(Agristis Stolonifera) and Pine trees *(Pinus Maritima)* to control soil erosion and provide shelter, but the pines did not do well, despite the thriving woodland further inland.

The 1866 deputation requested that the bathroom and lavatory arrangements at the *Clothworkers' Arms* should be improved (no doubt from first hand experience). It also asked Porter to make good the defects in some of the Waterside houses built in 1854. The deputation called for cases of gross overcrowding to be brought to the Companies' attention, so that better accommodation could be offered. Money was set aside for lodging houses as required by statute. Yet it still proved necessary to evict tenants for failure to pay rents. By this time, the Companies had followed others in building exemplar Model Cottages, and many new residences had sprung up all over the proportion. Those built in 1870 at Formoyle to the designs of Thomas Craig, the Companies' new Agriculturalist, received much favourable comment locally and won the Provincial Gold Medal of the Royal Agricultural Society of Ireland. The deputation admired the 'spectacular improvements to the hedgerows and plantations'[cc] achieved by Craig and agreed to build him a house. After his success at Formoyle, he was asked to design more labourers' cottages with guidance from Porter. Both Stronge and Craig recommended the enclosure of cottage gardens to provide allotments and orchards.

The 1870 deputation was proud of the Companies' achievements. 'The estate was thriving, the woodlands were maturing, the buildings were smart and well kept.'[dd] Stronge had followed Miller's practice on the Drapers' estate of building whitewashed stone gate piers with new iron gates to access newly fenced and enclosed agricultural land.

In 1866, the Merchant Taylors started to plan a major project in London to purchase the Charter House and rebuild a new Charterhouse School at Godalming. To provide finance for this, they hoped to sell their interest in the proportion. In 1870, there was an opportunity to sell to Bruce of Downhill, resulting in the Clothworkers also agreeing to sell. On 16 May 1871, the whole estate was sold for £150,000, of which the Merchant Taylors received £33,307 1s. 10d. towards the £91,600 cost of their school project. Quite extraordinarily, there were no arrears of rent at this time. Although the Clothworkers set up a trust to fund scholarships at Coleraine's Academical Institution, it disengaged completely from its former interest in Ulster. Their timing was remarkably astute in the light of all the anti-landlord agitation which followed in the 1870s. Their investment, during the thirty-one years that it was under their control, had paid off handsomely. The estate's agricultural land was properly drained, well planted with trees and properly enclosed. They left a good supply of model schools and cottages. Fine churches of all denominations had been built and assisted, not to mention a first-class hotel at Waterside.

Chapter 51

The Honourable The Irish Society

The arms of The Irish Society From the stained glass at Londonderry Guildhall.

It is Londonderry Cathedral that is recognised as the lasting memorial to the efforts of the Londoners in Ulster, despite it having to face much rebuilding and alteration since the laying of its foundation stone in 1628, so that little of the original structure remains. Following the siege in 1689, the roof needed extensive repair after its use as a platform for cannon. In 1740, it was damaged by fire. In 1778, the Earl-Bishop of Derry rebuilt its stone spire, surmounting it with a large gilt ball and weather vane, at a cost of £1,000. Unfortunately, the weight proved too much for the supporting arches and, in 1802, it was taken down to be replaced by a shorter one begun in 1803. The Irish Society contributed £200 and a further £2,400 was raised by Bishop Knox and local citizens. In 1813, eight new bells were added and, in 1818, funds were raised for the roof to be slated. At the same time, a cross was placed on the new spire. More elaborate and 'rather good' external refurbishment took place in the 19th

Century.[a] Unfortunately, Welland's interior was not so felicitous. He ripped out the 18th Century galleries from the aisles, panelled the entrance porch, and laid encaustic tiles on the floor. Most drastic of all, he destroyed the Georgian box-pews in the nave and aisles, designed and erected pews, poppy-heads, and lectern, and added a huge window at the east end.[b] To achieve this, the east end had to be remodelled, and its original round towers were crowned with 19th Century ornamentation. In 1885-87, Ferguson extended the nave into the old chancel, and built a new chancel reincorporating Welland's east window. He replaced the plaster vaulted ceilings of the old nave and aisles with trusses in a Perpendicular style. A new pulpit, organ, reredos and heating system were also added. In 1911, a new roof was again required, and, in 1925, the crenellations were renewed. In 1933, The Irish Society provided the churchyard with new wrought iron entrance gates to commemorate the cathedral's tercentenary. Almost continuous restoration has followed, and its 'stupendous' array of funerary monuments, in both the cathedral and churchyard, are often maintained by the Society.

The interior, Londonderry Cathedral looking towards Welland's fine window at the east end.

Londonderry Cathedral With its foundation stone laid in 1628, it remains the Londoners' lasting monument in Ireland, but it has been much altered and rebuilt since then.

The wrought iron entrance gates, Londonderry Cathedral provided by The Irish Society to commemorate the Cathedral's tercentenary in 1933.

The City of Londonderry has faced three major sieges; in 1641, when attacked by Irish insurgents, in 1648, when it faced Royalist forces and, in 1689, when besieged for one hundred and five days by the Jacobites. Much of the original was destroyed, including its arcaded Market House, the Cathedral's tower and roof, and much of the walls and gates. Reconstruction took time, but the old layout was retained. In 1690, Captain Francis Neville designed a new Market House (or Court House and Exchange), which was completed in 1692. Most houses were rebuilt, although parts of a few original properties have survived. In 1768, the Irish Society built an imposing town house as its offices in Bishop Street. As the population started to grow, gardens of the houses within the walls were built over, until expansion overflowed outside the walls. By the late 18th Century, there was a need for more gates through the walls to access the long rows of houses lining the main approach roads. In 1790, a new wooden bridge across the Foyle, pre-fabricated in America, was erected in thirteen months. It provided links to The Waterside on the south bank, where Quays and warehouses were erected to bring new prosperity to the City.

Bishop's Gate, Londonderry To allow Londonderry to expand it became necessary to extend Bishop's Street westward by pushing it through this ornamental arch at the walls.

The Court-House, Bishop Street, Londonderry This handsome Greek Revival-style building was built to designs by John Bowden in 1813-17.

Mid-19th Century lithograph of Bishop Street Londonderry by DS Buchanan, Glasgow This looks towards Bishop's Gate. *Courtesy of The Irish Society*

By the beginning of the 19th Century, a greater conscience to achieve architectural quality resulted in a number of distinguished buildings. In 1807, the Bishop of Derry initiated the rebuilding of Springhame's Free School (founded in 1617) with support from the Society. This was completed in 1814. It was renamed the Diocesan and Free Grammar School, and later Foyle College. A handsome Greek Revival style Court-House with an Ionic portico^c was built in Bishop Street in 1813-17. It was finished in Portland stone with panels of Dungiven sandstone. In 1828, a great Roman Doric column was erected on the Royal Bastion to Walker's memory, paid for by public subscription. The Irish Society contributed £50 towards the total of £4,200 raised. The Market House in the centre was almost entirely rebuilt in 1823-26 at a cost of £5,500 9s.11d. Its bowed front facing Bishop Street was surmounted by a clock tower. A new Deanery was provided in 1833, a 'marvellously reticent' late Georgian house, adjacent to The Irish Society premises.

The Deanery (left) and the former Irish Society Offices (right), Bishop Street, Londonderry These handsome Georgian houses were badly damaged in a bomb blast in 1988. Although fully restored, the Society has moved its headquarters to the Cutt (the Salmon Leap) above Coleraine.

Despite their poor condition, facades of other late Georgian houses can be seen elsewhere. 1835-37 saw the building of the Great James Street Presbyterian Church with its fine Ionic portico, and schoolhouses with residences for teachers were completed. In 1836-8, the Society commissioned William Tite²⁰⁵ from

---

²⁰⁵ Tite was 'spectacularly successful' and had been brought in to advise on the designs for the Royal Exchange architectural competition in the City of London in 1839, but was severely

London to design cottages for its estate peasantry and to make proposals for small farm houses and offices for cottiers. These were simply designed with slate roofs, whitewashed walls and earthen floors, 'well beaten and properly prepared'.[d] He also designed more refined semi-detached villas for people of substance, set in spacious grounds with curving drives. One of these was built at Pennyburn.

William Tite, PRIBA (1798-1873) As the pre-eminent London-based architect of his day, he was employed by The Irish Society to build a range of estate properties including Government house at Termonbacca.
John Prescott Knight 1858, oil on canvas RIBA Collections

Despite retaining its London base, The Irish Society was conscious of its status in Ulster and jealous of its authority in Civic Government and this was probably at the heart of the Court Case with the Skinners' Company. It maintained its representation at Westminster, and, before 1800, in the Irish House of Commons, and continued to advise those of its tenants with a right to vote to support its candidates. In the early days, the Society had followed the City of London in providing steadfast support for the Williamite and later Hanoverian cause. In 1696, it waited on the Lords of the Treasury to address William III on behalf of Londonderry and Coleraine to explain the sufferings caused by the siege. It saw it as its duty to forge links between Britain and Ireland, providing the connection between the Crown and the plantation, as evidenced on numerous Royal visits. By 1800, although Londonderry remained

---

criticised when he eventually built it himself. Yet he went on to be knighted in 1869 and became a Companion of the Bath in 1870.

an open constituency, the Society's authority in Coleraine was being challenged by the growing patronage of powerful families, such as the Beresfords and Jacksons. The Jacksons attempted to garner the Parliamentary franchise in Coleraine by controlling its Court of Common Council. Eventually, the Marquess of Waterford established personal control. When the Society tried to open up Coleraine's parliamentary representation, its deputation was barred from entering the Town Hall that it had helped to build. Yet, in 1831, it regained control and gained sufficient support for Alderman William Taylor Copeland of the City of London to be elected as Coleraine's Member of Parliament. 'Unedifying battles' between the interests of the Society and the Beresfords continued until 'Pocket Boroughs' were banned under the Reform Act of 1832.

St. Patrick's Parish Church, Coleraine was majorly restored in 1719 and again in 1777.

The interior, Coleraine Parish Church is full of fine memorial plaques.

The Irish Society had undertaken major maintenance work on the Coleraine Parish Church in 1719 and again in 1777. In 1735, George Dance Senior[206] was commissioned by the Coleraine Corporation (still dominated by the Beresfords and the Jacksons) to design a new Market House (or Town Hall) with a Court House above an arcaded ground floor. The Society offered £200 and 'a reasonable quantity of timber',[e] seeing it as a model for local residents to build better housing. Yet the start was delayed, and, in 1742, Dance provided revised plans, which were considered 'more agreeable'. This time, the Society offered £700 and 35 tons of timber free of charge. Work began in 1743 and was completed in the following year. The Society quickly became concerned about its maintenance, and threatened to ban the townspeople, until a proper scheme was put together. In 1787, when lightning cracked its tower from top to bottom, it had to be taken down, but Edward Mills's design for reconstruction incorporated much of Dance's original and added a weigh-house and store.

---

[206] Dance was a freeman of the Merchant Taylors' Company, who had designed the Mansion House in London.

The Town Hall, Coleraine In 1857, the Irish Society contributed £2,500 towards Thomas Turner's designs to rebuild this much altered structure. The eastern end was again altered in 1902.

Despite delays, it was completed in 1789, when the Society again exerted pressure to ensure a future maintenance plan. In 1830, a clock was provided by the Marquess of Waterford with a contribution from the Society, and the building was enlarged to provide a library, newsroom, ballast office, and a savings bank. It 1834, Tite visited Coleraine, and, after viewing the 'admirable works' on the Grocers' and Fishmongers' proportions, produced plans for semi-detached villas and houses with shops near the Market House. A street widening scheme was developed and the Society paid for drainage and other works. By the 1850s, the Market House had become inadequate for modern needs, and the Town Commissioners[207] approached the Society, who allocated £2,000 towards a new scheme designed by Thomas Turner[208]. The roof was completed by June 1858, by when the lower stages of the clocktower had been completed, but money was running out. The Society provided a further £500 of the £1,000 requested, and it was finished in 1859 at a cost of £4,146 19s. 10½d. It was

---

[207] In the 1840s the system of Local Government in Coleraine was changed with its Corporation being formed of Commissioners elected under what became the Towns Improvement (Ireland) Act of 1854. This limited The Irish Society's role in the control of Coleraine to its fishing and Admiralty interests, and it was no longer involved in the planning of the town, although it continued to contribute to schools and churches.

[208] Turner, who was in practice in Belfast, later joined into partnership with Richard Williamson, who, in 1860, succeeded as Surveyor to both the Society and the County, after Gordon's sudden death. Turner also designed the Northern Bank, built in 1866.

considered 'a fine conception',[f] but was again altered in 1902. In 1914, the Society added a stained-glass window to commemorate its tercentenary. In 1852, a fine new Methodist church with a Classical portico was built across the river at Killowen. In 1863, the Society decided to rebuild the Coleraine School.[209] In 1866, after several rejected plans, a Gothic style design was accepted, and its foundation stone was laid in the following year.

Outside Londonderry and Coleraine, the Society continued to make substantial contributions to both institutions and individuals, with regular payments for the upkeep of historic fortifications and churches. In 1819, it started to provide grants to maintain and rebuild Roman-Catholic and Presbyterian churches. By 1860, plans had been made to enlarge Clondermot Parish Church. Designs were provided for a school at Balloughry and for a house with a belfry for the superintendent at the Kilrea burial ground.

Clondermot (or Glendermot) Parish Church This was the plantation church on the Goldsmith's proportion, but was majorly enlarged by the Dean of Derry in 1861.

---

[209] The original Free School was built by the Society in 1705 and was revived in 1740. It was its 1821 replacement that now required rebuilding. It was again extended in 1935.

Balloughry school One of a number of local schools founded by The Irish Society, now administered by the National Board of Education.

During the 1800s a spirit of opulence prevailed within the Society. Its Admiralty Rights granted by the Charters of 1613 and 1662 gave it the privileges and profits of a Vice Admiralty. In 1835, it appointed a Vice Admiral and, five years later, acquired a yacht to salute each deputation with cannon on arrival. In 1846, having safely resolved the case brought by the Skinners, it commissioned Tite[210] to design Government House at Termonbacca as the official residence for its Agent and to house deputations on their annual visits, despite this being in the middle of the period of the Great Famine. Tite's 'elegant and substantial proposals' were always likely to exceed the budgeted allowance of £2,100. Stone was imported from Scotland, and chimney pieces, a kitchen range and stoves brought from London. Work began immediately and it was hoped that it would act as the catalyst for the building of villas nearby along the bank of the Foyle. When completed in 1848, the final cost was £5,814 3s. 11d. It is an extravagent property with 'fine cornices, mouldings and classical details',[g] and a superb marble chimney piece in its main room. Its gardens are full of mature trees and provide 'stunning' views over the Foyle. By the 1870s, with the Society following the Livery Companies in the long process of disengagement and disposal under the Land Purchase Acts, salutes for arriving deputations became inappropriate. By 1905, Government House had become superfluous and was sold. It is now a private residence.

---

[210] Tite was only chosen, after Gordon's designs failed to meet with approval.

Government House, Termonbacca This opulent property was designed by William Tite, and was built, somewhat insensitively, at the height of the Great Famine in 1846.

The 1860s were a busy time for the Society, as it took back control of the Culmore Estate, where the lease had expired. The fort, originally built in 1610 to protect the narrows below Londonderry, was repaired, although nothing remains but the original tower. Schemes were developed for a number of buildings, including eight model cottages, built between 1863 and 1864. With the Culmore School building being found to be defective, plans were made to rebuild it. On its completion in 1866, it was considered an 'ornament' and a 'credit to the officers'.[h] In 1866, the Ecclesiastical Commissioners built a new Parish Church at Culmore to replace the old plantation church. The Society provided the window for its west end. Yet removal of the 'interesting ruins of the original' sanctioned by the Commissioners was seen as 'an act of vandalism'.[i] A parsonage was provided by the Society in 1867, and the deputation planned more model cottages. These were built in 1875, but were two-up and two-down structures with back yards and external privies, hardly an advanced arrangement.

It was not just the maintenance and development of buildings. Sampson's criticisms had given impetus 'to ameliorate the condition of the inhabitants'.[j] By making itself responsible for the plantation's welfare, the Society became involved in a 'delicate relationship' with the Livery Companies.[k] In 1836, it supported plans to use unemployed labour to build an embankment to reclaim the slob-lands along the Bann. It also commissioned the establishment of a new route from Coleraine to Portrush, which the Grand Jury agreed to fund, if the Society would build the bridges. In 1858, plans were prepared 'for four double Cottiers' houses and seven farm-houses' at Molenan on the borders with Donegal and at Balloughry outside Londonderry.[l] In the following year, an elegant workers' house was built at Molenan.

The Society also believed that it had a role in supporting 'the civil government' of Londonderry and Coleraine; it established schools and promoted 'the civil and religious interests of the tenantry'.[m] It retained powers to inspect the accounts for dues at ports and bridges. From 1848 (after the Skinners' Case was resolved), it began making large annual grants for school improvement and to assist other charities. There were many officials on the Society's payroll, including the Chief Magistrate. It supported Londonderry's Mayor, Recorder, and officers of the Court. It constantly provided assistance at Quarter Sessions for making by-laws (which it was required to approve), with the common lands, for ferries, with jails and houses of correction, and to create freeholders. It encouraged tree planting and woodland care among its tenants to improve the countryside and to provide timber.

The Society had its problems with the Londonderry Corporation. Until 1790, it had owned the Foyle ferry, but this had been discontinued when the bridge was built. It leased the bridge site to the Corporation for £20 per annum, and, from 1790 to 1813, the Corporation generated £34,253 in tolls. At this point the bridge was badly damaged by ice and flood water. By Act of Parliament, the Government provided £15,000 to rebuild it. The Corporation was authorised to raise further money on the security of its future income, which it borrowed from the Society. After 'inefficiency and profligacy',[n] the Corporation reneged on its loan repayments, and, in 1828, the Society brought an action to require it to repay £500 annually. The Society has provided substantial funding for more recent bridges over both the Foyle and the Bann and, in 1919, it was still financing the Harbour Commissioners in Coleraine.

When the Corporation of Londonderry later fell into 'disrepute and bankruptcy',[o] the Society called for a new Constitution. In 1832, an Act of Parliament authorised its citizens to manage their own affairs and to raise local taxes. With the new Constitution in place, it was granted municipal privileges under the Municipal Reform Act of 1840, but forty-eight other Corporations, including Coleraine, were suppressed. Coleraine was now administered by a Board of Commissioners, but the Society's rights and duties were reaffirmed. In 1867, the Society made a substantial contribution to the £54,400 cost of improving the Bann's navigation, which involved the building of moles at the mouth of the river, and it has continued to contribute to the cost of embanking and reclaiming the slob-lands. In 1898, Coleraine became an Urban District Council, but, in 1926, this was reversed under the Municipal Corporations Act

(N. I.), and it regained its former status. In 1928, it was granted a new Royal Charter.

While the Society took a close interest in its political and civic responsibilities, it was less successful in maintaining tight control over its property leases. It did not always follow up to ensure that conditions applied to the granting of leases were adhered to. Tite was one of the first to complain about discrepancies between plans and finished buildings, which may have resulted from dishonesty among some of the Society's employees. He also pointed out that defects identified by earlier deputations were not always acted upon.

> This sort of thing appears to have been endemic, with the Society granting permission and the lessees cheating, cutting corners, and messing up every good intention.[p]

Tite recommended a tightening in controls, including repossession, to remedy shortcomings where lease conditions were not being acted upon. He wanted to see more frequent deputations from London.

Poaching of fish was a similar problem. 'The Society had lapsed into languid torpor, and its grip on things was loose, to be charitable.'[q] Although it maintained its lucrative salmon and eel fisheries, it had to resist pressure, from the middle of the 18th Century, to grant leases in perpetuity. Its rights to the salmon, eel and other fishings has caused controversy and much litigation, resulting in part from the confusion caused by the rights of other parties, and in part from usurpation by the Bishop of Derry.

Under the original agreement for the plantation, the Society had held the patronage of all Anglican churches throughout the County. After the Star Chamber case in 1635, the Bishops of Derry usurped their advowsons, and it was not until 1685-92 that the Society made attempts to recover them, but these proved unsuccessful, as it was deemed that the patronage of most of the livings was by then vested in the See. In 1838, the Society made another attempt to recover the advowson of Camus-juxta-Bann, but this was also turned down. Yet it retained its right of presentation to the Rectory of Coleraine, although, in 1869, this was removed by the Irish Church Act.

When horse racing was re-established in Londonderry, the Society did not have its ear very close to the ground and contributed fifty guineas per annum for a 'race plate'.

> This had to be discontinued when the Society received a petition signed by nearly 1,000 persons (including, naturally, all the clergy) stating that the race meetings were 'extremely prejudicial, subversive of decency and propriety, and destructive to the working classes and the peace of the community in general'.[r]

Such an attitude was symptomatic of growing puritanism.

Until late in the 19th Century, the Society still owned 29,900 acres of land, with 4,000 at Londonderry and 3,000 at Coleraine. Most of the rural area was then sold and part of its holdings in Londonderry was let to the Corporation. In 1887, in a final flourish, the Society funded the building of a new Guildhall after the earlier one in the Diamond had been burned down. The new building, in Victorian Gothic style, was built just outside the walls and was completed at a cost of £19,000 in 1890. Many of the Livery Companies contributed to its magnificent stained glass, depicting the arms of the various companies and scenes from Londonderry's turbulent history.

The Guildhall, Londonderry This Victorian Gothic building was funded by The Irish Society in 1885 at a cost of £19,000. Much of its fine stained glass was provided by the Livery Companies. It was rebuilt after a fire in 1908.

In 1891, tenants in Londonderry and Coleraine were offered leases in perpetuity if they would erect buildings to approved designs. Until then, the Society had continued to hold land at Pennyburn and the Larisks, part of the river bank including the quays, and land around the walls, on which housing and markets generated substantial rents. In 1903, it generated £99,207 from selling some of its properties, but all debts secured on the properties had to be discharged. Having paid these, the Society was left with £17,638.[s]

The interior of Londonderry's Guildhall showing part of its expanse of stained glass.

Chapter 52

The departure of the City of London Livery Companies from Ireland c.1870-20th Century

With calls for Home Rule and for radical changes in land ownership, it was inevitable that efforts would be made to disassemble the Dublin Establishment. In 1869, the Anglican Church of Ireland was disestablished. Despite the Livery Companies' more recent efforts to improve their estates and provide charity to the locality, they were a high profile target, and, throughout the second half of the 19th Century, faced criticism of the way they maintained control, despite their undoubted generosity. Scurrilous articles and pamphlets in the Press denounced their activities, intent on wearing The Irish Society down and there were rent strikes by tenants.

> Hatred was whipped up by agitators, rents were permanently in arrears, and a general lack of confidence made its presence felt in squalor, failure and decay. The tactics of the tenantry (which had been treated with open-handed generosity in most cases) and its political manipulators alienated the Londoners.

Eviction of tenants who failed to pay their rents was made very difficult and this only encouraged tenants, quite dishonourably, to defer payment in the hope that amounts due would be forgotten. In 1882, a Royal Commission on the City Livery Companies required so much detailed information that the tenants became even more unsettled and even further in arrears on rents. The atmosphere was not conducive to the Companies continuing their activities. They 'adopted a policy of gradual withdrawal of their grants for educational, religious and charitable bodies.'ª During the 1870s there were calls for major changes in Ireland's educational system and many of the Companies' schools were transferred as non-vested schools to the National Board of Education.

The Irish Society became exasperated at the amount of time it was having to spend in defending the Londoners' interests. It faced a series of attacks from Nationalist Members of Parliament with calls for a Select Committee to examine its affairs, culminating, in 1884, in proposed legislation for its abolition promoted by the Liberal Party. This caused a huge furore and the Bill was withdrawn, but

Parliamentary inquiries continued from 1889 to 1891. In 1889 a Select Committee was asked to examine the Charters and Articles under which the Londonderry estates were granted. When its report was published in 1890, there was no complaint on the way in which the Society had conducted its duties, but it was noted that its 'liberality' in making grants to churches, schools and other charitable purposes had diminished. This was hardly a surprise. New proposals were made for The Irish Society's Charter to be abolished by Act of Parliament. There was resentment that new by-laws of the Londonderry Corporation required its approval, which, it was claimed, caused delays. Yet the last by-law sent to the Society on 2 February 1878 was ratified within ten days.

As early as the 1870s, some Companies had discussed the advisability of selling their estates. With the Church of Ireland having been disestablished, it was realised that there was a majority of politicians committed to undoing all the policies begun in the reign of James I. The ground was being cut from under the Companies' feet. Six of the twelve Companies; the Grocers, Merchant Taylors, Goldsmiths, Haberdashers (or the partners who had bought from them), Vintners and Clothworkers, sold out before this, but the remainder tried to soldier on. The Fishmongers' considered selling in 1870, but the deal fell through. Meanwhile the political situation deteriorated, and the remaining Companies agreed to allow tenants to purchase their holdings. Sales had to be carried out in accordance with statutes.

A second Select Committee, made up largely of Home Rule activists, considered that the proceeds of land sales should be held in a fund to be used entirely for Irish purposes. This was tantamount to saying that the Livery Companies held their lands in trust and were not free to sell them 'without regard to those trusts'.[b] With the political climate favouring Irish Nationalism, progressive action was taken against the Londoners. On 5 January 1892, the Irish Attorney-General issued a writ summoning The Irish Society, the twelve Great Companies and the Corporation of London to appear in an action, which claimed they were acting as trustees of their Irish Estates and to force them to adopt a scheme for their future management. The result of the Skinners' case of 1830 was never questioned, and it was accepted that The Irish Society was a trustee for the public objects defined in its Charter. It was accountable to the Corporation of London and to the Crown but not to the Livery Companies, although it had discretionary powers to pay over part of any surplus profits to the Companies as a dividend on their original investment. In 1898, the new case came before the Irish Master of the Rolls. The Court found that the Companies had funded The Irish Society to purchase its estates and each had purchased its own proportion. The Companies thus had every right to profit from them and to sell them. There was no shred of evidence that the Companies were trustees or that they 'held their estates for public, charitable or other purposes'.[c] The Attorney-General's case was thus dismissed. It is probable that this litigation made those Companies, who still owned their estates, reticent about revealing the substantial recompense they received, which was, in practice, funded, by the British Government. Those that had invested in housing and fine buildings were amply repaid.

By 1903, at a time when most Livery Companies had already sold, Treasury loans were being granted to tenants to enable them to buy out their leases. The Irish Land Act (3 Edward VII. Cap. 37) clarified various anomalies in previous legislation. When a tenant agreed to buy, the land was transferred to Land Purchase Commissioners acting on their behalf, who funded a cash sum sufficient to provide the landlords with an income equivalent to the rents previously due, and they also repaid any arrears of rents. Yet bureaucracy delayed payment and created 'unnecessary vexation'.[d] This caused landlords to sell to anyone who would buy, and many tenants were evicted. At least the Land Commissioners were given powers to increase small uneconomic units to a realistic size by the addition of untenanted land. Matters were not fully wound up for some Livery Companies until immediately before the First World War and the Mercers retained interests until the 1960s, when they finally transferred the last holdings of their Kilrea estate to The Irish Society.

After the Companies' departure, there were efforts to persuade them to continue their largesse for the benefit of their erstwhile tenants and the locality. In the light of the 1898 judgement, the Companies felt no such obligation and when their ownership came to an end, 'the generous handouts for educational, charitable and other purposes' also ended. The Companies were bitter at the criticisms they had faced, and the Fishmongers referred to their tenants as 'an awful lot of ungrateful blackguards'. It took some of them until just before the First World War to extricate themselves. Their papers reveal degrees of bemused regret, exasperated relief, and more than a touch of righteous indignation.[e]

The Companies received small thanks for three centuries of trouble, which they had never sought and had been expected to fund when the State left them in the lurch. The original London settlers were the real sufferers. Livery Company and State assistance was always too little and too late. Yet The Irish Society remains in place and continued to provide funding for several primary and secondary schools in Coleraine and Londonderry until they were transferred to the Local Education Authority in 1948. Prizes, donations and annual visits take place to the present day and increasing numbers of schools of all religious denominations continue to be supported. It was only in 1955 tht the Society's responsibility for maintaining the walls of Londonderry was transferred to the City Council after a payment of £500.

Although the Home Rule Bill reached its third reading in 1914, the Government of Ireland (Amendment) Bill allowed parts of Ulster to be excluded from the scheme, and an Ulster Provisional Government met in Belfast. Although the First World War suspended negotiations, the Easter Rising of 1916 and the subsequent executions of its ringleaders swung Irish Roman-Catholic opinion behind the Republicans. Opinions became polarised 'with Irish Republicans being identified as allies of the Germans by one side and as martyrs dying for Ireland on the other'.[f] In the General Election in 1918, seventy-three Sinn Féin members were elected, and the *Dáil Éirann* met for the first time to declare independence. Yet disturbances continued with riots in Londonderry in the early summer of 1920 resulting in forty deaths. On 23 December, the Government of Ireland Act (10 and 11 George V, Cap. 67) provided for two subordinated Irish Parliaments. This was followed by partition and the formation of the Irish Free State, which included Donegal, Monaghan and Cavan from Ulster. Having lost half its hinterland, The City of Londonderry became hardly viable economically. Although the rest of Ulster was now separated from the south, one-third of its population had opposed it.

The legacy of the past just refused to go away. The Irish rebel objective was to remove any trace of the British, even where the British were providing assistance. With sectarian violence continuing, Northern Ireland faced considerable economic difficulties and unrest. Atrocities included the destruction, in 1973, of the Rev. Walker's statue in Londonderry. Yet Walker had been a Williamite hero against the Jacobites, and William had done a lot more good for Ireland than his Jacobite counterpart. The Guildhall in Londonderry has always been a focus for terrorist attack. It was badly damaged by fire in 1908. Only the clock tower remained intact, and the whole structure had to be rebuilt. In 1972, the building was badly damaged by two bombs causing almost all the magnificent stained glass to be destroyed. Restoration of the structure was completed in 1977 at a cost of £1.7 million but little of the glass was at that time replaced. In 1988, a bomb badly damaged the Society's handsome offices in Bishop Street. Although the building was fully restored, the Society, for purely operational reasons, moved its headquarters to the former fishery manager's residence at the Cutts (the Salmon Leap) on the River Bann south of Coleraine.

The Cutts at the Salmon Leap above Coleraine, the offices of The Irish Society on the edge of the River Bann.

Following the Foyle Fishery Case in 1948, the Government of Northern Ireland purchased the Irish Society's fishing rights in Lough Foyle and the River

504

Foyle for £100,000, resulting in a joint Fishery Commission being set up with the Republic in 1952. Yet the Society has continued to own the Bann fisheries. Despite frequent difficulties, some natural and some political, these have been conserved as a wonderful resource from profligate exploitation. Yet the decline in wild salmon over the last fifty years has meant that there is no longer netting on the river, but the Society receives £150,000 per annum from its commercial salmon angling operation.

The Society still receives income from the residue of its estates and investments, in addition to the fisheries on the Lower Bann. Having modernised its governance in the early 21st Century to become a Charity, almost all of its surplus income is disbursed in grants, administration of properties, and in the maintenance of its fisheries. Since the creation of a local charitable committee in the 1970s, an average of more than £100,000 has been granted annually to schools, charities and community improvement programmes in Londonderry and Coleraine, and grants are continuing to grow. With the local committee composed of all shades of political opinion, money is provided on a fully cross-community basis. The Society is a much leaner operation than in the past and its offices in London's Guildhall Yard Chambers were sold in 1991, although it still maintains a modest office in London's Guildhall.

In 1984, the elected members of the Londonderry City Council with its Nationalist majority, voted to remove the 'London' part of the Council's name. Despite this, the official name of the City remains Londonderry.[211] Some twenty years later, the Council funded the refurbishment of the many Livery Companies' cannon situated on the City walls. In 2010, it completed a full scale restoration of the Guildhall and its magnificent stained glass underlining its strong links with the City of London. The glass work was undertaken by Stephen Calderwood, whose family had provided the originals and had retained all the drawings. In 2011, the Guildhall was restored as the seat of local Government. As James Stevens Curl has written: 'Ireland was always a paradox; Ulster is no exception'.[g] At least since Curl was writing, concerted calls for reconciliation seem to be being heeded at last following the 'Peace Process' that culminated in the Stormont Agreement of 1998. This restored locally devolved Government to Northern Ireland under a power sharing deal between Unionists, Nationalists and Republicans. History may explain, but it cannot condone, 'the Troubles' between the late 1960s and mid 1990s, which remain stubbornly close to the surface.

---

[211] Most of the signage on roads to Londonderry have had the 'London' part of the name blanked out by graffiti writers.

To conclude this extraordinary story on a positive note, Londonderry remains the City of London's creation and the Society continues its deep involvement in maintaining its civic relationship. It also retains close ties with the Cathedral and with the County as a whole. There are only a few remains of the fine buildings in the proportions, but the walls, Cathedral and Guildhall in Londonderry bear witness to the Londoners' endeavour. Since the political settlement, a growing number of the Livery Companies, with the active assistance of The Irish Society, have offered support within the County of Londonderry through their charitable grant programmes. Once again, visits to the towns and Ulster's unparalleled countryside are helping to renew cultural and social links with London. At the same time, The Irish Society continues to foster its connections with the Corporation of the City of London, to bring its economic and cultural powerbase to the assistance of the needs of Northern Ireland as a whole.

Part of the Mercers' stained glass at the Londonderry Guildhall
This depicts the Royal Exchange in London, their most iconic investment property.

Main Sources

Dr Ian Archer *London-Derry Connections: The early years, 1613 – 1640,* 2013 'Archer'

Jonathan Bardon, *The Plantation of Ulster, The British Colonisation of the North of Ireland in the Seventeenth Century,* Gill & MacMillan, Dublin 2011 – 'Bardon'

John Betts, *The Story of The Irish Society*, 1913, The Honourable the Irish Society – 'Betts'

George Campbell, *The Irish Land*, 1869, Trübner and Co., London; Hodges, Foster and Co., Dublin – 'Campbell'

James Stevens Curl, *The Londonderry Plantation*, 1609-1914, Phillimore & Co. Limited, Chichester, 1986 – 'Curl 1986'

James Stevens Curl, *The Honourable The Irish Society and the Plantation of Ulster 1608 – 2000*, Philimore & Co. Limited, 2000 – 'Curl 2000'

James Stevens Curl, *The Livery Companies in Ireland,* 2001, The British Broadcasting Corporation – 'Curl 2001'

James Stevens Curl, *The City of London and the Plantation of Ulster*, BBCi History on Line, 2001 – 'Curl BBCi 2001'

Mary McNeill, *The Life and Times of Mary Ann McCracken*, 1960, Allen Figgis and Company Limited – 'McNeill'

Richard Robert Madden, *The United Irishmen, their lives and times*, 3 series, 1842, J. Madden & Co., London – 'Madden'

T. W. Moody, *Irish Historical Studies* Volume I No. 3 (March 1939) pp. 251- 273 – 'Moody'

Thomas Power O'Connor, MP, The Parnell Movement, 1891, Cassell Publishing Company, New York – 'O'Connor'

Fergus Whelan, *Dissent into Treason*, 2010, Brandon Books – 'Whelan'

References

Preface
a.   Bardon, p. 172

Part 1 The Historical background

Chapter 2 Early Ireland – the Celtic inheritance
a.   Curl 1986, p. 4
b.   Bardon, p. 7
c.   Curl 1986, p. 2
d.   Curl 1986, p. 5
e.   Curl 1986, p. 5
f.   Curl 1986, p. 5
g.   Madden, p. 4
h.   Bardon, p. 7
i.   Bardon, p. 13
j.   Bardon, p. 13
k.   Curl 1986, p. 5
l.   Bardon, p. 10
m.   Bardon, p. 11
n.   Bardon, p. 12
o.   Kenneth Nicholls, *Gaelic and Gaelicised Ireland in the Middle Ages,* Dublin, 1972, p. 68; cited in Bardon, p. 15
p.   Bardon, p. 12
q.   Bardon, p. 13
r.   Bardon, p. 13
s.   Bardon, p.13
t.   Bardon, p. 16
u.   Curl 1986, p. 5
v.   Cited in Bardon, p. 16
w.   Cited in Bardon, p. 17
x.   Cited in Bardon, p. 18
y.   Curl 1986, p. 5

Chapter 2 English efforts to bring Ireland to heel
a.   Curl 1986, p. 2
b.   Curl 1986, p. 2
c.   Curl 1986, p. 3

d.   Curl 1986, p. 3

e.   Constantina Maxwell, *Irish History from Contemporary sources (1509-1610),* London, 1923, p. 126; cited in Bardon, p. 5

f.   Curl 1986, p. 3

g.   Madden, p. 3

h.   Bardon, p. 5

i.   Curl 1986, p. 7

j.   Curl 1986, p. 7

k.   Curl 1986, p.7

l.   Bardon, p. 6

m.   Curl 1986, p. 7

n.   Bardon, p. 8

o.   Curl 1986, p. 18

p.   Bardon, p. 6

q.   Bardon, p. 6

r.   Bardon, p. 6

s.   Bardon, p. 7

t.   Curl 1986, p. 18

u.   Curl 1986, p. 8

v.   Curl 1986, p. 8

w.   Curl 1986, p. 8

x.   Curl 1986, p. 9

y.   Bardon, p. 23

z.   Bardon, p. 10

aa. G. Hill, *An Historical Account of the Macdonnells of Antrim, Including Notices of Some Other Septs, Irish and Scottish,* Belfast, 1873, p. 158; cited in Bardon, pp. 18-9

bb. Bardon, p. 18

cc. Richard Bagwell, *Ireland under the Tudors,* London, 1885-90, Vol. 2, p. 244; cited in Bardon, p. 18

dd. Curl 1986, p. 9

ee. Bardon, p. 1

ff. Bardon, p. 1

gg. David Beers Quinn, *The Elizabethans and the Irish,* Ithaca, NY, 1966, p. 108; cited in Bardon, p. 1

hh. Archer, p. 3

ii. Curl 1986, p. 10

jj. Colm Lennon, *Sixteenth-Century Ireland; The Incomplete Conquest,* Dublin, 1994, p. 280, cited in Bardon, p. 4

kk. Nicholas Canny, *The Elizabethan Conquest of Ireland: A Pattern Established, 1565-76,* Hassocks (Sussex), 1776, pp. 90-1; cited in Bardon, p. 4

ll. Bardon, p. 5

mm. Constantia Maxwell, *Irish History from Contemporary Sources (1509-1610),* London, 1923, pp. 170-1; cited in Bardon, p. 19

nn. Bardon, p. 19

oo. Bardon, p. 20

pp. Curl 1986, p. 6

qq. Curl 1986, p. 6

rr. Curl 1986, p. 6

ss. Curl 1986, p. 6

tt. Curl 1986, p. 11

uu. Curl 1986, p. 11

Chapter 3 The rise to pre-eminence of Hugh O'Neill, Earl of Tyrone

a. Richard Bagwell, *Ireland Under the Tudors,* London, 1885-90, Vol. 3, p.   224; cited in Bardon, p. 22

b. Curl 1986, p. 12

c. Curl 1986, p. 12

d. Curl 1986, p. 13

e. Curl 1986, p. 14

f. Bardon, p. 23

g. Archer, p. 3

h. *Paccata Hiberniae*, cited in Madden, pp. 362-3

i. Bardon, p. 25

j. Curl 1986, p. 1

k. Curl 1986, p. 1

l. Curl 1986, p. 1

m. Bardon, p. 28

n. Bardon, p. 36

o. Curl 1986, p. 16

p. Curl 1986, p. 16

Part 2 Plans to colonise Ulster

Chapter 4 Early steps in colonisation

a. Bardon, p. 63

b. Bardon, p. 52

c. Bardon, p. 55

d. Bardon, p. 56

e. Bardon, p. 56

f. Curl 1986, p. 18

g. Curl 1986, p. 18

h. Curl 1986, p. 17

i. Curl 1986, p. 17

j. Bardon, p. 56

k. Bardon, p. 57

l. Bardon, p. 60

m. Bardon, p. 60

n. Bardon, p. 60

o. Bardon, p. 60

p. Bardon, p. 60

q. Bardon, p. 61

r. Bardon, p. 67

s. Bardon, p. 262

t. H. C. O'Sullivan, *The Magennis Lordship of Iveagh in the early modern period, 1534-1691,* in Lindsay Proudfoot (ed.), *Down: History and Society,* Dublin 1997; cited in Bardon, p. 266

u. Madden, p. 5

v. M. Perceval-Maxwell, *The Scottish Migration to Ulster in the Reign of James I,* Belfast, 1973, p. 51; cited in Bardon, p.74

w. Curl 1986, p. 29

x. Bardon, p. 233

y. Bardon, p. 265

z. G. Hill, *An Historical Account of the MacDonnells of Antrim, Including Notices of Some Other Septs, Irish and Scottish,* Belfast, 1873, pp. 203-4; cited in Bardon, p.84

aa. Bardon, p. 267

bb. Bardon, p. 267

cc. Bardon, p. 268

Chapter 5 The flight of the Earls

a. Bardon p. 68

b. Bardon, p. 68

c. Bardon, p. 68

d. John McCavitt, *Sir Arthur Chichester, Lord Deputy of Ireland, 1605-16,* Belfast, 1998, p. 116; cited in Bardon, p. 68

e. *Calendar of State Papers, Ireland, 1606-8*, p. 270; cited in Bardon pp. 86-7

f. Robert J. Hunter, *Plantation in Donegal* in W. Nolan, L. Ronanyne and M. Donlevy (eds), *Donegal: History & Society,* Dublin, 1995, p.229; cited in Bardon, pp. 86-7

g. Bardon, p. 87

h. Robert J. Hunter, *Plantation in Donegal* in W. Nolan, L. Ronanyne and M. Donlevy (eds), *Donegal: History & Society*, Dublin, 1995, p. 241; cited in Bardon, p. 86

i. Bardon, p. 86

j. Bardon, p. 89

k. John McCavitt, *The Flight of the Earls,* Dublin, 2002, p. 88; cited in Bardon, p. 90

l. Bardon, p. 90

m. Bardon, p. 90

n. Bardon, p. 93

o. Micheline Kearney Walsh, *An Exile of Ireland: Hugh O'Neill, Prince of Ulster,* Dublin, 1996, p. 67; cited in Bardon, p. 95

p. Micheline Kearney Walsh, *An Exile of Ireland: Hugh O'Neill, Prince of Ulster,* Dublin, 1996, pp. 83-4; cited in Bardon, p. 106

Chapter 6 O'Doherty's rebellion

a. John McCavitt, *The Flight of the Earls,* Dublin, 2002, p. 113; cited in Bardon, p. 100

b. Bardon, p. 98

c. Bardon, p. 99

d. John McCavitt, *The Flight of the Earls,* Dublin, 2002, pp. 116-7; cited in Bardon, p. 99

e. Bardon, p. 101

f. John McCavitt, *The Flight of the Earls*, Dublin, 2002, pp. 147-8; cited in Bardon, p. 106

g. Curl 1986, p. 6

h. Curl 1986, p. 22

i. Bardon, p. 107

j. Micheline Kearney Walsh, *An Exile of Ireland: Hugh O'Neill, Prince of Ulster*, Dublin, 1996, p. 93; cited in Bardon, p. 108

Chapter 7 Planning of the plantation of Ulster

a. Curl 1986, p. 22

b. Bardon p. 112

c. *Calendar of State Papers, Ireland, 1608-10,* p. 17; cited in Bardon, p. 112

d. Bardon, p. 112

e. G. Hill, *An Historical Account of the Plantation of Ulster at the Commencement of the Seventeenth Century, 1608-20,* Belfast, 1877, p. 70; cited in Bardon, p. 112

f. John McCavitt, *Sir Arthur Chichester, Lord Deputy of Ireland, 1605-16*, Belfast, 1998, p. 151; cited in Bardon, p. 115

g. John McCavitt, *Sir Arthur Chichester, Lord Deputy of Ireland, 1605-16*, Belfast, 1998, p. 152; cited in Bardon, pp. 115-6

h. Bardon, p. 119

i. Curl 1986, p. 23

j. Curl 1986, p. 23

k. Curl 1986, p.23

l. Curl 1986, p. 24

m. Curl 1986, pp. 24-5

n. Curl 1986, p. 24

o. Curl 1986, p. 20

p. Curl 1986, p. 6

q. Curl 1986, p. 8

r. Madden, p. 6

s. Bardon, p. 217

t. Bardon, p. 218

u. Bardon, p. 145

v. Bardon, p. 149

w. G. Hill, *An Historical Account of the Plantation of Ulster at the Commencement of the Seventeenth Century, 1608-20,* Belfast, 1877, p. 134; cited in Bardon, p. 136

x. Curl 1986, pp. 22-3

y. G. Hill, *An Historical Account of the Plantation of Ulster at the Commencement of the Seventeenth Century, 1608-20,* Belfast, 1877, pp. 133-4; cited in Bardon, p. 136

Chapter 8 The plantation of the escheated lands of Ulster is begun

a. Bardon, p. 149

b. Cited in Bardon, p. 161

c. Nicholas Canny, *Making Ireland British, 1580-1650,* p. 213, Oxford, 2001; cited in Bardon, p. 237

d. Bardon, p. 237

e. Bardon, p. 237

f. Curl 1986, p. 28

g. Moody, p. 257

h. John McCavitt, *The Flight of the Earls, Dublin, 2002,* p. 160; cited in Bardon, p. 140

i.	Bardon, p. 145
j.	Bardon, p. 147
k.	Bardon, p. 148
l.	Bardon, p. 216
m.	Bardon, p. 217
n.	Bardon, p. 166
o.	Bardon, p. 218
p.	Bardon, p. 218
q.	Bardon, p. 219
r.	Bardon, p. 219
s.	Bardon, p. 220
t.	Bardon, p. 220
u.	Bardon, p. 220
v.	Bardon, p. 221
w.	Bardon, p. 221
x.	Bardon, p. 143
y.	Bardon, p. 143
z.	Bardon, p. 220
aa.	Bardon, p. 228
bb.	Bill Wilsden, *Plantation Castles on the Erne,* pp. 123-4, Dublin, 2010; cited in Bardon, p. 221
cc.	Bardon, p. 225
dd.	Bardon, p. 225
ee.	Bardon, p. 225
ff.	Bardon, p. 224
gg.	Bardon, p. 220
hh.	Bardon, p. 225
ii.	Bardon, p. 226
jj.	Bardon, p. 226
kk.	Bardon, p. 226
ll.	Bardon, p. 224
mm.	Bardon, p. 266
nn.	Bardon, p. 228
oo.	Bardon, p. 220
pp.	Bardon, p. 212
qq.	Bardon, p. 212
rr.	Bardon, p. 213
ss.	Bardon, p. 213

tt.　Bardon, p. 239

uu.　Bardon, p. 313

vv.　Bardon, p. 223

ww.　Bardon, p. 161

xx.　Bardon, p. 165

yy.　Curl 1986, p. 26

zz.　Curl 1986, p. 26

aaa.　Curl 1986, p. 30

bbb.　Bardon, p. 166

Part 3　The plantation of Londonderry

Chapter 9 Initial plans for a plantation by the City of London

a.　Archer, p. 3

b.　Bardon, p. 168

c.　Bardon, p. 169

d.　Curl 1986, p. 431

e.　Bardon, p. 169

f.　Betts, p. 13

g.　Curl 1986, p. 3

h.　Curl 1986, p. 3

i.　Archer, p. 3

j.　Archer, p. 3

k.　Archer, p. 3

l.　Gillespie, cited in Archer, p. 3

m.　Archer, p. 6

n.　Curl 1986, p. 28

o.　Curl 1986, p. 28

p.　Curl 1986, p. 31

q.　Rev. George Hill, *An Historical Account of the Plantation of Ulster at the Commencement of the Seventeenth Century, 1608-1620,* Belfast, 1877, p. 360; cited in Curl 1986, p. 31

r.　Curl 1986, p. 31

s.　T. W. Moody, *The Londonderry Plantation, 1609-1641. The City of London and the Plantation of Ulster,* p. 70, Belfast, 1939; cited in Curl 1986, p, 31

t.　Curl 1986, p. 32

u.　Betts, p. 17

v.　*Dictionary of National Biography, Vol.* II, p. 674; cited in Curl 1986, p. 30

w. Betts, p. 22

x. Bardon, p. 171

y. Betts, p. 28

z. Betts, pp. 24-5

aa. Archer, p. 4

bb. The Act of Common Council, cited in Betts, p. 30

cc. Archer, p. 4

dd. Archer, p. 4

ee. Curl 1986, p. 32

ff. Archer, p. 4

gg. Curl 1986, p. 35

hh. Curl 1986, p. 35

ii. Betts p. 43

Chapter 10   The formation of The Irish Society to supervise the Londoners' plantation

a.   Betts, p. 39

b.   Curl 1986, p. 36

c.   Curl 1986, p. 42

d.   Bardon, p. 172

e.   Phillips *MMS*, p. 155; cited in Curl 1986, p. 45

f.   Curl 1986, p. 43

g.   Phillips *MMS*, p. 155; cited in Curl 1986, p. 45

h.   Curl 1986, p. 45

i.   Curl 1986, p. 66
j.   Curl 1986, p. 37

k.   Curl 1986, p. 42

l.   Cited in Archer, p. 4

m.   T. W. Moody, *The Londonderry Plantation 1609-41, p. 107,* Belfast 1939; cited in Curl 1986, p. 57

n.   Curl 1986, p. 57

o.   Curl 1986, p. 57

p.   Bardon, p. 180

q.   Bardon, p. 180

r.   Bardon, p. 179

s.   Curl 1986, p. 57-8

t.   Bardon, p. 180

u.   Betts, p. 39

v.   T. W. Moody, *The Londonderry Plantation 1609-41,* p. 115, Belfast, 1939, cited in Curl 1986, p. 58

w.   Betts, p. 48

x.   Bardon, p. 179

y.   Bardon, p. 179

z.   Curl 1986, p. 56

aa.   Curl 1986, p. 56

bb.   Curl 1986, p. 58

cc.   Curl 1986, p. 58

dd.   Curl 1986, p. 59

ee.   Curl 1986, p. 59

ff.   Curl 1986, p. 58

gg.   Curl 1986, p. 58

hh.   Curl 1986, p. 58

ii.   Bardon, p. 180

jj.   Betts, p. 54

kk.   Curl 1986, p. 60

ll.   Curl 1986, p. 60

mm.   Curl 1986, p. 60

nn.   Curl 1986, p. 60

oo.   Curl 1986, p. 60

pp.   T. W. Moody, *The Londonderry Plantation 1609-41,* p. 146, Belfast 1939; cited in Curl 1986, p. 60

qq.   Bardon, p. 182

rr.   Curl 1986, p. 60

ss.   Bardon, p. 182

tt.   *Calendar of State Papers, Ireland, 1625-32*, p. 635; cited in Curl 1986, p. 61

uu.   Moody p. 263

vv.   Curl 1986, p. 63

ww.   Bardon, p. 185

xx.   Bardon, p. 185

yy.   Moody p. 263

zz.   Curl 1986, p. 63

aaa.   Bardon, p. 185

bbb.   Bardon, p. 185

ccc.   Bardon, pp. 185-6

ddd.   Curl 1986, p. 63

eee.   Curl 1986, p. 63

fff.   T. W. Moody, *The Londonderry Plantation, 1609-1641: The City of London and the Plantation of Ulster,* Belfast, 1939, p. 160; cited in Bardon, p. 186

ggg.   T. W. Moody, *The Londonderry Plantation, 1609-1641: The City of London and the Plantation of Ulster,* Belfast, 1939, p. 162; cited in Bardon, p. 186

hhh.   Cited in Betts, p. 64, and in Bardon, p. 244

iii.   Bardon, p. 187

jjj.   James I to Bodley; cited in Betts p. 65

kkk.   R. J. Hunter *The Fishmongers' Company of London and the Londonderry Plantation, 1609-41,* in O'Brien (ed.), 1999, pp. 219-20; cited in Bardon, p. 244-5

lll.   Curl 1986, p. 398

mmm. Curl 1986, p. 64

nnn.   Curl, p. 64

ooo.   Betts, p. 68

ppp.   Curl 1986, p. 65

qqq.   Curl 1986, p. 398

rrr.   Bardon, p. 209

sss.   Curl 1986, p. 398

ttt.   Curl 1986, p. 66

uuu.   Curl 1986, p. 66

vvv.   Curl 1986, p. 66

www. Curl 1986, p. 66

xxx.   Curl 1986, p. 70

Chapter 11 The resilience of the native Irish

a.   Bardon, p. 191

b.   John McCavitt, *Rebels, planters and conspirators: Armagh, 1594-1640* in A. J. Hughes and William Nolan (eds.) 2001 pp. 157-8; cited in Bardon, p. 192

c.   John McCavitt, *Rebels, planters and conspirators: Armagh, 1594-1640* in A. J. Hughes and William Nolan (eds.) 2001 pp. 255-7; cited in Bardon, p. 191)

d.   Bardon, p. 253

e.   Bardon, p. 253

f.   Bardon, p. 234

g.   Bardon, p. 262

h.   Bardon, p. 263

i.   Bardon, p. 263

j.   Bardon, pp. 263-5

k.   Bardon, p. 264

l.   Bardon, p. 198

m.   Bardon, p. 196

n.   Bardon, p. 197

o.   Bardon, p. 201

p.   Bardon, p. 197

q.   Bardon, p, 198

r.   Brian Mac Cuarta, *Catholic Revival in the North of Ireland, 1603-41,* Dublin, 2007; cited in Bardon, p. 198

s.   Bardon, p. 198

t.   Bardon, p. 199

u.   Bardon, p. 199

v.   Bardon, p. 199

w.   Bardon, p. 199

x.   Alan Ford, *The Protestant Reformation in Ireland, 1590-1641,* pp. 164-7, Dublin, 1997; cited in Bardon, p. 200

y.   Bardon, p. 200

z.   Brian Mac Cuarta, *Catholic Revival in the North of Ireland, 1603-41,* pp. 39-40, Dublin, 2007; cited in Bardon, p. 200

aa.   Bardon, p. 200

bb.   Bardon, p. 200

cc.   Alan Ford, *The Protestant Reformation in Ireland, 1590-1641*, p. 167, Dublin, 1987; cited in Bardon, p. 200

dd.   Bardon, p. 203

ee.   Bardon, p. 202

ff.   Alan Ford, *The Protestant Reformation in Ireland, 1590-1641*, pp. 74-9, Dublin, 1987; cited in Bardon, p. 202

gg.   Bardon, p. 202

hh.   Bardon, p. 202

ii.   Brian Mac Cuarta, *Catholic Revival in the North of Ireland, 1603-41*, pp. 57-8, Dublin, 2007; cited in Bardon, p. 203

jj.   Curl 1986, p. 64

kk.   *Phillips MMS*, p. 9; cited in Curl, p. 64

ll.   Bardon, p. 192

mm. *Phillips MMS*, p. 47; cited in Curl, p. 64

nn.   Curl 1986, p. 64

Chapter 12 The Livery Companies' poor management of their proportions

a.   Curl 1986, p. 73

b.   Bardon, p. 184

c. Bardon, p. 184

d. Curl 1986, p. 72

e. Archer, p. 5

f. Curl 1986, p. 66

g. Bardon, p. 186

h. Curl 1986, p. 64

i. Drapers' Company minutes; cited in Curl 1986, p. 64

j. Betts, p. 69

k. Curl 1986, p. 66

l. Curl 1986, p. 64

m. *Calendar of State Papers, Ireland, 1611-14,* pp. 309-10; cited in Curl 1986, p. 64

n. Curl 1986, p. 72

o. Goldsmiths' Company Records; cited in Curl 1986, p. 64

p. Bardon, p. 246

q. Curl 1986, p. 73

r. Curl 1986, p. 73

s. Curl 1986, p. 73

t. Bardon, pp. 209-10

u. Brian Lacy, *Siege City: The Story of Derry and Londonderry,* pp. 92-6, Belfast, 1990; Curl 2000, pp. 110-3; cited in Bardon, p. 210

v. Rev. George Hill, *An Historical Account of the Plantation in Ulster at the Commencement of the Seventeenth Century,* Belfast 1877, pp.451-590; cited in Curl 1986, p. 73

w. Curl 1986, pp. 73-4

x. Bardon, p. 243

y. Bardon, p. 246

z. Curl 1986, p. 74

aa. Curl 1986, p. 74

bb. Rev. George Hill, *An Historical Account of the Plantation in Ulster at the Commencement of the Seventeenth Century,* Belfast 1877, pp. 576-89; cited in Curl 1986, p. 74

cc. Archer, p. 5

dd. T. W. Moody, *The Londonderry Plantation, 1609-41 The City of London and the Plantation of Ulster,* p. 184, Belfast, 1939; cited in Bardon, p. 246

ee. Bardon, p. 255

ff. Curl 1986, p. 74

gg. T. W. Moody, *The Londonderry Plantation, 1609-41 The City of London and the Plantation of Ulster,* p. 192, Belfast, 1939; cited in Curl 1986, p. 74

hh.   Curl 1986, p. 74

ii.   Bardon, p. 248

jj.   Sampson's Memoir, p. 13, cited in *A Concise View of The Irish Society* fn. p. 16

kk.   Bardon, p. 214

ll.   Bardon, p. 252

mm.   The Rev. Andrew Stewart; cited in Bardon, p. 318

nn.   Bardon, p. 252

oo.   Bardon, p. 252

pp.   Bardon pp. 255-6

qq.   Bardon, p. 319

rr.   Bardon, p. 224

ss.   Philip Robinson *The Plantation of Ulster: British Settlement in an Irish Landscape, 1600-1670*, pp. 92-5, Dublin and New York, 1984; cited in Bardon, p. 236

tt.   *Records of The Irish Society: Collection of plantation documents, 1609-19,* compiled by Henry Carter, Goldsmiths' Clerk (1615-16), p. 560; cited in Moody, p. 264

uu.   Records of the Mercers' Company, Irish Minutes i, pp. 67-8; cited in Moody, p. 264

vv.   Archer, p. 6

ww.   Moody, p. 264

xx.   Bardon, p. 249

yy.   Archer, pp. 5-6

zz.   Bardon, p. 250; Curl 1986, pp. 74-5

aaa.   Bardon, p. 250

bbb.   Curl 1986, pp. 78-9

ccc.   Curl 1986, pp. 78-9

ddd.   Curl 1986, p. 79

eee.   Curl 1986, pp. 79-80

fff.   Bardon, p. 250

ggg.   Bardon, p. 250

hhh.   Victor Treadwell, (ed.) *The Irish Commission of 1622,* pp. 607-8, Dublin, 2006; cited in Bardon, p. 250

iii.   Curl 1986, p. 128

jjj.   Curl 1986, pp. 79-80

kkk.   Curl 1986, p. 79

lll.   T. W. Moody, *The Londonderry Plantation, 1609-41The City of London and the Plantation of Ulster,* p. 211, Belfast, 1939; cited in Curl 1986, p. 80

mmm.   Curl 1986, p. 82

nnn. Curl 1986, p. 82

ooo. Curl 1986, p. 82

ppp. *Phillips MMS,* p. 69; cited in Curl 1986, p. 81

qqq. A. H. Johnston, *The History of the Worshipful Companies of Drapers of London: preceded by an introduction on London and her Gilds up to the close of the XVth Century,* Oxford 1922, Vol. IV, p. 543; cited in Curl 1986, p. 80

rrr. Curl 1986, p. 82

sss. *Phillips MMS*, p. 67; cited in Curl 1986, p. 81

ttt. Curl 1986, p. 81

uuu. Curl 1986, p. 81

vvv. Curl 1986, p. 82

www. Curl 1986, p. 82

xxx. Curl 1986, p. 82

yyy. Curl 1986, p. 82

zzz. Curl 1986, p. 82

aaaa. Curl 1986, p. 82

Chapter 13 Charles I takes action against the Livery Companies

a. Curl 1986, p. 81

b. *Phillips MMS,* pp. 62-3; cited in Curl 1986, p. 81

c. Curl 1986, p. 82

d. Curl 1986, p. 83

e. Bardon, p. 257

f. Curl 1986, p. 83

g. *Calendar of State Papers, Ireland, 1625-1632,* pp. 205-7; cited in Curl 1986, p 83

h. *Phillips MMS*, p. 77; cited in Curl 1986, p. 83

i. Curl 1986, p. 83

j. Curl 1986, p. 83

k. Curl 1986, p. 83

l. Curl 1986, p. 83

m. Curl 1986, p. 83

n. Bardon, p. 256

o. Bardon, p. 256

p. Bardon, p. 256

q. Curl 1986, pp. 83-4

r. Curl 1986, p. 84

s. Curl 1986, p. 84

t. Curl 1986, p. 84

u. *Phillips MMS*, pp. 120-1; cited in Curl 1986, p. 84

v. Curl 1986, p. 398

w. Archer, p. 6

x. Curl 1986, p. 84

y. Curl 1986, p. 85

z. *Phillips MMS,* pp. 106-8; cited in Curl 1986, p. 85

aa. Curl 1986, p. 85

bb. Curl 1986, p. 85

cc. Phillips MMS, pp. 138-9

dd. Curl 1986, p. 84

ee. Curl 1986, p. 84

ff. *Phillips MMS*, pp. 104-5; cited in Curl 1986, p. 86

gg. Moody p. 266

hh. Moody, p. 266

ii. Moody, p. 266

jj. Curl 1986, p. 86

kk. Moody, p. 266

ll. Bardon, p. 258

mm. Archer, p. 5

nn. Archer, p. 5

oo. T. W. Moody, *The Londonderry Plantation, 1609-1641. The City of London and the Plantation of Ulster,* p. 339, Belfast, 1939; cited in Curl 1986, p, 156

pp. Archer, p. 1

qq. Archer, p. 5

rr. Curl 1986, p. 86

ss. *Phillips MMS*, pp. 1-29; cited in Curl 1986, p. 86

tt. Bardon, p. 258

uu. A. H. Johnston, *The History of the Worshipful Companies of Drapers of London: preceded by an introduction on London and her Gilds up to the close of the XVth Century,* Oxford 1922, Vol. IV, p. 593; cited in Curl 1986, p. 87

vv. Betts, p. 75

ww. Moody p. 267

xx. Archer, p. 6

yy. Betts, p. 78

zz. Betts, p. 78

aaa. Archer, p. 1

bbb. Moody pp. 271-2

ccc. Moody p. 272

ddd. Moody, p. 272

eee. Cited in Moody, p. 272

fff. Moody p. 271

ggg. Phillips to Bramhall, 1 March 1635 (*Knox MMS*); cited in Moody p. 269

hhh. Archer, p. 1

iii. Moody p. 272

jjj. Bardon, p. 254

kkk. Bardon, p. 254

lll. Curl 1986, p. 88

Chapter 14 Confrontation with Wentworth as Ireland's Lord Deputy

a. Bardon, p. 256

b. Archer, p. 1

c. Archer, p. 1

d. Curl 1986, p. 88

e. Archer, p. 6

f. Betts, p. 79

g. Curl 1986, p. 89

h. Bardon, p. 253

i. Curl 1986, p. 435

j. Curl 1986, p. 89

k. Bardon, p. 257

l. John Rushworth, *The Tryal of Thomas Earl of Strafford,* London, 1680, pp. 7-14; cited in Curl 1986, p. 89

m. Barton, p. 260

n. Bardon, p. 259-60

o. M. Perceval-Maxwell, *The Outbreak of the Irish Rebellion of 1641,* p. 43, Dublin,1994; cited in Bardon, p. 270

p. M. Perceval-Maxwell, *The Outbreak of the Irish Rebellion of 1641,* p. 41, Dublin, 1994; cited in Bardon, p. 269

q. Bardon, p. 322

r. Bardon, p. 269

s. Bardon, pp. 269-70

t. Archer, p. 1

u. Bardon, p. 261

v. Trevor Royle, *Civil War: The Wars of the Three Kingdoms, 1638 -1660,* p. 118, London, 2004, cited in Bardon, p. 261

w. Curl 1986, p.90

x. Archer, p. 1

Chapter 15 The Great Rebellion

a. Bardon, p. 271
b. M. Perceval-Maxwell, *The Outbreak of the Irish Rebellion of 1641,* p. 218, Dublin,1994; cited in Bardon, p. 275
c. Bardon, p. 273
d. Bardon, pp. 270-1
e. W. E. H. Lecky, *History of Ireland in the Eighteenth Century,* London, 1892, Vol. I, pp. 46-89; cited in Curl 1986, p. 91
f. Curl 1986, p. 90
g. Colonel Audley Mervyn; cited in Bardon, p. 275
h. Bardon, p. 280
i. Bardon, p. 275
j. Bardon, p. 276
k. Bardon, p. 276
l. Bardon, p. 281
m. Bardon, p. 275
n. *Trinity College Dublin MMS*, 866; cited in Curl 1986, p. 91
o. Bardon, p. 282
p. Bardon, p. 283
q. Bardon, p. 281
r. Whelan, p. 28
s. Bardon, p. 282
t. Bardon, p. 283

Part 4 The individual Livery Companies on their proportions (1)

Chapter 16 Mercers

a. Mathew Engel, *British Institutions: Livery Companies*
b. Curl 1986, p. 122
c. T. W. Moody, *The Londonderry Plantation, 1609-41The City of London and the Plantation of Ulster,* p. 86, Belfast, 1939; cited in Curl 1986, p. 122
d. Curl 1986, p. 123
e. Curl 1986, p. 123
f. Curl 1986, p. 124
g. Curl 1986, p. 128
h. Curl 1986, p. 126
i. *Acts of Court, Irish, 1609-1662,* p. 19; cited in Curl 1986, p. 126
j. Curl 1986, p. 126
k. Curl 1986, p. 127
l. T. W. Moody, *The Londonderry Plantation, 1609-41The City of London and the Plantation of Ulster,* p. 314, Belfast, 1939; cited in Curl 1986, p. 128

m. Curl 1986, p. 129

n. *Acts of Court, Irish 1609-1662,* pp. 131-2; cited in Curl 1986, p. 129

Chapter 17 Grocers

a. Curl 1986, p. 155

b. Curl 1986, p. 155

c. Heath Baron, *Some account of the Worshipful Companies of Grocers of London,* London, 1869, pp. 575-6; cited in Curl 1986, p. 157

d. Curl 1986, p. 155

e. Quoted in Heath Baron, *Some account of the Worshipful Companies of Grocers of London,* London, 1869, pp. 572-83; cited in Curl 1986, p. 156

f. T. W. Moody, *The Londonderry Plantation, 1609-41The City of London and the Plantation of Ulster,* p. 301, Belfast, 1939; cited in Curl 1986, p. 156

g. Curl 1986, p. 155

h. *Calendar of State Papers, Ireland, 1625-32,* pp. 643-5; cited in Curl 1986, p. 156

i. Curl 1986, p. 157

j. Curl 1986, p. 157

Chapter 18 Drapers

a. Curl 1986, p. 175

b. Bardon, p. 237

c. Curl 1986, p. 185

d. Philip Robinson, *Vernacular Housing in Ulster in the Seventeenth Century. Ulster folklife.* Vol. 25. 1979, pp. 1-28; cited in Curl 1986, p.186

e. Archer, p. 4

f. Curl 1986, p. 178

g. *Carew MMS.* 613, cited in Curl 1986, p. 180

h. Curl 1986, p. 180

Chapter 19 Fishmongers

a. Curl 1986, p. 232

b. Information provided by the Fishmongers' Company; cited in Curl 1986, p. 232

c. *Fishmongers' Court Ledgers, 1592-1610*; cited in T. W. Moody, *Irish Historical Studies Volume I No. 3,* March 1939, p. 70 and in Curl 1986, p. 232

d. *Fishmongers' Court Ledgers, 1592-1610,* pp. 573-9 and 606-11; cited in Curl 1986, p. 232

e. Curl 1986, p. 233

f. *Guildhall Library, City of London. M. S. 5570-2. 1610-31,* p. 248; cited in Curl 1986, p. 233

g. Carew *MMS.* 634; cited in Curl 1986, p. 233

h. Bardon, p. 241

i. Samuel Lewis, *A Topographical Dictionary of Ireland* ... (London 1850, Vol. I, p. 133

j. Curl 1986, p. 465

k. Curl 1986, p. 236

Chapter 20 Goldsmiths

a. Curl 1986, p. 278

b. Curl 1986, p. 278

c. Curl 1986, p. 278

d. Curl 1986, p. 280

Chapter 21 Merchant Taylors

a. *Merchant Taylors' Court Minutes, Vol. V*, pp. 420-38; cited in Curl 1986, p. 304

b. Curl 1986, p. 309

c. T. W. Moody, *The Londonderry Plantation, 1609-41 The City of London and the Plantation of Ulster,* p. 315, Belfast, 1939; cited in Curl 1986, p. 304

d. Archer, p. 4

e. *Merchant Taylors' Papers L. 5. M. S.,* pp. 419-20; cited in Curl 1986, p. 311

f. The Revd. John Joseph Ellis, *The History and Antiquities by the Worshipful Company of Merchant Taylors,* 1827; cited in Curl 1986, p. 305

g. *Merchant Taylors' Papers, L. 5. M. S.,* pp. 419-20; cited in Curl 1986, p. 311

Chapter 22 Skinners

a. Curl 1986, p. 285

b. *Skinners' Company Court Book 1551-1617*, Folios pp. 105-10; cited in Curl 1986, p. 285

c. Curl 1986, p. 285

d. T. W. Moody, *The Londonderry Plantation, 1609-41 The City of London and the Plantation of Ulster,* p. 96, Belfast, 1939; cited in Curl 1986, p. 285

e. *Skinners' Company Court Book 1551-1617*; cited in Curl 1986, p. 285

f. Curl 1986, p. 291

g. R. J. Hunter, *Towns in the Ulster Plantation. Studia Hibernica.* 1971. 11. pp. 40-9; cited in Curl 1986, p. 292

h. Curl 1986, p. 287

i. Phillips *MMS*, p. 163; cited in Curl 1986, p. 287

j. *Calendar of State Papers, Ireland, 1633-47*, p. 291; cited in Curl 1986, p. 291

Chapter 23 Haberdashers

a. Curl 1986, p. 314

b. *Letters to Beresford from Moore and Freeman, 2614, 1615*; cited in Curl 1986, p. 315
c. Curl 1986, p. 316
d. Curl 1986, p. 319
e. Curl 1986, p. 316
f. Curl 1986, pp. 318-9

Chapter 24 Salters

a. Phillips *MMS*; cited in Curl 1986, p. 321

Chapter 25 Ironmongers

a. Curl 1986, p. 350
b. T. W. Moody, *The Londonderry Plantation, 1609-41 The City of London and the Plantation of Ulster,* pp. 313-4, Belfast, 1939; cited in Curl 1986, p. 353
c. Curl 1986, p. 353
d. Curl 1986, p. 353
e. Archer, p. 4
f. Archer, p. 4
g. Archer, p. 4
h. Archer, p. 4
i. Curl 1986, pp. 353–4
j. Archer, p. 5
k. Archer, p. 5
l. R. J. Hunter *The Fishmongers' Company of London and the Londonderry Plantation, 1609-41,* in O'Brien (ed.), 1999, pp. 205-49; cited in Bardon, p. 243
m. Bardon, p. 242
n. Curl 1986, p. 355
o. Archer, p. 5
p. Archer, p. 5
q. Archer, p. 5

Chapter 26 Vintners

a. Curl 1986 p. 367
b. T. W. Moody, *The Londonderry Plantation, 1609-41 The City of London and the Plantation of Ulster,* p. 314, Belfast, 1939; cited in Curl 1986, p. 368
c. Phillips *MMS*, cited in Curl 1986, p. 371

Chapter 27 Clothworkers

a. Curl 1986, p. 374
b. Curl 1986, p. 375
c. Curl 1986, p. 378
d. Curl 1986, p. 381

e. Curl 1986, p. 378
f. Curl 1986, p. 378

Part 5 Control by Parliamentary forces

Chapter 28 The war of the Three Kingdoms
a. Bardon, p. 283
b. Bardon, p. 283
c. Bardon, p. 284
d. G. A. Hays-McCoy, *Irish Battles: A Military History of Ireland,* p. 193, London, 1969; cited in Bardon, p. 284
e. Bardon, p. 284
f. Bardon, p. 284
g. Bardon, p. 284

Chapter 29 Ireland under Parliamentary control
a. Whelan, p. 22
b. Curl 1986, p. 93
c. Bardon, p. 285
d. Bardon, p. 285
e. Bardon, p. 285
f. Curl 1986, p. 93
g. Bardon, p. 285
h. Gribben, p. 15, cited in Whelan p. 36

i. Bardon, p. 287
j. Bardon, p. 287
k. Bardon, p. 286
l. Bardon, p. 289
m. Colonel Richard Lawrence; cited in Bardon, p. 286
n. Bardon, p. 286
o. Madden, p. 15
p. Madden, p. 15
q. Bardon, p. 288
r. Bardon, p. 288
s. Bardon, p. 288
t. Bardon, p. 291
u. Bardon, p. 291
v. Bardon, p. 292
w. Bardon, p. 292
x. Curl 1986, p. 94

Part 6 The Restoration

Chapter 30 The restoration of Charles II and Ormonde's return to influence

a.   S. J. Connolly p. 124; cited in Whelan, p. 43
b.   Madden, p.16
c.   12 Charles II, Cap.11; cited in Curl 1986, p. 96
d.   Cited in Betts, p. 84
e.   Curl BBCi 2001, p. 7
f.   Bardon, p. 293
g.   Madden, p. 17
h.   Bardon, p. 294
i.   Bardon, p. 294
j.   Madden, p. 17
k.   Bardon, p. 295
l.   Whelan, p. 17
m.   Whelan, p. 23
n.   Whelan, p. 22
o.   Gregg, p. 160, cited in Whelan, p. 22
p.   Whelan, p.28
q.   Kilroy, p. 231, cited in Whelan, p. 48
r.   McNeill, p. 65
s.   Bardon, p. 295
t.   Bardon, p. 295
u.   Whelan, p. 49
v.   Whelan, p. 49
w.   Whelan, p. 49
x.   Whelan, p. 54
y.   Whelan, p. 53
z.   Curl 1986, p. 97
aa.   Curl 1986, p. 97
bb.   Curl 1986, p. 97
cc.   Curl 1986, p. 98
dd.   Bardon, p. 295

ee.   Bardon, p. 296
ff.   Curl 1986, p. 98
gg.   William Brooke; cited in Bardon, p. 297
hh.   Bardon, p. 297
ii.   William King, *The State of the Protestants,* London, 1691, p. 42; cited in Curl 1986, p. 98
jj.   Curl 1986, p. 98
kk.   William Brooke; cited in Bardon, p. 298
ll.   Richard Dobbs; cited in Bardon, p. 298
mm. Curl 1986, p. 98

Chapter 31

The Ulstermen's support for William of Orange

a. Whelan, p. 60
b. Houston, p. 8, cited in Whelan, p. 61
c. Whelan, p. 62
d. Whelan, p. 62
e. Curl 1986, p. 98
f. Curl 1986, p. 98
g. Bardon, p. 299
h. Curl 1986, p. 99
i. Curl 1986, p. 99
j. Whelan, p. 63
k. Pincus p. 141, cited in Whelan, p. 63
l. Bardon, p. 299
m. Bardon, p. 299
n. Bardon, p. 300
o. Madden, p. 18
p. Leyland, History of Ireland, cited in *A Concise View of The Irish Society*, Appendix, p. 3
q. Leland, History of Ireland, cited in *A Concise History of The Irish Society*, p. 12
r. Curl 1986, p. 101
s. Curl 1986, p. 102
t. Curl 1986, p. 102
u. Curl 1986, p. 102
v. From the *Apprentice Boys of Derry*
w. From the *Apprentice Boys of Derry*
x. Curl 1986, p. 105
y. Curl 1986, p. 102
z. Betts, p. 86
aa. Curl 1986, p. 101
bb. Curl 1986, p. 101
cc. Curl 1986, p. 101
dd. Bardon p. 300
ee. Curl 1986, p. 103
ff. Madden, p. 19
gg. Bardon, p. 300
hh. Madden, p. 18
ii. Curl 1986, p. 103
jj. Bardon, p. 300
kk. Curl 1986, p. 103
ll. Whelan, p. 68
mm. Curl 1986, p. 103

nn. Curl 1986, p. 104

oo. Curl 1986, p. 104

pp. Bardon, p. 301

qq. Curl 1986, p. 104

rr. Bardon, p. 300

ss. Curl 1986, p. 104

tt. Curl 1986, p. 104

uu. Bardon, p. 310

vv. Curl 1986, p. 104

ww. Curl 1986, p. 104

xx. Curl 1986, p. 105

yy. Bardon, p. 329

zz. Bardon, p. 330

aaa. Curl 1986, p. 108

Part 7 Domination of Irish Government by the Protestant Ascendancy

Chapter 32 The Protestant Ascendancy's assertion of authority

a. Whelan, p. 70

b. Whelan, p. 71

c. Whelan, p. 74

d. Whelan, p. 75

e. Curl 1986, p. 107

f. Madden, p. 21

g. Madden, p. 21

h. Whelan, p. 74

i. Whelan, p. 71

j. Curl 1986, p. 107

k. Curl 1986, p. 107

l. Curl 1986, p. 107

m. Bardon, p. 303

n. Bardon, p. 305

o. Bardon, p. 308

p. McNeill, p. 62

q. Madden, p. 22

r. McNeill, p. 62

s. J. Seaton Reid, *History of the Presbyterian Church in Ireland*, vol. 3, pp.68-70, Belfast, 1867; cited in Bardon p. 307

t. Curl BBCi 2001, p. 8

u. Bardon, p. 307

v. Bardon, p. 325

w. Madden, p. 29

Chapter 33 Efforts to control the Protestant Ascendancy

a. McNeill, p. 62
b. Madden, p. 42
c. Madden, p. 41
d. Curl 1986, p. 109
e. Curl 1986, p. 109
f. Madden, p. 41-2
g. McNeill, p. 63
h. Madden, p. 22
i. Madden, p. 24
j. Madden, p. 23
k. Curl 1986, p. 110

Chapter 34 The Londonderry plantations under William and the Hanoverians

a. *A Concise View of the Origin, Constitution, and Proceedings of ... The Irish Society,* London, 1842, p. 74; cited in Curl 1986, p. 105
b. Curl 1986, p. 105
c. Curl 1986, p. 106
d. Curl BBCi 2001, p. 8
e. *A Concise View of the Origin, Constitution, and Proceedings of ... The Irish Society,* London, 1842, p. 77; cited in Curl 1986, p. 107
f. Curl 1986, p. 107
g. Bardon, p. 315
h. Curl 1986, p. 108
i. Curl 1986, p. 108
j. Bardon, p. 324
k. Bardon, p. 324
l. Curl 1986, p. 131
m. Curl 1986, p. 111
n. Curl 2000, pp. 192-3
o. Curl 1986, p. 108
p. The Rev. Philip Skelton; cited in Bardon, p. 324
q. Cited in T. P. O'Connor, p. 22
r. Curl BBCi 2001, p. 8
s. Curl 1986, 109
t. Curl 1986, p. 107
u. Curl 1986, p. 109
v. Cecil Woodham-Smith, *The Great Hunger, Ireland 1845-1849*, Signet, New York, 1991, p. 22
w. Curl 2000, pp. 212-3
x. Curl 1986, p. 109
y. DNB (1917), ix, p. 732, cited in Curl 2000, pp. 212-3

Chapter 35 The development of the Irish linen industry

a. Madden, p. 22
b. Curl 1986, p. 98
c. Curl 1986, p. 107
d. Bardon, p. 330
e. McNeill, p. 64
f. Bardon, p. 322
g. Bardon, p. 331
h. Curl 1986, p. 107
i. Bardon, p. 331
j. Curl 1986, p. 113
k. Curl 1986, p. 195

Part 8 Ireland after 1800

Chapter 36 The Londonderry plantations

a. *A Concise View of the Origin, Constitution, and Proceedings of ... The Irish Society,* London, 1842; cited in Curl 1986, p. 110
b. Robert Slade, *Narrative of a Journey to the North of Ireland, in the year 1802,* p. cciii; cited in Curl 1986, p. 110
c. Robert Slade, *Narrative of a Journey to the North of Ireland, in the year 1802,* pp. cciii and cciv; cited in Curl 1986, p. 110
d. Curl 1986, p. 111
e. Curl 1986, p. 111
f. Curl 1986, p. 112
g. Curl BBCi 2001, pp. 8-9
h. Curl BBCi 2001, p. 9
i. Curl 1986, p. 113
j. Curl 1986, p. 113
k. Curl 1986, p. 114
l. Curl 1986, p. 132
m. James Stevens Curl, *The Life and Works of Henry Roberts (1803-76), Architect. The Evangelical Conscience and the Campaign for Model Housing and Healthy Nations,* London and Chichester, 1983
n. Curl 1986, p. 116
o. Curl 1986, p. 132
p. Curl 1986, p. 114
q. Curl BBCi 2001, p. 9
r. Curl BBCi 2001, p. 9
s. Curl BBCi 2001, p. 10
t. Curl 1986, p. 115
u. Curl 1986, p. 116

Chapter 37 Problems in Ireland outside Ulster

a. *Great Britain and the Irish Question 1798-1922*, Paul Adelmann and Robert Pearce, Hodder Murray, London, p. 33
b. Curl 1986, p. 115
c. Curl 1986, p. 114
d. O'Connor, p. 24
e. Healy, *Why there is a land question*, p. 55; cited in O'Connor, p. 24
f. Healy, *Why there is a land question*, p. 38, cited in O'Connor, p. 23
g. Cited in O'Connor, pp. 23-4
h. O'Connor, p. 16
i. O'Connor, p. 22
j. O'Connor, p.23
k. Cecil Woodham-Smith, *The Great Hunger, Ireland 1845-1849*, Signet, New York, 1991, p. 24
l. O'Connor, p. 16
m. O'Connor, p. 17
n. Helen Litton, *The Irish Famine: An Illustrated History*, Wolfhound Press, 2006, p. 95
o. O'Connor, p. 18
p. O'Connor, p.20
q. O'Connor, p. 18
r. O'Connor, p. 16
s. Robert Blake, *Disraeli,* University Paperbacks, St. Martin's Press, 1967, p. 179
t. Cecil Woodham-Smith, *The Great Hunger, Ireland 1845-1849*, Signet, New York, 1991, p. 31
u. Cited in O'Connor, p. 23
v. Cecil Woodham-Smith, *The Great Hunger, Ireland 1845-1849*, Signet, New York, 1991, p. 24
w. *The Commission Report,* p. 226, cited in O'Connor, p. 23
x. O'Connor, p. 26
y. O'Connor, p. 27
z. Cited in O'Connor, p. 27
aa. O'Rourke, p. 104, cited in O'Connor, p. 28
bb. O'Connor, p. 28
cc. Captain Wynne; cited in O'Connor, p. 31
dd. O'Rourke, p. 222; cited in O'Connor, p. 35
ee. *History of Ireland*, ii, p. 215; cited in O'Connor, p. 36
ff. A. M. Sullivan, New Ireland, p. 64; cited in O'Connor, p. 36
gg. *History of Ireland*, ii, p. 215; cited in O'Connor, p. 37
hh. *Census Commissioners*, p. 273; cited in O'Connor, p. 31
ii. O'Rourke pp. 390, 391; *Census Commissioners*, p. 243; cited in O'Connor, p. 31
jj. *Census Commissioners*, p. 310

kk. *Census Commissioners*, p. 277

ll. T. P. O'Connor, p.32

mm. Curl 1986, p. 115

nn. Cited in O'Connor, p. 27

oo. Helen Litton, The Irish Famine: An Illustrated History, Wolfhound Press, 2006, pp. 98-9

pp. Hansard lxxxiv, p. 694

qq. Curl 1986, p. 115

rr. Curl 1986, p. 116

ss. Curl 1986, p. 116

tt. Curl 1986, p. 117

uu. Curl 1986, p. 116

vv. Curl 1986, p. 117

ww. *Freeman's Journal*, 22 February, 1886, cited in Curl 1986, p. 118

Chapter 38 The seeds of growing unrest in Belfast

a. Bardon, p. 337

b. Bardon, p. 180

c. Rev. G. Hill, *An Historical Account of the Plantation of Ulster at the Commencement of the Seventeenth Century 1608-1620,* p. 590, Belfast,1877; cited in Bardon, p. 338

d. Bardon, p. 339

Part 9 The individual Livery Companies on their proportions (2) and those of The Honourable The Irish Society in Londonderry and Coleraine

Chapter 39 Mercers

a. Curl 1986, p. 130

b. Curl 1986, p. 130

c. Curl 1986, p. 130

d. Curl 1986, p. 130

e. Curl 1986, p. 131

f. Curl 1986, p. 131

g. Curl 1986, p. 132

h. Curl 1986, p. 132

i. Curl 1986, p. 132

j. Curl 1986, p. 132

k. Curl 1986, p. 132

l. Curl 1986, p. 133

m. Curl 1986, p. 133

n. Cited in Curl 1986, p. 132

o. Cited in Curl 1986, p. 135

p. Curl 1986, p. 135
q. Curl 1986, p. 135
r. Curl 1986, p. 135
s. Cited in Curl 1986, p. 135
t. Curl 1986, p. 144
u. Curl 1986, p. 144
v. Curl 1986, p. 144
w. Curl 1986, p. 134
x. Curl 1986, p. 134
y. Curl 1986, p. 138
z. Curl 1986, p. 138
aa. Curl 1986, p. 135
bb. Curl 1986, p. 147
cc. Curl 1986, p. 148
dd. Curl 1986, p. 148
ee. Curl 1986, p. 149
ff. Curl 1986, p. 148
gg. Curl 1986, p. 149
hh. Curl 1986, p. 149

Chapter 40 Grocers

a. Beresford to the Grocers' Company, November 1658; quoted in Heath Baron, *Some account of the Worshipful Companies of Grocers of London,* London, 1869, pp. 579-80; cited in Curl 1986, p. 157
b. Curl 1986, p. 158
c. Baron Heath, *Some account of the Worshipful Company of Grocers of the City of London,* London, 1869, p. 252; cited in Curl 1986, p. 158
d. Curl 1986, p. 158
e. Baron Heath, *Some Account of the Worshipful Company of Grocers of the City of London,* London, 1869, pp. 572-83; cited in Curl 1986, p. 158
f. *Guildhall Library, City of London. M.S.* 11642/1; cited in Curl 1986, p. 158
g. Curl, p. 158
h. Rev. G. Vaughan Sampson, *Memoir Explanatory of the Chart and Survey of the County of London-Derry, London 1814,* pp. 261-2; cited in Curl 1986, pp. 169-70
i. Cited in Curl 1986, p. 158
j. Curl 1986, p. 158
k. Curl 1986, p. 158
l. Baron Heath, *Some account of the Worshipful Company of Grocers of the City of London,* London, 1869, p. 253; cited in Curl 1986, p. 158
m. Curl, p. 163
n. *Guildhall Library, City of London. M.S.* 11642/3; cited in Curl 1986, p. 159
o. Curl 1986, p. 159

p.   Curl 1986, p. 162

q.   Curl 1986, p. 162

r.   Curl 1986, p. 159

s.   Curl 1986, p. 162

t.   Curl 1986, p. 163

u.   Curl 1986, p. 169

v.   Curl 1986, p. 167

w.   Curl 1986, p. 167

x.   Curl 1986, p. 170

y.   Cited in Curl 1986, p. 168

z.   Curl 1986, p. 168

aa.   *Grocers' Company Minutes M.S.* 11641; cited in Curl 1986, p. 168

bb.   Curl 1986, p. 169

M. S. 11642/5; cited in Curl 1986, p. 170

Chapter 42 Drapers

a.   Rev. A. H. Johnson, *The History of the Worshipful Company of the Drapers of London,* Oxford, 1922, Vol. IV, pp. 600-1; cited in Curl 1986, p. 187

b.   *Drapers' Company Records.* Ma. Dr. +134. pp. 280-2; cited in Curl 1986, p. 187

c.   Curl 1986, p. 188

d.   Curl 1986, p. 192

e.   *Reports of Deputations* … London, 1841, p. 2; cited in Curl 1986, p. 188

f.   *Reports of Deputations* … London, 1841, p. 3; cited in Curl 1986, p. 188

g.   *Report of the 1817 Deputation*, pp. 19-20; cited in Curl 1986, p. 190

h.   *Report of the Drapers' Deputation of 1818*, pp. 86-7; cited in Curl 1986, p. 195

i.   *Reports of Deputations … of the Drapers' Company of Jan. 23, 1817*, London, 1841, p. 24; cited in Curl 1986, p. 191

j.   *Reports of Deputations … of the Drapers' Company of Jan. 23, 1817*, London, 1841, p. 6; cited in Curl 1986, p. 189

k.   *Reports of Deputations … of the Drapers' Company of Jan. 23, 1817*, London, 1841, p. 60; cited in Curl 1986, p. 192

l.   Curl 1986, p. 195

m.   Curl 1986, p. 196

n.   Curl 1986, p. 196

o.   Curl 1986, p. 195

p.   *Reports of Deputations … of the Drapers' Company of Jan. 23, 1817*, London, 1841, p. 48; cited in Curl 1986, p. 192

q.   Curl 1986, p. 163

r.   *Report of the Deputation of 1819. London*, 1841, p. 106; cited in Curl 1986, p. 195

s.   *Report of the Drapers' Deputation of 1818,* p. 71; cited in Curl 1986, p. 193

t.   *Reports of Deputations ... of the Drapers' Company of Jan. 23, 1817*, London, 1841, pp. 51-2; cited in Curl 1986, p. 192

u.   *Report of the Drapers' Deputation of 1818*, p. 79; cited in Curl 1986, p. 195

v.   Curl 1986, p. 193

w.   *Report of the Deputation of 1818. London, 1841*, pp. 67-8; cited in Curl 1986, p. 193

x.   Curl 1986, p. 203

y.   Curl 1986, p. 198

z.   Curl 1986, p. 195

aa.   Curl 1986, p. 196

bb.   *Report of the Deputation of 1827. London, 1841*, p. 171; cited in Curl 1986, p. 205

cc.   Curl 1986, p. 205

dd.   *Reports of Deputations ... of the Drapers' Company of Jan. 23, 1817*, London, 1841, p. 58; cited in Curl 1986, p. 192

ee.   *Report of the Drapers' Deputation of 1818*, p. 84; cited in Curl, p. 195

ff.   *Report of the Deputation of 1827*. London, 1841, p. 159; cited in Curl 1986, p. 196

gg.   *Report of the Deputation of 1827. London, 1841*. Pp. 176-7; cited in Curl 1986, p. 205

hh.   Curl 1986, p. 203

ii.   *Reports of Deputations ... of the Drapers' Company ...* London, 1841, p. 223; cited in Curl 1986, p. 215

jj.   Curl 1986, p. 203

kk.   *Report of the Deputation of 1832, London, 1841*, p. 214; cited in Curl 1986, p. 209

ll.   *Report of the Deputation of 1832*, London, 1841, p. 217; cited in Curl 1986, p. 209

mm.   Curl 1986, p. 209

nn.   *Reports of Deputations ... of the Drapers' Company ...* London, 1841, pp. 258-9; cited in Curl 1986, p. 215

oo.   Curl 1986, p. 216

pp.   *Report of the Deputation Appointed by The Honorable The Irish Society ...* London, 1836, pp. 94-5; cited in Curl 1986, pp. 209-15

qq.   Curl 1986, p. 215

rr.   Curl 1986, p. 215

ss.   *Reports of Deputations ... of the Drapers' Company ...* London, 1841, p. 234; cited in Curl 1986, p. 215

tt.   *Report of Mr. Robert Forster ... Dated 29 th October, 1853.* London, p. 11; cited in Curl 1986, p. 223

uu.   Curl 1986, p. 223

vv.   Curl 1986, p. 223

ww.   Curl 1986, p. 226

xx.   *Report of Mr. Robert Forster ... Dated 29ᵗʰ October, 1853.* London, p. 21; cited in Curl 1986, p. 223

yy.   *Report of Mr. Robert Forster ... Dated 29ᵗʰ October, 1853.* London, p. 21; cited in Curl 1986, p. 223

zz.   *Report of the Deputation of 1862,* London 1868, p. 96; cited in Curl 1986, p. 226

aaa.   *Reports to the Court of Assistants of the Drapers' Company ...* London 1868, p. 33; cited in Curl 1986, p. 224

bbb.   Curl 1986, p. 226

ccc.   Curl 1986, p. 226

ddd.   Curl 1986, p. 226

eee.   Curl 1986, p. 226

fff.   Curl 1986, p. 227

ggg.   Curl 1986, p. 227

hhh.   *Report of the Deputation of 1875*, London, 1875, p. 5; cited in Curl 1986, p. 227

iii.   *Report of the Deputation of 1877,* London, 1877; cited in Curl 1986, p. 228

jjj.   *Report of the Deputation of 1875,* London, 1875, p. 7; cited in Curl 1986, p. 227

kkk.   *Report of the Deputation of 1878,* London, 1878, p. 39; cited in Curl 1986, p. 228

lll.   *Report of the Deputation of 1875,* London, 1875, p. 12; cited in Curl 1986, p. 228

mmm. Curl 1986, p. 223

nnn.   Curl 1986, p. 228

ooo.   Rev. A. H. Johnson, *The History of The Worshipful Company of Drapers of London.* Oxford, 1922. Vol. III, pp. 407-17; cited in Curl 1986, p. 229

ppp.   Curl 1986, p. 229

qqq.   Curl 1986, p. 231

rrr.   Curl 1986, p. 231

Chapter 42 Fishmongers

a. Curl 1986, p. 236

b. Robert Slade, *Narrative of a Journey to the North of Ireland, in the year 1802,* p. ccv; cited in Curl 1986, p. 110

c. Curl 1986, p. 240

d. Robert Slade, *Narrative of a Journey to the North of Ireland, in the year 1802,* p. ccxii; cited in Curl 1986, p. 240

e. Curl 1986, p. 243

f. Curl 1986, p. 271

g. Curl 1986, p. 248

h. Curl 1986, p. 245

i. Curl 1986, p. 248

j. Curl 1986, p. 242
k. Curl 1986, p. 242
l. Curl 1986, p. 249
m. Curl 1986, p. 258
n. Curl 1986, p. 242
o. Curl 1986, p. 262
p. Curl 1986, p. 262
q. Curl 1986, p. 262
r. *Fishmongers' Company Papers*, Fol. II. No. 19; cited in Curl 1986, p. 271
s. Curl 1986, p. 274
t. Curl 1986, p. 274
u. Curl 1986, p. 271
v. Curl 1986, p. 276
w. *Fishmongers' Company Papers, MS* 7273; cited in Curl 1986, p. 276
x. Curl 1986, p. 276
y. Curl 1986, p. 276
z. Curl 1986, p. 276
aa. Curl 1986, p. 277

Chapter 43 Goldsmiths

a. Curl 1986, p. 283
b. Curl 1986, p. 284

Chapter 44 Merchant Taylors

a. Curl 1986, p. 313

Chapter 45 Skinners

a. W. Shaw Mason, *A Statistical Account or Parochial Survey of Ireland.* Vol. 1. Dublin, 1814. Plate facing p. 302; cited in Curl 1986, p. 291
b. T. W. Moody, *The Londonderry Plantation, 1609-1641. The City of London and the Plantation of Ulster,* Belfast, 1939, p. 309; cited in Curl 1986, p. 294
c. Curl 1986, p. 294
d. Curl 1986, p. 294
e. Curl 1986, p. 294
f. Curl 1986, p. 294
g. Curl 1986, p. 294
h. Curl 1986, p. 294
i. Curl 1986, p. 294
j. Curl 1986, p. 294
k. Curl 1986, p. 294
l. Curl 1986, p. 294

m. Samuel Lewis, *A Topographical Dictionary of Ireland* etc. London, 1850, p. 568; cited in Curl 1986, p. 291

n. Curl 1986, pp.294-5

o. Curl 1986, p. 295

p. Curl 1986, p. 295

q. *Report of the Special Committee charged with the Sale of the Pellipar Estate*, London. 1911, p. 6; cited in Curl 1986, p. 296

r. Curl 1986, p. 296

s. Curl 1986, p. 296

t. Curl 1986, p. 296

u. *Skinners' Company Court Book I. Irish Estate 1873;* cited in Curl 1986, p. 295

v. Curl 1986, p. 303

w. Curl 1986, p. 303

Chapter 46 Haberdashers

a. Curl 1986, p. 318

Chapter 47 Salters

a.   Curl 1986, p. 325

b.   Curl 1986, p. 327

c.   Curl 1986, p. 327

d.   Curl 1986, p. 327

e.   W. H. Maitland, *History of Magherafelt.* Cookstown, 1916, p. 28; cited in Curl 1986, p. 325

f.   Curl 1986, p. 325

g.   Curl 1986, p. 334

h.   *Report of the Deputation ... of 1854,* p. 2; cited in Curl 1986, p. 327

i.   Curl 1986, p. 334

j.   *Report of the Deputation ... of 1854,* p. 3; cited in Curl 1986, p. 327

k.   *Report of the Deputation ... of 1854,* pp. 4-5; cited in Curl 1986, p. 328

l.   *Report of the Deputation ... of 1854,* p. 4; cited in Curl 1986, p. 327

m.   Curl 1986, p. 330

n.   *Report of the Deputation ... of 1854,* p. 6; cited in Curl 1986, p. 330

o.   Curl 1986, p. 334

p.   Curl 1986, p. 344

q.   *Report of the Deputation ... of 1854,* p. 8; cited in Curl 1986, p. 330

r.   *Report of the Deputation ... of 1854,* p. 16; cited in Curl 1986, p. 330

s.   Curl 1986, p. 334

t.   Curl 1986, p. 344

u.   Curl 1986, p. 330

v.   Curl 1986, p. 331

w.   *Report of the Deputation ... of 1854,* p. 6; cited in Curl 1986, p. 330

x.   Curl 1986, p. 340

y. *Report of the Deputation ... of 1854,* p. 24; cited in Curl 1986, p. 331
z. Curl 1986, p. 348
aa. Curl 1986, p. 335
bb. Curl 1986, p. 340
cc. Curl 1986, p. 348

Chapter 48 Ironmongers

a. John Nichol, *Some Account of the Worshipful Company of Ironmongers.* London; cited in Curl 1986, p. 357
b. John Nichol, *Some Account of the Worshipful Company of Ironmongers.* London; cited in Curl 1986, p. 357
c. *Report of the Deputation appointed by The Honourable The Irish Society.* London 1836, p. 78; cited in Curl 1986, p. 358
d. Robert Slade, *Narrative of a Journey to the North of Ireland, in the year 1802,* pp. ccviii-ccix; cited in Curl 1986, p. 358
e. Curl 1986, p. 358
f. Curl 1986, p. 360
g. Curl 1986, p. 360
h. *Guildhall Library. City of London. MS 17297*; cited in Curl 1986, p. 360
i. Curl 1986, p. 360
j. Curl 1986, p. 360
k. Curl 1986, p. 360
l. Curl 1986, p. 360
m. Curl 1986, p. 360
n. Curl 1986, p. 360
o. Curl 1986, p. 362
p. Curl 1986, p. 362
q. Curl 1986, p. 362
r. Curl 1986, p. 364
s. Guildhall Library ref. 16999/2; Company ledger 1896-1903, folio Z
t. Guildhall Library ref. 16999/2; Company ledger 1896-1903

Chapter 49 Vintners

a. Curl 1986, p. 372
b. Curl 1986, p. 372
c. Curl 1986, p. 373
d. Curl 1986, p. 372
e. Curl 1986, p. 372

Chapter 50 Clothworkers

a. Curl 1986, p. 384
b. Robert Slade, *Narrative of a Journey to the North of Ireland, in the year 1802,* p. ccxiii; cited in Curl 1986, pp. 111 and 384

c. Curl 1986, p. 384
d. Curl 1986, p. 385
e. Curl 1986, p. 385
f. Curl 1986, p. 385
g. Curl 1986, p. 385
h. Curl 1986, p. 394
i. Curl 1986, p. 388
j. Curl 1986, p. 387
k. *Clothworkers' Papers*; cited in Curl 1986, p. 387
l. Curl 1986, p. 387
m. Curl 1986, p. 388
n. Curl 1986, p. 387
o. Curl 1986, p. 387
p. Curl 1986, p. 387
q. Curl 1986, p. 390
r. *Minutes of the Irish Estates Committee*, fol. 500; cited in Curl 1986, p. 392
s. Curl 1986, p. 388
t. Curl 1986, p. 392
u. Curl 1986, p. 390
v. Curl 1986, p. 390
w. Curl 1986, p. 390
x. Curl 1986, p. 392
y. Curl 1986, p. 395
z. Curl 1986, p. 394
aa. Curl 1986, p. 392
bb. Curl 1986, p. 394
cc. Curl 1986, p. 394
dd. Curl 1986, p. 394

Chapter 51 The Honourable The Irish Society

a. Arthur C. Champneys *Irish Ecclesiastical Architecture* ... London. 1910, p. 202; cited in Curl, p. 399
b. Curl 1986, p. 399
c. Curl 1986, p. 407
d. Curl 1986, p. 412
e. Curl 1986, p. 419
f. Curl 1986, p. 422
g. Curl 1986, p. 412
h. Curl 1986, p. 414
i. Curl 1986, p. 414
j. *A Concise View of The Irish Society*. London, 1842, p. 188; cited in Curl 1986, p. 426
k. Curl 1986, p. 430

l. Curl 1986, p. 414

m. Raymond Smith, *The Irish Society, 1613-1963*, London. 1966, p. 63; cited in Curl 1986, p. 426

n. Curl 1986, p. 428

o. Curl 1986, p. 428

p. Curl 2000, p. 253

q. Curl 2000, p. 253

r. Irish Society (1841) 17; cited in Curl 2000, p. 260

s. Curl 2000, pp. 329-30

Chapter 52 The departure of the Livery Companies from Ireland

a. Curl 1986, p. 117

b. Curl 1986, p. 118

c. Curl 1986, p. 119

d. Curl 1986, p. 119

e. Curl BBCi 2001 pp. 9-10

f. Curl 2000, p. 312

g. Curl 1986, p. 121

MEN OF SUBSTANCE

INDEX